Communications in Computer and Information Science   1726

More information about this series at https://link.springer.com/bookseries/7899

Emmanuel Ahene · Fagen Li (Eds.)

Frontiers in Cyber Security

5th International Conference, FCS 2022
Kumasi, Ghana, December 13–15, 2022
Proceedings

 Springer

Editors
Emmanuel Ahene (iD)
Kwame Nkrumah University of Science
and Technology
Kumasi, Ghana

Fagen Li (iD)
University of Electronic Science
and Technology of China
Chengdu, China

ISSN 1865-0929   ISSN 1865-0937 (electronic)
Communications in Computer and Information Science
ISBN 978-981-19-8444-0   ISBN 978-981-19-8445-7 (eBook)
https://doi.org/10.1007/978-981-19-8445-7

This Springer imprint is published by the registered company Springer Nature Singapore Pte Ltd.
The registered company address is: 152 Beach Road, #21-01/04 Gateway East, Singapore 189721, Singapore

Preface

This volume comprises significant cyber security research papers from the fifth International Conference on Frontiers in Cyber Security (FCS 2022). The event was organized by the Department of Computer Science, Kwame Nkrumah University of Science and Technology (KNUST), in collaboration with the Center for Cyber Security, University of Electronic Science and Technology of China, and Huaiyin Institute of Technology (HYIT). FCS 2022 offered researchers with different directions in cyber security the avenue to contribute to science and exchange ideas. This proceedings provides valuable information on cutting-edge research and current topics in specific fields of cyber security.

Cyber security is an interdisciplinary field gaining increasing interest from academic and professional researchers worldwide. Recent cyber-attack behaviors expose everyday users to risks, including privacy leakage, property loss, etc. There is, therefore, the surging need to prevent various forms of cyber-attacks. This volume contains reasonable developments and contributions towards creating a cyber-safe world from multiple researchers within the cyber security paradigm. Specifically, after using the latest development trends and innovative technology, researchers and practitioners have proposed and discussed their research achievements in areas such as network security, system security, cryptography, trust management, privacy protection, information hiding, computer forensics, blockchain technology, AI security, content security, and their applications.

FCS 2022 was the fifth event of the Frontiers in Cyber Security (FCS) series. FCS keeps pace with international security innovation concepts and has provided theoretical and technical support for international cyberspace development since its inception in 2018. Hundreds of researchers have shared and explained their findings in a formal and to some extent informal setting. Participants have exchanged ideas at the FCS conference, promoting cyber security development over the past five years.

In 2022, FCS received 65 paper submissions and finally accepted 26 papers. This does not include any short articles. On average, each reviewer was assigned four papers and each paper received three reviews . The peer review process was double-blind to promote transparency and fairness. The conference gained significant attention worldwide, with participants coming from different countries, such as Ghana, Kenya, Rwanda, Namibia, China, Japan, Australia, etc. The format for participation was designed to be hybrid, allowing some participants with COVID-19 restrictions to comply with relevant epidemic prevention regulations by participating online.

This FCS 2022 volume is primarily organized according to the thematic directions of all the accepted papers. Specifically, the seven topics of FCS 2022, classified by reviewers, as follows: Internet of Things (IoT) Security, Artificial Intelligence and Cyber Security, Blockchain Technology and Applications, Cryptography, Database Security, Network Security, and Quantum Cryptography.

The proceedings editors wish to express their greatest appreciation to the team of dedicated Program Committee members and all the other reviewers for their contributions. We also thank Springer for their trust and for publishing the proceedings of FCS 2022.

October 2022   Emmanuel Ahene
                                                                                          Fagen Li

Organization

General Chairs

Leonard Kofitse Amekudzi	Kwame Nkrumah University of Science and Technology, Ghana
Xiaosong Zhang	University of Electronic Science and Technology of China, China

Program Committee Chairs

Emmanuel Ahene	Kwame Nkrumah University of Science and Technology, Ghana
Michael Asante	Kwame Nkrumah University of Science and Technology, Ghana
Fagen Li	University of Electronic Science and Technology of China, China

Publicity Chair

Abdul Salaam Gaddafi	Kwame Nkrumah University of Science and Technology, Ghana

Organizing Committee Chairs

Osei Akoto	Kwame Nkrumah University of Science and Technology, Ghana
Anyembe Andrew Omala	South Eastern Kenyan University, Kenya
Twum Frimpong	Kwame Nkrumah University of Science and Technology, Ghana
Chunhua Jin	Huaiyin Institute of Technology, China

Organizing Committee

Michael Eshun	Kwame Nkrumah University of Science and Technology, Ghana
Solomon Arthur	Kwame Nkrumah University of Science and Technology, Ghana

Israel Manu Debrah   Kwame Nkrumah University of Science and
                                      Technology, Ghana
Patrick Agyeman-Budu   Kwame Nkrumah University of Science and
                                      Technology, Ghana

Program Committee

Isaac Adjaye Aboagye   University of Ghana, Ghana
Peter Awonnatemi Agbedemnab   C. K. Tedam University of Technology and
                                      Applied Sciences, Ghana
Kwame Opuni-Boachie   Kwame Nkrumah University of Science and
  Agyemang   Technology, Ghana
Brighter Agyemang   University of Wollongong, Australia
Kwabena Agyemang   Kwame Nkrumah University of Science and
                                      Technology, Ghana
Emmanuel Kofi Akowuah   Kwame Nkrumah University of Science and
                                      Technology, Ghana
Ikram Ali   University of Electronic Science and Technology
                                      of China, China
Seth Alornyo   Koforidua Technical University, Ghana
Albert Kwaansah Ansah   University of Mines and Technology, Ghana
Edward Danso Ansong   University of Ghana, Ghana
Dominic Asamoah   Kwame Nkrumah University of Science and
                                      Technology, Ghana
Sarpong Kwadwo Asare   Emory University, USA
Edward Yellakour Baagyeri   C. K. Tedam University of Technology and
                                      Applied Sciences, Ghana
Jennifer Batamuliza   Adventist University of Central Africa, Rwanda
Rashad Elhabob   Karary University, Sudan
Nabeil Eltayab   Karary University, Sudan
Twum Frimpong   Kwame Nkrumah University of Science and
                                      Technology, Ghana
Kazeem Gbolagade   Kwara State University, Nigeria
Fuchen Guo   University of Wollongong, Australia
Charles Roland Haruna   University of Cape Coast, Ghana
Alzubair Hassan   University College Dublin, Ireland
Abdelrhman Hassan   University of Electronic Science and Technology
                                      of China, China
James Ben Hayfron-acquah   Kwame Nkrumah University of Science and
                                      Technology, Ghana
Chunhua Jin   Huaiyin Institute of Technology, China
Ferdinand Apietu Katsriku   University of Ghana, Ghana
Griffith Selorm Klogo   Kwame Nkrumah University of Science and
                                      Technology, Ghana

Chaoyang Li	Zhengzhou University of Light Industry, China
Hongwei Li	University of Electronic Science and Technology of China, China
Mingzhe Liu	Chengdu University of Technology, China
Xiaoguang Liu	Southwest Minzu University, China
Rongxing Lu	University of New Brunswick, Canada
Yaw Marfo Missah	Kwame Nkrumah University of Science and Technology, Ghana
Henry Nunoo-Mensah	Kwame Nkrumah University of Science and Technology, Ghana
Isaac Amankona Obiri	University of Electronic Science and Technology of China, China
Mark Ofori Oduro	Concordia University, Canada
Anyembe Andrew Omala	South Eastern Kenyan University, Kenya
Joseph Panford	Kwame Nkrumah University of Science and Technology, Ghana
Kwame Ofosuhene Peasah	Kwame Nkrumah University of Science and Technology, Ghana
Eric Osei Poku	Kwame Nkrumah University of Science and Technology, Ghana
Longjiang Qu	National University of Defense Technology, China
Nii Longdon Sowah	University of Ghana, Ghana
Bing Sun	National University of Defense Technology, China
Kate Takyi	Kwame Nkrumah University of Science and Technology, Ghana
Eric Tutu Tchao	Kwame Nkrumah University of Science and Technology, Ghana
Martha Teye	Universität Stuttgart, Germany
Najim Ussiph	Kwame Nkrumah University of Science and Technology, Ghana
Abubaker Wahaballa	University of Electronic Science and Technology of China, China
Joojo Walker	University of Electronic Science and Technology of China, China
Lei Wang	Shanghai Jiao Tong University, China
Jian Weng	Jinan University, China
Qianhong Wu	Beihang University, China
Ling Xiong	Xihua University, China
Haomiao Yang	University of Electronic Science and Technology of China, China
Hui Zhang	Chengdu University of Technology, China

Fangguo Zhang   Sun Yat-sen University, China
Mingwu Zhang   Hubei University of Technology, China
Liang Zhao   Sichuan University, China

Contents

IoT Security

Artificial Intelligence and Cyber Security

Blockchain Technology and Application

Cryptography

Database Security

Quantum Cryptography

Network Security

IoT Security

A Secure and Efficient Heterogeneous Signcryption Scheme for IIoT

Chunhua Jin$^{(\boxtimes)}$, Chenhao Li, Wenyu Qin, Xiaobing Chen, and Guanhua Chen

Faculty of Computer and Software Engineering, Huaiyin Institute of Technology, Huai'an 233003, China
xajch0206@163.com

Abstract. With the development of the Internet of Things (IoT), the Industrial Internet of Things (IIoT), as an extension of the IoT, has become more and more widely used in the industrial field. It collects various data in the IIoT environment through sensors. For security reasons, these data cannot be presented in plaintext. To ensure the security of these data, a signcryption primitive is presented. In practice, numerous sensors and servers are not in the same environment, so we need a heterogeneous signcryption scheme to solve this problem. In this paper, we introduce a heterogeneous signcryption scheme with the critical characteristic of allowing devices in certificateless cryptography (CLC) environments send messages to devices in identity-based cryptography (IBC) environments. In the random oracle model (ROM), for its security aspects, we present the relevant proofs. We also compared it with other schemes in terms of communication overhead. A comprehensive analysis has shown that our scheme improves efficiency and also increases security.

Keywords: IIoT · Secure communications · Signcryption · Heterogeneous · Certificateless cryptosystem · Identitybased cryptosystem

1 Introduction

Industrial Internet of Things (IIoT) are the application with extension of the IoT in the industrial field [1], which collects data in real time through various sensors, radio frequency identification technology, infrared sensors and other physical devices and technologies to achieve intelligent sensing and management of equipment, and has received wide attention from all walks of life for its ability to improve the utilization of equipment and reduce potential energy waste. In the fourth industrial revolution (Industry 4.0) [2–4], IIoT is an integral part of the transformation and enhancement of industrial equipment and production processes with big data and artificial intelligence. In the broader context of applications, IIoT plays an irreplaceable role in regulating the environment and ecosystem, such as the establishment of smart cities and smart factories [5], automotive industry [6].

Nowadays, IIoT provides us with great convenience and promotes the development of various industries, but the security issues of IIoT hinder its promotion [7,8]. The authenticity of the data collected through various sensors cannot be guaranteed effectively [9,10]. The collected data is transferred through an insecure channel in a typical application. As a result, this data can be easily attacked by adversaries (modification, interception, etc.), and the terminal collecting them is unable to discern whether the data have been tampered with. In identity-based systems, distinct information(e.g., Web Account) [11] can be generated directly from his or her public key. As for the private key, it is generated by the private key generator (PKG). Nonetheless, the problem of key escrow poses as a serious potential threat to the security of ID-based systems. Once PKG is compromised by a malicious adversary, then the malicious adversary will be able to use all the private keys. A compromised PKG can forge the signature of any user and remain undetected. To solve the above problem, a new system was proposed and named certificateless [12]. In CLC systems, key generator center (KGC) only generates partial private key, while the remaining private key (called secret value) is selected from the user himself [12,13]. By this way, the issue of key escrow can be settled more seamlessly. This also poses a problem. However, in CLC-based schemes, the user cannot obtain the required public key directly from the owner's identity, which causes an increased cost of generating and transmitting the user's public key. In IIoT, due to the importance of data, without a proper scheme to control and protect the critical data, these device data can be maliciously exploited by others. This can affect plant productivity and even have catastrophic consequences. Therefore, an effective signcryption scheme must be designed to protect the data.

Information security is crucial in protecting critical information in modern communication systems. Ensure the key data such as text, images, etc., that need to be kept private (confidentiality) know the message originator (authentication), modification protection (integrity) and availability when needed by legitimate users. Confidentiality is guaranteed by encryption procedures, whereas its integrity and authenticity are assured through the use of digital signature methods. But several disadvantages can be identified from the traditional approach. For example, excessive consumption of communication resources, etc. Due to some characteristics of IIoT, such as open communication channels, limited sensor resources, and lack of fixed infrastructure. Designing a cost-effective and secure signcryption scheme is still a challenging task.

1.1   Related Work

For the purpose of optimizing performance, Zheng [14] proposed another class of schemes, which he named signcryption. It can perform the role of signature and encryption in a single step. The scheme fully demonstrates its suitability for public key infrastructure (PKI) environments and suffers from the shortcomings of certificate distribution, storage and certificate generation difficulties. Therefore, in order to eliminate these shortcomings, Malone-Lee [15] created a ID-based signcryption (IBSC) scheme. This scheme combined the signature and encryption steps in a secure manner, after which many IBSC schemes [16–18] are introduced in Malone-Lee. However, IBSC scheme eliminates the public key certificate and allows a PKG generation of the user's full private key. This requires that the PKG must be trusted. To resolve the key escrow issue, Sattam [12] proposes a cryptography based on a certificateless environment. It circumvents the key custody problem inherent in ID-based cryptography, plus it does not need certificates to guarantee authenticity. It develops a new security model to resist an opponent who has the opportunity to be able to obtain the master key by utilizing an attack. This led to the introduction of a number of CLC signcryption schemes [19–21]. However, different cryptographic techniques may be used for different network systems.

In 2010, in order to solve the problem of heterogeneous communication, a two-way heterogeneous hybrid signcryption scheme was proposed by Sun [24] and others, However, this scheme only caters to external security and does not satisfy other cryptographic properties. In 2011, Huang [25] introduced a one-way heterogeneous signature scheme for IBC-TPKI, but this scheme is too complex and has high usage overhead. In 2016, Zhang [26] suggested a heterogeneous hybrid signcryption scheme with CLPKI-TPKI, but the efficiency of this scheme is low due to the presence of multiple bilinear pairs of operations in this scheme. In 2017, Wang [27] suggested a PKI-IBC heterogeneous scheme. This solution satisfies both confidentiality and two-way authentication. However, this scheme has very high transmission overhead and computation overhead during the signing and decryption process. In 2018, Niu [28] proposed a CLC-IBC heterogeneous signcryption scheme. This scheme was found to have passive attack vulnerability under CLPKG-KGC, in which the scheme could not satisfy unforgeability for sender signatures. In 2020, Liu [29] introduced a CLPKC-IDPKC heterogeneous authentication scheme. The scheme satisfies the confidentiality, unforgeability and anonymity of the signature encryption process. And it introduces a static measurement factors. Li [30] suggested a CLC-IBC scheme, solve the problem that only short messages can be encrypted in public key signing and improve the security of the scheme. In contrast, in some usage environment like IIoT, it is required that the signcryption scheme must have low computational and storage space consumption and high operational efficiency. Therefore, it is clear that the above scheme still has shortcomings in the different environment.

1.2 Motivation and Contribution

This paper aims to find a new heterogeneous signcryption scheme for IIoT. This solution should be able to solve the communication problems between different environments. The approach we used is CLC-IBC heterogeneous signcryption (CI-HSC). The contributions are stated as follows.

1. We construct an efficient CI-HSC scheme. In our proposed CI-HSC scheme, the sensor node is in CLC environment and the Internet server is in IBC environment.

2. Three polynomial time intractable assumptions are considered, named as q-bilinear Diffie-Hellman inversion (q-BDHI) assumption, q-strong Diffie-Hellman (q-SDH) assumption and modified inverse computational Diffie-Hellman (mICDH) assumption. We prove the confidentiality and unforgeability of the CI-HSC scheme under the problematic assumptions of the existence of q-BDHI, q-SDH and mICDH problems, respectively.
3. We compared our CI-HSC scheme with other competitive signcryption schemes. Then, we showed that our scheme is more efficient in terms of computational and communication costs compared to other schemes regarding the size of the symbolic encrypted text.
4. Our CI-HSC scheme is easier to implement, especially for those need confidentiality and unforgeability to provide secure communications.

1.3 Organization

Here we show the arrangement of the remainder of this paper. In Sect. 2, we present preliminaries. Then we show the HSC scheme we designed in Sect. 3. In Sect. 4, first we study the security of the scheme and second we analyze its performance. And finally, in Sect. 5, we made a summary of the scheme.

2 Preliminaries

Bilinear pairings concept are shown in this section.

2.1 Bilinear Pairings

Refer to the mapping $e : G_1 \times G_1 \to G_2$ between G_1 and G_2 as a bilinear pair. G_1 as well as G_2 have the same prime order p, G_2 is a cyclic multiplicative group of order p. It has these characteristics bellow.

1. Bilinearity: $e(aP, bQ) = e(P, Q)^{ab}$ for all $P, Q \in G_1$. $a, b \in Z_p^*$.
2. Non-degeneracy: There exists $P, Q \in G_1$ such that $e(P, Q) \neq 1$.
3. Computability: There is an efficient algorithm to compute $e(P, Q)$ for all $P, Q \in G_1$.

Definition 1. $(e, P, p, G_1, G_2, a, b)$ follows the same definitions as above.

1. The q-BDHI problem:
   Among the (G_1, G_2, e), choose $\alpha \in Z_p^*$ randomly and calculate $e(P, P)^{1/\alpha}$, where $(P, \alpha P, \ldots, \alpha^q P)$ is preset.
2. The q-SDH problem:
   Among the (G_1, G_2, e), finding pairs of $\left(\omega, \frac{1}{\alpha+\omega} P \right) \in Z_p^* \times G_1$, where $(P, \alpha P, \ldots, \alpha^q P)$, $\alpha \in Z_p^*$ is preset.
3. The mICDH problem:
   Among the G_1, compute $(a + b)^{-1} P$, calculate $(a + b)^{-1} P$, where (P, aP, b) is given.

3 CI-HSC

In this part, we first explain seven algorithms in this scheme, then demon strate that the scheme is resistant to two types of attacks, and finally detail our efficient heterogeneous signcryption scheme for transmitting data from a sender under CLC to a receiver under IBC. The scheme is briefly referred to CI-HSC.

3.1 Syntax

A generic CI-HSC is made up of the following seven algorithms.

- *Setup*: This is an initialization algorithm executed by registration center (RC), which takes as input the security parameter k and outputs the master key S and the system parameters containing the master public key P_{pub}.
- *CLC-PPKE*: The algorithm is started after entering the user's identity ID_u, S. KGC calculates the user's partial private key D_{IDu}.
- *CLC-UKG*: Algorithm to be performed by the sender in the CLC. The input is system parameter params and a secret value x, and the output is the user's public key PK_{ID_u}.
- *CLC-PKS*: The key is generated during this process. The input is the system parameters params, (D_{ID_u}, x), the algorithm output is the complete private key S_u of the user.
- *IBC-KG*: The algorithm generates a pair (PK_u, S_u). The input is 1^k, and the output is the public and private key pair (PK_u, S_u) is transmitted to ID_u. This is issued through the certificate of PKG.
- *SC*: This algorithm is executed by the sender and aims to encrypt the message before it is sent. Input is the system parameter params, ID_u and PK_u, also a message m, then output the ciphertext σ.
- *USC*: This algorithm is used to recover the σ and verify the identity of the receiver after receiving it. The input is the system parameter params, ID_u and S_u, and a ciphertext σ. The output is either message m or the error symbol "$\perp$". If an error symbol "$\perp$" is an output, then it means σ is not a legitimate cipher.
  Consistency requirements must be met by these algorithms, that means, if $\sigma = $ Signcrypt ($params, ID_u, PK_u, m$).
  Then $m = $ Unsigncrypt ($params, ID_u, S_u, \sigma$).

3.2 Security Notions

To achieve the requirement of unforgeability and confidentiality, the CI-HSC needs to resist two types attacks: indistinguishability against adaptive chosen ciphertext attacks (IND-CCA2) and existential unforgeability against adaptive chosen messages attacks (EUF-CMA).

Type I: An adversary is able to choose a (valid) public key to replace the target user's public key, and this operation holds when the adversary cannot obtain the KGC's master key.

Type II: An adversary has already obtained KGC's master key, in which case the adversary has no way of tampering with the user's public key.

Game-I: To maintain the confidentiality, the following games are conducted among the $\mathcal{A}$ and $\mathcal{C}$.

- *Initial*: $\mathcal{C}$ uses the safety parameters to operation of the *Setup* algorithm and dispatch the relevant parameters to $\mathcal{A}$.
- *Phase 1*: $\mathcal{A}$ adaptively issues the following query.
  1. Partial private key extraction queries: $\mathcal{A}$ sends the identity ID to $\mathcal{C}$. $\mathcal{C}$ sends the results to $\mathcal{A}$ after the algorithm is down.
  2. Private key queries: $\mathcal{A}$ selects the ID to send to $\mathcal{C}$, $\mathcal{C}$ runs the $CLC - PPKE, CLC - UKG, CLC - PKS$ algorithms in turn, and then sends the private key to $\mathcal{A}$.
  3. Public key queries: $\mathcal{C}$ executes the $CLC-UKG$ algorithm after $\mathcal{A}$ initiates a query against the ID, in this step $\mathcal{C}$ outputs the public key PK_{ID} to $\mathcal{A}$.
  4. Public key replacement queries: $\mathcal{A}$ replaces the PK_{ID} of any user with data from any specified range so that it becomes PK'_{ID}.
  5. Key extraction queries: $\mathcal{A}$ interrogates against the identity ID, $\mathcal{C}$ executes the $IBC - KG$ algorithm and returns the private key S_{ID} to $\mathcal{A}$.
  6. Unsigncryption queries: $\mathcal{A}$ presents the sender's identity ID, public key PK_i receiver ID' and ciphertext σ. $\mathcal{C}$ firstly obtains private key S_j of the receiver by $IBC - KG$ algorithm, and conveys the decrypted result to $\mathcal{A}$.
- *Challenge*: $\mathcal{A}$ decides determines a time to end phase 1 and enter the challenge phase, which produces two messages (m, m^*), two identities (ID_A, ID_B). Also, key extraction queries is not available for ID_B at phase 1. $\mathcal{C}$ export a random bit $\beta \in \{0,1\}$ and computes σ to $\mathcal{A}$.
- *Phase 2*: $\mathcal{A}$ the queries performed are consistent with Phase 1, but cannot make an (σ^*, ID_A, ID_B)-query to get the text m except $\mathcal{A}$ replace PK_A is performed at the end of the previous phase.
- *Guess*: $\mathcal{A}$ generates a bit a'. if $a' = a$, $\mathcal{A}$ win.

$\mathcal{A}$'s advantage is $Adv = |2P[a' = a] = 1|$.

Definition 2. A CI-HSC scheme is $(\epsilon, t, q_{ppk}, q_{sk}, q_{pk}, q_{pkr}, q_s)$-IND-CCA2 secure if no probabilistic polynomial time (PPT) adversary $\mathcal{A}$ who runs at most time t and has an advantage at least ϵ after at most q_{ppk} partial private key extraction queries, q_{sk} private key queries, q_{pk} public key queries, q_{pkr} public key replacement queries and q_u unsigncryption queries in Game-I.

Game-II: For unforgeability, this game is played between $\mathcal{C}$ and $\mathcal{A}_{\mathcal{I}}$:

- *Initial*: $\mathcal{C}$ consistency with Game-I.
- *Attack*: In addition to unsigncryption queries, $\mathcal{A}_{\mathcal{I}}$ performs the same queries as Game-I.

1. Signcryption queries: $\mathcal{A}_I$ submits a sender's identity ID_i, a receiver's identity ID_j and a ciphertext σ to $\mathcal{C}$. $\mathcal{C}$ After running algorithms $CLC - UKG$ and $CLC - PKS$ to get the sender's public and private keys(PK_i, S_i), executes $SC(m, ID_i, PK_i, S_i, ID_j)$ and send to $\mathcal{A}_I$.

- *Forgery*: $\mathcal{A}_I$ generates a new item $\left(\sigma^*, ID'_i, ID'_j\right)$ and succeeds if the following criteria are real:

1. USC $\left(\sigma^*, ID'_i, PK'_i, S'_i, ID'_j\right) = m^*$.
2. $\mathcal{A}_I$ has not requested a partial private key extraction queries and a public key replacement queries on ID'_s.
3. $\mathcal{A}_I$ has not requested a private key queries on ID'_s.
4. $\mathcal{A}_I$ has not requested a signcryption queries on $(\mathrm{m}^*, ID'_s, ID'_r)$.

The advantage of $\mathcal{A}_I$ has been defined as being the probability of his victory.

Definition 3. A CI-HSC scheme is $(\epsilon, t, q_{ppk}, q_{sk}, q_{pk}, q_{pkr}, q_s)$-Type-I-EUF-CMA secure if no PPT adversary $\mathcal{A}_I$ who runs at most time t and has an advantage at least ϵ after at most q_{ppk} partial private key extraction queries, q_{sk} private key queries, q_{pk} public key queries, q_{pkr} public key replacement queries and q_s signcryption queries in Game-II.

Game-III: For unforgeability, this game is played between $\mathcal{C}$ and $\mathcal{A}_{II}$.

- *Initial*: After $\mathcal{C}$ finishes *setup* the algorithm, the results are transferred to $\mathcal{A}_{II}$.
- *Attack*: $\mathcal{A}_{II}$ implementation queries like in Game-II, except for partial private key queries and public key replacement queries. Because $\mathcal{A}_{II}$ can know the master key S.
- *Forgery*: $\mathcal{A}_{II}$ generates a new item $\left(\sigma^*, ID'_i, ID'_j\right)$ and succeeds if the conditions below are true:
  1. USC $\left(\sigma^*, ID'_i, PK'_i, S'_i, ID_r\right) = m^*$.
  2. $\mathcal{A}_{II}$ has not requested a private key query on ID_s.
  3. $\mathcal{A}_{II}$ has not requested a signcryption query on (m^*, ID_s, ID_r).

The adversary $\mathcal{A}_{II}$'s advantage is the probability of his victory.

Definition 4. A CI-HSC scheme is $(\epsilon, t, q_{ppk}, q_{sk}, q_{pk}, q_{pkr}, q_s)$-Type-II-EUF-CMA secure if no PPT adversary $\mathcal{A}_{II}$ who runs at most time t and has an advantage at least ϵ after at most q_{sk} private key queries, q_{pk} public key queries, and q_s signcryption queries in Game-III.

From Definitions 3 and 4, the necessary condition for obtaining unforgeability is that the adversary has access to the receiver's private key. Furthermore, the unforgeability can be maintained even after the adversary gets the receiver's private key.

Table 1. Notations

Symbol	Description	Symbol	Description
G_1	An addition group	$\{0,1\}^*$	A string of arbitrary length
G_2	A multiple group	s	A master private key of KGC
P	A generator of G_1	P_{pub}	A master public key of KGC
p	The prime order of G_1 and G_2	g	A element in group G_1,in which $g = e(P,P)$
e	A bilinear pairing	ID	An identity of the entity (a client or a server)
r	A Commitment Value	H_i	A one way hash function(i=1,2,3,4)
x	A secret value of an entity with identity ID	T	A blinding operation
$\{0,1\}^n$	A string of n length	$\oplus$	The operation of XOR
D_{ID}	A partial private key of identity ID	PK_r	Receiver's public key
PK_s	Sender's public key	S_r	Receiver's private key
S_s	Sender's private key		

3.3   Our Scheme

The proposed scheme is specified as follows. Table 1 shows the major notations.

Setup: The definitions of (G_1, G_2, P, p, e) have been written in Sect. 2. H_1, H_2, H_3, H_4 are four hash functions, in which $H_1: \{0,1\}^* \to Z_p^*$, $H_2: G_1 \to Z_p^*$, $H_3: G_2 \to \{0,1\}^n$ and $H_4: \{0,1\}^n \times \{0,1\}^* \times G_1 \times G_2 \to Z_p^*$. $\mathcal{RC}$ selects a master key $s \in Z_p^*$ and sets $P_{pub} = sP$. At the same time in which it computes $g = \hat{e}(P,P)$.The $\mathcal{RC}$ make s confidential, then publishes system parameters (e, p, n, g, $G_1, G_2, P, P_{pub}, H_1, H_2, H_3, H_4$).

Keygeneration: This phase we discuss in two parts, sender and receiver. The details are as follows.

– *Sender:*
– *Partial-Private-Key-Extract*: Sender based on CLC environment sends its identity ID to $\mathcal{RC}$. The $\mathcal{RC}$ returns the partial private key.

$$D_{IDs} = \frac{1}{H_1(IDs) + s}P$$

– *Set-public-Key*: Select a $x \in Z_p^*$ as secret value, the Sender calculates its public key

$$PK_s = x(H_1(IDs)P + P_{pub})$$

– *Set-Private-Key*: Input (PK_s, x, D_{IDs}), the Sender calculates its full private key.

$$S_s = \frac{1}{x + H_2(PK_s)}D_{IDs}$$

– *Recevier:*
– *Set-public-Key*: Recevier based on IBC environment sends its identity ID to $\mathcal{RC}$. The $\mathcal{RC}$ returns the public key.

$$PK_r = H_1(IDr)P$$

- *Set-Private-Key*: Recevier sends its identity ID to $\mathcal{RC}$. The $\mathcal{RC}$ returns the Private-Key.

$$S_r = \frac{1}{H_1(IDr) + s}P$$

SC: Given a message m, a private key S_s of the sender, sender's public key PK_s and the identity information ID_r of the receiver. The detailed steps of the sincryption are as follows:

(1) Selects a random vaule $x \in Z_p^*$.
(2) Calculates Commitment Value $r = g^x$ and $c = m \oplus H_3(r)$.
(3) Calculates hath vaule $h = H_4(m, ID_s, PK_s, r)$.
(4) Calculates signatures $S = (x + h)S_s$.
(5) Calculates the blinded value $T = x(H_1(IDr)P + P_{pub})$.
(6) Output ciphertext $\sigma = (c, S, T)$.

USC: Given the identity ID_s of the sender, the public key PK_S, the private key S_r for receiver and a ciphertext σ. The specific steps are as follows.

(1) Receiver recovery commitment value $r = e(T, S_r)$.
(2) The recipient recovers the plaintext $m = c \oplus H_3(r)$.
(3) Calculates hash value $h = H_4(m, ID_s, PK_s, r)$.
(4) Verifying the equation

$$r = e(S, PK_s + H_2(PK_s)(H_1(IDs)P + P_{pub}))g^{-h}$$

The receiver uses the above information for verification. If its holds, then the verification is passed and the plaintext m is output. If it is not equal, then the verification fails and the message is rejected and the error symbol $\perp$ is returned (Fig. 1).

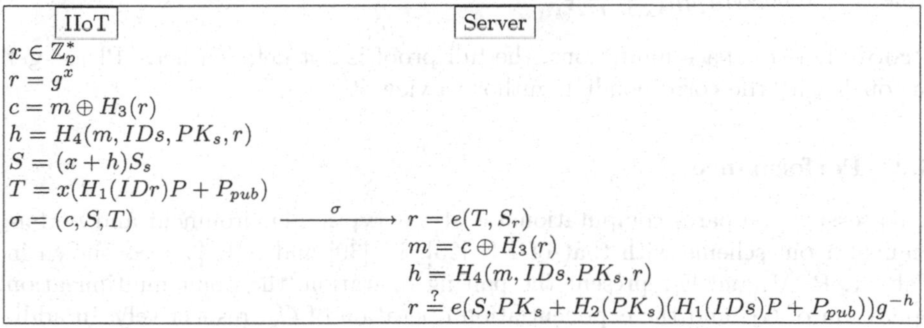

IIoT	Server
$x \in Z_p^*$	
$r = g^x$	
$c = m \oplus H_3(r)$	
$h = H_4(m, IDs, PK_s, r)$	
$S = (x + h)S_s$	
$T = x(H_1(IDr)P + P_{pub})$	
$\sigma = (c, S, T)$ $\xrightarrow{\quad \sigma \quad}$	$r = e(T, S_r)$
	$m = c \oplus H_3(r)$
	$h = H_4(m, IDs, PK_s, r)$
	$r \overset{?}{=} e(S, PK_s + H_2(PK_s)(H_1(IDs)P + P_{pub}))g^{-h}$

Fig. 1. CLC-IBC signcryption communication

4 Security and Performance

This section analyzes security and performance for proposed CI-HSC scheme.

4.1 Security

Theorems I, II provide security proof for CI-HSC.

Theorem I. Under the q-BDHI assumption, in ROM, if an attacker $\mathcal{A}$ is against the security of Definition 2 who has an advantage ϵ', an algorithm $\mathcal{C}$ can settle the q-BDHI problem for an advantage $\epsilon' \geq \frac{\epsilon}{q_{H_1}\left(q_{H_3}+2q_{H_4}\right)} \left(1 - \frac{q_u}{2^k}\right)$ in time $t' \leq t + O\left(q_u\right) t_p + 0\left(q_u q_{H_4}\right) t_e$, in which t_e is the time for an exponentiation operation in G_2 and t_p is the time for one pairing operation.

Proof: Due to space limitations, the full proof is not detailed here. Please get in touch with the corresponding author to view it.

Theorem II. Under the ROM, our scheme is EUF-CMA secure under q-SDH and mICDH assumptions.

Lemma 1. Under the q-SDH assumption, in ROM, if an attacker $\mathcal{A}_{\mathcal{I}}$ is against the security of Definition 3 who has an advantage ϵ, an algorithm $\mathcal{C}$ can settle the q-SDH problem for an advantage $\epsilon \geq 10\left(q_s + 1\right)\left(q_s + q_{H_4}\right)/2^k$ in time $t' \leq 120686 q_{H_1} q_{H_4} \frac{t+O(q_s t_p)}{\epsilon(1-1/2^k)(1-q/2^k)} + O\left(q^2 t_m\right)$.

Proof: Due to space limitations, the full proof is not detailed here. Please get in touch with the corresponding author to view it.

Lemma 2. Under the mICDH assumption, in ROM, if an attacker $\mathcal{A}_{II}$ is against the security of Definition 4 who has an advantage ϵ', an algorithm $\mathcal{C}$ can settle the mICDH problem for an advantage $\epsilon \geq 10(q_s + 1)(q_s + q_{H_4})/2^k$ in time $t' \leq 120686 q_{H_1} q_{H_4} \frac{t+O(q_s t_p)}{\epsilon(1-1/2^k)}$.

Proof: Due to space limitations, the full proof is not detailed here. Please get in touch with the corresponding author to view it.

4.2 Performance

This session compares computational cost, encryption environment and performance of our scheme with that of XU [23], LI [30] and NIU [31], as shown in Table 1. P, M, and E represent the pairing operation, the point multiplication operation of G_1, and the exponentiation operation of G_2, respectively. In addition, since the other calculations have been too simplistic, they are omitted here. As can be seen from Table 1, compared to LI and NIU, we have more superiority regarding communication consumption. The computational cost was similar to our scheme in XU, and we have an advantage in terms of computational cost (Table 2).

Table 2. Performance comparison

Schemes	Signcryption			Unsigncryption			Communication cost	Energy cost	Environment
	P	M	E	P	M	E			
XU [23]	1	2	1	3	0	0	$|m| + 2|G_1|$	106.08	CLC
LI [30]	1	4	1	1	5	1	$|m| + |G_1| + 2Z_P^*$	144.96	IBC-CLC
NIU [31]	1	5	1	3	2	0	$|m| + 4|G_1|$	164.4	IBC-CLC
Ours	0	3	1	2	2	1	$|m| + 2|G_1|$	79.92	CLC-IBC

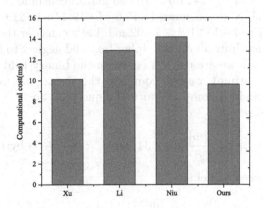

Fig. 2. Computational cost comparison.

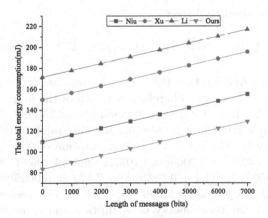

Fig. 3. Energy consumption.

We give a quantitative analysis for XU [23], LI [30], NIU [31] and our scheme. We have operated four schemes on an supersingular curve with a embedding degree of 4 and 80 bits q on the ATmega128 [32]. From [32], we can find out that P takes 1.9 s and E takes 0.9 s. Moreover, from [33], we can find out that M takes 0.81 s. Summarize the above, the computational time of sender, XU, LI, NIU and our scheme are $1 * 1.9 + 2 * 0.81 + 1 * 0.9 = 4.42$ s, $1 * 1.9 + 4 * 0.81 + 1 * 0.9 = 6.04$ s, $1 * 1.9 + 5 * 0.81 + 1 * 0.9 = 6.85$ s, and $3 * 0.81 + 1 * 0.9 = 3.33$ s. The specific data comparison is shown in Fig. 2. The receiving side, the calculation times are: $3 * 1.9 = 5.7$ s, $1 * 1.9 + 5 * 0.81 + 1 * 0.9 = 6.85$ s, $3 * 1.9 + 2 * 0.81 = 7.32$ s, and $2 * 1.9 + 2 * 0.81 + 1 * 0.9 = 6.32$ s.

For energy consumption, based on [34,35], one P, M, E operation requires 45.6 mJ, 19.44 mJ, 21.6 mJ of energy respectively. From this it is clear that XU consumes $2 * 19.44 + 1 * 45.6 + 2 * 21.6 = 106.08$ mJ, LI consumes $1 * 45.6 + 4 * 19.44 + 1 * 21.6 = 144.96$ mJ, NIU consumes $1 * 45.6 + 5 * 19.44 + 1 * 21.6 = 164.4$ mJ and ours consumes $3 * 19.44 + 1 * 21.6 = 79.92$ mJ. Let's consider the communication cost, in which we just think about the cipher text and neglect to include identities and public keys. Since we are using a curve on the binary field $\mathbb{F}_{2^{271}}$ (where G_1 is of order 252 bits prime), we can compress the size of the elements in G_1 to 34 bytes by the standard compression technique [32]. So in XU and ours, the senders need to deliver

$$|m| + 2|G_1| = \frac{|m|}{8} + 2 * 34 \text{ bytes } = \frac{|m|}{8} + 68 \text{ bytes}$$

In LI, the senders need to deliver

$$|m| + |G_1| + 2|Z_P^*| = \frac{|m|}{8} + 1 * 34 + 2 * 32 \text{ bytes } =$$

$$\frac{|m|}{8} + 98 \text{ bytes}$$

In NIU, the senders need to deliver

$$|m| + 4 * |G_1| = \frac{|m|}{8} + 4 * 34 \text{ bytes } = \frac{|m|}{8} + 136 \text{ bytes}$$

From [32], we can find out that the IIoT consumes $3 * 27 * 8 / 12400 = 0.052$ mJ to transmit one byte messages. Therefore, for each of the four schemes, XU and ours required $0.052 * (|m|/8 + 68) = 0.0065|m| + 3.536$ mJ. LI,NIU required $0.052 * (|m|/8 + 98) = 0.0065|m| + 5.096$ mJ, $0.052 * (|m|/8 + 136) = 0.0065|m| + 7.072$ mJ, respectively. The total energy consumption of XU, LI, NIU, ours are $106.08 + 0.0065|m| + 3.536 = 0.0065|m| + 109.616$ mJ, $144.96 + 0.0065|m| + 5.096 = 0.0065|m| + 150.056$ mJ, $164.4 + 0.0065|m| + 7.072 = 0.0065|m| + 171.472$ mJ, and $79.92 + 0.0065 |m| + 3.536 = 0.0065|m| + 83.456$ mJ, respectively.

In Figs. 2 and 3, the total energy consumption and computational cost are presented. From Fig. 2, we offer that our scheme is 24.6, 44.9 and 51.3% less in computation time compared to XU, LI and NIU, respectively. Let $|m| = 100$, comparing the four schemes, the energy consumption of our scheme is lower than the other schemes by $24.3, 44.6, 51.5\%$, respectively. Due to the minimal energy of sensor nodes, our CL-HSC scheme is more suitable for data transmission from IIoT.

5 Conclusion

This paper proposes a secure, effective HSC scheme that permits the sender to be in a CLC environment and still securely deliver the message to a receiver in an IBC environment. We prove that the CI-HSC scheme can be secured within the q-BDHI, q-SDH and mICDH problems of ROM. Our performance results show that the structure can be guaranteed to be reliable and efficient.

References

1. Xiong, H., Wu, Y., Jin, C., Kumari, S.: Efficient and privacy-preserving authentication protocol for heterogeneous systems in IIoT. IEEE Internet Things J. **7**(12), 11713–11724 (2020)
2. Wu, Y., Dai, H.N., Wang, H.: Convergence of blockchain and edge computing for secure and scalable IIoT critical infrastructures in industry 4.0. IEEE Internet Things J. **8**(4), 2300–2317 (2020)
3. Jayaram, A.: Lean six sigma approach for global supply chain management using industry 4.0 and IIoT. In: 2016 2nd International Conference on Contemporary Computing and Informatics (IC3I), pp. 89–94. IEEE (2016)
4. Chen, B., Wan, J., Lan, Y., Imran, M., Li, D., Guizani, N.: Improving cognitive ability of edge intelligent IIoT through machine learning. IEEE Netw. **33**(5), 61–67 (2019)
5. Ho, T.M., et al.: Next-generation wireless solutions for the smart factory, smart vehicles, the smart grid and smart cities. arXiv preprint arXiv:1907.10102 (2019)
6. Yerra, V.A., Pilla, S.: IIoT-enabled production system for composite intensive vehicle manufacturing. SAE Int. J. Engines **10**(2), 209–214 (2017)
7. Zhang, Y., Huang, X.: Security and privacy techniques for the industrial internet of things. In: Alcaraz, C. (ed.) Security and Privacy Trends in the Industrial Internet of Things. ASTSA, pp. 245–268. Springer, Cham (2019). https://doi.org/10.1007/978-3-030-12330-7_12
8. Abomhara, M., Køien, G.M.: Security and privacy in the internet of things: Current status and open issues. In: 2014 International Conference on Privacy and Security in Mobile Systems (PRISMS), pp. 1–8. IEEE (2014)
9. Kaci, A., Bouabana-Tebibel, T., Rachedi, A., Yahiaoui, C.: Toward a big data approach for indexing encrypted data in cloud computing. Secur. Priv. **2**(3), e65 (2019)
10. Kaci, A., Rachedi, A.: Toward a machine learning and software defined network approaches to manage miners' reputation in blockchain. J. Netw. Syst. Manage. **28**(3), 478–501 (2020)
11. Shamir, A.: Identity-based cryptosystems and signature schemes. In: Blakley, G.R., Chaum, D. (eds.) CRYPTO 1984. LNCS, vol. 196, pp. 47–53. Springer, Heidelberg (1985). https://doi.org/10.1007/3-540-39568-7_5

12. Al-Riyami, S.S., Paterson, K.G.: Certificateless public key cryptography. In: Laih, C.-S. (ed.) ASIACRYPT 2003. LNCS, vol. 2894, pp. 452–473. Springer, Heidelberg (2003). https://doi.org/10.1007/978-3-540-40061-5_29
13. Zhang, Z., Wong, D.S., Xu, J., Feng, D.: Certificateless public-key signature: Security model and efficient construction. In: Zhou, J., Yung, M., Bao, F. (eds.) ACNS 2006. LNCS, vol. 3989, pp. 293–308. Springer, Heidelberg (2006). https://doi.org/10.1007/11767480_20
14. Zheng, Y.: Digital signcryption or how to achieve cost(signature & encryption) << cost(signature) + cost(encryption). In: Kaliski, B.S. (ed.) CRYPTO 1997. LNCS, vol. 1294, pp. 165–179. Springer, Heidelberg (1997). https://doi.org/10.1007/BFb0052234
15. Malone-Lee, J.: Identity-based signcryption. Cryptology ePrint Archive (2002)
16. So, H.K.H., Kwok, S.H., Lam, E.Y., Lui, K.S.: Zero-configuration identity-based signcryption scheme for smart grid. In: 2010 First IEEE International Conference on Smart Grid Communications, pp. 321–326. IEEE (2010)
17. Karati, A., Islam, S.H., Biswas, G., Bhuiyan, M.Z.A., Vijayakumar, P., Karuppiah, M.: Provably secure identity-based signcryption scheme for crowdsourced industrial internet of things environments. IEEE Internet Things J. $5(4)$, 2904–2914 (2017)
18. Ashibani, Y., Mahmoud, Q.H.: An efficient and secure scheme for smart home communication using identity-based signcryption. In: 2017 IEEE 36th International Performance Computing and Communications Conference (IPCCC), pp. 1–7. IEEE (2017)
19. Li, F., Han, Y., Jin, C.: Cost-effective and anonymous access control for wireless body area networks. IEEE Syst. J. $12(1)$, 747–758 (2016)
20. Ullah, S.S., Hussain, S., Alroobaea, R., Ali, I., et al.: Securing NDN-based internet of health things through cost-effective signcryption scheme. Wirel. Commun. Mob. Comput. 2021, 1–13 (2021)
21. Li, F., Hong, J.: Efficient certificateless access control for wireless body area networks. IEEE Sens. J. $16(13)$, 5389–5396 (2016)
22. Nayak, B.: A secure id-based signcryption scheme based on elliptic curve cryptography. Int. J. Comput. Intell. Stud. $6(2-3)$, 150–156 (2017)
23. Xu, G., Dong, J., Ma, C., Liu, J., Cliff, U.G.O.: A certificateless signcryption mechanism based on blockchain for edge computing. IEEE Internet Things J. (2022). https://doi.org/10.1109/JIOT.2022.3151359
24. Sun, Y., Li, H.: Efficient signcryption between TPKC and IDPKC and its multi-receiver construction. Sci. China Inf. Sci. $53(3)$, 557–566 (2010)
25. Huang, Q., Wong, D.S., Yang, G.: Heterogeneous signcryption with key privacy. Comput. J. $54(4)$, 525–536 (2011)
26. Zhang, Y.L., Zhang, L.G., Zhang, Y.J., Wang, H., Wang, C.F.: CLPKC-to-TPKI heterogeneous signcryption scheme with anonymity. Acta Electon. Sin. $40(10)$, 2432 (2016)
27. Wang, C., Liu, C., Niu, S., Chen, L., Wang, X.: An authenticated key agreement protocol for cross-domain based on heterogeneous signcryption scheme. In: 2017 13th International Wireless Communications and Mobile Computing Conference (IWCMC), pp. 723–728. IEEE (2017)
28. Niu, S., Li, Z., Wang, C.: Privacy-preserving multi-party aggregate signcryption for heterogeneous systems. In: Sun, X., Chao, H.-C., You, X., Bertino, E. (eds.) ICCCS 2017. LNCS, vol. 10603, pp. 216–229. Springer, Cham (2017). https://doi.org/10.1007/978-3-319-68542-7_18
29. Liu, Q., Gong, B., Ning, Z.: Research on CLPKC-IDPKC cross-domain identity authentication for IOT environment. Comput. Commun. 157, 410–416 (2020)

30. Shijin, L., Tao, F., Ting, S.: Security analysis and improvement of hybrid signcryption scheme based on heterogeneous system. In: 2019 14th International Conference on Computer Science & Education (ICCSE), pp. 840–845. IEEE (2019)
31. Niu, S., Yang, X., Wang, C., Tian, M., Du, X.: Hybrid group signcryption scheme based on heterogeneous cryptosystem. J. Electron. Inf. Technol. **41**(5), 1180–1186 (2019)
32. Shim, K.A., Lee, Y.R., Park, C.M.: Eibas: An efficient identity-based broadcast authentication scheme in wireless sensor networks. Ad Hoc Netw. **11**(1), 182–189 (2013)
33. Gura, N., Patel, A., Wander, A., Eberle, H., Shantz, S.C.: Comparing elliptic curve cryptography and RSA on 8-bit CPUs. In: Joye, M., Quisquater, J.-J. (eds.) CHES 2004. LNCS, vol. 3156, pp. 119–132. Springer, Heidelberg (2004). https://doi.org/10.1007/978-3-540-28632-5_9
34. Shim, K.A.: S2drp: Secure implementations of distributed reprogramming protocol for wireless sensor networks. Ad Hoc Netw. **19**, 1–8 (2014)
35. Ma, C., Xue, K., Hong, P.: Distributed access control with adaptive privacy preserving property for wireless sensor networks. Secur. Commun. Netw. **7**(4), 759–773 (2014)

A Federated Learning Based Privacy-Preserving Data Sharing Scheme for Internet of Vehicles

Yangpeng Wang, Ling Xiong$^{(\boxtimes)}$, Xianhua Niu, Yunxiang Wang,
and Dexin Liang

School of Computer and Software Engineering, Xihua University, Chengdu, China
lingdonghua99@163.com

Abstract. The data analysis in the process of vehicle collaboration for the Internet of Vehicles (IoV) environment improves the driving experience and service quality. However, the privacy issue is becoming one of the problems of obstructing the development of data sharing among vehicles. To overcome the disadvantage, in this work, we propose a privacy-preserving data sharing scheme based on federated learning by the collaboration of participants, which can resist gradient leakage, poisoning attacks, etc. Firstly, the gradient data is encrypted by random masking to protect the privacy of training data. Then, the Pearson correlation coefficient is utilized to distinguish the correctness of the model parameters uploaded from the vehicle at uplink. Finally, the proposed scheme can verify the correctness of the global model distributed from AS at downlink using the Lagrange interpolation The experimental results show that the proposed privacy-preserving data sharing scheme provides higher learning accuracy by eliminating malicious gradients.

Keywords: Federated learning · Privacy-preserving · IoV · Data sharing

1 Introduction

With the rapid development of intelligent transportation system, new computing methods have been widely deployed on Internet of Vehicles. In particular, the integration of IoV and artificial intelligence has led to a trend of sharing data among vehicles and infrastructure. The shared data usually includes trajectories, surrounding information and operation information, etc. To improve the driving experience and service quality, vehicles could utilize the shared data. For example, vehicles could generate a region traffic flow model according to the shared data. However, in the process of sharing data, the data privacy of the vehicles will be damaged, which may lead to serious consequences.

In the privacy-sensitive scenario of the IoV, to avoid privacy disclosure caused by sharing data, the federated learning(FL) [1,2] mechanism is applied to the

Supported by the National Natural Science Foundation of China (No. 62171387, No.62202390).

E. Ahene and F. Li (Eds.): FCS 2022, CCIS 1726, pp. 18–33, 2022.
https://doi.org/10.1007/978-981-19-8445-7_2

IoV. The existing achievements [3–5] have well implemented the scheme that the vehicle privacy data is not sent directly in the public channel. However, as previous work [6] had shown that, the private information of vehicle can also be leaked from the gradient. Considering such security vulnerabilities, if a aggregation server and other entities obtain sufficient gradients, the privacy data(e.g. vehicle position information and trajectories information) of participants will be seriously threatened. Another concern is that the gradient may come from malicious participants. On the one hand, the malicious vehicles upload incorrect gradients to lead to a decline in the accuracy of the model, and even make the final global model unavailable. On the other hand, the AS may forge the aggregation model parameters, if the participant cannot recognize the modified global model, the entire FL process will be destroyed, even leading to a serious threat to traffic safety.

In this paper, we address the data privacy leakage issue by integrating federated learning into IoV, on this basis, we use masks to encrypt the model gradient and remove the incorrect gradients without knowing the gradient. Finally we verify the correctness of the global model. The contributions of the paper can be summarized as follows.

- The proposed scheme divides the vehicles into multiple groups containing an appropriate number of vehicles, and vehicles in the same group use the negotiated mask to encrypt the model gradient. Moreover, secret share is adopt to recover the mask of leaved vehicles.
- The proposed scheme distinguishs the correctness of gradients by using the Pearson correlation coefficient when receiving the uploaded gradients from vehicle. Then the Lagrange interpolation is adopted to verify the global aggregation result at the downlink from AS to RSU.
- The convolution neural network (CNN) with the MNIST dataset is uesed to evaluate the performance of the proposed scheme. The experimental results demonstrate that the proposed scheme shows a higher accuracy with the acceptable overhead for the FL participants.

The remainder of the paper is organized as follows. Section 2 presents related work and Sect. 3 presents background knowledge include the system model, cryptography primitives and federated learning. Section 4 introduces the mechanism details. Analysis including correctness, privacy and performance evaluation are presented in Sect. 5. Section 6 concludes the paper.

2 Related Work

In recent years, given the rising popularity of IoV [7–10], the data privacy of vehicles has increasingly become the focus of attention. Several studies have been proposed to solve related issues.

Traditional privacy protection schemes mainly combined cryptography to encrypt or hide the collected data and send it to the center. Hui Li et al. [11] designed an Architecture for identity and location privacy protection in

VANET base on k-anonymity and dynamic threshold encryption. Han et al. [12] designed a vehicle privacy-preserving algorithm based on a local differential privacy to minimize the possibility of exposing the regional semantic privacy of the k-location set. Ma et al. [13] performed homomorphic encryption on the sensitive part of the data and keep the ciphertext at the blockchain to preserve IoV data privacy. Zhang et al. [14] encrypted traffic flow data by BGN homomorphic encryption to protect the travel direction when arriving at T-junctions or crossroads.

Although these approaches do solve the issue of data privacy to a certain extent, still have two issues: (1) based on differential privacy, the noise will affect the availability of data. Based on homomorphic encryption, the computational overhead is not suitable in IoV. (2) a large amount of collected data needs to be sent, which will lead to the potential threat of leaking sensitive data and high network bandwidth usage.

FL, as a distributed artificial intelligence approach, allows participant trains local models on local privacy database and then the center aggregates the local model to construct a global model. Compared with traditional privacy protection schemes, FL could enhance communication efficiency and privacy preservation [15]. Lu et al. [16] designed a secure data sharing scheme based on asynchronous FL and blockchain, which could improve efficiency. A hierarchical FL algorithm with a multi-leader and multi-player game for knowledge sharing is proposed in [17]. Wu et al. [18] proposed a Traffic-Aware FL framework to enhance motion control of vehicles. Although the above FL-based schemes avoid directly uploading a large amount of privacy data, the uploaded gradient is not protected, and the privacy data is still likely to be exposed [6].

To prevent the leaking of privacy from the gradient, some studies are proposed. Phong et al. [19] bridged deep learning and homomorphic encryption to ensure that the server can not get user privacy and the accuracy is kept intact. Liu et al. [20] presented a privacy-enhanced FL (PEFL) framework by using homomorphic encryption, in process of FL, In the whole process, the gradient is only processed in the form of ciphertext. Although homomorphic encryption is useful for privacy-preserving, it is not suitable for IoV as the time cost. The scheme of adding mask to gradient was proposed in [21], two types of masks would be added in gradient, the participant only reply one mask recover request from the center, which Effectively protects privacy gradient. Further, a more efficient scheme [22] based on [21] is proposed, which only needs logarithmic overhead. To verify global aggregation result in FL, Fu et al. [23] designed a verifiable FL scheme by using Lagrange interpolation. Guo et al. [24] proposed a verifiable aggregation scheme for FL by using Linear homomorphic hash and Cryptographic commitment. To achieve the privacy-preserving, we propose a privacy-enhanced federated learning scheme based on gradient encryption by the mask.

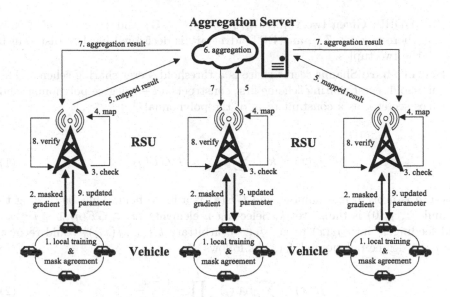

Fig. 1. Proposed Federated Learning Framework in IoV

3 Preliminaries

3.1 System Model

As shown in Fig. 1, the proposed scheme consists of some vehicles, some Roadside Units(RSUs) and one Aggregation Server(AS).

The vehicle executes federated learning to generate the local gradient on local privacy data set. During the whole process, the vehicle transmits the gradient instead of privacy data. RSU is a kind of wireless infrastructure, as relay node, RSU is responsible for organizing vehicles to execute the mask agreement and checking the correctness of received model parameters. AS is responsible for constructing a global model. In the proposed scheme, AS may return forged global model parameters to other participants.

3.2 Cryptography Block

- **Hard problem** Let $\mathbb{G}$ denotes a cyclic group, $g \in \mathbb{G}$ denotes a generator of group $\mathbb{G}$, and q is the prime order of group $\mathbb{G}$. Then the computational hard problems named Discrete Logarithm Problem (DLP), Decisional Diffie Hellman Problem (DDHP),Computational Diffie-Hellman Problem(CDHP) can be described as follows.
  - (1) DLP: Given one tuple {P, Q}$(P, Q \in \mathbb{G})$, where $Q = P^x$, $x \in \mathbb{Z}_q^*$, the advantage for any probabilistic polynomial time (PPT) adversary to calculate x is negligible.
  - (2) CDHP: Given one tuple $\{g, g^x, g^y \in \mathbb{G}\}$, where $x, y \in \mathbb{Z}_q^*$, the advantage for any PPT adversary to calculate $g^{xy} \in \mathbb{G}$ is negligible.

(3) DDHP: Given two tuples $\{g, g^x, g^y, g^{xy} \in \mathbb{G}\}$ and $\{g, g^x, g^y, g^z \in \mathbb{G}\}$, where $x, y, z \in \mathbb{Z}_q^*$, any PPT adversary is decisional hard to distinguish the two tuples.

- **Secret share** Shamir secret share is a threshold secret sharing scheme. The threshold secret sharing scheme first constructs a $t-1$ degree polynomial and takes secret k as a constant term of the polynomial

$$f_k(x) = k + \sum_{j=1}^{t-1} a_j x^j, a_j \in GF(q) \tag{1}$$

where q is a big prime number and $GF(*)$ is a finite field. Thus, according to formula 1, $f_k(0)$ is the secret k. Selecting n elements $\{x_i \in GF(q), 1 \leq i \leq n\}$ and feeding x_i into $f_k(x)$ to get $f_k(x_i)$, arbitrary t $\{(x_i, f(x_i))\}$ could recover the $t-1$ degree polynomial $f_k(x)$ as follows

$$f_k(x) = \sum_{i=1}^{t} f_k(x_i) \prod_{j=1, j \neq i}^{t} \frac{x - x_i}{x_i - x_j} \tag{2}$$

Therefore, secret k is secure if malicious participants can not obtain t or more sub-secrets $\{x_i, f_k(x_i)\}$.

3.3 Federated Learning

We leverage federated learning to protect the privacy data of vehicle. Assume there are N vehicles in proposed scheme, Vehicle $v_i(0 \leq i \leq N-1)$ participates in the FL and cooperatively trains a model $\mathcal{M}$ on private data set $D_i = \{(x_j, y_j), 0 \leq j \leq d_i - 1\}$, where d_i is the size of D_i A loss function quantifies the difference between estimated values and real values of samples in D_i, defined as follows:

$$E_i(\mathcal{M}) = \frac{1}{d_i} \sum_{j=0}^{d-1} L(\mathcal{M}, x_j, y_j) \tag{3}$$

where $L(\mathcal{M}, x_j, y_j)$ is the loss function on data sample (x_j, y_j), and y_j is the label of x_j. The global loss function $E(\mathcal{M})$ could be calculated.

$$E(\mathcal{M}) = \frac{1}{N} \sum_{i=0}^{N-1} E_i(\mathcal{M}) \tag{4}$$

In FL, each vehicle trains the model on the training set by a back propagation algorithm, and gets the private gradient $\omega_i = \frac{\partial E_i}{\partial \mathcal{M}}$. Vehicles and RSUs synchronously upload gradients to the AS to aggregate. Then AS returns the result to RSUs, vehicles download the result.

4   The Proposed Scheme

We assume that most vehicles are honest, but a small number of malicious gradients generated by malicious vehicles will still affect the aggregation results of FL. In the proposed scheme, RSUs could check the correctness of gradients uploaded by local region vehicles and eliminate malicious gradients. AS may forge global aggregation result, to verify the correctness of the global aggregation result, RSUs would perform the Lagrange interpolation function on the local region gradients. RSUs are regarded as honest participants, but during the whole process, all RSUs also can not learn vehicles' privacy data and gradients. The CA is used to generate public parameters for the registered vehicles and RSUs. The vehicle generates a private-public key pair which are used for negotiating masks respectively, the RSU generates a private-public key pair which is used for negotiating a common integer sequence as the Lagrange interpolation function points.

4.1   Initialization

In this phase, CA initializes all necessary system parameters and publishs the parameters to participants. RSU calculates common sequence as the necessity of verifying global parameter.

Algorithm 1: sequence generation algorithm

   Result: Three integer sequences $SeqA, SeqB, SeqS$

1   Initialization: $R - RSU_0, RSU_1, \cdots, RSU_{K-1}$;

2   **for** $RSU_i = RSU_0 \rightarrow RSU_{K-1}$ **do**

3      $r_i \leftarrow$ random select integer in Z_q ;

4   broadcast $Z_i = g^{r_i}$ to R/RSU_i ;

5   calculate $X_i = (\frac{Z_{i+1}}{Z_{i-1}})^{r_i}$;

6   broadcast X_i to R/RSU_i ;

7   calculate $ComKey = (Z_{i-1})^{nr_i} \cdot X_i^{n-1} \cdot X_{i+1}^{n-2} \cdots X_{i-2}$;

8   broadcast $t_i = Enc(ComKey, 1)$ to R/RSU_i ;

9      $T = \{t_0, t_1, \cdots, t_{K-1}\}/\{t_i\}$;

10   **for** $t \in T$ **do**

11   **if** $Dec(ComKey, t)$!= 1 **then**

12   abort

13   **end**

14   **end**

15      $SeqA, SeqB, SeqS = h1(ComKey||1), h1(ComKey||2), h2(ComKey||3)$;

16      $h1(*)$ or $h2(*)$: map $*$ to a integer sequence

17 **end**

The CA generates a cyclic group $\mathbb{G}$ with prime order q, chooses randomly a group generator g as a public parameter which is used for calculating vehicles' agreement key and RSUs' public key. The CA also generates $m+1$ positive integer $P = \{p, p_1, p_2, \cdots, p_m\}$, where $gcd(p_i, p_j) = 1, (i \neq j), 1 \leq i, j \leq m$ and p is large enough. Vehicles and RSUs receive public parameters $PP = \{\mathbb{G}, q, g, P\}$ to generate a private-public key, for example, vehicle v_i chooses $SK_i \in \mathbb{Z}_q^*$ and calculates $PK_{z,i} = g^{SK_i}$, RSU gets the private-public pair with the same operations with vehicle.

RSUs should calculate three common sequences $SeqA$, $SeqB$ and $SeqS$ as Algorithm 1 which are confidential to other entities to achieve the verifiability of the aggregated result from AS. Let $R = \{RSU_0, RSU_1, \cdots, RSU_{K-1}\}$,

---

Algorithm 2: FL algorithm

Output: global modelω

1 Initialization $groups = \{g_0, g_1, \cdots, g_{n_g-1}\}$ in each RSU ;
2 $\qquad\qquad R = \{RSU_0, RSU_1, \cdots, RSU_{K-1}\}$;
3 **for** *each local epoch* **do**
4 $\quad$ **for** *group $\in$ groups in parallel* **do**
5 $\qquad$ **for** *$v_i \in$ group in parallel* **do**
6 $\qquad\quad$ learning local model $\omega_i = \omega_i - \alpha \cdot \nabla E_i(\mathcal{M}, x, y)$;
7 $\qquad\quad$ upload $\omega_{k,z,i}^{(M)} = \omega_i + m_{k,z,i}^{(R)} + m_i^{(V)}$ to RSU_k ;
8 $\qquad$ **end**
9 $\quad$ **end**
10 $\quad$ **for** *each $RSU_k \in R$* **do**
11 $\qquad$ $\{\omega_k\} \leftarrow$ eliminate incorrect gradients ;
12 $\qquad$ upoad CRT(*) $\leftarrow$ Lagrange Interpolation on ω_k ;
13 $\quad$ **end**
14 $\quad$ distribute $\omega^{(G)} \leftarrow$ AS aggregates CRT(*) from RSUs ;
15 $\quad$ $\omega^{(G')} \leftarrow$ RSU calculates real model parameter from $\omega^{(G)}$;
16 $\quad$ return $\omega^{(G')}$ to vehicles ;
17 **end**

4.2 Gradient Encryption

- **Mask agreement.** In the proposed scheme, for any RSU_k, $0 \leq k \leq K - 1$, we divide the vehicles in the RSU area into multiple groups, each group contains $h = \frac{N_k}{n_k}$ vehicles, where N_k is the number of vehicles in RSU_k and n_k is the number of the groups in RSU_k. In a group, every vehicle negotiates mask with the neighbor vehicles. To describe the mask agreement process, we denote the vehicles that have joined the mask agreement process as ordered sequence $\{v_0, v_1, \cdots, v_{h-1}\}$ in every group. In followed phases, we introduce the agreement process.

Vehicle $v_i(0 \leq i \leq h - 1)$ in group $g_z(0 \leq z \leq n_k - 1)$ sends $PK_{z,i}$ to RSU_k when enters the communication range of RSU_k. RSU_k transmits all other public keys to a vehicle v_i to execute the secret share in the group. Once a group is generated, then calculates the first mask code(FMC) $m_{k,z,i}^{(R)}$ between RSU_k and vehicle v_i as follows:

$$m_{k,z,i}^{(R)} = Hash(PK_{z,i}^{SK_k})$$ (5)

where $Hash(*)$ is the function that map $*$ to a integer sequence with the same size as $|\omega|$.

Then RSU_k sends $\{PK_k||PK_{z,<i+1>}||c_{i,<i+1>}||PK_{z,<i-1>}||c_{i,<i-1>}||\{PK_u\}\}$ to $\{v_i, |i = 0, 1, \cdots, h - 1\}$, where $< \cdot > = \cdot \pmod{h}$, $c_{i,<\cdot>} = -c_{<\cdot>,i}$, $\{PK_u\}$ is a set include other participants' information exclude $PK_{z,<i+1>}$ and $PK_{z,<i-1>}$.

After receiving message, vehicle v_i calculates FMC $m_{k,z,i}^{(R)} = Hash(PK_k^{SK_{z,i}})$, and calculates $k_1 = PK_{z,<i+1>}^{SK_{z,i}}$ and $k_2 = PK_{z,<i-1>}^{SK_{z,i}}$. To calculate second mask code(SMC), vehicle v_i executes $m_{i,<i+1>}^{(V)} = Hash(k_1)$ and $m_{i,<i-1>}^{(V)} = Hash(k_2)$, SMC could be calculated as follows.

$$m_i^{(V)} = c_{i,<i+1>} \cdot m_{i,<i+1>}^{(V)} + c_{i,<i-1>} \cdot m_{i,<i-1>}^{(V)}$$ (6)

Notice that both $m_i^{(V)}$ and $m_{k,z,i}^{(R)}$ would be added to the gradient to ensure the confidentiality of the gradient.

Vehicle v_i executes secret share to share k_1 and k_2 with the vehicle v_j, $j = 0, 1, \cdots, h - 1$. In the proposed scheme, the Shamir algorithm is used for secret share. Vehicle v_i constructs two polynomials $f_{k_1}(x)$ and $f_{k_2}(x)$ as formula 1 and generates sub-secret $s_j = \{f_{k_1}(x_j)||f_{k_2}(x_j)||x_j\}$ for vehicle v_j. Then v_i encrypts sub-secrets

$$s_{i,j} = Enc(PK_j, s_j)$$

where $Enc(\cdot, *)$ is the encryption function such as RSA, $\cdot$ and $*$ are the public key and the plaintext. Vehicle v_i sends $s_{i,j}$ to RSU_k for forwarding to vehicle v_j.

- **Local training.** The local training is implemented with distributed gradient descent. In the training process, we iteratively improve the accuracy of model $\mathcal{M}$ by minimizing the global loss function 4.

For every vehicle in IoV, the goal of training the model is to find the gradient to update $\mathcal{M}$ for minimizing the value of the loss function 3.

Vehicle $v_i(0 \leq i \leq h-1)$ in $RSU_k(0 \leq k \leq K-1)$ calculates $\omega_i = \frac{\partial E_i}{\partial \mathcal{M}}$, where ω_i is a vector with dimension $d = |\omega_i|$. Then vehicle v_i masks ω_i as follows:

$$\omega_{k,z,i}^{(M)} = \omega_i + m_i^{(V)} + m_{k,z,i}^{(R)}$$ (7)

4.3   Region Verification

The difference between the malicious gradient and correct gradient is perceptible. Actually, the low similarity with the correct gradients means that the gradient is malicious with high probability. So the Pearson correlation coefficient between gradients could be calculated to make a distinction between the correct gradients and the malicious gradients. Pearson correlation coefficient is defined as follows:

$$\rho_{XY} = \frac{Cov(X,Y)}{\sigma(X)\sigma(Y)} \tag{8}$$

where $Cov(X,Y)$ is covariance between random variables X and Y, $\sigma()$ is the standard deviation.

- **Verification** $RSU_k(0 \le k \le K-1)$ calculates the gradients sum of group $g_z(0 \le z \le n_k - 1)$ if all vehicles upload masked gradients. And we set

$$\omega_{k,z} = \sum_{i=0}^{h-1} \omega_{k,z,i}^{(M)} - m_{k,z,i}^{(R)} \tag{9}$$

If a vehicle (suppose v_i) leaves RSU_k's communication range, because of the lack of $\omega_{k,i}^{(M)}$, the sum of the gradients could not be recovered. To eliminate the mask, RSU_k sends a recover request to the rest vehicles in the group to get v_i's sub-secrets. The rest vehicle $v_j(0 \le j \le h-1, j \ne i)$ sends $dc_{i,j} = Dec(SK_j, s_{i,j})$ to RSU_k, where $Dec(\cdot, *)$ is decryption algorithm corresponding to encryption algorithm $Enc(\cdot, *)$. After receiving enough sub-secrets, RSU_k extracts $\{x_j, f_{k_1}(x_j), f_{k_2}(x_j)\}$ from $dc_{i,j}$ and executes formula 2 to get k_1 and k_2, further RSU_k calculates $m_{i,i+1}^{(V)} = Hash(k_1)$ and $m_{i,i-1}^{(V)} = Hash(k_2)$ to get the SMC of v_i as formula 6. Then RSU_k adds the recovered SMC to uploaded gradients to eliminate masks as follows.

$$\omega_{k,z,i} = \sum_{c=0, c \ne i}^{h-1} (\omega_{k,z,c}^{(M)} - m_{k,z,c}^{(R)}) + m_i^{(V)} \tag{10}$$

Note that, the value of $\omega_{k,z,i}$ is the gradients sum $\omega_{k,z}$ of group g_z, the RSU can not attain the specific gradients when recovering the SMC.

To calculate the Pearson correlation coefficient, the gradients coordinate-wise medians $(\bar{\omega}_k)(0 \le k \le K-1)$ should be calculated as the benchmark.

$$\bar{\omega}_k = \frac{1}{n_k} \sum_{r=0}^{n_k - 1} \omega_{k,r}$$

RSU_k randomly selects $X = \omega_{k,x}$ and $Y = \omega_{k,y}(0 \le x, y \le n_g - 1)$, and calculates ρ_{XY} according to $\bar{\omega}_k$ and formula 8. RSU_k discards $\omega_{k,x}$ if $\rho_{XY} \le l$, where l is the limiting value of correlation coefficient, The number of rest gradients sum is $n_{k,re}$. Then RSU_k broadcasts $n_{k,re}$ to R. Before uploading gradients to AS, RSU_k will process the gradients sum with Lagrange interpolation.

- **Interpolation** RSU_k would convert the sum of gradients $\omega_k = \sum_{r=0}^{n_{k,re}-1} \omega_{k,r}$ from float number to finite field as follows:

$$\omega_k = \begin{cases} \lfloor \lambda \cdot \omega_k \rceil, & \lfloor \lambda \cdot \omega_k \rceil \geq 0 \\ p + \lfloor \lambda \cdot \omega_k \rceil, & \lfloor \lambda \cdot \omega_k \rceil < 0 \end{cases}$$

where $\lfloor * \rceil$ is the rounding method, λ is a large integer (i.e. 10^6) used to control accuracy. And in this phase, the data uploaded by RSU_k to AS is not gradients, but the Lagrange function results. First, RSU_k randomly selects $m - 1$ arrays $U_k = \{u_{k,i}, | i = 1, 2, \cdots, m - 1\}$ that satisfies that the sum of U_k is equql to ω_k, note that, each element in U_k is an array with the dimension d. RSU_k has parameters $SeqS = [s_0, s_1, \cdots, s_{d-1}]$ and $SeqA = [a_0, a_1, \cdots, a_{m-1}]$, according to $(U_k, SeqA, SeqS)$, we have points $P_j = \{(a_i, u_{k,i,j}), | i \in \{0, 1, \cdots, m - 2\}\} \cup \{(a_{m-1}, s_j)\}$, where $u_{k,i,j}$ is the j-th element in $u_{k,i}$. Therefore Lagrange interpolation function could be executed on P_j to generate $m - 1$ degree polynomial $F_{k,j}(x)$ as formula 2. RSU_k sends $Pack_{k,j} = CRT[F_{k,j}(b_0), \cdots, F_{k,j}(b_{m-1})]$ on $SeqB = [b_0, b_1, \cdots, b_{m-1}]$, where CRT is the Chinese remainder theorem as [23].

4.4 Aggregation and Update

After receiving $\{(Pack_{k,0}, \cdots, Pack_{k,d-1}), | k = 0, 1, \cdots, K - 1\}$, AS executes aggregation as follows:

$$\omega^{(G)} = (\sum_{k=0}^{K-1} Pack_{k,0}, \sum_{k=0}^{K-1} Pack_{k,1}, \cdots, \sum_{k=0}^{K-1} Pack_{k,d-1})$$

Because AS does not know the x-coordinate $SeqA$ and $SeqB$ corresponding to packaged function values $Pack_{k,*}$, AS couldn't forge an aggregation result that can be verified successfully by RSU. Then AS distributes $\omega^{(G)}$ to each RSU. After receiving $\omega^{(G)}$ from AS and $n_{re} = \sum_{i=0}^{K-1} n_{i,re}$ from other RSUs, to verify $\omega^{(G)}$, For any $j = 0, 1, \cdots, d - 1$, RSU_k should unpack $\omega^{(G)}$ as follows:

$$F_j(b_i) \equiv \sum_{k=0}^{K-1} Pack_{k,j} \pmod{p_i}$$

As mentioned before, there are points $\{(b_0, F_j(b_0)), \cdots, (b_{m-1}, F_j(b_{m-1}))\}$, RSU_k applies the Lagrange interpolation to calculate corresponded function expression $F_j(x)$. Then RSU_k calculates $F_j(a_{m-1})$, the aggregation result is correct if $K \cdot s_j = F_j(a_{m-1})$ holds. Next, RSU_k calculates aggregation gradient as follows:

$$\omega^{(G')} = (C(\sum_{c=0}^{m-2} F_1(a_c)), C(\sum_{c=0}^{m-2} F_2(a_c)), \cdots, C(\sum_{c=0}^{m-2} F_d(a_c)))$$

where

$$C(x) = \begin{cases} x, & x \in [0, \dfrac{p-1}{2}) \\ x - p, & x \in [\dfrac{p-1}{2}, p) \end{cases} \tag{11}$$

Then RSU_k sends global model parameters $\omega^{(G')}$ and n_{re} to each vehicle in communication region. The vehicle updates the local model as follows:

$$\mathcal{M} = \mathcal{M} - \alpha \frac{\omega^{(G')}}{n_{re}} \tag{12}$$

where α is the learning rate. Then vehicles iteratively perform local training until global model $\mathcal{M}$ is available. The proposed FL algorithm is illustrated in Algorithm 2.

5   Analysis

5.1   Correctness and Privacy

The masks FMC and SMC are added into the gradient, after receiving the masked gradient, RSU performs formula 9 to get the sum of gradients. For any group r in RSU_k the correctness of the formula is as follows.

$$
\begin{aligned}
\omega_{k,r} &= \sum_{i=0}^{h-1} \omega_{k,r,i}^{(M)} - m_{k,r,i}^{(R)} \\
&= \sum_{i=0}^{h-1} \omega_i + c_{i,i+1} \cdot m_{i,i+1}^{(V)} + c_{i,i-1} \cdot m_{i,i-1}^{(V)} \\
&= \sum_{i=0}^{h-1} \omega_i
\end{aligned}
$$

If the vehicle $v_i (0 \le i \le h-1)$ leaves, RSU performs formula 10, and the correctness of the formula is as follows.

$$
\begin{aligned}
\omega_{k,r} &= \sum_{j=0, j \ne i}^{h-1} (\omega_{k,r,j}^{(M)} - m_{k,r,j}^{(R)}) + m_i^{(V)} \\
&= \sum_{j=0}^{h-1} \omega_{k,r,j}^{(M)} - \sum_{j=0}^{h-1} m_{k,r,j}^{(R)} - \omega_{k,r,i}^{(M)} + m_{k,z,i}^{(R)} + m_i^{(V)} \\
&= \sum_{j=0, j \ne i}^{h-1} \omega_j
\end{aligned}
$$

In the proposed scheme, to achieve the privacy-preserving of vehicle's data, we adopt FL to keep raw privacy data locally, Furthermore, the mask is used to protect gradients.

We combine h vehicles $\{v_0, v_1, \cdots, v_{h-1}\}$ to form a group. If the vehicle only masks uploaded gradients ω_i with SMC $m_i^{(V)}$, the vehicle's privacy gradient may leak. Because the vehicle may be curious about neighbor vehicle's privacy gradient, especially if the two side neighbors of a vehicle conspire, the SMC may be eliminated. To address the problem of gradient leakage caused by neighbor vehicles collusion, We add FMC $m_{k,z,i}^{(R)}$ and SMC $m_i^{(V)}$ to the gradient. The FMC is only known between RSU and vehicle, so malicious neighbor vehicles can not get v_i's privacy gradient without knowing the FMC. In the meantime, we also avoid the RSU from knowing the specific gradient of the vehicle by adding the SMC, so the RSU only knows the sum of h vehicles' gradients. As mentioned above, the privacy gradient is only known by itself. And according to the computational or decisional hard problems mentioned before, it is difficult to calculate the FMC and SMC without knowing corresponding private key. hence, during the whole FL process, the privacy data and gradient of the vehicle will not be leaked.

5.2 Performance

In this section, we give the performance analysis of our proposed scheme. Our simulation experiment is conducted on Intel(R) Core(TM) i7-10875H,2.30GHz and 16 GB memory.

- **Performance of RSUs setup and agreement** RSUs should perform Lagrange interpolation with some points, RSUs' common sequence is regarded as the x-coordinate only known by itself. In the experiment, we use the JPBC library in Java JDK8 to execute the Algorithm 1.

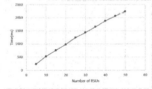 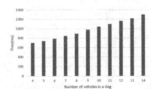 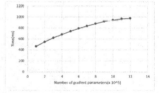

Fig. 2. The sequence generation overhead of RSU

Fig. 3. The mask agreement overhead of vehicle

Fig. 4. the mask agreement overhead with different number of gradient parameter

We measure the computing overhead of our proposed algorithm under different number of RSUs. The computation overhead is shown in Fig. 2, with the number of RSU increasing, the overhead increases linearly. The frequency of RSU updating the common sequence can maintain at a low value, in the condition, the cost of calculating common sequences is acceptable. Next we measure the cost of agreement phase, we set $h = 4, 5, \cdots, 14$ and fix gradient length10^6. The computational overhead is shown in Fig. 3. With the number of gradients increasing, the computational overhead increases approximately linearly. A vehicle shares secrets K_1, K_2 with the vehicles within the group, the share operation cost is low as the number of vehicles in a group is small. And the most time-consuming operation at this phase is to calculate the masks as the length of the gradient is generally the time of 10^5. Meanwhile, We set the number of CNN model parameters from 10^5 to $12 * 10^5$ and set $h = 9$. The computational overhead of different length of gradient as Fig. 4. The computational overhead increases approximately linearly with the increase of gradient length.

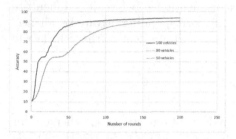

Fig. 5. The accuracy with various numbers of vehicles

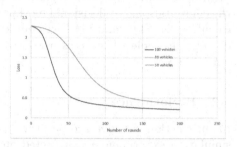

Fig. 6. The loss with various numbers of vehicels

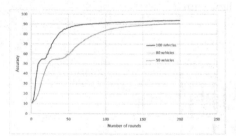

Fig. 7. The accuracy in various numbers of groups with low correlation coefficient

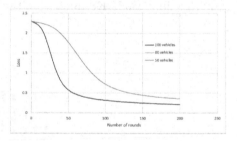

Fig. 8. The loss in various numbers of groups with low correlation coefficient

- **Performance of FL** We use the MNIST dataset to evaluate the proposed scheme. We divided the dataset into $50, 80, 100$ parts and assigned them to $50, 80, 100$ vehicles, and the number of vehicles in a group is $h = 5$, that is, $10, 16, 20$ groups would join in FL. Each vehicle executes the local train with a splited dataset. The Convolutional Neural Network (CNN) is used in the training process. The result of accuracy and loss are shown in Figs. 5 and 6. We set a various number of vehicles and 0 low correlation group, 100 vehicles that joined FL could provide the highest accuracy and the lowest loss, 50 and 80 vehicles could achieve almost the same accuracy and loss. The proposed scheme could achieve a satisfactory result with no malicious vehicles.

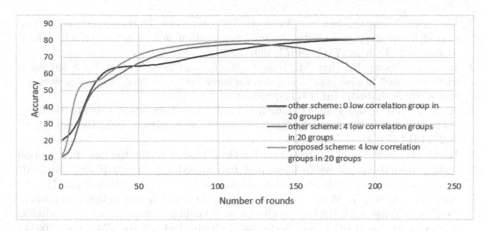

Fig. 9. The performance with malicious gradient between scheme [23] and the proposed scheme

To measure the result with the malicious vehicles joined, we execute FL with 100 data providers(20 groups) with different proportions of low correlation groups. The result of accuracy and loss are shown in Figs. 7 and 8. The accuracy has a reduction and the loss is not as good as Fig. 6. And as shonw in Fig. 9, compared with [23], we have better performance in the presence of malicious vehicles.

6   Conclusion

In this paper, we propose the privacy-preserving FL scheme. The proposed scheme addresses the vehicle data privacy and gradient privacy, and the malicious participants' gradient could be removed at RSU by calculating the Pearson correlation coefficient. Meanwhile, we use Lagrange interpolation to verify the correctness of the returned result from AS. To reduce the overhead, We form a small number of vehicles as a group to negotiate the mask. Numerical results confirm the effectiveness of our proposed scheme in terms of accuracy. In future work, we plan to reduce data waste in the process of eliminating malicious gradients.

References

1. Konecny, J., McMahan, H.B., Yu, F.X., Richtarik, P., Suresh, A.T., Bacon, D.: Federated learning: Strategies for improving communication efficiency. In: NIPS Workshop on Private Multi-Party Machine Learning (2016)
2. Reisizadeh, A., Mokhtari, A., Hassani, H., Jadbabaie, A., Pedarsani, R.: Fedpaq: A communication-efficient federated learning method with periodic averaging and quantization. In: International Conference on Artificial Intelligence and Statistics, pp. 2021–2031 (2020)

3. Liang, F., Yang, Q., Liu, R., Wang, J., Sato, K., Guo, J.: Semi-synchronous federated learning protocol with dynamic aggregation in internet of vehicles. IEEE Trans. Veh. Technol. **71**(5), 4677–4691 (2022)
4. Kong, X., Wang, K., Hou, M., Hao, X., Shen, G., Chen, X., Xia, F.: A federated learning-based license plate recognition scheme for 5g-enabled internet of vehicles. IEEE Trans. Industr. Inf. **17**(12), 8523–8530 (2021)
5. Ayaz, F., Sheng, Z., Tian, D., Guan, Y.L.: A blockchain based federated learning for message dissemination in vehicular networks. IEEE Trans. Veh. Technol. **71**(2), 1927–1940 (2022)
6. Hitaj, B., Ateniese, G., Perez-Cruz, F.: Deep models under the gan: Information leakage from collaborative deep learning. In: Proceedings of the 2017 ACM SIGSAC Conference on Computer and Communications Security, pp. 603–618 (2017)
7. Xiong, L., Xiong, N., Wang, C., Yu, X., Shuai, M.: An efficient lightweight authentication scheme with daptive resilience of asynchronization attacks for wireless sensor networks. IEEE Trans. Syst. Man Cybern. Syst. **51**(9), 5626–5638 (2021)
8. Xiong, L., Li, G., He, M., Liu, Z., Peng, T.: An efficient privacy-aware authentication scheme with hierarchical access control for mobile cloud computing services. IEEE Trans. Cloud Comput. (2020). https://doi.org/10.1109/TCC.2020.3029878
9. Gong, C., Xiong, L., He, X., Niu, X.: Blockchain-based conditional privacy-preserving authentication scheme for vehicular ad hoc networks. J. Ambient. Intell. Humaniz. Comput. **2022**, 1–14 (2022)
10. Shuai, M., Xiong, L., Wang, C., Yu, N.: A secure authentication scheme with forward secrecy for industrial internet of things using Rabin cryptosystem. Comput. Commun. **16**(1), 215–227 (2020)
11. Li, H., Pei, L., Liao, D., Sun, G., Xu, D.: Blockchain meets vanet: An architecture for identity and location privacy protection in vanet. Peer-to-Peer Netw. Appl. **12**(5), 1178–1193 (2019)
12. Han, W., Cheng, M., Lei, M., Xu, H., Qian, L.: Privacy protection algorithm for the internet of vehicles based on local differential privacy and game model. Comput. Mater. Continua **64**(2), 1025–1038 (2020)
13. Ma, Z., Wang, L., Zhao, W.: Blockchain-driven trusted data sharing with privacy protection in iot sensor network. IEEE Sens. J. **21**(22), 25472–25479 (2021)
14. Zhang, C., Zhu, L., Ni, J., Huang, C., Shen, X.: Verifiable and privacy-preserving traffic flow statistics for advanced traffic management systems. IEEE Trans. Veh. Technol. **69**(9), 10336–10347 (2020)
15. Tan, K., Bremner, D., Kernec, J.L., Imran, M.: Federated machine learning in vehicular networks: A summary of recent applications. In: 2020 International Conference on UK-China Emerging Technologies (UCET), pp. 1–4 (2020)
16. Lu, Y., Huang, X., Zhang, K., Maharjan, S., Zhang, Y.: Blockchain empowered asynchronous federated learning for secure data sharing in internet of vehicles. IEEE Trans. Veh. Technol. **69**(4), 4298–4311 (2020)
17. Chai, H., Leng, S., Chen, Y., Zhang, K.: A hierarchical blockchain-enabled federated learning algorithm for knowledge sharing in internet of vehicles. IEEE Trans. Intell. Transp. Syst. **22**(7), 3975–3986 (2021)
18. Wu, T., Jiang, M., Han, Y., Yuan, Z., Li, X., Zhang, L.: A traffic-aware federated imitation learning framework for motion control at unsignalized intersections with internet of vehicles. Electronics **10**(24), 3050 (2021)
19. Phong, L.T., Aono, Y., Hayashi, T., Wang, L., Moriai, S.: Privacy-preserving deep learning via additively homomorphic encryption. IEEE Trans. Inf. Forensics Secur. **13**(5), 1333–1345 (2018)

20. Liu, X., Li, H., Xu, G., Chen, Z., Huang, X., Lu, R.: Privacy-enhanced federated learning against poisoning adversaries. IEEE Trans. Inf. Forensics Secur. **16**, 4574–4588 (2021)
21. Bonawitz, K., et al.: Practical secure aggregation for privacy-preserving machine learning. In: Proceedings of the 2017 ACM SIGSAC Conference on Computer and Communications Security, pp. 1175–1191 (2017)
22. Bell, J.H., Bonawitz, K.A., Gascon, A., Lepoint, T., Raykova, M.: Secure Single-Server Aggregation with (Poly)Logarithmic Overhead, pp. 1253–1269. Association for Computing Machinery (2020)
23. Fu, A., Zhang, X., Xiong, N., Gao, Y., Wang, H., Zhang, J.: Vfl: A verifiable federated learning with privacy-preserving for big data in industrial iot. IEEE Trans. Industr. Inf. **18**(5), 3316–3326 (2022)
24. Guo, X., Liu, Z., Li, J., Gao, J., Hou, B., Dong, C., Baker, T.: Verifl: Communication-efficient and fast verifiable aggregation for federated learning. IEEE Trans. Inf. Forensics Secur. **16**, 1736–1751 (2021)

LightGBM-RF: A Hybrid Model for Anomaly Detection in Smart Building

Otuekong Ekpo$^{(\boxtimes)}$, Kate Takyi, and Rose-Mary Owusuaa Mensah Gyening

Department of Computer Science, Kwame Nkrumah University of Science and Technology,
Kumasi, Ghana
ooekpo@st.knust.edu.gh

Abstract. Smart building uses sophisticated and integrated building technology and allows numerous IoT systems to interact as well as provide convenience to its users. Unfortunately, smart buildings have become a point of attraction for cybercriminals. Due to the fact that the majority of these IoT devices lack the memory and computing power required for robust security operations, they are inherently vulnerable. IoT devices are consequently vulnerable to various attacks. Therefore, a single attack on network systems or devices can cause serious harm to the security of data as well as privacy in a smart building.

This paper presents LightGBM-RF, a machine learning model that accurately detects anomalies in a smart building by utilizing a combination of Light Gradient Boosting Machine and Random Forest algorithms. The model detects anomalies with an accuracy of 99.19%, thereby providing an effective scheme for detecting different attack families, and the potential to significantly improve security in smart buildings.

Keywords: Internet of Things (IoT) · Smart building · Anomaly detection · Machine learning algorithms

1 Introduction

1.1 Background

Due to the Internet of Things' (IoT) rapid evolution and application across all spheres of human endeavor, ongoing research efforts in the IoT and its related components are necessary. While the IoT industry's rapid growth has brought enormous benefits to humanity, it has also sparked a number of security concerns. Cybercrime has been on the increase as criminals and hackers seek to exploit the security loophole and weaknesses of IoT devices.

Globally, the number of Internet of Things (IoT) devices is projected to triple by 2030, rising from 8.74 billion in 2020 to well above 25.4 billion [1]. The Internet of Things will pervade all facets of life, with applications ranging from home automation to smart buildings, connected cars, precision agriculture, wearable technology, and e-health. IoT devices are an easy target for bad actors and malware to manipulate due to

E. Ahene and F. Li (Eds.): FCS 2022, CCIS 1726, pp. 34–47, 2022.
https://doi.org/10.1007/978-981-19-8445-7_3

their vulnerabilities. Additionally, several devices in smart buildings are mostly linked to the internet and these devices can seamlessly become a threat and lead to serious consequences that can disrupt a user's experience. Many of the exploits can be difficult to detect since the threat actors are smart or utilize the same tools that legitimate users do [2].

1.2 Motivation and Contribution

Numerous academic disciplines, including statistics, earth sciences, chemistry, engineering, and data mining, have long been involved in anomaly detection research. Data that is abnormal can be very helpful and hold the key to new discoveries, or it can be useless, as when it results from measurement errors. As a result, the study of anomaly detection has many applications in a variety of fields today and has gained popularity among researchers both locally and internationally. Examples of such applications include but not limited to damage detection and industrial fault [3–7] and intrusion detection in cybersecurity [8–10]. Additionally, there have been more applications in the fields of medical diagnosis [11–14], Infrastructure monitoring [15, 16], bioinformatics [17], astronomy [18], and detection in the earth sciences [19–21].

Therefore, our research findings would be useful in advancing knowledge of the security threats as well as anomalies in smart buildings, and hence, devising a model that can serve to improve their security. Consequently, this study will yield a probe into identified security threats and their likely ramifications, remedies, and security recommendations for smart buildings. Overall, the outcomes of this work can be used in the enhancement of the deployment of IoT technology in smart buildings. The main contribution of this paper is a novel accurate machine learning technique for detecting anomalies in smart building networks.

The remainder of this paper is as follows: Sect. 2 introduces related work in this area; Sect. 3 details the LightGBM-RF method; Sect. 4 tests and evaluates the method; and Sect. 5 summarizes the paper's content.

2 Related Work

Malik et al. [22] proposed a detection engine for intrusion based on a Deep Belief Network (DBN). The DBN Classifier model was tested utilizing the TON_IOT Weather dataset [23]. The experiments demonstrated that their approach surpassed other existing methods with an accuracy of 86.3%. The limitation of their research is its failure to identify novel threats, and its achieved performance will require further improvement to be effective for IoT systems.

Khorasgani and Biswas [24] proposed an integrated diagnosis technique that combined a diagnostic residual-based method with an unsupervised anomaly detection approach for tracking and defect detection in smart buildings. The researchers used the tree-augmented naive Bayesian learning algorithm (TAN) to create a classification model for fault isolation and identification. The strength of this work stems from the fact that TAN model can adapt some measurement dependencies, thereby enhancing the diagnosis reference model by uncovering additional monitor-fault-mode relationships. The method used to learn the TAN classifier for fault isolation and detection had a limitation in that it uses historical data. As a result, it is expected that the classifier will not be able to identify and extract new faults precisely.

Dhamor et al. [25] investigated detection DDoS in IoT devices. In their work, they present a novel technique to preprocess data on a dataset called CICDDoS2019 [26]. The performance of the selected machine learning techniques for the detection of DDoS traffic was tested on their preprocessed dataset. It is also observed that machine learning (ML) techniques were valuable in identifying DDoS attacks, and Random Forest, with an accuracy of 99.24%. On the scope of this research was limited to detecting DDoS traffic and did not empirically investigate other attack families within the IoT environment.

A couple of traditional and hybrid ML algorithms were compared by Sumathi and Karthikeyan [27]. On the KDDcup99 [28] and DARPF datasets [29], where they tested these algorithms, they discovered that Decision Trees and Fuzzy C-Means outperform the others. With a detection time of 0.15 s and an accuracy of 98.7%, the fuzzy C-Mean algorithm could better identify DDoS activity. Similarly, Ajeetha and Madhu Pryia [30] proposed a DDoS detection technique using ML and traces of traffic flow. They assessed the Random Forest and Nave Bayes algorithms on the datasets gotten from the SANS and IANA website [31], of which the malicious ports and the genuine ports are gathered. This dataset contains a collection of genuine and malware traffic data. It was observed that the Nave Bayes algorithm, achieved a 90.90% accuracy, and was considered better than the Random Forest algorithm, which had an accuracy of 78.18%.

Wehbi et al. [32] surveyed previous research on the detection of DDoS attack in the IoT ecosystem and afterwards proposed three novel approaches based on Linear Discriminant Analysis (LDA), K-Nearest Neighbor (KNN), Support Vector Machine (SVM), and Quadratic Discriminant Analysis (QDA) algorithms. They evaluated these algorithms on a dataset generated and simulated by the authors. The strength of this work was a novel feature extraction classification and the development of a seven-layer framework for detecting DDoS. They also added two new criteria to avoid misclassifying regular traffic as DDoS attack, which is quite a common issue with ML-based DDoS attack detection. Eventually, they observed that the three approaches performed adequately, with Random Forest outperforming others, with a 99.99% accuracy. This study was however limited to DDoS attack detection.

Soe et al. [33] presents a ML-based botnet intrusion detection framework with sequential detection architecture utilizing an attribute selection technique on the N-BaIoT dataset [34] for attacks detection. To achieve an accuracy of 99%, they used three machine learning techniques: Nave Bayes, Artificial Neural Network (ANN), J48 decision tree. However, the research failed to investigate normal traffic trends on the different types of IoT devices in order to extend the anomaly-sub-engine for unknown attacks detection.

In summary, the smart building contains a wide range of IoT devices, systems, and software, which increases the attack surface for most organizations because they mostly deal with multiple vendors. This poses a risk to these organizations because supply chain (in)security can lead to a variety of vulnerabilities. To our knowledge, no previous study has used machine learning to identify anomalies in an intelligent building using a standard dataset with novel threats such as denial of service (DoS), distributed denial of service

(DDoS), ransomware, backdoors, injection, password compromise, cross site scripting and man in the middle attacks. Hence, the research sought to close the knowledge gap by investigating potential threats in smart building ecosystems and detecting any anomalies that may arise.

In all the reviewed papers, machine learning-based approaches, which are frequently utilized in the IoT security area, have been shown to be beneficial for generating viable models for identifying IoT risks. However, most of the approaches are not sufficient due to the diversity and sophistication of new cyber-attack categories, as well as the lack of heterogeneous data sources to prepare and verify predictive models. To close this existing gap, we leveraged a standard dataset generated through a novel smart building architectural testbed and publicly available at [23]. In the dataset, the IoT and network devices make up the edge tier; virtual machines and gateways make up the fog layer; and cloud offerings like data analytics and visualization are included in the cloud layer and are connected to the other layers [35]. Because most threats in the IoT paradigm happen in real time, a rapid anomaly detector with improved accuracy is necessary hence a model called the Light Gradient Boosting Machine and Random Forest (LightGBM-RF) is proposed. This is a combined ML model for anomaly detection in smart buildings to address these new attack families. This innovation is critical for IoT-based anomaly detection since literature is currently generally lacking in the smart building ecosystem with industrial internet of things (IIoT) and internet of things (IoT) features.

3   Methods

The hybrid method proposed for anomaly detection in smart building is called LightGBM-RF. We outline the phases of our proposed approach in a flow chart (Fig. 1), with subsections describing each stage. In our approach, the TON_IoT dataset [23] was downloaded, preprocessed, and data cleaning was performed to eliminate duplicate values. Next, the Random Forest (RF) algorithm was used for feature selection. This is primarily because there are a lot of features in our training set; therefore, there is a need to find the relevant features in order to form the optimal feature subset. Thus, the multiplicity of the TON_IoT dataset is reduced from 115 to 40 features that is relevant to the problem which we sought to address using our proposed LightGBM-RF method.

Furthermore, the dataset was separated into the matrix of features and the target variable. The labelled variable is used as the target variable to gain a deeper understanding of the dataset. It indicates if the network traffic is normal or an attack where 0 represents normal network traffic, while 1 represents attack network traffic. Furthermore, the dataset was divided into validation and training sets, of which 75% was for training and 25% was for validation. Finally, the LightGBM-RF model was developed to assess the performance in detecting anomalies in a smart building.

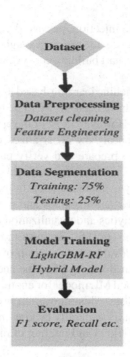

Fig. 1. Workflow diagram of the proposed model

3.1 Dataset Acquisition

The research considered the TON_IoT dataset [23] to detect anomalies. As one of the most recent datasets published in 2019, the TON_IoT is made up of data from a real-time and large-scale network developed at the University of New South Wales Canberra's Cyber Range and Internet of Things (IoT) Labs [36].

It is developed using an interconnection of IoT systems in the cloud, edge, and fog layers to model the realistic integration of recent real-world IoT networks. This entailed using operating systems and sensory devices as the infrastructure for customizing virtualized resources and cloud solutions at the fog and cloud layers, respectively. A couple of Internet of Things/Industrial Internet of Things devices, like light bulb sensor systems and Modbus, gadgets, and smart televisions, were utilized, as well as host devices, such as servers and workstations, that were also used to link up the devices, physical gateways (switches and routers), and hypervisors to the internet.

3.2 Data Preprocessing

In the preprocessing phase, Pandas, ScikitLearn, and Numpy libraries were used. The dataset was imported and loaded into memory using the Numpy and Pandas libraries. A variety of tasks such as removing invalid, missing, or duplicated data and converting data into the correct format were undertaken. The TON_IoT dataset [23] contains 461043 rows, 45 columns, and 11071 duplicate values. The missing values in the dataset are also denoted by "-." Columns with a high number of '-' values were thus identified for cleanup. The duplicate values were also removed. The ts variable, which represents the time of the first packet, has high cardinality and therefore has a weak relationship to the 'label' column. Also, the 'src_ip' representing the source internet protocol address, 'src_port' representing the source port address, 'dst_ip' representing the destination internet protocol address, and 'dst_port' representing the destination port are the addresses and port numbers of the devices in use and thus will not be helpful in detecting attacks.

It is critical to encode non-numerical values to numerical values in order to prepare the dataset for experimental operations. This was also taken into consideration during data cleaning. One-Hot encoding transforms categorical data variables to binary forms, and aids in improving a model's prediction and classification accuracy. Since our data is categorical and the aim is class prediction, it is chosen over other encoding approaches. Thus, it is applied to the proto and conn_state variables. The proto variable has 3 unique values: tcp – transmission control protocol, udp – user datagram protocol, and icmp – internet control message protocol all of which are network communication protocols.

The random forest algorithm was used for feature selection. Due to the number of features in the training set, we needed to find the most important features that will help detect normal and attack network traffics. The random forest model was trained on the data and extracted the top 11 important features. The feature importance chart shown in Fig. 2 below is used to rank and visualize the important features from the dataset that are considered to be essential for developing the model.

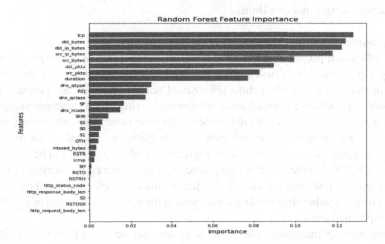

Fig. 2. Feature importance chart

3.3 Data Segmentation

Here, the dataset was divided into validation and training sets, and 75% of the data was used for training while the other 25% was for validation. The training set contained 140,125 records, while the validation set contained 46,709 records.

3.4 Model Training

The following algorithms is used in our hybrid model in detecting anomalies in a smart building system. The evaluation metrics are provided in the next section, but our algorithm and its features are explained below.

Random Forest Algorithm
Random forest (RF) is an effective ML algorithm, popular for its accuracy and independent fast learning over diverse datasets. It uses the bootstrap (bagging) method to resample trees [37]. A bootstrap subset generated for training is used to train the trees in a forest. In RF, each node is divided with the help of the best predictor, which is randomly selected at the node level. The additional random layer helps it to overcome overfitting. To enhance the bagged trees, a small de-correlating strand is applied. By bagging on bootstrap sets of training data, numerous decision tree algorithms could be developed. Out of the entire set of predictors, a random sample of 'n' predictors is chosen as a splitting candidate. As the number of trees in the forest grows, the random forest's generalization error reaches a limit.

Light Gradient Boosting Machine (LightGBM) Algorithm
In 2017, Microsoft proposed the LGBM boosting model [38]. LGB is a gradient-based elevating algorithm that is distributed, fast, and high performing. It is derived from popular machine learning algorithms [39]. Small gradient samples are properly trained (occasionally generating a small error in training), while large gradient samples are undertrained. Hence, this technique broadens leaf-wise rather than node-wise, and also for leaf-wise augmentation, the optimum delta function is selected. A lot of machine learning problems, such as classification, regression, and prediction, can be solved using this approach [40]. Furthermore, training is accelerated by the task of sorting continuous attributes into discrete bins. As a result, this feature improves efficiency as it uses the leaf-wise split method rather than the level-wise split method which can result in significantly more complicated trees.

During the implementation phase, the programming language Python was used, and the software application's pseudo-code was developed. Hence, the flow in which our hybrid algorithm was implemented is summarized in the LightGBM-RF pseudocode that is provided in Table 1.

Table 1. Pseudocode of the LightGBM-RF algorithm.

Algorithm 1: Pseudocode of the LightGBM-RF Algorithm
Import VotingClassifier
Import RandomForestClassifier
Import LightGBM
Set random forest n_estimators=200
Set random forest criterion='entropy'
Add random forest and lightgbm to ensemble model
Set voting classifier to hard voting
Set voting classifier weight to [1,1]
Fit ensemble model (X_train, y_train)
Get the prediction of anomaly detection
Print accuracy, precision, recall and f1-score
Print classification report
Print confusion matrix

3.5 Evaluation Metrics

To determine how well the proposed model will perform, specific metrics are evaluated. This is necessary to analyze our experimental findings. Thus, the model is assessed using four metrics: Recall, Accuracy, F1-score, Precision.

4 Experimental Results

The experimental results are based on the original test data. The hold out approach was used for dividing the dataset. The validation set results of the LightGBM-RF algorithm and its confusion matrix are shown in Sects. 4.2 and 4.3, respectively.

4.1 Experimental Settings

The experiments are performed on an eight generation HP Envy PC with Nvidia GeForce MX150 GPU, Intel(R) Core (TM) i7, with processor speed of 2.0 GHz, and a 16.0 GB RAM memory on Windows 10 operating system. It also made use of the different applications and packages like Anaconda Jupyter Notebook, Google Colab, Scikit Learn (Sklearn), Panda library, Numpy library, Seaborn library, Matplotlib, and Python 3.9 language.

4.2 Performance Metrics

After selecting features with RF and classifying these using LightGBM-RF, some statistical measures are performed to assess the performance of the proposed method. Figure 3 depicts a bar chart displaying the LightGBM-RF model's validation set results. While Table 2 provides a tabular representation of the model's performance metrics.

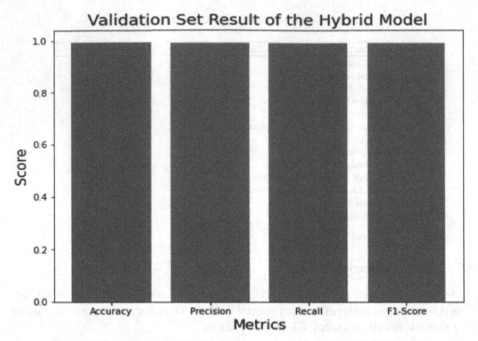

Fig. 3. The bar chart of the validation set results of the LightGBM-RF model.

Table 2. Validation set results of the LightGBM-RF

Algorithm	Accuracy (%)	Precision (%)	F1-Score (%)	Recall (%)
LightGBM-RF	99.1950	98.9145	98.9258	98.9371

4.3 Confusion Matrix

A confusion matrix is a table that enables the conception and presentation of a model by outlining the values that the model asserts to correspond to different classifications as shown in Fig. 4. It has a size of N × N, where n corresponds to the number of classes, with the rows representing the predicted classes and the columns representing the actual classes. The confusion matrix displays the number of false positives, true negatives, false negatives, and true positives.

From Fig. 4, it is evident that the results from the study show that there are 17313 predicted anomalies in total that turned out to be anomalous. This means that the model's true positive (TP) value is:

$$TP = 17313$$

There are 29020 instances of predicted normal traffic that are actually normal. As a result, the model's true negative (TN) value is:

$$TN = 29020$$

There is a total of 190 predicted anomalies that turned out to be normal. The model's false positive (FP) value is thus:

$$FP = 190$$

There is a total of 186 instances where the expected normal traffic turned out to be anomalous. Consequently, the model's false negative (FN) value is:

$$FN = 186$$

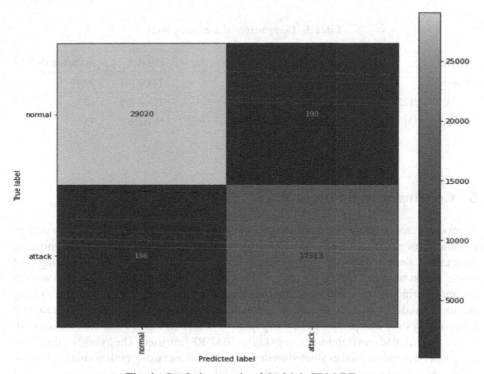

Fig. 4. Confusion matrix of the LightGBM-RF

4.4 Performance Comparison with Other Studies

The accuracy and false positive rate of anomaly detection models define them. However, this is not to assert that other performance indicators aren't equally important. Nonetheless, the hybrid model for detecting IoT anomalies has demonstrated 99.19% accuracy in identifying normal and anomalous trends in IoT data. This accuracy rate suggests that combining RF with LightGBM can result in a high-accuracy anomaly detection approach. Furthermore, it has been demonstrated that using the random forest algorithm for feature engineering and classification results in a high accuracy.

As compared to other scholars' work in this area, the actual accuracy of the model, which equals 99.19%, performed better than Soe et al. [33] and Malik et al. [22] in terms of accuracy and other metrics. A tabular analysis is provided below in Table 3. Additionally, this study investigated anomalies in the fog, edge, and cloud layers and performed admirably in detecting threats in the smart building system, thus emphasizing our contributions to the study. We conducted a series of investigations to assess this model's capacity to discern and identify anomalous attacks as well as detect various attacks accurately.

As a consequence of the study findings, the proposed model appears to be a good candidate for developing an anomaly detection system in smart buildings.

Table 3. Comparison with existing work

Reference	Technique	Dataset	Accuracy (%)
Proposed	LightGBM-RF	TON-IoT	99.19
Malik et al. [22]	Deep belief network	TON-IoT	86.3
Soe et al. [33]	Nave Bayes, ANN & J48 decision tree	N-BaIoT	99

5   Conclusion and Future Work

In modern environment of complex systems, controlling and managing system performance is an essential task. With hundreds or even thousands of objects to monitor, anomalous detection can help figure out where a deviation is arising, improving root cause assessment and obtaining technical support quickly. Anomaly detection aids in the monitoring of the cause of chaos engineering by discovering patterns and alerting the individuals responsible for taking action. A hybrid machine learning-based anomaly detection system was presented in this paper. To detect anomalies and analyze network traffic, LightGBM and Random Forest (LightGBM-RF) are used. The hybrid LightGBM-RF model was trained and evaluated on the TON-IoT dataset using both normal and attack traffic, and it achieved an overall accuracy of 99.19% in detecting anomalies. We also conducted extensive empirical investigation on standard machine learning problems, thus justifying our algorithm's versatility and superior performance when compared to existing state-of-the-art methods.

The fundamental significance of this research is the robust and accurate integration of the Random Forest (RF) algorithm and the Light Gradient Boosting Machine (LightGBM) algorithm in detecting anomalies in a smart building. Given that it is a lightweight model, particularly in comparison to other anomaly detection models, the model makes for an excellent anomaly detection technique in smart buildings for researchers and the industry to adapt. Additionally, it is essential that security be built into the process of design and development of smart buildings and their IoT products and services should have a high-level security requirement as well as security boundaries.

In the future, we intend to improve the model's accuracy by experimenting with deep learning algorithms, comparing its performance to recent real-world datasets, and adapting it in a production environment to detect new types of IoT threats.

References

1. Statista. https://www.statista.com/statistics/471264/iot-number-of-connected-devices-wor
   ldwide/. Accessed 11 Sep 2022
2. Kuyucu, M.K., Bahtiyar, serif, Ince, G.: Security and privacy in the smart home: a survey of
   issues and mitigation strategies. In: 2019 4th International Conference on Computer Science
   and Engineering (UBMK) (2019). https://doi.org/10.1109/ubmk.2019.8907037
3. Atha, D.J., Jahanshahi, M.R.: Evaluation of deep learning approaches based on convolutional
   neural networks for corrosion detection. Struct. Health Monit. **17**, 1110–1128 (2017). https://
   doi.org/10.1177/1475921717737051
4. Hundman, K., Constantinou, V., Laporte, C., Colwell, I., Soderstrom, T.: Detecting spacecraft
   anomalies using LSTMs and nonparametric dynamic thresholding. In: Proceedings of the 24th
   ACM SIGKDD International Conference on Knowledge Discovery & Data Mining (2018).
   https://doi.org/10.1145/3219819.3219845
5. Lopez, F., et al.: Categorization of anomalies in smart manufacturing systems to support the
   selection of detection mechanisms. IEEE Robot. Autom. Lett. **2**, 1885–1892 (2017). https://
   doi.org/10.1109/lra.2017.2714135
6. Ramotsoela, D., Abu-Mahfouz, A., Hancke, G.: A survey of anomaly detection in industrial
   wireless sensor networks with critical water system infrastructure as a case study. Sensors **18**,
   2491 (2018). https://doi.org/10.3390/s18082491
7. Zhao, R., Yan, R., Chen, Z., Mao, K., Wang, P., Gao, R.X.: Deep learning and its applications
   to machine health monitoring. Mech. Syst. Signal Process. **115**, 213–237 (2019). https://doi.
   org/10.1016/j.ymssp.2018.05.050
8. Kwon, D., Kim, H., Kim, J., Suh, S.C., Kim, I., Kim, K.J.: A survey of deep learning-based
   network anomaly detection. Clust. Comput. **22**(1), 949–961 (2017). https://doi.org/10.1007/
   s10586-017-1117-8
9. Malaiya, R.K., Kwon, D., Kim, J., Suh, S.C., Kim, H., Kim, I.: An empirical evaluation of
   deep learning for network anomaly detection. In: 2018 International Conference on Computing, Networking and Communications (ICNC) (2018). https://doi.org/10.1109/iccnc.2018.
   8390278
10. Xin, Y., et al.: Machine learning and deep learning methods for cybersecurity. IEEE Access
    6, 35365–35381 (2018). https://doi.org/10.1109/access.2018.2836950
11. Iakovidis, D.K., Georgakopoulos, S.V., Vasilakakis, M., Koulaouzidis, A., Plagianakos, V.P.:
    Detecting and locating gastrointestinal anomalies using deep learning and iterative cluster
    unification. IEEE Trans. Med. Imaging **37**, 2196–2210 (2018). https://doi.org/10.1109/tmi.
    2018.2837002
12. Latif, S., Usman, M., Rana, R., Qadir, J.: Phonocardiographic sensing using deep learning for
    abnormal heartbeat detection. IEEE Sens. J. **18**, 9393–9400 (2018). https://doi.org/10.1109/
    jsen.2018.2870759
13. Schlegl, T., Seeböck, P., Waldstein, S.M., Schmidt-Erfurth, U., Langs, G.: Unsupervised
    anomaly detection with generative adversarial networks to guide marker discovery. In:
    Niethammer, M., et al. (eds.) IPMI 2017. LNCS, vol. 10265, pp. 146–157. Springer, Cham
    (2017). https://doi.org/10.1007/978-3-319-59050-9_12
14. Seebock, P., et al.: Exploiting epistemic uncertainty of anatomy segmentation for anomaly
    detection in retinal OCT. IEEE Trans. Med. Imaging **39**, 87–98 (2020). https://doi.org/10.
    1109/tmi.2019.2919951

15. Borghesi, A., Bartolini, A., Lombardi, M., Milano, M., Benini, L.: Anomaly detection using autoencoders in high performance computing systems. Proc. AAAI Conf. Artif. Intell. **33**, 9428–9433 (2019). https://doi.org/10.1609/aaai.v33i01.33019428
16. Sipple, J.: Interpretable, multidimensional, multimodal anomaly detection with negative sampling for detection of device failure. In: International Conference on Machine Learning, pp. 9016–9025 (2020)
17. Min, S., Lee, B., Yoon, S.: Deep learning in bioinformatics. Brief. Bioinform. (2016). https://doi.org/10.1093/bib/bbw068
18. Reyes, E., Estevez, P.A.: Transformation based deep anomaly detection in astronomical images. In: 2020 International Joint Conference on Neural Networks (IJCNN) (2020). https://doi.org/10.1109/ijcnn48605.2020.9206997
19. Fisher, W.D., Camp, T.K., Krzhizhanovskaya, V.V.: Anomaly detection in earth dam and levee passive seismic data using support vector machines and automatic feature selection. J. Comput. Sci. **20**, 143–153 (2017). https://doi.org/10.1016/j.jocs.2016.11.016
20. Flach, M., et al.: Multivariate anomaly detection for earth observations: a comparison of algorithms and feature extraction techniques. Earth Syst. Dyn. **8**, 677–696 (2017). https://doi.org/10.5194/esd-8-677-2017
21. Jiang, T., Li, Y., Xie, W., Du, Q.: Discriminative reconstruction constrained generative adversarial network for hyperspectral anomaly detection. IEEE Trans. Geosci. Remote Sens. **58**, 4666–4679 (2020). https://doi.org/10.1109/tgrs.2020.2965961
22. Malik, R., Singh, Y., Sheikh, Z.A., Anand, P., Singh, P.K., Workneh, T.C.: An improved deep belief network IDS on IOT-based network for traffic systems. J. Adv. Transp. **2022**, 1–17 (2022). https://doi.org/10.1155/2022/7892130
23. The TON_IoT datasets. https://research.unsw.edu.au/projects/toniot-datasets. Accessed 11 Sep 2022
24. Khorasgani, H., Biswas, G.: A methodology for monitoring smart buildings with incomplete models. Appl. Soft Comput. **71**, 396–406 (2018). https://doi.org/10.1016/j.asoc.2018.06.018
25. Dhamor, T., Bhat, S., Thenmalar, S.: Dynamic approaches for detection of DDoS threats using machine learning. Ann. Rom. Soc. Cell Biol. **25**, 13663–13673 (2021)
26. DDoS Evaluation Dataset (CIC-DDoS2019). https://www.unb.ca/cic/datasets/ddos2019.html. Accessed 11 Sep 2022
27. Sumathi, S., Karthikeyan, N.: Search for effective data mining algorithm for network-based intrusion detection (NIDS)-DDOS attacks. In: 2018 International Conference on Intelligent Computing and Communication for Smart World (I2C2SW) (2018). https://doi.org/10.1109/i2c2sw45816.2018.8997522
28. KDD cup 1999 data, the UCI KDD archive information and computer science University of California. http://kdd.ics.uci.edu/databases/kddcup99/kddcup99.html. Accessed 11 Sep 2022
29. DARP dataset. https://www.data.world/datasets/darp. Accessed 11 Sep 2022
30. Ajeetha, G., Madhu Priya, G.: Machine learning based DDOS attack detection. In: 2019 Innovations in Power and Advanced Computing Technologies (i-PACT) (2019).https://doi.org/10.1109/i-pact44901.2019.8959961
31. Internet Assigned Numbers Authority: Service name and transport protocol port number registry. https://www.iana.org/assignments/service-names-port-numbers/service-namesport-numbers.xhtml. Accessed 11 Sep 2022
32. Wehbi, K., Hong, L., Al-salah, T., Bhutta, A.A.: A survey on machine learning based detection on DDoS attacks for IOT systems. In: 2019 SoutheastCon (2019). https://doi.org/10.1109/southeastcon42311.2019.9020468
33. Soe, Y.N., Feng, Y., Santosa, P.I., Hartanto, R., Sakurai, K.: Machine learning-based IOT-botnet attack detection with sequential architecture. Sensors **20**, 4372 (2020). https://doi.org/10.3390/s20164372

34. UCI Machine Learning Repository: Detection_of_IoT_botnet_attacks_N_BaIoT data set.   https://archive.ics.uci.edu/ml/datasets/detection_of_IoT_botnet_attacks_N_BaIoT. Accessed 11 Sep 2022
35. Moustafa, N.: A new distributed architecture for evaluating AI-based security systems at the edge: network ToN_IoT datasets. Sustain. Cities Soc. **72**, 102994 (2021). https://doi.org/10.1016/j.scs.2021.102994
36. Moustafa, N.: New generations of internet of things datasets for cybersecurity applications-based machine learning: ToN_IoT datasets. In: Proceedings of the eResearch Australasia Conference, Brisbane, Australia, pp. 21–25 (2019)
37. Lee, T.-H., Ullah, A., Wang, R.: Bootstrap aggregating and random forest. In: Fuleky, P. (ed.) Macroeconomic Forecasting in the Era of Big Data. ASTAE, vol. 52, pp. 389–429. Springer, Cham (2020). https://doi.org/10.1007/978-3-030-31150-6_13
38. Ke, G., et al.: LightGBM: a highly efficient gradient boosting decision tree. In: Advances in Neural Information Processing Systems 30 (2017)
39. Jin, D., Lu, Y., Qin, J., Cheng, Z., Mao, Z.: SwiftIDS: Real-time intrusion detection system based on LIGHTGBM and parallel intrusion detection mechanism. Comput. Secur. **97**, 101984 (2020). https://doi.org/10.1016/j.cose.2020.101984
40. Xiaosong, Z.H.A.O., Qiangfu, Z.H.A.O.: Stock prediction using optimized LIGHTGBM based on cost awareness. In: 2021 5th IEEE International Conference on Cybernetics (CYBCONF) (2021). https://doi.org/10.1109/cybconf51991.2021.9464148

Enabling Hidden Frequency Keyword-Based Auditing on Distributed Architectures for a Smart Government

Jingting Xue[1,2]([✉]) [iD], Shuqin Luo[1]([✉]) [iD], Lingjie Shi[1] [iD], Xiaojun Zhang[1,3] [iD], and Chunxiang Xu[2] [iD]

[1] School of Computer Science, Research Center for Cyber Security, Southwest Petroleum University, Chengdu 610599, China
jtxue@swpu.edu.cn, shuqin_luo0108@163.com
[2] School of Computer Science and Engineering, University of Electronic Science and Technology of China, Chengdu 610097, China
[3] School of Cyber Science and Engineering, Shanghai Jiao Tong University, Shanghai 200030, China

Abstract. Public auditing checks the integrity of outsourced data via random sampling and verifying sample data blocks. In practice, however, users do not pay attention to the entire data set but focus on the integrity of only the part of the data containing keywords of interest. Therefore, the keyword-based auditing paradigm is proposed; it depends entirely on the subjective choice or access habits, which makes it possible for malicious storage servers to analyze the auditing frequency, or reduce redundant backups. For government data, auditing frequency privacy leakage or corruption of any file could be catastrophic. In this paper, we propose a hidden frequency keyword-based auditing scheme for a smart government named HFKA, which is compatible with distributed storage architecture. HFKA leverages a Bloom filter, which adjusts the false positive rate to consider auditing files corresponding to specified keywords and auditing random files obtained via fuzzy matching. To obtain privacy-preserving fuzzy matching, HFKA constructs an index table embedded with update times to retrieve a wide range of files to be audited. This approach is secure against the replay attack and supports the index table update through structure iteration instead of recalculation. HFKA provides storage robustness, privacy protection of hidden frequencies, and data security. Additionally, HFKA can reduce audit computation overhead by 32.6% compared to the probabilistic public auditing.

Keywords: Keyword-based auditing · Frequency hiding · Distributed architecture · Smart government · Fuzzy matching

1 Introduction

With the emergence of information islands and the increasing volume of government data, a smart government [1] is being developed to facilitate the integration

© The Author(s), under exclusive license to Springer Nature Singapore Pte Ltd. 2022
E. Ahene and F. Li (Eds.): FCS 2022, CCIS 1726, pp. 48–68, 2022.
https://doi.org/10.1007/978-981-19-8445-7_4

of government management services, as evidenced by the realization of data sharing between government departments at all levels. The cloud [2] is the available intermediate carrier for data storage and sharing, and the public integrity auditing [3,5–7,9,10] paradigm can be used to check the integrity of outsourced data to support its availability. However, for massive and targeted government data, the existing probabilistic public auditing (PPA) model directly applied to smart government scenarios has the following two limitations. (i) The PPA model does not support targeted auditing of government data. Specifically, civil servants in different departments pay attention to the integrity of only those files about their own departments rather than the entire outsourced database. The challenge information in the PPA model cannot completely cover the involved data, and therefore, cannot complete integrity auditing of the specified data. (ii) PPA, which evenly selects data to be audited, is not economical for government data verification. In each audit, PPA consumes unnecessary computation resources to check irrelevant randomly selected files in addition to the department files. In summary, for smart government, the proposed public keyword-based auditing (PKA) model [4] that determines the challenge information according to users' wishes could be a better choice.

In the PKA model, the third-party auditor (TPA) periodically verifies the users' data of interest integrity by retrieving specific keywords and performing verifications, thereby reducing the overall cost of auditing while satisfying their needs. Unfortunately, the PKA model cannot fully meet the security requirements of data auditing and sharing in smart government. In general, various departments' keyword setting is a long-term and business-related process to a certain extent, which results in the files selected for auditing being relatively fixed. The probability of these kinds of unrelated files being audited is negligible. In this case, malicious cloud servers can infer privacy contexts such as department information or file types, based on the auditing frequency and may even delete files that are rarely retrieved to save storage space. Undoubtedly, the value of government data is enormous. Either a privacy leak or a file corruption can expose a government to a major security crisis.

To ensure the security requirements of government data in integrity auditing, we propose HFKA that combines PPA and PKA. Specifically, the contributions of this work are as follows:

- We propose the first hidden frequency keyword-based auditing scheme for a smart government, named HFKA. In HFKA, a Bloom filter is introduced to achieve fuzzy matching between user-specified keywords and files to be audited. According to the degree of confidentiality requirements, HFKA sets Bloom filter modes with different fuzziness levels. The generated verifiable challenge information can not only cover the files that users are interested in but also randomly select some low-frequency auditing files. HFKA is well-suited for scenarios where users perform differential targeted auditing on specific data in a shared dataset.
- We design an index table label (ITL) to support the implementation of fuzzy matching that can protect keyword contents from storage servers and resist

two lazy behaviors. The ITL aggregates the serial numbers of all files corresponding to a defined keyword, so the aggregated value determines whether a storage proof covers all the involved files in the challenge information. In addition, a global variable indicating the update time is embedded in the ITL. When a storage server does not perform update operations according to the storage protocol, HFKA can identify replay attacks on proofs in a new round of auditing.

– We demonstrate the storage robustness, privacy protection regarding auditing frequency and data security of HFKA. The performance evaluation shows that HFKA maintains the computation complexity and communication complexity at $O(1)$ in terms of the total number of files n during the integrity auditing phase. Furthermore, we design a comparative experiment to observe the auditing frequency of *Type-A* files (files corresponding to the predefined high-frequency keywords from all extracted keywords) and *Type-B* files (files corresponding to the other keywords). The experimental results show that it is negligible to distinguish user-specified high-frequency files from randomly selected low-frequency files. Our scheme achieves the auditing frequency hiding and satisfies the security requirements of government data.

Organization. The remainder of this paper is organized as follows. Section 2 reviews the related work. Section 3 covers the system model, threat model and definitions, and briefly introduces design goals of HFKA. Section 4 presents a detailed construction of HFKA. Section 5 provides a security analysis, and Sect. 6 presents the performance evaluation. Finally, Sect. 7 concludes the paper and gives directions for future work.

2   Related Work

Data integrity auditing enables users to verify the integrity of outsourced data. In 2007, Juels et al. [6] proposed the proofs of retrievability (PoR) protocol to enable a user to recover complete data from partial data provided by a server. Ateniese et al. [5] introduced a probabilistic data possession (PDP) proof generation model that can ensure overall data integrity by randomly sampling certain data. Considering the computation overhead and economic burden of users to verify data in a cloud environment, Wang et al. [7] achieves public verifiability by introducing a TPA based on the PoR model to complete auditing work. Then, Wang et al. [9] implemented storage correctness assurance and error localization based on a homomorphic token and an erasure-coded approach [8]. In [10], to resist an honest but curious TPA with malicious behavior, based on a homomorphic linear authenticator with a masking technique, TPA was designed to audit user outsourced data integrity without knowing the data content. Similarly, masking was used to improve the system decentralization and storage efficiency in [13–15]. To protect conditional identity privacy in medical data, Zhang et al. [12] designed an identity-based aggregated signature to protect patients' real identity and used Ethereum blockchain to record TPA's auditing results, thereby preventing a dishonest TPA from performing malicious auditing behaviors. To address the authenticity of big data streams in untrusted environments, a novel data structure, P-ATHAT, was constructed based on the BLS signature and Merkle hash tree to achieve real-time authentication of data streams in [16]. Li et al. [17] proved that the security of P-ATHAT is unable to resist forgery attacks on cloud servers. Shen et al. [19] focused on identity privacy using the user's biological data to verify their identity; the method can perform integrity auditing under the condition that there is no hardware token to store the private key. Zheng et al. [20] protected a user's private key by updating it. To reduce the burden of recalculating the private key, a TPA participates in generating part of the private key. Zhou et al. [11] discussed the use of certificateless signatures to avoid the management and computation problems of certificates in the case of multicopy storage. Notably, these schemes all use the probabilistic auditing model of PDP to audit the integrity of the user's private data.

For integrity verification of shared data, different auditing models should be selected depending on the specific scenario. Take smart government as an example. Users in different departments have different concerns about outsourced shared data, and the probabilistic auditing model cannot meet the individual needs. In 2021, Gao et al. [4] proposed a keyword-based auditing paradigm that determined the scope of audited data based on keywords selected by users. In addition, a feasible keyword-based auditing scheme was achieved using the privacy-preserving keyword-file index table designed by Ge et al. in [21] and referred to the trapdoors in [22]. As a result of the index table design, which adopted a linked-list structure with an index vector and generated an authentication label for each keyword, storage space is saved and it is easier for the user to detect malicious behavior of the cloud server based on the authentication label. The content in trapdoor in [22] is ciphertext, meaning that without access to user's encrypted key, no one can forge an efficient trapdoor or crack the information included in the trapdoor. It also supported multiple keywords submitted into a trapdoor.

However, since users have attention preferences for certain data, semihonest cloud servers can infer user privacy by considering how often certain data are audited. Therefore, we need a new paradigm to address the challenge of auditing frequency privacy in this particular scenario. Bringer et al. [23] first used the locality-sensitive hash (LSH) algorithm to allow fuzzy search. LSH has been used in many schemes as a basic technique for fuzzing keywords [25–28]. Li et al. [24] chose to use edit-distance to measure the similarity between keywords for imprecise fuzzy search. Furthermore, the Bloom filter is a widely used fuzzy tool. In 2021, Indra et al. [30] designed a two-dimensional bloom matrix to achieve fast matching of similar words. Tong et al. [31] designed a twins Bloom filter with LSH in 2022 that combined the above approaches. The coin has two sides, and the fuzzy operations of the above schemes aim to narrow down the trapdoor search and improve the keyword search accuracy, which is the opposite of our intended effect of amplifying the hidden keyword frequency in the search results. Only the application of a Bloom filter by Gervais et al. [32] to fuzzy user's address in the process of simple payment verification fits the intended purpose perfectly.

There has recently been a high frequency of centralized storage accidents, but in smart government, any corruption of shared data is unacceptable. Consequently, distributed storage architecture is available. The distributed storage system, Hyperledger Fabric, is an ideal architecture for data storage designed by Cachin et al. [39]. Furthermore, Xu et al. [18] proved the feasibility of Hyperledger Fabric architecture when discussing how to achieve distributed storage integrity auditing. More privacy-preserving schemes are summarized in [40].

3 Preliminaries

3.1 System Model

On the basis of previous work [4], combined with the *Hyperledger Fabric* architecture[1], HFKA introduces the *Fabric certificate authority* and optimizes the traditional single cloud storage server into a scalable distributed storage structure. In addition, HFKA introduces a retrieval server to modularize the entity's functionality.

The system model of HFKA involves five entities as illustrated in Fig. 1: *Fabric Certificate Authority* ($\mathcal{FCA}$), *User* ($\mathcal{U}$), *Third-Party Auditor* ($\mathcal{TPA}$), *Retrieval Server* ($\mathcal{RS}$), *Storage Node* ($\mathcal{SN}$).

- *Fabric Certificate Authority.* The $\mathcal{FCA}$ is a trusted institution that generates and determines digital certificates on the basis of public key infrastructure (PKI). According to the auditing requirements of smart government, the $\mathcal{FCA}$

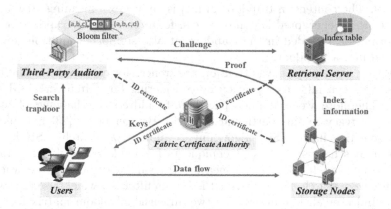

Fig. 1. System model of HFKA

---

[1] Hyperledger Fabric architecture is a scalable architectural design, an open interface style, and pluggable components. It first introduced authority management into the blockchain field, and its authority management function was completed by its independent Fabric certificate authority module. Hyperledger Fabric provides an important architectural reference for the design and implementation of distributed platforms.

mainly issues identity certificates of various entities and generates the signature key pairs for $\mathcal{U}$.

- *User*. Each $\mathcal{U}$ is a collator and uploader of some government outsourced data. According to the construction goal of the smart government platform, $\mathcal{U}$s of each department outsource files to a distributed storage network, involving many $\mathcal{SN}$s. To ensure the recoverability and confidentiality of outsourced data, each $\mathcal{U}$ completes data preprocessing, such as redundancy and encryption. During the auditing phase, each $\mathcal{U}$ generates authenticators and index information.
- *Third-Party Auditor*. The $\mathcal{TPA}$ performs audit tasks on behalf of $\mathcal{U}$s, with expertise and corresponding computing resources. The $\mathcal{TPA}$ completes the fuzzy matching of the specified keywords, challenges the $\mathcal{RS}$ in the auditing phase, and finally checks the validity of the proof information fed back by $\mathcal{SN}$s.
- *Retrieval Server*. The $\mathcal{RS}$ assists the $\mathcal{TPA}$ in completing the generation of the audited files set, specifically including saving index information and retrieving corresponding files according to the keyword trapdoor.
- *Storage Node*. Each $\mathcal{SN}$ is a storage unit in the distributed storage architecture that stores redundantly processed data blocks and calculates storage proofs based on challenge information.

Here, we briefly describe the relationships among the various entities in the system model of HFKA. To free up local storage space and realize data sharing, the involved $\mathcal{U}$s outsource the preprocessed (encrypted and redundantly processed) data to a distributed storage architecture with multiple $\mathcal{SN}$s. The $\mathcal{TPA}$ is authorized to perform periodic integrity auditing tasks, aiming to determine the integrity of outsourced data with the least amount of user-side communication and computational overhead. The $\mathcal{RS}$ assists $\mathcal{SN}$s with completing the serial number confirmation of the audited data during the challenge phase. The $\mathcal{FCA}$ creates signature keys for $\mathcal{U}$s and offers ID certificate management for each entity to assist the security of distributed storage systems.

3.2   Threat Model

In the threat model, $\mathcal{RS}$ and $\mathcal{U}$ are assumed to be completely trusted, but $\mathcal{SN}$ is considered to be semihonest and $\mathcal{TPA}$ is considered to be curious. The above security assumptions are consistent with the situation of the interests in the actual smart government.

Semihonest $\mathcal{SN}$. The $\mathcal{SN}$ may detect data privacy by utilizing keyword-based auditing or a replay storage proof with exited proof to reduce the computational overhead of data updating. The details of the malicious behavior of a semihonest $\mathcal{SN}$ are as follows: (i) *Frequency analysis attack*. In the challenge generating phase, the $\mathcal{TPA}$ and the $\mathcal{RS}$ select the auditing target data based on the search trapdoor input by the $\mathcal{U}$. $\mathcal{U}$'s subjectivity makes the auditing distribution concentrated in a small number of files. A curious $\mathcal{SN}$ can analyze the auditing frequency of certain data and delete those data that are rarely audited to save storage space. Additionally, a curious $\mathcal{SN}$ can combine these data with external information (such as $\mathcal{U}$'s department) to guess the value and types of files with high auditing frequency. (ii) *Replay attack.* When the $\mathcal{U}$ updates the outsourced data, a lazy $\mathcal{SN}$ does not perform the updating operation. The generation of a storage proof is computed by the $\mathcal{SN}$ completely, even though the $\mathcal{SN}$ does not generate storage proofs based on the challenge information. Because the verified proof has the verification logic, it can pass the $\mathcal{TPA}$'s verification. In fact, the random number selection range of the $\mathcal{TPA}$ is also limited. Although it is extremely unlikely that two groups of challenge information are exactly the same, the probability becomes nonnegligible after multiple rounds of auditing. It is more difficult to be distinguished in this case. Once the attack occurs, whether due to hardware/software failures or to reduce computational costs, the behavior violates cloud storage principles.

Curious $\mathcal{TPA}$. A curious $\mathcal{TPA}$ does not initiate attacks, but will eavesdrop on all kinds of private data. (iii) *Privacy speculation.* In HFKA, a curious $\mathcal{TPA}$ may guess the type of outsourced files and further infer a $\mathcal{U}$'s identity based on the keywords in the $\mathcal{U}$'s search trapdoor. As the number of auditing rounds increases, the $\mathcal{TPA}$ learns more information. Based on the $\mathcal{U}$'s identity and the keywords entered in the search trapdoor, the $\mathcal{TPA}$ can detect the general content of the files. This level of confidentiality leakage is unacceptable for government data.

Based on the above discussion, we provide three relevant definitions for the security of HFKA.

Definition 2 (*Storage Robustness.*) *Storage robustness means that HFKA can resist $\mathcal{SN}$'s replay attack and frequency analysis attack.*

Definition 3 (*Privacy Protection.*) *Privacy protection means that not only outsourced data context privacy, as well as keywords specified by user, index and keyword-file relation privacy can be guaranteed.*

Definition 4 (*Data Security.*) *Data security means that any adversary cannot detect original files in a direct or indirect manner, such as via brute force attack or ciphertext-chosen attack.*

3.3   Design Goals

To achieve a secure and efficient application of keyword-based auditing for smart government, HFKA aims to achieve the following goals: (i) *Privacy preserving.* HFKA hides information about files, keywords, keyword-file index table and trapdoor using encryption and other processing methods so that $\mathcal{SN}$s and $\mathcal{RS}$ cannot obtain sensitive information about files. Even if the data are intercepted by an adversary in the middle of network transmission, no information can be leaked, even the correspondence between files and keywords. (ii) *Even auditing.* Even auditing makes it impossible for adversaries to capture file auditing regularity, which is an important feature to protect data integrity. For the traditional PPA auditing model, the probabilistic auditing framework aims to achieve even auditing. However, the considerable auditing overhead is unacceptable for smart government due to its absolute evenness. HFKA overcomes the limitations of the above models and achieves relatively even auditing of the files that are and are not of concern to $\mathcal{U}$ and is suitable for the smart government scenario. (iii) *Replay attack resistance*. To further ensure data security, HFKA resists replay attacks, focusing on resisting the replay of stored proofs of updated data. The $\mathcal{TPA}$ can verify whether the storage proofs come from the updated data instead of the old data, which prevents $\mathcal{SN}$s from not updating the data to reduce computational overhead or because of hardware/software failures. Meanwhile, the calculation of the design for replay attack resistance is constant.

4   The Proposed Scheme

An $\mathcal{FCA}$, multiple $\mathcal{U}$s, a $\mathcal{TPA}$, an $\mathcal{RS}$ and multiple $\mathcal{SN}$s in the distributed storage architecture are involved in HFKA. For readability, we show a $\mathcal{U}$ and an $\mathcal{SN}$ that interact with other entities, as shown in Fig. 2.

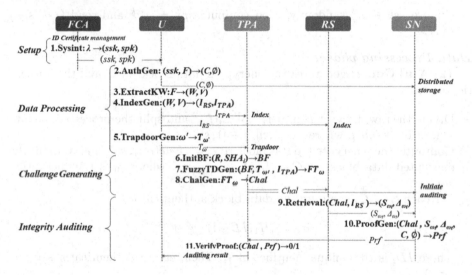

Fig. 2. Procedure of HFKA

Setup phase.

(1) **SysInit**. Given a secure parameter λ, $\mathcal{FCA}$ chooses the public parameters and issues identification certificates for all entities and generates signature key pairs for $\mathcal{U}$.

- Initialize the public parameters: choose two multiplicative cyclic groups of q-order $G_1(g), G_2(u)$; a bilinear pairing $e : G_1 \times G_1 \rightarrow G_2$; three hash functions $H_1, H_2, H_3 : \{0,1\}^* \rightarrow G_1$; secure hash functions $SHA_i : \{0,1\}^* \rightarrow Z_q^*, i \in \{1, 2, ..., \mathcal{R}\}$; a symmetric encryption algorithm: $Enc(\cdot, key)$; a pseudo random permutation PRP: $\pi(\cdot, key)$ and a pseudo random function PRF: $f(\cdot, key)$.
- Issue the identification certificates for $\mathcal{U}$s, $\mathcal{RS}$, $\mathcal{SN}$s and $\mathcal{TPA}$. There is an example to illustrate the structure of each entity's certificate as shown in Fig. 3.

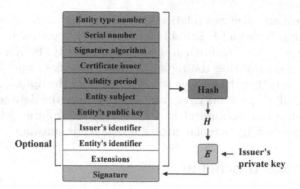

Fig. 3. Certificate issued by $\mathcal{FCA}$.

- Choose $ssk \in Z_q^*$ randomly, then compute $spk = g^{ssk}$ and send (ssk, spk) to $\mathcal{U}$.

Data Processing phase.

(2) **AuthGen**. $\mathcal{U}$ generates the encrypted data block set C and the authenticator set ϕ.

- Divide the raw data set F into $f_1 \| f_2 \| ... \| f_n$ [2] and split the processed file into s data blocks m_{ij}, where $i \in [1, n], j \in [1, s]$.
- Compute the encrypted data block $c_{ij} = Enc(m_{ij}, k_0)$ and obtain the encrypted data block set $C = \{c_{ij}\}_{i \in [1,n], j \in [1,s]}$, where k_0 is the encryption key.
- For each $c_{ij} \in C$, compute the data block authenticator

$$\sigma_{ij} = [H_1(ID_i \| j) \cdot g^{c_{ij}}]^{ssk},$$

where ID_i is the unique identifier of f_i. Then, create authenticator set $\phi = \{\sigma_{ij}\}_{i \in [1,n], j \in [1,s]}$.
- Send $\{C, \phi\}$ to certain $\mathcal{SN}$s randomly and record these $\mathcal{SN}$s' certificates.

(3) **ExtractKW**. Based on F, $\mathcal{U}$ generates the keyword set W and the index vector set V.

- Extract top-$\mathcal{K}$ ranked keywords $\{\omega_t\}_{t=1,2,...,\mathcal{K}}$ from the files using the *time frequency inverse document frequency*[3] text keyword extraction method. Then, create the keyword set $W = \{\omega_t\}_{t=1,2,...,\mathcal{K}}$.

---

[2] The *Reed Solomon* erase-code technique is chosen to redundantly segment F, and its security and efficiency have been widely proven.

[3] Time frequency inverse document frequency is a keyword extraction technology that sorts all words according to the frequency of each word in the document, which is used to extract the top-$\mathcal{K}$ words as the keywords of a file in HFKA.

– For ω_t, set up an n-bit binary array as the index vector v_{ω_t} and initialize $v_{\omega_t} = 0$. For each file $f_i \in F$, set $v_{\omega_t}[i] = 1$ if f_i contains the keyword ω_t (e.g., $v_{\omega_t} = \{0, 1, 0, 0, ..., 0\}$ when only the file f_2 contains ω_t). Create the index vector set $V = \{v_{\omega_1}, v_{\omega_2}, ..., v_{\omega_\mathcal{K}}\}$.

(4) **IndexGen**. Based on (W, V), $\mathcal{U}$ generates the encrypted index table I_{RS} and challenge generating auxiliary index I_{TPA}.

– For ω_t, compute the index address $f_{\omega_t} = f(\omega_t, k_1)$ via PRF and then update the original index vector v_{ω_t} to $v_{f_{\omega_t}}$, where k_1 is the key of the PRF implementation.
– Compute the encrypted permutation $\pi_{\omega_t} = \pi(v_{f_{\omega_t}}, k_2)$ via PRP, where k_2 is the key of the PRP implementation.
– Compute the encrypted index vector $e_{\omega_t} = v_{f_{\omega_t}} \oplus \pi_{\omega_t}$ to facilitate the restoration of the original index vector.
– Create a set $S_{\omega_t} = \emptyset$ to record the subscripts of files containing ω_t and add i to S_{ω_t} if f_i contains ω_t. Then, compute the index table label

$$\Delta_{\omega_t,j} = [H_2(Z)^{-1} \cdot H_3(f_{\omega_t} \| j) \cdot \prod_{i \in S_{\omega_t}} (H_1(ID_i \| j)^{-1})]^{ssk},$$

where Z is the number of file updates with an initial value of 1. Let $\Delta_{\omega_t} = \{\Delta_{\omega_t,j}\}_{j=1,2,...,s}$ be the ITL set.
– Set the encrypted index table $I_{RS} = \{(f_{\omega_t}, e_{\omega_t}, \Delta_{\omega_t})\}_{\omega_t \in W}$ and challenge generating auxiliary index $I_{TPA} = \{(f_{\omega_t}, \pi_{\omega_t})\}_{\omega_t \in W}$. Send I_{RS} and I_{TPA} to RS and TPA, respectively.

(5) **TrapdoorGen**. Based on the searched keyword ω', $\mathcal{U}$ generates the search trapdoor $T_{\omega'}$.

– Compute the search index address $f_{\omega'} = f(\omega', k_1)$ and the encrypted permutation $\pi_{\omega'} = \pi(v_{f_{\omega'}}, k_2)$. Set the search trapdoor $T_{\omega'} = (f_{\omega'}, \pi_{\omega'})$.

Challenge Generating phase.

(6) **InitBF**. TPA initiates the Bloom filter and sets its parameters tuple BF.

– Compute $Len = \frac{\ln 2 \cdot |T_{\omega'}|}{\mathcal{R}}$. Create a Len-bit array $\mathcal{B}$ and make $\mathcal{B}[i] = 0$, where $i \in [0, Len - 1]$. Build $BF = (\mathcal{B}, \{SHA_i\}_{i=1,2,...,\mathcal{R}})$.

(7) **FuzzyTDGen**. Based on $T_{\omega'}$ and I_{TPA}, TPA updates BF and generates the fuzzy search trapdoor FT_ω. The pseudo-code is shown in **Algorithm 1**.

– When $T_{\omega'}$ is verified to be legitimate with I_{TPA}, extract the index address $f_{\omega'}$ from $T_{\omega'}$ and then update BF: $\mathcal{B}[SHA_i(f_{\omega'}) \bmod Len]_{i=1,2,...,\mathcal{R}} = 1$.
– Create a set $F_{\omega'}$ and then take the all files' index address as the input of BF. Write $f_{\omega''}$ into $F_{\omega'}$ if $\mathcal{B}[SHA_i(f_{\omega''}) \bmod Len] = 1$.
– Search $\pi_{\omega''}$ with $f_{\omega''}$ from I_{TPA}, and set $\Pi_{\omega'} = \{\pi_{\omega''}\}$. Let $FT_\omega = (F_{\omega'}, \Pi_{\omega'})$ be the fuzzy search trapdoor.

Algorithm 1: FuzzyTDGen

Input: Bloom filter data tuple BF, search trapdoor $T_{\omega'}$, challenge generating auxiliary index I_{TPA};

Output: Fuzzy search trapdoor FT_ω;

```
 1  for ∃f_ω' ∈ {T_ω'} is not checked do      12  for each f_ω_i ∈ I_TPA do
 2      search (f_ω, π_ω) according to f_ω';   13      for j ∈ (0, R) do
 3      if π_ω == π_ω' then                    14          data' = SHA_j(f_ω_i);
 4          continue;                          15          if B[data' mod Len] == 1
 5      else                                                then
 6          return "The search trapdoor  16              continue;
            from U                         17          else
 7          exits problem!";                18              break;
 8  for each i ∈ (0, R) do                 19      add f_ω_i into F_ω', π_ω_i into Π_ω';
 9      for each f_ω' ∈ {T_ω'} do          20  return FT_ω = (F_ω', Π_ω');
10          data = SHA_i(f_ω');
11          B[data mod Len] = 1;
```

---

(8) **ChalGen**. Based on FT_ω, TPA generates the challenge information $Chal$.

- Randomly choose a c-element subset $Q = \{q_1, q_2, ..., q_c\} \subseteq [1, s]$ and $v_j \in Z_q^*$ for each element of Q.
- Generate $Chal = (FT_\omega, Q, \{v_1, v_2, ..., v_j\})$ and send it to RS and SN.

Integrity Auditing phase.

(9) **Retrieval**. Based on $Chal$ and I_{RS}, RS selects the challenged file set S_{ω_t} and corresponding index table label Δ_{ω_t}.

- Take $f_{\omega''}$ from FT_ω and retrieve $f_{\omega_t} = f_{\omega''}$ in I_{RS}. Then, remove the e_{ω_t} and Δ_{ω_t} corresponding to f_{ω_t} from I_{RS} and remove the $\pi_{\omega''}$ corresponding to $f_{\omega''}$ from FT_ω.
- Compute $v_{\omega_t} = e_{\omega_t} \oplus \pi_{\omega''}$.
- Initiate the challenged file set $S_{\omega_t} = \emptyset$. When $v_{\omega_t}[i] = 1, i \in [1, n]$, write i into S_{ω_t} and send $(S_{\omega_t}, \Delta_{\omega_t})$ to SN.

(10) **ProofGen**. Based on $Chal, S_{\omega_t}, \Delta_{\omega_t}, C$ and ϕ, SN generates the storage proof Prf.

- With $Chal = (FT_\omega, Q, \{v_1, v_2, ..., v_j\})$ from TPA, $S_{\omega_t}, \Delta_{\omega_t}$ from RS and $C = \{c_{ij}\}, \phi = \{\sigma_{ij}\}$ from U, compute

$$T = \prod_{i \in S_{\omega_t}} \prod_{j \in Q} \sigma_{ij}^{v_j} \cdot \prod_{j \in Q} \Delta_{\omega_t, j}^{v_j},$$

$$\mu = \sum_{i \in S_{\omega_t}} \sum_{j \in Q} c_{ij} \cdot v_j,$$

and then set $Prf = (T, \mu)$.

(11) **VerifyProof**. Based on $Chal$ and Prf, $\mathcal{TPA}$ verifies the validity of Prf.

– Verify whether Prf is valid via the following equation:

$$e(T,g) \overset{?}{=} e(g^{\mu} \cdot \prod_{j \in Q} [H_2(Z)^{-1} \cdot H_3(f_{\omega_t} \| j)]^{v_j}, spk).$$

5 Security Analysis

Theorem 1. *HFKA achieves storage robustness, i.e., semihonest storage nodes are unable to launch successful auditing frequency analysis attacks and auditing proof replay attacks using stored data.*

Proof. We design two games to prove why HFKA can resist the above two attacks.

  Game 1. We assume that adversary $\mathcal{M}_1$, a malicious $\mathcal{SN}$ that proactively counts the frequency of stored files being audited and attempts to delete files with a minimal auditing frequency to free storage space for other users. M is the number of files stored in $\mathcal{M}_1$ for a $\mathcal{U}$, A is the number of files selected by $\mathcal{U}$ in each round, and R is the number of auditing rounds. In the original keyword-based auditing paradigm, as the number of auditing rounds increases, $\mathcal{M}_1$ can calculate the probability of each file being audited based on the law of large numbers, i.e., knowing $\mathcal{U}$'s preference of files as shown in the following equation: $P_i = \lim\limits_{R \to \infty} \frac{\sum_{j=1}^{R} X_{ij}}{A \cdot R}$, where $X_{ij} = 1$ if f_i is selected in the j-th round, else $X_{ij} = 0$. Given the calculated P_i of each file being audited, $\mathcal{M}_1$ can delete files with P_i close to 0 and hardly be detected by the $\mathcal{U}$. In HFKA, as a result of the Bloom filter, additional $A \cdot p$ files are chosen randomly in each round, where p is the false positive rate of the Bloom filter. As a result, the files not selected by $\mathcal{U}$ have a probability of $\frac{A \cdot p}{M-A}$ of being selected by the Bloom filter in each round. The probability of P_i analyzed by $\mathcal{M}_1$ becomes as follows: $P_i = \lim\limits_{R \to \infty} \frac{\sum_{j=1}^{R} X_{ij}}{A(1+p) \cdot R} + \frac{A \cdot p}{M-A} = P_i' + \frac{A \cdot p}{M-A}$, where $X_{ij} = 1$ if f_i is selected in j-th round, else $X_{ij} = 0$. From the above equation, we can see that even if the probability of a file being selected by a $\mathcal{U}$ tends toward 0, the probability of it being audited is still not less than $\frac{A \cdot p}{M-A}$. It is worthwhile for $\mathcal{SN}$ to delete $\mathcal{U}$'s data with $\frac{A \cdot p \cdot 100}{M-A}\%$ risk.

  Game 2. We assume that the adversary $\mathcal{M}_2$ is a lazy $\mathcal{SN}$. It does not perform the update operation to save its own computing resources when $\mathcal{U}$ requests a data update. Furthermore, it attempts to use the original data to pass the auditing verification. We analyze whether $\mathcal{M}_2$ can forge proof with nonupdated data according to the auditing verification formula as follows: $e(T,g) = e(g^{\mu} \cdot \prod_{j \in Q} [H_2(Z)^{-1} \cdot H_3(f_{\omega_t} \| j)]^{v_j}, spk)$. In this formula, except for the T and μ provided by $\mathcal{M}_2$, Z, spk is public, and f_{ω_t} and $(j, v_j)_{j \in Q}$ are generated by $\mathcal{TPA}$ itself. However, only T and μ are computed under data block c_{ij}, which suggests that $\mathcal{M}_2$ can pass the verification with nonupdated data. We provide more details to support the following analysis: $T = \prod\limits_{i \in S_{\omega_t}} \prod\limits_{j \in Q} \sigma_{ij}^{v_j} \cdot \prod\limits_{j \in Q} \Delta_{\omega_t,j}^{v_j}, \sigma_{ij} = [H_1(ID_i||j) \cdot g^{c_{ij}}]^{ssk}, \Delta_{\omega_t,j} = [H_2(Z)^{-1} \cdot H_3(f_{\omega_t}||j) \cdot \prod\limits_{i \in S_{\omega_t}} (H_1(ID_i||j)^{-1})]^{ssk}, \mu = \sum\limits_{i \in S_{\omega_t}} \sum\limits_{j \in Q} c_{ij} \cdot v_j$. Ignoring challenge information $(j, v_j)_{j \in Q}$ and challenged file set $S_{\omega_t} = \{i\}$, μ is related to only c_{ij}, but T also implies Z. We make Z' be $\mathcal{M}_2$'s update times; then, the system updates data z times after $\mathcal{M}_2$ does not perform an update operation. That is, the global number of updates is $Z = Z' + z$. The probability of $H(Z) = H(Z')$ can be ignored due to the anticollision property of the hash function.   ∎

Theorem 2. *HFKA achieves privacy protection, i.e., no entities other than users can obtain specific content about outsourced data or users through the Bloom filter and the index table while executing auditing tasks.*

Proof. We analyze how HFKA achieves privacy protection to resist a semihonest $\mathcal{SN}$ or a curious $\mathcal{TPA}$.

There are two strategies to undermine $\mathcal{U}$'s privacy for a semihonest $\mathcal{SN}$: (i) It deciphers ω_t and then infers the file's type and even the content from ω_t. (ii) It does not decipher ω_t but speculates the importance of files based on the frequency of selected f_{ω_t} and the audited files in each round. For the first strategy, HFKA adopts PRF to protect ω_t. Only $\mathcal{U}$ knows its keyword ω_t; other entities know only the keyword index address: $f_{\omega_t} = f(\omega_t, k_1)$. Because of the backward unpredictability of PRF, $\mathcal{SN}$ cannot invert ω_t by any subsequence of f_{ω_t}. For the second strategy, HFKA resists $\mathcal{SN}$'s privacy attacks in two aspects. Before formally analyzing the measures, we show how $\mathcal{SN}$ violates $\mathcal{U}$'s privacy. By asking the $\mathcal{TPA}$ or $\mathcal{RS}$, the $\mathcal{SN}$ can easily obtain f_ωs in the auditing trapdoor of each round. After accumulating enough rounds of data, $\mathcal{SN}$ can easily guess the documents corresponding to certain high-frequency keywords, as well as the connections between keywords. Two measures are taken to cope with such a situation, firstly using the Bloom filter to make the mapping relationships more ambiguous for each round, and secondly adopting distributed storage so that the audit information received for a certain $\mathcal{SN}$ is not complete and the relationships between keywords and documents and between keywords and keywords are further weakened. Hence, HFKA blocks the adversary attack from the frequency distribution. $\mathcal{TPA}$ faces the same difficulty regarding $f_{\omega_t} \to \omega_t$. When users are anonymous and PRF is backward unpredictable, a curious $\mathcal{TPA}$ can do nothing.   ∎

Theorem 3. *HFKA achieves data security, which means that no external adversary can obtain any details about the data in the event that outsourced data are intercepted in transit.*

Proof. In the whole process of information interaction, the data involved can be classified as follows: keyword searchable data (index address f_{ω_t}, search vector π_{ω_t}, encrypted index vector e_{ω_t}, ITL $\Delta_{\omega_t,j}$), auditing information (encrypted data c_{ij} and data authenticator σ_{ij}). The security of f_{ω_t} is based on PRF, and the security of π_{ω_t} is based on PRP. PRF is indistinguishable and its proof is detailed in [36]; that is, in the face of an attack, the attacker cannot determine whether the same PRF function is selected, i.e., the attacker cannot further guess the function input. PRP also achieves indiscernibility using computationally difficult mathematical problems. Since e_{ω_t} is designed to recover the original index vector v_{ω_t}, its security is off the table. The security of c_{ij} is based on AES-128. AES can resist differential cryptanalysis, linear cryptanalysis and other basic attacks; more details are provided in [38]. Moreover, AES with a 128-bit key has the same safety strength as RSA-3072 and ECC-256, which is estimated to be available until 2040. The security of σ_{ij} and $\Delta_{\omega_t,j}$ is based on a discrete logarithm problem (DLP) [37], which is stated as follows: For $a, g \in G$, $\exists\ b$ such that $g^b = a$; finding such b is computationally complex, where G is a cyclic group. For σ_{ij}, $\mathcal{M}$ must solve the DLP twice to obtain the data block c_{ij}, which is still protected by AES-128.   ∎

6   Performance Evaluation

In this section, we evaluate the performance of HFKA on a Lenovo desktop computer equipped with an Intel Core i5 CPU and 8 GB of RAM. All cryptographic operations in HFKA, such as PRP, PRF, Bloom filter and bilinear pairing, are performed using the PBC library. We conduct detailed experiments to demonstrate the unique function of HFKA by balancing the auditing distribution to hide the files' audited frequency.

6.1   Auditing Distribution

The Bloom filter plays an important role in HFKA, which hides the frequency distribution properties of keyword-based auditing. We elaborate how it plays in HFKA from experiments in three perspectives. **Experiment 1** investigates the factors influencing the false positive rate of the Bloom filter and finds the most suitable parameters of it to assist the implementation of HFKA. **Experiment 2** shows the results of implementing the frequency hiding function of HFKA. **Experiment 3** further improves the fuzzing capability of the Bloom filter. It is assumed that the distribution of $\mathcal{K}$ keywords in n files is uniform. That is, the distribution of keywords can represent the auditing distribution of files.

Based on the original introduction of the Bloom filter in [34], we know that its false positive rate p is equal to $(1 - e^{\frac{-k \cdot m}{n}})^k$, where k is the number of hash functions, m is the size of the input, and n is the length of the BF array. In **Experiment 1**, we construct the Bloom filter and control its false positive rate by adjusting the parameters. Figure 4 shows the variation in the false positive rate with different parameters. Comparing the four small plots (a), (b), (c), (d) in Fig. 4, it was found that the larger the input size is, the larger the false positive rate is. For any of the small plots, we found that both of the number of hash functions and the size of the BF array are inversely proportional to the false

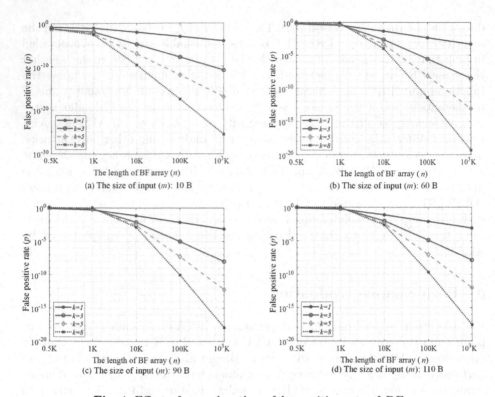

Fig. 4. Effect of array length on false positive rate of BF

positive rate. Here, we set the size of each keyword index address to 10 B, so an input size of 60 B means that the user selects 6 keywords in a search trapdoor. According to the fuzzy requirements of HFKA and the specific experimental data, it is most suitable when the input size is between 90 B and 110 B, the array length is 1000 bits, and the hash function number is 3 so that the false positive rate can be approximately 55%.

In **Experiment 2**, we use keywords from the simulated dataset to perform fuzzy matching experiments. We select several keywords to update the Bloom filter in each round, and then input all keywords for matching, and then finally collect these matching results. The total number of keywords is 50, and 9 or 10 keywords are chosen in each round. The false positive rate means that there would be 4 or 5 additional chosen keywords. Figure 5 shows the distribution of the selected keywords after 20 rounds of experiments. Horizontally, the false positive rate of the Bloom filter in each round can be seen, with red ● being the keywords selected by $\mathcal{U}$ and blue ✖ being the fuzzy keywords selected by the Bloom filter. Vertically, the frequency of each keyword that was selected can be seen. The more red ● there are in a column, the higher probability of the keyword would be selected by $\mathcal{U}$, such as ω_{10}, ω_{24}, while blue ✖ balances the probability of the other keywords being selected, such as ω_{20}, ω_{40}. The frequency of each

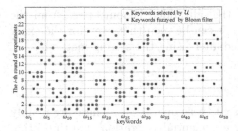

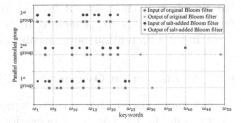

Fig. 5. The keyword distribution of Experiment 2

Fig. 6. The use of salt-hashing BF in Experiment 3

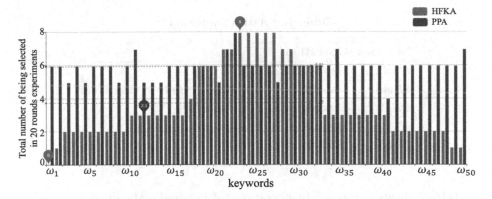

Fig. 7. The auditing frequency comparison between HFKA and PPA

keyword is counted and compared with traditional auditing in Fig. 7. HFKA represents high and low frequencies, which are evenly distributed in itself, while PPA are all evenly distributed. Moreover, we discuss the total auditing overhead. To guarantee detection confidence of 99% probability, TPA needs to select 460 files from 10,000 files randomly in the PPA model. However, in the PKA model [4], the user is only concerned about 2% probability of the total files, i.e., select 200 files from 10,000 files. In HFKA, due to the 55% false positive of the Bloom filter, there are additional 110 files to be selected, i.e., a total of 310 files are selected in each round. Therefore, HFKA audits 150 files less than PPA each time, which saves 32.6% probability of auditing overhead.

In **Experiment 3**, we fix the configuration of the Bloom filter and the search trapdoor, but add different salt to the hash functions in each round. We adopt the control method to verify the efficacy of salted hash functions. To avoid the coincidence of one experimental group, we set three parallel experimental groups, where the 1st, 2nd and 3rd groups have different Bloom filter parameter settings. As shown in the Fig. 6, the red ● in each group indicates the input of the original Bloom filter, while the dark-blue ● indicates the input of salt-added Bloom filter, which must be consistent with the red ●. Correspondingly, the light-blue ✖ indicates the keywords fuzzied by the original Bloom filter, while the purple ✖ is the keyword fuzzied by the salt-added Bloom filter. From the results of the above experimental groups, it can be seen that even for the exact same input, different outputs are obtained after using the salting method.

6.2   Computation Overhead

Table 1 shows the symbols used to represent these operations. There are mainly calculations in HFKA: hash operation, exponential operation, multiplication operation and bilinear pairing operation. We ignore the *XOR, PRF, PRP, addition* operations, which have minimal computational cost.

Table 1. Notation description

Notation	Operation
$HASH_{G_1}$	Map a value to G_1
$SHA_{Z_q^*}$	Map a value to Z_q^* with a secure hash algorithm
EXP_{G_1}	Exponentiation operation in G_1
MUL_{G_1}	Multiplication operation in G_1
$PAIR$	Bilinear pairing with G_1, G_2

Table 2 shows the concrete operations of involved data in each phase of HFKA. The data preprocessing phase includes data authenticator generation and index label generation. The challenge generation phase includes Bloom filter updating and fuzzy matching. The integrity auditing phase includes proof generation and verification. Compared to the method of Gao et al. [4], HFKA only increases the Bloom filter updating and the fuzzy matching process, which increase $\mathcal{R}\cdot(|F_{\omega'}|+\mathcal{K})$ HMAC operations in each round of auditing. We assess the run time of SHA operations with 128-bit keys and 1024 bytes input in Python, and the experimental results show that it is only 0.03 ms, which is negligible due to the whole system.

Table 2. Computation overhead

Processing phase	Computation overhead
Authenticator generation	$n \cdot s \cdot (HASH_{G_1} + MUL_{G_1} + EXP_{G_1})$
ITL generation	$\mathcal{K} \cdot s \cdot [(|S_{\omega_t} + 2|)HASH_{G_1} + (|S_{\omega_t}| + 1)MUL_{G_1} + EXP_{G_1}]$
BF updating	$\mathcal{R} \cdot |F_{\omega'}| \cdot SHA_{Z_q^*}$
Fuzzy matching	$\mathcal{K} \cdot \mathcal{R} \cdot SHA_{Z_q^*}$
Proof generation	$c \cdot (2 \cdot |S_{\omega_t}| + 1) \cdot EXP_{G_1} + c \cdot |S_{\omega_t}| \cdot MUL_{G_1}$
Proof verification	$2 \cdot PAIR + (c+1) \cdot MUL_{G_1} + (c+1) \cdot EXP_{G_1} + 2c \cdot HASH_{G_1}$

6.3 Storage Overhead

Here, we consider the storage overhead in HFKA. Due to the involvement of the keyword-file index, HFKA has some additional storage overhead compared to PPA. We list the additional data structures and the storage space they consume as the number of files sampled increases in Table 3. According to the experimental results, when there are 100 files, $\mathcal{RS}$ requires only 0.37 MB of space to store $I_{\mathcal{RS}}$, and $\mathcal{TPA}$ requires only 0.368 MB of space. When there are 1000 files, these values become 16.64 MB and 16.62 MB. Even when the number of files increases to 10,000, the size of $I_{\mathcal{RS}}$ is only 466.51 MB, and the size of $I_{\mathcal{TPA}}$ is 466.31 MB. Notably, the size of a Bloom filter with a 55% false positive rate is always 1K bits, as will be elaborated in Sect. 6.1. Furthermore, the size of $I_{\mathcal{RS}}$ and $I_{\mathcal{TPA}}$ are related to the number of files. In fact, $I_{\mathcal{RS}}$ and $I_{\mathcal{TPA}}$ are directly related to the number of keywords, and the number of files affects the number of keywords.

Table 3. Storage overhead

The number of files	$I_{\mathcal{RS}}$ storage	$I_{\mathcal{TPA}}$ storage	Bloom filter (55%)
100	0.37 MB	0.368 MB	1000 bit
1000	16.64 MB	16.62 MB	1000 bit
10,000	466.51 MB	466.31 MB	1000 bit

7 Conclusion and Future Work

In this paper, we propose a keyword-based auditing scheme, HFKA, to address the auditing frequency leakage problem for a smart government. We utilize the Bloom filter to achieve a specified keyword fuzzy matching. Meanwhile, we design an index table label to resist replay attacks by lazy server nodes and generate storage proofs without exposing any keyword-file privacy. We also separate the retrieval work from the storage work using a special retrieval server to improve the retrieval efficiency, reduce the storage cost and computing cost of the storage node, and further maintain the keyword privacy. Finally, the security of the scheme is proven by rigorous security analysis, and the feasibility of the scheme is proven by performance evaluation.

In future work, we will examine the security protection and economic viability of the keyword-based auditing paradigm in real world applications and strengthen the integration of the auditing model and smart government. First, in order to allow batch auditing and dynamic auditing of various storage nodes, we will enhance the data label construction of outsourced data. Second, we will attempt to store massively outsourced and more finely partitioned data via a directed acyclic graph (DAG). The difficulties of implementing smart government affairs will then be examined, and we will work to overcome security issues and performance bottlenecks in data sharing and integrity auditing.

Acknowledgements. This work was supported in part by the Southwest Petroleum University "Set Sail" Project (Grant No.0202667680-2021QHZ017); in part by the National Natural Science Foundation of China (Grant No.61902327); in part by the China Postdoctoral Science Foundation (Grant No.2020M681316); in part by the Chengdu Key R & D project (Grant No.2021-YF05-00965-SN); and in part by the Southwest Petroleum University Graduate Teaching and Research Reform Project (Grant No.JY20ZD06).

References

1. Mellouli, S., Luna, R., Luis, F.: Smart government, citizen participation and open data. Inf. Polity **19**(1–2), 1–4 (2014)
2. Wu, J., Ping, L., Ge, X., Wang, Y., Fu, J.: Cloud storage as the infrastructure of cloud computing. In: International Conference on Intelligent Computing and Cognitive Informatics, pp. 380–383 (2010)
3. Yang, K., Jia, X.: Data storage auditing service in cloud computing: Challenges, methods and opportunities. World Wide Web **15**(4), 409–428 (2012)
4. Gao, X., Yu, J., Chang Y., Wang, H., Fan, J.: Checking only when it is necessary: Enabling integrity auditing based on the keyword with sensitive information privacy for encrypted cloud data. IEEE Trans. Dependable Secure Comput., 1 (2021). https://doi.org/10.1109/TDSC.2021.3106780
5. Ateniese, G., et al.: Provable data possession at untrusted stores. In: Proceedings of the 14th ACM Conference on Computer and Communications Security, pp. 598–609. ACM, Alexandria, VI (2007)
6. Juels, A., Kaliski, B.: Proofs of retrievability for large files. Proc. Comput. Commun. Secur. Alexandria: AcMPress **584**, 597 (2007)
7. Wang, Q., Wang, C., Li, J., Ren, K., Lou, W.: Enabling public verifiability and data dynamics for storage security in cloud computing. In: Backes, M., Ning, P. (eds.) ESORICS 2009. LNCS, vol. 5789, pp. 355–370. Springer, Heidelberg (2009). https://doi.org/10.1007/978-3-642-04444-1_22
8. Merkle, R.C.: Secrecy, Authentication, and Public Key Systems, 2nd edn. Stanford University, Stanford (1979)
9. Wang, C., Wang, Q., Ren, K., Lou, W.: Privacy-preserving public auditing for data storage security in cloud computing. In: 2010 IEEE INFOCOM, pp. 1–9. IEEE, San Diego, CA (2010)
10. Wang, C., Chow, S.S.M., Wang, Q., Ren, K., Lou, W.: Privacy-preserving public auditing for secure cloud storage. IEEE Trans. Comput. **62**(6), 362–375 (2013)
11. Zhou, L., Fu, A., Yang, G., Wang, H., Zhang, Y.: Efficient certificateless multi-copy integrity auditing scheme supporting data dynamics. IEEE Trans. Dependable Secur. Comput. **19**(2), 1118–1132 (2022)
12. Zhang, X., Zhao, J., Xu, C., Li, H., Wang, H., Zhang, Y.: CIPPPA: Conditional identity privacy-preserving public auditing for cloud-Based WBANs against malicious auditors. IEEE Trans. Cloud Comput. **9**(4), 1362–1375 (2021)
13. Rashmi, K V., Shah, N B., Kumar, P V.: Enabling node repair in any erasure code for distributed storage. In: 2011 IEEE International Symposium on Information Theory, pp. 1235–1239. IEEE, St. Petersburg (2011)
14. Perard, D., Lacan, J., Bachy, Y., Detchart, J.: Erasure code-based low storage blockchain node. In: Proceedings of 2018 IEEE International Conference on Internet of Things (iThings) and IEEE Green Computing and Communications (GreenCom) and IEEE Cyber, Physical and Social Computing (CPSCom) and IEEE Smart Data (SmartData), pp. 1622–1627. IEEE, Halifax, Canada (2018)

15. Jin, H., Luo, R., He, Q., Wu, S., Zeng, Z., Xia, X.: Cost-effective data placement in edge storage systems with erasure code. IEEE Trans. Serv. Comput., 1 (2022). https://doi.org/10.1109/TSC.2022.3152849
16. Sun, Y., Liu, Q., Chen, X., Du, X.: An adaptive authenticated data structure with privacy-preserving for big data stream in cloud. IEEE Trans. Inf. Forensics Secur. 15(2020), 3295–3310 (2020)
17. Li, S., Zhang, Y., Xu, C., Chen, K.: Cryptoanalysis of an authenticated data structure scheme with public privacy-preserving auditing. IEEE Trans. Inf. Forensics Secur. 16, 2564–2565 (2021)
18. Xu, S., Cai, X., Zhao, Y., Ren, Z., Du, L., Wang, Q., Zhou, J.: zkrpChain: Towards multi-party privacy-preserving data auditing for consortium blockchains based on zero-knowledge range proofs. Futur. Gener. Comput. Syst. 128, 490–504 (2022)
19. Shen, W., Qin, J., Yu, J., Hao, R., Hu, J., Ma, J.: Data integrity auditing without private key storage for secure cloud storage. IEEE Trans. Cloud Comput. 9(4), 1408–1421 (2019)
20. Zheng, W., Lai, C.F., He, D., Kumar, N., Chen, B.: Secure storage auditing with efficient key updates for cognitive industrial IoT environment. IEEE Trans. Industr. Inf. 17(6), 4238–4247 (2020)
21. Ge, X., Yu, J., Hu, C.: Enabling effifficient verififiable fuzzy keyword search over encrypted data in cloud computing. IEEE Access 6, 45725–45739 (2018)
22. Miao, Y., Tong, Q., Deng, R., Choo, K.K.R., Liu, X., Li, H.: Verifiable searchable encryption framework against insider keyword-guessing attack in cloud storage. IEEE Trans. Cloud Comput. 10, 835–848 (2020)
23. Bringer, J., Chabanne, H., Kindarji, B.: Error-tolerant searchable encryption. In: IEEE International Conference on Communications, pp. 1–6 (2009)
24. Li, J., Wang, Q., Wang, C., Cao, N., Ren, K., Lou, W.: Fuzzy keyword search over encrypted data in cloud computing. In: 2010 Proceedings IEEE INFOCOM, pp. 1–5. IEEE, Cape Town (2010)
25. Wang, Q., et al.: Searchable encryption over feature-rich data. IEEE Trans. Dependable Secure Comput. 15(3), 496–510 (2016)
26. Zhong, H., Li, Z., Cui, J., Sun, Y., Liu, L.: Efficient dynamic multi-keyword fuzzy search over encrypted cloud data. J. Netw. Comput. Appl. 149, 102469 (2020)
27. Liu, Q., Peng, Y., Pei, S., Wu, J., Peng, T., Wang, G.: Prime inner product encoding for effective wildcard-based multi-keyword fuzzy search. IEEE Trans. Serv. Comput. 15, 1799 (2020)
28. Li, X., et al.: VRFMS: verifiable ranked fuzzy multi-keyword search over encrypted data. IEEE Trans. Serv. Comput., 1 (2022). https://doi.org/10.1109/TSC.2021.3140092
29. Sahu, I.K., Nene, M.J.: Identity-based integrity verification (IBIV) protocol for cloud data storage. In: 2021 International Conference on Advances in Electrical, Computing, Communication and Sustainable Technologies (ICAECT), pp. 1–6. IEEE, Bhilai (2021)
30. Yoosuf, M.S., Anitha, R.: LDuAP: Lightweight dual auditing protocol to verify data integrity in cloud storage servers. J. Ambient. Intell. Humaniz. Comput. 13(8), 3787–3805 (2022)
31. Tong, Q., Miao, Y., Weng, J., Liu, X., Choo, K.K.R., Deng, R.: Verifiable fuzzy multi-keyword search over encrypted data with adaptive security. IEEE Trans. Knowl. Data Eng., 1 (2022). https://doi.org/10.1109/TKDE.2022.3152033
32. Gervais, A., Capkun, S., Karame, G.O., Gruber, D.: On the privacy provisions of bloom filters in lightweight bitcoin clients. In: Proceedings of the 30th Annual

Computer Security Applications Conference, pp. 326–335. ACM, New Orleans, Louisiana (2014)

33. Pagh, A., Pagh, R., Rao, S.: An optimal bloom filter replacement. In: Proceedings of the Sixteenth Annual ACM-SIAM Symposium on Discrete Algorithms, pp. 823–829. SODA, Vancouver, BC (2005)

34. Kiss, S.Z., Hosszu, E., Tapolcai, J., Ronyai, L., Rottenstreich, O.: Bloom filter with a false positive free zone. IEEE Trans. Netw. Serv. Manage. **18**(2), 2334–2349 (2021)

35. Kamara, S., Papamanthou, C., Roeder, T.: Dynamic searchable symmetric encryption. In: Proceedings of the 2012 ACM Conference on Computer and Communications Security, pp. 965–976. ACM, Raleigh, NC (2012)

36. Bellare, M., Impagliazzo, R.: A tool for obtaining tighter security analyses of pseudorandom function based constructions, with applications to PRP to PRF conversion. IACR Cryptol. ePrint Arch. **1999**, 24 (1999)

37. McCurley, K S.: The discrete logarithm problem. In: Proceedings of Symposium in Applied Mathematics, pp. 49–74 (1990)

38. Daemen, J., Rijmen, V.: AES proposal: Rijndael (1999)

39. Cachin, C.: Architecture of the hyperledger blockchain fabric. In: Workshop on Distributed Cryptocurrencies and Consensus Ledgers, pp. 1–4. Chicago (2016)

40. Qu, Y., Nosouhi, M.R., Cui, L., Yu, S.: Existing privacy protection solutions. In: Personalized Privacy Protection in Big Data. DA, pp. 5–13. Springer, Singapore (2021). https://doi.org/10.1007/978-981-16-3750-6_2

A Lightweight Certificateless Searchable Public Key Encryption Scheme for Medical Internet of Things

Xiaoguang Liu[1,2(✉)], Yingying Sun[2,3], and Hao Dong[2,3]

[1] School of Mathematics, Southwest Minzu University, Chengdu 610041, Sichuan, People's Republic of China
21700128@swun.edu.cn
[2] Guangxi Key Laboratory of Cryptography and Information Security, Guilin University of Electronic Technology, Guilin 541004, Guangxi, People's Republic of China
[3] School of Computer Science and Engineering, Southwest Minzu University, Chengdu 610041, Sichuan, People's Republic of China

Abstract. To ensure the confidentiality of medical data, the medical information is usually encrypted before outsourcing to a third party for processing. Encryption technology can ensure the privacy of data, but it limits the search for data. The problem is usually solved using public key encryption with keyword search (PEKS). Recently, a few certificateless PEKS (CPEKS) schemes have been proposed. However, they rely on the high-consuming bilinear pairing, and some of them are vulnerable to inside keyword guessing attacks (IKGA). To solve these problems, we propose a lightweight CPEKS scheme for the Medical Internet of things (IoMT), which does not contain bilinear pairing. The scheme is proved to be secure in the random oracle model. The analysis results show that it has better comprehensive performance than the existing schemes according to the security property, the computation cost, and the communication cost.

Keywords: Certificateless · Searchable public key encryption · Pairing-free · Privacy protection · Security · IoMT

1 Introduction

The Internet of Things (IoT) links a lot of objects to exchange and share information through Internet Protocol, it plays an irreplaceable role in the era of

This work is supported by the Fundamental Research Funds for the Central Universities of Southwest Minzu University (No: ZYN2022077), the Fund of Guangxi Key Laboratory of Cryptography and Information Security (No: GCIS202121), the Foreign Experts Program of Ministry of Science and Technology of China (No: DL2022186001L), and the Sichuan Science and Technology Program (No: 2021ZYD0021).

E. Ahene and F. Li (Eds.): FCS 2022, CCIS 1726, pp. 69–86, 2022.
https://doi.org/10.1007/978-981-19-8445-7_5

the interconnection of all things [1]. In particular, IoMT has rapid development, such as electronic medical records, AI-assisted diagnosis and treatment, etc. [2,3]. During the fight against COVID-19, many things in the hospital can be interconnected under 5G coverage, and massive data on epidemic prevention and control are collected, analyzed, transmitted, and shared in real-time. So it can reduce the infection probability of medical staff and solve the problem of resource shortage.

IoMT is a patient-centered medical model that uses advanced information technologies to realize medical resource sharing, remote diagnosis, and real-time monitoring [4]. Figure 1 shows the typical network architecture for IoMT data processing. In this architecture, patients' physical information is collected through medical sensing devices and then uploaded to the cloud server via the Internet. The cloud server will be responsible for the computing and storage of data for the IoMT system. Thus, some users, such as legitimate doctors, can obtain the data from the cloud server after their requests are approved. However, medical data not only contains the patient's signature but also contains much private information. The uploaded data may be leaked and tampered with since the cloud server is not completely trusted. Therefore, how to ensure data security while using it legally is the core issue in IoMT [5].

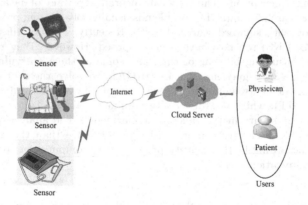

Fig. 1. Typical network architecture for IoMT data processing.

As we all know, encryption technology can enhance the security of data, but how to efficiently search and share encrypted data is a hot potato. To solve the problem, searchable encryption (SE) schemes based on symmetric encryption have been proposed [6,7]. However, an awkward problem that these schemes face is how to secretly distribute keys to authorized users [8]. In 2004, Boneh et al. [9] gave the first PEKS scheme. The case involved three entities: the sender, the server, and the receiver. The sender extracts the keyword from the message and encrypts it with the public key of the receiver to generate the keyword ciphertext. The receiver uses its private key to encrypt the keyword to generate a trapdoor. Then, the server tests the received keyword ciphertext and trapdoor. If both contain the same keyword, the server will return the message containing the keyword to the receiver. After that, there are many works based on PEKS, such as [10,11]. Recently, Miao et al. [12] pointed out that most existing PEKS schemes are still vulnerable to IKGA, and they proposed an authenticated search encryption scheme. However, many proposed schemes are based on traditional public key infrastructure (PKI) or identity encryption. These schemes involve certificate management and key escrow problems. Lu et al. [13] proposed a CPEKS scheme. It not only effectively solves the above problems but also prevents IKGA. Unfortunately, the scheme relies on bilinear pairing.

In this paper, we will propose a lightweight pairing-free CPEKS scheme. The contributions of this paper can be summarized as follows:

1. We give a lightweight CPEKS scheme. It avoids the problems of certificate management and key escrow, and can realize efficient keyword search. Novelly, the scheme does not involve high-consuming bilinear pairing.
2. To enhance the security, we input not only the public key of the data receiver but also the public key of the data owner in the encryption scheme, so that the data receiver can verify the identity of the data owner.
3. The random numbers are added to the trapdoor generation to improve the security, and the scheme is proved to be secure in the random oracle model.

The structure of the paper is as follows. In Sect. 2, we introduce some related works. In Sect. 3, the preliminaries are given. In Sect. 4, we introduce the details of the proposed CPEKS scheme. In Sects. 5 and 6, we give the security proof and performance analysis respectively. Finally, some conclusions are given in Sect. 7.

2   Related Works

As mentioned above, to ensure that medical information can be safely stored on the cloud, the data is usually encrypted. To realize ciphertext search without disclosing any plaintext information, Boneh et al. [9] proposed the first PEKS scheme. Baek et al. [14] pointed out that the scheme in [9] needs to transmit the trapdoor through an unrealistic secure channel to ensure that it cannot be acquired by the adversary. Therefore, they proposed a secure channel-free PEKS scheme. However, Yau et al. [15] pointed out that [14] is vulnerable to offline keyword guessing attacks. This is because the keyword is selected in a small space, and users usually use common keywords to search [16].

To solve this problem, Hu et al. [17] proposed a PEKS scheme with the designated server. However, Yau et al. [18] pointed out that [17] is vulnerable to keyword guessing attacks by malicious servers. Then, Chen [19] proposed an enhanced designated server searchable encryption scheme, but the problem in [17] is still not effectively solved. Later, Peng et al. [20] proposed the fuzzy keyword search public key encryption. However, this scheme can only prevent attacks from external adversaries. After that, Ma et al. [21] proposed the PEKS scheme with authorization. Huang et al. [22] pointed out that the scheme in [21] cannot resist IKGA initiated by internal adversaries. In addition, to resist offline keyword guessing attacks, Chen et al. [23] defined dual-server public key encryption with a keyword search for secure cloud storage, which uses two servers to resist IKGA. However, the limitation of this scheme is that the servers cannot cooperate. Later, Lu et al. [24] proposed a new certificate-based searchable encryption scheme. Because it is based on PKI, there is a cumbersome certificate management problem. Liu et al. [25] proposed a new framework called identity-certifying authority-assisted identity-based searchable encryption, but it has the key escrow problem.

In 2003, Al-Riyami and Paterson [26] introduced the concept of certificateless public key encryption (CLPKE). Peng et al. [27] combined PEKS with CLPKE to propose a CPEKS scheme. This scheme effectively solves the problems of certificate management and key escrow. After, Ma et al. [28] proposed a CPEKS scheme for the industrial internet of things (IIoT). However, the keyword is encrypted only by the receiver's public key, and the adversary can impersonate the sender to encrypt the keyword and initiate IKGA. Zhang et al. [29] proposed a verifiable CPEKS scheme, which can resist IKGA by verifying the identity of the sender. Recently, He et al. [30] proposed a CPEKS scheme for IIoT, which is provably secure against IKGA. It is a pity that many of the existing CPEKS schemes all rely on high-consuming bilinear pairing. Therefore, Lu et al. [31] proposed a privacy-preserving and pairing-free multirecipient CPEKS scheme. In the trapdoor algorithm, $t_2 = (\text{sk}_{i,1} + \text{sk}_{i,2}) H_2(\text{id}_S, \text{id}_i, k', w')$. Since H_2 mapping is an integer, the malicious server can easily calculate the private key of the receiver by accessing trapdoor. Subsequently, Lu et al. [32] proposed a pairing-free PKI-based searchable encryption. But it has the certificate management problem and is still not suitable for the resource-limited IoMT equipment.

3   Preliminaries

3.1   Eliptic Curve Diffie-Hellman Problem

Let G be an additive cyclic group with the order of prime q, and P is the generator of the group G.

1. *Eliptic Curve Diffie-Hellman Problem (CDH)*: Given the triple $(P, aP, bP) \in G$, where $a, b \in Z_q^*$. It is difficult to calculate abP.
2. *Decisional Curve Diffie-Hellman Problem (DDH)*: Given the quad $(P, aP, bP, cP) \in G$, where $a, b, c \in Z_q^*$. It is difficult to determine whether c equals ab.

3.2 System Model

The system model of the CPEKS scheme is mainly composed of four entities: Key Generation Center (KGC), cloud server, data owner, and data receiver. Each entity works as follows:

1. *KGC*: It is a semi-trusted third party, which can generate the system master key and the partial private keys of the data owner and data receiver. At the same time, KGC publishes system parameters.
2. *Data owner*: His/Her encrypted information is divided into two parts. First, he/she uses a traditional encryption algorithm to encrypt patient privacy data and generate the ciphertext. In addition, keywords are extracted from patient privacy data. Then, he/she uses the proposed CPEKS scheme to encrypt keywords to generate keyword ciphertext. Finally, he/she uploads ciphertext to the cloud server.
3. *Data receiver*: He/she uses its private key and the data owner's public key to generate a trapdoor for the keywords he/she wants to search for. Then, the trapdoor is sent to the cloud server.
4. *Cloud server*: It is also a semi-trusted third party for storing and processing medical data. It compares the keyword ciphertext sent by the data owner with the trapdoor sent by the data receiver. If they both contain the same keyword, it returns the corresponding information to the data receiver.

4 The Proposed CPEKS Scheme

The proposed CPEKS scheme consists of the following eight polynomial-time algorithms. We define the identity of the data owner as ID_O and the identity of the data receiver as ID_R.

1. *Setup*: Given a security parameter λ, KGC first selects the cyclic additive group G with order of prime q, and P is the generator of G. Then, KGC randomly selects $s \in Z_q^*$ as the system master key, calculates $P_{pub} = sP$ as the system public key, and chooses three different secure hash functions: $H_1 : \{0,1\}^* \times G \to Z_q^*$, $H_2 : \{0,1\}^* \to Z_q^*$, and $H_3 : \{0,1\}^* \times G \to Z_q^*$. Finally, KGC publishes the system parameters $params = \{\lambda, G, q, P, P_{pub}, H_1, H_2, H_3\}$ and keeps s secretly.
2. *Partial-Private-Key-Extract*: KGC will perform the following steps:
   (a) KGC first takes the identity of the data owner $ID_O \in \{0,1\}^*$ as input, and selects a random value $r_{ID_O} \in Z_q^*$. Then KGC calculates $Q_{ID_O}=r_{ID_O}P$, $\mu_{ID_O}=H_1(ID_O, Q_{ID_O})$, $d_{ID_O}=r_{ID_O}+s\mu_{ID_O} \pmod q$, and returns Q_{ID_O} and d_{ID_O} to the data owner.
   (b) Takes the identity of the data receiver $ID_R \in \{0,1\}^*$ as input, KGC selects a random value $r_{ID_R} \in Z_q^*$, and calculates $Q_{ID_R}=r_{ID_R}P$, $\mu_{ID_R}=H_1(ID_R, Q_{ID_R})$, $d_{ID_R}=r_{ID_R} + s\mu_{ID_R} \pmod q$. KGC returns Q_{ID_R} and d_{ID_R} to the data receiver.
3. *Set-Secret-Value*: Takes $ID_O \in \{0,1\}^*$ and $ID_R \in \{0,1\}^*$ as input:

(a) The data receiver chooses a random value $x_{ID_O} \in Z_q^*$ as its secret value.

(b) The data owner chooses a random value $x_{ID_R} \in Z_q^*$ as its secret value.

4. *Set-Private-Key*:

   (a) Sets $SK_{ID_O} = (x_{ID_O}, d_{ID_O})$ as the private key of the data owner.

   (b) Sets $SK_{ID_R} = (x_{ID_R}, d_{ID_R})$ as the private key of the data receiver.

5. *Set-Public-key*: Takes the parameter *params*, the secret value x_{ID_O} of the data owner and the secret value x_{ID_R} of the data receiver as input.

   (a) The data owner calculates $Y_{ID_O} = x_{ID_O}P$ and sets $PK_{ID_O} = (Y_{ID_O}, Q_{ID_O})$ as the public key of the data owner.

   (b) The data receiver calculates $Y_{ID_R} = x_{ID_R}P$ and sets $PK_{ID_R} = (Y_{ID_R}, Q_{ID_R})$ as the public key of the data receiver.

6. *CPEKS*: Takes *params*, ID_O, ID_R, SK_{ID_O} and PK_{ID_R} as input. The data owner encrypts the keyword w as follows:

   (a) The data owner randomly selects number $r_1 \in Z_q^*$.

   (b) The data owner calculates $\beta_{ID_O} = H_3(ID_O, ID_R, x_{ID_O}Y_{ID_R})$, and
   $$C_1 = r_1P \;,\; C_2 = \left(H_2(w) + r_1\beta_{ID_O}^{-1}\right)(x_{ID_O} + d_{ID_O})^{-1},$$
   $$C_3 = \beta_{ID_O}\left(Y_{ID_R} + Q_{ID_R} + \mu_{ID_R}P_{pub}\right).$$
   The data owner returns ciphertext $C = (C_1, C_2, C_3)$.

7. *Trapdoor*: Takes *params*, SK_{ID_R} and PK_{ID_O} as input. The data receiver calculates T_w as follows:

   (a) The data receiver randomly selects number $r_2 \in Z_q^*$.

   (b) The data receiver calculates $\beta_{ID_R} = H_3(ID_O, ID_R, x_{ID_R}Y_{ID_O})$, and
   $$T_1 = r_2P, \; T_2 = (r_2 + \beta_{ID_R}H_2(w))(x_{ID_R} + d_{ID_R})^{-1} + \beta_{ID_R},$$
   $$T_3 = \beta_{ID_R}\left(Y_{ID_O} + Q_{ID_O} + \mu_{ID_O}P_{pub}\right).$$
   The data receiver returns trapdoor $T_w = (T_1, T_2, T_3)$.

8. *Test*: Takes *params*, T_w and ciphertext C as input. The cloud server verifies whether $T_2\left(Y_{ID_R} + Q_{ID_R} + \mu_{ID_R}P_{pub}\right) - C_3 - T_1 = C_2T_3 - C_1$ is ture. If the equation is true, it outputs "1", Otherwise, the cloud server outputs "0".

Correctness: $T_{w'}$ is the trapdoor for the keyword w', and w is the keyword contained in the ciphertext C. If $w = w'$, we have: $x_{ID_O}Y_{ID_R} = x_{ID_O}x_{ID_R}P = x_{ID_R}Y_{ID_O}$, $\beta_{ID_o} = \beta_{ID_R}$,

$$
\begin{aligned}
&C_2T_3 - C_1 \\
&= \left(H_2(w) + r_1\beta_{ID_O}^{-1}\right)(x_{ID_O} + d_{ID_O})^{-1}\beta_{ID_R}(Y_{ID_O} + Q_{ID_O} + \mu_{ID_O}P_{pub}) - C_1 \\
&= \beta_{ID_R}\left(H_2(w) + r_1\beta_{ID_O}^{-1}\right)(x_{ID_O} + d_{ID_O})^{-1}(x_{ID_O} + d_{ID_O})P - C_1 \\
&= \beta_{ID_R}H_2(w)P + r_1P - C_1 \\
&= \beta_{ID_R}H_2(w)P.
\end{aligned}
$$

$$\tag{1}$$

and

$$
\begin{aligned}
&T_2\left(Y_{ID_R} + Q_{ID_R} + \mu_{ID_R}P_{pub}\right) - C_3 - T_1 \\
&= \left(\beta_{ID_R} + (r_2 + \beta_{ID_R}H_2(w))(x_{ID_R} + d_{ID_R})^{-1}\right)(Y_{ID_R} + Q_{ID_R} + \mu_{ID_R}P_{pub}) \\
&\quad -C_3 - T_1 \\
&= \beta_{ID_R}(x_{ID_R} + d_{ID_R})P + (r_2 + \beta_{ID_R}H_2(w))(x_{ID_R} + d_{ID_R})^{-1}(x_{ID_R} + d_{ID_R})P \\
&\quad -C_3 - T_1 \\
&= \beta_{ID_R}(x_{ID_R} + d_{ID_R})P + r_2P + \beta_{ID_R}H_2(w)P - C_3 - T_1 \\
&= \beta_{ID_R}H_2(w)P.
\end{aligned}
$$

$$\tag{2}$$

Therefore

$$T_2 \left(Y_{\mathrm{ID}_R} + Q_{\mathrm{ID}_R} + \mu_{\mathrm{ID}_R} P_{\mathrm{pub}}\right) - C_3 - T_1 = C_2 T_3 - C_1. \tag{3}$$

5 Security Analysis

In this section, the security model of the proposed CPEKS scheme is given. Then, we will prove that the scheme can effectively resist IKGA in this security model.

5.1 Security Model

In the adaptive choice ciphertext attack game of certificateless cryptography, there are two types of adversaries. Type 1 adversary $\mathcal{A}_1$, that is an external adversary. It can arbitrarily replace the user's public key, but cannot obtain the system master key s. Type 2 adversary $\mathcal{A}_2$, that is an internal adversary, generally refers to the semi-trusted cloud server. It can obtain the system master key s, but cannot replace the user's public key. According to the different adversaries, we define two attack games between the challenger $\mathcal{C}$ and the adversaries.

Game 1. *The game is an interaction between $\mathcal{C}$ and $\mathcal{A}_1$.*

1. *Setup*: Given the security parameter l, $\mathcal{C}$ executes the algorithm to generate the system master key s and system parameters *params*. Then, the system master key s is kept secret and the system parameters *params* are sent to $\mathcal{A}_1$.
2. *Queries*:
   (a) *Hash query*: $\mathcal{C}$ allows $\mathcal{A}_1$ to query the hash oracles and get the hash value.
   (b) *Extract-Partial-Private-Key-Query*: $\mathcal{A}_1$ selects an identity ID, $\mathcal{C}$ calculates the partial private key d_{ID} of the identity ID and returns it to $\mathcal{A}_1$.
   (c) *Extract-Private-Key-Query*: When $\mathcal{C}$ receives $\mathcal{A}_1$'s query, $\mathcal{C}$ calculates the corresponding private key $\mathrm{SK}_{\mathrm{ID}}$ and returns it to $\mathcal{A}_1$.
   (d) *Request-Public-Key-Query*: $\mathcal{A}_1$ selects an identity ID, $\mathcal{C}$ calculates the public key $\mathrm{PK}_{\mathrm{ID}}$ of the identity ID and returns it to $\mathcal{A}_1$.
   (e) *Replace-Public-Key-Query*: $\mathcal{A}_1$ can select a new public key $\mathrm{PK}'_{\mathrm{ID}}$ to replace the original public key $\mathrm{PK}_{\mathrm{ID}}$.
   (f) *Trapdoor-Query*: When $\mathcal{C}$ receives the keyword w query of $\mathcal{A}_1$, $\mathcal{C}$ calculates the corresponding keyword trapdoor T_w and returns it to $\mathcal{A}_1$.
3. *Challenge*: The adversary $\mathcal{A}_1$ with identity ID selects w_0 and w_1 as challenge keywords, and they have not executed Trapdoor-Query. The challenger $\mathcal{C}$ randomly selects $b \in \{0,1\}$ and then generates keyword ciphertext of w_b by executing the algorithm.
4. *More-Queries*: The adversary $\mathcal{A}_1$ can continue to execute all polynomial bounded adaptive queries as in the Queries phase, except that it cannot execute the Trapdoor-Query for w_0 and w_1.

5. *Guess*: The adversary $\mathcal{A}_1$ gives its guess $b' \in \{0, 1\}$, if $b' = b$, indicating that the $\mathcal{A}_1$ challenge is successful. (the advantage of $\mathcal{A}_1$ challenge success is defined as $\text{Adv}(\mathcal{A}_1) = |\Pr[b' = b] - 1/2|$).

Game 2. *The game is an interaction between $\mathcal{C}$ and $\mathcal{A}_2$.*

1. *Setup*: Given the security parameter l, $\mathcal{C}$ executes the algorithm to generate the system master key s and system parameters *params* and then sends them to $\mathcal{A}_2$.
2. *Queries*: In addition to Extract-Private-Key-Query and Replace-Public-Key-Query, the adversary $\mathcal{A}_2$ can execute the same queries in the Queries phase of game 1.
3. *Challenge*: The adversary $\mathcal{A}_2$ with identity ID selects w_0 and w_1 as challenge keywords, and they have not executed Trapdoor-Query. The challenger $\mathcal{C}$ randomly selects $b \in \{0, 1\}$ and then generates keyword ciphertext of w_b by executing the algorithm.
4. *More-Queries*: The adversary $\mathcal{A}_2$ can continue to execute all polynomial bounded adaptive queries as in the Queries phase, except that it cannot execute the Trapdoor-Query for w_0 and w_1.
5. *Guess*: The adversary $\mathcal{A}_2$ gives its guess $b' \in \{0, 1\}$, if $b' = b$, indicating that the $\mathcal{A}_2$ challenge is successful. (the advantage of $\mathcal{A}_2$ challenge success is defined as $\text{Adv}(\mathcal{A}_2) = |\Pr[b' = b] - 1/2|$).

Definition 1. *If no adversary can win the above games with non-negligible advantages $\text{Adv}(\mathcal{A}_1)$ and $\text{Adv}(\mathcal{A}_2)$, it shows that the proposed CPEKS scheme is semantically secure against IKGA.*

5.2   Security Proof

Theorem 1. *Assuming the CDH problem is an intractable problem, the proposed CPEKS scheme is semantically secure against IKGA in the random oracle model. The theorem will be proved based on the following two lemmas.*

Lemma 1. *Suppose that there is an adversary $\mathcal{A}_1$ of type 1 to win the CPEKS scheme with a non-negligible advantage of ε. Then, we must construct an algorithm $\mathcal{C}$ to solve the CDH problem with a non-negligible advantage:*

$$\varepsilon' \geq \frac{1}{eq_{H3}q_T}\left(1 - \frac{1}{q_{H1}}\right)^{q_S + q_E}. \tag{4}$$

where q_{H_1}, q_{H_3}, q_T, q_E and q_S respectively represent the maximum number of queries H_1- Query, H_3- Query, Trapdoor-Query, Extract-Partial-Private-Key-Query and Extract-Private-Key-Query.

Proof: Suppose that (P, aP, bP) is an instance randomly generated by the CDH problem, then algorithm $\mathcal{C}$ simulates the challenger and calculates abP by interacting with adversary $\mathcal{A}_1$.

1. *Setup*: $\mathcal{C}$ randomly selects ID_I $(1 \leq I \leq q_{H_1})$ as the challenge identity. Then $\mathcal{C}$ executes the algorithm to calculate the system public key $P_{\mathrm{pub}} = aP$ and system parameters $params = \{\lambda, G, q, P, P_{\mathrm{pub}}, H_1, H_2, H_3\}$. Finally, $\mathcal{C}$ returns $params$ to $\mathcal{A}_1$.

2. *Queries*:

   (a) H_1-*Query*: $\mathcal{C}$ maintains a L_{H_1} list containing tuple $\langle \mathrm{ID}_i, Q_{\mathrm{ID}_i}, \mu_i \rangle$. When receiving the query about $(\mathrm{ID}_i, Q_{\mathrm{ID}_i})$ from adversary $\mathcal{A}_1$, if the tuple $\langle \mathrm{ID}_i, Q_{\mathrm{ID}_i}, \mu_i \rangle$ exists in L_{H_1} list, $\mathcal{C}$ returns μ_i. Otherwise, $\mathcal{C}$ selects a random value $\mu_i \in Z_q^*$ and returns it to $\mathcal{A}_1$. In addition, the tuple $\langle \mathrm{ID}_i, Q_{\mathrm{ID}_i}, \mu_i \rangle$ is added to the L_{H_1} list.

   (b) H_2-*Query*: $\mathcal{C}$ maintains a L_{H_2} list containing tuple $\langle w_i, c_i, \tau_i, \psi_i, H_{2i} \rangle$. When receiving the query about w_i from adversary $\mathcal{A}_1$, if the tuple $\langle w_i, c_i, \tau_i, \psi_i, H_{2i} \rangle$ exists in L_{H_2}, $\mathcal{C}$ returns H_{2i}. Otherwise, $\mathcal{C}$ generates a random coin $c_i \in \{0, 1\}$, where $\Pr[c_i = 0] = \frac{1}{q_T + 1}$. In addition, $\mathcal{C}$ selects random values $\tau_i, \psi_i \in Z_q^*$ and calculates $H_{2i} = (1 - c_i) \tau_i + \psi_i$. Finally, $\mathcal{C}$ returns H_{2i} to $\mathcal{A}_1$ and adds the tuple $\langle w_i, c_i, \tau_i, \psi_i, H_{2i} \rangle$ to the L_{H_2} list.

   (c) H_3-*Query*: $\mathcal{C}$ maintains a L_{H_3} list containing tuple $\langle \mathrm{ID}_i, \mathrm{ID}_j, x_{\mathrm{ID}_i} Y_{\mathrm{ID}_j}, \beta_i \rangle$. When receiving the query about $(\mathrm{ID}_i, \mathrm{ID}_j, x_{\mathrm{ID}_i} Y_{\mathrm{ID}_j})$ from adversary $\mathcal{A}_1$, if the tuple $\langle \mathrm{ID}_i, \mathrm{ID}_j, x_{\mathrm{ID}_i} Y_{\mathrm{ID}_j}, \beta_i \rangle$ exists in L_{H_3}, $\mathcal{C}$ returns β_i. Otherwise, $\mathcal{C}$ selects a random value $\beta_i \in Z_q^*$ and returns it to $\mathcal{A}_1$. In addition, the tuple $\langle \mathrm{ID}_i, \mathrm{ID}_j, x_{\mathrm{ID}_i} Y_{\mathrm{ID}_j}, \beta_i \rangle$ is added to the L_{H_3} list.

   (d) *Extract-Partial-Private-Key-Query*: $\mathcal{C}$ maintains a L_{p_1} list containing tuple $\langle \mathrm{ID}_i, Q_{\mathrm{ID}_i}, d_{\mathrm{ID}_i} \rangle$. When receiving the query about ID_i from adversary $\mathcal{A}_1$, $\mathcal{C}$ aborts the algorithm if $\mathrm{ID}_i = \mathrm{ID}_I$ (this process is indicated by E_1). Otherwise, $\mathcal{C}$ selects random values $\mu_i, d_{\mathrm{ID}_i} \in Z_q^*$ to calculate $Q_{\mathrm{ID}_i} = d_{\mathrm{ID}_i} P - \mu_i P_{pub}$, then returns d_{ID_i} and Q_{ID_i} to $\mathcal{A}_1$. In addition, the tuples $\langle \mathrm{ID}_i, Q_{\mathrm{ID}_i}, d_{\mathrm{ID}_i} \rangle$ and $\langle \mathrm{ID}_i, Q_{\mathrm{ID}_i}, \mu_i \rangle$ are added to the L_{p_1} list and L_{H_1} list, respectively.

   (e) *Extract-Private-Key-Query*: $\mathcal{C}$ maintains a L_{p_2} list containing tuple $\langle \mathrm{ID}_i, Y_{\mathrm{ID}_i}, x_{\mathrm{ID}_i} \rangle$. When receiving the query about ID_i from adversary $\mathcal{A}_1$, if $\mathrm{ID}_i = \mathrm{ID}_I$, $\mathcal{C}$ aborts the algorithm (this process is indicated by E_2). Otherwise, $\mathcal{C}$ selects a random value $x_{\mathrm{ID}_i} \in Z_q^*$ and calculates $Y_{\mathrm{ID}_i} = x_{\mathrm{ID}_i} P$. Then $\mathcal{C}$ recovers $\langle \mathrm{ID}_i, Q_{\mathrm{ID}_i}, d_{\mathrm{ID}_i} \rangle$ from the L_{p_1} list and returns $\mathrm{SK}_{\mathrm{ID}_i} = (x_{\mathrm{ID}_i}, d_{\mathrm{ID}_i})$ to $\mathcal{A}_1$. In addition, the tuple $\langle \mathrm{ID}_i, d_{\mathrm{ID}_i}, x_{\mathrm{ID}_i} \rangle$ is added to the L_{p_2} list.
   guuyugyugh

   (f) *Request-Public-Key-Query*: When the adversary $\mathcal{A}_1$ queries the identity of ID_i, $\mathcal{C}$ queries tuples $\langle \mathrm{ID}_i, Q_{\mathrm{ID}_i}, d_{\mathrm{ID}_i} \rangle$ and $\langle \mathrm{ID}_i, Y_{\mathrm{ID}_i}, x_{\mathrm{ID}_i} \rangle$ from the L_{p_1} list and L_{p_2} list, respectively. Then $\mathcal{C}$ calculates $\mathrm{PK}_{\mathrm{ID}_i} = (Y_{\mathrm{ID}_i}, Q_{\mathrm{ID}_i})$ and returns it to $\mathcal{A}_1$.

   (g) *Replace-Public-Key-Query*: When receiving the adversary $\mathcal{A}_1$' s query about $(\mathrm{ID}_i, Q_{\mathrm{ID}_i}, Y_{\mathrm{ID}_i})$, $\mathcal{C}$ uses Y'_{ID_i} and Q'_{ID_i} to replace Y_{ID_i} and Q_{ID_i} respectively. Then, the tuple $(\mathrm{ID}_i, Q_{\mathrm{ID}_i}, Y_{\mathrm{ID}_i})$ is updated.

   (h) *Trapdoor-Query*: When receiving $\mathcal{A}_1$'s Trapdoor-Query about w_i (the identity is ID_i), $\mathcal{C}$ queries the tuple $\langle w_i, c_i, \tau_i, \psi_i, H_{2i} \rangle$ from the L_{H_2} list. If

$c_i = 0$, $\mathcal{C}$ aborts the algorithm (this process is indicated by E_3). Otherwise, $\mathcal{C}$ selects the random value $r_{1i} \in Z_q^*$ and calculates $T_{1i} = r_{1i}P$. Then $\mathcal{C}$ queries tuples $\langle w_i, c_i, \tau_i, \psi_i, H_{2i} \rangle$ and $\langle \text{ID}_i, \text{ID}_j, x_{\text{ID}_i} Y_{\text{ID}_j}, \beta_i \rangle$ from the L_{H_2} list and L_{H_3} list, calculates $T_{2i} = \beta_i + (r_{1i} + \beta_i\psi_i)(x_{\text{ID}_i} + d_{\text{ID}_i})^{-1}$ and $T_{3i} = \beta_i(Y_{\text{ID}_O} + Q_{\text{ID}_O} + \mu_{\text{ID}_O}P_{\text{pub}})$. $\mathcal{C}$ returns $T_{wi} = (T_{1i}, T_{2i}, T_{3i})$ to $\mathcal{A}_1$.

3. *Challenge:* The adversary $\mathcal{A}_1$ gives challenge keywords w_0 and w_1, which identity is ID*. $\mathcal{C}$ queries tuples $\langle w_0, c_0, \tau_0, \psi_0, H_{20} \rangle$ and $\langle w_1, c_1, \tau_1, \psi_1, H_{21} \rangle$ from the L_{H_2} list. If $c_0 = c_1 = 1$, $\mathcal{C}$ aborts the algorithm (this process is indicated by E_4). Otherwise, $\mathcal{C}$ selects a random value $r_{2i} \in Z_q^*$ and calculates $C_{1i} = r_{2i}P$. Then, $\mathcal{C}$ respectively queries tuples $\langle w_i, c_i, \tau_i, \psi_i, H_{2i} \rangle$ and $\langle \text{ID}_i, \text{ID}_j, x_{\text{ID}_i} Y_{\text{ID}_j}, \beta_i \rangle$ from the L_{H_2} list and L_{H_3} list, calculates $C_{2i} = (\tau_i + \psi_i + r_{2i}\beta_i^{-1})(x_{\text{ID}_O} + d_{\text{ID}_O})^{-1}$. Finally, $\mathcal{C}$ queries the tuple $\langle \text{ID}_i, Q_{\text{ID}_i}, \mu_i \rangle$ from the L_{H_1} list and calculates $C_{3i} = \beta_i(Y_{\text{ID}_i} + Q_{\text{ID}_i} + \mu_{\text{ID}_i}P_{\text{pub}})$, then $\mathcal{C}$ returns $C = (C_{1i}, C_{2i}, C_{3i})$ to $\mathcal{A}_1$.

4. *More-Queries:* The adversary $\mathcal{A}_1$ can continue to execute queries except w_0 and w_1 (this process is indicated by E_5).

5. *Guess:* The adversary $\mathcal{A}_1$ gives a guess $b' \in \{0, 1\}$. Then $\mathcal{C}$ sets $C_{1i} = bP$. If the $(b(\beta_i^{-1}C_{3i} - Q_{\text{ID}_i}) - x_{\text{ID}_i}C_{1i})\mu_{\text{ID}_i}^{-1} = abP$ holds, it means that $\mathcal{C}$ can solve the CDH problem.

We construct an algorithm to solve the CDH problem. We need to prove that $\mathcal{C}$ has at least ε' advantage in correctly solving this problem. Next, we first summarize the definition of five events E_i ($i = 1, 2, 3, 4, 5$).

1. E_1: The adversary $\mathcal{A}_1$ uses identity ID_I to perform Extract-Partial-Private-Key-Query.
2. E_2: The adversary $\mathcal{A}_1$ uses identity ID_I to perform Extract-Private-Key-Query.
3. E_3: The challenger $\mathcal{C}$ aborts the algorithm during the Trapdoor-Query phase.
4. E_4: The challenger $\mathcal{C}$ aborts the algorithm during the Challenge phase.
5. E_5: The adversary $\mathcal{A}_1$ does not perform More-Queries for w_0 and w_1.

The following is an analysis of advantage ε' for $\mathcal{C}$. Clearly,

$$\varepsilon' \geq \frac{1}{eq_{H3}q_T}\left(1 - \frac{1}{q_{H1}}\right)^{q_S + q_E}, \tag{5}$$

$$\Pr[\neg E_3] = \left(1 - \frac{1}{q_T + 1}\right)^{q_T} \geq \frac{1}{e}, \tag{6}$$

and

$$\Pr[\neg E_4] = \left(1 - \left(1 - \frac{1}{q_T + 1}\right)^2\right) \geq \frac{1}{q_T}. \tag{7}$$

Therefore, we have

$$\Pr[\neg E_1 \wedge \neg E_2 \wedge \neg E_3 \wedge \neg E_4] \geq \left(1 - \frac{1}{q_{H1}}\right)^{q_S + q_E} \frac{1}{eq_T}. \tag{8}$$

Next, we prove that $pr(\neg E_5) \geq 2\varepsilon$,

$$pr[b'=b]= pr[b'=b|\neg E_5]pr[\neg E_5] + pr[b'=b|E_5]pr[E_5]$$

$$\leq pr[b'=b|E_5]pr[E_5] + pr[\neg E_5] \tag{9}$$

$$=\tfrac{1}{2}+\tfrac{1}{2}pr[\neg E_5],$$

so we have $pr[b'=b]-\tfrac{1}{2} \leq \tfrac{1}{2}pr[\neg E_5]$. Similarly, we can infer that $\Pr[b' = b] \geq \tfrac{1}{2} - \tfrac{1}{2}\Pr[\neg E_5]$. Because $\mathcal{A}_1$ wins the game with advantage $|\Pr[b' = b] - \tfrac{1}{2}| \geq \varepsilon$, therefore $\varepsilon \leq |\Pr[b' = b] - \tfrac{1}{2}| \leq \tfrac{1}{2}\Pr[\neg E_5]$. Then we can know that $pr(\neg E_5) \geq 2\varepsilon$. In addition, $\mathcal{C}$ will select the correct tuple from the L_{H_3} list with a probability of $\frac{1}{q_{H3}}$. Therefore

$$\varepsilon' \geq \tfrac{1}{2} \cdot \Pr[\neg E_5] \cdot \frac{1}{q_{H3}} \cdot \Pr[\neg E_1 \wedge \neg E_2 \wedge \neg E_3 \wedge \neg E_4]$$

$$= \tfrac{1}{2} \cdot 2\varepsilon \cdot \frac{1}{q_{H3}}\left(1 - \frac{1}{q_{H1}}\right)^{q_S+q_E} \frac{1}{eq_T} \tag{10}$$

$$= \frac{1}{eq_{H3}q_T}\left(1 - \frac{1}{q_{H1}}\right)^{q_S+q_E}.$$

Lemma 2. *Suppose that there is an adversary $\mathcal{A}_2$ of type 2 to win the CPEKS scheme with a non-negligible advantage of ε. Then, we can construct an algorithm $\mathcal{C}$ to solve the CDH problem with a non-negligible advantage:*

$$\varepsilon' \geq \frac{1}{eq_{H3}q_T}\left(1 - \frac{1}{q_{H1}}\right)^{q_E} \tag{11}$$

where q_{H_1}, q_{H_3}, q_T and q_E respectively represent the maximum number of queries H_1-query, H_3-query, Trapdoor-Query and Extract-Partial-Private-Key-Query.

Proof: Suppose that (P, aP, bP) is an instance randomly generated by the CDH problem, then algorithm $\mathcal{C}$ simulates the challenger and calculates abP by interacting with adversary $\mathcal{A}_2$.

1. *Setup*: $\mathcal{C}$ randomly selects $\text{ID}_I (1 \leq I \leq q_{H_1})$ as the challenge identity. Then $\mathcal{C}$ executes the algorithm to randomly select $s \in Z_q^*$ as the system master key and calculates $P_{\text{pub}} = sP$. Finally, $\mathcal{C}$ returns system parameters $params = \{\lambda, G, q, P, P_{\text{pub}}, H_1, H_2, H_3\}$ and s to $\mathcal{A}_2$.
2. *Queries*:
   (a) H_1-*Query*: $\mathcal{C}$ maintains a L_{H_1} list containing tuple $\langle \text{ID}_i, Q_{\text{ID}_i}, \mu_i \rangle$. When receiving the query about $(\text{ID}_i, Q_{\text{ID}_i})$ from adversary $\mathcal{A}_2$, if the tuple $\langle \text{ID}_i, Q_{\text{ID}_i}, \mu_i \rangle$ exists in L_{H_1} list, $\mathcal{C}$ returns μ_i. Otherwise, $\mathcal{C}$ selects a random value $\mu_i \in Z_q^*$ and returns it to $\mathcal{A}_2$. In addition, the tuple $\langle \text{ID}_i, Q_{\text{ID}_i}, \mu_i \rangle$ is added to the L_{H_1} list.

(b) H_2-*Query*: $\mathcal{C}$ maintains a L_{H_2} list containing tuple $\langle w_i, c_i, \tau_i, \psi_i, H_{2i} \rangle$. When receiving the query about w_i from adversary $\mathcal{A}_2$, if the tuple $\langle w_i, c_i, \tau_i, \psi_i, H_{2i} \rangle$ exists in L_{H_2}, $\mathcal{C}$ returns H_{2i}. Otherwise, $\mathcal{C}$ generates a random coin $c_i \in \{0, 1\}$, where $\Pr[c_i = 0] = \frac{1}{q_T+1}$. In addition, $\mathcal{C}$ selects random values $\tau_i, \psi_i \in Z_q^*$ and calculates $H_{2i} = (1 - c_i)\tau_i + \psi_i$. Finally, $\mathcal{C}$ returns H_{2i} to $\mathcal{A}_2$ and adds the tuple $\langle w_i, c_i, \tau_i, \psi_i, H_{2i} \rangle$ to the L_{H_2} list.

(c) H_3-*Query*: $\mathcal{C}$ maintains a L_{H_3} list containing tuple $\langle \mathrm{ID}_i, \mathrm{ID}_j, x_{\mathrm{ID}_i} Y_{\mathrm{ID}_j}, \beta_i \rangle$. When receiving the query about $(\mathrm{ID}_i, \mathrm{ID}_j, x_{\mathrm{ID}_i} Y_{\mathrm{ID}_j})$ from adversary $\mathcal{A}_2$, if the tuple $\langle \mathrm{ID}_i, \mathrm{ID}_j, x_{\mathrm{ID}_i} Y_{\mathrm{ID}_j}, \beta_i \rangle$ exists in L_{H_3} list, $\mathcal{C}$ returns β_i. Otherwise, $\mathcal{C}$ selects a random value $\beta_i \in Z_q^*$ and returns it to $\mathcal{A}_2$. In addition, the tuple $\langle \mathrm{ID}_i, \mathrm{ID}_j, x_{\mathrm{ID}_i} Y_{\mathrm{ID}_j}, \beta_i \rangle$ is added to the L_{H_3} list.

(d) *Extract-Partial-Private-Key-Query*: $\mathcal{C}$ maintains a L_{p_1} list containing tuple $\langle \mathrm{ID}_i, Q_{\mathrm{ID}_i}, d_{\mathrm{ID}_i} \rangle$. When receiving the query about ID_i from adversary $\mathcal{A}_2$, $\mathcal{C}$ aborts the algorithm if $\mathrm{ID}_i = \mathrm{ID}_I$ (this process is indicated by E_1). Otherwise, $\mathcal{C}$ selects a random value $r_{\mathrm{ID}_i} \in Z_q^*$, and calculates $Q_{\mathrm{ID}_i} = r_{\mathrm{ID}_i} P$. Then $\mathcal{C}$ queries the tuple $\langle \mathrm{ID}_i, Q_{\mathrm{ID}_i}, \mu_i \rangle$ from the L_{H_1} list, calculates $d_{\mathrm{ID}_i} = r_{\mathrm{ID}_i} + s\mu_i$ and returns d_{ID_i} and r_{ID_i} to $\mathcal{A}_2$. In addition, the tuple $\langle \mathrm{ID}_i, Q_{\mathrm{ID}_i}, d_{\mathrm{ID}_i} \rangle$ is added to the L_{p_1} list.

(e) *Request-Public-Key-Query*: $\mathcal{C}$ maintains a L_{p_2} list containing tuple $\langle \mathrm{ID}_i, Y_{\mathrm{ID}_i}, x_{\mathrm{ID}_i} \rangle$. When receiving the query about ID_i from adversary $\mathcal{A}_2$. If Y_{ID_i} exists in L_{p_2} list, then $\mathcal{C}$ queries the tuple $\langle \mathrm{ID}_i, Q_{\mathrm{ID}_i}, d_{\mathrm{ID}_i} \rangle$ from the L_{p_1} list and returns $\mathrm{PK}_{\mathrm{ID}_i} = (Y_{\mathrm{ID}_i}, Q_{\mathrm{ID}_i})$ to $\mathcal{A}_2$. Otherwise, $\mathcal{C}$ selects a random value $x_{\mathrm{ID}_i} \in Z_q^*$ and calculates $Y_{\mathrm{ID}_i} = x_{\mathrm{ID}_i} P$. In addition, the tuple $(\mathrm{ID}_i, Y_{\mathrm{ID}_i}, x_{\mathrm{ID}_i})$ is added to the L_{p_2} list.

(f) *Trapdoor-Query*: When receiving $\mathcal{A}_2$'s Trapdoor-Query about w_i (the identity is ID_i), $\mathcal{C}$ queries the tuple $\langle w_i, c_i, \tau_i, \psi_i, H_{2i} \rangle$ from the L_{H_2} list. If $c_i = 0$, $\mathcal{C}$ aborts the algorithm (this process is indicated by E_2). Otherwise, $\mathcal{C}$ selects a random value $r_{1i} \in Z_q^*$ and calculates $T_{1i} = r_{1i} P$. Then $\mathcal{C}$ queries tuples $\langle w_i, c_i, \tau_i, \psi_i, H_{2i} \rangle$ and $\langle \mathrm{ID}_i, \mathrm{ID}_j, x_{\mathrm{ID}_i} Y_{\mathrm{ID}_j}, \beta_i \rangle$ from the L_{H_2} list and L_{H_3} list, calculates $T_{2i} = \beta_i + (r_{1i} + \beta_i \psi_i)(x_{\mathrm{ID}_i} + d_{\mathrm{ID}_i})^{-1}$ and $T_{3i} = \beta_i (Y_{\mathrm{ID}_O} + Q_{\mathrm{ID}_O} + \mu_{\mathrm{ID}_O} P_{\mathrm{pub}})$. $\mathcal{C}$ returns $T_{wi} = (T_{1i}, T_{2i}, T_{3i})$ to $\mathcal{A}_2$.

3. *Challenge*: The adversary $\mathcal{A}_2$ gives challenge keywords w_0 and w_1, which identity is ID^*. $\mathcal{C}$ queries tuples $\langle w_0, c_0, \tau_0, \psi_0, H_{20} \rangle$ and $\langle w_1, c_1, \tau_1, \psi_1, H_{21} \rangle$ from the L_{H_2} list. If $c_0 = c_1 = 1$, $\mathcal{C}$ aborts the algorithm (this process is indicated by E_3). Otherwise, $\mathcal{C}$ selects the random value $r_{2i} \in Z_q^*$ and calculates $C_{1i} = r_{2i} P$. After that, $\mathcal{C}$ respectively queries tuples $\langle w_i, c_i, \tau_i, \psi_i, H_{2i} \rangle$ and $\langle \mathrm{ID}_i, \mathrm{ID}_j, x_{\mathrm{ID}_i} Y_{\mathrm{ID}_j}, \beta_i \rangle$ from the L_{H_2} list and L_{H_3} list, calculates $C_{2i} = (\tau_i + \psi_i + r_{2i} \beta_i^{-1})(x_{\mathrm{ID}_0} + d_{\mathrm{ID}_0})^{-1}$, queries the tuple $\langle \mathrm{ID}_i, Q_{\mathrm{ID}_i}, \mu_i \rangle$ from the L_{H_1} list and calculates $C_{3i} = \beta_i (Y_{\mathrm{ID}_i} + Q_{\mathrm{ID}_i} + \mu_{\mathrm{ID}_i} P_{\mathrm{pub}})$. Then $\mathcal{C}$ sends $C = (C_{1i}, C_{2i}, C_{3i})$ to $\mathcal{A}_2$.

4. *More-Queries*: The adversary $\mathcal{A}_2$ can continue to execute queries except w_0 and w_1 (this process is indicated by E_4).

5. *Guess*: $\mathcal{A}_2$ gives guess $b' \in \{0, 1\}$. $\mathcal{C}$ sets $Q_{\mathrm{ID}_i} = aP$ and $C_{1i} = bP$. If the $b(\beta_i^{-1} C_{3i} - \mu_i P_{\mathrm{pub}}) - x_{\mathrm{ID}_i} C_{1i} = abP$ holds, it means that $\mathcal{C}$ can solve the CDH problem.

We construct an algorithm to solve the CDH problem. We need to prove that $\mathcal{C}$ has at least ε' advantages in correctly solving this problem. Next, we summarize the definition of four events E_i $(i = 1, 2, 3, 4)$.

1. E_1: The adversary $\mathcal{A}_2$ uses identity ID_I to perform Extract-Partial-Private-Key-Query.
2. E_2: The challenger $\mathcal{C}$ aborts the algorithm during the Trapdoor-Query phase.
3. E_3: The challenger $\mathcal{C}$ aborts the algorithm during the Challenge phase.
4. E_4: The adversary $\mathcal{A}_2$ does not perform More-Queries for w_0 and w_1.

The following is an analysis of advantage ε' for $\mathcal{C}$. Clearly,

$$\Pr\left[\neg E_2\right] = \left(1 - \frac{1}{q_T + 1}\right)^{q_T} \geq \frac{1}{e}, \tag{12}$$

and

$$\Pr\left[\neg E_3\right] = \left(1 - \left(1 - \frac{1}{q_T + 1}\right)^2\right) \geq \frac{1}{q_T}. \tag{13}$$

Therefore, we have

$$\Pr\left[\neg E_1 \wedge \neg E_2 \wedge \neg E_3\right] \geq \left(1 - \frac{1}{q_{H1}}\right)^{q_E} \frac{1}{eq_T}. \tag{14}$$

Next, we prove that $\mathrm{pr}(\neg E_4) \geq 2\varepsilon$,

$$\mathrm{pr}[b'{=}b] = \mathrm{pr}[b'{=}b|\neg E_4]\mathrm{pr}[\neg E_4] + \mathrm{pr}[b'{=}b|E_4]\mathrm{pr}[E_4]$$

$$\leq \mathrm{pr}[b'{=}b|E_4]\mathrm{pr}[E_4] + \mathrm{pr}[\neg E_4] \tag{15}$$

$$= \tfrac{1}{2} + \tfrac{1}{2}\mathrm{pr}[\neg E_4].$$

so we have $\mathrm{pr}[b'{=}b] - \frac{1}{2} \leq \frac{1}{2}\mathrm{pr}[\neg E_4]$. Similarly, we can infer that $\Pr[b' = b] \geq \frac{1}{2} - \frac{1}{2}\Pr\left[\neg E_4\right]$. Because $\mathcal{A}_1$ wins the game with advantage $\left|\Pr\left[b' = b\right] - \frac{1}{2}\right| \geq \varepsilon$, therefore $\varepsilon \leq \left|\Pr[b' = b] - \frac{1}{2}\right| \leq \frac{1}{2}\Pr\left[\neg E_4\right]$. Thus we can know that $\mathrm{pr}(\neg E_4) \geq 2\varepsilon$. In addition, $\mathcal{C}$ will select the correct tuple from the L_{H_3} list with a probability of $\frac{1}{q_{H3}}$. Therefore

$$\varepsilon' \geq \tfrac{1}{2} \cdot \Pr\left[\neg E_4\right] \cdot \frac{1}{q_{H3}} \cdot \Pr\left[\neg E_1 \wedge \neg E_2 \wedge \neg E_3\right]$$

$$= \tfrac{1}{2} \cdot 2\varepsilon \cdot \frac{1}{q_{H3}}\left(1 - \frac{1}{q_{H1}}\right)^{q_E} \frac{1}{eq_T} \tag{16}$$

$$= \frac{1}{eq_{H3}q_T}\left(1 - \frac{1}{q_{H1}}\right)^{q_E}.$$

6 Performance Analysis

In this section, we will compare the proposed scheme with schemes [12, 28, 30, 31] and [32] in terms of security property, computation cost and communication cost.

6.1 Security Property

Table 1 shows the comparison of the security property of the six schemes. We express no key escrow, certificate-based, CLPKE, authentication, outside keyword guessing attack and IKGA with NE, CB, CL, AU, OK and IK respectively. From Table 1, We can find that scheme [12] has the key escrow problem. Scheme [32] has the problem of certificate management. Schemes [28, 30] and ours are based on CLPKE without the above two problems. However, scheme [28] lacks an authentication function, and the adversary can initiate IKGA. In particular, schemes [12, 28] and [30] all rely on high-consuming bilinear pairing. Scheme [31] cannot avoid OKGA and IKGA. Therefore, only our scheme considers the six security properties and pairing-free.

Table 1. The comparison of security properties

Scheme	Security properties						Bilinear pairing
	NE	CB	CL	AU	OK	IK	
[12]	×	√	×	√	√	√	Pairing-based
[28]	√	√	√	×	√	×	Pairing-based
[30]	√	√	√	√	√	√	Pairing-based
[31]	√	√	√	√	×	×	Pairing-free
[32]	√	×	×	√	√	√	Pairing-free
Ours	√	√	√	√	√	√	Pairing-free

√−supported, ×−not supported.

6.2 Computation Cost

In this section, we will use the test results of scheme [13] to estimate the computation cost of the five schemes. T_{hm}, T_{sa}, T_b, T_{sp} and T_h respectively indicate a hash-to-point operation, a scalar addition operation, a bilinear pairing operation, a scalar multiplication operation and a general hash operation. The running time is 4.362 ms, 0.013 ms, 4.154 ms, 1.631 ms, and 0.004 ms respectively.

In Table 2, we estimate the computation cost of the six schemes from KeyGen, Encryption, Trapdoor, and Test respectively. It can be found that the running time of our scheme in the KeyGen algorithm is reduced by 57.16%, 20.19% compared with schemes [28] and [32] respectively. Our scheme has the least running time in the Encryption algorithm, which is reduced by 56.98%, 79.56%, 47.79%, 19.77% and 19.95% respectively compared with [12, 28, 30, 31] and [32]. The running time of Trapdoor algorithm is reduced by 13.93%, 51.20% respectively compared with [12, 30]. The running time of Test algorithm is reduced by 85.48%, 65.87% and 57.24% respectively compared with [12, 28] and [30]. In addition, the running time of scheme [28] in the Trapdoor algorithm is reduced by 8.47% compared with our scheme, but the overall running time of our scheme is reduced by 63.73% compared with [28]. The reason is that our scheme uses curve $y^2 \equiv x^3 + ax + b$ and scalar multiplication instead of high-consuming bilinear pairing. In particular, although our scheme runs slightly longer than scheme [31] and [32] in Trapdoor and Test algorithms. It is worth noting that our scheme is based on CLPKE, which avoids certificate management and IKGA problems. Therefore, our scheme has higher efficiency compared with other schemes.

Table 2. Computation cost (ms)

Scheme	KeyGen	Encryption	Trapdoor	Test
[12]	$4T_{sp} = 6.542$	$4T_{sp} + 2T_{hm} + T_h$ $= 15.252$	$2T_{sp} + T_{hm} = 7.624$	$6T_b + 3T_{sp} + T_{hm}$ $+T_h = 34.183$
[28]	$2T_{hm} + 4T_{sp}$ $= 15.248$	$4T_{sp} + 3T_{hm} + T_h$ $+3T_b + T_{sa} = 32.098$	$T_{sp} + T_{hm} + T_{sa}$ $= 6.006$	$T_b + T_{sp} + 2T_{hm}$ $+T_h + 2T_{sa} = 14.539$
[30]	$2T_h + 4T_{sp}$ $= 6.532$	$5T_{sp} + T_{hm} + 3T_h$ $+3T_{sa} = 12.568$	$3T_{sp} + T_{hm} + 2T_{sa}$ $+3T_h T_b = 13.447$	$2T_b + 2T_{sp} + 2T_h$ $+2T_{sa} = 11.604$
[31]	$2T_h + 4T_{sp}$ $= 6.532$	$5T_{sp} + 4T_h + 2T_{sa}$ $= 8.179$	$2T_{sp} + 2T_{sa} + 2T_h$ $= 3.296$	$2T_{sp} + 2T_h = 3.27$
[32]	$4T_h + 5T_{sp}$ $+T_{sa} = 8.184$	$4T_h + 5T_{sp} + 2T_{sa}$ $= 8.197$	$2T_h + 2T_{sp} + 2T_{sa}$ $= 3.296$	$2T_h + 2T_{sp} = 3.27$
Ours	$2T_h + 4T_{sp}$ $= 6.532$	$4T_{sp} + 3T_h +$ $2T_{sa} = 6.562$	$4T_{sp} + 3T_h + 2T_{sa}$ $= 6.562$	$3T_{sp} + T_h + 5T_{sa}$ $= 4.962$

6.3 Communication Cost

We compare the communication cost of the five schemes from the size of PK, EN and TD respectively (PK, EN, TD indicate public key, encryption, trapdoor). In addition, we assume the size of points in group G, the cyclic multiplication group G_1 and Z_p^* as 1024bit, 512bit and 160bit respectively for the security. Table 3 shows that for PK, our scheme has the same communication cost with [12,28,30] and [31]. But the communication cost of our scheme is reduced by 33.33% compared with scheme [32]. For EN and TD, our scheme is reduced by 31.68% and 13.75% respectively compared with scheme [12].

Table 3. Communication cost (bits)

Schemes	Size of PK	Size of EN	Size of TD	Total
[12]	$2|G| = 2048$	$3|G| + |Z_q^*| = 3232$	$2|G| + |G_1| = 2560$	7840
[28]	$2|G|=2048$	$|G| + |Z_q^*| = 1184$	$|G| = 1024$	4256
[30]	$2|G|=2048$	$2|G| =2048$	$|G_1| = 512$	4608
[31]	$2|G| = 2048$	$|G| + |Z_q^*| = 1184$	$|G| + |Z_q^*| = 1184$	4416
[32]	$3|G| = 3072$	$|G| + 3|Z_q^*|=1504$	$|G| + |Z_q^*| = 1184$	5760
Ours	$2|G| = 2048$	$2|G| + |Z_q^*| = 2208$	$2|G| + |Z_q^*| = 2208$	6464

Overall, the communication cost of our scheme is slightly higher than other schemes except for [12]. Scheme [12] is identity-based encryption, which cannot avoid the problem of key escrow. Scheme [32] is based on PKI, which has the problem of certificate management. Fortunately, our scheme is based on CLPKE and can solve these problems. In addition, our scheme is pairing-free, which is necessary for IoMT. Compared with scheme [28] and [31] our scheme can effectively resist IKGA. Therefore, our scheme is more secure, efficient, and in line with the actual application scenario.

7   Conclusion

The emergence of IoMT gradually replaces traditional medicine, realizes telemedicine and other technologies, and provides a broad development space for modern medicine. The emergence of cloud services not only promotes the development of IoMT but also brings some challenges to medical data privacy. To ensure data security and an effective search for encrypted data, some PEKS schemes have been proposed. However, many of these schemes have some drawbacks. In this paper, we propose a pairing-free CPEKS scheme. It not only solves the secure storage and search for encrypted data but also has no certificate management and key escrow problems. Novelly, the proposed scheme CPEKS does not rely on high-consuming bilinear pairing. The analysis results show that our scheme has better comprehensive performance and is in line with the actual application scenario of IoMT.

References

1. Srinadh, V., Srinivasa Rao, M., Ranjan Sahoo, M., Rameshchandra, K.: An analytical study on security and future research of internet of things. Materials Today: Proceedings (2021). https://www.sciencedirect.com/science/article/pii/S2214785320400586
2. Zhang, T., Liu, M., Yuan, T., Al-Nabhan, N.: Emotion-aware and intelligent internet of medical things toward emotion recognition during covid-19 pandemic. IEEE Internet Things J. 8(21), 16 002–16 013 (2021)
3. Daoud, M.K., Otair, M.: The role of artificial intelligence and the internet of things in the development of medical radiology (an experimental study on magnetic resonance imaging). In: Proceeding 2020 International Conference on Intelligent Computing and Human-Computer Interaction (ICHCI), Sanya, China, 2020, pp. 17–20 (2020)
4. Liu, X., Yang, X., Luo, Y., Zhang, Q.: Verifiable multi-keyword search encryption scheme with anonymous key generation for medical internet of things. IEEE Internet Things J. (2021). https://ieeexplore.ieee.org/document/9344688
5. Ghubaish, A., Salman, T., Zolanvari, M., Unal, D., Al-Ali, A., Jain, R.: Recent advances in the internet-of-medical-things (IOMT) systems security. IEEE Internet Things J. 8(11), 8707–8718 (2021)
6. Song, D.X., Wagner, D., Perrig, A.: Practical techniques for searches on encrypted data. In: Proceeding: IEEE Symposium on Security and Privacy. Berkeley, CA, USA 2000, pp. 44–55 (2000)

7. Ryu, E.-K., Takagi, T.: Efficient conjunctive keyword-searchable encryption. In: Proceeding 21st International Conference on Advanced Information Networking and Applications Workshops, Niagara Falls, ON, Canada, 2007, pp. 409–414 (2007)
8. Zhang, Q.: An overview and analysis of hybrid encryption: The combination of symmetric encryption and asymmetric encryption. In: Proceeding 2021 2nd International Conference on Computing and Data Science (CDS), Stanford, CA, USA, 2021, pp. 616–622 (2021)
9. Boneh, D., Crescenzo, G. Di., Ostrovsky, R., Persiano, G.: Public key encryption with keyword search. In: Proceeding International Conference on the Theory and Applications of Cryptographic Techniques, Interlaken, Switzerland, 2004, pp. 506–522 (2004)
10. Chen, Y.C., Horng, G.: Timestamped conjunctive keyword-searchable public key encryption. In: Proceeding 2009 Fourth International Conference on Innovative Computing, Information and Control, Kaohsiung, Taiwan, 2009, pp. 729–732 (2009)
11. Ohtaki, Y.: Partial disclosure of searchable encrypted data with support for Boolean queries. In: Proceeding 2008 Third International Conference on Availability, Reliability and Security, Barcelona, Spain, 2008, pp. 1083–1090 (2008)
12. Miao, Y., Tong, Q., Deng, R., Choo, K.-K., R., Liu, X., Li, H.: Verifiable searchable encryption framework against insider keyword-guessing attack in cloud storage. IEEE Trans. Cloud Comput. (2020). https://ieeexplore.ieee.org/document/9075374
13. Lu, Y., Li, J.: Lightweight public key authenticated encryption with keyword search against adaptively-chosen-targets adversaries for mobile devices. IEEE Trans. Mob. Comput. (2021). https://ieeexplore.ieee.org/document/9423618
14. Baek, J., Safavi-Naini, R., Susilo, W.: Public key encryption with keyword search revisited. In: Proceeding International Conference on Computational Science and Its Applications (2008)
15. Yau, W.-C., Heng, S.-H., Goi, B.-M.: Off-line keyword guessing attacks on recent public key encryption with keyword search schemes. In: Proceeding International Conference on Autonomic and Trusted Computing, Oslo, Norway, 2008, pp. 100–105 (2008)
16. Byun, J.W., Rhee, H.S., Park, H.-A., Lee, D.H.: Off-line keyword guessing attacks on recent keyword search schemes over encrypted data. In: Proceeding Workshop on Secure Data Management, Seoul, Korea, pp. 75–83 (2006)
17. Hu, C.Y., Liu, P.T.: A secure searchable public key encryption scheme with a designated tester against keyword guessing attacks and its extension. In: Proceeding International Conference on Computer Science, Environment, Ecoinformatics, and Education, Wuhan, China, 2011, pp. 131–136 (2011)
18. Yau, W.-C., Phan, C.-W., Heng, S.-H., Goi, B.-M.: Keyword guessing attacks on secure searchable public key encryption schemes with a designated tester. Int. J. Comput. Math. **90**, 2581–2587 (2013)
19. Chen, Y.-C.: Speks: secure server-designation public key encryption with keyword search against keyword guessing attacks. Comput. J. **58**(4), 922–933 (2015)
20. Xu, P., Jin, H., Wu, Q., Wang, W.: Public-key encryption with fuzzy keyword search: a provably secure scheme under keyword guessing attack. IEEE Trans. Comput. **62**(11), 2266–2277 (2013)
21. Ma, S., Huang, Q., Zhang, M., Yang, B.: Efficient public key encryption with equality test supporting flexible authorization. IEEE Trans. Inf. Forensics Secur. **10**(3), 458–470 (2015)

22. Huang, Q., Li, H.: An efficient public-key searchable encryption scheme secure against inside keyword guessing attacks. Inf. Sci. **403–404**, 1–14 (2017)
23. Chen, R., Mu, Y., Yang, G., Guo, F., Wang, X.: Dual-server public-key encryption with keyword search for secure cloud storage. IEEE Trans. Inf. Forensics Secur. **11**(4), 789–798 (2016)
24. Lu, Y., Li, J., Zhang, Y.: Secure channel free certificate-based searchable encryption withstanding outside and inside keyword guessing attacks. IEEE Trans. Serv. Comput. **14**(6), 2041–2054 (2021)
25. Liu, Z.-Y., Tseng, Y.-F., Tso, R., Chen, Y.-C., Mambo, M.: Identity-certifying authority-aided identity-based searchable encryption framework in cloud systems. IEEE Syst. J. **16**, 1–12 (2021)
26. Al-Riyami S.-S., Paterson, K.-G.: Certificateless public key cryptography. In: Proceeding International Conference on the Theory and Application of Cryptology and Information Security, Taipei, China, 2003, pp. 452–473 (2003)
27. Peng, Y., Cui, J., Peng, C., Ying, Z.: Certificateless public key encryption with keyword search. China Commun. **11**(11), 100–113 (2014)
28. Ma, M., He, D., Kumar, N., Choo, K.-K.R., Chen, J.: Certificateless searchable public key encryption scheme for industrial internet of things. IEEE Trans. Ind. Inform. **14**(2), 759–767 (2018)
29. Zhang, Y., Liu, X., Lang, X., Zhang, Y., Wang, C.: Vclpkes: verifiable certificateless public key searchable encryption scheme for industrial internet of things. IEEE Access **8**, 20 849–20 861 (2020)
30. He, D., Ma, M., Zeadally, S., Kumar, N., Liang, K.: Certificateless public key authenticated encryption with keyword search for industrial internet of things. IEEE Trans. Industr. Inf. **14**(8), 3618–3627 (2018)
31. Lu, Y., Li, J., Zhang, Y.: Privacy-preserving and pairing-free multirecipient certificateless encryption with keyword search for cloud-assisted IIoT. IEEE Internet Things J. **7**(4), 2553–2562 (2020)
32. Lu, Y., Li, J., Wang, F.: Pairing-free certificate-based searchable encryption supporting privacy-preserving keyword search function for IIoTs. IEEE Trans. Industr. Inf. **17**(4), 2696–2706 (2021)

Artificial Intelligence and Cyber Security

Cross-site Scripting Threat Intelligence Detection Based on Deep Learning

Zhonglin Liu⬤, Yong Fang, and Yijia Xu⁽✉⁾

School of Cyber Science and Engineering, Sichuan University, Chengdu, Sichuan, China
jungleforsa@gmail.com, yfang@scu.edu.cn, xuyijia@stu.scu.edu.cn

Abstract. In an increasingly complex cyber environment, where the role of traditional protection tools is increasingly limited, intelligence is the key point in the battle. Through the information monitoring of Internet social platforms, potential cyberattack threats to enterprises, governments, and other institutions could be analyzed. Twitter, the world's largest social media platform, spreads news and shares tweets about cybersecurity-related events and technologies daily, with cross-site scripting attacks being one of them. In the status quo, this paper proposes a cross-site scripting threat intelligence detection model based on deep learning, which can detect tweets involving threats related to cross-site scripting attacks. We utilized a variety of word vector extraction tools blended with topic word extraction techniques to construct a word vector matrix with multi-dimensional features. Then, the threat event detection model is trained using a bidirectional recurrent convolutional neural network with a self-attentive mechanism. In the experiment, the accuracy rate of our proposed model exceeds 0.96, and through multiple sets of control experimental data results, it is proved that the structure designed in the model is conducive to improving the performance of the model and that the model is effective in detecting tweets that involve cross-site scripting threats.

Keywords: Neural networks · Cross-site scripting · Threats · Deep learning

1 Introduction

As Internet technology becomes more popular, cyber threats are happening all the time. According to the report of the World Economic Forum in 2021, the frequency of data fraud, theft, and cyberattacks has greatly increased economic and social risks [1]. Therefore, the ability to detect cyber threats in time can effectively reduce the losses of related departments and provide reliable evidence and clues for prosecutors [2].

The Twitter social platform is one of the most visited social media in the world. There are a large number of news and personal tweets posted every day, which contain a wide range of information, including security-related events and news [3]. There are also many cybersecurity practitioners sharing information

E. Ahene and F. Li (Eds.): FCS 2022, CCIS 1726, pp. 89–104, 2022.
https://doi.org/10.1007/978-981-19-8445-7_6

about new vulnerabilities, exploit codes, and related security incident details they understand or research on social media [4]. In this way, this cybersecurity data generator can be used to help researchers investigate the identification of short-text content threats.

Cross-site scripting attack is a very common script injection attack. It is the top three vulnerabilities in web security threats in the OWSAP report all year round [5]. It enables the victim's browser to load and execute malicious JavaScript scripts after visiting a website or page containing malicious code, thereby being controlled and attacked by the malicious script code. So we set cross-site scripting threat intelligence as the research object of this paper.

Deep learning is currently one of the core technologies leading the development of artificial intelligence and is widely used in the field of pattern recognition and text classification [6]. In this paper, we took advantage of natural language processing to analyze text and proposed a multi-dimensional text feature detection model based on deep learning to detect related threats that appeared on Twitter. Our main contributions are as follows:

- We proposed a multi-dimensional method to obtain word-level feature vectors. It is a combination of a variety of pre-training word vector tools so that our model can obtain more features and context-related information from tweets.
- We used the Latent Dirichlet Allocation (abbreviated as LDA) algorithm to extract relevant topic words in the tweets to obtain text-level features. These features can improve the performance of the model in discriminating tweets.
- We have designed a state-of-the-art detection model. This model is based on the Bi-LSTM neural network, which learns the context and various features, and then uses the self-attention mechanism to improve the learning efficiency, so that our detection model has a better classification effect. The final model has an accuracy rate of over 0.96 under actual data.

The rest of the paper is organized as follows. In Sect. 2, the research results are introduced on threat intelligence detection in recent years. In Sect. 3, We will introduce the specific details and key technologies of the detection model. The results of our experiment and evaluation will be shown in Sect. 4. Section 5 is the summary of the work.

2   Related Work

A large amount of real-time data on social platforms has attracted many researchers to study related security incidents. Cyber threat incidents are always a hot topic and it can be seen as a dichotomous problem. Researchers usually use machine learning methods to find the trigger words of the event and then classify the text. Willett et al. proposed a framework for network assessment, which extracts threat events and assesses the degree of damage, which is used to assist the security personnel in better understanding the global network situation [7]. Qiu et al. performed a detailed parsing of sentence features and used the obtained feature information to classify cyber-attack events, while also pointing out that the detection of event types is best suited to the trigger-matching method, and that the performance of word embedding feature models trained on large corpora is also superior to that of other models [8]. Khandpur et al. proposed a query strategy based on convolution kernel and dependency analysis to detect various types of network attack events, such as data leakage, account hijacking, and code injection [9]. However, due to the high training cost and computational cost of the autoencoder, it is not conducive for other researchers to expand and adjust on this basis. Le et al. proposed a keyword seed-based learning framework for threat event detection [10], a scheme that is good at detecting known threats but does not discriminate well against unknown kinds of threats. The unsupervised learning scheme proposed by Bose et al. selects and extracts key terms in the text [11], calculates a threshold for the weight of the term in the threat event, and then ranks its severity. However, the processing of its text features is too narrow, and it is easy to make the model over-fitting. In some specific cases, it cannot be classified accurately. The supervised learning method proposed by Ji et al. [12] used a multi-task learning model to detect security threats in tweets. The feature processing method is too complicated and the final experimental effect is mediocre. Trong et al. used a manually labeled data set to use security event trigger words to detect events, which is not efficient [13]. Shin et al. considered the detection of threat events through repeated words and new words [14]. This scheme can theoretically effectively identify new threat events. Balakrishna et al. proposed a high-level text representation method to learn contextual features in samples [15], and detect threat events through high-dimensional and deep text features.

Given the problems and shortcomings of the above research, we start from the text feature vector representation method, through the fusion of different dimensional vector representations, and with the help of the deep neural network to extract high-dimensional features, we propose a multi-dimensional text based on deep learning feature detection model.

3   Methodology

3.1   Overview

Aiming at the identification of cross-site scripting threats, we designed a scientific and effective detection model based on the data obtained on Twitter. The overall architecture of the model is shown in Fig. 1 and is divided into three parts: data collection, Multi-dimensional feature vector fusion, and deep neural network.

i) **Data collection.** The purpose is to provide data for training the deep neural network model. We used a crawler to obtain a large amount of tweet data containing related threats and not containing threats from Twitter. It is hoped that the meaning of the entire tweet can be obtained from the terms of the tweet, contextual content, topic words, etc., to detect tweets involving threats. In addition, to facilitate feature extraction and deep neural network training, we clean and de-duplicate the collected data, delete punctuation marks, emoticons, and other interference information in tweets, and mark positive and negative samples.

ii) **Multi-dimensional feature vector fusion**. Traditional event detection needs to consider event trigger words in the text, which is inefficient. To achieve a better model detection effect, we have carried out better-vectorized expressions for short text content such as tweets. The existing pre-training models are Word2Vec, GloVe, and FastText, each of which has different characteristics. We used these three pre-training models to train and vectorize the representation of this paper respectively and then concatenate it so that the text is converted into a feature vector with multiple encoding features. In addition, we not only considered the vector features of the words themselves, but we used LDA (Latent Dirichlet Allocation), which implies Dirichlet distribution, to extract the topic words of tweets so that we can obtain text-level feature vectors. Finally, the feature vector obtained by the fusion of the text feature and the word feature can fully express the meaning of the tweets in multiple dimensions and also serve as the input of the deep neural network model.

iii) **Deep neural network**. Aiming at the acquired feature vectors of tweets, and considering that the text content has the characteristics of contextual relevance, we used Bi-directional Long Short-Term Memory neural network (abbreviated as Bi-LSTM) to train the content threat detection model. The definition of a threat event is usually determined by the trigger word and the elements that appear in certain specific events. In a tweet, different tweet fragments contribute differently to the definition of the entire event. Therefore, a self-attention mechanism is introduced into the detection model, it can weigh the importance of different lexical units, adjust the feature weight value, reduce a certain data dimension, make the detection model pay attention to the key information of the current content, and improve the accuracy of the model.

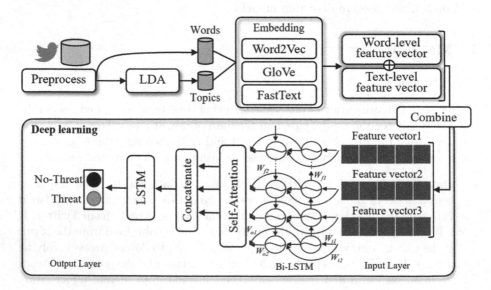

Fig. 1. The overall framework of the threat event detection model

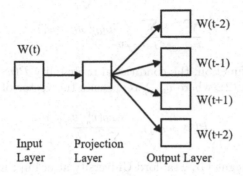

Fig. 2. Skip-Gram model structure

3.2   Feature Integration

Tweets are made up of words, but this cannot be directly applied to our model as training parameters, so we have to convert the words of the tweets into a vector representation via a word vector model. The three most effective word vector models are Word2Vec, GloVe, and FastText. In addition, to obtain text-level tweet features, we use the LDA model to extract the topic words of the tweet and combine them with the tweet vector, so that the deep neural network can learn more information.

Word-Level Features. Word2Vec. Although traditional One-hot vectors are easy to understand, the resulting vector matrix becomes very sparse when encountering a large collection of data with a large lexicon, which does not represent the information contained in the text well, nor does it represent contextual associations. In addition, the One-hot method generates a huge matrix when calculating, which will reduce the computational efficiency of the model [16]. Therefore, the deep learning research team under Google proposed the Word2Vec word vector model in 2013. This model can reduce the dimensionality of the data generated by the original One-hot model, and calculate the cosine similarity of the word vector space to establish the correlation between the upper and lower questions in this article [17]. The common training models of the Word2Vec tool are CBOW and Skip-Gram. The Skip-Gram model is used in this paper.

The structure of the Skip-Gram model is shown in Fig. 2. Set up a window with adjustable width, use the word in the center of the window as the output, slide from the beginning of the sentence to the end in turn, and then adjust the parameters through the neural network gradient descent method. After the training is complete, the words can be represented as vectors in the network using the weight matrix. Assuming that Wt represents the central word, then $W_{t-c}, W_{t-c+1}, ..., W_{t+c}$ represents the context of the central word, the objective function of Skip-Gram is shown in Eq. (1), and c represents the window size:

$$\frac{1}{T}\sum_{t=1}^{T}\sum_{-c\leqslant j\leqslant c, j\neq 0} logp(w_{t+j}|w_t) \tag{1}$$

Using the Softmax function, the conditional probability $P(w_t|w_{t+j})$ is obtained as shown in formula (2), where $v_{w_{t+j}}$ represents the vector of the word w_{t+j}.

$$P(w_t|w_{t+j}) = \frac{exp(v_{w_t}^t v_{c_{t+1}})}{\sum_{c=1}^{C}(v_{c_t}^T v_c)} \tag{2}$$

GloVe. GloVe is designed by Stanford University after improving the Word2Vec encoding model [18]. It is characterized by using the co-occurrence information characteristics of words and words, fitting the differences between co-occurring words of different word pairs so that the word vector model can obtain the global information of the text. In terms of formula description, the probability of word j appearing in the environment of the word i is shown in formula (3):

$$P_{ij} = P(j|i) = \frac{x_{ij}}{x_i} \tag{3}$$

At the same time, a constraint condition is needed to make the formula hold, that is, the distance between words, for example, the distance between words does not exceed 3 words. The main contribution of GloVe is to establish the association between the co-occurrence probability and the word vector. Then there is the co-occurrence probability Pij, the word i and the word j respectively represent the central word and the background word, and the corresponding vectors are represented by V and $\widetilde{v}$.

$$f(v_i, v_j, \widetilde{v_k}) = \frac{p_{ik}}{p_{jk}} \tag{4}$$

For the symmetry of any pair of words, that is, $v_i = \widetilde{v_j}$, and $X_{ij} = \widetilde{X_{ji}}$, then:

$$f((v_i - v_j)^T \widetilde{v_k}) = \frac{f(v_i^T \widetilde{v_k})}{f(v_j^T \widetilde{v_k})} \tag{5}$$

$$f(x) = exp(x) \tag{6}$$

available:

$$v_i^T \widetilde{v_k} = log(x_{ik}) - log(x_i) = log(x_i k) - b_i - b_k \tag{7}$$

The loss function is defined as:

$$Loss = \sum_{i,j=1}^{V} f(x_{ij})(v_i^T \widetilde{v_j} + b_i + b_j - log(x_{ij}))^2 \tag{8}$$

The vector of the final word is represented by the sum of the vector of the center word and the background word.

FastText. This is a fast text classifier and word vector tool proposed by Facebook, which provides efficient feature representation and text classification, and is mainly used in synonym mining and text classification systems in the company's systems [19]. Due to the simple structure of the model, it is very convenient and fast to represent word features. This model is also based on the improved Word2vec vector model, which proposes a subword embedding approach based on the original, taking into account additional features of the character-level N-gram. For short textual word vector training, the model can combine the internal structure information of words with short textual character features more quickly. The FastText structure is shown in Fig. 3.

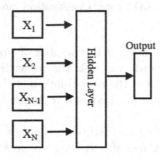

Fig. 3. FastText structure

X_1, X_2, X_N represent N-gram vectors corresponding to different texts. For a phrase w, combined with the sub-word information, the sub-word with a length of 3–6, that is, the N-gram character set is expressed as $G_w \subset \{1, ..., G\}$. Assuming that the sub-word vector in the dictionary is denoted as z_g and the word vector of the vocabulary w is denoted as v_w, then there is an objective function as shown in formula 9.

$$v_w = \sum_{g \in G_w} z_g \qquad (9)$$

Text-level Features and Integration. The representation of word features can be enhanced by integrating the features obtained from the three different pre-trained models in 3.2.1. The focus of these word embedding models is still on the words themselves, which are word-level features. The description of an event must have the theme it wants to express. Most sentences of the same type of event have similar expressions. Therefore, we introduced the LDA topic classification model to enhance the expression of text features, obtain the topic keywords of a tweet, and get text-level features.

The LDA topic word generation model was originally a three-layer Bayesian production model proposed by Blei et al. [20], which created the association from text to topic and then to words. The basic scheme is to treat the document as the probability distribution of the topic described by the keyword. The topic words can be used as the text clustering center, and the texts of the same topic can be aggregated. Topic words can also be used for feature generation, and the LDA model to obtain the topic distribution of the text and extract keywords. So that the feature space of the text can be dimensioned down and can be used for a variety of prediction tasks. The model design framework is shown in Fig. 4.

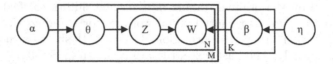

Fig. 4. LDA topic classification model

M is the number of texts and N is the number of words, which are associated with K topics. W is each word, and Z is the topic distribution of its word, α is the hyperparameter of θ, β is the probability distribution of word and topic, θ is the probability distribution of text and topic, and η is the hyperparameter expression of β.

To transform each tweet into a feature vector that has enough feature information for deep learning, we merge text-level features with word-level features. That is, the text-transformed word vector feature matrix is stitched with the topic word vector matrix, and the topic words obtained through the LDA model are used as global additional feature words. Finally, the tweets are passed through the word vector tool of the same dimension, combined with the text-level features, and the encoding process of the feature vector matrix is shown in Fig. 5.

3.3   Deep Learning Algorithm

Recurrent Neural Network. Recurrent neural network (referred to as RNN) in deep learning is an important branch of it, and its main feature is the ability to obtain contextual feature information [21]. Researchers have improved their long-term dependence and built a long and short-term memory neural network referred to as LSTM. It can solve the problem of gradient disappearance and gradient explosion in the process of model training, making it perform better in tasks that rely on contextual information. Compared with a simple RNN, the repetitive module of LSTM is much more complicated. This repetitive module is called a cell.

Inside the cell, the LSTM network will go through three stages [25]. The first stage is the forgetting stage. Whether to discard the output content of the previous node, is also called the forget gate; The second stage is to select the memory part, and the input content can be selectively memorized after calculation; The last stage is used to control the output, which can control

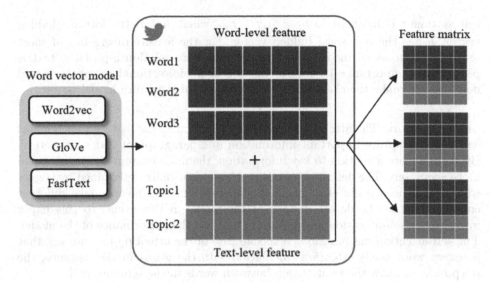

Fig. 5. Text feature vector combination process

whether the cell outputs the results of the current round of calculations. The calculation process is shown in the following Eqs. 10-15.

$$f_t = \sigma(W_f[h_{t-1}, x_t] + b_f) \tag{10}$$

$$i_t = \sigma(W_i[h_{t-1}, x_t] + b_i) \tag{11}$$

$$\widetilde{C_t} = tanh(W_C[h_{t-1}, x_t] + b_C) \tag{12}$$

$$C_t = f_t * C_{t-1} + i_t * \widetilde{C_t} \tag{13}$$

$$o_t = \sigma(W_o[h_{t-1}, x_t] + b_o) \tag{14}$$

$$h_t = o_t * tanh(C_t) \tag{15}$$

In the formula, α represents the Sigmoid activation function, W is the weight of the layer, and b represents the deviation. f_t represents the forget gate, i_t is the input gate, h_t represents that the selective forgetting function at time t is implemented by the sigmoid layer, mainly referring to the output of the previous stage and the input of the current stage, and then implementing selective forgetting. In the second stage, the information stored in the LSTM network cell is determined by using the $tanh$ function to obtain the candidate vector, multiplying the previous state value by the corresponding forgetting gate, and adding the product of the input gate and the candidate value to obtain the final cell state Value C.

Researchers had proposed bi-directional recurrent neural networks to improve LSTM into Bi-LSTM (Bi-directional Long Short-Term Memory) to better use forget gates and memory gates to capture contextual relationships and obtain features that are not limited to sequential inputs [22]. The output of Bi-LSTM cell at time t is updated to $h_t = \overrightarrow{h_tf} + \overrightarrow{h_tb}$, where $\overrightarrow{h_tf}$ is the forward hidden vector, $\overrightarrow{h_tb}$ is the backward hidden vector. For the feature divergence of short text corpus in social media, the contextual feature relationship of the text is particularly important. Therefore, the use of a bidirectional recurrent neural network will make the classification performance of the entire model better.

Self-attention. The attention mechanism is similar to the feature that humans can quickly capture important information in a paragraph of text or a picture. By paying more attention to key information, the main content can be obtained more accurately. The definition of a threat event is usually determined by trigger words or some specific elements [23]. Different text fragments make different contributions to the detection task of the model in this event, so this paper introduces a self-attention mechanism to improve the performance of the model. The self-attention mechanism is a special case of the attention mechanism, that is, every word needs attention calculation with the words in the sentence, the purpose is to learn the relationship between words in the sentence [24].

The attention mechanism can weigh different grammatical units, which can reduce the data dimension and improve the accuracy of the model. Solve the long-distance dependence problem by calculating the mutual influence between words. The data source is generally represented by a series of key-value pairs, such as <k,v>, where k represents the key, and v is the corresponding value. When calculating the attention value, we need to calculate the similarity between the sequence and each key in the data, denoted by S. Common similarity calculations are dot product and multi-layer perception forms, as shown in equation (16).

$$S(k_i, q) = \begin{cases} k_i^T q & dot \\ V_a^T tanh(Wk_i + Uq) & preceptron \end{cases} \tag{16}$$

Then the obtained similarity S is normalized using the Softmax function, and the weight a of the sequence value is expressed by formula 17.

$$a_i = softmax(S(k_i, q)) \tag{17}$$

Finally, after the weights are obtained, they can be weighted and summed to obtain the corresponding attention value. The self-attention mechanism makes q, k, and v equal in the attention mechanism. The expression of the attention value is shown in Eq. 18.

$$Attention = \sum_{t=1}^{t} a_i * v_i \tag{18}$$

Network Structure. The neural network structure of the entire model is shown in Fig. 6. Three different word vector models are used for word embedding for a piece of the tweet, and then Bi-LSTM and self-attention mechanism are used for text feature extraction on the embedding results. Then the three output vectors

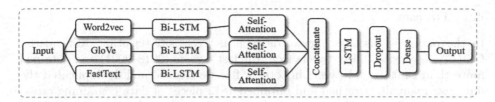

Fig. 6. Details of the detection model

are concatenated and passed into the LSTM for further feature extraction. The Dropout layer is used to prevent over-fitting, and finally the prediction result is output through the fully connected layer.

4 Experiment

To verify the reliability and effectiveness of the threat event detection model based on deep learning, we built a detector based on the overall framework of Fig. 1. First, use the collected samples to train the model and optimize the parameters, and then use the test sample set to evaluate the detection effect of the model.

4.1 Environment

The experimental environment designed in this paper is all running under the Windows 10 64-bit operating system, and all the functional modules in the content are developed and run under the Python 3.6 environment. All the involved Python libraries and their versions are shown in Table 1.

Table 1. Environment and configuration

Type	Content
Configuration	CPU: i7-10700F, RAM: 16G GPU: GeForce GTX1060 6G
Python Library	Genism 3.8.3, FastText 0.9.2, Keras 2.2.4, Keras-self-attention 0.50.0, Scikit-learn 0.24.2, Seaborn 0.9.0, Matplotlib 3.3.4, Numpy 1.19.5, Nltk 3.6.5, Pandas 1.1.5, Tensorflow-gpu 1.13.1, Tensorboard 1.13.1, Tensorflow-estimator 1.13.1

4.2   Dataset

In the paper, we used the keywords such as "cross site-scripting, XSS, alert(, CSRF" as seeds to collect tweets from the last 4 years (2018–2021) and obtained more than 24,000 valid tweets in total. After we cleaned and de-duplicated the data, we manually screened and obtained 1812 pieces of data containing cross-site scripting threats. These tweets are usually the authors sharing vulnerabilities discovered by them or reposting some exploit methods. At the same time, we also extracted 2000 tweets that did not contain threats from the data. These tweets are often advertisements containing relevant keywords or other abbreviations of the same name. Therefore, this type of control sample is highly confusing. We label the tweets that contain threats and the tweets that are not, which can be used for neural network model training.

4.3   Experiment and Analysis

The main characteristics of the threat event detection model are its multi-dimensional coding feature representation and attention mechanism. In the experiment, different parameters will affect the detection performance of the model. After comparison, we set the loss function loss of the neural network to Categorical_Crossentrop, Adam as the optimization function; the number of neurons in the Bi-LSTM hidden layer is 200, the number of neurons in the LSTM hidden layer is 128, the Batch-size is 32, and the epoch is 30; The dimension of the word vector pre-training model is 128, the window is set to 5, the number of iterations is 5, and 2 subject words are obtained through LDA. At the same time, to make the experimental results more objective, we conducted multiple sets of controlled experiments in the experiment to verify the effectiveness of the method.

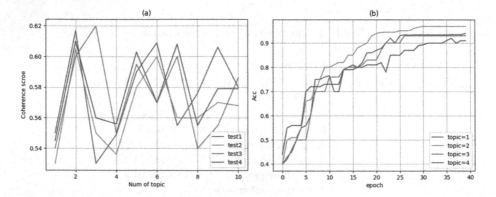

Fig. 7. (a) The number of topic words and the corresponding coherence score; (b) The influence of the number of topic words on the detection accuracy

Table 2. Results of threat event detection

	Accuracy	Recall	**F1 score**
Contains threat events	0.969	0.977	0.973
No threats included	0.970	0.975	0.972
Contains threat events (without keywords)	0.932	0.953	0.942
No threats included (without keywords)	0.940	0.952	0.946

a) **Threat event detection** The first experiment is mainly to evaluate the accuracy, recall, and F1 value of threat event detection in the dataset to prove the effectiveness of the model in detecting threat tweets. In the experiment, 1812 tweets containing threat information were used as positive samples, 2000 tweets that did not contain threat were used as negative samples, and a 10-fold crossover was used for verification experiments. In addition, because the experimental data was searched by some special keywords, we considered that the detection model of threatening tweets may be affected by some trigger words, so we deleted the keyword seeds in the 900 positive samples (such as xss, XSS, CSRF) as a control group to verify the robustness of the entire detection model. The experimental results are shown in Table 2.

It can be seen from Table 2 that the tweet detection model related to cross-site scripting threats has a good classification effect, and can accurately identify both positive and negative samples. Moreover, after we remove the keyword seeds with strong features, the detection accuracy, and recall of our model can exceed 93%, although the accuracy drops slightly. This indicates that these keywords are indeed more informative in terms of semantic representation and that the detection model we designed is robust.

Table 3. Results of control experiment

id	Model component	Accuracy	Recall	F1 score
1	Word2vec+BiLSTM	0.864	0.843	0.853
2	Word2vec+BiLSTM+Self-Att	0.898	0.890	0.894
3	Word2vec+LDA+BiLSTM+Self-Att	0.912	0.910	0.911
4	Mult-W2V+BiLSTM	0.940	0.934	0.935
5	Mult-W2V+BiLSTM+Self-Att	0.959	0.954	0.956
6	Mult-W2V+LDA+BiLSTM+Self-Att	**0.969**	**0.976**	**0.972**

b) **Number of topics** In the process of multi-dimensional feature fusion, we have introduced topic words. Only the appropriate number of topic words have better coherence and feature expression meaning. Too many or too few topics will affect the performance of the model. The Coherence Score is used to indicate the interpretability, meaning, and semantic coherence of the selected topic. The higher the score, the better. The result of the experiment is shown in Fig. 7.

The influence of the number of topic words on the detection accuracy. As shown in Fig. 7(a), we have done several experiments on the coherence score, and selected part of the data for graphing. It can be seen that the score reaches the highest when the number of topic words is 2 to 3. Our sample data is only aimed at cross-site scripting types of threats, with fewer topics, so it is more appropriate to choose 2 topic words as the multi-dimensional feature fusion segment; In addition, from (b), it can be seen that the number of different subject words has a certain influence on the accuracy of model detection. Too few or too many subject words will affect the recognition of the model. When the model topic=2, the accuracy rate is relatively highest. And as the number of training iterations increases, the accuracy of the model increases the fastest.

c) **Model component** For the same data set (without removing the keyword seed), to verify the impact of different feature engineering and neural network structures on the event threat detection model. We used the controlled variable method in the experiment and conducted multiple sets of controlled experiments to prove that the combination of multi-dimensional feature fusion, recurrent neural network, attention mechanism and other methods we used is effective and can improve the accuracy of model detection. The experimental results are illustrated in Table 3.

In Table 3, Mult-W2V represents the combination of three different word embedding methods (Word2vec, GloVe, FastText), and Self-Att represents the self-attention mechanism. It can be seen from Table 3 that we used Word2vec as a control group. From the results of experiments 1, 2, and 3, the self-attention mechanism can effectively improve the detection efficiency of the model. Compared with experiments No. 1 to No. 3 and No. 4 to No. 6, the use of multi-dimensional coding can enable the model to obtain more features and significantly improve detection accuracy. Compared with experiments No. 2, 3, and No. 5, 6, the addition of topic words can be more conducive to obtaining the information characteristics that the author intended to express from the tweets, thereby improving the performance of the model. Therefore, the third experiment uses multiple control groups to prove that the model components used in our proposed model are meaningful and can effectively help the model detect tweets involving threats.

5   Conclusion

In this paper, aiming at the growing threat information on the Internet, we propose a threat event detection model based on deep learning. By using real data on Twitter to train the model, it proves that threats such as cross-site scripting attacks can be effectively detected. To extract feature information in short texts, the model adopts the fusion of multi-type word vector features and tweet topic words to obtain the hidden information as comprehensively as possible. Then use the bidirectional recurrent neural network and self-attention mechanism to train the data. Ultimately, experiments are designed according to the characteristics of threat event detection. In the results of multiple sets of comparative experiments, it is proved that the detection model proposed in this paper has good performance in terms of parameter selection, model robustness, and detection accuracy. In future work, the threat scope of model detection can also be extended to other aspects, not just limited to cross-site scripting threats, we believe that they are essentially the same.

Acknowledgements. This work was supported in part by National Natural Science Foundation of China (U20B2045).

References

1. Marsh, M,. et al.: The Global Risks Report 2021, 21 December 2021. https://www.oliverwyman.com/content/dam/mmc-web/insights/publications/2021/january/global-risks-report/The-Global-Risks-Report-2021-small-FINAL.pdf
2. Noor, U., Anwar, Z., Amjad, T., Choo, K.K.R.: A machine learning-based Fin-Tech cyber threat attribution framework using high-level indicators of compromise. Future Gener. Comput. Syst. **96**, 227–242 (2019)
3. Yagcioglu, S., et al.: Detecting Cybersecurity Events from Noisy Short Text. arXiv (2019). arXiv:1904.05054
4. Internet Security Center. 2020 Global Advanced Persistent Threat APT Research Report, February 2021. https://zt.360.cn/1101061855.php?dtid=1101062360&did=211138962
5. OWASP, OWASP Top 10 2021. https://owasp.org/Top10/. 2021-12-21
6. Ruder, S.: An overview of multi-task learning in deep neural networks. arXiv (2017). arXiv:1706.05098
7. Willett, P.K., Kirubarajan, T.: System diagnosis and prognosis: security and condition monitoring issues III. In: System Diagnosis and Prognosis: Security and Condition Monitoring Issues, vol. III, p. 5107 (2003)
8. Qiu, X., Lin, X., Qiu, L.: Feature representation models for cyber attack event extraction. In: 2016 IEEE/WIC/ACM International Conference on Web Intelligence Workshops (WIW), pp. 29–32. IEEE (2016)
9. Khandpur, R.P., Ji, T., Jan, S., et al.: Crowdsourcing cybersecurity: cyber attack detection using social media. In: Proceedings of the 2017 ACM on Conference on Information and Knowledge Management, pp. 1049–1057 (2017)
10. Le Sceller, Q., Karbab, E.M.B., Debbabi, M., et al.: Sonar: automatic detection of cyber security events over the twitter stream. In: Proceedings of the 12th International Conference on Availability, Reliability and Security, pp. 1–11 (2017)
11. Bose, A., Behzadan, V., Aguirre, C., et al.: A novel approach for detection and ranking of trendy and emerging cyber threat events in twitter streams. In: 2019 IEEE/ACM International Conference on Advances in Social Networks Analysis and Mining (ASONAM), pp. 871–878. IEEE (2019)
12. Ji, T., Zhang, X., Self, N., et al.: Feature driven learning framework for cybersecurity event detection. In: Proceedings of the 2019 IEEE/ACM International Conference on Advances in Social Networks Analysis and Mining, pp. 196–203 (2019)

13. Trong, H.M.D., Le, D.T., Veyseh, A.P.B., et al.: Introducing a new dataset for event detection in cybersecurity texts. In: Proceedings of the 2020 Conference on Empirical Methods in Natural Language Processing (EMNLP), pp. 5381–5390 2020)

14. Shin H, Shim W C, Moon J, et al. Cybersecurity Event Detection with New and Re-emerging Words. In: Proceedings of the 15th ACM Asia Conference on Computer and Communications Security, pp. 665–678 (2020)

15. Simran, K., Balakrishna, P., Vinayakumar, R., Soman, K.P.: Deep learning approach for enhanced cyber threat indicators in twitter stream. In: Thampi, S.M., Martinez Perez, G., Ko, R., Rawat, D.B. (eds.) SSCC 2019. CCIS, vol. 1208, pp. 135–145. Springer, Singapore (2020). https://doi.org/10.1007/978-981-15-4825-3_11

16. Cassel, M., Lima, F.: Evaluating one-hot encoding finite state machines for SEU reliability in SRAM-based FPGAs. In: 12th IEEE International On-Line Testing Symposium (IOLTS 2006). IEEE (2006). 6 pp

17. Mikolov, T., Sutskever, I., Chen, K., Corrado, G., Dean, J.: Distributed representations of words and phrases and their compositionality. Adv. Neural. Inf. Process. Syst. **26**, 3111–3119 (2013)

18. Pennington, J., Socher, R., Manning, C.D.: Glove: global vectors for word representation. In: Proceedings of the 2014 Conference on Empirical Methods in Natural Language Processing (EMNLP), pp. 1532–1543 (2014)

19. Joulin, A., Grave, E., Bojanowski, P., et al.: Bag of tricks for efficient text classification. In: Proceedings of the 15th Conference of the European Chapter of the Association for Computational Linguistics: Volume 2, Short Papers, vol. 2, pp. 427–431

20. Sun, F., Chen, H.: Feature extension for Chinese short text classification based on LDA and word2vec. In: 2018 13th IEEE Conference on Industrial Electronics and Applications (ICIEA), pp. 1189–1194. IEEE 2018

21. Sutskever, I., Vinyals, O., Le Quoc, V.: Sequence to sequence learning with neural networks. In: Proceedings of the 28th Annual Conference on Neural Information Processing Systems-NIPS, Montreal, QC, Canada, 8–13 December 2014, pp. 3104–3112 (2014)

22. Graves, A., Schmidhuber, J.: Framewise phoneme classification with bidirectional LSTM and other neural network architectures. Neural Netw. **18**(5–6), 602–610 (2005)

23. Li, X., Zhang, W., Ding, Q.: Understanding and improving deep learning-based rolling bearing fault diagnosis with attention mechanism. Signal Process. **161**, 136–154 (2019)

24. Zhao, H., Jia, J., Koltun, V.: Exploring self-attention for image recognition. In: Proceedings of the IEEE/CVF Conference on Computer Vision and Pattern Recognition, pp. 10076–10085 (2020)

25. Yin, X., Zhao, H., Zhao, J.B.: Military named entity recognition based on multi-neural network cooperation. Tsinghua Univ. J. (Nat. Sci. Ed.) **60**(8), 648–655 (2020)

Power Analysis Attack Based on Lightweight Convolutional Neural Network

Xiang Li[1], Ning Yang[1], Aidong Chen[2,4]([✉]), Weifeng Liu[3], Xiaoxiao Liu[4], and Na Huang[2,4]

[1] Beijing Key Laboratory of Information Service Engineering, Beijing 100101, China
[2] College of Robotics, Beijing Union University, Beijing 100101, China
aidong@buu.edu.cn
[3] Institute of Semiconductors, Chinese Academy of Sciences, Beijing 100083, China
[4] Research Centre for Multi-intelligent Systems, Beijing 100101, China

Abstract. Since the beginning of the 21st century, modern information technology and electronic integrated circuit technology have developed rapidly. In the chip industry, the ability to resist side-channel attacks has become an important indicator for international mainstream evaluation agencies to evaluate chip security. This paper proposes an improved method for side channel analysis based on the CNN_{best} model, incorporating a lightweight combined channel and space convolutional attention module, optimising the position of the attention module, improving the learning efficiency of key features of the power consumption curve, and effectively reducing the number of traces used by the attack model. The addition of dropout layer network structure solves the problem that the model is prone to rapid overfitting. The optimal value of drop rate is sought through comparative experiments to speed up the convergence of the model and reduce the number of traces required for a successful attack. The experimental results show that the number of traces required by the method in this paper for side-channel attacks is reduced by 88% compared with the original model, which significantly improves the attack performance and can meet the requirements of side-channel modeling and analysis.

Keywords: Side channel analysis · Power consumption attacks · Deep learning · Attention mechanisms

1 Introduction

With the development of cryptography and information technology, the current cryptographic algorithm itself is strong enough. People cannot live without embedded devices, such as smart cards, routers for door locks, etc. A large part of the security of embedded devices relies on cryptographic algorithms to protect them, and mature cryptographic algorithms have been mathematically proven, so brute force attacks are unlikely to break

This work was supported by the Academic Research Projects of Beijing Union University (SK160202103).

them with current levels of computing power, but side channel attacks target the device, focusing on using physical information leaked during device operation to bypass cryptographic algorithms. This is often an easily overlooked security risk, and research into side channeling can help to remedy these security risks and strengthen device security. Due to the process characteristics of the device itself, the device will leak side channel information such as power consumption, electromagnetism and time during operation, as shown in Fig. 1. If an attacker is able to obtain data on the changes in the energy consumption of the circuit operation, using certain methods to analyse this data, he will be able to obtain some information on the key. The leaked information is directly related to the key or a part of the subkey, and the operations related to this information are called sensitive operations, and the operation obtained is called a sensitive intermediate value. Thereby, the intermediate value leakage model portrays the mapping relationship between the intermediate value of the cryptographic algorithm to the actual leaked value and is an assumption made by the attacker against the cryptographic device [1].

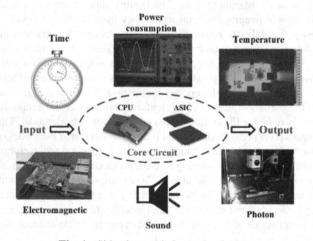

Fig. 1. Side channel information leakage.

Side channel analysis (SCA) can be divided into two categories according to different methods. The first category is the Non-Profiling SCA analysis method, and the second category is the Profiling SCA analysis method. The Non-Profiling SCA analysis method does not require additional equipment, directly collects power consumption on the target chip, and recovers the key by means of statistical analysis. Common Non-Profiling SCA analysis methods include Differential Power Analysis (DPA) [2], Correlated Power Analysis (CPA) [3] and Mutual Information Analysis [4]. In contrast, the Profiling SCA analysis method uses a large number of tagged (plaintext and key) power consumption profiles on a target device that is fully consistent with the target device and then models the power consumption before the key, using this model to attack the target device. Common modeling and analysis methods include Template Attack (TA) [5] and linear regression analysis models [6, 7]. The modeling attack capability of the side channel combined with deep learning is relatively strong. In the attack scenario, if the deep learning technique trains lightweight and easily trained models with good performance, it is even greatly enhanced the comprehensive attack capability of this technique, which can effectively improve the security testing capability in terms of side channels.

In recent years an increasing number of scholars have concluded that the use of deep learning for side channel modelling is effective, as the greatest advantage of deep learning is that it can learn the feature extraction process to a certain extent and can extract more complex and high-level abstract features. In recent years, the current state of research in the modelling class of side channel analysis using deep learning can be divided into four parts: improved network design or training methods, optimised loss functions, data augmentation and other research directions. With regard to improving network design, in 2020, Ryad et al. used VGG-16 as a starting point to give the effect of hyperparameters on the modelling and attack process, and proposed the CNN_{best} architecture, which provided a great help for further extensive research in this field [8]. In 2021, Lu et al. proposed a neural network architecture that can get rid of the manual extraction of traces on the mask-protected original feature point step and obtain intermediate values by directly analyzing the raw power consumption curve end-to-end [9]. In 2022, Wu et al. proposed a deep learning-assisted template attack, based on a similarity learning approach, using a triadic model for implementation [10]. The evaluation metrics of deep learning models and side-channel attack models are not consistent, with deep learning using accuracy and precision, while side-channel analysis is most commonly used for guessing entropy and success rate. Thus, in 2020, Zhang et al. proposed an evaluation metric CER for the side-channel attack scenario applicable to deep learning, where minimizing $Loss_{CER}$ is equivalent to simultaneously maximizing the score corresponding to the correct key and minimizing the score of the incorrect key [11]. In 2021, Zaid et al. proposed Ranking Loss, where the evaluator uses a prediction function to estimate which intermediate value is processed and uses the power consumption curve to calculate the score, thus computing L_{RKL} [12]. Regarding data augmentation, in 2019, Picek et al. use the data balancing technique SMOTE to analyse minority class samples and manually synthesise new samples to add to the dataset based on minority class samples, reducing the low performance associated with data imbalance [13]. In 2022, Perin et al. investigate the importance of different feature selection, where optimising points of interest leads to better attacks and greater workload [14].

The main contributions of this paper:

(1) Integrate the Convolutional Block Attention Module (CBAM) into the CNN_{best} model, and conduct five insertion position experiments so that to get the optimal insertion position. At the meatime, we modify the feature extraction part, and assign greater weights to the feature points of the power consumption traces, so that the network can learn better Features in the power traces that have strong operational dependencies and strong data dependencies with the encryption step;

(2) A dropout layer is added to our modified CBAM model, and three sets of parameter optimization experiments are carried out to seek the optimal parameter of the drop probability, which solves the problem of rapid over-fitting that is prone to occur in the model, significantly accelerates the speed of model convergence, and effectively improves the accuracy of guessing the correct key.

2 Background Knowledge

2.1 Convolutional Neural Network

Convolutional neural network (CNN) is a variant of MLP. CNN was proposed by Yann Lecun [15], and its essence is an MLP. Each layer in the convolutional neural network has multiple feature maps, each feature map extracts a feature of the input through a convolution filter, and each feature map has multiple neurons, as shown in Fig. 2. The convolutional layer and the pooling layer of the hidden layer are the core modules to realize the feature extraction function of the convolutional neural network. The network model uses the gradient descent method to minimize the loss function to reversely adjust the weight parameters in the network layer by layer, and improve the accuracy of the network through frequent iterative training. The input of the first fully connected layer is the feature image obtained by feature extraction by the convolutional layer and the subsampling layer. The last output layer is a classifier that can use logistic regression, Softmax regression or even a support vector machine to classify the input image.

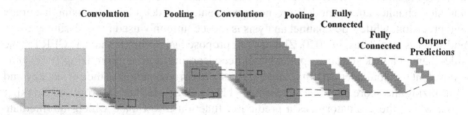

Fig. 2. CNN structure.

2.2 Side Channel Attack Principle

After modeling, the analyst obtains a model $F(\cdot) : X \rightarrow P(Y)$, which can be assimilated into a probability function (possibly normalized). In the attack phase, the analyst tries to recover a fixed k^* and the power consumption profile measured from the target device as $D = \{(x_i^n)\}_{i=1}^n$ can calculate the log-likelihood function score $d[k] = \sum_{i=1}^n log(F(x_i)[f(p_i, k)])$ for all attack power consumption profiles for each $k \in K$. The analyst then selects the key k_{guess} that leads to the highest score in the log-likelihood function, $k_{guess} = argmax_{k \in K} d[k]$. If $k_{guess} = k^*$, the attack succeeds.

2.3 CNN_{best}

IN 2020, the Researchers Detail the Principles of Combining Deep Learning with Template Attacks and How This Works in Practice, Using VGG-16 as a Starting Point, Giving the Impact of Hyperparameters on the Modelling Process and the Attack Process, and Proposing the CNN_{best} Architecture [8]. The Model is Defined as a CNN Architecture with 5 Blocks and 1 Block-By-Block Convolution, a Number of Filters Equal to 64, 128,

256, 512 and 512, a Kernel Size of 11, and a Fill Method of Same-Using ReLU Activation Function and Average Pooling. Two Final Fully Connected Layers, Consisting of 4096 Units. By Using an RMSprop Optimiser with an Initial Learning Rate of 10. This Network Structure is Shown in Fig. 3.

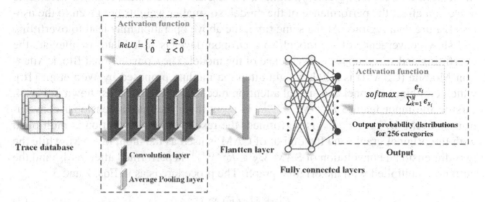

Fig. 3. CNN_{best} structure.

2.4 Evaluation Indicators

Two different metrics were chosen to evaluate the performance of the model: the rank function and the accuracy.

(1) *The rank function*

The *key* used during the acquisition of dataset $D_{profiling}$ using $k^* \in K$. The rank function corresponding to the model trained using dataset D_{train} and tested using dataset D_{test} is defined as $rank(\hat{g}, D_{train}, D_{test,n}) = |\{k \in K | d_{n[k]} > d_{n[k^*]}\}|$. If k^* has the highest (lowest) score, its rank is $0(|K| - 1)$.

(2) *The accuracy*

y_i denotes $|K|$ dimensional output $\hat{g}(l_i, p_i)$, D_{test} may be of unbounded size, as defined in Eq. 1.

$$acc(\hat{g}, D_{train}, D_{test}) = \frac{|\{(l_i, p_i, k^*) \in D_{test} | k^* = argmax_{k \in K} y_{i[k]}\}|}{|D_{test}|} \quad (1)$$

3 Methodology

3.1 Convolutional Block Attention Mechanism

In order to improve CNN performance, in addition to studying depth, width and cardinality factors, researchers have also studied increasing the representational power of the network by focusing on important features and suppressing unnecessary features through the attention mechanism, which is one way to achieve adaptive attention in the network. The data-dependent or operation-dependent time periods required for power consumption curve analysis tend to be a relatively small portion of the entire power consumption curve, meaning that there are small regions with physical information leakage, so to improve the ultimate performance of the model, this paper hopes to give more useful feature data regions greater weight in the useless feature data regions. Electronic noise can affect the performance of the model, so smaller weights are given to the useless feature data regions. At the same time, the above operation may lead to overfitting and slow convergence of the model, so a Dropout layer is added later to alleviate the overfitting and speed up the convergence of the model. The Convolutional Block Attention Module (CBAM) is a lightweight attention module proposed by Woo et al. [16], which combines channel and spatial attention mechanism modules, as shown in Fig. 4. Firstly, the input feature $F \in R^{C \times H \times W}$ is input, then the one-dimensional convolution of CAM $M_C \in R^{C \times 1 \times 1}$ is performed, the result of the convolution is multiplied with the original graph, and the output of CAM is used as the input of SAM, while the two-dimensional convolution of SAM $M_S \in R^{1 \times H \times W}$ is performed afterwards, and the output is multiplied with the original graph. The procedure is as in Eqs. 2 and 3.

$$F' = M_C(F) \otimes F \tag{2}$$

$$F'' = M_S(F') \otimes F' \tag{3}$$

Among them, F represents the input of the feature map ($C \times H \times W$), M_C is the one-dimensional ($C \times 1 \times 1$) channel attention map, M_S is the two-dimensional $1 \times H \times W$ channel attention map, $\otimes$ represents the multiplication operation, F' represents the intermediate output ($C \times H \times W$), and F'' represents the final output ($C \times H \times W$).

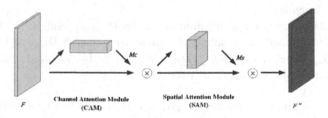

Fig. 4. CBAM structure.

CBAM is generally used for feature extraction of images with two-dimensional convolution, but in this paper one-dimensional convolution is used, so the channel space attention module in this paper is designed for one-dimensional data. And with different insertion positions, the MLP hyperparameters in the channel attention module are slightly different.

Firstly, the Channel Attention module, which uses a global one-dimensional maximum pooling operation and a global one-dimensional average pooling operation to obtain two sets of data. Each channel in the two sets of data has now been compressed into a number, and then two convolutional layers with *kernel size* $= 1$ are used to act as the fully connected layer, the activation function is the ReLU function. The last two sets of data are summed by the corresponding indexes and the final result is presented by the Sigmoid activation function, as shown in Fig. 5.

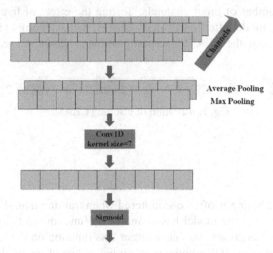

Fig. 5. 1-d Channel attention module.

Secondly is the Spatial Attention module, which first separately conducts average pooling and max pooling operations on the values of each element of the input data on the current channel so that to get two sets of data. And then using a one-dimensional convolution of *kernel size* =7 to convert the two sets of data into a set of data, which should be consistent with the size of the input data. Finally, by the Sigmoid activation function, the output of this part can be down, as shown in Fig. 6.

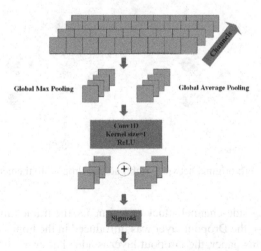

Fig. 6. 1-d Spatial attention module.

The insertion positions of five CBAMs are designed in this paper respectively, at the interval of each layer of the five layers of convolution and behind the fifth layer of convolution, where the MLP neurons number of the channel attention module are set to 0.5 times the number of input channels. Testing the effect of five positions on the performance of the model after insertion of CBAM, and selecting the best performing model for the next step, the CBAM insertion position is shown in Fig. 7.

Fig. 7. Location of inserting CBAM.

3.2 Dropout

The problem of overfitting is often encountered when training neural networks. This is reflected in the fact that the model has a small loss function on the training data and has a high prediction accuracy, but has a larger loss function on the test data and has a lower prediction accuracy. If the model is overfitted, the resulting model is almost unusable. Hinton proposed Dropout [17], which tends to cause overfitting when a complex feedforward neural network is trained on a small data set. To prevent overfitting, the performance of a neural network can be improved by blocking the coaction of feature detectors. Subsequently, there have been a number of articles on Dropout [18, 19]. A normal feed-forward neural network is shown in left panel of Fig. 8.

Letting the activation value of a certain neuron stop working with a certain probability p during forward propagation makes the model more generalizable as it does not rely too much on certain local features, dropout principle as shown in right panel of Fig. 8.

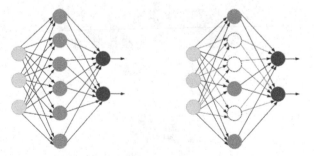

Fig. 8. Left: original network; right: adding dropout to the network.

When performing side-channel attack experiments, the trained model is very prone to rapid overfitting, so the Dropout layer was introduced in the hope of solving the rapid overfit problem. In this paper, the Dropout layer is added after the first fully connected layer in the experiment, and the overall structure is shown in Fig. 9.

Fig. 9. Location of adding dropout.

4 Experiment

4.1 Experimental Platform and Data Set

The experiment is conducted in the CentOS 8 operating system on python 3.6 + pytorch 1.10 and executed by the processor Intel(R) Xeon(R) gold 5218 CPU, memory 128GB, graphics card Nvidia Geforce RTX 2080 Ti, hard disk 512GB SSD + 4TB HDD workstation for training model.

The dataset mainly uses ASCAD public datasets [8], 50,000 training set data, 10,000 test set data, each data contains the power consumption of the third byte for the first round of S-box encryption that has been synchronously aligned, a total of 700 data points.

4.2 Feature Extraction Network Integrated into CBAM

First, in order to verify the performance of the model inserting CBAM at different insertion locations, the experiment trained five models with different insertion locations for testing and comparing them with the original model. These models are all "accuracy optimal" models in the training set to simulate the choices that a model might make in a real attack environment. And in later experimental tests, it may be found that these models may not be the best choice for the attack dataset.

Depending on the insertion location, these models are labeled CBAM1, CBAM2, CBAM3, CBAM4 and CBAM5, respectively, with the number following the tag name referring to Fig. 10, and the original model is labeled No CBAM. The experiment measures the quality of the model from the rank traces of the model and the number of traces required to attack the correct key, so as to select the model for the next experiment.

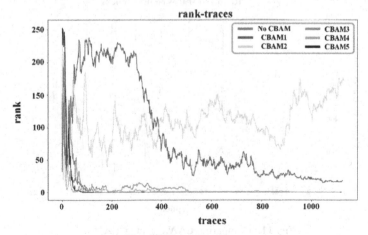

Fig. 10. Rank line chart.

It can be seen from the experimental test rank line chart results that both CBAM3 and CBAM5 predict the correct key earlier than the original model. The CBAM5 performs the best output. The CBAM4 also model performs well in the early stage, but the rank of the model is stable at 1 for a long time, and always cannot be lowered to 0. Finally the rank is successfully lowered to 0 until 913 traces are reached. Besides, CBAM1 and CBAM2 cannot infer the correct key within the 1200 traces, so CBAM1 and CBAM2 are directly abandoned.

Table 1 shows the number of traces required when the correct key rank is stable to 0 when each model was attacking.

Table 1. Number of traces required for each method.

Model	No CBAM	CBAM3	CBAM4	CBAM5
Number of traces	520	128	913	83

In order to understand the change law of the specific performance of the model during each epoch training and compare the changes of the model in the training process between the original model and CBAM5, this paper tests the model generated by each epoch. And using the number of traces required to reduce the rank to 0 for measuring the quality of the model, as shown in Fig. 11. In the experiment, when the number of traces required exceeds 800, this paper regards it as the model cannot attack the true key, and it appears as a peak reaching 1000 in the line chart. It can be seen from the test result curve that although the performance of the CBAM5 model is better than that of the original model, based on the above results, the CBAM5 model is selected for the next experiment.

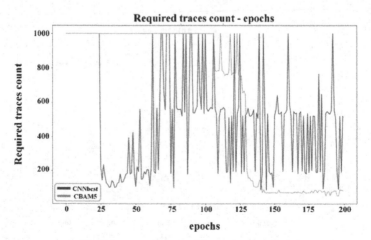

Fig. 11. Comparing CNN_{best} and CBAM5.

4.3   Add Dropout to the Model

Figure 11 shows that the performance of the model inserted with the attention module is improved compared to the original model, and it is also more stable, but the convergence speed is not as fast as the original model, and the index quickly drops to less than 100 after 125 epochs. At the same time, the trend of rapid overfitting of the original model can be clearly seen in this figure.

In order to improve the above problems, this paper conducts an experiment of adding a Dropout layer. The experiment finally selects $p = 0.3$ as the dropout rate added by the improved model. The final experimental results are shown in Fig. 12. Although the accuracy of the classification model is not an effective indicator to measure the performance of the side channel model, the final performance is related to the accuracy of the classification model. The accuracy on the test data set is shown in Table 2. The table is a selection of epochs where each model has the best performance when the rank drops to 0 during training, where the minimum number of traces is needed for comparison.

Table 2. Acc of three models.

Model	NO CBAM/%	CBAM5/%	CBAM + Dropout0.3/%
Acc	0.49	0.5	0.57

Figure 12 clearly shows that after adding Dropout to the model with the attention module, the model converged significantly faster and showed better performance in the subsequent epochs. The model with Dropout added is the model with the highest accuracy.

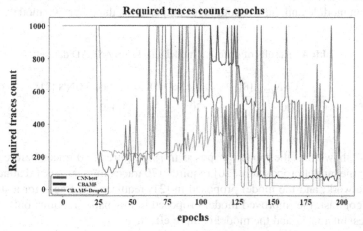

Fig. 12. Compare CNN_{best}, the model with the CBAM5 and the model with both the CBAM5 and the dropout.

Table 3 clearly shows the performance comparison of the three, demonstrating the improved convergence speed and performance results with CBAM5.

Table 3. Minimum number of traces required for different models.

Model	NO CBAM	CBAM5	CBAM5 + Dropout0.3
Number of traces	88	53	10
Epochs	140	187	129

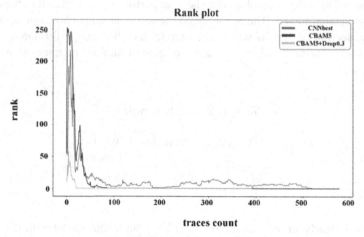

Fig. 13. Rank of three models.

In order to verify the three models more clearly, a comparison of the rank curves of the "best trained" models is shown in Fig. 13, where it is clear that the model with both the attention module and the Dropout layer outperforms the other two models.

Table 4. Results of different model attacks on ASCAD dataset.

Model	CNN_{best} [8]	SincNet [20]	Zaid's CNN [21]	Ours
Number of traces	520	170	191	17

Table 4 shows that the model proposed in [8] requires 520 traces before the rank drops to 0; the model proposed in [20] requires 170 traces for a successful attack on the SincNet network; and the model proposed in [21] requires 191 traces for a successful attack. In contrast, the improved model proposed in this paper requires only 10 traces for a successful attack, and the model is more effective.

5 Conclusion

Information security is the backing of national development. It is an important research direction to organically integrate deep learning theory and technology with classical side-channel attacks, and to explore new analysis methods and evaluation indicators. At present, with the rapid development of science and technology, side-channel attacks can find vulnerabilities in cryptographic algorithms, and can also prompt researchers to improve the defense capabilities of cryptographic algorithms. The two are interdependent and jointly promote the development of cryptographic algorithms and information security. This paper proposes an improved side-channel modeling attack method based on the CNN_{best} network. By introducing the CBAM in the best position, the feature extraction network is optimized to suppress noise features and improve the learning of key features; adding a dropout layer can effectively alleviate the over-modeling. The fitting phenomenon occurs, helping to reduce the number of power consumption traces used by the attack. The experimental results show that the model proposed in this paper can effectively improve the modeling side channel analysis method based on neural network. Considering the power consumption traces collected in reality, due to hidden countermeasures or device settings, an offset power consumption traces, that is, an asynchronous power consumption traces, will be generated. This is the direction we need to improve the network adaptation.

References

1. Mangard, S., Oswald, E., Standaert, F.X.: One for all–all for one: unifying standard differential power analysis attacks. IET Inf. Secur. **5**(2), 100–110 (2011)
2. Kocher, P., Jaffe, J., Jun, B., Rohatgi, P.: Introduction to differential power analysis. J. Cryptogr. Eng. **1**(1), 5–27 (2011)
3. Brier, E., Clavier, C., Olivier, F.: Correlation power analysis with a leakage model. In: Joye, M., Quisquater, J.-J. (eds.) CHES 2004. LNCS, vol. 3156, pp. 16–29. Springer, Heidelberg (2004). https://doi.org/10.1007/978-3-540-28632-5_2
4. Batina, L., Gierlichs, B., Prouff, E., Rivain, M., Standaert, F.X., Veyrat-Charvillon, N.: Mutual information analysis: a comprehensive study. J. Cryptol. **24**(2), 269–291 (2011)
5. Chari, S., Rao, J.R., Rohatgi, P.: Template attacks. In: Kaliski, B.S., Koç, çK., Paar, C. (eds.) CHES 2002. LNCS, vol. 2523, pp. 13–28. Springer, Heidelberg (2003). https://doi.org/10.1007/3-540-36400-5_3
6. Doget, J., Prouff, E., Rivain, M., Standaert, F.X.: Univariate side channel attacks and leakage modeling. J. Cryptogr. Eng. **1**(2), 123–144 (2011)
7. Schindler, W.: Advanced stochastic methods in side channel analysis on block ciphers in the presence of masking. J. Math. Cryptology **2**(3), 291–310 (2008)
8. Benadjila, R., Prouff, E., Strullu, R., Cagli, E., Dumas, C.: Deep learning for side-channel analysis and introduction to ascad database. J. Cryptogr. Eng. **10**(2), 163–188 (2020)
9. Lu, X., Zhang, C., Cao, P., Gu, D., Lu, H.: Pay attention to raw traces: a deep learning architecture for end-to-end profiling attacks. IACR Trans. Cryptographic Hardware Embed. Syst. **2021**(3), 235–274 (2021)
10. Wu, L., Perin, G., Picek, S.: The best of two worlds: deep learning-assisted template attack. IACR Trans. Cryptographic Hardware Embed. Syst. **2022**(3), 413–437 (2011)

11. Zhang, J., Zheng, M., Nan, J., Hu, H., Yu, N.: A novel evaluation metric for deep learning-based side channel analysis and its extended application to imbalanced data. IACR Trans. Cryptographic Hardware Embed. Syst. **2020**(3), 73–96 (2020)
12. Zaid, G., Bossuet, L., Dassance, F., Habrard, A., Venelli, A.: Ranking loss: maximizing the success rate in deep learning side-channel analysis. IACR Trans. Cryptographic Hardware Embed. Syst. **2021**(1), 25–55 (2021)
13. Picek, S., Heuser, A., Jovic, A., Bhasin, S., Regazzoni, F.: The curse of class imbalance and conflicting metrics with machine learning for side-channel evaluations. IACR Trans. Cryptographic Hardware Embed. Syst. **2019**(1), 1–29 (2019)
14. Perin, G., Wu, L., Picek, S.: Exploring feature selection scenarios for deep learning-based side-channel analysis. IACR Trans. Cryptographic Hardware Embed. Syst. **2022**(4), 828–861 (2022)
15. Krizhevsky, A., Sutskever, I., Hinton, G.E.: Imagenet classification with deep convolutional neural networks. Commun. ACM **60**(6), 84–90 (2017)
16. Woo, S., Park, J., Lee, J.-Y., Kweon, I.S.: CBAM: convolutional block attention module. In: Ferrari, V., Hebert, M., Sminchisescu, C., Weiss, Y. (eds.) ECCV 2018. LNCS, vol. 11211, pp. 3–19. Springer, Cham (2018). https://doi.org/10.1007/978-3-030-01234-2_1
17. Hinton, G.E., Srivastava, N., Krizhevsky, A., Sutskever, I., Salakhutdinov, R.R.: Improving neural networks by preventing coadaptation of feature detectors. arXiv preprint arXiv:1207. 0580 (2012)
18. Srivastava, N., Hinton, G., Krizhevsky, A., Sutskever, I., Salakhutdinov, R.: Dropout: a simple way to prevent neural networks from overfitting. The J. Mach. Learn. Res. **15**(1), 1929–1958 (2014)
19. Bouthillier, X., Konda, K., Vincent, P., Memisevic, R.: Dropout as data augmentation. arXiv preprint arXiv:1506.08700 (2015)
20. Chen, P., Wang, P., Dong, G., Hu, H.: SincNet-based side channel attack. J. Cryptologic Res. **7**(5), 583–594 (2020)
21. Zaid, G., Bossuet, L., Habrard, A., Venelli, A.: Methodology for efficient CNN architectures in profiling attacks. IACR Trans. Cryptographic Hardware Embed. Syst. **2020**(1), 1–36 (2020)

Enhancing Port Scans Attack Detection Using Principal Component Analysis and Machine Learning Algorithms

Emmanuel Kwesi Baah[1]([✉]) [iD], Steven Yirenkyi[2] [iD], Dominic Asamoah[2] [iD],
Stephen Opoku Oppong[3] [iD], Edward Opoku-Mensah[4] [iD], Benjamin Tei Partey[2] [iD],
Anthony Kingsley Sackey[5] [iD], Oliver Kornyo[2] [iD], and Evans Obu[1] [iD]

[1] Christian Service University College, Kumasi, Ghana
ekbaah@csuc.edu.gh
[2] Kwame Nkrumah University of Science and Technology, Kumasi, Ghana
[3] University of Education, Winneba, Ghana
[4] HEC Montréal, Montreal, Canada
[5] Ho Technical University, Ho, Ghana

Abstract. Port scanning attacks remain one of the major penetration testing schemes attackers employ to undertake maliferous intentions. With the increasingly sophisticated nature of cyber criminals and advanced technology and the failure of traditional network intrusion detection systems, the challenge of effectively detecting open ports with much efficiency in minimal time continues to linger. Thus, several recent studies, particularly those that employed machine learning approaches, have attempted to resolve and address the issue of enhancing this intrusion detection technique, yet suffer many performance challenges demanding further investigation. This paper employed seven machine learning classifiers to detect port scanning attacks after successfully using principal component analysis to resolve the relevant component and enhance the results. Comparison is made between the outcome of the various models and previous studies using accuracy, precision, recall, area-under-curve, f1-score, false-positive rate, and training time as performance metrics. Our results indicate that XGBoost was the best classifier with the highest accuracy of 99.98%, no false positive detected, a precision of 99.99%, a recall of 99.98, and an area-under-curve of 99.99% compared with the other classifiers and previous studies on port scan attack detection.

Keywords: Port scanning · Intrusion detection system · Machine learning · Principal component analysis · Network attacks

1 Introduction

In most organizations, a single occurrence of cybercrime is enough to cripple their business and close them down. As the strings of the internet become increasingly entwined with business processes, the rate of cybercrime has increased exponentially. Cybercrime is profitable because organizations rely on computers to facilitate their business processes. A malicious actor can profit by denying access to data or stealing data to sell

E. Ahene and F. Li (Eds.): FCS 2022, CCIS 1726, pp. 119–133, 2022.
https://doi.org/10.1007/978-981-19-8445-7_8

on secondary markets. Increased computer literacy and lower computing cost are other global factors that have led to the proliferation of cybercrime. All cyberattacks begin with the reconnaissance stage. In this phase, malicious actors search for exposed or unsecured endpoints they use to gain unauthorized access to an organization's resources. Increased computer proficiency and lower computing costs have resulted in a world where everything is directly or indirectly connected to the internet. Cybersecurity has never been more critical than now, as businesses move their resources on the internet to save money and facilitate employee collaboration. Over the years, cybercrime has evolved. People are not hacking into servers solely to modify a website's content any longer. Today's network assaults are sophisticated and may cause victims irreversible harm [1]. The Cyber Kill Chain architecture [2] illustrates hackers' stages to accomplish their goals. In the Cyber Kill structure, the reconnaissance phase is the initial stage. One of the most common types of reconnaissance is port scanning [3].

Port scanning is one of the most popular methods used in the reconnaissance stage. It systematically scans computers on a network to identify open ports, determines the type and version of software listening on a particular open port, and submits payloads through the open port to exploit the vulnerable software. By locating open ports on the target host, port scanning is used to uncover vulnerabilities. Attackers can plan and develop their assault model based on the information collected through open ports. The attacker sends malformed packets to all of a target host's ports and waits for a response from the open ports. An Intrusion Detection System (IDS) may flag the malicious packets, or an Intrusion Prevention System (IPS) may discard or block them (IPS). Both approaches notify network administrators when port scanning occurs, allowing them to take preventive actions. As a result, monitoring port scan attempts would make it easier to prevent network resources from being overburdened. Attackers exploit flaws in communication protocols like UDP and TCP by delivering streams of packets to all ports on the target system with a certain flag set and receiving replies from open ports [4].

Port scanning is not a new problem, and many port scanning detection methods have been proposed over the years; Bhuyan [5] classified port scan detection techniques into two major categories: single-source and distributed scan detection approach. Sridharan [3] evaluated two intrusion detection tools: SNORT and the TRW algorithm. The authors proposed the TAPS algorithm that outperformed them all. Nisa and Kifayat [4] proposed a simple, efficient, abstract framework to detect real-time slow port scans. However, owing to the rapid advancement of technology, there are always new forms of network attacks that would easily slip past IDSs and IPSs. Most IDS are signature-based in that they have a signature database of well-known attacks that incoming packets are compared against. Thus, if an attacker employs a new attack form, the IPS and IDS cannot stop it. The rapid development of attacks and the vast amount of network data makes machine learning appreciable and highly applicable to the problem of port scanning detection.

With the increased occurrence of network-based cyberattacks and validated network datasets, machine-learning models have been employed to identify and classify malicious network requests. It has been proven by researchers [6, 7] that machine learning can enhance the anomaly detection efficiency of Intrusion Detection Systems. However, as network infrastructure becomes more distributed with the increasing dependency on the internet and the shortage of security experts [8], researchers need to keep improving the accuracy of machine learning models. There are two basic approaches to machine learning: supervised and unsupervised learning. While supervised learning uses labelled data to forecast outcomes, the latter does not. This study deployed seven classification machine-learning algorithms to detect malicious packets. One of the well-known and most recent datasets in network security research: the Intrusion Detection Evaluation Dataset (CIC-IDS2017), was used to train and test the machine learning models. Because of the high dimensionality of the CIC-IDS2017 dataset, it presents various challenges to machine learning algorithms. It is computationally expensive to model, which further decreases the predictive performance of a model. Hence, the Principal Component Analysis was used for dimensionality reduction purposes.

Our major contribution is to improve the existing port scanning detection models using the known performance metrics with the use of PCA as one factor that enhance the detection of the port scan when employing machine learning algorithms.

The rest of the study is sectioned as follows. The background of the problem and related works are presented in Sect. 2. The proposed methodology is presented in Sect. 3, while Sect. 4 discusses the results and findings from the experiments. Lastly, conclusions are drawn, and future works are presented.

2   Background and Related Works

2.1   Detecting Port Scan Attempts with Comparative Analysis of Deep Learning and Support Vector Machine Algorithms

Computer crimes are becoming more sophisticated, and the number of crimes keeps increasing yearly. Reconnaissance is the first step in a cyber-attack, hence the need to detect and stop attackers at this stage. Aksu and Aydin [9] used deep learning and support vector machines (SVM) machine learning algorithms to create Intrusion Detection Systems models to detect port scans. In this study, the researchers focused on port scan attempts in the CICIDS2017 datasets. Two hundred eighty-six thousand four hundred sixty-seven records (286,467), consisting of 158,930 port scan attempts and 127,537 normal traffic, were taken from the dataset for preprocessing. Redundant, unrelated, and non-variant features were removed from the dataset. Non-numeric features were encoded into numeric forms. 67% of the dataset was used to train the model, while 33% was used to test the model. The SVM and deep learning models were evaluated using accuracy, precision, recall, and f1-score metrics. The deep learning model outperformed the SVM model by scoring 97%, 99%, 99%, and 99% for the accuracy, precision, recall, and f1-score metrics, respectively. Using a deep learning model achieves great results; however, no mention of the overhead concerning the training time used by the model is stated, which is of key relevance to the detection of port scans.

2.2   Detection of Slow Port Scans in Flow-Based Network Traffic

Most security systems are signature-based and are inefficient in detecting new attack strategies. Port scans usually send large requests to different ports within a short time. It is easy to detect such port scans. In slow port scans, requests are made every fifteen seconds or five minutes. Detecting slow port scans is relatively difficult. Ring et al. [10] attempt to solve the problem of detecting slow port scans in flow-based network data by proposing an approach where preprocessed flow-based data is used to detect such scans. The researchers used two approaches: unsupervised using sequential hypothesis testing and supervised using machine learning classification algorithms. The CIDDS-001 dataset was used for the evaluation of the two approaches. It consists of two parts: traffic observed within an OpenStack environment and traffic observed on an external server on the internet. Only the OpenStack records were used in this research. The OpenStack traffic data consists of four weeks of network traffic. The first two weeks of data referred to as week 1 and week 2, which contain several attacks, were used in the experiments. All attacks, except port scanning attacks, were removed. The dataset also indicated that the time interval between port scan requests and time intervals δ were restricted for the division of the dataset. One network-based event is calculated for each source IP address in each time window. These network-based events are used as data for the detection algorithms. A network-based event is an aggregation of connections based on a source IP address. It is important because a flow describes one connection, whilst port scans cause multiple connections.

In the supervised port scanning detection (SPSD) approach, $\delta = 60$. Decision Tree (DT) and Support Vector Machines (SVM) are used to classify port scans. The classifiers are trained on week 1 to classify week 2 and vice versa. For DT, the Gini index was used as the split criterion. For SVM, the researchers used a Radial Basis Function (RBF) kernel with $C = 100$ and $\gamma = 1.0$. The approaches were evaluated on the number of detected attacks and false alarms. In both cases, the SPSD approach achieved the best results; however, their study rate increase with the false-positive rate in the SPSD with the Decision is alarming, creating uncertainty with the increasing weeks opening up a better approach to detection of port scanning attacks and the dataset used is subject obsolete.

2.3 Artificial Intelligence Managed Network Defense System Against Port Scanning Outbreaks

Kumar et al. [11] attempted to solve the detection of malicious port scans by creating an Artificial Intelligence Managed Network Defense System. The authors placed the organization's network infrastructure behind a conventional Intrusion Detection System (IDS) connected to an Intelligent Layer. The Intelligent Layer consists of the machine learning model, which analyzes the network traffic and then uses the results to update the rules in the IDS. The authors used the NSL-KDD benchmark dataset in training the machine learning model. The NSL-KDD dataset is one of the most well-known informational indexes created by the MIT Lincoln Lab. The types of modules in the NSL-KDD dataset can be classified into five 5 types, normal traffic and four types of attacks, namely DoS, Probing, U2R, and R2L. To extract port scan attributes, they extracted two types of datasets from the NSL-KDD dataset: Packet-Level Dataset and the Flow-based dataset. These two sub-datasets were used to train the machine learning model. The authors then did an empirical study on different machine learning algorithms and finally landed on the decision tree algorithm. The decision tree algorithm picks the most important features of the training dataset, thus letting parallel estimation of each feature. Kumar et al. [11] proposed an interesting way of detecting port scans using machine learning which learns itself and constantly updates the rules in a conventional IDS. However, they trained their model on an old dataset. The NSL-KDD dataset is based on the KDD'99 dataset in 1999. The authors also failed to state how long it takes to train their model. Given that the model learns and updates the rules in the IDS in real-time, it is paramount for the model to have a short training time and still produce accurate results. Thus, they did not specify what metrics they used to evaluate their machine-learning model's effectiveness over a conventional IDS.

2.4   Machine Learning-Driven Intrusion Detection for Contiki-NG-Based IoT Networks Exposed to NSL-KDD Dataset

Liu et al. [12] sought to implement a machine learning-based IDS for IoT devices by generating a custom dataset based on the types of attacks in the NSL-KDD dataset. The researchers employed supervised and unsupervised machine learning algorithms to detect network attacks, including port scans. The IoT network setup for this study consisted of four types of nodes, three of which were legitimate. The packets flowing through the network were collected into a PCAP file and passed through a feature extractor to generate the intrusion dataset. The authors opted for evaluation metrics such as Matthews Correlation Coefficient (MCC) to train and evaluate the machine learning models because the dataset generated was remarkably imbalanced; benign packets accounted for 74.6% of the dataset. The accuracy, true positive rate, false-positive rate, precision, recall, F measure, MCC, and AUC metrics were used to evaluate the supervised machine learning models. The XGBoost model surpassed all other models trained in the study. Generally, tree-based algorithms perform better and attain 96% or higher accuracy, which is good considering IoT devices have limited resources, and tree-based algorithms are high-performing simple solutions. However, this study suffers the challenge of using an obsolete dataset set for port scan attacks and the performance of the models used greatly needs improvements.

2.5   Port-Scanning Attack Detection Using Supervised Machine Learning Classifiers

Algaohali et al. [13] classified malicious port scans using soft computing, which uses approximate calculations to provide imprecise but usable solutions to complex computational problems. Machine learning falls under soft computing.

The CICIDS2017 intrusion detection dataset was used in training five machine learning models: Decision Trees, Random Forest, AdaBoost, K-Nearest Neighbors, and SVM. The CICIDS2017 dataset was used because it includes various attacks that have recently been carried out on networks, it is up to date, it is a labelled dataset made up of flow-based features that have been statistically expanded by measuring some parameters, and it possesses real-time network traffic. The dataset was cleaned by filling empty instances with 0 and deleting repeated columns. The categorical values for certain features were converted to numerical values. The important features that helped determine the target variable were filtered out using the Lasso algorithm. Four features out of the seventy-eight (78) had the best chances of classifying a port scanning attack: Total Length of Fwd

Packets, Fwd Packet Length Max, Flow IAT Mean, and Total Length of Bwd Packets. The Total Length of Fwd Packets and Packet Length Max features were the most significant determiners of port scanning attacks. Thus, because the attacker sent packets with a header only to check the ports' status, there was no need to add data inside the packets. The CICIDS2017 dataset was then divided into training data and testing data. The models were trained 10 times. The final result was the average of the repeated operation. The authors evaluated the machine learning algorithms based on Accuracy, Precision, Recall, F-Measure, and Area Under Curve (AUC) metrics. The decision tree obtained the following results, Accuracy 99.84%, Precision 99.82%, Recall 99.95%, F-Measure 99.89%, and AUC 99.76%. The random forest algorithm obtained the following results, Accuracy 99.97%, Precision 99.75%, Recall 99.89%, F-Measure 99.82%, and AUC 99.64%. The AdaBoost algorithm obtained the following results, Accuracy 99.64%, Precision 99.62%, Recall 99.87%, F-Measure 99.75%, and AUC 99.47%. The KNN algorithm obtained the following results: Accuracy 99.64%, Precision 99.62%, Recall 99.87%, F-Measure 99.89%, and AUC 99.79%. The SVM (kernel = linear) algorithm obtained the following results, Accuracy 89.61%, Precision 99.73%, Recall 85.62%, F-Measure 92.14%, AUC 92.52%.

The F-Measure and AUC metrics were used in comparing the models. The time taken to predict an attack was also used in the comparison. The decision tree, random forest, and K Nearest Neighbours (KNN) had accuracies and an AUC of almost 100%. However, the decision tree algorithm was the best model for predicting attack traffic because it took the smallest amount of time to predict attack traffic. However, although Algaohali et al. [4] were able to produce good results; however there remains the need to explicitly validate the false-positive rates of all of the models used and with a justifiable training time owing to the advanced technology and evolving implementation of networks.

2.6 Detecting Port Scan Attacks Using Logistic Regression

Port scanning is a precursor to launching network attacks as it identifies vulnerable machines that will enable the attacker to gain access to a network. Al-Hajia et al. [14] proposed a new inclusive discovery scheme to evaluate six supervised machine learning algorithms and select the best-performing algorithm. The machine learning algorithms used in this research are Logistic Regression, Fine Decision Tree, Linear, Quadratic Discriminant, Naive Bayes, and Ensemble Boosted Trees. Their objective was to develop a machine learning model to predict port scanning attacks; hence different models were created using different algorithms to build a comparative study and gain more insights. The paramount model would then be deployed as an intrusion detection system. The PSA-2017 dataset by Loughborough University, UK, was used as training and testing data. The dataset was assembled from a network in a research lab and contained 700,848 samples of normal traffic and port scanning attacks. There were nine (9) features in the dataset. The dataset was preprocessed by encoding the target variable binary values: 0 for port scanning attack and 1 for normal traffic. The dataset was randomly shuffled to avoid any bias. Finally, it was split into training and testing datasets. The researchers employed a 5-fold cross-validation in training and testing the models. The resultant models were then evaluated based on the two-class confusion matrix, accuracy, precision, recall, harmonic average (F1), and the prediction overhead (PT). The accuracy metric was used to determine the best-performing algorithm. The accuracy scores for each of the six algorithms are as follows: Logistic Regression, 99.4%; Fine Decision Tree, 99.2%; Linear Discriminant Classifier, 99.0%; Quadratic Discriminant Classifier, 97.3%; Naive Bayes, 96.9%; Ensemble Boosted Trees, 78.2%. The Logistic Regression model was selected to be deployed and predict port scanning attacks. Aside from having the highest accuracy, the Logistic Regression model is highly precise and sensitive to port scan attacks, recording 99.9% for the precision metric and 99.4 for the recall metric. The model also uses the least amount of time to detect malicious port scans, with an overhead of 0.454 microseconds. The Logistic Regression model was compared to models in the same study area. The researcher's proposed model created with the Logistic Regression algorithm, based on the PSA-2017 dataset, had the highest accuracy of all the models. The proposed model had improved detection accuracy by beating other compared models with the least detection overhead. However, compared to the work done by Algaohali et al. [4] in the same year, though different datasets were used, the performance of the models used was better, and the overhead for the chosen classifier was computationally not advisable considering how fast and sophisticated cybercriminal can be, opening up room for improvement in this case.

2.7 An End-To-End Framework for Machine Learning-Based Network Intrusion Detection System

Securing communication between IoT devices and Cyber-physical systems (CPS) imposes a constantly evolving characteristic on networks. This characteristic, along with the massive amount of data generated, makes machine learning suitable for solving this security problem. The reconnaissance stage in the Cyber-kill-chain is responsible for identifying vulnerable hosts. Therefore, the ability to shield devices from being identified in the first place is of great importance. The problem is that the datasets used in studies to train machine learning (ML) models to detect such attacks are outdated regarding background and attack traffic. De Carvalho Bertoli et al. [15] proposed the use of the AB-TRAP (Attack, Bonafide, Train, RealizAtion, and Performance) framework to develop a Network Intrusion Detection System (NIDS). The AB-TRAP framework defines steps to build Attack and Bonafide datasets, use the datasets to train for machine learning models, assess the model's performance, and finally, deploy the model on a NIDS. Their objective of generating attack datasets was to solve challenges in currently available datasets, which include not containing the most recent attacks, not being reproducible, and not being properly labelled. The bonafide dataset contains normal traffic. It was essential for both supervised and unsupervised learning algorithms, and it can be obtained from open-data traffic providers, public datasets, and the deployment environment.

Since the constituents of the bonafide traffic depended on the deployment environment, the third option was the most appropriate way of obtaining the dataset. The attack and bonafide datasets are combined to form the AB-TRAP dataset. The machine learning models are evaluated based on the F1-score, precision, recall, and ROC/AUC metrics. The best-performing model is selected and implemented in an environment similar to the deployment environment. For software-defined networks (SDN), the model can be deployed in multiple stages, from the cloud to IoT gateways. SDNs have higher computational resources for complex processing. Machine learning models must use network stacks lightly in IoT devices where computational resources are constrained. IoT devices using Linux can use Linux Kernel Modules with Netfilter to filter packets or eBPF/XDP (extended Berkeley Packet Filter/eXpress Data Path), which allows safe execution of byte-code in a virtual machine. The model was evaluated in the deployment environment.

The authors presented a case study using the AB-TRAP framework in port scanning detection. The case study was done in a Local Area Network (LAN) and Cloud Environment. In the LAN version of the case study, the researchers generated the attack dataset using virtual machines (VM) on Kali Linux. An attacker VM used port scanning tools and a shell script that executed all combinations of attacks on a target VM. The IP address for each attack was used to label the data. Two VMs with static routes were used to interconnect the subnets, and router0 captured traffic between both subnets. Packets in the MAWILab dataset of 11th November 2019, with anomalous and suspicious traffic, were filtered out, and the remaining packets were used as the bonafide dataset. The attack and bonafide datasets were combined to form the AB-TRAP dataset. In the preprocessing stage, the target variable was encoded in binary: 0 for the attack, 1 for bonafide. All features except TCP/IP features were removed, and all redundant and non-variant features were removed. IP source and destination features were removed to avoid using them in predicting port scanning. The final dataset had 15 features. Naïve Bayes (NB), Logistic Regression (LR), Random Forest (FR), and Decision Tree (DT) algorithms were used to create the models.

The models were evaluated with the F1-score metric. The DT algorithm was selected for the next stage since it had the best F1 score. The shallow version of the decision tree was selected to avoid overfitting. The DT model was deployed on Raspberry Pi 4. The DT model was implemented as a Loadable Kernel Module (LKM)/Netfilter. The model was evaluated with two scenarios: with and without the LKM loaded on the Raspberry Pi. The researchers used the iPerf3 tool to generate TCP/IP traffic from a computer to the Raspberry Pi with a sampling rate of 1 Hz of the CPU and RAM usage. The results showed that the LKM did not overuse the RAM and had negligible CPU usage.

The researchers generated the attack dataset using cloud instances in the Cloud Environment version of the case study. One instance was used to perform port scanning attacks against the other instances. For each attack, the target instance receives two messages from the attacker. The first message is to start the tcpdump. After performing the port scanning, the attacker sends the second message to stop the tcpdump. After running the attacker instance, the researchers compiled files from all target instances into a single CSV file. The dataset used in the LAN case study was merged with the MAWILab dataset of 10th November 2020 to create the bonafide dataset of this case study. The dataset was preprocessed in the same manner as in the LAN case study, except that the TCP TTL and source port features were kept. Multi-Layer Perceptron (MLP), Support Vector Machine (SVM), k-Nearest Neighbors (kNN), and XGBoost machine learning algorithms were evaluated in addition to those evaluated in the LAN case study. MLP, KNN, XGB, RF, and DT had an F1 score of 1.00, indicating overfitting. The models were deployed in the userspace, allowing the researchers to abstract the complexities and implement them in kernel space.

TCP packets flow to the machine learning model from kernel to user space. Each model becomes a byte stream, and a Python application executes these models in the userspace with NFQUEUE. NIDS relies on the IPtables firewall using Netfilter NFQUEUE to make decisions about packets. The machine learning models were deployed and evaluated on a Raspberry Pi. The iPerf3 tool was used to generate TCP/IP traffic and 1 Hz sampling with each of the 8 trained models loaded at once. CPU and RAM were used as the performance metrics to evaluate the models. KNN, RF, and XGB required the most processing power. KNN and RF used the most memory in predicting port scanning attacks. The file size of each model was also used as a metric to help measure the trained model's deployment feasibility. Though the study proposed a novel approach to intrusion detection, yet does not explicitly employ this in detecting port scan attacks. Again, the study also suffered from the challenge of overfitting the model as no cross-validation was done on the dataset obtained.

2.8 Research Gap

From the review of existing literature, we can establish that the most recent studies on the detection of port scanning attacks have either used a novel approach or machine learning or deep learning technique have faced challenges with performance metrics with accuracies, false-positive rates, precision, recall or reducing the training time. Others have also been challenged with using an obsolete dataset for the technique. At the same time, some also have modelled which were not cross-validated and unavoidably encountered the challenge of overfitting the model. Therefore, this study enhances the previous works as it employs machine learning models that best enhance the detection of port scans with a minimal false-positive rate, better accuracies, precision, recall, and f1-score, as well as minimal training time.

3 Materials and Methods

The proposed conceptual framework expresses the research methodology followed to detect port scans on a network effectively. Figure 1 expresses the details of the entire process of how this study was conducted. In the first stage, extracting the relevant features from the chosen dataset. The dataset was explored before applying the Principal Component Analysis (PCA) algorithm. The final dataset was tested and trained on multiple machine-learning classifiers similar to other researchers' approaches. The results were evaluated and compared with previous studies.

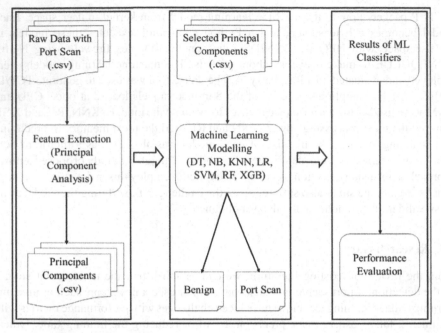

Fig. 1. Research design framework for port scan attack detection.

3.1 Dataset and Pre-processing

Owing to the challenge expressed with the obsolete dataset, the Canadian Institute for Cyber Security dataset on Intrusion Detection System, CICIDS2017. Several authors consider this dataset one of the current datasets used to detect port scans, reflecting the modern network infrastructure. In a paper by Sharafaldin et al. [16], this dataset was generated from real network traffic that hides the behaviour of human activities and creates a benign naturalistic background with a benign profile system. The port scans captured from the live network traffic were used for this study though the CICFlowMeter tool harnessed other forms of network intrusion attacks which is beyond the scope of this study. A total of 286467 records were found, with 79 features, including backward packets, fwd packets, flow duration, destination port, and source IP. After dropping all rows with relative infinity values, a total of records of 127292 were considered benign, while 158804 were port scans. The final dataset used for the feature extraction was reduced to 78 features. The CICIDS2017 dataset is used in our study. Table 1 shows the distribution of the network flows for the port scanning dataset with a label encoded as 0 for benign and 1 for port scan records.

Table 1. Distribution of the CICFlowMeter capture for port scans dataset.

Flow type label	Indicator	Number of flows
Port scans	1	158804
Benign	0	127292

3.2 Feature Extraction with Principal Component Analysis

PCA is a linear transformation model that maximizes the variance of the data and creates new features called components [17]. PCA lowers data by geometrically projecting it onto smaller dimensions known as principal components (PCs) to obtain the best data summary with the fewest possible PCs. As a feature extraction technique, PCA selects the most relevant features that take the maximum information from the dataset as it converts high-dimensional data to low-dimensional data. Thus, it determines the feature having the highest explaining variance as the first principal component, followed by the other components with reducing explaining variance as the subsequent component.

Using the PCA on the 78 features, 18 principal components were extracted, as depicted in Fig. 2. The variance of the other principal components diminishes after the eighteenth component. Thus, summing these 18 components represented 90% of the entire information obtained from the dataset.

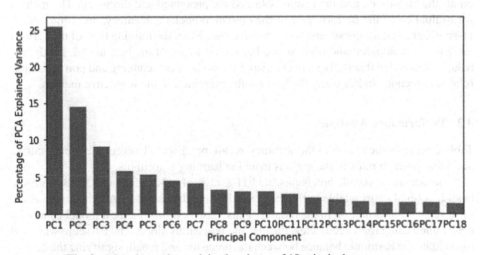

Fig. 2. PCA shows the explained variance of 18 principal components.

3.3 Machine Learning Algorithms for Port Scan Detection

Since machine learning algorithms have played a key role in building efficient intrusion detection systems, employing a machine learning classifier that can categorically distinguish between objects of different classes was ideal. The learning algorithms used on the dataset categorize the labels based on the model built. From the review conducted, a total of seven (7) supervised classifiers were deployed for the detection; taking insight from the works of Liu et al. [12], Algaohali et al. [13], Al-Hajia et al. [14], and De Carvalho Bertoli et al. [15]. Hence, the Random Forest (RF), Decision Tree (DT), Naïve Bayes (NB), K-Nearest Neighbors (KNN), Logistic Regression (LR), Support Vector Machines (SVM), and Extreme Gradient Boosting (XGB). The primary motivation for developing prediction models using various learning approaches is to conduct a comparison study. 80% of the dataset was used to train the models; the remaining 20% was used to test the accuracy of the models. 10-fold cross-validation was used to train the models to avoid overfitting was used for the experiments.

As done in several intrusion detection studies, this study adopts the same performance metrics for evaluating the results obtained. The classification algorithms' precision, accuracy, recall, f1-score, area-under-curve(AUC), and false-positive rate will be evaluated to select the best-performing one. The training time, which is not always considered in all port scan detection studies, was added to the performance metrics.

4   Results and Discussion

4.1   Experiments

The experiments were conducted to detect the port scans using 10-*fold* cross-validation on all the classifiers, and the results obtained are presented and discussed. The metrics for evaluation of the performance of the classifiers include accuracy, precision, recall, f1-score, area-under-curve, and false-positive rate. Next, the training time of the various models was compared and used as another metric to select the best model. Lastly, the results obtained in this study were compared with other port scanning and port scanning-related detection studies using the best results presented in the respective metrics.

4.2   Performance Analysis

Table 2 presents the results of the accuracy, recall, precision, f1-score, area-under-curve, and false-positive rates of the various machine learning algorithms.

The accuracy, recall, precisions, and f1-scores of KNN, RF, and XGB were the best. It is highly attributable to the data cleaning and the use of PCA, which retains the most relevant information in the dataset. Thus, based on this, the best model cannot be determined using their accuracies, recalls, and precisions alone. The F1-score was used to evaluate the harmonic balance between the precision and recall, signifying the quality of the classifier deployed.

The area-under-curve(AUC) was used as a performance measure to validate the model's accuracy and ensure that it does not deliver a false sense of prediction strength and avoids overfitting. The results show that none of the models was overfitted.

The false-positive rate is another key measure in many malware detection schemes, as it expresses the model's ability to misclassify a benign record or packet as a port scan. It reduces the impact of having to mistake benign records for port scans. Our results indicate that the XGBost did not misclassify any of the records. However, this could be suspicious. Random forest is the closest to this and offers the confidence that makes it the next likely option. Decision Tree follows the RT with a 1% false positive rate and KNN with 2%. Thus, considering these results, the three models, KNN, RF, and XGB, the XGB would be preferred in this regard for port scanning attack detection.

Table 2. Performance measure of machine learning models used.

Metric	DT	NB	KNN	LR	RF	SVM	XGB
Accuracy	0.9996	0.9181	**0.9998**	0.9966	**0.9998**	0.9985	**0.9998**
Precision	0.9996	0.8834	0.9998	0.9954	**0.9999**	0.9985	**0.9999**
Recall	0.9997	0.9823	**0.9998**	0.9986	0.9997	0.9989	0.9997
F1-score	0.9997	0.9302	**0.9998**	0.9970	**0.9998**	0.9987	**0.9998**
AUC	0.9996	0.9812	**0.9999**	0.9995	**0.9999**	0.9995	**0.9999**
False-positives	0.0118	16.484	0.0236	0.595	0.0039	0.0787	**0.0000**

However, each classifier's training time is another relevant metric for evaluating port scanning attacks. Though logical regression (LR) is considered less performing in terms of the other metrics discussed above, yet had the fastest training time for the prediction. Nevertheless, it cannot be concluded as the best since the differences it makes between the two other better-performing classifiers, DT and XGB, is only 0.04 microseconds, as shown in Table 3.

Table 3. Training timing of machine learning models used.

Model	DT	NB	KNN	LR	RF	SVM	XGB
Time (in seconds)	0.085	0.048	515.48	**0.023**	0.173	13.960	0.073

From the discussions and considering the work by Liu et al. [12], the XGBoost is voted in our study as the best-performing model for detecting port scans on a network, though it places second in terms of training time.

The results were compared with previous studies on port scanning attack detection. In all measures shown in Table 4, our study outperforms current studies except for the recall, which is a minor difference.

Table 4. Performance metric comparison of accuracy, precision, recall, and AUC of existing models with the proposed model.

Reference	Accuracy	Precision	Recall	F1-score	AUC
Aksu and Aydin [9]	0.9780	0.99	0.990	0.990	-
Kumar and Lim [18]	0.9444	0.92	**1.000**	0.960	-
Liu et al. [12]	0.9700	0.97	0.968	0.968	0.996
Algaohali et al. [13]	0.9990	**0.99**	0.999	0.998	0.998
Al-Hajia et al. [14]	0.9984	**0.99**	0.994	0.997	-
De Carvalho Bertoli et al. [15]	-	-	-	0.960	0.980
Proposed model	**0.9998**	**0.99**	0.999	**0.999**	**0.999**

5 Conclusion and Future Works

An enhanced machine learning model is presented to detect port scanning attacks efficiently with Principal Component Analysis. The study investigated seven machine learning algorithms used by other researchers and selected the best model for the prediction. The results obtained are valid since they were cross-validated. Three of the chosen classifiers performed extremely well in all the assessment metrics. However, the XGBoost was the best model for the detection, with a zero (0%) false positive rate, 99.98% score for accuracy, 99.99% precision, 99.98 recall, and 99.99% AUC with 0.07 s of training time. Compared to other studies, this study greatly enhanced the previous results in many aspects, as proven.

A further study on what has been achieved so far would consider running the models on a GPU, as it may aid in reducing the training time. Again, testing the models on other datasets and the new CICIDS2018 dataset, which might have new resilience to port scans, would contribute greatly to existing knowledge. Other researchers also used some more machine learning and deep learning algorithms; hence, trying how they perform against the machine learning model remains to be done.

References

1. Mell, P.: Understanding intrusion detection systems. Auerbach Publications (2003)
2. Cyber Kill Chain®, https://www.lockheedmartin.com/en-us/capabilities/cyber/cyber-kill-chain.html. Accessed 05 Aug 2022
3. Sridharan, A., Ye, T., Bhattacharyya, S.: Connectionless port scan detection on the backbone. In: 2006 IEEE International Performance Computing and Communications Conference, pp. 567–576. IEEE, Phoenix, AX, USA (2006)
4. Nisa, M.u., Kifayat, K.: Detection of slow port scanning attacks. In: 2020 International Conference on Cyber Warfare and Security (ICCWS), pp. 1–7. IEEE, Islamabad (2020)
5. Bhuyan, M.H., Bhattacharyya, D.K., Kalita, J.K.: Surveying port scans and their detection methodologies. Comput. J. **54**(10), 1565–1581 (2011)
6. Saranya, T., Sridevi, S., Deisy, C., Chung, T.D., Khan, M.K.A.A.: Performance analysis of machine learning algorithms in intrusion detection system: a review. Procedia Comput. Sci. **171**, 1251–1260 (2020)

7. Saidi, F., Trabelsi, Z., Ghazela, H.B.: Fuzzy logic based intrusion detection system as a service for malicious port scanning traffic detection. In: 2019 IEEE/ACS 16th International Conference on Computer Systems and Applications (AICCSA), pp. 1–9. IEEE, Abu Dhabi (2019)

8. Camacho, J., Theron, R., Garcia-Gimenez, J.M., Macia-Fernandez, G., Garcia-Teodoro, P.: Group-wise principal component analysis for exploratory intrusion detection. IEEE Access **7**, 113081–113093 (2019)

9. Aksu, D., Ali Aydin, M.: Detecting port scan attempts with comparative analysis of deep learning and support vector machine algorithms. In: 2018 International Congress on Big Data, Deep Learning and Fighting Cyber Terrorism (IBIGDELFT), Ankara, Turkey, pp. 77–80 (2018)

10. Ring, M., Landes, D., Hotho, A.: Detection of slow port scans in flow-based network traffic. PLoS ONE **13**(9), e0204507 (2018)

11. Kumar, M.S., Ben-Othman, J., Srinivasagan, K.G., Krishnan, G.U.: Artificial intelligence managed network defense system against port scanning outbreaks. In: 2019 International Conference on Vision Towards Emerging Trends in Communication and Networking (ViTECoN), Vellore, India, pp. 1–5 (2019)

12. Liu, J., Kantarci, B., Adams, C.: Machine learning-driven intrusion detection for Contiki-NG-based IoT networks exposed to NSL-KDD dataset. In: Proceedings of the 2nd ACM Workshop on Wireless Security and Machine Learning, pp. 25–30. ACM, Linz (2020)

13. Algaolahi, A.Q.M., Hasan, A.A., Sallam, A., Sharaf, A.M., Abdu, A.A., Alqadi, A.A.: Port-scanning attack detection using supervised machine learning classifiers. In: 2021 1st International Conference on Emerging Smart Technologies and Applications (eSmarTA), pp. 1–5. IEEE, Sana'a (2021)

14. Al-Haija, Q. A., Saleh, E., Alnabhan, M.: Detecting port scan attacks using logistic regression. In: 2021 4th International Symposium on Advanced Electrical and Communication Technologies (ISAECT), pp. 1–5. IEEE, Alkhobar (2021)

15. Bertoli, G.D.C., et al.: An end-to-end framework for machine learning-based network intrusion detection system. IEEE Access **9**, 106790–106805 (2021)

16. Sharafaldin, I., Lashkari, A. H., Ghorbani, A. A.: Toward generating a new intrusion detection dataset and intrusion traffic characterization. In: Proceedings of the 4th International Conference on Information Systems Security and Privacy, pp. 108–116. IEEE, Funchal (2018)

17. Ibrahimi, K., Ouaddane, M.: Management of intrusion detection systems based-KDD99: analysis with LDA and PCA. In: 2017 International Conference on Wireless Networks and Mobile Communications (WINCOM), pp. 1–6. IEEE, Rabat (2017)

18. Kumar, A., Lim, T. J.: EDIMA: Early detection of iot malware network activity using machine learning techniques. In: 2019 IEEE 5th World Forum on Internet of Things (WF-IoT), pp. 289–294. IEEE, Limerick (2019)

SVFLS: A Secure and Verifiable Federated Learning Training Scheme

Yi Liu[1(✉)], Guoxiong Hu[1], Yudi Zhang[1], and Mingwu Zhang[1,2]

[1] School of Computers, Hubei University of Technology, Wuhan 430068, China
byliuyi@163.com
[2] Xiangyang Industrial Institute of Hubei University of Technology,
Xiangyang 441100, China

Abstract. Federated learning has received extensive attention in recent years since the clients only need to share their local gradients with the servers without directly sharing their datasets to train the model. However, the existing research shows that the attackers can still reconstruct private information from shared gradients, resulting in privacy leakage. In addition, the aggregated results could be tampered with by servers or attackers. In this paper, we propose a secure and verifiable federated learning training scheme (SVFLS) to protect the privacy of data owners and verify aggregated results. Specifically, we employ threshold paillier encryption to protect the local gradients of data owners and use the bilinear aggregate signature to verify the correctness (or integrity) of aggregated results. Furthermore, our scheme can tolerate data owners dropping out during the training phase. We conduct extensive experiments on real datasets and demonstrate that our scheme is effective and practical.

Keywords: Homomorphic encryption · Bilinear aggregate signature · Privacy-preserving · Verifiable federated learning

1 Introduction

Deep learning is widely used in many scenarios in our life, such as medical prediction [1,2], smart grid [3,4] and autonomous driving [5,6], etc. These applications have penetrated into many aspects of our lives and gradually changed our lifestyle. Deep learning requires large amounts of data to train models, however, these data could be sensitive. For example, patients could be reluctant to provide information such as their medical records to the third-party service providers in the healthcare system. Therefore, the traditional centralized deep learning faces many challenges with security and privacy issues.

Federated learning [7] has received extensive attention from academia and industry since it was proposed by Google in 2016. It only requires data owners to share their local gradients instead of raw data to cloud servers. Compared with centralized deep learning, federated learning avoids the direct processing of raw data and thus effectively reduces the risk of privacy leakage.

ⓒ The Author(s), under exclusive license to Springer Nature Singapore Pte Ltd. 2022
E. Ahene and F. Li (Eds.): FCS 2022, CCIS 1726, pp. 134–148, 2022.
https://doi.org/10.1007/978-981-19-8445-7_9

Recent studies have shown that federated learning still faces many risks of privacy breaches. For example, attackers can still reconstruct their private information based on the local gradients uploaded by data owners, leading to privacy leakage [8]. Furthermore, cloud servers and attackers may tamper with aggregated results sent to data owners [9]. Malpractice can occur in a healthcare system if a healthcare institution uses the wrong aggregated results to train the model. Therefore, it has important practical significance to effectively protect the privacy of data owners and prevent the aggregated results from being tampered with. In a real-world scenario, data owners may drop out for some reason, which is also a challenge.

We employ threshold paillier encryption to protect data privacy and bilinear aggregate signature to verify aggregated results. Our scheme also supports data owners to drop out during the training phase without privacy leakage. Specifically, our main contributions are as follows:

- We use threshold paillier encryption to protect the local gradient, which can effectively prevent the privacy leakage of data owners.
- We use bilinear aggregate signature to verify the integrity of aggregated results, which can effectively prevent tampering by cloud servers and attackers.
- Our scheme allows data owners to drop out at any stage of training without revealing their privacy.
- We provide a comprehensive security analysis of our SVFLS. We claim that the cloud server and other participants do not obtain any useful information of the local gradients and the aggregated results cannot be tampered with. Furthermore, we conduct extensive experiments on real datasets, demonstrating that our SVFLS is effective and practical.

The rest of this article is organized as follows. Section 2 briefly introduces related works. Section 3 describes the problem statement. Section 4 gives preliminaries. Section 5 gives a detailed description of SVFLS. Section 6 provides the security analysis of SVFLS. After that, performance evaluation is given in Sect. 7. Finally, conclusions are provided in Sect. 8.

2 Related Works

2.1 Homomorphic Encryption

In the existing homomorphic encryption schemes, Paillier [17] and other encryption techniques are used to protect messages. Li et al. [10] proposed a deep learning scheme that uses multiple secret keys to protect privacy in cloud computing, and realized the combination of fully homomorphic encryption and double decryption mechanism, enabling cloud servers to train on ciphertext. Hardy et al. [20] used homomorphic encryption and entity resolution to protect the privacy of vertically distributed datasets.

2.2 Differential Privacy

Differential privacy can protect the privacy by adding noise to the parameters. Shokri et al. [11] proposed a deep learning privacy protection scheme based on differential privacy, which achieves a balance between security and accuracy. Melis et al. [21] added Laplace noise to the gradient data, and Wu et al. [22] adopted Gaussian noise.

2.3 Secure Multi-party Computation

Secure multi-party computation is used to solve the problem of a group of mutually distrustful parties, each holding secret data, working together to compute a given function. Bell et al. [23] and Mohassel et al. [24] adopted secret sharing to protect the privacy of training data, which is a representative technology to achieve secure multi-party computing. Bonawitz et al. [12] proposed a federated learning training scheme based on secure multi-party computation, which realizes the protection of data owners' gradients and supports data owners to drop out.

2.4 Verifiability

During the training process of deep learning, the cloud server may return a wrong aggregated result to the data owners. Tramèr et al. [13] designed a verifiable deep learning scheme called Slalom, but it requires additional hardware support. Ghodsi et al. [14] proposed a framework named SafetyNets, but it only supports a small number of activation functions. Compared with existing methods, we propose a secure and verifiable federated learning training scheme (SVFLS). We use threshold paillier encryption to protect the local gradients of data owners and bilinear aggregated signatures to verify the correctness of aggregated results. Additionally, data owners are allowed to drop out at any stage of training without revealing their privacy in our scheme.

3 Problem Statement

3.1 System Overview

As shown in Fig. 1, there are three entities in our scheme, i.e., *Trusted Authority*, *Cloud Server* and *Data Owners*. We assume that the cloud server and data owners are semi-honest, which means they will execute the protocol honestly but try to infer additional information from other members.

- *Trusted Authority(TA):* The main job of TA is to initialize the system, and to generate public parameters, functions and private keys. Then TA sends the corresponding parameters to the cloud server and data owners through a secure channel.

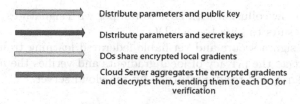

Distribute parameters and public key

Distribute parameters and secret keys

DOs share encrypted local gradients

Cloud Server aggregates the encrypted gradients and decrypts them, sending them to each DO for verification

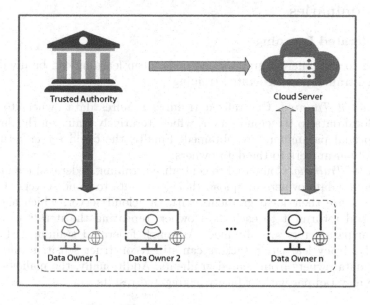

Fig. 1. System overview.

- *Cloud Server:* The cloud server is responsible for aggregating encrypted gradients and signed gradients sent from data owners. In addition, when a threshold number of data owners' secret shares are merged, the cloud server can decrypt the encrypted aggregated gradients and return the aggregated results to each data owner for verification.
- *Data Owners(DOs):* DOs encrypt and sign the local gradients after training on their local dataset. After verifying the correctness of the aggregated results, DOs update their model parameters.

3.2 Threat Model and Design Goal

In our threat model, we consider DOs and the cloud server to be honest but curious. Specifically, each DO executes the protocol honestly, but is also curious about the local gradients of other DOs out of business interests. The cloud server will honestly execute the aggregation protocol, but may also try to infer the privacy of other DOs. In particular, we allow collusion between DOs below a threshold number, and also allow the cloud server to tamper with signatures (here we do not allow collusion with DOs to tamper with signatures) and modify the aggregated results to send to each DO.

We aim to design a secure and verifiable federated learning training scheme that mainly protects the privacy of local gradients and verifies the integrity and correctness of aggregated results returned by the cloud server.

4 Preliminaries

4.1 Federated Learning

According to the different training methods, deep learning can be divided into centralized training and federated training.

1. *Centralized Training.* Centralized training requires data owners to upload their local data to the cloud server, which iteratively trains on the data until the optimal parameters are obtained. Finally, the cloud server returns the optimal parameters to the data owners.
2. *Federated Training.* Compared to centralized training, federated training does not require data owners to upload their local data to cloud servers. The data owners share their local gradients with the cloud server, which aggregates them and returns it to each data owner, repeating the iteration until the optimal parameters are obtained. Although federated training reduces the risk of privacy leakage, attackers can still reconstruct sensitive information about data owners from shared gradients. Additionally, the malicious cloud server may tamper with or falsify aggregated results.

4.2 Threshold Paillier Encryption

The (N, T)-threshold Paillier encryption [15] is adopted by our scheme due to its not only additive homomorphism but also threshold property, which enables secure aggregation of the plaintexts of the data owners.

Each DO holds a unified public key pk, and the private key is divided into N shares $(s_1, s_2, ..., s_N)$, which are distributed to N DOs.

1. *Key Generation:* We choose two primes p and q, taking $n = pq$ as the public key, denoted as pk. Then, we select two primes p' and q' that satisfies $p = 2p' + 1$ and $q = 2q' + 1$. We set $n' = p'q'$. To acquire a private key s_i, we randomly pick a_j (for $0 < j < N$) from $\{0, ..., n*n'-1\}$. Particularly, $a_0 = d$ is picked to satisfy $d = 0 \bmod n'$ and $d = 1 \bmod n$. Finally, we obtain the private key $s_i = \sum_{j=0}^{T-1} a_j(i)^j \bmod nn'$ $(1 \leq i \leq N)$.
2. *Encryption:* To encrypt a plaintext m, each DO_i calculates with the public key pk as follows:

$$C = Enc_{pk}(m) = (1 + n)^m r_i^n \bmod n^2$$

where r_i is a random number picked by each DO_i from $Z_{n^2}^*$.
Given two plaintexts of m_1, m_2 and a constant b, the homomorphic property can be described as follows:

$$Enc_{pk}(m_1 + m_2) = Enc_{pk}(m_1) \cdot Enc_{pk}(m_2)$$
$$= (1+n)^{m_1+m_2}(r_1 r_2)^n \bmod n^2$$

$$Enc_{pk}(b \cdot m_1) = (Enc_{pk}(m_1))^b$$
$$= (1+n)^{bm_1} r_1^{bn} \bmod n^2$$

where $r_1, r_2 \in Z_{n^2}^*$, are the private random numbers.

3. *Decryption:* Each DO_i uses the private key s_i to encrypt C to obtain a secret share C_i as follows:

$$C_i = C^{2\Delta s_i}, where \Delta = (N!).$$

If T shares of C_i are combined, the plaintext m will be obtained through the "extraction algorithm" [15].

4.3   Bilinear Aggregate Signature

Bilinear aggregated signatures [16] can verify multiple distinct signatures generated by different data owners. There are two groups G_1 and G_2 whose generators are g_1 and g_2 respectively. The bilinear map $e : G_1 \times G_2 \to G_3$. Given a message m, the hash function $h\colon m \to G_2$. In general, it consists of five algorithms as follows:

1. **KeyGen:** Each DO randomly chooses x and compute $u \leftarrow g_1^x$. Therefore, each DO will hold a public key $u \in G_1$, and a secret key $x \in Z_p$.
2. **Sign:** Given a secret key x, a message m, compute $h(m) \to h$, and $h^x \to \sigma$. The signature is $\sigma \in G_2$.
3. **Verify:** Given the public key u, a message m and a signature σ, compute $h(m) \to h$. Accept it if $e(g_1, \sigma) = e(u, h)$holds.
4. **AggSign:** Suppose there are N data owners $DO_i(1 \le i \le N)$. Each DO_i has a message m_i. Then, each DO_i computes a signature $\sigma_i \in G_2$ on a message m_i. Compute $\sigma \leftarrow \prod_{i=1}^{N} \sigma_i$. The aggregated signature is $\sigma \in G_2$.
5. **AggVerify:** Suppose each DO's $(1 \le i \le N)$ secret key is x_i, then its public key is $u_i \in G_1.DO_i$ computes $h(m_i) \to h_i$. Then accept the result if $e(g_1, \sigma) = \prod_{i=1}^{N} e(v_i, h_i)$holds.

5   Proposed Scheme

In this section, we give a detailed description of our scheme. To protect the privacy of the local gradients of each DO, we employ threshold paillier encryption to implement secure aggregation of the gradients. In addition, to prevent the cloud server from tampering with the aggregated results, we employ bilinear aggregate signature to verify the correctness of the aggregated results returned by the cloud server.

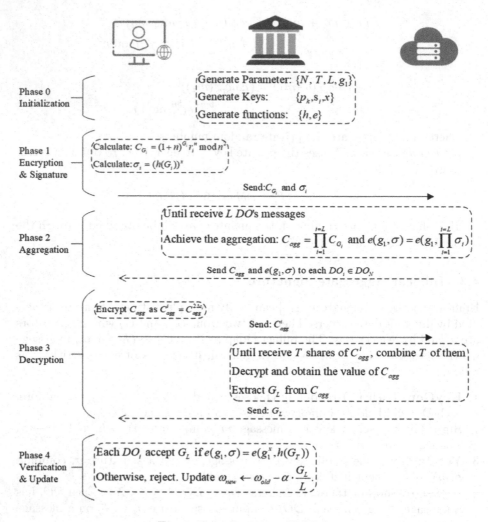

Fig. 2. Overview of our SVFLS.

As shown in Fig. 2, five phases are concluded in SVFLS. In phase 0, TA is responsible for initializing the system, generating parameters, keys and functions. In phase 1, each DO encrypts their own local gradients while signing the local gradients, and then sends them to the cloud server. In phase 2, the cloud server aggregates the encrypted gradients and signatures sent from each DO and returns them to each DO. In phase 3, after each DO receives the ciphertext of the aggregated result, they encrypt it with their own private key to obtain a secret share and sends it to the cloud server. After receiving T secret shares, the cloud server decrypts them and extracts the plaintext of the aggregated result. Finally, the aggregated result is sent to each DO. In phase 4, each DO verifies the correctness of the aggregated result returned by the cloud server and updates the parameter if the result is correct, otherwise rejects it.

5.1   Initialization

TA initializes the whole system in phase 0. The main work contains four parts:

1. *Parameter Generation:* We assume there are N data owners constituting the set DO_N. Considering that only L data owners out of N data owners are able to complete the uploading task due to factors such as network and devices, these L data owners form the set DO_L and their gradients form the sum of the gradients. In addition, TA will also generate a generator g_1 of a multiplicative cyclic group G_1. Generally, TA will generate N, T, L, g_1. It should be pointed out that $T < L \leq N$.
2. *Key Generation:* In the threshold paillier encryption system, the public key p_k will be set as $n = pq$, where n is a large positive integer, p and q are two primes. The private key s_i will be generated for each $DO_i \in DO_N$, as depicted in Sect. 4.2. In the bilinear aggregate signature scheme, the private key is x, and $u \leftarrow g_1^x$ is the public key.
3. *Functions Generation:* TA will generate two functions include a homomorphic hash function h and a bilinear map $e : G_1 \times G_2 \rightarrow G_3$. Given two messages m_1 and m_2, the homomorphic function h satisfies: $h(m_1) \in G_2$ and $h(m_1 + m_2) = h(m_1) \cdot h(m_2)$.
4. *Data Distribution:* The public parameter group (N, T, L, g_1) and the public key p_k are open for the data owners and the cloud server, while the private keys s_i and x, the homomorphic hash function h and the bilinear map e are known only to the data owners and are confidential to the cloud server.

5.2   Gradient Encryption and Signature

In phase 1, each $DO_i \in DO_N$ will encrypt their local gradient G_i with the public key $p_k = n$ as follows:

$$C_{G_i} = Enc_{pk}(G_i) = (1+n)^{G_i} r_i^n \bmod n^2 \tag{1}$$

where $n = pq$, and r_i is a random number chosen by each DO_i from the multiplicative group $Z_{n^2}^*$.

Meanwhile, each DO_i calculates their signature σ_i with the private key x as follows:

$$\sigma_i = (h(G_i))^x \tag{2}$$

where h is a homomorphic hash function. Finally, each DO_i uploads C_{G_i} and σ_i to the cloud server.

5.3   Secure Aggregation

In phase 2, only L data owners uploaded their results due to factors such as network or devices, which constitute a group DO_L. The cloud server achieves the aggregation with each DO's C_{G_i} and σ_i as follows:

$$C_{agg} = \prod_{i=1}^{i=L} C_{G_i} = (1+n)^{\sum_{i=1}^{i=L} G_i} \left(\prod_{i=1}^{i=L} r_i\right)^n \bmod n^2 \tag{3}$$

$$e(g_1, \sigma) = e(g_1, \prod_{i=1}^{i=L} \sigma_i) \tag{4}$$

where e is a bilinear map : $G_1 \times G_2 \rightarrow G_3$, and g_1 is the generator of a multiplicative cyclic group G_1.

We denote $G_L = \sum_{i=1}^{i=L} G_i$ as the sum of these L DO's gradients. Then, C_{agg} and $e(g_1, \sigma)$ will be sent to each $DO_i \in DO_N$.

5.4   Decryption

In phase 3, the cloud sever will obtain the sum of DOs' gradients G_L with decryption.

Before decrypting the ciphertext of the sum of the gradients, each $DO_i \in DO_N$ will first encrypt C_{agg} with their private key s_i to obtain a secret share C_{agg}^i as follows:

$$C_{agg}^i = C_{agg}^{2\Delta s_i} \tag{5}$$

where $\Delta = N!$. Then, each DO's C_{agg}^i will be sent to the cloud server again.

After at least T DOs' C_{agg}^i are received by the cloud server, T DOs' C_{agg}^i will be randomly chosen as a set DO_T, and be combined as follows:

$$C'_{agg} = \prod_{i \in DO_T} C_{agg}^{i \ 2\lambda_{(0,i)}^{DO_T} \bmod n^2}$$

where

$$\lambda_{(0,i)}^{DO_T} = \Delta \cdot \prod_{i' \in DO_T \backslash i} \frac{-i'}{i - i'} \tag{6}$$

Then, the value of C'_{agg} will have the form $C'_{agg} = C^{4\Delta^2 d}$. For obtaining the plaintext G_L, the Lagrange interpolation algorithm is used to conclude that $C'_{agg} = (1 + n)^{4\Delta^2 G_L} \bmod n^2$, then we can obtain $4\Delta^2 G_L$ through the "extraction algorithm" proposed in [15]. Finally, we can get the value of G_L by multiplying $(4\Delta^2)^{-1} \bmod n$.

5.5   Verification and Update

In phase 4, each $DO_i \in DO_N$ will receive the sum of gradients G_L from the cloud server. Then they will verify whether the aggregated result G_L is reliable. Accept G_L if the follow equation holds:

$$e(g_1, \sigma) = e(g_1^x, h(G_L)) \tag{7}$$

Otherwise, they will reject G_L. Finally, they will calculate the newest global weight ω to update their local models as follows:

$$\omega_{new} \leftarrow \omega_{old} - \alpha \cdot \frac{G_L}{L} \tag{8}$$

where α denotes the learning rate.

Phase 1–4 will be executed iteratively until the optimal parameter is acquired.

6 Security Analysis

In this section, we will discuss the security of our SVFLS. We consider the confidentiality and verifiability of the proposed scheme, which means that the private data and local gradients of data owners should not be leaked to arbitrary entities, and the aggregated results should not be tampered with. We assume the cloud server and all data owners are semi-honest.

6.1 Data Privacy

In our scenario, the security threats mainly come from the cloud server and the data owners themselves. We assume that both the cloud server and the data owners are honest and curious, but we allow the cloud server to falsify the aggregated results and allow collusion between data owners below a threshold. Considering that the (N, T)-threshold paillier encryption [15] adopted in our scheme is secure through the decisional composite residuosity assumption (DCRA) [17] proposed by Paillier, which is a difficult problem based on composite residual classes, we can prove that our encryption method is secure and can effectively protect the gradient of the data owners from being leaked.

For *the cloud server*, its main task is to aggregate the ciphertexts and decrypt the aggregated result. In the process of aggregation, the cloud server will get the sum of the gradients of the data owners through multiplying the ciphertexts of C_{G_i}. Since the threshold paillier scheme we adopted was proven to be secure, it is impossible for the cloud server to infer DOs' local gradients. Similarly, since the homomorphic hash function h is one-way and irreversible, and x is confidential to the cloud server, it still cannot get G_i through $\sigma_i = (h(G_i))^x$. In the process of decryption, the cloud server must combine at least T secret shares sent by DOs to decrypt the plaintext of the final aggregated result. Therefore, The cloud server knows nothing but the sum of the gradients $G_L = \sum_{i \in DO_L} G_i$.

For *the data owners*, each DO will perform the process of encryption twice and send the ciphertext to the cloud server. In the first process of encryption, each DO will use a uniform public key to encrypt its local gradient. In the first process of encryption, each DO will encrypt their own local gradient with a unified public key. Since each DO holds a different private key to decrypt the ciphertext, at least T secret shares need to be combined. Therefore, it is impossible for a single data owner or $T-1$ data owners to infer the private gradients of others. In the second process of encryption, each DO will encrypt the ciphertext of the sum of the gradients with their private key, even if information leakage occurs, the attackers can only obtain the sum of the gradients and cannot infer the private gradient of each DO.

6.2 Verification

The cloud server may falsify the results of aggregated gradients, but SVFLS can detect this malicious behavior. If the cloud server tries to forge G_L, σ should be modified as well to make the following equation hold:

$$e(g_1, \sigma) = e(g_1, \prod_{i=1}^{i=L} (h(G_i))^x)$$

$$= e(g_1, (\prod_{i=1}^{i=L} h(G_i)))^x \qquad (9)$$

$$= e(g_1^x, h(\sum_{i=1}^{i=L} G_i))$$

$$= e(g_1^x, h(G_L))$$

The cloud servers can obtain the encrypted local gradient C_{G_i} and signature σ_i. Since x and h are confidential to the cloud server, for a forged $C_{G_i'}$, the cloud server cannot forge it corresponding signature $\sigma_i' = (h(G_i'))^x$. Namely, the cloud server also cannot forge the aggregated signature $\sigma' = \sum_{i=1}^{i=L} \sigma_i'$. In addition, g_1^x on the right side of the equation is confidential for cloud servers. Therefore, our SVFLS can effectively verify the correctness of aggregation results.

7 Performance Evaluation

In this section, we analyze the performance of SVFLS under different conditions. We perform performance analysis and evaluation of our scheme in terms of computation overhead and communication overhead. We implement the scheme on real datasets, demonstrating the effectiveness and practicality of the scheme.

7.1 Experimental Environment and Settings

The simulation experiment is conducted on Windows 11 operating system, with AMD Ryzen 7 4800H 2.90 GHz and 16G RAM. We evaluate the performance of our scheme using the MNIST handwritten digits dataset, which contains 60000 examples, and the test set 10000 examples. In addition, we apply $(N, \lfloor N/2 \rfloor)$-threshold paillier encryption with the key size set as 512 bits in the experiment. There are three important influencing factors, including the number of DOs online, the number of gradients per DO and the dropout rate, denoted as $|L|$, $|G|$ and $|R|$, respectively. We evaluate our experimental performance in terms of computation overhead and communication overhead. Finally, we compare the functions with some existing schemes.

7.2 Computation Overhead

1. *Single data owner:* The computation overhead of a single DO consists of three parts: 1) encrypting their gradients, which takes $O(|G|)$ time; 2) generating the signatures, which takes $O(|L| \cdot |G|)$ time; 3) generating shares with private key, which takes $O(|L| \cdot |G|)$ time. Therefore, the computation overhead of a single data owner is $O(|L| \cdot |G|)$.

Figure 3(a) shows that, with 100 gradients per data owner, the running time of a single data owner increases linearly with the number of data owners. Because each data owner will calculate the value of $C_{agg}^i = C_{agg}^{2\Delta s_i}$, where $\Delta = N!$.

Figure 3(b) shows that in the case of 100 data owners, the running time of a single data owner increases linearly with the number of gradients owned by each data owner. Because each data owner needs to perform exponential operations to encrypt gradients, as the number of gradients increases, so does the runtime per data owner. Finally, the running time of each data owner is not affected at different dropout rates, because the running time of a single data owner is not related to the dropout rate but to the total number of data owners.

As shown in Fig. 3, the computation overhead of a single data owner keeps constant under different dropout rates.

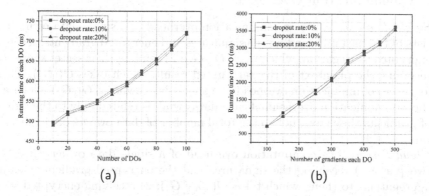

Fig. 3. Total running time of each DO. (a) $|G| = 100$ (b) $|L| = 100$

2. *Cloud Server:* The computation overhead of the server consists of: 1) aggregating encrypted gradients and signatures from each DO, which takes $O(|L| \cdot |G|)$; 2) achieving the plaintext of the aggregated result, which takes $O(|L|)$.

Figure 4 shows that the server runtime increases linearly with the number of data owners or the number of gradients per data owner. Because as the number of data owners or the number of gradients per data owner increases, the server needs to aggregate more gradients.

Figure 4 also shows that as the dropout rate increases, the computational overhead of the server decreases, because the higher the dropout rate, the fewer online data owners, and the fewer gradients the server needs to aggregate.

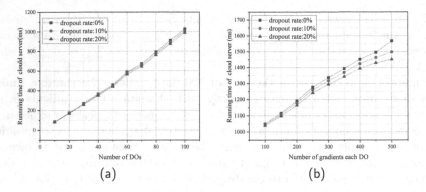

Fig. 4. Total running time of cloud server. (a) $|G| = 100$ (b) $|L| = 100$

7.3 Communication Overhead

1. *Single data owner:* The communication overhead of a single data owner consists of two parts: 1) sending the signatures and encrypted gradients, receiving encrypted aggregation, which takes $O(|G|)$; 2) sending their secret shares and receiving the plaintext of the aggregated result, which takes $O(|G|)$. Therefore, the communication overhead of a single data owner is $O(|G|)$. Generally, the communication overhead of each data owner is related only to the number of gradients they have, not to the total number of data owners or the dropout rate.

2. *Cloud Server:* The computation overhead of a single data owner consists of two parts: 1) receiving the signatures and the encrypted gradients, sending aggregations to them, which takes $O(|L| \cdot |G|)$; 2) receiving encrypted secret shares from L data owners and sending the plaintext of aggregation to them, which takes $O(|L| \cdot |G|)$. Therefore, the communication overhead of the cloud server is $O(|L| \cdot |G|)$. The communication overhead of the server increases with the number of data owners or the number of gradients per data owner, as the server needs to aggregate more gradients.

7.4 Comparison with Existing Schemes

As can be seen from Table 1, we make a functional comparison with PPML [18], PPDL [19] and SafetyNets [14], whose main work is similar to our SVFLS. Specifically, both PPML [18] and PPDL [19] support protecting the privacy of data, but they do not support the verifiability of aggregated results. Moreover, PPDL [19] also does not support the data owners drop out during the training. Although SafetyNets [14] supports verifiability, it does not take into account data privacy leakages and data owners drop out during training. Compared to them, our SVFLS supports the protection of data privacy and also supports the verifiability of aggregated result. In addition, our SVFLS also supports some data owners to drop out during the training process.

Table 1. Comparison with existing schemes

	Data privacy	Robustness to drop out	Verifiability
PPML	✓	✓	✗
PPDL	✓	✗	✗
SafetyNets	✗	✗	✓
SVFLS	✓	✓	✓

8 Conclusion

In this paper, we have proposed SVFLS, a secure and verifiable federated learning training scheme. The private data and local gradients of data owners are effectively protected, and the correctness and integrity of the aggregated results can be effectively verified. Furthermore, even if the data owners drop out during the training phase, their privacy will not be leaked. Finally, experiments on real datasets also show the effectiveness and practicality of our scheme.

Acknowledgements. This work is supported by the National Natural Science Foundation of China under grants 62072134 and U2001205, and the Key projects of Guangxi Natural Science Foundation under grant 2019JJD170020, and the Key Research and Development Program of Hubei Province under Grant 2021BEA163.

References

1. Ahiska, K., Ozgoren, M.K., Leblebicioglu, M.K.: Autopilot design for vehicle cornering through Icy roads. IEEE Trans. Veh. Technol. **67**(3), 1867–1880 (2017)
2. Xu, G., Li, H., Lu, R.: Practical and privacy-aware truth discovery in mobile crowd sensing systems. In: Proceedings of the 2018 ACM SIGSAC Conference on Computer and Communications Security, pp. 2312–2314 (2018)
3. Zhao, L., et al.: Shielding collaborative learning: mitigating poisoning attacks through client-side detection. IEEE Trans. Depend. Secure Comput. **18**(5), 2029–2041 (2020)
4. Saxena, N., Grijalva, S., Chukwuka, V., Vasilakos, A.V.: Network security and privacy challenges in smart vehicle-to-grid. IEEE Wirel. Commun. **24**(4), 88–98 (2017)
5. Mohassel, P., Zhang, Y.: SecureML: a system for scalable privacy-preserving machine learning. In: 2017 IEEE Symposium on Security and Privacy (SP), pp. 19–38. IEEE (2017)
6. Zhang, Y., Xu, C., Li, H., Yang, K., Zhou, J., Lin, X.: HealthDep: an efficient and secure deduplication scheme for cloud-assisted ehealth systems. IEEE Trans. Industr. Inf. **14**(9), 4101–4112 (2018)
7. McMahan, H.B., Moore, E., Ramage, D., y Arcas, B.A.: Federated learning of deep networks using model averaging. arXiv preprint arXiv:1602.05629 (2016)
8. Liu, Y., et al.: Trojaning attack on neural networks (2017)

9. Fu, A., Chen, Z., Mu, Y., Susilo, W., Sun, Y., Wu, J.: Cloud-based outsourcing for enabling privacy-preserving large-scale non-negative matrix factorization. IEEE Trans. Services Comput. **15**(1), 266–278 (2022). https://doi.org/10.1109/TSC.2019.2937484

10. Li, P., Li, J., Huang, Z., Li, T., Gao, C.Z., Yiu, S.M., Chen, K.: Multi-key privacy-preserving deep learning in cloud computing. Futur. Gener. Comput. Syst. **74**, 76–85 (2017)

11. Shokri, R., Shmatikov, V.: Privacy-preserving deep learning. In: Proceedings of the 22nd ACM SIGSAC Conference on Computer and Communications Security, pp. 1310–1321 (2015)

12. Bonawitz, K., et al.: Practical secure aggregation for privacy-preserving machine learning. In: proceedings of the 2017 ACM SIGSAC Conference on Computer and Communications Security, pp. 1175–1191 (2017)

13. Tramer, F., Boneh, D.: Slalom: Fast, verifiable and private execution of neural networks in trusted hardware. arXiv preprint arXiv:1806.03287 (2018)

14. Ghodsi, Z., Gu, T., Garg, S.: SafetyNets: verifiable execution of deep neural networks on an untrusted cloud. Adv. Neural Inf. Process. Syst. **30**, 4675–4684 (2017)

15. Damgård, I., Jurik, M.: A generalisation, a simplification and some applications of Paillier's probabilistic public-key system. In: International Workshop on Public Key Cryptography, pp. 119–136. Springer (2001). https://doi.org/10.1007/3-540-44586-2_9

16. Boneh, D., Gentry, C., Lynn, B., Shacham, H.: Aggregate and verifiably encrypted signatures from bilinear maps. In: International Conference on the Theory and Applications of Cryptographic Techniques, pp. 416–432. Springer (2003). https://doi.org/10.1007/3-540-39200-9_26

17. Paillier, P.: Public-key cryptosystems based on composite degree residuosity classes. In: International Conference on the Theory and Applications of Cryptographic Techniques, pp. 223–238. Springer (1999). https://doi.org/10.1007/3-540-48910-X_16

18. Bonawitz, K., et al.: Practical secure aggregation for privacy-preserving machine learning. In: proceedings of the 2017 ACM SIGSAC Conference on Computer and Communications Security, pp. 1175–1191 (2017)

19. Aono, Y., Hayashi, T., Wang, L., Moriai, S., et al.: Privacy-preserving deep learning via additively homomorphic encryption. IEEE Trans. Inf. Forensics Secur. **13**(5), 1333–1345 (2017)

20. Hardy, S., et al.: Private federated learning on vertically partitioned data via entity resolution and additively homomorphic encryption. arXiv preprint arXiv:1711.10677 (2017)

21. Melis, L., Danezis, G., De Cristofaro, E.: Efficient private statistics with succinct sketches. arXiv preprint arXiv:1508.06110 (2015)

22. Wu, X., Li, F., Kumar, A., Chaudhuri, K., Jha, S., Naughton, J.: Bolt-on differential privacy for scalable stochastic gradient descent-based analytics. In: Proceedings of the 2017 ACM International Conference on Management of Data, pp. 1307–1322 (2017)

23. Bell, J.H., Bonawitz, K.A., Gascón, A., Lepoint, T., Raykova, M.: Secure single-server aggregation with (poly) logarithmic overhead. In: Proceedings of the 2020 ACM SIGSAC Conference on Computer and Communications Security, pp. 1253–1269 (2020)

24. Mohassel, P., Zhang, Y.: SecureML: a system for scalable privacy-preserving machine learning. In: 2017 IEEE Symposium on Security and Privacy (SP), pp. 19–38. IEEE (2017)

A Pragmatic Label-Specific Backdoor Attack

Yu Wang[✉], Haomiao Yang, Jiasheng Li, and Mengyu Ge

School of Computer Science and Engineering (School of Cyberspace
Security),University of Electronic Science and Technology of China,
Chengdu 610000, China
202021081812@std.uestc.edu.cn

Abstract. Backdoor attacks, as an insidious security threat to deep
neural networks (DNNs), are adept at injecting triggers into DNNs. A
malicious attacker can create a link between the customized trigger and
the targeted label, such that the prediction of the poisoned model will be
manipulated if the input contains the predetermined trigger. However,
most existing backdoor attacks define an obvious trigger (eg: conspicuous pigment block) and need to modify the poisoned images' label, causing these images seems to be labeled incorrectly, which leads to these
images can not pass human inspection. In addition, the design of the
trigger always needs the information of the entire training data set, an
extremely stringent experiment setting. These settings above remarkably
restrict the practicality of backdoor attacks in the real world.

In our paper, the proposed algorithm effectively solves these restrictions of existing backdoor attack. Our Label-Specific backdoor attack
can design a unique trigger for each label, while just accessing the images
of the target label. The victim model trained on our poisoned training
dataset will maliciously output attacker-manipulated predictions while
the poisoned model is activated by the trigger. Meanwhile victim model
still maintains a good performance confronting benign data samples.
Hence, our proposed backdoor attack approach must be more practical.

Keywords: Deep neural network · Backdoor attack · Label-specific
trigger

1 Introduction

Deep learning has shown increasing performance advantages in many real-world
tasks with the development of computing resources and enrichment of training
data [1,2], so many industries are more willing to make deep neural networks the
foundational mean for solving practical challenges. Therefore, the security issue
of deep neural networks is more remarkable than before. In common, a security system needs to consider three main aspects: availability, confidentiality,
and integrity, where availability and confidentiality refer to the possible software vulnerabilities in the deep learning system framework as well as its dependent libraries, such as overflow attacks and DDos attacks, and the possibility

© The Author(s), under exclusive license to Springer Nature Singapore Pte Ltd. 2022
E. Ahene and F. Li (Eds.): FCS 2022, CCIS 1726, pp. 149–162, 2022.
https://doi.org/10.1007/978-981-19-8445-7_10

of the model's own parameters and data being stolen by an attacker during the inference phase [3,4], respectively. As for integrity-related security issues, they mainly refer to the interference in the process of model learning and prediction, which makes the output results not conform to the normal performance of the model, which can be divided into two categories: Evasion Attacks [5] and Data Poisoning Attacks [6,7]. Among them, data poisoning attacks occur during the model training phase, where attackers exploit vulnerabilities in data collection to manipulate training data so that downstream machine learning models contain exploitable behavior. Some attacks degrade the inference capability of the entire sample [8], while targeted data poisoning attacks induce false outputs on specific target samples [9].

Backdoor attacks, a classic representation of targeted data poisoning attacks, compromise the integrity of a model by poisoning a portion of the training data during the training phase of the model. Since deep learning systems often require large amounts of training data to support model training and high-quality training sets are expensive to collect and collate, practitioners seek larger and larger data sets to train their data-hungry models. Due to the surge in demand for training data and increased accessibility through the web, data curation efforts are also ongoing and the process of data curation is increasingly automated, which allows malicious attackers to control or poison training datasets.

A backdoor attack manifests itself in the form of a poisoned neural network model that outputs the same results as a normal model when confronted with benign data inputs but changes its output to a target label specified by the attacker when confronted with data with a trigger set by the attacker. Since a successful backdoor attack does not lead to any degradation in the overall task performance of the model, and the malicious attacker is free to select target labels and triggers, it is difficult to detect the backdoor attack. However, partial backdoor attack defense and backdoor removal techniques have been proposed and have yielded good results for partial backdoor attacks. So the concealment of backdoor attacks has received great questions.

A series of approaches to generating triggers have occurred in the existing works on backdoor attacks. The initial mean of backdoor attacks is to directly inject randomly generated triggers into the training data, so that the model trained on that data relies on triggers for inference, while the threat model of such attack methods usually includes label flipping, in which the poisoned images are often easily inspected because they belong to the incorrect class and contain a trigger that is placed in a visible location. In addition, there is a class of work that investigates invisible triggers, and to provide stealth in backdoor attacks, they make the trigger unobtrusive to the naked eye through different backdoor generation strategies, but the label-image inconsistency problem is still left behind. Subsequent work related to clean-label backdoor attacks emerged, which ensure that the labels of the poisoned data appear to human reviewers to be consistent with the category of the image itself.

In order to address these severe shortcomings and limitations in the above-mentioned backdoor attacks, we proposes a new backdoor attack scheme that is more likely to be implemented in practical scenarios, and our contribution can be mainly concluded in the following three points:

- **Clean-label backdoor attack:** In our scheme, the user does not modify the label of the poisoned image as in a standard backdoor attack, so that the attack can effectively avoid the defense of human inspection and does not need to access data of different labels.
- **Less data information:** Compared with other backdoor attack methods and existing clean-label attack methods, the malicious attacker in our attack method needs extremely little information, only the data of the target label is indispensable in the trigger generation phase. The information about the structure of the victim model, and training process settings is not needed at all.
- **Low data poisoning rate:** Our attack method, as one of the clean-label backdoor attack, only need to poison a very small portion of the target label to achieve a very good attack effect. Concretely, we only need 0.5% of the overall dataset to achieve close to 100% of the attack effect, e.g.: 250 pictures in Cifar-10 dataset containing a total of 50000 pieces of images.

2 Related Work

2.1 Image Classification

Image Classification is a fundamental task that attempts to comprehend an entire image as a whole. The goal is to classify the image by assigning it to a specific label. Typically, Image Classification refers to images in which only one object appears and is analyzed. The backdoor attack scenarios considered in this thesis all take place in the image classification task, where the inputs $x \in X$ and label $y \in Y$ are mainly included, where the combination of (x, y) is the samples in the dataset (X, Y). The model can then be defined as the equation $f_\theta : X{\rightarrow}Y$, θ represents the parameters of the model (including the weights and bias in the neural network). To evaluate the performance of the model, a loss function $L(x,y,\theta)$ is often defined. The objective of the image classification task is to improve the accuracy of the model for image classification, which is equivalent to minimizing the loss function. Therefore, the model parameter θ^* corresponding to the smallest value of the loss function is what we want.

$$\theta^* = \arg\min_{\theta} \frac{1}{n}\sum_{i=1}^{n} L(x,y,\theta)$$

Here the minimization of the loss function is usually done by using various gradient descent strategies, such as SGD, Adam, etc.

2.2 Data Poisoning Attack

Data poisoning attacks [10] mainly refers to a kind of attack where an attacker manipulates training samples or model architecture, aiming at impairing the functionality of the model such as wrong predictions of data from all classes (an indiscriminate attack) or misclassification of subsequent input data associated with a specific label (a targeted attack).

As for untargeted data poisoning attacks, the goal of such attacks is to degrade the performance of a model so that it can no longer provide services. From the previous work presented [10], such attacks first act on simple machine learning models, like SVMs [8], logistic regression models [11], and linear classifiers [12], and then use methods like gradient descent strategy to reduce the overall effectiveness of the model. This series of attacks often render the final poisoned model incapable of completing its task and functionally paralyzed, which is discernible to anyone using it. As a result, this attack must be disposable, after which the poisoned model is quickly taken offline and modified. Moreover, the prerequisites required for the success of such an attack are stringent, which compel the attacker to have control over most of the training data. However, another collection of data poisoning attacks, targeting certain labels instead of the entire dataset, has substantial existing works and they can be divided into several categories. The following sections will specifically introduce Standard Backdoor Attack, Invisible Backdoor Attack, and Clean-Label Backdoor Attack and analyze their characteristics.

2.3   Backdoor Attack

Due to the uniqueness of backdoor attacks in terms of attack purpose, the comprehensive performance of backdoor attacks can be concluded with three aspects: attack success rate (ASR), attack stealthiness, and the model performance on the benign dataset. More specifically, the attack stealthiness can be assessed from two perspectives: whether the trigger is conspicuous and whether the label of the poisoned data is modified.

As shown in Table 1, we summarize the characteristics of some classical backdoor attack algorithms here, mainly comparing the adversary capabilities assumed by different methods and the visibility of generated triggers. 'Obvious trigger' refers to whether its trigger is visible, and 'label flipping' refers to whether an attacker needs label poisoning operations. The "low poisoning rate" also refers to whether the poisoning rate of attackers is low as well as the "entire dataset information" indicates whether the attacker needs information on the complete training dataset.

Table 1. Backdoor attack features

	BadNets [13]	SSBA [14]	HTBA [15]	Ours
Obvious Trigger	✓	×	×	×
Label Flipping	✓	×	×	×
Low Poisoning Rate	✓	✓	✓	×
Entire dataset information	✓	✓	✓	×

Standard Backdoor Attack. The original backdoor attack scheme against DNNs is BadNets [13], the representative of Standard Backdoor Attack. In this attack scheme, the attacker would specify an attack target label t, then implant conspicuous triggers in parts of the image data with non-target labels, after which modify the labels of these images to target label t. The combination of poisoned data, image data injected with trigger, and benign dataset will be fed into the victim model, which will be successfully injected with the backdoor after a normal training procedure. Meanwhile, there are many similar backdoor attacks, [16] uses the combination of sample features belonging to non-target labels in the training dataset to generate a trigger, [17] generates a separate trigger for each input image, and [18] reduce the possibility of detection by backdoor detection techniques through adversarial regularization. In general, all these approaches require conspicuous triggers and label flipping to conduct the connections between target label and trigger, which greatly reduces the stealthiness of backdoor attacks. In addition, backdoor attack methods that require label flipping operations always assume that the attacker has information about the complete dataset and can make changes to the entire dataset, which is unrealistic in practical scenarios.

Invisible Backdoor Attack. In order to improve the conspicuousness of backdoor attacks, [19] mentions the conspicuousness of the trigger for the first time, specifically that the trigger set in a backdoor attack should not be too visible, or the image data with the trigger will be easily recognized in front of the human inspector. Therefore, [19] proposes a backdoor attack method based on a blended strategy. Meanwhile, [20] used image-scaling attack to hide the trigger and SSBA [21] proposed a sample-specific backdoor attack method. Although such trigger generation approaches can help the backdooring attacks evade human inspector detection, these methods still require the attacker to do label-flipping operations on non-target data and to maintain information about the entire dataset.

Clean-Label Backdoor Attack. The most distinctive feature of this type of backdoor attack is just like its name itself, 'clean-label' means that there is no label poisoning in the method. In this series of approaches, even the image data provided by the malicious attacker remains consistent with their semantic label, and the label-flipping operation no longer exists in the attack procedures. The HTBA [15] minimizes the distance between the non-target label data and the target-label data in the feature space by using the PGD algorithm to add the trigger so that the victim model will misclassify the data with the trigger. So at the same time, a feature extractor obtained on the complete training dataset has to be known to the attacker. Similar work has been done on [21–23], all of these attack methods assume that the attacker has access to the entire dataset information.

3 Method

We first briefly introduce the threat model and the problem setup parts and then show the detailed procedure of the proposed method.

3.1 Threat Model

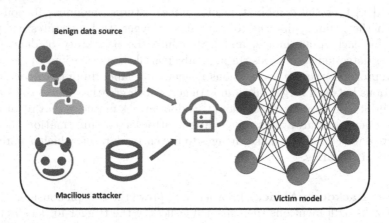

Fig. 1. Threat model

We consider a practical scenario: a model owner would like to use the data collected from multiple sources to assist in training their model and only the data collection phase is open to the public. Hence throughout all model training phases, any malicious attacker can only interfere with the model during the data collection phase. Therefore, we will define two main parts in Fig. 1: the attacker and the victim model, where the attacker is one of the many data providers and the victim model is the model with the backdoor trigger. As a result, the attacker can control only a limited part of the training dataset while having no information about the data from other providers.

The essential goal of the attacker is to successfully implant the trigger of the backdoor attack into the victim model. More concretely, the attacker wants to manipulate the model's output when confronting data patched with the trigger, whose output label will be the attacker's pre-specified label instead of the original label of the image data, and ensure the model's performance on clean data at the same time (classification accuracy).

The attacker's knowledge and capabilities: We divide the practical scenario into three phases: data collection phase, model training phase, and model deployment phase. In the data collection phase, the attacker is one of the many data providers. We assume that the attacker is responsible for providing data for a certain label and has only limited knowledge about the model training task, not the specific information about the whole training task, such as the number of labels and the meaning of each label for the multi-category task. However, the attacker can find some relevant additional publicly available datasets to assist in training the alternative model based on the basic information available, but we assume here that there is no overlap of sample labels between the publicly available alternative datasets and the training dataset. As for the attacker's manipulation of the poisoned data, our assumptions are more stringent. The attacker is required not to do label flipping (poisoning) on the data, and the percentage of poisoned data is also limited to a small range. Based on previous work settings, the attacker to modify the data range is also limited in the l norm range, making the trigger to add will not cause a sharp change of the original image.

In the training phase of the model, the attacker has no information about the parameters used in the training phase of the victim model and the structure of the model, and cannot directly modify the model parameters of the model training to control the model training process. In the deployment phase of the model, it is also impossible to do any modification to the trained model, but in this phase, it is possible to control the output of the model by putting data with a trigger into the victim model. This adversary capability is common and feasible in realistic scenarios and is weaker than the adversary capability mentioned in the existing work [13].

3.2   Proposed Attack

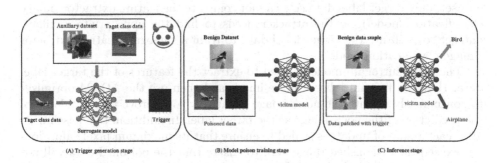

Fig. 2. Backdoor attack workflow

In this section, we will mainly introduce our attack method with a complete illustration(label-specific backdoor attack). The exact attack workflow will be divided into three stages: trigger generation stage, model poisoning stage, and inference stage (model deployment stage) (Fig. 2).

Trigger Generation Stage: At this stage, our main goal is to generate the target-label-specific trigger and the specific algorithm for this part is shown in ALGORITHM 1. Because of the characteristics of the clean-label backdoor and the limitation of our ability to the adversary, our method is different from

---

Algorithm 1. Trigger generation algorithm

Input: Auxiliary dataset D_{aux}, targeted label data D_t, target label t, *limited pixal range of trigger ρ, total train epoch N_{train}, trigger generation epoch $N_{trigger}$;*
Output: *Pretrained surrogate model $f_{surrogate}$, Trigger τ;*
Begin:
1. *Surrogate dataset $D_{surrogate} \in (X, Y) \leftarrow$ combine the Auxiliary dataset D_{aux} and targeted label data D_t*
2. *$f_{surrogate} \leftarrow$ random initialization*
For $i \in range(0, N_{train})$: **do**
  $loss = CrossEntropy(f_{surrogate}(X), Y)$
  compute gradient and update $f_{surrogate}$
For $i \in range(0, N_{trigger})$: **do**
  $loss = CrossEntropy(f_{surrogate}(\rho), t)$
  compute gradient and update trigger image ρ
Output *trigger image ρ and Pretrained surrogate model $f_{surrogate}$*

---

the previous work, which directly establishes a connection between the trigger and the target label through label reversal operation. Rather, by reinforcing the connection between the victim Model and the characteristics of the target label data itself.

Therefore, we first need an extractor that can extract the features of the target label data, and a well-trained target classification model is an ideal feature extractor because a high-performance classification model must be a good feature extractor. However, due to the attacker can not access the complete training dataset, only target label data sets cannot complete the feature extractor (image classification model), so the attacker needs to find the appropriate auxiliary dataset to facilitate the target label data to train a surrogate feature extractor (image classification model).

Then, the surrogate model is used to extract the features of the target label data. Here, we first initialize a noise image and then use the ADAM optimizer to continuously update the noise image iteratively to improve the confidence of the prediction of the noise image as the target label. In addition, the noise image after each round of update is scaled to ensure that its maximum pixel value does not exceed the established range, and to ensure that the poisoned data will not change too much from the original image. Otherwise, the model will be overfitted to the trigger image on the target label, which will not only affect the overall performance of the model, especially the accuracy of the clean data of the target label but also lead to the reduction of the concealability of the backdoor attack.

After several rounds of iterative optimization, the noise image finally obtained is the trigger corresponding to our ideal target label, because it will be super-imposed on any image to make it possess certain characteristics of the target label. The subsequent Model poisoning training phase will have Victim Model strengthen the connection between the trigger and the target label.

Model Poisoning Stage: After the completion of the trigger generation stage, a very small portion of the target label dataset can be selected with a trigger as the poisoned data. It should be noted here that we only add a trigger to the image data but do not change any label corresponding to the data, and then fuse it together with the benign dataset as the poisoned dataset. The subsequent model training process is the same as the normal machine learning model training process, and the attacker does not exercise any control over the training process. The final trained model is the poisoned model with the backdoor implanted.

Inference Stage: This stage is the stage when the backdoor attack works after the actual deployment of the victimization model on the ground. The attacker can add the triggers generated in the previous stage to any non-target labeled data to generate test data with triggers, which feeds the victim model and outputs the target labels specified by the attacker.

4   Experiment

4.1   Experiment Settings

This experiment mainly uses 2 GTX3090 Ti GPUs, 12th Gen Intel(R) Core(TM) i9-12900K and 128G RAM as the hardware base. As for the machine learning framework, we use Pytorch for all experiments, including comparison (ablation) experiments.

Datasets and Models: The experiments here mainly focus on the classification task of image datasets. We use CIFAR-10 dataset containing 10 classes [24], and Tiny ImageNet dataset containing 200 classes, a subset of ImageNet dataset [25], which are both classical datasets for image classification tasks. CIFAR-10 dataset is used as the training dataset of the victim model. Tiny Imagenet is a helper dataset used by attackers to generate Surrogate Models. It is worth noting that the two datasets do not coincide in the setting of labels, which is consistent with our setting in the threat model.

As for the model selection, all experiments have been conducted on Resnet-18 and GoogleNet models, and the backdoor attack effect is evaluated when the structures of the surrogate model and victim model are inconsistent.

Attack Setup: Our experiment is mainly divided into the trigger generation stage, poison model stage, and Inference stage. In Trigger Generation Stage, our experimental process is mainly to train surrogate models and generate triggers for target label datasets. Therefore, in this part, we specify that the target label is Label 0 in the CIFAR-10 dataset – the size of the airplane and the corresponding trigger, which is equal to the size of the original image($3 \times 32x32$). The 5000 images corresponding to the target label Airplane were then merged with the auxiliary dataset Tiny ImageNet into the surrogate dataset, which was used to train the surrogate Model.

In the subsequent model poisoning stage, the data poison rate γ in backdoor attack varies in different experiments. More specifically, we set the highest data poisoning rate as $\gamma = 0.5\%$, 200 training rounds, and the way of implanting backdoor as directly stacking the trigger with the original image. Meanwhile, we also tested the experimental effects of different data poisoning rates.

Here we define three datasets: poison training data set, poison test data set, and clean test dataset. The poison training dataset is used to implant a backdoor into the victim Model. Therefore, 250 images randomly selected from data belonging to the airplane label are superimposed with trigger images to generate backdoor data and put into the original dataset as the poison training dataset.

The poison test dataset and clean test dataset are used to measure the success rate of backdoor attacks and the Benign accuracy of models, respectively. Therefore, the clean test dataset is the original test dataset in the CIFAR-10 dataset (10000 images with 10 classes), and the poison test dataset is generated by modifying the dataset in the clean test dataset with non-target labels.

During the training process, we also recorded the attack success rate and Benign accuracy of the model. It is worth noting that to prove that our backdoor attack method does not require information from the Victim Model Architecture, we also tested the experimental effects of the Surrogate Model when it is different from the Victim Model.

In the Inference stage, we test the attack success rate of the final victim model, the Benign accuracy of the model, and other indicators (Fig. 3).

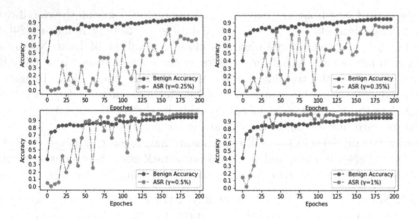

Fig. 3. Benign accuracy and attack success rate via epoch under different poisoning rate

Evaluation Metric: Here, we use two indexes, attack success rate and Benign accuracy to jointly measure the effect of the backdoor attack.

Attack success rate (ASR): recorded here is the proportion of the data of non-target labels that are successfully misclassified as target labels after being put into the victim model. This index directly reflects the effectiveness of the backdoor attack.

Benign accuracy refers to the performance of the victim model on Benign data sets. This index can also measure the stealthiness of backdoor attack methods to a certain extent.

4.2 Main Results

Table 2. Comparison between existing clean-label backdoor attack performance with ours under different poison budgets(the proportion of images that are poisoned). PB: Poison Budget, BA: Benign Accuracy, ASR: Attack Success Rate, TA: Target-label Accuracy

Approach	Ours					HTBA	SSBA
PB	125	150	175	250	500	500	500
BA (%)	95.36	95.35	95.41	95.33	95.32	94.52	94.41
ASR(%)	66.11	75.53	84.57	99.08	99.53	41.37	83.31
TA (%)	93.33	93.41	93.54	93.37	93.74	96.31	95.87

Attack Effectiveness

As shown in Table 2, our attack can successfully implant the backdoor into the Victim Model as the backdoor attack success rate is more than 99% with only 250 samples (0.5% of the training dataset). More specifically, we record experimental effects on different poison budgets in backdoor attacks. When poison samples occupy only 0.25% of the overall training dataset (125 pieces of poisoned images), the attack success rate can reach above 66%. In the meantime, during the improvement of the poisoning rate, Not only is the attack success rate on the rise, but the other two indexes that we pay attention to in the experiment are Benign accuracy and target-label accuracy, which have been kept around 95%. Benign accuracy remains a high effect. It can be seen that our scheme does not cause model performance degradation on the main task. Target-label accuracy also maintaines at a high level, indicating that our trigger generation algorithm can actually extract the intrinsic features of the target label data. This is because only by strengthening the connection between the label and its inherent features can the model's performance on the clean data of the target label not be degraded.

In addition, Table II also shows the attack performance of two classical clean-label backdoor attack schemes under the same experimental settings. Benign accuracy and target-label accuracy of HTBA and SSBA programs are almost consistent with ours, but it is obvious that when the poisoning rate has reached 1%, The attack success rate of our scheme is almost 100%, but the effect of HTBA and SSBA is far worse than our scheme.

In addition, to verify that our attack scheme does not depend on the structural knowledge of the victim model, we conduct corresponding experiments on the different pairs of surrogate model and victim model, and it can be concluded from the results that no matter whether the structure of surrogate Model and victim Model is constant or not, our attack maintain a high attack success rate (Table 3).

Table 3. The ASR with pairs of surrogate model and victim model on Cifar-10 dataset and data poisoning rate $\gamma = 0.5\%$

Surrogate model	Victim model	
	ResNet-18	GoogLeNet
ResNet-18	99.08	95.46
GoogLeNet	96.35	99.26

Time Analysis

Although the generation method of our trigger is different from the random setting of the standard backdoor attack method, which needs to be generated by the surrogate model, our approach can iteratively generate the trigger of the corresponding category within 10s using the trained surrogate model while this trigger can complete the poisoning training and output manipulation for a target label.

5 Conclusion

In this paper, we propose a backdoor attack scheme that is most likely to be implemented in real scenarios. As a kind of clean-label backdoor attack, the attacker does not need to perform any label poisoning operation and has no information on non-target label data. As far as we know, the attacker's ability and knowledge are the weakest among these existing works. At the same time, we only need the data poisoning rate of 0.5% of the overall training dataset to achieve 99.53% success rate of backdoor attacks. Therefore, we believe that such a real-world backdoor attack scheme is enough to reveal a remarkable hidden danger in DNNs. Our work wants to indicate that relevant workers need to research the defense scheme against this kind of attack to protect the deep learning system.

Besides, to urge the development of the backdoor attack defense method, we will concentrate on research about backdoor attack techniques, which can escape the existing defense method, including human inspection and AI-based approaches.

References

1. He, K., Zhang, X., Ren, S., Sun, J.: Deep residual learning for image recognition. In: Proceedings of the IEEE Conference on Computer Vision and Pattern Recognition, pp. 770–778 (2016)

2. Li, X., Ma, C., Wu, B., He, Z., Yang, M.H.: Target-aware deep tracking. In: Proceedings of the IEEE/CVF Conference on Computer Vision and Pattern Recognition, pp. 1369–1378 (2019)
3. Tramèr, F., Zhang, F., Juels, A., Reiter, M.K., Ristenpart, T.: Stealing machine learning models via prediction {APIs}. In: 25th USENIX Security Symposium (USENIX Security 16), pp. 601–618 (2016)
4. Shokri, R., Stronati, M., Song, C., Shmatikov, V.: Membership inference attacks against machine learning models. In: 2017 IEEE Symposium on Security and Privacy (SP), pp. 3–18. IEEE (2017)
5. Moosavi-Dezfooli, S.M., Fawzi, A., Frossard, P.: DeepFool: a simple and accurate method to fool deep neural networks. In: Proceedings of the IEEE Conference on Computer Vision and Pattern Recognition, pp. 2574–2582 (2016)
6. Li, B., Wang, Y., Singh, A., Vorobeychik, Y.: Data poisoning attacks on factorization-based collaborative filtering. In: Advances in Neural Information Processing Systems, vol. 29 (2016)
7. Alfeld, S., Zhu, X., Barford, P.: Data poisoning attacks against autoregressive models. In: Proceedings of the AAAI Conference on Artificial Intelligence, vol. 30 (2016)
8. Biggio, B., Nelson, B., Laskov, P.: Poisoning attacks against support vector machines. arXiv preprint arXiv:1206.6389 (2012)
9. Shafahi, A., et al.: Poison frogs! targeted clean-label poisoning attacks on neural networks. In: Advances in Neural Information Processing systems, vol. 31 (2018)
10. Goldblum, M., et al.: Dataset security for machine learning: data poisoning, backdoor attacks, and defenses. IEEE Trans. Pattern Anal. Mach. Intell. (2022)
11. Muñoz-González, L., et al.: Towards poisoning of deep learning algorithms with back-gradient optimization. In: Proceedings of the 10th ACM Workshop On Artificial Intelligence and Security, pp. 27–38 (2017)
12. Steinhardt, J., Koh, PW., Liang, P.S.: Certified defenses for data poisoning attacks. In: Advances in Neural Information Processing Systems, vol. 30 (2017)
13. Tianyu, G., Liu, K., Dolan-Gavitt, B., Garg, S.: BadNets: evaluating backdooring attacks on deep neural networks. IEEE Access **7**, 47230–47244 (2019)
14. Souri, H., Goldblum, M., Fowl, L., Chellappa, R., Goldstein, T.: Sleeper agent: scalable hidden trigger backdoors for neural networks trained from scratch. arXiv preprint arXiv:2106.08970 (2021)
15. Saha, A., Subramanya, A., Pirsiavash, H.: Hidden trigger backdoor attacks. In: Proceedings of the AAAI Conference on Artificial Intelligence, vol. 34, pp. 11957–11965 (2020)
16. Lin, J., Xu, L., Liu, Y., Zhang, X.: Composite backdoor attack for deep neural network by mixing existing benign features. In Proceedings of the 2020 ACM SIGSAC Conference on Computer and Communications Security, pp. 113–131 (2020)
17. Nguyen, T.A., Tran, A.: Input-aware dynamic backdoor attack. In: Advances in Neural Information Processing Systems, vol. 33, pp. 3454–3464 (2020)
18. Shokri, R., et al. Bypassing backdoor detection algorithms in deep learning. In: 2020 IEEE European Symposium on Security and Privacy (EuroS&P), pp. 175–183. IEEE (2020)
19. Chen, X., Liu, C., Li, B., Lu, K., Song, D.: Targeted backdoor attacks on deep learning systems using data poisoning. arXiv preprint arXiv:1712.05526. (2017)
20. Quiring, E., Rieck, K.: Backdooring and poisoning neural networks with image-scaling attacks. In: 2020 IEEE Security and Privacy Workshops (SPW), pp. 41–47. IEEE (2020)

21. Li, Y., Li, Y., Wu, B., Li, L., He, R., Lyu, S.: Invisible backdoor attack with sample-specific triggers. In: Proceedings of the IEEE/CVF International Conference on Computer Vision, pp. 16463–16472 (2021)
22. Barni, M., Kallas, K., Tondi, B.: A new backdoor attack in CNNs by training set corruption without label poisoning. In: 2019 IEEE International Conference on Image Processing (ICIP), pp. 101–105. IEEE (2019)
23. Liu, Y., Ma, X., Bailey, J., Lu, F.: Reflection backdoor: a natural backdoor attack on deep neural networks. In: Vedaldi, A., Bischof, H., Brox, T., Frahm, J.-M. (eds.) ECCV 2020. LNCS, vol. 12355, pp. 182–199. Springer, Cham (2020). https://doi.org/10.1007/978-3-030-58607-2_11
24. Krizhevsky, A., Hinton, G., et al.: Learning multiple layers of features from tiny images (2009)
25. Deng, J., Dong, W., Socher, R., Li, L.J., Li, K., Fei-Fei, L. ImageNet: a large-scale hierarchical image database. In: 2009 IEEE Conference on Computer Vision and Pattern Recognition, pp. 248–255. IEEE (2009)

Threat Landscape Across Multiple Cloud Service Providers Using Honeypots as an Attack Source

Samuel Kelly Brew and Emmanuel Ahene$^{(\boxtimes)}$ (ID)

Computer Science Department, College of Science, Kwame Nkrumah University of Science and Technology, Kumasi, Ghana
{kelly_brew,aheneemmanuel}@knust.edu.gh

Abstract. As the number of users of cloud services increases, so does the frequency of attacks against cloud infrastructure and systems. Cloud service providers do possess some control over the security of their systems. Nonetheless, these measures are only partially effective. End-users and clients should be informed of which cloud service provider delivers the best security for their services. This study aims to investigate the threat landscape of three cloud service providers: Google Cloud Services, Linode, and Amazon Web Services. Honeypots have been added to adequately monitor attacks and the attack sequence, allowing for a more thorough examination of the attack procedure. This research will clearly lay out the statistics regarding the Cloud service provider with the least threat landscape, as well as provide supporting information for all stakeholders in the cloud computing industry's cyber threat awareness and provide recommendations for the base security configurations of all public-facing infrastructure.

Keywords: Cloud service provider · Honeypots · Cloud computing · Cyber attacks · GCP · AWS · Linode

1 Introduction

Gartner Inc. expects that global end-user spending on public cloud services would climb by 20.4% between 2021 and 2022, from $410.88 billion to $494.70 billion [5]. Obviously, this is owing to the ease with which cloud service providers facilitate setup and access, as all that is required to connect to such a service is an end-user device with an internet connection [12]. Even though these cloud computing assets offer immense benefits to enterprises, they may also serve as backdoors for cyber-criminals to engage in a variety of nefarious actions [20].

In the current threat landscape, threat actors are continuously engaged on a global scale, seeking to exploit both new and existing vulnerabilities, many of which are decades old. In 2017, a recent big data breach affecting Alteryx clients exposed their personal information. This vulnerability occurred on a misconfigured Amazon Web Services Compute [4].

Consequently, it is crucial to comprehend and investigate how hackers scan and interact with public systems. Honeypots, which may impersonate a wide

E. Ahene and F. Li (Eds.): FCS 2022, CCIS 1726, pp. 163–179, 2022.
https://doi.org/10.1007/978-981-19-8445-7_11

variety of services across a system or network to tempt potential attackers into initiating inter-action, are widely employed to monitor such activity [25]. These honeypot data will provide a complete picture of all attacker contacts, aiding the cyber-security and cloud computing communities in understanding hacker behaviour and locating system vulnerabilities.

Honeypots are intended to offer minute value pertinent to the primary operation of an organization. They do not manage client information, transaction processing, or logistics and in most instances, honeypots are inactive until someone communicates with them [21]. Here, these communications are monitored and analyzed to discover the attacker's motivation and ultimate objective [23]. It is assumed that only an attacker will communicate with honeypots, as it is uncommon for normal users or programs to exploit the services offered by honeypots [21].

Typically, honeypots work in three modes. These include detection of intrusions, technique and proliferation research, and resource exhaustion [17]. All these modes aim to provide enterprises using honeypots with alerts, information, and some form of security [16].

The data obtained, such as source of attacks via IP address information and geolocation, commands executed by attackers, passwords used, etc., enables security teams at diverse enterprises to enhance their security posture. Honeypots' detection accuracy is free of false positives, as any communication with honeypots is judged malicious [13].

This study investigates honeypot attacks against cloud service providers (CSPs) such as Amazon Web Services (AWS), Google Cloud Platform (GCP), and Linode Cloud Services across four specific regions namely London, Sydney, Singapore and Tokyo. Based on the numerous signs of compromise specified in the honeypot frameworks, this study will evaluate which CSP has a more severe threat landscape by area by evaluating data from these CSPs.

This study will provide a thorough picture of all attacker interactions, supporting the cybersecurity and cloud computing communities in comprehending hacker behaviour and identifying system flaws.

1.1   Motivation and Contribution

Organizations engage in cloud computing not only because it is essential for company operations, but also because it offers true economic value, and is thus heavily influenced by industry-level trends [18]. As a result, information technology and cloud computing have become an integral part of the operations of businesses that offer specific services to internet users and consumers. To access a larger portion of the worldwide population, some firms construct infrastructure on-premises, while others utilize cloud solutions [2].

To ensure that the event reaches a global audience, enterprises must realize that they are opening their systems to malicious actors who are constantly searching for vulnerabilities to cause havoc. Even though cloud service providers have defence mechanisms in place, there is a high probability that current security tools will miss new attack techniques, especially zero-day assaults [6].

Establishing IT infrastructure on-premises requires a substantial financial investment to cover, among other things, the price of processing power or servers, electrical power, cooling, and a leased connection to an internet exchange [19]. In contrast, cloud solutions are more cost-effective because firms only pay for computing space and are relieved of the responsibility of providing power, cooling, and connectivity [10]. Consequently, cloud services are the most desired solution for all businesses.

It is reasonable to emphasize the need for a study on the attack pattern across various cloud service providers to educate the cyber community on specific cybersecurity issues affecting each CSP. Given the global reach of cloud service solutions, this is a reasonable course of action to take.

The collected intelligence will not only provide us with information on the severity of the attack on each CSP, but it will also be essential in the process of refining and upgrading the security policies and processes that are in place to ensure the efficient running of the system. Because of this, enterprises will be able to make timely decisions based on accurate information to improve the level of system protection they provide for their customers.

In addition, businesses can create a complete intelligence database on attack vectors by replicating this solution on their own self-hosted internet-facing infrastructure. Because of this, they can conduct an analysis of the attack data and make well-informed decisions on the security of their systems.

1.2   Related Works

In 2016, La [9] proposed a technique for defending honeypot-enabled networks against attacks whilst examining a game-theoretic model of deception involving an attacker and a defender. The attacker may attempt to deceive the defender using several methods ranging from the suspicious to the commonplace, whereas the defender may deploy honeypots as a deception weapon to trap attackers. The test results reveal that there is a threshold for active attackers over which both parties will participate in dishonest behaviour and a threshold below which the defence can modify its tactics while keeping the attacker's low success rate. During the reconnaissance phase of the cyber kill chain, the attacker gathers intelligence on the target and its attack methods. This could involve collecting data from social media accounts and other sources.

In 2017, Paradise [14] proposed a methodology for administering social network honeypots in order to detect APTs during their reconnaissance phase. Following a thorough review, the honeypot accounts were successfully incorporated into the organisation's social network and began to receive strange friend requests and e-mails, signalling the possibility of a potential future attack.

Promise [15], in 2018 conducted a real-world threat analysis on the Ghana Education Service's network by deploying a hybrid honeypot consisting of a Valhalla honeypot and a honeyd. The honeypots were attacked using port scanning, SQL injection, SSH brute force, and spam.

Bove and Muller [1], in 2019 set up honeypots on several public cloud infrastructures, including Amazon Web Services, Microsoft Azure, and Google

Cloud Platform. These honeypots were dispersed throughout multiple continents, including North America, Asia, and Europe. According to their research, attacks originated from 216 countries and utilized 268,614 unique IP addresses, with China accounting for 25.83 per cent of all attacks.

In 2020, Al-Mohannadi [11] deployed two low-interaction honeypots on AWS EC2 in China and the United States, dubbed Kippo and Dionaea, respectively. In the configuration, Elasticsearch, Logstash, and Kibana were utilized. Their findings indicated that most attacks were "Root trying auth none" attacks, which occur when an attacker tries to gain root access but fails.

Finally, in 2021, Kelly [7] established multiple honeypots on well-known cloud providers, such as AWS, Google Cloud Platform, and Microsoft Azure, each of which operates in a different region. In this study, North Virginia, London, and Singapore were the regions examined. There was regional distribution, but it was inconsistent. There was no outline of all the attack techniques employed by cybercriminals to determine precisely what type of data or information was requested.

1.3   Organization

The rest of this paper follows in this order. In Sect. 2, there is a breakdown of honeypots with regards to their classification based on the level of interaction and objectives. Section 3 will talk about the design of the honeypot system and its implementation on the various cloud service providers. The results are evaluated in Sect. 4 and the paper is concluded in Sect. 5.

2   Background

From a layperson's perspective, a honeypot offers no value that is directly relevant to the core function of a business [21]. It does not manage customer information, transaction processing, or logistics. It does not contain any processes or legitimate data interpretations used by an organization or its customers. In most instances, a honeypot remains inactive until it receives communication. Because no legitimate users or applications utilize the provided resources, any attempt to communicate with a honey-pot is suspicious.

The definition of honeypots as a security resource is purposefully vague because there are numerous types with distinct functions. Classifying honeypots involves describing their level of interaction with malicious actors and their objectives.

2.1   Low-Interaction Honeypots

Low-interaction honeypots that are simple to deploy grant the attacker very restricted access [24]. The adversary will have limited ability to communicate with the decoy system [22]. Low-interaction honeypots may not be effective enough because they only simulate a system in its most fundamental form.

Their objective is to gather information about access levels. Honeyd is an example of a low-interaction honeypot because it simulates the networks, hosts, and services that would run from a single host. Honeyd's ability to mirror specific operating system versions is a further advantage.

2.2   Medium-Interaction Honeypots

Medium-interaction honeypots are more advanced than low-interaction honeypots because they provide the attacker with more information [3]. This interaction makes it possible for the attacker to obtain significantly more information from the attacks, as more vulnerabilities are made available [22].

Medium-interaction honeypot examples include Mwcollect, Honeytrap, and Nepenthes.

2.3   High-Interaction Honeypots

High-interaction honeypots are the most sophisticated honeypot type. These honeypots contain an operating system, allowing an attacker to launch any type of attack on the honeypot, even though their setup is more difficult and time-consuming [8, 22].

Due to its highly interactive nature, this type provides large volumes of logs and data. The honeynet is an example of a high-interaction honeypot.

2.4   Intrusion Detection Honeypots

Figure 1 depicts an example of an intrusion detection goal: when an attacker gains access to a variety of database servers, including a honeypot, the attacker will eventually interact with both the honeypot and the legitimate servers.

Alert on interaction with the honeypot system serves as a notification because it is not anticipated that anything will occur there [17].

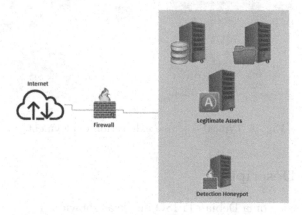

Fig. 1. Typical intrusion detection honeypot deployment

2.5   Technique and Proliferation Research Honeypots

As depicted in Fig. 2, honeypots have no true production value, so most businesses utilize them as research tools. Honeypots can provide valuable insights and data for further analysis, particularly honeypots with a high interaction rate.

Honeypots can contribute to the study of cyber-attacks by tracking and monitoring the attacker's attack process [17].

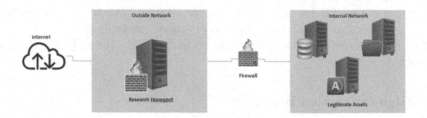

Fig. 2. Typical research honeypot deployment

2.6   Resource Exhaustion Honeypots

As shown in Fig. 3, The purpose of Resource Exhaustion honeypots is to waste as much of the attacker's time as possible by deploying many honeypots that allow interaction to appear real and keep the bad actors interested [17].

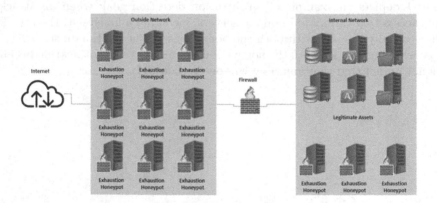

Fig. 3. Typical resource exhaustion deployment

3   System Description

The system is based on a Debian 11 ISO image as shown in Fig. 4. Docker is used to paravirtualize the honeypot daemons and additional support components. This allowed the running of multiple honeypot daemons simultaneously on the same network interface, resulting in a system that required minimal maintenance. The containerization of honeypot daemons in Docker provided adequate isolation of runtime environments and simplified update procedures.

Existing honeypots (Glastopf, kippo, honeytrap, and Dionaea) were merged with the network intrusion detection and prevention system Suricata, data monitoring and visualisation triple elasticsearch-logstash-kibana, and a data submission system ewsposter, which now supports hpfeeds honeypot data sharing.

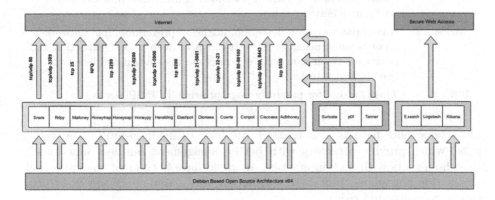

Fig. 4. System framework

3.1   System Components

Table 1. Honeypot and Functions

Honeypot	Function
Dionaea	This is a modular low-interaction honeypot that incorporates Python as a scripting language
Cowrie	This is an SSH, and Telnet honeypot designed to log attacks such as brute force attacks
Honeytrap	This is a security platform that was created to keep an eye on UDP and TCP services for attacks
Mailoney	An SMTP honeypot containing various modules
Heralding	A honeypot that supports a variety of protocols now, including FTP, telnet, HTTP, ssh, socks5, HTTPS, PostgreSQL, vnc, IMAP, imaps, SMTP, vnc, and pop3
Conpot	This is an Industrial Control Systems honeypot
Adbhoney	This is a honeypot intended for use with the Android Debug Bridge via TCP/IP

Table 2. Framework Tools and Functions

Tools	Function
EWSPoster	This is a tool, written in Python, to collect logs and alerts from different honeypots also network IDS and transmit them to InfluxDb, JSON, Hpfeed, or a Honeypot backend
Tanner	This service examines HTTP requests and composes the response that Snare then serves. Tanner responds to Snare by simulating the weaknesses of numerous applications. Tanner also provides Dorks for Snare's enticing skills
Suricata	It contains intrusion detection, intrusion prevention, and network security monitoring features. It excels at deep packet inspection and pattern matching, making it a priceless instrument for detecting threats and attacks
P0f	This is a tool for passively fingerprinting TCP/IP stacks

Most honeypots used in this research are low- to medium-interaction honeypots, which provide attackers with better engagement but less functionality than honeypots with high interaction. It would have been great to deploy high-interaction honeypots, but their installation and maintenance are exceedingly time-consuming and risky.

3.2 System Provisioning

The systems were installed for a period of seven (7) days and each system had a minimum of four CPUs and sixteen gigabytes of memory which were required to run the honeynet systems without encountering problems with the respective ELK stacks. The ratio of CPUs to RAM varied, but the optimal configuration was a four-processor system with sixteen gigabytes of RAM, as stated.

All compute nodes were configured with firewall rules that permitted connections from any Internet location, port, and protocol as shown in Table 3. This was done to make vulnerable ports and protocols accessible to everyone, thereby enabling unrestricted attacks.

Table 3. Applied System Firewall Rules

Rule name	Direction	IP range	Ports	Protocol	Action
allow_udp_ingress	Ingress	0.0.0.0/24	0 - 65535	UDP	Allow
allow_tcp_ingress	Ingress	0.0.0.0/24	0 - 65535	TCP	Allow

4 Results and Discussion

4.1 Time for First Failed Login Attempt

As soon as the systems went online, malicious actors discovered the ssh service provided by the Cowrie honeypot. As depicted in Fig. 5, the Sydney GCP node was attacked in a mere six seconds. Additionally, it took nearly two hours for the Sydney Linode instance to be attacked. However, once the onslaught began against all nodes in each site, it persisted mercilessly.

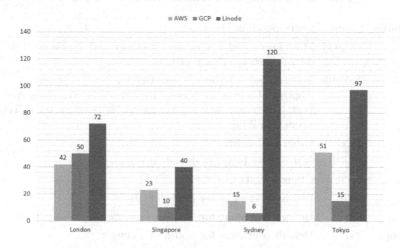

Fig. 5. Time for first failed login attempt

4.2   Passwords Used in Attacks with Corresponding Devices

Table 4. Password Count and Corresponding Devices

Password	Count	Corresponding devices
Admin	188,296	IoT devices including 3Com, Belkin, BenQ, D-Link, Digicom, Linksys, Netgear, Sitecom, Asus, Synology, Arris, Dell, Netcomm, Netstar, Sigma, SUN, Telco Systems, Tenda, Zcom and ZTE.
1234	123,315	IoT devices including GANZ PixelPro CCTV Cameras
123456	29,942	IoT devices including Lacie NAS devices, Hikvision, Panasonic, Samsung CCTV devices and Seagate
root	25,788	root 25,788 IoT devices including devices by D-Max
(Blank)	22,491	Used on IoT devices such as 3com, Acer, Adtran, Aironet, Alcatel and Ascend. Also, on HP Printers
User	17,766	Default password for Compaq insight manager, Dlink and Terayon devices
Passsword	16,725	IoT devices such as 3Com, Brocade, Flowpoint, IBM and Netgear devices
Changeme	23	Default password for Cisco BBSM Administrator and Network Registar

4.3   Usernames Used in Attacks with Corresponding Devices

Table 5. Username Count and Corresponding Devices

Username	Count	Corresponding Devices
Root	320,943	Most Linux and IoT devices. Seagate and Synology NAS devices also use this username
Admin	205,205	IoT devices including 3Com, Belkin, BenQ, D-Link, Digicom, Linksys, Netgear, Sitecom, Asus, Synology, Arris, Dell, Netcomm, Netstar, Sigma, SUN, Telco Systems, Tenda, Zcom and ZTE
User	62,179	Other IoT devices
Sa	26,315	SQL Server Instance default username
Ubuntu	1,435	Ubuntu 12.04 Live CD
Postgres	996	Default username for PostgreSQL
Nagios	261	Default username for Nagios Network Monitoring Tool
Hadoop	237	Default username for nodes in a cluster

4.4   Attack Distribution by Cloud Service Provider - London (England)

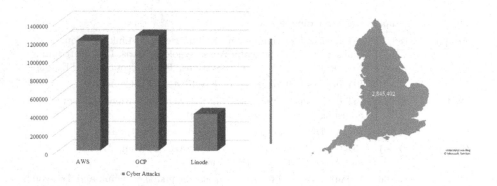

Fig. 6. Attack distribution by CSP - London

As shown in Fig. 6, the London simulation reported a total of 2,845,402 cyber-attacks, with GCP and AWS logging the majority. Linode, on the other side, experienced the fewest attacks, 400.007.

4.5 Attack Distribution by Cloud Service Provider - Singapore (Republic of Singapore)

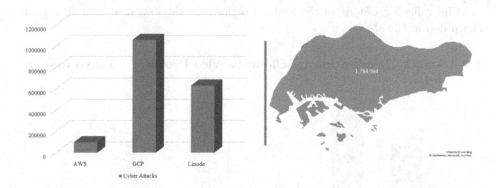

Fig. 7. Attack distribution by CSP - Singapore

With the Singapore simulation, a total of 1,784,004 cyberattacks were documented as shown in Fig. 7, the majority of which were recorded by GCP with a value of 1,058,212. Following this came Linode, who had an attack value of 628,296.

AWS's third-place finish, with a measly 97,496 points, was a surprise. This may explain why AWS computing machines in the Singapore area are not particularly enticing to malicious actors.

4.6 Attack Distribution by Cloud Service Provider - Sydney (Australia)

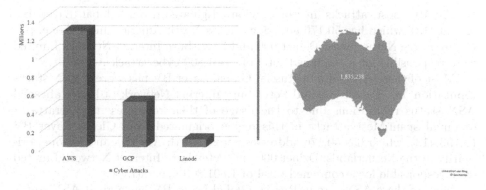

Fig. 8. Attack distribution by CSP - Sydney

Sydney ranked third in terms of cyber-attack data, with a total of 1,835,338 attacks. As shown in Fig. 8, AWS experienced 68.61% of attacks with a total value of 1,259,064. Then GCP and Linode followed with 492,053 and 84,121 respectively.

The value for Linode in the Sydney region was the lowest among all regions examined in the study.

4.7   Attack Distribution by Cloud Service Provider - Tokyo (Japan)

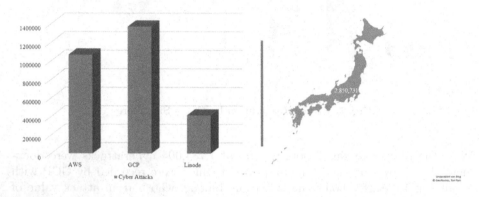

Fig. 9. Attack distribution by CSP - Tokyo

As shown in Fig. 9, Tokyo had the greatest number of cyberattacks with a total value of 2,850,731. GCP had the highest number of attacks in the region, with a total value of 1,370,793, followed by AWS with a total value of 1,067,223.

Linode, like the other regions, had the fewest attacks with a total value of 412,715.

4.8   Top ASN Source Attacks

In Fig. 10, most attacks in this region originated from Global Layer BV (2,193,413), which has 50,176 addresses across North America and Europe, primarily in the Netherlands. Dzinet 000 and Petersburg Internet Network Limited were responsible for a combined total of 1,601,800 cyberattacks.

Most of these ASNs are in Russia. Global Layer BV has a great ASN status reputation, but Dzinet 000 and Petersburg Internet Network Ltd have abysmal ASN status reputations due to the usage of their resources in cyberattacks or email spam.Most attacks in this region originated from Global Layer BV (2,193,413), which has 50,176 addresses across North America and Europe, primarily in the Netherlands. Dzinet 000 and Petersburg Internet Network Limited were responsible for a combined total of 1,601,800 cyberattacks.

Most of these ASNs are in Russia. Global Layer BV has a great ASN status reputation, but Dzinet 000 and Petersburg Internet Network Ltd have abysmal ASN status reputations due to the usage of their resources in cyberattacks or email spam.

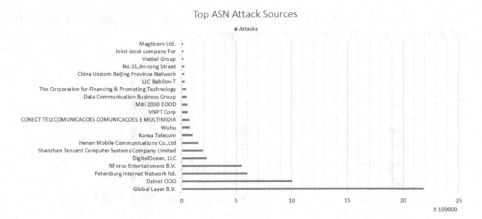

Fig. 10. Top ASN source attacks

4.9 Top Country Source Attacks

Contrary to research studies, most of the attack traffic emanated from Ireland (2,195,147), Russia (1,906,912), and China (982,053) as shown in Fig. 11. Some attackers hide their origin to prevent detection by utilising compromised hosts, hence the sources of attacks may be false positives. Additionally, VPNs can be utilised to mask attack sources and promote backbone hopping.

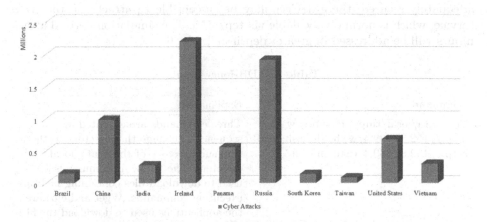

Fig. 11. Top county source attacks

4.10 Source OS Attack Distribution

Most operating systems utilised in the attack were a combination of Linux and Windows-based systems as shown in Fig. 12. Most attacks sourced from Windows 7 or 8, followed by Linux kernel versions 3.11 and higher. These Windows 7 or 8 hosts are potentially compromised hosts that are being used as attack pivots.

After the end of support, several Windows OS types are vulnerable to exploitation due to the lack of security updates.

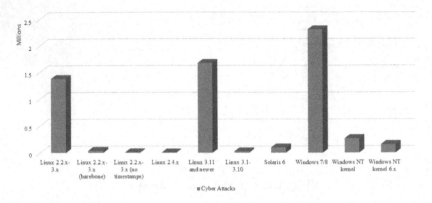

Fig. 12. Source OS attack distribution

4.11   Adbhoney Inputs

By default, attackers can weaponize the Android Debug Bridge, which helps developers debug Android applications. Other IoT products, such as smart TVs, smart refrigerators, and smart automobiles, utilise Android-compatible mother-boards at present. Multiple of these IoT gadgets operate on Android. If not adequately secured, these devices may be susceptible to attacks on the ADB service, which is normally available via tcp/5555. The simulation-derived attack inputs will be addressed in greater depth in Table. 6.

Table 6. ADBHoney Inputs

Command	Explanation
Cd /data/local/tmp/; busybox wget http://152.89.239.4/w.sh; sh w.sh; curl http://152.89.239.4/c.sh; sh c.sh	Three commands are executed in sequence to change the directory to the tmp subdirectory of the /data/local directory. The following commands are used to download files containing malware execution commands. Wget and curl are the applications used to download the files
Rm -rf /data/local/tmp/*	A command that ensures that the temporary directory is completely empty. This command completely deletes the contents of the temp folder
Chmod 0755 /data/local/tmp/nohup	This command grants everyone read and execute access, but only the owner of the file nohup in the temp folder has write access

4.12   Cowrie Inputs

The cowrie honeypot, which emulates the telnet and ssh protocols, gathered interesting inputs which are explained into detail in Table. 7

Table 7. Cowrie Inputs

Command	Explanation
Enable	This command is used in Cisco device configurations to enter global configuration mode. An attacker might believe that the vulnerable ssh or telnet port was connected to a network device
Uname - a	This command (Unix Name) displays critical system information such as the operating system kernel name, hostname, kernel release, machine architecture, and details about the operating system
Config terminal	This command enters Global mode on Cisco network devices, allowing the user to create system-wide resources
Cat/proc/cpuinfo — grep name — wc -l	This command displays the number of CPUs installed on a Linux host. This is merely a reconnaissance phase
Crontab -l	This displays a list of commands that are scheduled to execute at a specified time
W	This command is used to display logged-in user information on Linux distributions. User, tty, source connection, and login time etc

5   Conclusion

Using honeypots, we have undertaken a comparative investigation of cyber attacks against cloud systems, including Google Cloud Compute, Linode, and Amazon Web Services. We also revealed that the Linode Cloud Service is the least vulnerable to attack across all four regions examined in this study. Our analysis also delivers cyberspace-awareness-related information that is valuable to its stakeholders.

Our future work will incorporate additional Cloud Service Providers and locations, as well as the extending of the simulation time across all CSPs for a more comprehensive examination. In addition, we plan to employ high-interaction honeypots in future simulations to further deduce the patterns and sequences of attacks.

References

1. Bove, D., Muller, T.: Investigating characteristics of attacks on public cloud systems. In: Proceedings - 6th IEEE International Conference on Cyber Security and Cloud Computing CSCloud 2019 5th IEEE International Conference on Edge Computing Scalable Cloud, EdgeCom 2019, pp. 89–94 (2019). https://doi.org/10.1109/CSCloud/EdgeCom.2019.00-13

2. Dillon, T., Wu, C., Chang, E.: Cloud computing: issues and challenges. In: Proceedings - International Conference Advanced Information Networking Applications AINA, pp. 27–33 (2010). https://doi.org/10.1109/AINA.2010.187

3. Fraunholz, D., Pohl, F., Schotten, H.D.: Towards basic design principles for high- and medium-interaction honeypots. In: European Conference Information Warfare Security ECCWS, pp. 120–126 (2017)

4. Hackett, R.: Data breach exposes 123 million U.S. Households (2017)

5. Hurst, A.: Global public cloud end-user spending to grow 20.4% in 2022 - gartner (2022)

6. Iqbal, S., et al.: On cloud security attacks: a taxonomy and intrusion detection and prevention as a service. **08**, 016 (2016). https://doi.org/10.1016/j.jnca.2016

7. Kelly, C., et al.: A comparative analysis of honeypots on different cloud platforms. Sensors **21**(7), 2433 (2021). https://doi.org/10.3390/s21072433

8. Khan, I., Durad, H., Alam, M.: Data analytics layer for high-interaction honeypots. In: Proceedings 2019 16th International Bhurban Conference on Applied Sciences and Technology IBCAST 2019, pp. 681–686 (2019). https://doi.org/10.1109/IBCAST.2019.8667132

9. La, Q.D., et al.: Deceptive attack and defense game in honeypot-enabled networks for the internet of things. IEEE Internet Things J. **3**(6), 1025–1035 (2016). https://doi.org/10.1109/JIOT.2016.2547994

10. Marston, S., et al.: Cloud computing - the business perspective. Decis. Support Syst. **51**(1) 176–189 (2011). https://doi.org/10.1016/j.dss.2010.12.006

11. Al-Mohannadi, H., Awan, I., Al Hamar, J.: Analysis of adversary activities using cloud-based web services to enhance cyber threat intelligence. Ser. Oriented Comput. Appl. **14**(3), 175–187 (2020). https://doi.org/10.1007/s11761-019-00285-7

12. Morag, A.: Exploitable hosts used in cloud native cyber attacks. Netw. Secur. **2020**(10), 6–10 (2020). https://doi.org/10.1016/S1353-4858(20)30116-1

13. Nawrocki, M., Wählisch, M., Schmidt, T.C., Keil, C., Schönfelder, J.: A survey on honeypot software and data analysis. arXiv:1608.06249 (2016)

14. Paradise, A., et al.: Creation and management of social network honeypots for detecting targeted cyber attacks. IEEE Trans. Comput. Soc. Syst. **4**(3) 65–79 (2017). https://doi.org/10.1109/TCSS.2017.2719705

15. Promise R., Twum, F.: Mitigating computer attacks in a corporate network using honeypots: a case study of ghana education service. Int. J. Comput. Appl. **180**(32), 18–22 (2018). https://doi.org/10.5120/ijca2018916836. http://www.ijcaonline.org/archives/volume180/number32/agbedanu-2018-ijca-916836.pdf

16. Sahoo, S., et al.: A stealth cyber-attack detection strategy for dc microgrids. IEEE Trans. Power Electron. **34**(8), 8162–8174 (2019). https://doi.org/10.1109/TPEL.2018.2879886

17. Sanders, C.: Intrusion detection honeypots : detection through deception, vol. 1, Chris Sanders, Oakwood, first edition (2020)

18. Sether, A.: Cloud computing benefits. SSRN Electron. J. (2016). https://doi.org/10.2139/ssrn.2781593

19. Shilpashree, S., Patil, R.R., Parvathi, C.: Cloud computing an overview. Int. J. Eng. Technol. **7**(4), 2743–2746 (2018)
20. Singh, A., Chatterjee, K.: Cloud security issues and challenges: a survey. J, Netw. Comput. Appl. **79**, 88–115 (2017)
21. Spitzner, L.: Honeypots: catching the insider threat. In: Proceedings - Annual Computer Security Applications Conference ACSAC 2003-Janua (Acsac), pp. 170–179 (2003). https://doi.org/10.1109/CSAC.2003.1254322
22. Tiwari, A., Kumar, D.: Comparitive study of various honeypot tools on the basis of their classification and features. SSRN Electron. J. 1556-5068 (2020). https://doi.org/10.2139/ssrn.3565078
23. Veena, R.C., Brahmananda, S.H.: Analysis of honeypot data utilizing elastic search for cyber threat intelligence. Int. J. Control Autom. **13**(2), 634–645 (2020)
24. Zakari, A., Lawan, A.A., Bekaroo, G.: Towards improving the security of low-interaction honeypots: insights from a comparative analysis. In: Fleming, P., Vyas, N., Sanei, S., Deb, K. (eds.) ELECOM 2016. LNEE, vol. 416, pp. 314–321. Springer, Cham (2017). https://doi.org/10.1007/978-3-319-52171-8_28
25. Zhuge, J.W., Tang, Y., Han, X.H., Duan, H.X.: Honeypot technology research and application. Ruan Jian Xue Bao/J. Softw. **24**(4), 825–842 (2013). https://doi.org/10.3724/SP.J.1001.2013.04369

Blockchain Technology and Application

AP-HBSG: Authentication Protocol for Heterogeneous Blockchain-Based Smart Grid Environment

Egide Nkurunziza[1]([✉]), Tandoh Lawrence[2], Elfadul Issameldeen[1], and Gervais Mwitende[3]

[1] School of Computer Science and Engineering, University of Electronic Science and Technology of China, Chengdu 611731, China
nkurunzizaegide@gmail.com
[2] University of Development Studies, Tamale, Ghana
[3] Pivot Access Ltd, Kigali, Rwanda

Abstract. In the past, more research has been undertaken on the security of the smart grid (SG), with the aim of securing the SG in a manner that takes into account devices with limited resources, e.g., smart meters (SM). Consequently, several protocols for authenticating communicating participants in the SG and safeguarding the transfer of their keys have been devised over the years. However, most existing protocols work in a homogeneous context, which means that different entities operate in the same cryptographic settings. In addition, the majority of them are subject to a single point of failure, meaning that if a central device fails, all connected devices fail as well. To mitigate the previously mentioned issues and maintain the security of the SG network, an authentication protocol for heterogeneous blockchain-based smart grid environment (AP-HBSG) is designed. In the first part, an anonymous and heterogeneous certificateless authentication protocol is designed to secure and execute the session key agreement process. In addition, one participant belongs to a certificateless public cryptography (CL-PKC) whereas the other participant belongs to a public key infrastructure (PKI). In the second part, a blind signature is used to add authentication security within the blockchain nodes. Besides, a random oracle model (ROM) is used for the security analysis of the proposed protocol and we prove that it is secure under discrete logarithm (DL) problem and computational Diffie-Hellman (CDH) problem. The performance analysis shows that our proposed protocol has a lower computational and communication cost than other recently proposed protocols.

Keywords: Heterogeneous · Authentication · Key agreement · Blockchain · Smart grid

1 Introduction

The conventional electricity grid is the result of rapid global urbanization and infrastructure development over the past century. Its architecture consists of

© The Author(s), under exclusive license to Springer Nature Singapore Pte Ltd. 2022
E. Ahene and F. Li (Eds.): FCS 2022, CCIS 1726, pp. 183–197, 2022.
https://doi.org/10.1007/978-981-19-8445-7_12

power generation, transmission, and distribution systems. It is hierarchical, whereby the electricity is from the power source and delivered to the customer/consumer at the bottom. The conventional grid does not have real-time data from the consumer. Despite the fact that the traditional electricity system has made a substantial contribution to the current country's development, there is a growing need to update it for various compelling reasons stated below. It contributes to environmental pollution. There is a gap between electricity production and the increasing demand for electricity [1].

Nevertheless, with the emerging smart grid (SG), the abovementioned difficulties that have plagued the electric power industry for decades will be effectively resolved. With the help of the SG, green energies like tides, wind, and solar power are integrated into the grid. These renewable energy sources contribute to lessening both environmental degradation and the expanding demand for electricity. Additionally, the SG has made it possible for customers and the utility company to have two-way communication. Besides, the smart meter is an essential device of the smart grid that collects customers' data, including how much electricity they consume, notifications for power outages and restorations, and remote power on and power off functionality, etc. These data are all transmitted to the service provider. After receiving the data, the service provider can plan the power production and balance the amount of electricity used during peak and off-peak hours [2].

The adversary can, however, eavesdrop on communications between the utility provider and the smart meter in order to obtain customers' secret information and learn about their daily routines, including whether the client is at home, and then plot a burglary attempt. [3]. A well-equipped attacker can also infiltrate the SG communication infrastructure and bring the entire system down, as in the case of the cyberattack on the Ukrainian power grid, which affected 225,000 customers. [4].

1.1   Motivation

Most designed authentication protocols are homogenous, meaning that the communicating entities share the same cryptographic settings. The majority of the protocols are susceptible to a single point of failure. In addition, several of them have high computing costs and are therefore unsuitable for devices with limited resources, such as smart meters in a smart grid. Moreover, they don't satisfy fundamental authentication and key agreement requirements, such as perfect forward secrecy. All of these challenges prompted us to design an authentication protocol for the heterogeneous blockchain-based smart grid (AP-HBSG) to avoid a single point of failure. Also, this suggested protocol enables entities with different cryptographic settings to communicate and guarantees basic security and privacy features for authentication and key agreement protocol.

1.2   Contribution

The contributions of the suggested AP-HBSG protocol are described in the subsequent part.

First, the suggested protocol is able to function in a heterogeneous environment, meaning it enables communication between entities with different cryptographic settings. In this proposed protocol, for instance, the smart meter uses certificateless public key cryptography (CL-PKC), whereas the Node M uses public key infrastructure (PKI).

Second, the proposed protocol offers mutual authentication and key agreement. Also, it can't be broken by attacks like man-in-the-middle, DoS, replay, and modification attacks. Additionally, a decentralized system is designed, and a consensus mechanism is introduced where the blockchain nodes need authorization from SM to use smart meter data. Moreover, a blind signature is used to introduce authentication from node M to the rest of the nodes.

Third, the designed protocol AP-HBSG is lightweight and does not strain the smart meter with intensive computations, as compared to the most recent related published protocol.

Fourth, The security of the provided protocol is evaluated using the random oracle model, and it is shown to be secure under the elliptic curve discrete logarithm (ECDL) problem and Computational Diffie-Hellman (CDH) problem.

1.3   Organization of the Paper

The remaining sections are organized as follows. The related work is presented in Sect. 2. The preliminary information is presented in Sect. 3. In Sect. 4, we presented the proposed protocol in full. Section 5 provides an exhaustive security analysis. In addition, Sect. 6 demonstrates the performance analysis of the suggested protocol. The conclusion to AP-HBSG is provided in Sect. 7 of our paper.

2   Related Work

According to the foregoing discussion, the privacy and security of the SG communication system must be safeguarded against malevolent agents. Therefore, presenting authentication and communication protocols is a fascinating topic that has attracted considerable scholarly interest. In 2011, Fouda et al. [5] came up with a scheme for key sharing and authentication that uses Diffie-Hellman exchange and a hash-based authentication code. They stated that their system has reduced latency and fewer message exchanges. Moreover, they assert that their method meets the fundamental requirements for the SG communication architecture. Wu and Zhou [6] suggested a robust, secure key management system based on public key settings and the Needham-Schroeder authentication system. In addition, it employs a rigorous one-time usage rule and on-the-fly key generation to prevent certain problems with session keys. Xia and Wang [7] came up with a scheme for a secure key distribution for the smart grid so that SG network connectivity could be kept secure. They did a cryptanalysis of Wu and Zhou's proposed protocol and showed that it can be completely destroyed by a man-in-the-middle attack. The scheme provided is secure against the afore-mentioned issue. Additionally, it can facilitate the duplication of a third party during power outages. Part et al. [8] investigated the security of a protocol proposed by Xia and Wang and determined that it is susceptible to the unknown key share attack. In addition, they asserted that the heuristic analysis employed against this attack is invalid. In addition, they found that the responder to initiator communication can be impersonated. Tsai and Lo [9] proposed a novel key distribution scheme for the smart grid. The developed scheme combines identity-based signature and identity-based encryption to provide anonymity for the SM and mutual authentication between the SM and the service provider (SP). Using a single private key, an SM can also get services from an SP anonymously and without the help of a trusted third party (TTP). Odelu et al. [10] conducted a cryptanalysis on Tsai and Lo's scheme and concluded that it does not meet the requirements for secret key (SK) security and credential privacy for SM. They have therefore presented a new scheme that satisfies the aforementioned security requirements. Also, their scheme enables smart grid key agreement and authentication. In 2018, Mahmood et al. [11] proposed an authentication scheme to safeguard smart grid communication infrastructure. They assert that their scheme is secure against replay, impersonation, insider, and man-in-the-middle attacks. Furthermore, their scheme provides perfect forward secrecy and mutual authentication. Abbasinezhad and Nikooghadam [12] demonstrated in the same year that Mahmood et al.'s scheme had security flaws, i.e., once ephemeral secrets are leaked, the private key and shared session key of the participants can be easily compromised. In response, they proposed an authentication scheme capable of addressing the aforementioned problems. Chen et al. [13] discovered faults in [11,12] in 2019. The first does not provide perfect forward secrecy and private key privacy, whereas the second does not withstand replay attacks. In addition, they have presented an authentication system that eliminates the aforementioned issue. Li et al. [14] have suggested a new message authentication scheme, which they assert is anonymous and provably secure. They asserted that their scheme satisfies essential security requirements for SG, such as impersonation attack resistance. In addition, the proposed protocol guarantees forward secrecy and is resistant to tracking attacks. In 2019, Wu et al. [15] discovered that Li et al.'s scheme is unable to provide mutual authentication and cannot withstand denial of service and impersonation attacks. Then, they proposed an anonymous and efficient authentication scheme capable of mitigating the aforementioned flaws. Besides, in 2021 Wu et al. [16] perform cryptanalysis on Chen et al. [13] and discover that it contains several flaws, including known session-specific temporary information attacks and impersonation attacks. The security evaluation was carried out using the CK adversary model. Then, they proposed an alternative authentication scheme that is more robust and resistant to the aforementioned vulnerabilities. Nkurunziza et al. [17] presented an authentication protocol for smart grid entities in 2021 that employs blockchain and elliptic curve. The designed protocol satisfies the requirements for authentication and key agreement between smart grid communication architectures.

2.1 Blockchain Overview

In 2008, an unknown person identified as Satoshi Nakomoto invented a blockchain system [18]. Initially, it was invented for decentralized digital money, called Bitcoin. From that time, people did further researches to see other areas of its application [19], and they developed several other blockchain-based applications, e.g., Ethereum [18]. Actually, a blockchain is described as a database that deploys peer-to-peer networks for nodes communication, and it utilizes cryptographic technology for security. Additionally, blockchain has an important feature called consensus mechanism, which enables each node that is engaged in the network to agree on the ledger's modification. Nodes in blockchain store and write transactions in a decentralized manner without third party intervention. The blockchain has a ledger where transactions are written down, and it can be simulated to a company's book where all financial transactions are recorded. The newly created transaction is considered valid by every node after verifying if the right signature is applied to it. Then, the verified transactions are compiled in a block by nodes, which participated in the mining process [20]. Nodes that participated in the mining process are named miners. The reader can check Fig. 1 to understand the basic functionality of blockchain, and six steps are used to explain it. The main advantages of blockchain technology are decentralization, verifiability, immutability, and consensus mechanisms [19,21].

2.2 Traditional AMI Communication Settings and Proposed Blockchain-Based Settings

Bidirectional information exchange in the SG is enabled by the advanced metering infrastructure (AMI) [22]. This makes AMI an important part of the SG. In AMI communication, there is a crucial component named MDMS, which is a database that performs a permanent storage of data and processes data from smart meter. MDMS works in a centralized environment [22,23], where it connects and serves the outage management systems (OMS), geographical information systems (GIS), customer information systems (CIS), and distribution management systems (DMS). Nevertheless, the traditional architecture presents an inconvenience, when MDMS is broken, the dependent services are unavailable. This is caused by the centralized settings of the traditional system, as it is susceptible to a single point of failure and a single point of management. Consequently, a blockchain architecture is recommended as a solution to the aforementioned issue.

3 Preliminaries

In this section, we discuss elliptic curve cryptography (ECC) and the hard assumptions, followed by a list of notations used in our protocol.

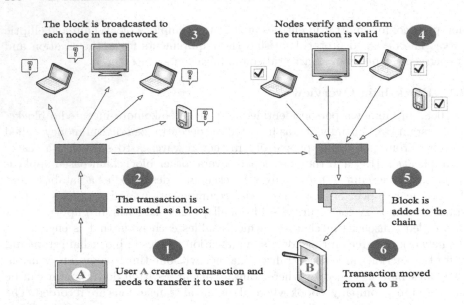

Fig. 1. Blockchain workflow.

3.1 Elliptic Curve Cryptography

Since its invention in 1986, ECC has attracted enterprises and academics with diverse perspectives, for example, designing protocols and proving security. ECC's primary benefit over related technologies such as RSA is its smaller key size. Consequently, it is utilized in components (e.g., smart meters) with restricted processing power, memory capacity, and bandwidth [24]. The equation for ECC is $E_p(a, b) : y^2 = x^3 + ax + b$ with a discriminant of $4a^3 + 27b^2 \neq 0$. This equation represents the elliptic curve over the prime field (E/F_p). The preceding equation is defined by $a, b \in F_p$, and the elliptic curve contains the points (x, y) and zero. The expression for scalar multiplication is $\kappa P = P + P + P + P + \cdots + P$ (κ times)), $\kappa \in Z_q^*$. As noticed, this form of the equation is a repeated addition of the point P on the elliptic curve.

3.2 Hard Assumptions

– **Definition 1.** ECDL problem assumption: Here we have elements $(P, V = wP)$ and w is randomly selected. Additionally, we suppose that G is a group with order q, where q is a large prime number and P is the group's generator. According to the ECDL problem, it is hard to derive w from V in polynomial time.

– **Definition 2.** CDH problem assumption: Here we have elements (P, bP, cP), where b and c are values chosen at random. Moreover, we assume that G is an additive group of order q, where q is a large prime number and P is the generator of the group. According to the CDH problem, it is impossible to calculate bcP.

3.3 Notations

The following table describes the AP-HBSG protocol's notations and their meanings.

3.4 Syntax

AP-HBSG consists of the three algorithms described below.

1. **Initialization:** In this phase, the registration center (RC) gets the security parameter φ as input. The RC produces a master secret key s along with the system public parameters prs. The RC keeps the secret master key s, whereas the prs is made public.
2. **Registration:** During this phase, SM submits ID_{sm} to RC, which then returns to SM the partial private key d_{sm}. On the other hand, node M provides its identity ID_m and public key PK_m to the RC, and then the RC generates a digital certificate $[Crt]$. Here, RC functions as key generation center (KGC) and certificate authority (CA).
3. **Authentication and session key agreement:** In this phase, the authentication algorithm is provided with SM's keys, which are PR_{sm} and PK_{sm}. Also, the secret key $sk = z$ and public key PK_m of node M are provided. The algorithm is then processed. If it returns true, SM and node M mutual authentication was successful. Otherwise, it terminates. After authentication is done successfully, the equal session keys $ek_{sm} = ek_m = ek_i$ are computed.

3.5 System Model

Our system model, consists of three components: the RC, SM, and node M. The SM and node M have to register with RC before initiating communication. Note that RC performs a function comparable to that of a KGC in a CL-PKC environment and a CA in PKI settings. For further explanation, node M is selected by the remaining nodes as a collector node based on the proof of work results among blockchain nodes. The remaining nodes, such as node U, node C, node V, and node W, represent mobile workers at various locations who can now access real-time outage information transmitted by smart meters. Moreover, the mobile personnel can find the outage and resolve the issue. In addition, smart meter notifications can inform them that the reported issue has been resolved before they leave the location. This architecture does not suffer from a single point of failure or a single point of management.

Table 1. Notations

Notation	Meaning
RC	Registration center
s	A master key of KGC
KGC	Key generation center
P_{pub}	A public key of KGC
CA	Certificate authority
d_{sm}	A partial private key of entity SM
SM	A smart meter
$r_{sm}, g_{sm}, a_{sm}, b_m$	Secret values
ID_{sm}	Identity of SM
$PR_{sm} = (g_{sm}, d_{sm})$	A full private key of SM
ID_m	Identity of node M
$PK_{sm} = (G_{sm}, R_{sm})$	A public key of SM
φ	Security parameter
G	A cyclic additive group
q	An order of group G
ek_i	A shared session key
P	A generator of G
TS	Time stamp
F_p	A prime field
Enc	Symetric encryption
E/F_p	An elliptic curve E over a prime field
Dec	Symetric decryption
$\oplus$	A system of binary computation XOR
prs	Public parameters
H_i	An ith Hash function
sk	secret key of node M
PK_m	public key of node M

3.6 Security Model

Before demonstrating the security of our protocol, we must create the security model. The CL-PKC adversarial model was initially suggested by Al-Riyami [25], who categorized adversaries as Type 1 adversary $\mathcal{A}_1$ and Type 2 adversary $\mathcal{A}_2$. $\mathcal{A}_1$ is considered an external adversary because he has no knowledge of any entity's master key or private key. Since there is no certificate utilized in CL-PKC, $\mathcal{A}_1$ can substitute any value for the public key of any entity. $\mathcal{A}_2$ is a malicious KGC since it has access to any entity's partial private key and possesses the master secret key. However, $\mathcal{A}_2$ cannot substitute any entity's public key. Several more researchers [26–28] contributed to and worked on the formal security model CL-PKC. Moreover, Huang et al. [28] have categorized the two categories of adversaries into three security levels based on their attacking strength: normal, strong, and super adversary. The technique that resists super adversaries is superior to the other two since it can also endure attacks from normal and strong enemies. In addition, the CL-PKC approach, which is only effective against attacks from normal adversaries, is impractical for the IoT internet. In contrast, a number of authentication and key agreement security models [29–31] are created. Additionally, we have chosen security model [32] by Wu et al. since it is suitable to our protocol. Since it is certificateless, our protocol is robust to attacks from both $\mathcal{A}_1$ and $\mathcal{A}_2$ adversaries. In the following part, we illustrate the security of the proposed protocol using two games. Θ_i^k represents the instance k of the entity i.

Game 1: This game comprises two players: the challenger $\mathbb{C}_1$ and the Type 1 adversary $\mathcal{A}_1$. Described below is the communication between the two parties:

- **Setup.** $\mathbb{C}_1$ conducts a setup algorithm to generate the master secret key msk and the prs, then retains s and transmits prs to $\mathcal{A}_1$.
- **Query** (ID_i): $\mathcal{A}_1$ submits queries to the following oracles of his or her choosing.
- **Create-user** (ID_i): When $\mathbb{C}_1$ gets this query on ID_i, it contacts C^{lst} and then verifies that ID_i has been created. Then, $\mathbb{C}_1$ executes the subsequent algorithm: Extract-Partial-Private Key to get d_i, Extract-Private Key to get $PR_i = (d_i, g_i)$, and Request-Public Key to get $PK_i = (G_i, R_i)$. In addition, $\mathbb{C}_1$ adds (ID_i, d_i, g_i, PK_i) tuple to a C^{lst} and outputs PK_i to $\mathcal{A}_1$ (We suppose other queries follow the created query).
- **Extract-Partial-Private-Key** (ID_i): $\mathcal{A}_1$ is capable of deducing a partial private key for any ID_i outside that of the target identity ID_I. $\mathbb{C}_1$ calculates the associated partial private key d_i and returns it to $\mathcal{A}_1$.
- **Extract-Private-Key** (ID_i): $\mathcal{A}_1$ is capable of deducing a private key for any ID_i, excluding the identity ID_I of the target. $\mathbb{C}_1$ generates the related private key PR_i and forwards it to $\mathcal{A}_1$.
- **Request-Public Key** (ID_i): $\mathcal{A}_1$ is capable of requesting a public key for any ID_i besides the target identity ID_I. $\mathbb{C}_1$ computes the related public key PK_i and transmits it back to $\mathcal{A}_1$.
- **Replace-Public Key** (ID_i, PK_i'): The adversary $\mathcal{A}_1$ possesses the capacity to replace the original public key PK_i with the new public key PK_i'.
- **Send** (Θ_i^k, M): This send query mimics the active attack. According to the proposed protocol, when $\mathbb{C}_1$ receives message M from $\mathcal{A}_1$, the challenger performs calculations and delivers responses to $\mathcal{A}_1$.
- **Reveal** (Θ_i^k, M): This type of query allows $\mathcal{A}_1$ to obtain the session key ek_i. Adversary submits a request to reveal the session key if the oracle accepts ek_i is transmitted to $\mathcal{A}_1$, else $\perp$ is returned.
- **Corrupt** (ID_i): $\mathcal{A}_1$ transmits a demand for the private key of the entity i identified as ID_i, and $\mathbb{C}_1$ responds with the private key.
- **Test** (Θ_i^k): The purpose of this query is to evaluate the semantic security of the session key. When $\mathcal{A}_1$ presents the test query to $\mathbb{C}_1$, the challenger selects a random bit $b \in \{0,1\}$ if $b = 1$ sends ek_i to $\mathcal{A}_1$. Otherwise, $\mathbb{C}_1$ generates a random string and sends it to $\mathcal{A}_1$.

Game 2. This game requires two parties: the challenger $\mathbb{C}_2$ and the super Type 2 adversary $\mathcal{A}_2$. The following describes their interaction:

- **Setup:** Similar to the first game, $\mathbb{C}_2$ creates the master secret key msk and prs using the setup algorithm. Then, $\mathbb{C}_2$ transmits prs and msk to $\mathcal{A}_2$.
- **Query:** $\mathcal{A}_2$ conducts the next oracle queries in accordance with his or her intentions. Create-user(ID_i) query, Extract-Private-Key (ID_i) query, Request-Public Key (ID_i) query, Send (Θ_i^k, M) query, Reveal (Θ_i^k, M) query, Corrupt (ID_i) query and Test (Θ_i^k) query. Moreover, $\mathbb{C}_2$ replies to queries identically to game 1.

As a guess for the value of b in the test query, the adversary $\mathcal{A}_2$ returns b'. The value of b can be accurately guessed by $\mathcal{A}_2$ with $\mathrm{Adv}(\mathcal{A}_2) = |\Pr[b' = b] - 1/2|$ probability. In addition, $\mathcal{A}_2$ has the capacity to perform Extract-Partial-Private-Key queries at any time, but cannot perform Replace-Public-Key queries on the target identity ID_I. $\mathcal{A}_2$ can do the following queries based on the key exchange properties without authentication [33]: Send, Reveal, Corrupt, and Test queries. Respectively, adversaries $\mathcal{A}_1$ and $\mathcal{A}_2$ are able to execute queries under adaptive chosen message attacks [34]. A reader can check [35] for additional information on mutual authentication and key exchange.

Definition 3. If no polynomially-bounded adversary $\mathcal{A}_1$ has a non-negligible advantage ε in game 1, $\mathcal{A}_1$ has no capacity to build a valid login message $\mathcal{M}_1$ without accessing the KGC's master key s. This means that the authentication check could not be passed.

Definition 4. If no polynomially-bounded adversary $\mathcal{A}_2$ has a non-negligible advantage ε in game 2, $\mathcal{A}_2$ has no capacity to build a valid login message $\mathcal{M}_1$ without accessing the smart meter's secret value g_{sm}. This means that the authentication check could not be passed.

3.7   Design Goal

The design goal is to achieve anonymity, mutual authentication, man-in-the-middle attack resistance, modification attack resistance, modification attack resistance, key agreement, perfect forward secrecy, DoS attack resistance, key escrow, key control, replay attack, ephemeral secret attacks, and key compromise impersonation attacks.

4   Proposed Protocol

We have two parts in this section. In the first part, we presented a heterogeneous certificateless authentication scheme. In this part, we describe how SM and node M authenticate each other and then exchange a session key. It consists of three steps: initialization, registration, and authentication. In the second part, we utilized blind signature with message recovery [36] for authenticating node M to the rest of the nodes.

4.1   Heterogeneous Certificateless Authentication Scheme

- **Initialization:** RC collects preliminary parameters, specifically the $E_p(a, b)$ elliptic curve, during the initialization step. Then, a point P is selected as a generator alongside a hash function $H_i : \{0,1\}^* \to Z_q^*$ $i = \{1, 2, 3, 4, 5, 6\}$. In addition, RC chooses $s \in Z_q^*$ as the master key and generates the public key $P_{pub} = sP$. RC finally outputs $prs = (E_p(a, b), P, H_i)$.

- **Registration:** Before engaging in data exchange, SM and node M have to register with RC. Entity SM sends its identity ID_{sm} to RC for registration. RC computes $R_{sm} = r_{sm}P$, where $r_{sm} \in Z_q^*$ is chosen at random, and also computes the hash function $h_1 = H_1(ID_{sm}, R_{sm})$. R_{sm} represents the partial public key for SM. Also, $d_{sm} = r_{sm} + sh_1 \pmod{q}$ is the partial private key for SM. Furthermore, SM calculates its private key $PR_{sm} = (g_{sm}, d_{sm})$. The SM public key is also calculated as $PK_{sm} = (G_{sm}, R_{sm})$, and $G_{sm} = g_{sm}P$. Moreover, $g_{sm} \in Z_q^*$ is the secret value for SM, and it is determined at random. On the other side, node M selects $z \in Z_q^*$, establishes the secret key $sk = z$, and computes $PK_m = zP$. Then, node M transmits its identity ID_m and public key PK_m to the RC. The RC generates the Crt and transmits it to node M. In this instance, the RC uses the elliptic curve digital algorithm (ECDSA) [37] to generate the Crt, which is a recommended method. Remember that Crt can be transmitted on a public channel.

- **Authentication and session key sharing** In this step, SM and node M share a session secret key. However, prior to this step, SM and node M must authenticate each other. In addition, SM calculates $B_{sm} = a_{sm}P$ and $A_{sm} = a_{sm}PK_m$, where $a_{sm} \in Z_q^*$ is chosen at random. Note that SM computes B_{sm} and A_{sm} offline. The SM then calculates the hash functions $h_2 = H_2(ID_{sm}, A_{sm}, B_{sm}, PK_{sm}, TS, P_{pub})$ and $h_3 = H_3(ID_{sm}, A_{sm}, B_{sm}, PK_{sm}, TS, P_{pub}, h_2)$. In addition, the signature $\eta = a_{sm}^{-1}(h_2g_{sm} + h_3d_{sm}) \bmod q$ and symmetric encryption $c = (ID_{sm} \| B_{sm} \| \eta \| TS) \oplus H_4(A_{sm})$ are computed. At the end, SM transmits the message $\mathcal{M}_1 = \{B_{sm}, c\}$ to node M over a public channel.
  Node M computes $A_m = zB_{sm}$ upon receiving the message $\mathcal{M}_1$ from SM and retrieves $ID_{sm} \| B_{sm} \| \eta \| TS = c \oplus H_4(A_m)$. In addition, it computes the hash functions $h_1 = H_1(ID_{sm}, R_{sm})$, $h_2 = H_2(ID_{sm}, A_m, B_{sm}, PK_{sm}, TS, P_{pub})$, and $h_3 = H_3(ID_{sm}, A_m, B_{sm}, PK_{sm}, TS, P_{pub}, h_2)$ and verifies if $\eta B_{sm} = h_2G_{sm} + h_3(R_{sm} + h_1P_{pub})$ holds, else terminates. In addition, node M computes $B_m = b_mP$ and $\Lambda = B_{sm}b_m$, where $b_m \in Z_q^*$ is chosen at random. node M computes the session secret key $ek_m = H_5(ID_{sm} \| ID_m \| A_m \| \Lambda)$, the instances $v = H_4(A_m)$, and $\omega = Enc_v(H_6(ID_m \| B_m \| A_m))$. Finally, node M sends $\mathcal{M}_2 = \{ID_m, B_m, \omega\}$ to SM through a public channel.
  Upon receiving $\mathcal{M}_2$, SM calculates $v = H_4(A_{sm})$ and $Dec_v(\omega)$, and then verifies that $H_6(ID_m^t \| B_m^t \| A_m) = H_6(ID_m \| B_m \| A_m)$ holds. If true, the message $\mathcal{M}_2$ is from node M and its contents have not been altered during transmission. Here, ID_m^t and B_m^t are received as plaintext on the public channel. Additionally, SM calculates $\Lambda = B_ma_{sm}$ and $ek_{sm} = H_5(ID_{sm} \| ID_m \| A_m \| \Lambda)$. The shared session secret key consists of the elements $ek_{sm} = ek_m = ek_i$.

Correctness

In the following equations, we prove the consistency of signature computations.

$$\eta B_{sm} = a_{sm}^{-1}(h_2 g_{sm} + h_3 d_{sm}) B_{sm}$$
$$= a_{sm}^{-1}(h_2 g_{sm} + h_3 d_{sm}) a_{sm} P$$
$$= (h_2 g_{sm} + h_3 d_{sm}) P$$
$$= h_2 g_{sm} P + h_3 d_{sm} P$$
$$= h_2 G_{sm} + h_3 (r_{sm} + h_1 s) P$$
$$= h_2 G_{sm} + h_3 (r_{sm} P + h_1 s P)$$
$$= h_2 G_{sm} + h_3 (R_{sm} + h_1 P_{pub})$$

4.2 Authentication Scheme from Collector Node to Other Blockchain Nodes

The description that follows pertains to a blind signature with message recovery [36]. This is used to verify node M with the other nodes. Details about the blind signature is left off due to page limitations.

4.3 Consensus Mechanism in Blockchain Nodes

Using the computed shared session key ek_{sm}, SM sends an encrypted message $ME = ENC_{ek_{sm}}(m)$ to node M as a consensus message. Hence, if node M is able to decrypt $m = DEC_{ek_m}(ME)$ using ek_m, hence it is authorized to use the data. Furthermore, node M uses the signature [36] for authentication then consensus message m is broadcasted to the blockchain nodes. Moreover, blockchain nodes can verify the originality of the consensus message, then insert m into their ledger.

5 Analysis of the Proposed Protocol

In comparison to existing protocols, we analyze the proposed protocol's security, communication, and computational efficiency.

5.1 Security Analysis

Due to page limitations, details about both formal and informal analysis are left off.

6 Performance Analysis

Recent related schemes MCNKLS [11], CMCL [13], LWKXSC [14], WWZH [15], and WLCTA [16] are chosen to be compared with the proposed scheme AP-HBSG. The comparison is based on security features (Table 2), computation costs, and communication costs (Table 3). Due to page limitations, details about how computation and communication costs are obtained are left off.

F1: Provides Anonymity. F2: Provides mutual authentication. F3: Resists Man-in-the-middle attack resistance. F4: Free from key escrow problem.

Table 2. Protocol security features comparison

Scheme	F1	F2	F3	F4
MCNKLS [11]	✗	✓	✓	✗
CMCL [13]	✗	✓	✓	✓
LWKXSC [14]	✓	✓	✗	✓
WWZH [15]	✓	✓	✓	✗
WLCTA [16]	✗	✓	✓	✓
Ours	✓	✓	✓	✓

Table 3. Costs of computation and communication are compared.

Protocols	Computation costs (ms)	Communication costs (bytes)	Messages rounds
MCNKLS [11]	$5T_m = 67.5$	438	2
CMCL [13]	$4T_m + 1T_{bp} + 1T_{sh} = 113.5$	389	2
LWKXSC [14]	$4T_{exp} = 63.2$	308	2
WWZH [15]	$4T_{exp} = 63.2$	268	2
WLCTA [16]	$6T_m + 2T_{bp} + T_{sh} = 157.9$	568	2
Ours	$3T_{pm} = 40.5$	214	2

7 Conclusion

We have proposed the AP-HBSG protocol. It enabled two heterogeneous systems to communicate. The smart meter in the CL-PKC environment and the node M in PKI settings. Next, the proposed protocol has less computation cost in comparison with the recent related protocol. Moreover, the basic requirements such as mutual authentication and key agreement are provided.

Acknowledgment. This work is supported by the Sichuan Science and Technology Program (grant no. 2021YFG0157).

References

1. Farhangi, H.: The path of the smart grid. IEEE Power Energ. Mag. **8**(1), 18–28 (2009)
2. Guan, Z., Zhang, Y., Zhu, L., Wu, L., Yu, S.: Effect: an efficient flexible privacy-preserving data aggregation scheme with authentication in smart grid. Sci. Chin. Inf. Sci. **62**(3), 1–14 (2019)
3. Fan, C.I., Huang, S.Y., Lai, Y.L.: Privacy-enhanced data aggregation scheme against internal attackers in smart grid. IEEE Trans. Industr. Inf. **10**(1), 666–675 (2013)
4. Case, D.U.: Analysis of the cyber attack on the ukrainian power grid. Electricity Inf. Sharing Anal. Cent. (E-ISAC) **388**, 1–29 (2016)

5. Fouda, M.M., Fadlullah, Z.M., Kato, N., Lu, R., Shen, X.S.: A lightweight message authentication scheme for smart grid communications. IEEE Trans. Smart Grid **2**(4), 675–685 (2011)
6. Wu, D., Zhou, C.: Fault-tolerant and scalable key management for smart grid. IEEE Trans. Smart Grid **2**(2), 375–381 (2011)
7. Xia, J., Wang, Y.: Secure key distribution for the smart grid. IEEE Trans. Smart Grid **3**(3), 1437–1443 (2012)
8. Park, J.H., Kim, M., Kwon, D.: Security weakness in the smart grid key distribution scheme proposed by Xia and Wang. IEEE Trans. Smart Grid **4**(3), 1613–1614 (2013)
9. Tsai, J.L., Lo, N.W.: Secure anonymous key distribution scheme for smart grid. IEEE Trans. Smart Grid **7**(2), 906–914 (2015)
10. Odelu, V., Das, A.K., Wazid, M., Conti, M.: Provably secure authenticated key agreement scheme for smart grid. IEEE Trans. Smart Grid **9**(3), 1900–1910 (2016)
11. Mahmood, K., Chaudhry, S.A., Naqvi, H., Kumari, S., Li, X., Sangaiah, A.K.: An elliptic curve cryptography based lightweight authentication scheme for smart grid communication. Futur. Gener. Comput. Syst. **81**, 557–565 (2018)
12. Abbasinezhad-Mood, D., Nikooghadam, M.: Design and hardware implementation of a security-enhanced elliptic curve cryptography based lightweight authentication scheme for smart grid communications. Futur. Gener. Comput. Syst. **84**, 47–57 (2018)
13. Chen, Y., Martínez, J.F., Castillejo, P., López, L.: A bilinear map pairing based authentication scheme for smart grid communications: Pauth. IEEE Access **7**, 22633–22643 (2019)
14. Li, X., Wu, F., Kumari, S., Xu, L., Sangaiah, A.K., Choo, K.K.R.: A provably secure and anonymous message authentication scheme for smart grids. J. Parallel Distrib. Comput. **132**, 242–249 (2019)
15. Wu, L., Wang, J., Zeadally, S., He, D.: Anonymous and efficient message authentication scheme for smart grid. Secur. Commun. Netw. **2019**, 4836016 (2019)
16. Wu, T.-Y., Lee, Y.-Q., Chen, C.-M., Tian, Y., Al-Nabhan, N.A.: An enhanced pairing-based authentication scheme for smart grid communications. Journal of Ambient Intelligence and Humanized Computing **2021**, 1–13 (2021). https://doi.org/10.1007/s12652-020-02740-2
17. Nkurunziza, E., Mwitende, G., Tandoh, L., Li, F.: Certificateless authentication and consensus for the blockchain-based smart grid. In: Cao, C., Zhang, Y., Hong, Y., Wang, D. (eds.) FCS 2021. CCIS, vol. 1558, pp. 134–151. Springer, Singapore (2022). https://doi.org/10.1007/978-981-19-0523-0_9
18. Crosby, M., Pattanayak, P., Verma, S., Kalyanaraman, V., et al.: Blockchain technology: beyond bitcoin. Appl. Innov. **2**(6–10), 71 (2016)
19. Ozyilmaz, K.R., Yurdakul, A.: Designing a blockchain-based IoT with Ethereum, swarm, and LoRa: the software solution to create high availability with minimal security risks. IEEE Consum. Electron. Mag. **8**(2), 28–34 (2019)
20. Huang, J., Kong, L., Chen, G., Wu, M.Y., Liu, X., Zeng, P.: Towards secure industrial IoT: blockchain system with credit-based consensus mechanism. IEEE Trans. Industr. Inf. **15**(6), 3680–3689 (2019)
21. Golosova, J., Romanovs, A.: The advantages and disadvantages of the blockchain technology. In: 2018 IEEE 6th Workshop on Advances in Information, Electronic and Electrical Engineering (AIEEE), pp. 1–6. IEEE (2018)
22. Strategy, N.M.G.: Advanced metering infrastructure. US Department of Energy Office of Electricity and Energy Reliability (2008)

23. Zhou, J., Hu, R.Q., Qian, Y.: Scalable distributed communication architectures to support advanced metering infrastructure in smart grid. IEEE Trans. Parallel Distrib. Syst. **23**(9), 1632–1642 (2012)
24. Koblitz, N.: Elliptic curve cryptosystems. Math. Comput. **48**(177), 203–209 (1987)
25. Al-Riyami, S.S., Paterson, K.G.: Certificateless public key cryptography. In: Laih, C.-S. (ed.) ASIACRYPT 2003. LNCS, vol. 2894, pp. 452–473. Springer, Heidelberg (2003). https://doi.org/10.1007/978-3-540-40061-5_29
26. Du, H., Wen, Q., Zhang, S., Gao, M.: A new provably secure certificateless signature scheme for internet of things. Ad Hoc Netw. **100**, 102074 (2020)
27. Huang, X., Mu, Y., Susilo, W., Wong, D.S., Wu, W.: Certificateless signature revisited. In: Pieprzyk, J., Ghodosi, H., Dawson, E. (eds.) ACISP 2007. LNCS, vol. 4586, pp. 308–322. Springer, Heidelberg (2007). https://doi.org/10.1007/978-3-540-73458-1_23
28. Huang, X., Mu, Y., Susilo, W., Wong, D.S., Wu, W.: Certificateless signatures: new schemes and security models. Comput. J. **55**(4), 457–474 (2012)
29. Canetti, R., Krawczyk, H.: Analysis of key-exchange protocols and their use for building secure channels. In: Pfitzmann, B. (ed.) EUROCRYPT 2001. LNCS, vol. 2045, pp. 453–474. Springer, Heidelberg (2001). https://doi.org/10.1007/3-540-44987-6_28
30. LaMacchia, B., Lauter, K., Mityagin, A.: Stronger security of authenticated key exchange. In: Susilo, W., Liu, J.K., Mu, Y. (eds.) ProvSec 2007. LNCS, vol. 4784, pp. 1–16. Springer, Heidelberg (2007). https://doi.org/10.1007/978-3-540-75670-5_1
31. Hassan, A., Eltayieb, N., Elhabob, R., Li, F.: An efficient certificateless user authentication and key exchange protocol for client-server environment. J. Ambient. Intell. Humaniz. Comput. **9**(6), 1713–1727 (2018)
32. Wu, T.Y., Tseng, Y.M.: An efficient user authentication and key exchange protocol for mobile client-server environment. Comput. Netw. **54**(9), 1520–1530 (2010)
33. Jakobsson, M., Pointcheval, D.: Mutual authentication for low-power mobile devices. In: Syverson, P. (ed.) FC 2001. LNCS, vol. 2339, pp. 178–195. Springer, Heidelberg (2002). https://doi.org/10.1007/3-540-46088-8_17
34. Choon, J.C., Hee Cheon, J.: An identity-based signature from gap Diffie-Hellman groups. In: Desmedt, Y.G. (ed.) PKC 2003. LNCS, vol. 2567, pp. 18–30. Springer, Heidelberg (2003). https://doi.org/10.1007/3-540-36288-6_2
35. Boneh, D., Franklin, M.: Identity-based encryption from the weil pairing. In: Kilian, J. (ed.) CRYPTO 2001. LNCS, vol. 2139, pp. 213–229. Springer, Heidelberg (2001). https://doi.org/10.1007/3-540-44647-8_13
36. James, S., Gayathri, N., Reddy, P.V.: Pairing free identity-based blind signature scheme with message recovery. Cryptography **2**(4), 29 (2018)
37. Johnson, D., Menezes, A., Vanstone, S.: The elliptic curve digital signature algorithm (ECDSA). Int. J. Inf. Secur. **1**(1), 36–63 (2001)

Blockchain-Based Patient-to-Patient Health Data Sharing

Sandro Amofa[1(✉)], Jianbin Gao[1], Maame Gyamfua Asante-Mensah[2,3],
Charles Roland Haruna[1,3], and Xia Qi[1]

[1] University of Electronic Science and Technology of China,
Chengdu, People's Republic of China
ikwame.amofa@gmail.com
[2] The Skolkovo Institute of Science and Technology, Moscow, Russia
[3] University of Cape Coast, Cape Coast, Ghana

Abstract. The Covid-19 pandemic catalyzed many exciting forms of health data sharing. Aside from the institution-to-institution health data sharing among cooperating institutions for research and discovery of insights in healthcare, individual-to-many and individual-to-individual health data sharing also came to the fore. However, the security risks involved here are substantial since health data disclosures can lead to privacy and security breaches or complications. In this research, we present a scheme to enable individuals to share details of medical experiences with other individuals or interested groups. Our system provides the sharing entities with anonymity and thus, facilitates rapid dissemination of empirical insights during public health emergencies like Covid-19.

Keywords: Blockchain · Health data sharing · Data protection · Privacy · Data control

1 Introduction

Researchers and key stakeholders will not soon forget the rapidity with which the Covid-19 pandemic spread across the globe, overwhelmed health authorities, and destabilized national economies [10, 12, 13, 22]. Though the SARS-CoV-2 variant is only one of several coronaviruses, it proved to be more virulent, with higher infection rates. Even industrialized countries with advanced and robust healthcare systems recorded higher death tolls [8]. The pandemic was notable for the scope and scale of collaborations between governments, health institutions and authorities, technology companies, and the general public. The partnership was evident in the number of contact tracing APIs released to aid developers craft solutions for the labor-intensive task of tracing contacts of a single infected individual [2, 21, 27]. As the pandemic slowly ends, fears of future public health crises involving more lethal strains of the virus abound [20, 25]. These fears raise significant concerns that researchers must address in preparation for speedy control of subsequent regional or global pandemics. The Covid-19 pandemic established new standards for Institution-to-Institution and Individual-to-Institution health data sharing to reduce infection rates and identify trends that helped control the virus' spread [9]. Thus, the attempt to prevent the spread of the pandemic through modern digital communications technology transformed sensitive personal data into a by-product of contemporary life and gave impetus to a new trend of Individual-to-Individual health data sharing. While this is not entirely novel, the many individuals who shared details of their infection and treatment with significant numbers via personal contact and online digital platforms [7] raised several hard questions regarding the privacy of individual location data and the security of personal health information. Thus, sharing health data has reached an inflection point that all stakeholders must manage diligently to reap benefits for already well-defined public and personal healthcare goals. Fortunately, healthcare applications already leverage rapid advancements in Internet of Things (IoT) technologies, Ubiquitous/Pervasive Computing, and their application to manage data-analytic architectures that facilitate the secure sharing of health data between willing participants [3]. However, important questions that emerge with this exploding form of health data sharing concern the privacy of individuals and the security of the data. The challenges are presented as below:

1. Allow patients to access data and experience from other patients while remaining anonymous,
2. Guarantee that input data actually comes from patients in the group,
3. Maintain a secure log of network actions for audit purposes, and
4. Prove identity of users in case of dispute.

First, an entity must establish an uncontested proof of associating an individual with a particular medical condition before sharing can be permitted. Second, the data must remain adequately secure before and after sharing as alteration can affect the utility of the data. And finally, there must be a valid mechanism that provides incontrovertible proof of details of sharing transactions. The sequence of events, requirements for security, and the non-repudiation of data transactions lend the management of such a situation to blockchain technology. The blockchain is a mechanism that encompasses a distributed system of networked peer nodes, a consensus protocol, and a cryptographically secure, continuously extending list of all transactions in the network [28].

This paper proposes a blockchain-based mechanism to facilitate secure individual-to-individual health data sharing. To participate in the system, the individuals first register in the system. They then receive unique identities for conducting data exchange transactions. A set of smart contracts are developed and deployed to automate some aspects of interactions in the system. The list of our main contributions is as follows:

1. We provide an architecture for securely sharing health data between individuals anonymously.
2. Using the secure architecture, we provide proof of an association between a given individual and a specified medical condition.
3. We provide the limitations of the architecture and the possible means of minimizing their effects.

After the brief introduction we proceed with Related Works, and continue with the Preliminaries of blockchain technology, smart contracts, and Bilinear Maps. After these we present the System Overview and Design which highlight the system entities and interactions. Consequently, a Discussion and Evaluation section presents the analysis and results of experiments. The last section presents a conclusion on the research.

2 Related Works

One challenge of modern healthcare is patient engagement and support to achieve the desired outcomes of improved health and better quality of life. Patient engagement can be facilitated by the quality of information received from trusted sources to aid decisions made for the management of chronic conditions like diabetes. This section considers some of the literature discussing health data sharing paradigms.

In this [5] research the authors are primarily interested in controlling data after it is shared with requesters. It focuses on secure health data sharing using smart contracts to automate the period for which the data can be accessed by the requesting party. It achieves security by combining user-generated acceptable use policies with smart contracts. However, while it does provide an architecture for the secure exchange, it does not provide rigorous mathematical proofs for any of the security mechanisms.

The authors in this research [15] identified privacy, risks minimization, data security, control, transparency, trust, and accountable use among the many barriers to information sharing. While the research reviewed empirical evidence for the patient's views and public attitudes toward health data sharing, it did not propose a method to address the privacy/security threats or advocate blockchain technology to address the trustless environment within which health data sharing usually occurs.

Here [14], the researchers admit the growing necessity of health data sharing and the challenges stakeholders have to address to make the data available and useful while keeping data and identities still secure. Although they analyse five key aspects of health data sharing, they do not focus their attention on individual-to-individual sharing. Again, they made no attempt at providing rigorous mathematical security for the positions they take in the research.

We also considered [1,4,6,24] for the their appreciation of health data sharing. Even though we agree with their perception of various paradigms they do not focus on individual-to-individual health data sharing. Although several researchers agree to the growing importance of health data sharing there are few proposals on secure, privacy-guaranteed health data sharing between individuals. The following sections present a scheme to secure the proposed sharing paradigm.

3 Preliminaries

This section presents brief description of the blockchain, smart contracts and the security foundations of our work.

3.1 Blockchain

The blockchain is a technology that combines a linked-list data structure with a consensus protocol on a peer-to-peer network environment. It was initially created to solve the double spending problem in the Bitcoin cryptocurrency. Each block b on the blockchain B can be viewed as a distinct list of individual transaction data. The blockchain maintains a continuously extending list of transactions such that each node stores duplicate copies of network-approved transactions. The blockchain record is permanent and

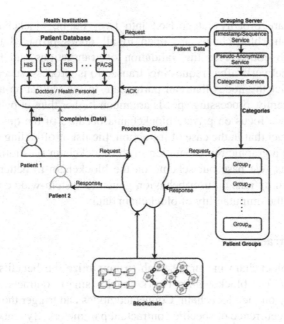

Fig. 1. A conceptual overview of the Patient-to-Patient Health Data Sharing.

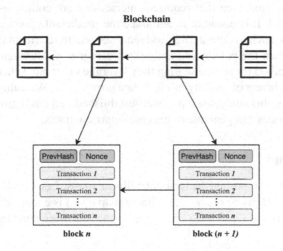

Fig. 2. A simplified view of the blockchain depicting the link between consecutive blocks.

obfuscated, and users can generate a unique account for each transaction to achieve convincing anonymity on the network. Nodes cooperate to validate transactions through a consensus protocol to maintain one consistent interpretation of events as the foundation for all subsequent transactions. This distinguishing feature of the blockchain makes its data longitudinal and suitable for managing transactions on patient health data.

Blockchains are broadly categorised into two: Public blockchains and Private blockchains. Public blockchains are open to all nodes provided they have sufficient resources to compete in the validation of transactions and transmit data to the blockchain network after requesting transactions process successfully. Private blockchains restrict the nodes that can participate in the validation and transmission process. Consequently, processing speeds are much higher than in public blockchains. In this research, we focus on private blockchains because of the quick processing of requests and the fact that in the case of infraction, the list of offending nodes is limited. Figure 2 provides a graphic representation of the blockchain illustrating the unbroken list of transactions. We base our scheme on the blockchain to better take advantage of preemptive assumptions on user behavior, generate system-wide consistent view of transactions, and the immutability of blockchain data.

3.2 Smart Contracts

We incorporate blockchain in our research to maximize the benefits of Smart Contract functionality. The blockchain network enables smart contracts: scripts that execute automatically on the blockchain. Connected nodes can trigger the execution of the scripts upon the occurrence of specific contractual parameters. By embedding desirable behaviors as responding scripts on the blockchain without specifying which node can execute it, we can guarantee that required interactions are collusion-resistant with a very high likelihood. It is essential to automate the predictable portions of health data sharing operations, such as data storage and requests, and to restrict manual interactions by anyone other than the patient and authorized caregivers. Although smart contracts are not the sole method for secure sharing they leverage other blockchain capabilities to provide additional layers of security through data provenance. We utilized the Ethereum blockchain [26] for this study since it is well-established and has a growing worldwide user base where nodes can generate or execute smart contracts.

3.3 Bilinear Maps

Here, we review the important facts about bilinear maps. Let $\mathbb{G}_1, \mathbb{G}_2$ and $\mathbb{G}_T$ denote three cyclic groups of prime order p. A bilinear map $e(.,.)$ is a map of $\mathbb{G}_1 \times \mathbb{G}_2 \rightarrow \mathbb{G}_T$. With any generators $g \in \mathbb{G}_1, h \in \mathbb{G}_2$ and $x, y \in \mathbb{Z}_p^*$ the following conditions are satisfied:

1. $e(g^x, h^y) = e(g, h)^{xy}$ (Bilinearity)
2. $e(g^x, h^y) \neq 1$ ((Non-degeneracy)

Let B represent a bilinear map group system such that $B = (p, \mathbb{G}_1, \mathbb{G}_2, \mathbb{G}_T, e(.,.))$. B's description could also include group generators. All group operations and the bilinear map $e(.,.)$ must be computable efficiently, i.e. in time $\text{poly}(|p|)$. In our construction, we consider symmetric case such that $e(g^y, h^x) = e(g^x, h^y)$. Refer to [11, 16, 18] for a comprehensive overview on bilinear maps.

4 System Overview and Design

This section presents an overview of the proposed blockchain-based patient-to-patient health data sharing scheme. We show the overall architecture in Fig. 1. Below, we briefly describe the system entities and their functions.

1. **Patients**: In this scheme, a patient is a participant who registers in the system to receive medical treatment and contributes the resulting electronic medical records personal data to the system.
2. **Health Institution**: These are participating hospitals and other healthcare providers that keep patient's electronic medical records. They participate in the scheme by providing nodes for processing requests or hosting patient databases. It is the first entity in the scheme to receive data from patients and make it available to other units.
3. **Processing Cloud**: This is a network of nodes that receive requests for data and process it by assisting the Query Manager to validate the requests. The processing nodes assist in the creation of blocks from requests and replies. They also create packages containing the replies to requests.
4. **Grouping server**: The grouping server receives data from connected patient databases and abstracts larger categories and passes the data to the downstream entity Patient Groups . It has a Timestamp/Sequence Service that orders patient data and an Anonymizer Service that removes personal identifiers from data.
5. **Blockchain**: The Blockchain network receives and stores transaction details that have been processed into blocks. The blockchain stores the transaction logs of sharing patient data. For this scheme the blockchain is a distributed database of a times-tamped list of records linked by placing the hash of the previous block on the next one in the chain.

4.1 Multi-receiver Identity-Based Signcryption(mIBSC)

Setup$(\lambda, N) \rightarrow (params, MSK)$. The scheme's security parameter is λ, and the maximum size of the collection of receivers is N. $\mathbb{G}_1, \mathbb{G}_2$ are two prime groups of order p such that $|p| = \lambda$. $g \in \mathbb{G}_1$ and $h \in \mathbb{G}_2$ such that a bilinear map $e : \mathbb{G}_1 \times \mathbb{G}_2 \rightarrow \mathbb{G}_T$. Let call the number of bits required to indicate an identity and a message n_0 and n_1, respectively. Three hash functions are used: $H_1 : \{0,1\}^{n_0} \rightarrow \mathbb{Z}_p^*, H_2 : \{0,1\}^{n_1} \times \mathbb{G}_2 \rightarrow \mathbb{Z}_p^*$, and $H_3 : \mathbb{G}_2 \rightarrow \{0,1\}^{(n_1)+|\mathbb{G}_1|}$. The PKG selects $\gamma \xleftarrow{\$} \mathbb{Z}_p^*$ and calculates $w = g^\gamma$ and $u = e(g,h)$. The public parameters are as follows:

$$\&params \leftarrow (w, u, h, h^\gamma, \dots, h^{\gamma^N})$$

The Master Secret Key is
$$MSK = (g, \gamma).$$

Extract$(ID_i, MSK) \rightarrow SK_{ID_i}$. The PKG runs the Extract algorithm with the input of the user identity ID_i and master secret key $MSK = (g, \gamma)$. Upon successful validation of the ID_i, the PKG computes the public key and private key as $SK_{ID_i} = g^{\left(\frac{1}{H_1(ID_i)+\gamma}\right)}$ respectively.

As a patient medical data is stored in Electronic Medical Records (EMR) to provide greater access, it is critical that the data is stored chronologically. Hence, a doctor may be confident that the data in the patient's EMR is accurate, and all computational results on the data are correct. Before outsourcing medical data to a cloud server, the hospital employs a smart contract to establish blockchain proof to achieve immutable sequential order.

Signcryption. Suppose a hospital with an identity ID_{Sender}, and a private key $SK_{sender} = g^{\left(\frac{1}{H_1(sender)+\gamma}\right)}$ wants to signcrypt a patient's health data and EMR which are denoted here as m such that t healthcare providers of the identities $ID_1, \ldots, ID_t$ can access the data, it performs the following:

- Select $k \xleftarrow{\$} \mathbb{Z}_p^*, \leftarrow \{0,1\}^n$.
- Compute the following:
  - $C_1 = w^{-k}$
  - $C_2 = h^{k \cdot \Pi_{i=1}^S (\gamma + H_1(ID_i))}$
  - $C_3 = m \cdot u^k$.
  - $f = H_2(m, C_1, C_2, C_3)$
  - $v = SK_{sender}^{-kf}$
- Output signcryption of m as $\sigma = (C_1, C_2, C_3, v, L)$, where L is the list of the recipients who can be authorized to designcrypt σ.

Designcryption$(S, \sigma, ID_{sender}, SK_{ID_i}, ID_i, params)$. To recover the message m from the ciphertext σ, a data user with the private key $SK_{ID_i} = g^{\left(\frac{1}{H_1(ID_i)+\gamma}\right)}$ and identity ID_i ($ID_i \in S$) performs the following:

1. Compute
$$R = (e(C_1, h^{p_{i,s}(\gamma)}) \cdot e(SK_{ID_i}, C_2))^{\frac{1}{\Pi_{j=1,j\neq1}^S H_1 ID_j}} \text{ with } p_{i,s}(\gamma) = \frac{1}{\gamma} \cdot (\Pi_{j=1,j\neq i}^S (\gamma + H_1(ID_j)) - \Pi_{j=1,j\neq i}^S H_1(ID_j)).$$
2. Recover the message as $m = C_3/R$ and compute $f = H_2(m, C_1, C_2, C_3)$
3. Accept the message m if $e(v, h^\gamma h^{H_1(ID_{sender})}) \cdot R^f == 1$; otherwise output the error symbol $\perp$.

4.2 Interaction

In this section, we present the interaction of entities and component functions to secure health data sharing between patients. We also outline the system structures that preserve the privacy of data on the platform.

Registration: To set up the system, a new patient goes through the steps of registering with the Health Institution to store their details in the Patient Database and setting up policies for secure data sharing and acceptable use by other entities. After the patient sends the Health Institution a request to participate in the scheme, the HI formulates a set of parameters and generates an identity, ID_i as shown in Section IV subsection A. It then generates a SHA256 hash of the key and forwards the hash to the Processing Cloud, which acts as a query manager. It also delivers the ID_i to the patient with some parameters to form a key pair for signing and verifying actions on the network. The Processing Cloud sends an acknowledgment message to the Health Institution to complete the registration process.

Request: The patient sends a request for data signed and encrypted as determined by the signcryption detailed in Section IV subsection A (Signcryption). The Processing Cloud acquires the the message and commences the verification process. It first generates a SHA256 hash of the id provided. If it matches the hash received from the Health Institution in which the patient first registered, the request is assumed to proceed from a user legitimately recorded in the systems and proceeds to the subsequent step. The Processing Cloud then retrieves the necessary parameters from the Patient Database and verifies the signature on the request. If the signature verification is successful, the Processing Cloud then fetches the policies set created at the timestamp the patient registered in the system. It reads the permissions to determine if an identity, ID_i can receive the data and what operations the requester can run with the data received. After completing this, the requisite node forwards the request to the appropriate nodes which interface with the Patient Groups entity.

Processing/Reply: Two patients registered in the system with identities ID_1 and ID_2 can exchange data using the scheme as detailed in the overall architecture. Patient ID_1 first gets treated for a disease with details $D = d_1, d_2, ..., d_n$. The supervising caregivers transfer these details to the Patient Database initially and subsequently to the the Grouping Server for detailed analysis, timestamping, categorisation and anonymisation. Finally, the Groping Server transmits the categories for D to the Patient Groups entity. Patient ID_2, as well as any other patient can receive the list of patient groups in order to determine which one would be more appropriate for them to receive data from. Patient ID_2 can then initiate a request to Patient ID_1 for information on the category $Group_i$ that they both belong to. The request/reply cycle is routed through the Processing Cloud to ensure that transaction details between the transacting parties can be captured and transmitted to the blockchain for provenance in the event of unanticipated malicious activity.

4.3 Smart Contracts

With a focus on automation, we developed smart contracts to execute four predetermined transactions. These transactions are the StoreData contract, RequestData contract, Individual-to-individual contract and the Individual-to-Many contract. A patient, $Patient_1$, who gets treated in a hospital for a medical condition such as Covid-19 infection can register to provide data on their experience. After successful registration, $Patient_1$ sets up three smart contracts:

– **StoreData:** The system invokes this contract with every transaction $Patient_1$ makes in the network. Supervising caregivers record the data associated with the treatment of *Patient*₁. From the Patient Database, the new data is transmitted to the Grouping Server and finally to the Patient Groups. The log is events is prepared as a block and forwarded to the blockchain.

- **OnetoOneSharing:** To setup the OnetoOneSharing contract, $Patient_1$ requests a placeholder identity from a given Hospital. $Patient_1$ then sets a policy to share data $D = d_1, d_2, ..., d_n$. The data, D can then be shared with any single entity, $Patient_n$ after a properly formatted request is received. A log of events is prepared for each transaction and transmitted to the blockchain.

- **OnetoManySharing:** Similar to the OnetoOneSharing contract, $Patient_1$ requests a list of placeholder identities from a given Hospital. The details in D can then be shared with those identities and subsequently to any number of requesters who meet the security requirements of the network. For every request/reply cycle that invokes this contract, a transaction is recorded on the blockchain.

- **RequestData:** A patient, $Patient_2$ after success registration in the system first provides details of their conditions/treatment to the Patient Database. A script in the Database then executes to retrieve identities with similar details from the Patient Groups entity. Upon a successful match with $Patient_n$, $Patient_2$ can begin to receive details of their medical condition, treatments, etc.

5   Discussion and Evaluation

This section evaluates the performance of our scheme using scenarios where health data is shared between pairs of cooperating entities. The data used in the analysis is the result of simulations executed on single computer running Ubuntu 18.04 operating system. All security patches and updates were applied to ensure noted vulnerabilities did not affect the running of our scripts that were written in python for the simulations and solidity for the smart contracts. Figure 4 shows the results of costs of executing smart contracts on the network. This patient-centric approach to data sharing has many benefits including improved care and safety for patients and empirically-based decisions for medical personnel. Thus a key metric we evaluated was the latency in the network with increasing numbers of users on the network. The results are displayed in Fig. 3.

In our tests, we simulate 2000 to 10000 concurrent users for varying periods. We recorded data for average response time, and latency in the network. The data patients can transmit in the system is restricted to text files that describe symptoms, test results, diagnoses, etc. Thus, transmissions occur with less latency and data sizes remain small because even the largest individual messages transmitted are in Kilobytes. From the results we conclude that the scheme can handle a sufficiently large number of users at low latency which shows the system is efficient. We also performed a comparative performance analysis taking into account the research we considered in the related works. We focused on properties such as blockchain-basis and privacy guarantees. Table 1 lists the results of the analysis.

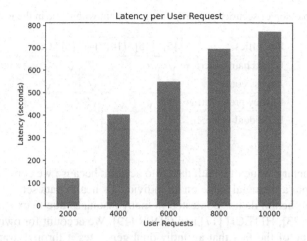

Fig. 3. A graph of the latency (in seconds) per user request in the system.

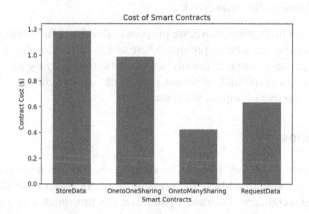

Fig. 4. A graph of the costs of executing smart contracts in the system.

5.1 Limitations

The following are the limitations we encountered in the course of the research:

1. The subject of personal health data sharing is still a sensitive issue outside the well-orchestrated confines of the research environment. Thus we did not have access to actual individuals to test out the system. When we complete the system fully, we will recruit individuals to test it out fully.
2. Patient access to their data as contained in hospital hosted databases is still a difficult challenge. Administrators restrict access based on security, privacy and economic grounds. In the full system, we hope to include an incentive that allows access while guaranteeing optimum security. Unfortunately its scope is too wide for this research.
3. The ability to own and exercise control over personal health data has precipitated a new economy where interested entities can buy and sell health data. We did not

Table 1. Comparison of security properties of our system with those in the Related Works.

Properties	[5]	[15]	[14]	[4]	[6]	Ours
Blockchain-based	✓	×	×	✓	✓	✓
Access control	✓	✓	×	✓	✓	✓
Privacy preservation	✓	✓	✓	✓	✓	✓
Individual-centered	×	×	×	×	×	✓

take the monetary value of health data into account because we could not justify any methods to put a financial value on an individual's health data set.

4. Ownership of health data is contested in many instances due to existing regulations like HIPAA [23], HITECH [17] and GDPR [19]. We account for ownership of data only by virtue of the fact that an individual generates it through transactions with healthcare institutions. We do not account for data ownership in terms of regulatory, ethical or administrative frameworks.

To mitigate the limitations above, we propose to develop a fully operational version of the health data sharing scheme presented here and to systematically recruit a preliminary group of patients who are incentivised to participate fully by allowing access to their data so we can empirically determine the limits of our scheme, while observing the factors that improve or impede the system.

6   Conclusions

Health data sharing remains integral to effective healthcare management and has evolved in many forms to address the pressing needs of patients, healthcare personnel, and other stakeholders. The recent pandemic has precipitated two notable forms, namely many new ones. Patient-to-patient health data sharing came to the fore strongly due to the willingness of those infected to create awareness of the pandemic, enabling the general public to prepare for the challenge of surviving the infection through possession of concrete details of actual sufferer's medical ordeals. In this paper, we presented a network-based scheme to assist individuals in sharing their medical details with others with guaranteed privacy. Our system relies on the blockchain to mediate access to data and protect data integrity. We employ two smart contracts to automate the sharing and eliminate some aspects of the human agency required in the scheme. We assert this scheme to be reliable and relevant to possible future pandemics and other public health emergencies.

References

1. Aggarwal, R., et al.: Patient perceptions on data sharing and applying artificial intelligence to health care data: cross-sectional survey. J. Med. Internet Res. 23(8), e26162 (2021)
2. Ahmed, N., et al.: A survey of COVID-19 contact tracing apps. IEEE Access 8, 134577–134601 (2020)

3. Albesher, A.A.: IoT in health-care: recent advances in the development of smart cyber-physical ubiquitous environments. IJCSNS **19**(2), 181 (2019)
4. Amofa, S., Gao, J., Amankona, I.O., Qi, X., Su, X.: Complementary blockchain-based privacy protection for COVID-19 contact tracing. In: 2021 IEEE 21st International Conference on Communication Technology (ICCT), pp. 1455–1460. IEEE (2021)
5. Amofa, S., et al.: A blockchain-based architecture framework for secure sharing of personal health data. In: 2018 IEEE 20th International Conference on e-Health Networking, Applications and Services (Healthcom), pp. 1–6. IEEE (2018)
6. Cao, B., Zhang, L., Peng, M., Imran, M.A.: Wireless blockchain: principles, technologies and applications. John Wiley & Sons (2021)
7. Chandrasekaran, R., et al.: Topics, trends, and sentiments of tweets about the COVID-19 pandemic: temporal infoveillance study. J. Med. Internet Res. **22**(10), e22624 (2020)
8. Ciminelli, G., Garcia-Mandicó, S.: COVID-19 in Italy: an analysis of death registry data. J. Public Health **42**(4), 723–730 (2020)
9. Dagliati, A., Malovini, A., Tibollo, V., Bellazzi, R.: Health informatics and EHR to support clinical research in the COVID-19 pandemic: an overview. Brief. Bioinform. **22**(2), 812–822 (2021)
10. Douglas, M., Katikireddi, S.V., Taulbut, M., McKee, M., McCartney, G.: Mitigating the wider health effects of COVID-19 pandemic response. BMJ **369**, m1557 (2020)
11. Goh, E.J.: Encryption schemes from bilinear maps. In: CiteSeer (2007)
12. Gursoy, D., Chi, C.G.: Effects of COVID-19 pandemic on hospitality industry: review of the current situations and a research agenda. J. Hospitality Mark. Manage. **29**(5), 527–529 (2020)
13. Haleem, A., Javaid, M., Vaishya, R.: Effects of COVID-19 pandemic in daily life. Curr. Med. Res. Pract. **10**(2), 78 (2020)
14. Hulsen, T.: Sharing is caring-data sharing initiatives in healthcare. Int. J. Environ. Res. Public Health **17**(9), 3046 (2020)
15. Kalkman, S., van Delden, J., Banerjee, A., Tyl, B., Mostert, M., van Thiel, G.: Patients and public views and attitudes towards the sharing of health data for research: a narrative review of the empirical evidence. J. Med. Ethics **48**(1), 3–13 (2022)
16. Libert, B.: New secure applications of bilinear maps in cryptography, Ph. D. thesis, CiteSeer (2006)
17. Mennemeyer, S.T., Menachemi, N., Rahurkar, S., Ford, E.W.: Impact of the hitech act on physicians adoption of electronic health records. J. Am. Med. Inform. Assoc. **23**(2), 375–379 (2016)
18. Okamoto, T.: Cryptography based on bilinear maps. In: Fossorier, M.P.C., Imai, H., Lin, S., Poli, A. (eds.) AAECC 2006. LNCS, vol. 3857, pp. 35–50. Springer, Heidelberg (2006). https://doi.org/10.1007/11617983_3
19. Phillips, M.: International data-sharing norms: from the OECD to the general data protection regulation (GDPR). Hum. Genet. **137**(8), 575–582 (2018)
20. Rahman, F.I., Ether, S.A., Islam, M.R.: The delta plus COVID-19 variant has evolved to become the next potential variant of concern: mutation history and measures of prevention. J. Basic Clinical Physiol. Pharmacol. **33**(1), 109–112 (2022)
21. Raskar, R., Pahwa, D., Beaudry, R.: Contact tracing: holistic solution beyond bluetooth. IEEE Data Eng. Bull. **43**(2), 67–70 (2020)
22. Rume, T., Islam, S.D.U.: Environmental effects of COVID-19 pandemic and potential strategies of sustainability. Heliyon **6**(9), e04965 (2020)
23. Solove, D.J.: HIPAA turns 10: analyzing the past, present, and future impact (2013)
24. Sri, P.A., Bhaskari, D.L.: Blockchain technology for secure medical data sharing using consensus mechanism. Mater. Today Proc. **2020**, 2214-7853 (2020)

25. Thakur, V., et al.: Waves and variants of *SARS-CoV-2*: understanding the causes and effect of the COVID-19 catastrophe. Infection **50**(2), 309–325 (2021). https://doi.org/10.1007/s15010-021-01734-2

26. Vujičić, D., Jagodić, D., Ranić, S.: Blockchain technology, bitcoin, and Ethereum: a brief overview. In: 2018 17th international symposium infoteh-jahorina (infoteh), pp. 1–6. IEEE (2018)

27. Wen, H., Zhao, Q., Lin, Z., Xuan, D., Shroff, N.: A study of the privacy of COVID-19 contact tracing apps. In: Park, N., Sun, K., Foresti, S., Butler, K., Saxena, N. (eds.) SecureComm 2020. LNICST, vol. 335, pp. 297–317. Springer, Cham (2020). https://doi.org/10.1007/978-3-030-63086-7_17

28. Xia, Q., Sifah, E.B., Smahi, A., Amofa, S., Zhang, X.: BBDS: blockchain-based data sharing for electronic medical records in cloud environments. Information **8**(2), 44 (2017)

Efficient and Automatic Pseudonym Management Scheme for VANET with Blockchain

Xiangsong Zhang[1], Ming Yuan[2], and Zhenhua Liu[2,3(✉)]

[1] Xi'an Technological University, Xi'an 710021, China
[2] School of Mathematics and Statistics, Xidian University, Xi'an 710071, China
zh_liu@mail.xidian.edu.cn
[3] State Key Laboratory of Cryptology, P.O. Box 5159, Beijing 100878, China

Abstract. As a product of the development of intelligent transportation system, vehicular ad hoc network (VANET) has been widely studied in recent years, where the vehicles would utilize many pseudonyms to achieve conditional privacy protection. With the increasing number of pseudonyms, the management of pseudonyms would become a new challenge. In this paper, we investigate pseudonym management in VANET based on blockchain. Firstly, an efficient and automatic pseudonym management scheme is proposed to realize the registration, update and revocation of vehicle's pseudonyms. At the same time, the voting system is applied to the pseudonym revocation protocol, which can provide a solution of the legal vehicle's pseudonym being revoked wrongly. Then, security analysis shows that the proposed scheme can meet the security requirements of VANET. Finally, the performance of the proposed scheme is analyzed through the experiments and simulations. The experimental results show that the automatic pseudonym management scheme is practical and superior to the existing schemes in terms of storage and computational overhead.

Keywords: VANET · Blockchain · Pseudonym management · Smart contract

1 Introduction

Recent advances in wireless communication technologies and automobiles have fueled the growth of intelligent transport system (ITS) that can address various vehicular traffic issues, such as traffic congestions, information disseminations, and accidents. VANET is an integral component of ITS, where the moving vehicles are connected and communicated by wireless [15]. Each participating vehicle is equipped with an on-board unit (OBU) that can communicate with nearby

Supported by by the Natural Science Basic Research Plan in Shaanxi Province of China under Grant No. 2022JZ-38 and the National Natural Science Foundation of China under Grants No. 61807026.

vehicles and roadside units (RSUs). Furthermore, RSUs can connect to the backbone network for data exchange or sharing via the Internet [12].

In such an open access VANET, the vehicle communication system is vulnerable, which would threaten the privacy of vehicles [17]. The technical specifications represented by IEEE WAVE 1609.2 [5] and ZETSI 102 [6] have proposed some security and privacy solutions. For instance, vehicle public key infrastructure (VPKI) can provide multiple short-term certificates (pseudonymes) for legitimate vehicles [16], which can switch from one pseudonym to another to realize the unlinkability. If a vehicle's pseudonym certificate expires, the pseudonym and the certificate need to be revoked. Therefore, pseudonym management becomes one of serious security issues in VANET [18]. Currently, there are many solutions to pseudonym management based on PKI technology, which can realize authentication and anonymity [2, 11, 13, 19, 20, 23, 26–28].

Furthermore, these schemes from PKI adopted the centralized management model, i.e. Trust Authority (TA). Obviously, there are some limitations, such as the single point of failure [1], the massive communication overhead [2], and the false revocation [17]. Recently, based on a distributed platform blockchain, some key management schemes [8, 9, 14] had been proposed for VANET. Unfortunately, these schemes cannot support the automatic key management. Specially, Lei et al.'s scheme [9] cannot support key update, and the other schemes [8, 14] cannot realize the key agreement that is a key protocol to protect data transmission directly. Actually, the blockchain technology can be viewed as a double-edged sword for key management in VANET. On one hand, the tamper-proof property of blocks can be used to construct a trust chain for public key. On the other hand, the property brings some troubles on key management such as key update and revocation. In order to realize efficient key management in VANET, Ma et al. [15] used smart contract [21] to manage the vehicles' key in an automatic way and proposed a decentralized key management mechanism based on blockchain. Thus blockchain technology would be applied to key management that gives a new direction to pseudonym management in VANET.

In order to realize efficient and secure pseudonym management for VANET, we propose an automatic pseudonym management scheme. The major contributions of the paper are as follows.

- **Distributed storage of pseudonym**. The decentralized pseudonym management scheme frees VANET from the dependence on PKI by using the blockchain-based tamper-proof and distributed storage of pseudonym. The distributed storage based on blockchain is suitable for a distributed VANET, and also makes VANET more robust against the single point of failure compared with the existing centralized models. In addition, since each RSU can know the anonymity of each vehicle through the blockchain, cross-regional anonymous authentication can be achieved among the vehicles.
- **Automatic pseudonym management**. Based on the smart contract technique, the decentralized pseudonym management scheme can implement automatic registration, update and revocation of the vehicle's pseudonyms. At

the same time, the application of smart contract can improve the efficiency of pseudonym management.

- **Pseudonym update and revocation**. The blockchain technique is applied to accelerate the dissemination of the updated or revoked pseudonym to the entire network. The decentralized pseudonym management scheme can employ a blockchain and smart contract based on the decentralized voting mechanism to detect some malicious vehicles with adversarial behaviors.

2 System Framework

2.1 System Model

As shown in Fig. 1, an automatic pseudonym management scheme includes three entities: Register authority (RA) , blockchain network [15] and on-board unit.

- **RA**. The tasks include the deployment of blockchain network and smart contract, the issuance of transaction data, and the verification of vehicle identity. RA is also responsible for generating the initial pseudonym for vehicle.
- **OBU**. As a processing unit embedded in the vehicle, OBU is responsible for V2V and V2I communications. In addition, a hardware security module is installed to securely store cryptographic materials. Through OBU during driving, all vehicles can regularly send some security information that consists of the driving speed, the driving direction, the vehicle position, and so on. Furthermore, the security information is collected by RSUs.
- **Blockchain network**. It is a peer-to-peer network constructed by RSUs. Each RSU sends the transactions and runs the mining function. Blockchain network can accelerate the transactions and the synchronization of blocks. As the miners, some RSU nodes need to use proof of work and proof of stake consensus mechanism to create new blocks. In addition, RSUs can generate the pseudonyms, pseudonym certificates, as well as the corresponding public and private keys for the legal vehicles according to the anonymous credentials submitted by the vehicles. When a pseudonym is revoked, RSU is responsible for distributing the revocation information of pseudonym certificate.

2.2 Attack Model

Assume that RA, RSUs and vehicles are equipped with hardware security modules that are responsible for securely storing cryptographic materials, and RA is honest-but-curious and executes faithfully any programming protocol.

In a pseudonym management scheme there exist two types of attacks, i.e. internal attacks and external attacks [15]. Internal attacks can be performed by an adversary Adv_1, whose goals are to decrypt the ciphertexts to obtain the other vehicles' private data and services with the following capabilities:

1. Adv_1 can eavesdrop on all communications in VANET to obtain the encrypted data.

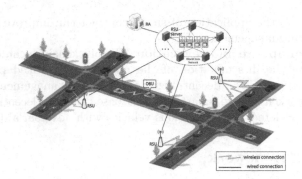

Fig. 1. System model

2. Adv_1 can compromise RSUs to guess the traffic contents between the vehicles and RSUs.

On the other hands, an adversary Adv_2 can execute the external attacks, and enable the unauthorized users to login, enjoy services and even destroy VANET with the following capabilities:

1. Adv_2 can eavesdrop on all communication in VANET to obtain the encrypted data and guess the plaintexts.
2. Adv_2 can compromise the vehicle or RSU to guess the legal identity.
3. Adv_2 can tamper or masquerade the messages from the legal participants.

2.3   Design Goals

We will propose an efficient and automatic pseudonym management scheme for VANET by using of blockchain. According to the security requirements and attack model, the proposed scheme should satisfy the following design goals:

- **Distributed storage and automatic management**. Our scheme can utilize blockchain to support the distributed storage of the vehicle's pseudonyms, and use smart contract to automatically manage these pseudonyms [15].
- **Authentication**. The proposed scheme can support the authentication between RSU and OBU by negotiating a shared session key. After successful authentication, a secure channel for communication will be created [15].
- **Pseudonym update and revocation**. When a pseudonym is expired, the proposed scheme can use smart contract to update the vehicle's pseudonym. Furthermore, our scheme can realize the pseudonym revocation by using the decentralized voting mechanism on smart contract [17].

3   Efficient and Automatic Pseudonym Management Scheme

3.1   System Setup Phase

RA executes the initialization and generates the public/secret keys PK_{RA}, SK_{RA}, and each RSU computes its public/secret keys PK_{RSU}, SK_{RSU}. A smart contract managing pseudonyms will be established on blockchain. RA creates a blockchain account for each blockchain network node through the account generation tools and then uses the account address to create a smart contract. After RA deploys the smart contract successfully, blockchain network will create automatically a contract address. Only RA and blockchain network nodes can send a transaction to trigger the execution of smart contract that offers four functions, including *RegisterPseudonym*, *UpdatePseudonym*, *VotePseudonym* and *RevokePseudonym*, to manage the pseudonyms of the vehicles.

3.2   Registration Phase

OBU holds a long-term certificate (LTC) containing identity information ID and completes the initial registration process with RA through a secure channel to access VANET. At the same time, OBU will receive IP_{cert_v} issued by RA. As shown in Table 1, OBU and RA execute the registration protocol as below.

- **Step 1:** OBU registers through a secure channel, and sends the long-term certificate and $[t_s, t_e]$ to RA, where $[t_s, t_e]$ is a pseudonym request interval.
- **Step 2:** RA encrypts OBU's identity ID to generate an initial pseudonym IP_v and the corresponding ipk_v, isk_v according to the system parameters. After that, a "credential identifiable key" $(IK_{IP_{cert_v}})$ is created to bind the credential to the vehicle's certificate: $IK_{IP_{cert_v}} = h(C||t_s||t_e||Rnd_{IK_{IP_{cert_v}}})$, where $C = Enc_K(IP_v, exp)$, $Rnd_{IK_{IP_{cert_v}}}$ is a random number generated by RA for this credential, and exp is the expiration of the long-term certificate. Then RA generates IP_{cert_v} that includes χ and $Sign_{SK_{RA}}(\chi)$, where $\chi \leftarrow (C, IK_{IP_{cert_v}}, t_s, t_e)$. RA sends $IP_v, ipk_v, isk_v, IP_{cert_v}, IK_{IP_{cert_v}}, Rnd_{IK_{IP_{cert_v}}}$ to OBU through the secure channel.
- **Step 3:** OBU stores $IP_v, ipk_v, isk_v, IP_{cert_v}, IK_{IP_{cert_v}}, Rnd_{IK_{IP_{cert_v}}}$.

3.3   Authentication Phase

After receiving IP_v, ipk_v, isk_v and $IPcert_v$, OBU interacts with RSU to execute the V2I authentication as shown in Table 2. Then a secure channel is established.

- **Step 1:** When OBU moves to the wireless communication range of the accessible RSU, the V2I authentication protocol will be executed. RSU randomly selects x_R, calculates $h_R = g^{x_R}$, and generates a signature $\sigma_1 = Sign_{SK_{RSU}}(h_R, TS_1)$, where TS_1 is the time-stamp. RSU periodically broadcasts $\{R_{ID}, \sigma_1, h_R, TS_1\}$.

Table 1. Registration protocol

OBU		RA
	Send $LTC, [t_s, t_e]$ $\longrightarrow$	
		Generate IP_v, ipk_v, isk_v
		Compute C, IK_{IPcert_v}
		Generate $IPcert_v$
	Send $IP_v, isk_v, IK_{IPcert_v},$ $IPcert_v, Rnd_{IK_{IPcert_v}}$ $\longleftarrow$	
Store $IP_v, isk_v, IK_{IPcert_v},$ $ipk_v, IPcert_v, Rnd_{IK_{IPcert_v}}$		

– **Step 2:** After receiving the broadcasting messages, OBU first checks whether TS_1 is fresh. If TS_1 is fresh, OBU uses R_{ID} to verify σ_1. If the verification is successful, OBU selects randomly y_V, computes $h_V = g^{y_V}$, and generates a signature $\sigma_2 = Sign_{isk_v}(h_V, TS_2)$, where TS_2 is the time-stamp.. Then OBU calculates a shared key $K_{V-R} = h_R{}^{y_V}$ with RSU. OBU uses K_{V-R} to generate $c = Enc_{K_{V-R}}(IP_v)$. OBU sends c, σ_2, h_V, TS_2 to RSU.
– **Step 3:** After receiving the data, RSU checks if TS_2 is fresh. If it is fresh, RSU calculates the shared key $K_{V-R} = h_V{}^{x_R}$, uses K_{V-R} to decrypt c to obtain IP_v, and uses IP_v to verify σ_2. If the verification holds, OBU is regarded as a legal one. Otherwise, RSU will reject the access request from OBU.

If the verification is successful, RSU and OBU can establish a secure channel by negotiating a shared key that is created by Diffie-Hellman key agreement.

Table 2. V2I authentication protocol

RSU		OBU
Select x_R, compute h_R		
Generate σ_1	Send $R_{ID}, \sigma_1, h_R, TS_1$ $\longrightarrow$	
		Check TS_1, verify σ_1
		Compute h_V, generate σ_2
		Compute K_{V-R}, generate c
	Send c, σ_2, h_V, TS_2 $\longleftarrow$	
Check TS_2, compute K_{V-R},		
Decrypt c, obtain IP_v		
Verify σ_2		

3.4 Pseudonyms Generation Phase

By using the secure channel, RSU sends the pseudonyms, the pseudonym certificates, and the corresponding public and secret keys to OBU. As shown in Table 3, the steps of pseudonym generation protocol are listed as follows.

- **Step 1:** OBU generates a pseudonym request message $m = (Rnd_{IK_{IPcert_v}}, IPcert_v, [t'_s, t'_e])$, where t'_s and t'_e are the start time-stamp and the end time-stamp of the actual pseudonym request interval. Then OBU sends $\{ID_{req}, m, n, TS_3\}$ to RSU, where ID_{req} is the pseudonym request identity, n is a freshly random value, and TS_3 is the time-stamp.
- **Step 2:** After receiving the request, RSU first uses the shared key with OBU to decrypt the request message and verifies the validity of IP_{cert_v}: $Verify_{PK_{RA}}(IP_{cert_v})$. If OBU's credential is valid, RSU checks whether the actual period of the requested pseudonyms (i.e., $[t'_s, t'_e]$) is within the period specified in the credential (i.e., $[t_s, t_e]$) and OBU indeed has the credential by verifying if the equation $IK_{IP_{cert_v}} = h(C\|t_s\|t_e\|Rnd_{IK_{IPcert_v}})$ holds. RSU chooses random numbers to generate public/secret keys (pk_v^i, sk_v^i) and the corresponding public key certificates $Cert_v^i$ ($i = 1, \cdots, n$) for OBU, where n is the number of pseudonyms distributed by RSU each time, and the public key certificates are signatures generated by RSU with its secret key SK_{RSU}. Then RSU generates "pseudonym identifiable key" $IK_{P_v^i}$ to bind pseudonyms to OBU's credential: $IK_{P_v^i} = h(IK_{IP_{cert_v}}\|pk_v^i\|t_s^i\|t_e^i\|h^i(Rnd_v))$. RSU implicitly associates a batch of pseudonyms belonging to each OBU by calculating the pseudonym sequence number SN, i.e., $SN^1 = h(IK_{P_v^1}\|h^1(Rnd_v))$, and $SN^i = h(SN^{i-1}\|h^i(Rnd_v)), i = 2, \cdots, n$. Afterwards RSU generates pseudonyms for OBU: $P_v^i \leftarrow (SN^i, IK_{P_v^i}, t_s^i, t_e^i)$, $PS = \{(P_v^1, pk_v^1, sk_v^1, Cert_v^1), \cdots, (P_v^n, pk_v^n, sk_v^n, Cert_v^n)\}$. RSU encapsulates the binding data $\{IP_{cert_v}, PS\}$ in JSON format and then encodes as hexadecimal embedded into the data field of the transaction. Then RSU sends the transaction to blockchain network and triggers the smart contract function $RegisterPseudonym$. After smart contract is executed and the mining is successful, the transaction record is added to the blockchain. RSU sends $\{ID_{res}, PS, Rnd_v, n+1, TS_4\}$ to OBU by a secure channel, where ID_{res} is a pseudonym response message.
- **Step 3:** After receiving the response message from RSU, OBU first recovers the message with the shared key, and then verifies $IK_{P_v^i}$ by verifying whether the equation $h(IK_{IP_{cert_v}}\|pk_v^i\|t_s^i\|t_e^i\|h^i(Rnd_v)) == IK_{P_v^i}$ holds. If the verification is successful, OBU stores PS.

Table 3. Pseudonym generation protocol

OBU		RSU
Prepare m	Send ID_{req}, m, n, TS_3 $\longrightarrow$	
		Verify IP_{cert_v}, check $IK_{IP_{cert_v}}$
		Generate Rnd_v, compute P_v^i
		Generate PS, trigger SC
	$\longleftarrow$ Send $ID_{res}, PS, Rnd_v, n+1, TS_4$	
Verify $IK_{P_v^i}$		
Store PS		

3.5 Pseudonyms Update Phase

The pseudonyms update requires RSU to issue new pseudonyms by using of smart contracts. If the pseudonym request time in the credential is about to expire, OBU sends the current IP_{cert_v} and the new request time interval $[t'_s, t'_e]$ to RA to apply for a new credential through RSU. After RA validates IP_{cert_v}, a new credential is generated to replace IP_{cert_v} that will soon be unavailable. As shown in Table 4, the steps are described in detail as follows.

- **Step 1:** OBU sends $\{\sigma_3, IP_{cert_v}, h_V, TS_5\}$ to the nearby RSU, where $\sigma_3 = Sign_{isk_v}(IP_{cert_v}, h_V, TS_5)$.
- **Step 2:** After receiving $\{\sigma_3, IP_{cert_v}, h_V, TS_5\}$, RSU temporarily saves h_V and then forwards them from OBU to RA.
- **Step 3:** After getting the data, RA checks the validity of IP_{cert_v} and verifies σ_3. If the verifications are both successful, RA generates a new credential $IP_{cert'_v}$ for OBU by selecting a new $Rnd_{IK_{IP_{cert'_v}}}$ and using its private key SK_{RA} to generate a signature, and returns $IP_{cert'_v}$, $Rnd_{IK_{IP_{cert'_v}}}$ to RSU.
- **Step 4:** After receiving the return message, RSU temporarily saves $IP_{cert'_v}$, $Rnd_{IK_{IP_{cert'_v}}}$, and sends $\{R_{ID}, \sigma_4, h_R, TS_6\}$ to OBU, where $h_R = g^{x_R}$, $\sigma_4 = Sign_{SK_{RSU}}(h_R, TS_6)$. Then, RSU calculates a shared key $K_{V-R} = h_V{}^{x_R}$.
- **Step 5:** After receiving $\{R_{ID}, \sigma_4, h_R, TS_6\}$, OBU first checks whether TS_6 is fresh. If TS_6 is fresh, OBU continues to verify σ_4. If the verification is successful, OBU calculates a shared key $K_{V-R} = h_R{}^{y_V}$.

After the above steps, OBU and RSU can establish a secure channel. RSU encapsulates the binding data $\{IP_{cert'_v}, PS'\}$ in JSON format and then encodes as hexadecimal embedded into the data field of the transaction. Then RSU sends the transaction to blockchain network and triggers SC function $UpdatePseudonym$. After smart contact is executed and the mining is successful, the transaction record is added to blockchain. RSU sends $\{IP_{cert'_v}, PS', Rnd_{IK_{IP_{cert'_v}}}\}$ to OBU through the secure channel.

3.6 Pseudonyms Revocation Phase

When OBU has been found to have some malicious behaviors in VANET, such as reading disloyal traffic information, the pseudonyms of OBU should be revoked in time. The process of pseudonym revocation is described in detail as follows.

- **Step 1:** If OBU_j receives a false message m from OBU_i, OBU_j will generates a *report*, including m, the pseudonym, and pseudonym certificate.
- **Step 2:** OBU_j sends the *report* to the nearest RSU. *RSU* checks whether the message m is malicious. If so, RSU encapsulates a voting transaction and sends to blockchain network for triggering smart contact and adding a ticket to $VotePseudonym_{OBU_i}$. If OBU_i continues to perform some malicious operations, RSU adds another ticket to $VotePseudonym_{OBU_i}$. Once the vehicle's $VotePseudonym_{OBU_i}$ exceeds a threshold Thr, i.e., $VotePseudonym_{OBU_i} \geq Thr$, smart contact will notify RSU.

- **Step 3:** RSU sends a revocation transaction to blockchain and triggers *RevokePseudonym* to remove OBU's pseudonym and certificate. In addition, RSU periodically checks the validity period of the unrevoked OBU's pseudonym and sends the transaction for triggering smart contact to remove the user pseudonym when it is expired. RSU broadcasts the revocation information, and further transfers it to RA. RA can directly recover the real identity of OBU through the decryption, and then revoke LTC of the vehicle.

In the proposed scheme, each RSU releases the revocation information at any time to notify the vehicles in any new revocation event. The vehicles can receive the latest certificate revocation list timely through RSUs.

Table 4. Pseudonym update protocol

OBU		RSU		RA
Send $\sigma_3, h_V,$ IP_{cert_v}, TS_5 $\longrightarrow$				
		Save h_V		
			Send $\sigma_3, h_V,$ IP_{cert_v}, TS_5 $\longrightarrow$	
				Verify $\sigma_3, IP_{cert_v},$ h_V, TS_5 Select $Rnd_{IK_{IPcert'_v}}$ Generate $IP_{cert'_v}$
			Send $IP_{cert'_v},$ $Rnd_{IK_{IPcert'_v}}$ $\longleftarrow$	
		Save $Rnd_{IK_{IPcert'_v}},$ $IP_{cert'_v}$ Generate σ_4, h_R Compute K_{V-R}		
	Send $R_{ID}, \sigma_4,$ h_R, TS_6 $\longleftarrow$			
Check TS_6 Verify σ_4 Compute K_{V-R}				
		Trigger SC		
	Send $IP_{cert'_v}, PS',$ $Rnd_{IK_{IPcert'_v}}$ $\longleftarrow$			
Store $IP_{cert'_v}, PS'$ $Rnd_{IK_{IPcert'_v}}$				

4 Security Analysis

We only discuss the ability of automatic pseudonym management scheme against typical attacks towards VANET.

1. **Resisting Internal Attacks:** Adv_1 eavesdrops on the communication data between OBU and RSU. However, since the data are encrypted by them, Adv_1 cannot decrypt the data without the session key. In addition, the session key is calculated securely between OBU and RSU. Furthermore, if Adv_1 wants to decrypt, it needs to obtain RSU's secret key, but these parameters are securely stored in HSM, and thus it is very difficult to realize the goal. Even if RSU is compromised, Adv_1 cannot obtain the secrets in HSM and affect the vehicle.
2. **Resisting External Attacks:** According to the attack model, we enumerate several important attacks, such as replay attacks, DoS attacks and collusion attacks, launched by Adv_2. These attacks can be prevented effectively.
   (a) **Replay Attack:** Adv_2 uses network listening or other means to steal the authentication credentials, and then re-send them to RSU. In the proposed scheme, OBU and RSU use in conjunction with nonce and time-stamp TS checking, which can effectively thwart replay attacks.
   (b) **DoS Attack:** Adv_2 is compromised by malicious organizations to act irrationally (e.g., initiate DoS attacks). Adv_2 sends a large number of intercepted message to VANET, which causes some legitimate requests to fail to respond. In the proposed scheme, we add time-stamps TS to ensure the freshness of the messages and prevent the expiring messages from Adv_2. In addition, it is impossible that Adv_2 compromises the legitimate users to launch DoS attacks, since the cryptographic materials of all legitimate users are protected by HSM.
   (c) **Collusion Attack:** Adv_2 can collude with the other compromised users to disrupt VANET or obtain the private data by stealing the session key. After the mutual authentication between OBU and RSU, RSU issues multiple anonymous identities and the corresponding signing keys to OBU. The keys and pseudonyms will be encrypted with the shared session key K_{V-R}, which effectively prevents the keys from being stolen by attackers during the key transmission. Key leakage can not occur at this time, thus the entire network is secure. Thus, the proposed scheme can defense collusion attacks in the actual VANET.

5 Performance Evaluation

5.1 Implementation and Gas Cost

To analyze the practicality of the proposed automatic pseudonym management scheme, a prototype of smart contact is compiled and deployed on the testnet of the Ethereum network, Rinkeby. Here, Rinkeby not only provides a free request of funds, but also designs a user friendly web interface for a convenient block explorer. Smart contact is deployed on the Rinkeby Testnet with the addresses:

- **RA's account address:**

  $0x8c29789a5017e77b9e00634536b288a9085a4d44,$

- **RSU's account address:**

  $0xeec732d6b74f9354b8a12da9ace819418066918b.$

The details of this implementation are presented as follows.

1. Firstly, we use MyEtherWallet to generate two accounts for our test, switch to RA's account, and request 3 Ethers from Rinkeby such that RA can publish the transactions.
2. Then, we execute the followings as RA's identity. We deploy the smart contract into Rinkeby using Remix. The creation of smart contact is only performed once and the cost is $0.2576.
3. Next, we simulate RSU to add the anonymity of the vehicle to blockchain. We switch to RSU's account and trigger the smart contact functions $Register$ $-Pseudonym$ and $UpdatePseudonym$. The cost of $RegisterPseudonym$ and $UpdatePseudonym$ operation are $0.0259 and $0.0093, respectively.
4. Finally, RSU sends a revocation transaction to the blockchain and triggers $RevokePseudonym$. The cost of $RevokePseudonym$ operation is $0.0158.

The costs measured by the experiment are shown in Table 5. We compare the proposed scheme with PKI-based solutions [22,25]. According to [22], the initial setup cost of traditional PKI infrastructure is about $10,000, and the annual management fee is about $45,000. Assume that the proposed initial setup and annual overhead are the same as the traditional PKI. The approximate cost of managing a car based on a traditional PKI is $20 per year, but the approximate cost of managing a car based on a blockchain is $0.30 per year. The results in Fig. 2 show that Display POWER MANAGEMENT Signalling is practical in application.

Table 5. Costs of the different functions in the SC

Functionalities	Gas used	Actual cost (Ether)	USD
Smart Contract Creation	1302525	0.001302525	0.2579
$RegisterPseudonym$	130808	0.000130808	0.0259
$UpdatePseudonym$	46970	0.000046970	0.0093
$RevokePseudonym$	797979	0.000797979	0.0158

5.2 Storage Overhead

The storage overhead of the proposed scheme depends on the amount of vehicle and RSU storage pseudonyms. According to the IEEE standard [4], the size of the certificate is 126 bytes, the public key size of RSU is 29 bytes, and the pseudonym of vehicle is 32 bytes. By implementing the smart contract on Ethereum and analyzing results, it is concluded that the size of a transaction data is 100 bytes, one block contains about 15 transactions, and the block header is about 200 bytes. Assuming there are 1 million vehicles in the network, the amount of data that needs to be stored by each RSU is 30 Mbytes. If there are 100000 RSUs deployed in the network, the amount of data that is maintained by each vehicle is equal to 2.8 Mbytes. Table 6 shows the comparisons of the storage overhead. Since smart contract is used to manage pseudonyms, the storage overhead of RSU in the proposed scheme is smaller.

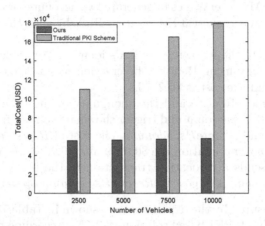

Fig. 2. Cost comparison with traditional PKI schemes

Table 6. Comparisons of storage overhead

Schemes	Standard	Ours
Vehicle	1.2 MB	2.8 MB
RSU	132 MB	30 MB

5.3 Computation Overhead

Due to the rapid change in the vehicle location and network topology, the computational overhead of RSU and OBU will affect the performance of VANET. On the one hand, RSU has a wealth of computing overhead, so we do not consider the impact of RSU's computing overhead on VANET. On the other hand, the computing power of OBU is limited, so we mainly analyzes the computing overhead of OBU. The sum of the computation overhead of V2I authentication and V2V authentication is the computation overhead of the proposed scheme.

In order to evaluate the computational cost of various cryptographic operations, the simulation platform used in the experiment is MIRACL. Each operation is performed 10,000 times on a 16 GB 64-bit Windows 10 system on an Intel(R) Core(TM) i5-1135G7@ 2.40 GHz workstation. The definition and execution time of various operations are summarized in Table 7. Compared with the calculations summarized in Table 7, the calculation cost of hash function (T_h), point addition (T_{pa}), RSA verification (T_{R_v}) and RSA encryption (T_{R_e}) can be omitted according to [24], and according to [3], the computational overhead of RSA encryption is the same as that of RSA verification.

In the V2I authentication protocol of the proposed scheme, OBU verifies the signature of RSU and generates a signature. During the verification process, OBU needs to calculate the shared key, which is equivalent to two RSA encryption operations. Therefore, the computational cost of the proposed scheme in the V2I authentication process is $T_{bp} + 2T_{pm} + 2T_{ep2} + T_{mul} + 2T_{R_e}$.

During the V2V authentication process, all OBUs use pseudonyms for communication, so OBU first verifies whether RSU's signature on the pseudonyms is valid. Next, if the pseudonym signature is valid, OBU will perform a RSA verification operation on the signed message. OBU also needs to perform RSA encryption to generate its own signed message. Finally, the computational cost of the proposed scheme in the V2V authentication process is $T_{bp} + T_{pm} + T_{ep2} + T_{mul} + T_{R_\sigma} + T_{R_v}$.

In this section, we compare the performance of the proposed scheme with other three schemes in terms of computational overhead. The computational costs of the four schemes are evaluated and summarized in Table 8. The comparative analysis shows that in the V2I and V2V authentication process, the proposed scheme owns the lower computational cost than the other three schemes.

Table 7. The definition and execution time of related operations

Operations	Definitions	Time (ms)
T_{bp}	Bilinear pairing operation (bp)	1.6
T_{mtp}	Map-to-point hash operation (mtp)	0.8
T_{ep2}	Exponentiation in G2 of the bilinear pairing (ep2)	0.6
T_{mul}	Scale multiplication (mul)	0.533
T_{R_σ}	RSA sign (R_σ)	0.533

Table 8. Computational cost in the V2I and V2V authentication

Schemes	V2I Authentication	V2V Authentication	Computational Time (ms)
PACE [3]	$5T_{bp} + 17T_{pm}$ $+2T_{ep2} + T_{mul}$	$5T_{bp} + 15T_{pm}$ $+2T_{ep2} + T_{mul}$	45.06
CPAS [7]	$3T_{mtp} + 3T_{bp}$ $+7T_{pm}$	$3T_{mtp} + 3T_{bp}$ $+5T_{pm}$	24
ACPN [10]	$5T_{mtp} + 5T_{bp}$ $+4T_{pm} + T_{R_e}$	$2T_{mtp} + T_{bp}$ $+3T_{pm}$	20.8
Ours	$T_{bp} + 2T_{pm} + 2T_{ep2}$ $+T_{mul} + 2T_{R_e}$	$T_{bp} + T_{pm} + T_{ep2}$ $+T_{mul} + T_{R_\sigma} + T_{R_v}$	9

6   Conclusions

In the paper, we have proposed an efficient and automatic pseudonym management scheme for VANET. By using blockchain technology to manage users' anonymous credential and pseudonym materials, the proposed scheme can reduce the cost and improve the efficiency compared to the traditional certificate-based PKI scheme for VANET. When a vehicle is driving across domains, a pseudonymous certificate can be used for cross-domain authentication at a nearby RSU, which effectively protects the privacy of the vehicle. In addition, when RSU discovers that a vehicle reports incorrect traffic information, it will trigger a smart contract to vote on the vehicle, so that the anonymity of the vehicle can be revoked more reasonably. Security and performance analysis shows that the proposed scheme is secure and practical. The future work is to present a more effective pseudonym generation and dynamic mechanism for VANET.

References

1. Albarqi, A., Alzaid, E., Al Ghamdi, F., Asiri, S., Kar, J.: Public key infrastructure: a survey. J. Inf. Secur. **6**(1), 31–37 (2015)
2. Calandriello, G., Papadimitratos, P., Hubaux, J.P., Lioy, A.: Efficient and robust pseudonymous authentication in VANET. In: Proceedings of the fourth ACM international Workshop on Vehicular Ad Hoc Networks (VANET2007), pp. 19–28, ACM (2007). https://doi.org/10.1145/1287748.1287752
3. Huang, D., Misra, S., Verma, M., Xue, G.: PACP: an efficient pseudonymous authentication-based conditional privacy protocol for VANETs. IEEE Trans. Intell. Trans. Syst. **12**(3), 736–746 (2011)
4. Intelligent Transportation Systems Committee of the IEEE Vehicular Technology Society. In: IEEE Trial-Use Standard for Wireless Access in Vehicular Environments-security Services for Applications and Management Messages, IEEE Standard, 1609.2-2006, pp. 1–105, IEEE (2006). https://doi.org/10.1109/IEEESTD.2006.243731
5. Intelligent Transportation Systems Committee of the IEEE Vehicular Technology Society. In: IEEE Standard for Wireless Access in Vehicular Environments-Security Services for Applications and Management Messages, IEEE Standard, 1609.2-2016, pp. 1–240, IEEE (2016). https://doi.org/10.1109/IEEESTD.2016.7426684
6. European Telecommunications Standard Institute: Intelligent Transport Systems (ITS) Security; Trust and Privacy Management; Release 2 ETSI Standard, ETSI-TS 102 941, pp. 1–83, ETSI (2021). https://standards.globalspec.com/std/14474013/TS%20102%20941
7. Shim, K.A.: CPAS: an efficient conditional privacy-preserving authentication scheme for vehicular sensor networks. IEEE Trans. Veh. Technol. **61**(4), 1874–1883 (2012)
8. Lasla, N., Younis, M., Znaidi, W., Arbia, D.B.: Efficient distributed admission and revocation using blockchain for cooperative ITS. In: 9th IFIP International Conference on New Technologies, Mobility and Security (NTMS'18), pp. 1–5, IEEE (2018). https://doi.org/10.1109/NTMS.2018.8328734
9. Lei, A., Cruickshank, H., Cao, Y., Asuquo, P., Ogah, C.P.A., Sun, Z.: Blockchain-based dynamic key management for heterogeneous intelligent transportation systems. IEEE Internet of Things J. **4**(6), 1832–1843 (2017)

10. Li, J., Lu, H., Guizani, M.: ACPN: a novel authentication framework with conditional privacy-preservation and non-repudiation for VANETs. IEEE Trans. Parallel Distrib. Syst. **26**(4), 938–948 (2015)
11. Lin, X., Sun, X., Ho, P.H., Shen, X.: GSIS: a secure and privacy preserving protocol for vehicular communications. IEEE Trans. Veh. Technol. **56**(6), 3442–3456 (2007)
12. Lin, C., He, D., Huang, X., Kumar, N., Choo, K.R.: BCPPA: a blockchain-based conditional privacy-preserving authentication protocol for vehicular Ad hoc networks. IEEE Trans. Intell. Trans. Syst. **22**(12), 7408–7420 (2020)
13. Lin, X., Li, X.: Achieving efficient cooperative message authentication in vehicular ad hoc networks. IEEE Trans. Veh. Technol. **62**(7), 3339–3348 (2013)
14. Lu, Z., Liu, W., Wang, W., Qu, G., Liu, Z.: A privacy-preserving trust model based on blockchain for VANETS. IEEE Access **6**, 45655–45664 (2018)
15. Ma, Z., Zhang, J., Guo, Y., Liu, Y., Liu, X., He, W.: An efficient decentralized key management mechanism for VANET with blockchain. IEEE Trans. Veh. Technol. **69**(6), 5836–5849 (2020)
16. Papadimitratos, P., et al.: Secure vehicular communication systems: design and architecture. IEEE Commun. Mag. **46**(11), 100–109 (2008)
17. Qi, J., Gao, T.: A privacy-preserving authentication and pseudonym revocation scheme for VANETs. IEEE Access **8**, 177693–177707 (2020)
18. Qu, F., Wu, Z., Wang, F.Y., Cho, W.: A security and privacy review of VANETs. IEEE Trans. Intell. Trans. Syst. **16**(6), 2985–2996 (2015)
19. Raya, M., Hubaux, J.P.: Securing vehicular ad hoc networks. J. Comput. Secur. **15**(1), 39–68 (2007)
20. Shao, J., Lin, X., Lu, R.X., Zuo, C.: A threshold anonymous authentication protocol for VANETs. IEEE Trans. Veh. Technol. **65**(3), 1711–1720 (2016)
21. Tikhomirov, S., Voskresenskaya, E., Ivanitskiy, I., Takhaviev, R., Alexandrov, Y.: Smartcheck: static analysis of Ethereum smart contracts. In: 2018 IEEE/ACM 1st International Workshop on Emerging Trends in Software Engineering for Blockchain (WETSEB'18), pp. 9–16, IEEE/ACM (2018). https://doi.org/10.1145/3194113.3194115
22. VeriSign.: total cost of ownership for public key infrastructure, Patent (2005). http://www.imaginar.org/sites/ecommerce/index_archivos/guias/G_tco.pdf
23. Vijayakumar, P., Chang, V., Deborah, L.J., Balusamy, B., Shynu, P.G.: Computationally efficient privacy preserving anonymous mutual and batch authentication schemes for vehicular ad hoc networks. Future Gener. Comput. Syst. **78**, 943–955 (2018)
24. Vijay, S., Sharma, S.C.: Threshold signature cryptography scheme in wireless ad-hoc computing. Contemp. Comput. **40**(7), 327–335 (2009)
25. The costs of managed PKI: in-house implementationof PKI vs. traditional managed PKI vs. on-demand PKI, patent (2006). https://azslide.com/the-costs-ofmanaged-pki_59892e9b1723dda4299be2/36.html
26. Zhang, L., Wu, Q., Qin, B., Domingo-Ferrer, J., Liu, B.: Practical secure and privacy-preserving scheme for value-added applications in VANETs. Comput. Commun. **71**, 50–60 (2015)
27. Zhong, H., Huang, B., Cui, J., Li, J., Sha, K.: Efficient conditional privacy-preserving authentication scheme using revocation messages for VANET. In: 27th International Conference on Computer Communication and Networks (ICCCN2018), pp. 1–8. IEEE (2018). https://doi.org/10.1109/ICCCN.2018.8487337
28. Zhu, X., Jiang, S., Wang, L., Li, H.: Efficient privacy-preserving authentication for vehicular ad hoc networks. IEEE Trans. Veh. Technol. **63**(2), 907–919 (2014)

Ethereum Contract Honeypot Risk Analysis

Motoya Ishimaki[1]([✉]) and Kazumasa Omote[1,2]

[1] University of Tsukuba, Tennodai 1-1-1, Tsukuba 305-8573, Japan
s2120527@s.tsukuba.ac.jp, omote@risk.tsukuba.ac.jp
[2] National Institute of Information and Communications Technology,
4-2-1 Nukui-Kitamachi, Koganei, Tokyo 184-8795, Japan

Abstract. In recent years, smart contracts on the Ethereum platform have attracted considerable attention, and smart contracts have increasingly become targets of cyberattacks for the purpose of stealing cryptoassets. One of the emerging attack methods is to intentionally deploy contracts that appear to contain vulnerabilities but have backdoors, and that, lure attackers who are targeting vulnerable contracts to steal cryptoassets. These are called smart contract honeypots (henceforth referred to simply as "contract honeypots"). Torres et al. analyzed contract honeypots for the first time at USNIX Security 2019. In this study, we look at eight types of contract honeypots organized by Torres et al. and calculate the damages caused by each of them. We also analyze the code of contract honeypots by focusing on the arguments of the money transfer process, and we discovered a new type of contract honeypot. This analysis suggests that smart contracts with "this.balance" in the money transfer process may be contract honeypots. Furthermore, we discuss the impact of contract honeypots on general users.

Keywords: Blockchain · Ethereum · Smart contract · Honeypot · Risk analysis

1 Introduction

In recent years, blockchain has been attracting attention as a technology that can decentralize assets, the two most famous blockchains being Bitcoin [9] and Ethereum [1]. In addition to cryptoasset, various services that use block-chain technology have emerged, and they utilize Ethereum. Smart contracts are important for these services. Smart contracts are systems that can automatically execute contracts without the intervention of a third party. They are also decentralized, and they can offer tamper-proof services.

However, the anonymity of cryptoassets makes them an inviting target for cyberattacks. Smart contracts, which are a feature of the Ethereum blockchain, are usually implemented using a programming language such as Solidity. This software, like other common software, can contain vulnerabilities due to bugs. Some smart contracts have already been attacked in the past; one example of

E. Ahene and F. Li (Eds.): FCS 2022, CCIS 1726, pp. 226–240, 2022.
https://doi.org/10.1007/978-981-19-8445-7_15

an attack is the DAO incident [15], which resulted in a loss of approximately 6 billion yen. In addition, because smart contracts leverage the blockchain, it is quite difficult to modify the code once it has been deployed and stored on the blockchain, as well as difficult to modify the results of its execution. For these reasons, attackers have begun to look for vulnerable smart contracts and to target the theft of cryptoassets. Various approaches have been studied to counteract this [4, 7, 8].

However, attackers are not limited to the above tactics, they have searched more sophisticated trick. Torres et al. [10] revealed that attackers do not look for vulnerable contracts, but rather dare to be on the installation side in order to steal assets from attackers who are more vulnerable than they are. This is called a smart contract honeypot (hereafter simply referred to as contract honeypots.). Torres et al. proposed a tool called HoneyBadger that can detect contract honeypots.

In this study, we target eight types of contract honeypots organized by Torres et al. The number of victims and the dollar amount of damage were clarified for each, and new characteristics of contract honeypots were analyzed to discover a new species of contract honeypots. We focused on the argument of the money transfer process ("msg.sender.transfer") and found that the argument "this.balance" is a characteristic of contract honeypots. Furthermore, this study conducted a risk analysis for the general users who are exposed to the risk, which had not been done in previous studies.

2 Preparation

2.1 Smart Contract

By realizing this on the Ethereum platform, it is possible to build a system in which exchange contracts between service providers and users are programmed on the blockchain, and transactions are automatically executed when the contract terms are met. Smart contracts have the following advantages.

- The contents of the transaction are resistant to fraud and tampering.
- The transparency of transaction details is high.
- De-centralized service operation is possible, which reduces the risk of system downtime.

Despite these advantages, the need to manage the cryptoassets involved at the time the contract is executed has motivated to attack and has become a target for general users.

2.2 Solidity

Solidity is a high-level language that is intended for writing contracts. The user compiles the contract, stores it in a transaction in the form of byte code, and then deploys it as a smart contract. It is not possible to check the pre-compiled Solidity source code after storage. However, because the creators of smart contracts aim

Table 1. Contract honeypot

Trap door	Technique	Content
Balance Disoder (BD)	EVM	- Take advantage of fluctuating balances prior to contract execution
Inheritance Disoder (ID)	Solidity Compiler	- Use specifications for when a contract inherits from another contract
Skip Empty String Literal (SESL)		- Take advantage of the language property that empty character literals are skipped
Type Deduction Overflow (TDO)		- Use compiler's type inference function
Uninitialised Struct (US)		- Use the structure mechanism
Hidden State Update (HSU)	EtherScan Explorer	- Use a specification that internal messages containing empty transaction values are not displayed
Hidden Transfer (HT)		- Use the specification that the code will not be displayed if the code length exceeds a certain number
Straw Man Contract (SMC)		- Make them appear vulnerable to reentrant attacks

to make their contracts known and used, they may register their source code on a website called EtherScan[1], which allows users to check the status of the Ethereum blockchain using a GUI. Contract honeypot creators also need other attackers to discover the existence of vulnerabilities, so they usually register their contracts.

2.3 Contract Honeypot

Attackers who are on the installation side of contract honeypots are trying to steal assets from attackers who are more vulnerable than they are. They include Solidity code in a contract that can be exploited by anyone, and they intentionally deploy the contract with a trapdoor hidden in it to lure other attackers who target exploitable contracts. The attacker who are on the installation side of contract honeypots then uses this technique to cheat the lured attacker out of cryptoassets. Thus, a contract honeypot is Solidity code that contains a trapdoor and that looks easy to exploit but is in fact cleverly designed so that it cannot be exploited. Table 1 shows the details of contract honeypots. According to Torres et al. [10], there are eight major types of contract honeypots, and each contract honeypot uses a different technique to exploit vulnerabilities.

---

[1] https://etherscan.io/apis.

3   Related Research

Luu et al. [8] tried a symbolic execution-based approach to search vulnerable smart contracts. They found that 8,833 out of 19,366 smart contracts were potentially vulnerable. However, such symbolic execution-based detection methods have the disadvantages of slow detection time and the need for predefined patterns. In addition, this research has not analyzed the risk of contract honeypots for general users.

Torres et al. [10] presented a tool called HoneyBadger[2]. By visually checking smart contracts, Torres et al. have published information on labels and eight types of honeypot trapdoor methods to determine whether each contract is a contract honeypot or not. The details of this information are shown in Table 1. However, they use a symbolic execution-based detection scheme proposed by Luu et al. [8] which has the disadvantages of slow detection time due to the need to examine executable paths and the need for predefined patterns. Furthermore, they have not yet analyzed the risk of contract honeypots for general users. Chen et al. [3] used EVM bytecode to detect smart contract honeypots. The features they used for detection were the "CALLER" and "BALANCE" features. However, these features are not detectable before the theft of cryptoassets occurs because they use features that are not known without executing smart contracts, such as features related to checking account balances and features related to checking account addresses. Therefore, it is difficult to prevent the theft of cryptoassets from occurring. In addition, Chen et al. does not mention the risks posed by contract honeypots for general users.

To overcome the slow detection time due to symbolic execution, Camino et al. [2] proposed a contract honeypot detection method based on machine learning which uses the characteristics of smart contract transaction histories. Camino. et al. used the same features as were used by Torres et al. [10] Therefore, they could not be used to actually reduce the damage. On the other hand, based on the work by Camino et al., Hara et al. [5] constructed a model that examined detection before contract execution using bytecode features in order to detect contracts before they were executed, However, because it only detects XGBoost, it must be compared with other machine learning algorithms. In addition, Teng et al. [6] studied the detection of transaction-based contract honeypots, their works may also detect self-destructing contract honeypots. Self-destructed contracts do not function as transactions and cannot be detected in real-time. All of these studies have yet to analyze the risk to ordinary users.

4   Contract Honeypots

In the study by Torres et al. [10], eight types of contract honeypots were classified. In this section, we describe the eight contract honeypots, based on their code characteristics.

---

[2] https://github.com/christoftorres/HoneyBadger.

Balance Disorder (BD). The attacker is attempting to exploit the entire balance and remittance by transferring more Ether than is contained in the contract honeypot. However, in this contract honeypot, the remittance is added to the balance before the contract is executed, so the conditions for remittance do not match and the remittance that is stolen.

Inheritance Disorder (ID). This is a contract that exploits inheritance in Solidity and requires changing the ownership of the contract in order to steal it. The scope of the variable is abused so that the process of changing the contract ownership cannot be accessed, and the Ether is exploited with no change to the contract owner.

Skip Empty String Literal (SESL). This is a contract honeypot that embeds an empty string in a function argument, thereby skipping the Solidity compiler's encoding process and shifting the argument of the subsequent function by 32 bytes. This function ensures that the Ether is not returned, and that the Ether is stolen by the installer of the contract honeypot.

Type Deduction Overflow (TDO). This is a contract honeypot that exploits the variable type to gain Ether when the loop termination condition is reached, and the loop termination condition is 255 wei. However, the maximum Ether that can be obtained is 255 wei, which is necessarily much lower than the amount transferred.

Uninitialised Struct (US). This contract honeypot allows users to guess a random number stored in the contract. However, The random number values can be easily retrieved by anyone. So the user is induced to guess a random number by activating a guessNumber written in Solidity code and placing a wager. The first variable in the structure, however, the location of the first variable in the structure maps to the location of the random number, and makes it difficult to satisfy the remittance conditions.

Hidden State Update (HSU). The variable used to withdraw the Ether is set to True or False. The attacker overwrites the variable by implicitly executing a function. The victims who are unaware of the change in variables are unknowingly drawn out of Ether by the attacker.

Hidden Transfer (HT). Previously, Etherscan had horizontal and vertical scrolling capabilities in a scrollbox that displayed Solidity code. It is a contract honeypot that exploits the scrolling functionality of EtherScan. If a very long space after the source code were inserted, the code displayed on Etherscan could effectively be hidden. This is a contract honeypot technique that aims to deceive the victim by hiding a trap.

Straw Man Contract (SMC). This is a contract honeypot that exploits a reentry vulnerability. By including the string "CashOut" in the money transfer process, the caller is limited to the user who installed the contract honeypot. This process causes an exception for users other than the contract honeypot installer, so the attack fails, and the amount of Ether transferred to the contract is stolen.

5   Analysis

The purpose of this study is to calculate the damage of contract honeypots to the users, which has not been done in previous studies, and to inform blockchain users about the dangers of contract honeypots. We also extract the class names contained in Solidity, which is used in contract honeypots, and the arguments of "msg.sender.transfer", a function that transfers Ether, to understand the attacker's intentions.

5.1   Data Used in the Analysis

The contract honeypots that are the subject this study comprise a total of 323 contract honeypots from 2017 to 2019 that were detected by HoneyBadger [10]. We consider the contracts not detected by HoneyBadger as legitimate contracts, and we collect a total of 263,007 contracts for January-February 2018, which were the most affected months. The 771 contracts having "msg.sender.transfer" in the collected source code are considered legitimate contracts in this analysis.

5.2   Contract Honeypot Damage

Purpose of Analysis. The Torres et al. [10] study analyzes eight types of contract honeypots and proposes a detection method, but it is unclear whether any of the contract honeypots have actually caused damage, and if so, how much damage they caused. Therefore, in this analysis, we clarify the actual number of victims and the actual dollar amount of victims for contracts that were determined to be contract honeypots by HoneyBadger [10].

Analysis Methodology

1. Collect contract addresses determined to be honeypots by HoneyBadger using EtherScanAPI[3] for the period from January 2018 to April 2019.
2. If one remittance transaction is confirmed for a single contract honeypot address, it is calculated as one case of damage, and the amount of damage is calculated based on the amount of remittances made. If the sender is the address of the contract honeypot creator, it is excluded from the damage count.

Analysis Results. The breakdown of the total victims of contract honeypots is shown in Table 2. The time-series analysis of the number of victims and dollar amount of victims to contract honeypots are shown in Fig. 1 and Fig. 2, and the average amount of damage per contract honeypot is shown in Fig. 3. According to Table 2, HSU has the highest total damage amount of all contract honeypots of about 60 ETH, and the highest number of cases of damage (74 cases). The

---

[3] https://etherscan.io/apis.

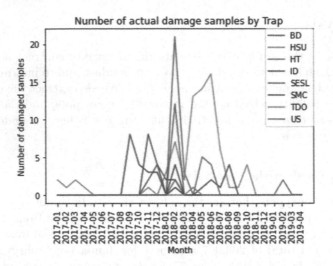

Fig. 1. Number of victims of each contract honeypot

Table 2. Breakdown of total damage to contract honeypots

Trap door	Number of victims	Total amount of damage (Ether)
Balance Disoder (BD)	10	4.5101
Inheritance Disorder (ID)	27	18.22660389
Skip Empty String Literal (SESL)	12	6.599685965
Type Deduction Overflow (TDO)	1	1.00E-07
Uninitialised Struct (US)	35	7.036012884
Hidden State Update (HSU)	74	59.93716123
Hidden Transfer (HT)	2	1.1
Straw Man Contract (SMC)	16	7.664034233

number of TDO was 1, and the amount of damage was 1.00 E-07 ETH. According to Fig. 3, ID honeypots were significantly different from the other contract honeypots, with a maximum damage amount of approximately 7 ETH per case. Furthermore, the overall number of victims in contract honeypots became sparse after 2018/03, and the number and amount of damages for HSU showed a dramatic updown from 2018/03 to 2018/11 (Fig. 1, Fig. 2).

5.3   Analysis of Contract Honeypot Features

Purpose of Analysis. In the Torres et al. [10] study, machine learning was used to analyze the code of the contract honeypots to extract features. However, the names used in the contracts and the argument names used in the money transfer process ("msg.sender.transfer") were considered to be the most

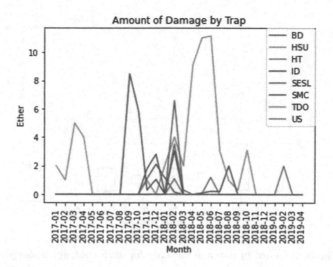

Fig. 2. Amount of damage caused by per type of contract honeypot

Table 3. Contract honeypots undetected by HoneyBadger

Contract address	Deployed date and time	Amount of damage (Ether)
0x31FD6...	2018/1/31 12:53	1.01
0x5ABb8...	2018/1/31 15:59	–
0x2BB5B...	2018/1/31 16:26	–
0x55Bec...	2018/2/1 3:52	–
0x61dc3...	2018/2/1 4:55	–
0x66385...	2018/2/1 19:29	1.01
0xf414b...	2018/2/2 10:01	–
0xcfebf...	2018/2/2 10:28	1.05
0x0b82b...	2018/2/6 7:35	–

likely to show the characteristics of contract honeypots without code analysis. "msg.sender.transfer" is a function used for transferring Ether, so the arguments of this function are of interest. Therefore, in this analysis, we identify frequently used contract names and "msg.sender.transfer" argument names.

Analysis Methodology

1. The source code was obtained from a contract address detected as a honeypot by HoneyBadger using EtherScanAPI.
2. Extract the argument names as its arguments as many times as "msg.sender. transfer" is included in the source code of a single contract honeypot. For example, if a single "msg.sender.transfer" is included in the source code of a contract honeypot, it is calculated as one argument name.

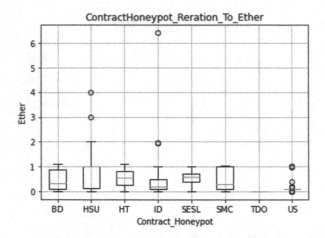

Fig. 3. Amount of damage per case for each contract honeypot

Table 4. List of contracts that have been active since May 2019

Transaction hash	Contract address	Trap door	Solidity method	Date and time of behavior check	Transaction sender	Victimization amount (Ether)
0x456ca...	0x68af0...	HSU	SetPwd	2022/5/29 06:42	0x328eb...	1.000001
0x61909...	0x68af0...	HSU	SetPwd	2022/5/29 06:36	0x328eb...	1.0
0x06cd2...	0x68af0...	HSU	CashOut	2022/5/28 01:37	0x48088...	1E−18
0x2b129...	0x68af0...	HSU	SetPwd	2022/5/28 01:33	0x48088...	1E−18
0x54983...	0x413c8...	US	play	2022/05/23 09:10	0x48088...	0.1
0x54983...	0x413c8...	US	play	2022/05/23 07:33	0x48088...	0.11
0x42009...	0x3e784...	ID	Kill	2021/1/19 22:18	0x80028...	–
0x5e179...	0x3e784...	ID	Withdraw	2021/1/19 22:16	0x80028...	–
0xc036f...	0x3bafb...	BD	Withdraw	2021/1/19 21:54	0x125d6...	–
0x53bf9...	0x4dc76...	ID	TakeAll	2021/1/19 21:43	0x80028...	–
0xbfa13...	0x96830...	US	Kill	2020/12/28 22:09	0xfc8c5...	–
0xa95ef...	0x9f54d...	BD	Kill	2020/9/20 11:14	0x4ef20...	–
0x5098e...	0xc0c7d...	ID	Withdrawfunds	2019/6/23 0:52	0xa5b8f...	–
0x1be0b...	0x68af0...	HSU	CashOut	2019/5/29 17:35	0x7d902...	–

Analysis Results. Figure 4 shows the calculated frequency of the names that are included in contracts, and Fig. 5 shows the calculated frequency of msg.sender. transfer arguments that are included in all contracts. Figure 4 shows that the five contract honeypots BD, HSU, ID, SESL, and US commonly use "ownable" as the contract name. From Fig. 5, we also found that "this.balance" is frequently used as the argument of "msg.sender.transfer" in 7 out of 8 types of contract honeypots.

This is common to most of the contract honeypots, which tend to use this. balance as "msg.sender.transfer" argument to associate with all Ether balances that have been transferred and to indicate that Ether can be obtained. In addition, contract names such as "ownable", which also indicates that Ether can be obtained, were frequently used.

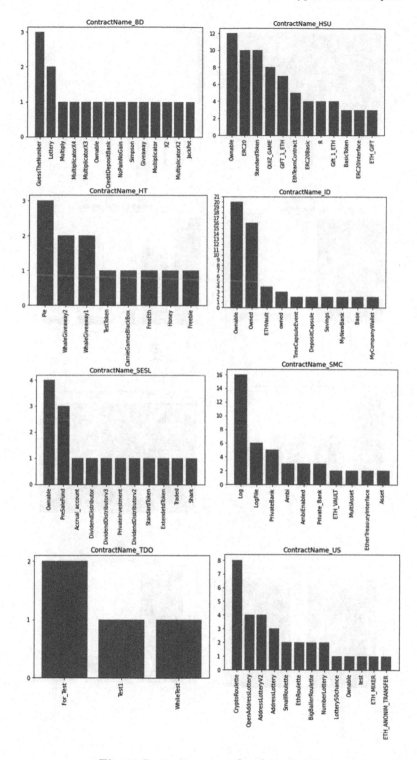

Fig. 4. Contract names of each contract

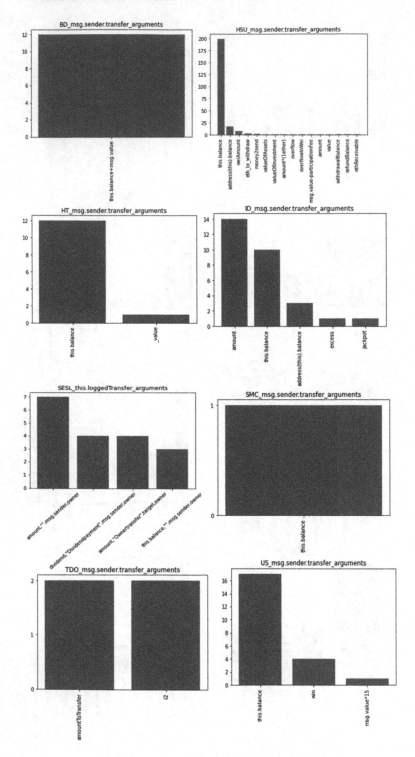

Fig. 5. Contract names of each contract

5.4   Detection of New Contract Honeypots

Purpose of Analysis. In the previous section, it was found that "this.balance" was frequently used as an argument in the contract honeypot's money transfer process ("msg.sender.transfer"). Therefore, we examine if this argument can be used to detect contract honeypots that HoneyBadger could not detect.

Analysis Procedure. The analysis procedure is shown below.

1. Collect smart contracts from January 2018 to February 2018 using Ether-ScanAPI. The collected contracts are those that are determined to be non-honeypots by HoneyBadger in order to check the extent to which "this.balance" is included in regular contracts.
2. Extract the argument names as its arguments as many times as "msg.sender.transfer" is included in the source code of a single contract honeypot. For example, if a single "msg.sender.transfer" is included in the source code of acontract honeypot, it is calculated as one argument name.

Analysis Results. In this analysis, we found 50 legitimate contracts that included "this.balance" as an argument of "msg.sender.transfer" call, 3 of which were written in the same Solidity file. Thus we included 47 legitimate contracts in our analysis. We found 9 contract honeypots out of 47 cases that could not be detected by HoneyBadger using "this.balance" as an indicator (Table 3). The contents of the contracts in three and two of the nine cases were all the same, which suggests that they were copied. We also identified three contract honeypots that appeared to be HT and three contract honeypots that combined the functions of HT and HSU. In addition, we found three contract honeypots with if(1==2) in the remittance process on Solidity code. These three cases are considered to be new contract honeypots because none of them fit the classification method by Torres et al. [10]. Note that these contracts were determined by the author with reference to existing honeypot traps. We also found a total of 3.07 ETH damages in 3 of the 9 contracts. Those damages were also observed on 1/31/2018 at 13:57, 2/2/2018 at 7:15, and 2/6/2018 at 10:14.

5.5   Regular Contracts

Purpose of Analysis. Determine the extent to which "this.balance" appears in regular contracts and what the contents of these regular contracts are.

Analysis Procedure. The analysis procedure checks the type of Solidity code, such as whether it is a game-type contract or a trap-type contract.

Analysis Results. Figure 6 shows the results of "msg.sender.transfer" argument investigation for normal contracts. It was found that the argument "balance" was the most frequently used argument in normal contracts. This argument can be roughly divided into two types: an argument for the total amount of

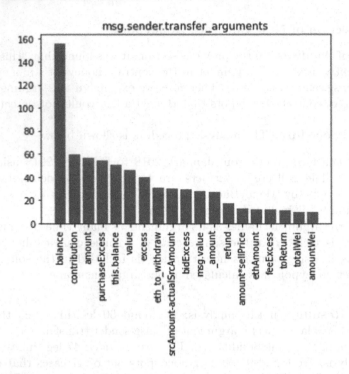

Fig. 6. Arguments of "msg.sender.transfer" function in regular contracts

the sender's stake in a game-type contract, and an argument for the amount of money paid by the contract setter to the game participants. The latter argument has a different meaning from "this.balance" and represents the total balance of the contract. In addition, the use of argument names that are reminiscent of balances, such as "this.balance", was also noticeable, but we found that most of them were variables that were related to the amount of money paid by the sender or the amount of Ether withdrawn, and we do not believe that they can be used as indicators of contract honeypots.

Of the 47 contracts, 38 were considered legitimate and included "this.balance" in "msg.sender.transfer". Of these 38, 23 were contracts whose purpose was unknown or that could have been involved in crimes. Specifically, 14 were game-type contracts, such as gambling and number-guessing, 1 was a pyramid scheme-type contract, 3 were contracts related to the sale and purchase of smart contract ownership, and 5 were money transfer-type contracts. For the remaining 15 contracts, we found that there were five money exchange-type contracts, one crowdfunding-type contract, four contracts related to buying and selling tokens, and five NFT-type contracts. From the above, we believe that "this.balance" indicator is effective as a feature for detecting suspicious contracts.

6   Discussion

6.1   Contract Honeypots Tracking

The analysis in Sect. 5.3 shows that the damage inflicted by contract honeypots did not decrease over in the period from January 2017 to May 2019, and that contract honeypots may continue to be a threat in the future. Therefore, we analyze the damage caused by contract honeypots for the period after May 2019.

First, we visually check the Method column in the Transaction section on EtherScan for contract honeypots that used some Solidity function in May 2019 or later. Next, we capture detailed behavior, such as Ether remittance processing and contract self-destruction.

The results of the follow-up survey after May 2019 are shown in Table 4. Six new cases were identified after May 2019, all of which were tricked by the contract honeypots. The total amount of damage was approximately 2.11 ETH. In addition, the following two activities were also identified: (1) management by the contract honeypot installer (specifically, withdrawing the funds accumulated in the wallet and deleting the contract), and (2) withdrawing Ether stored in the contract by the Ethereum user.

6.2   Difference Between the Presence and Absence of Damage

In this section, we focus on three types of contract honeypots (HSU, ID, and SESL) that are distinctive. In particular, we focus on HSU, which suffered the most damage, ID, which caused damages up to a 7 ETH per case, and SESL, whose inflicted damage was confirmed to be sudden (refer to Fig. 1) and whose traps had special characteristics (multiple arguments for remittance processing, unique definition of remittance processing, and trap intractability) relative to other contract honeypots. The number of contracts used in this study was 172. In particular, there were 112 cases in which contract honeypots failed in their attacks. The reasons are as follows: (1) No one accessed the contract honeypot; (2) An Ethereum user confirmed contract honeypot with 0 ETH; and (3) In the HSU, Ethereum users stole ether because the contract installers did not know how to use the traps or forgot to install the traps.

6.3   Damage of Legitimate Users

In this section, we focus on 172 cases of three types of contract honeypots (HSU, ID, and SESL), The contracts were confirmed to be of two types: 124 were game-like contracts that lure victims, and 48 were contracts that were intentionally made to appear vulnerable. In particular, in the former case, because the contract was a game contract, it is not necessarily the case that only the attackers accessed the contract honeypot. Legitimate users could access it regardless of whether the contract was a vulnerable honeypot or not, and legitimate users could be harmed.

7   Conclusion

In addition to understanding the scale of damage caused by contract honeypots, this study calculated the contract names commonly used by contract honeypots and the actual damages of contract honeypots based on the contract names code and "msg.sender.transfer" argument in Solidity code. In an analysis based on contract names and arguments, we presented the characteristics of honeypot class names that could easily be confirmed on EtherScan and the characteristics of "msg.sender.transfer" function arguments that should be carefully. We suggested the possibility of detecting unknown contract honeypots using "this.balance". In addition, we analyzed the damage caused by transaction-based contract honeypots, as well as the damage to legitimate users.

Acknowledgements. This work was supported by JSPS KAKENHI Grant Number JP22H03588.

References

1. Buterin, V.: A next-generation smart contract and decentralized application platform. White Paper (2014)
2. Camino, R., Torres, C.F., Baden, M., State, R.: A data science approach for detecting honeypots in Ethereum. In: IEEE ICBC 2020, pp. 1–9. IEEE (2020)
3. Chen, W., et al.: Honeypot contract risk warning on Ethereum smart contracts. In: IEEE JCC (2020)
4. Gogineni, A.K., et al.: Multi-class classification of vulnerabilities in smart contracts using AWD-LSTM, with pretrained encoder inspired from natural language processing. arXiv:2004.00362 (2020)
5. Hara, K., Takahashi, T., Ishimaki, M., Omote, K.: Machine-learning approach using solidity bytecode for smart-contract honeypot detection in the Ethereum. In: IEEE QRS-C (2021)
6. Hu, T., et al.: Transaction-based classification and detection approach for Ethereum smart contract. Inf. Process. Manag. **58**(2021), 102462 (2021)
7. Liao, W., Tsai, T.T., He, C.K., Tien, C.W.: SoliAudit: smart contract vulnerability assessment based on machine learning and fuzz testing. In: IOTSMS 2019, pp. 458–465. IEEE (2019)
8. Luu, L., et al.: Making smart contracts smarter. In: CCS 2016, pp. 254–269 (2016)
9. Nakamoto, S.: Bitcoin: a peer-to-peer electronic cash system (2008)
10. Torres, C.F., et al.: The art of the scam: demystifying honeypots in Ethereum smart contracts. In: USENIX Security 2019, pp. 1591–1607 (2019)
11. Coincheck. https://coincheck.com/ja/. Accessed 5 Sept 2022
12. Cryptocurrency Market Research. https://coinmarketcap.com/ja/. Accessed 5 Sept 2022
13. Cryptocurrency Penetration. https://www.finder.com/jp/finder-cryptocurrency-adoption-index. Accessed 5 Sept 2022
14. EVM. https://github.com/CoinCulture/evmtools/blob/master/analysis/guide.md. Accessed 20 Sept 2021
15. The DAO. https://www.gemini.com/cryptopedia/the-dao-hack-makerdao. Accessed 5 Sept 2022

A Gas Cost Analytical Approach Based on Certificateless Key Encapsulation Protocol for Medicalized Blockchains

Abigail Akosua Addobea[1]($\boxtimes$) (iD), QianMu Li[1] (iD), Isaac Amankona Obiri[2] (iD), and Jun Hou[3] (iD)

[1] Nanjing University of Science and Technology, Nanjing 210094, Jiangsu, China
abigailaddobea@njust.edu.cn, abigailaddobea@ymail.com, qianmu@njust.edu.cn
[2] University of Electronic Science and Technology, Chengdu 611731, Sichuan, China
obiriisaac@gmail.com
[3] Nanjing Vocational University of Industry Technology, Nanjing 21000, Jiangsu, China
houjunnjust@163.com

Abstract. The emergence of blockchain decentralization has garnered considerable interest from the scientific and scholarly communities since it addresses scalability issues and provides security for its users. Since its inception, numerous encryption methods have adopted its methodology to develop medically applicable schemes. However, most proposed schemes involve time-consuming operations, while others rely on standard pairing libraries. Both approaches cause complexity delays, affecting the blockchain's execution speed. In the case of blockchain digital signatures, participants' cryptographic keys are tied to their assets instead of their identities. This contradicts the non-repudiation feature of public key digital signatures. Therefore, this article proposes a lightweight hybrid encryption protocol employing the key encapsulation technique to generate encapsulated keys for blockchain network participants. The proposed method allows users to generate encapsulated keys linked to their identities. In order to increase the speed of cryptographic execution on the blockchain, we evaluate the computational overhead of the proposed model using the pairing Ethereum library (Py-eth library). In addition, the Ethereum Improvement Proposals (EIPs) library measures the consumption of gas costs on the blockchain. Our performance analysis demonstrates that the proposed protocol achieves a lower computational cost with less gas consumption, accelerating blockchain transaction executions.

Keywords: Blockchain · Key encapsulation · Gas cost · Elliptic curve cryptography · Eip library

This work was supported in part by The 4th project "Research on the Key Technology of Endogenous Security Switches" (2020YFB1804604) of the National Key R&D Program.

1 Introduction

In the public key encryption paradigm, message sizes are assumed to be of fixed length. Nevertheless, this assumption does not hold in reality. It becomes a cumbersome process when transferring bulk messages through a public channel to the cloud server. Key management is of ultimate concern in the medical-cloud domain, so user keys to establish communication must be protected. Not only that but the transmission data must also be secured. However, problems with key attacks occur when transmitting large messages without proper encryption mechanisms. Not only that, the transmission data must also be secured. However, problems with key attacks occur when transmitting large messages without utilizing proper encryption mechanisms. An attack on a user's private/public key pair can further aggravate the situation, resulting in a breach of medical data. Hybrid encryption has shown to be an efficient method since it incorporates both symmetric and asymmetric algorithms.

However, these activities occur in centralized settings, liable to the single point of failure (SPOF). In the same vein, cloud providers cannot be fully trusted to ensure the security of user medical data, including their respective private keys. An honest-but-curious cloud server may compromise the private keys of users. Hence, integrating the blockchain method while adopting the hybrid encryption method will mitigate the centralization and security problems in cloud centralization models. Since the inception of blockchain, a lot of decentralized public key encryption methods applicable to healthcare have been proposed in literature [5,12,21,25]. Nonetheless, the majority of these schemes built use time-consuming operations such as pairing operations. Another noticeable downside is the lack of appropriate pairing-based blockchain simulation libraries used for scheme implementation [5,12,21,25].

Another noticeable downside is the lack of appropriate pairing-based blockchain simulation libraries used for scheme implementation [5,12,25]. With reference to the latter, the standard simulation libraries such as MIRACL,jPBC [2,8,11] have higher execution run times making it unfeasible for blockchain transactions. Similar to the former, the use of time-consuming cryptographic operations causes higher transaction complexities, leading to higher gas costs, which delays the speed of transaction executions on the blockchain [19]. While digital signatures have been widely applied to blockchains, public blockchains do not bind the identity of the participant to their signature; rather, the identity is tied to the participant's address, which breaks the non-repudiation feature [20]. In such a case, the signature keys are not protected, but only the assets. Therefore, any vulnerability in the blockchain system can lead to a compromise of cryptographic keys. Based on these identified problems, the proposed article presents its contributions in the following bulleted points:

(i) The suggested article proposes a lightweight hybrid encryption mechanism adopting a Key Encapsulation (KEM) approach for medical settings based on blockchain. Each participant derives an encapsulated key that is tied to their respective identities.

(ii) We prove the hardness of the proposed method in the random oracle model (ROM), which is indistinguishable against chosen ciphertext attack (IND-CCA1) and satisfies computational Diffie-Hellman (CDH) assumptions.

(iii) The proposed method is lightweight since it does not involve time-consuming operations in the algorithm generation. Moreover, the performance of the proposed method is tested with a pairing-Ethereum library with lesser running times than the standard libraries(MIRACL and PBC). Finally, a further comparative analysis is performed with eip-1108 from the Ethereum Improvement Proposals (EIPs) library to evaluate the gas cost consumption.

(iv) Results from the performance analysis have shown the proposed method to have a lesser computational overhead with the least gas cost complexity on the blockchain, which avoids complexity delays of transaction execution on the medicalized blockchains.

Paper Organisation. The remaining parts of the paper are categorized into the following sections. Section 2 summarizes the state-of-the-art key management blockchain schemes. Section 3 presents the preliminaries, the underlying hardness assumptions and the generic model of the proposed method. Section 4 introduces the proposed protocol. Section 5 analyzes the proof of the proposed protocol according to the hardness assumption stated in Sect. 3.2. The performance of the proposed method is evaluated in Sect. 6. Finally, Sect. 7 presents the conclusion of the proposed article.

2 Summary of Existing Research

Blockchain technology, as introduced by Satoshi Nakamoto [16] is a decentralized platform that runs on a distributed ledger that uses cryptographically hashed blocks to record network transactions. With its initial introduction of bitcoin, the blockchain paradigm developed into other domains such as healthcare, agriculture and entertainment. Regarding health care, Nguyen et al. [17] utilized blockchain to offload EHR health data to enable data sharing through smart contracts. Consequently, Abudnadi et al. [1] introduced a BBPM approach to curb coronavirus diffusion by leveraging blockchain networks on people's mobile devices. El Majdoubi et al. [9] also applied the concept of blockchain to design an end-to-end (E2E) encryption privacy-preserving framework to establish an effective data sharing system in the smart healthcare system. Their framework relied on a Hyperledger fabric by storing encrypted data on an Interplanetary File System (IPFS), with high resiliency and scalability. Similarly, Hylock et al. [10] also presented a patient centric blockchain framework named HealthChain to strengthen patient engagement in an interoperable environment. The authors used a proof-of-concept tool to evaluate the performance of the patients blocks.

Badr et al. [5] proposed a novel protocol based on pseudonym encryption to provide privacy-preservation to patients on the blockchain. The pseudonym encryption approach will enable patients to anonymously access, check and update their sensitive data on eHealth Records (EHRs) system.

Authors in [14] also conducted a literature survey to address existing blockchain issues and vulnerabilities such as mining incentives, mining attacks, and key management in the health sector.

Concerning other blockchain aspects, Badshah et al. [6] constructed a lightweight authenticated key exchange scheme for smart grids in which secure communication is established between service providers (SP) and energy smart grids (SG). Consequently, Yao et al. [24] also used a homomorphic hash function to design a key exchange protocol in the blockchain that provides privacy protection to social network participants. Similarly, Mwitende et al. [15] designed CLAKA a Certificateless authenticated key agreement scheme for decentralized wireless body area networks (WBANs) to mitigate single point of failure and escrow vulnerabilities typical in cloud based identity based AKA (Authenticated key agreement) systems. One disadvantage of the scheme is that it is computationally costly due to excessive pairings in the scheme.

Similarly, authors in [18] addressed the issue of private key protection for bitcoin wallets. The authors introduced a group key management scheme to ensure transaction confidentiality amongst group communicators on the blockchain network. Zhao et al. [27] also used the concept of blockhain to design an efficient key management scheme to protect private physiological data in the body sensor networks (BSN). Although, the authors used a biosensor nodes to design a backup and efficient recovery scheme, research shows that the algorithm in the existing work is not concretely sound to achieve health data protection in BSN. Moreover, Hylock et al. [10] also presented a patient centric blockchain framework named HealthChain to strengthen patient engagement in an interoperable environment. The authors used a proof-of-concept tool to evaluate the performance of the patients blocks.

Despite the various application of blockchain systems, the authors design a key encapsulation model that relies on certificateless cryptography with a concentration on the blockchain. The proposed approach allows participants exchange derived encapsulated keys to access medical information stored on the blockchain. The proposed method is advantageous since it is constructed in a certificateless setting. Therefore, the total reliance on the Key Generation Server (KGS) to derive full private keys for users is obviated. Thus, the proposed method avoids the key escrow effect prevalent in identity-based systems. The proposed method is lightweight and does not entail intensive cryptographic operations such as pairings, making it very applicable for medical blockchains.

3   Preliminaries

This section describes the fundamental theories and key concepts that are applicable to this work.

3.1   Elliptic Curve Cryptography

The proposed protocol is based on the underlying concept of the Elliptic Curve Cryptography (ECC). This curve is chosen due to its shorter key sizes and faster execution. According to [7], a 160-bit ECC is considered to be as secure as 1024-bit RSA key. Therefore, an elliptic curve is a non-singular curve $E_q(a, b)$ is defined over F_q where q is a large prime number. An elliptic curve equation is of the form in Eq. 1

$$y^2 = (x^3 + ax + b) mod q; \tag{1}$$

where $a, b, x, y \in F_q$ and $4a^3 + 27b^2 mod q \neq 0$. Considering an additive cyclic group $\mathbb{G}_q$, given $k \in G_q$ and a point $P \in E_q(a, b)$, kP becomes the scalar multiplication over $E_q(a, b)$ with $\mathcal{O}$ being the point at infinity.

3.2 Complexity Assumptions

The proposed method relies on the following hardness assumption.

Definition 1. *Computational Diffie-Hellman Problem (CDH): The computational Diffie-Hellman (CDH) problem is defined as the following: Given $(Q = xP, R = yP) \in \mathbb{G}_q$ for any $x, y \in \mathbb{Z}_q^*$, xyP can effectively be computed. Thus, according to the CDH problem it is intractable for a polynomial bounded adversary $\mathcal{A}$ to solve difficult for an adversary $\mathcal{A}$ to solve $xyP \in \mathbb{G}_q$.*

3.3 Generic Model of a Certificateless Key Encapsulation (CL-KEM) Method

This section presents the formal definition of certificateless key encapsulation system. A certificateless key encapsulation protocol comprises of 7 polynomial time algorithms namely Setup, User key Generation, Partial-private-key-Extract, Set-Private-Key, Set-Public-Key, Encapsulation and Decapsulation.

(i) Setup: The Key Generation Server (KGS) initializes the system by taking a security parameter $k \in \mathbb{Z}_q^*$ to set up the system parameters *params*, the master public and master secret key respectively (mpk, msk). It publicly publishes *params* and *mpk* and keeps the *msk* secret.

(ii) User-key-Generation: Each user to the system runs this algorithm to generate the secret value and its corresponding public value. Taking *params* and the user's identity U_{ID}, it generates public/secret key (p_k, s_k) pair.

(iii) Partial-private-Key Extract: The user takes its identity U_{ID}, and its corresponding public value p_k, *params*, master secret key msk as inputs. The Key generation server (KGS) runs this algorithm and returns the partial private key D_{ID} and partial public key R_{ID} and securely sends it to the user.

(iv) Set Private key: Each user runs this algorithm by taking *params*, partial private key D_{ID}, and his/her secret value x_{ID}, to derive its full private key as S_{ID}.

(v) Set public key: The user runs this algorithm by taking *params*, the user's secret value x_{ID}, partial public key R_{ID}, the user's public value p_k, and returns the user's public key as P_{ID}.

(vi) Encapsulation: This deterministic algorithm is executed by the sender $user_A$ by taking the sender's identity ID_A, the public key P_{ID_A} as inputs and returns the encapsulated key pair k, c where $(k, c) \in (K, C)$, where c is the encapsulation of key k.

(vii) Decapsulation: The decapsulation algorithm is performed by the receiver $user_B$ by taking the encapsulation c, the sender's identity ID_A, the public key P_{ID_A}, the receiver's public key and private key (P_{ID_B}, S_{ID_B}) as inputs and returns the key or an invalid encapsulation $\perp$.

Table Description. Table 1 describes the symbols and notations used in the work.

Table 1. Descriptions of symbols and notations.

Symbols	Notations	Symbols	Notations
KGS	Key Generation Server	R_D	Doctor's partial public key
$\mathbb{G}_q$	Group element of prime order q	R_P	Patient's partial public key
α	KGS Master secret key	S_D	Doctor's private key
Ω	Proposed protocol system parameters	S_P	Patient's private key
γ	KGS master public key	$Encap_A$	Encapsulation algorithm for doctor
(p_D, s_D)	Doctor's Key generated value	$Encap_B$	Encapsulation algorithm for patient
(p_p, s_p)	Patient's Key generated value	K_1	Session key computed by patient
φ	KGS computed value	K_2	Session key computed by doctor
D_D	Doctor's partial private key	$\parallel$	Concatenation operation
D_P	Patient's partial private key	w.r.t	with respect to

3.4 Adversarial Model

Al-Riyami and Patterson [3] firstly proposed the certificateless public Key algorithm and established the security model for the certificateless public key algorithm by which it considers two adversaries Type I adversary modeled as $\mathcal{A}_I$ and Type II adversary modeled as $\mathcal{A}_{II}$. The Type I adversary represents the dishonest user who does not have access to the KGS's master key, but is able to replace public keys of its choice. Likewise, the Type II adversary represents a malicious but curious KGS that possesses the master secret key, msk who can request for private keys of its choice but is incapable of replacing the user's public key.

A CL-KEM must fully achieve the confidentiality feature. Therefore, the proposed protocol is indistinguishable against chosen ciphertext attack (IND-CCA1), if no polynomial time bounded adversaries $\mathcal{A}_I$ and $\mathcal{A}_{II}$ having a non-negligible advantage ε is capable of making queries to the following oracles by playing a request-response game with the challenger, $\mathcal{C}$.

4   Proposed Protocol

This section presents the construction of the proposed certificateless key encapsulated protocol that considers three entities namely the KGS, the patient and the doctor.

4.1   Protocol Construction

(a) Setup: The KGS, initially selects $k \in \mathbb{Z}_q^*$ as input and derives a list of system parameters, ξ, a master public and private key pair as (mpk, msk). Given k, KGS makes the following computations:
   - Selects a security parameter a k-bit prime q and establishes the system parameters $\Omega = \langle F_q, E/F_q, \mathbb{G}_q, P \rangle$, where P is the generator of $\mathbb{G}_q$.
   - Chooses the master secret key $\alpha \in \mathbb{Z}_q^*$ uniformly at random and compute the master public key $\gamma = aP$.
   - Selects two cryptographic hash functions $H_0 : \{0,1\}^* \times \mathbb{G}_q^2 \to \{0,1\}^*$, $H_1 : \{0,1\}^m \times \mathbb{G}_q^2 \to \mathbb{Z}_q^*$, $H_2 : \{0,1\}^m \times \{0,1\}^m \times \{0,1\}^m \to \mathbb{Z}_q^*$. Publishes the system parameters as $\Omega = \{F_q, E/F_q, \mathbb{G}_q, P, \gamma, H_0, H_1, H_2\}$ and keeps α, the master key secret. Hence, the master public and secret key pair $(mpk, msk) = (\gamma, a)$.
(b) User Key Generation:
   - Doctor Key Generation: The doctor picks $y \in \mathbb{Z}_q^*$ and computes yp. It sets $Y = yP$. and returns $(s_P, p_p) = (y, Y) = (y, yP)$.
   - Patient Key Generation: The patient picks $z \in \mathbb{Z}_q^*$. Computes $Z = zP$ and sets $Z = zP$. He returns $(s_D, p_D) = (z, Z) = (z, zP)$.

(c) Partial private Key Extract: The state information (φ) is first computed by choosing $s \in \mathbb{Z}_q^*$ and computes $\varphi = sP$. The KGS continues to generate the partial private key for both doctor and patient by doing the following:
   - The partial private key for the patient is computed as $d_P = s + \alpha H_1(ID_P \parallel \varphi \parallel p_p)$. It returns the partial private key as $(R_P, D_P) = (\varphi, d_P)$.
   - The partial private key for the doctor is computed as $d_D = s + \alpha H_1(ID_D \parallel \varphi \parallel p_D)$. It returns the partial private key as $(R_D, D_D) = (\varphi, d_D)$.
(d) Set Private Key: The patient takes d_P and a $z \in \mathbb{Z}_q^*$ to obtain its private key S_P. Thus, $S_P = (s_P, D_P) = (z, d_P)$. The doctor computes its private key S_D by taking d_D and $y \in \mathbb{Z}_q^*$. It returns $S_D = (s_D, D_D) = (y, d_D)$.
(e) Set Public Key: The patient sets its public key as $P_P = (p_P, R_P) = (z, \varphi)$. Similarly, the doctor also computes its public key as $P_D = (p_D, R_D) = (y, \varphi)$.
(f) Encapsulation: At this stage, both the patient and the doctor perform the encapsulation algorithm as follows:
   $Encap_A$: The patient performs the below encapsulation algorithm:
   - Picks $u \in \mathbb{Z}_q^*$ and computes $c = uP$
   - Picks Z and computes $c_1 = u(Z + \varphi + \gamma H_1(ID_P) \| \varphi \| p_p)$ and $c_2 = uZ = uzP = zuP = zc$.
   - Derives the corresponding session key $K_1 = H_2(ID_P \| P_p \| c \| c_1 \| c_2)$ and sends it to the doctor through a secure channel.
   $Encap_B$: The doctor performs the below encapsulation algorithm:
   - Picks $x \in \mathbb{Z}_q^*$ and computes $c' = xP$.
   - Picks Y, and computes $c_1' = x(Y + \varphi + \gamma H_1(ID_D) \| \varphi \| p_D)$ and $c_2' = xY = xyP = c'y$

- Derives the corresponding session key as $K_2 = H_2(ID_D||P_D||c'||c_1'||c_2')$ and sends it to the doctor through a secure channel. Both parties exchange the encapsulated keys K_1 and K_2 through a secure channel.

(g) Decapsulation: After successfully exchanging the encapsulated keys, both parties perform the decapsulation algorithm to obtain the encapsulators c_1 and c_1'. Both parties decipher keys K_1 and K_2 as follows:

$$K_1 = H_2(ID_P||P_p||c||(z + d_p)c||uZ)$$

$$(z + d_p)c = (z + (s + aH_1(ID_P||\varphi||P_p)))c$$

$$= zc + (s + aH_1(ID_P||\varphi||P_p))c$$

$$= zuP + (suP + auPH_1(ID_P||\varphi||P_p))$$

$$= u(zP + sP + aPH_1(ID_P||\varphi||P_p))$$

$$= u(Z + \varphi + \gamma H_1(ID_P||\varphi||P_p)) = c_1$$

$$K_2 = H_2(ID_D||P_D||c||(y + d_D)c'||xP)$$

$$(y + d_D)c' = (y + (s + aH_1(ID_D||varphi||P_D)))c'$$

$$= yc' + (s + aH_1(ID_D||\varphi||P_D))c'$$

$$= yxP + (sxP + axPH_1(ID_D||\varphi||P_D))$$

$$= x(Y + \varphi + \gamma H_1(ID_D||\varphi||P_D)) = c_1'$$

5   Security Proofs and Analysis

This section provides analyzes the security proof the proposed protocol in the random oracle model (ROM). Theorem 1 shows the proposed model is secure against the Type-I and Type II adversary.

Theorem 1. *In the ROM, the proposed protocol is IND-CCA1 (INDistinguishability under Chosen Ciphertext Attack) secure under the assumption that the CDH problem is intractable to be solved by any polynomial time bounded adversary. The basis of Theorem 1 is proven in Lemma 1.*

Lemma 1. *Assuming there are two resistant collision hash functions H_1 and H_2 existing as random oracles. If there exists and adversary $\mathcal{A}_I$ against IND-CCA1 with a non-negligible advantage ε capable of making the following queries: q_{H_i} to the random hash oracles, q_{par} queries to the Partial-Key-Extract oracle, q_u queries to the Create User (ID_i), q_{pri} queries to the Private key request oracle, q_{pub} queries to the Public Key request oracle and q_D queries to the decapsulation oracle to the random oracle, q_{pubR} queries to the Public Key replacement, q_{sv} queries to the secret value extraction. Then there exists an algorithm $\mathcal{G}$ that solves the CDH problem with the following advantage $\varepsilon' \geq$*

$$\varepsilon \cdot \left(1 - \frac{q_{par}}{q_{HO}}\right) \cdot \left(1 - \frac{q_{sv}}{q_{HO}}\right) \cdot \left(1 - \frac{q_{pubR}}{q_{H1}}\right) \cdot \left(\frac{1}{q_{HO} - q_{par} - q_{sv} - q_{pubR}}\right) \cdot \left(\frac{1}{q_{H1}}\right)$$

Proof. We let a Type-I adversary acts as an "outsider" adversary, who replaces the public key of random entities of its choice but cannot replace the master key. In our .... Algorithm, a challenger$\mathcal{C}$ is tasked with the instance of been able to compute the CDH problem (P, aP, bP) with an advantage ε' by interacting with the adversary $\mathcal{A}_1$. $\mathcal{C}$ maintains a public list L_i $(0 \leq i \leq 2)$, with the corresponding hash functions H_i $(0 \leq i \leq 2)$ being the random oracles. $\mathcal{C}$ also keeps a list of publicized private and public keys in the list L_w. $\mathcal{C}$ randomly picks a token t, with $(0 \leq t \leq q_{H_0})$ and sets ID_t as the challenged identity.

The algorithm $\mathcal{G}$ simulates the challenger to run the algorithm through the following oracles:

Phase 1: $\mathcal{A}_1$ can issue a series of polynomial bounded number of queries to random oracles H_i with $(0 \leq i \leq 2)$ with $\mathcal{C}$ responding with the following:

1. **Create-User (ID):** The adversary $\mathcal{A}_I$ creates a challenged identity ID_t, where $(1 \leq t \leq q_{H_0})$. If $ID_i = ID_t$, the challenger $\mathcal{C}$ develops a tuple $H_0(ID_t, \varphi_t, Y_t)$ into the list L_o and maintains an initial list $L_w = \langle ID_t, \perp, Y_t \rangle$. If $ID_i \neq ID_t$, $\mathcal{C}$ generates a tuple $H_0(ID_i, \varphi_i, Y_i)$ and inserts it into the list L_o and $\langle ID_i, \varphi_i, Y_i \rangle$ into L_w.

2. **Setup:** The Challenger sets the master public key $X = bP$, where $b \in_R \mathbb{Z}_q^*$ is the master secret key and generates the system parameters $\Omega = \{F_q, E/F_q, \mathbb{G}_q, P, X, H_0, H_1, H_2\}$. Publishes the system parameters publicly and queries the hash oracles in the following manner:

3. **H_0Queries:** $\mathcal{A}_I$ submits a query to H_0 with a randomly chosen identity, the challenger $\mathcal{C}$searches the list, L_0 containing the tuples $\langle (ID_i, \varphi_i, Y_i), v_i \rangle$. On receiving the query, $\mathcal{C}$ checks for the following:
   - If the tuple $\langle (ID_i, \varphi_i, Y_i), v_i \rangle$ already exits in the list L_0, the challenger returns v as a response.
   - Otherwise, it randomly chooses $v \in \mathbb{Z}_q^*$ and updates the tuple $\langle (ID_i, \varphi_i, Y_i), v_i \rangle$ in L_0 and returns v as an answer.

4. **H_1Queries:** $\mathcal{A}_I$ submits a query to the simulator H_1 containing the tuples $\langle U_i, T_i, Y_i, ID_i, P_i, V_i \rangle$ with the following queries $\langle aP, U_i, V_i \rangle$ from the adversary $\mathcal{A}_I$. $\mathcal{C}$ runs the simulator and checks the simulator if it returns the value 1. If it does, $\mathcal{C}$ returns T_i and aborts the simulation. Else, $\mathcal{C}$ scans the list L_1 with entries $\langle U_i, *, Y_i, ID_i, P_i, V_i \rangle$ for different values of V_i for the simulator to return 1 with the queried tuples $\langle aP, U_i, V_i \rangle$ from the adversary $\mathcal{A}_I$. If the tuples exist, it returns V_i and replaces the symbol $*$ with T_i. Otherwise, $\mathcal{C}$ chooses $V \in_R \{0, 1\}^n$ and updates the list L_1 and returns V_i to $\mathcal{A}_I$.

5. **H_2 Queries:** $\mathcal{C}$ analyzes the following tuple and verifies if it exists in the list L_2. If it exists, $\mathcal{C}$ responds the query with $H = h_i$ to the adversary $\mathcal{A}_I$. Otherwise, $\mathcal{C}$ picks $h_i \in_R \mathbb{Z}_q^*$, adds it to the tuple $\langle U, V, \varphi_i, ID_P, P_P, ID_D, P_D, h_i \rangle$ and updates the list L_2 and returns h_i to $\mathcal{A}_I$.

6. **Extract Partial-Key Queries:** To respond to the queries for the partial private key of the user with identityID_i, the challenger $\mathcal{C}$,computes the following: If, $ID_i = ID_t$, $\mathcal{C}$ halts the simulation. However, if $ID_i \neq ID_t$, $\mathcal{C}$ recovers the tuple $\langle ID_i (\varphi_i, d_i) \rangle$ from the list L_w, and answers the query with (φ_i, d_i). Else, it picks $u_i, v \in \mathbb{Z}_p^*$ and computes $\varphi_i = d_i P - vX$. L_w is

updated with (ID, φ_i, v) and adds $\langle ID, (\varphi_i, d_i) \rangle$ to the list partial-private-key list, and answers the query with (φ_i, d_i).

7. **Extract- Secret- Value:** $\mathcal{A}_I$ present ID_i to $\mathcal{C}$ and requests for the secret value of submitted ID_i. $\mathcal{C}$ checks L_w if the public key of the requested ID_i has been replaced whereas $ID_i \neq ID_t$, $\mathcal{C}$ picks y and submits as a response to $\mathcal{A}_I$. Otherwise, if ID_i has been replaced and $ID_i = ID_t$, $\mathcal{C}$ halts the operation.

8. **Extract Public key Queries:** $\mathcal{C}$ tosses a *coin* $P \in \{0,1\}$ and returns 0 with probability ε and $1 - \varepsilon$. $\mathcal{C}$ maintains a public-key List consisting of the following tuples $\langle ID_i (\varphi_{ID}, Y), P \rangle$. On receiving a query on a chosen identity ID_i, the challenger $\mathcal{C}$ responds with the following:
   - If the tuple $\langle ID_i, (\varphi_i, Y), P \rangle$ exist in the public-key list, the challenger responds with $P_i = (\varphi_i, Y)$.
   - Else, $\mathcal{C}$ tosses a coin $P \in \{0,1\}$, if $Pr[coin\ P = 0] = \varepsilon$.
   - If $Pr[coin\ P = 0]$, $\mathcal{C}$ does the following: $\mathcal{C}$ searches the partial key list L_{ppke} if the following tuple $\langle ID, (\varphi_{ID}, d_i) \rangle$ exists and chooses $y \in_R Z_p^*$ and compute $Y = yP$ and then update the private key list and the public key list with $\langle ID, (y, d_i) \rangle$ and $\langle ID_i, (\varphi_i, Y), P \rangle$ respectively and finally returns $P_i = (\varphi_i, Y)$ as the public key.
   - If not, $\mathcal{C}$ runs the partial key extract algorithm to obtain the partial keys (φ_i, d_i). Then picks $y \in_R Z_p^*$ at random and computes $Y = yP$. It updates the private-key and public-key lists with the tuples $\langle ID_i, (\varphi_i, d_i) \rangle$ and $\langle ID_i, (\varphi_i, Y), coin\ P \rangle$ respectively and returns the pubic key $P_i = (\varphi_i, Y)$. Otherwise, if $(coinP = 1)$, randomly pick $x_i, y_i \in Z_p^*$ and computes $\varphi_i = x_i P, Y_i = y_i P$, it then updates the private key list with $\langle ID_i, (y_i, \omega) x_i \rangle$ and $\langle ID_i, (\varphi_i, Y_i), coin\ P \rangle$ to the public key list, and returns $P_i = (\varphi_i, Y_i)$ where ω is a state information.

9. **Extract Private key Queries:** The adversary $\mathcal{A}_I$ throws a challenge to $\mathcal{C}$ with a chosen arbitrary identity, ID_i to request for its private key. If the public key of the chosen identity ID_i has not been replaced and $ID_i \neq ID_t$, then $\mathcal{C}$ responds with (y_i, d_i). If the identity has already been replaced, $ID_i = ID_t$, $\mathcal{C}$ does not provide the private key to $\mathcal{A}_I$, but it finally aborts the operation.

10. **Public key Replacement Queries:** For $\mathcal{A}_1$ to replace any public key with a new value it may choose arbitrary values $P_i' = (p_i', R_i')$ for the replacement of the public keys of a user ID_i.

11. **Encapsulation key Queries:** $\mathcal{A}_1$ produces the sender's identity (patient's ID) ID_P, it's corresponding public key $P_P = (p_P, R_P)$, the receiver's (doctor's) identity ID_D, it's corresponding public key $P_D = (p_D, R_D)$ and sends them to $\mathcal{C}$. The full private key of the sender $S_P = (s_D, D_D)$ is obtained from the private key list. $\mathcal{C}$ checks if the tuple $\langle ID, (y, d_D) \rangle$.
   - If the tuple does not exist, it aborts the execution.
   - If the tuple exists and $ID_D \neq ID_t$, then $\mathcal{C}$ computes
   - as the session key or reject if otherwise

12. **Decapsulation Queries:** The adversary $\mathcal{A}_1$ submits a query $(ID_D, P_D, c) (ID_D', P_D, c')$ where ID_D is a randomly chosen identity of a doctor, its corresponding public key P_D where $P_D = (p_D, R_D) = (y, \varphi)$

and an encapsulation value c' to the challenger $\mathcal{C}$. $\mathcal{C}$ checks the tuple $\langle ID_i, (\varphi_i, Y_i), coin\ P \rangle$ from the public key list if the tuple exists. If the tuple exists and $coin\ P = 0$, and $ID_i \neq ID_D$, it searches the private key list for the tuple $\langle ID_D, (y, \varphi_D) \rangle$ and further computes $K_2 = H_2 (ID_D \parallel P_D \parallel c \parallel (y + d_D) c' \parallel c')$ where $c' = xP$. Otherwise, if the tuple exits, $coin\ P = 1$, then $\mathcal{C}$ computes the following:

- Executes H_1queries to get a tuple $\langle ID_D, (\varphi_D, Y), u \rangle$.
- If there exists $\langle (ID, U), V \rangle$ where $V = H_2 (ID \parallel U)$ and outputs V as the session key or reject if otherwise.
- If the tuple $\langle ID_i, (\varphi_i, Y), coin\ P \rangle$ does not exist that means the public key of the challenged user (the randomly chosen identity of the doctor) has been replaced by $\mathcal{A}_1$. Thus, $ID_i = ID_D$, then $\mathcal{C}$ checks $(y + d_D) c' = x (y + s + aH_1 (ID_P \parallel \varphi \parallel P_D)) P$ if the equality holds.

Challenge: At the end of Phase I, $\mathcal{A}_1$ puts out a challenge on identity ID_i^* and the challenger $\mathcal{C}$ responds to the query as follows:

The algorithm runs the public key request queries on the challenged identity ID_i^*, to obtain the tuple $\langle ID_i^*, (\varphi_i, Y^*), coin \rangle$ in the public key list. If the $coin = 0$, the execution aborts and terminate. If $coin \neq 0$, the algorithm does the following:

Checks the tuple $\langle ID_i^*, (y^*, \omega), x_i \rangle$ in the private key list but the following is already precomputed $\varphi_i = x_i^* P$, $Y_i^* = y_i^* P$, $\varphi_i = d_i P - vX$.

(a) Selects $a \in_R Z_p^*$ and sets $c^* = aP$, $c_1^* = a(Y_i^* + \varphi_i^* + XH_1 (ID_i^* \parallel \varphi_i^* \parallel Y_i^*))$ and $c_2^* = aY_i^*$.

(b) Compute $\Gamma = a\varphi_i^* P$ and $v^* = H_1(ID_i^* \parallel \varphi_i^* \parallel Y_i^*)$ and pick $k_i \in_R K$ where $(i = 1 \ldots .n.)$ and K is the key space.

(c) Computes $K_1 = H_2 (ID_i^* \parallel (\varphi_i^*, Y_i^*) \parallel c^* \parallel c_1^* \parallel c_2^*)$.

(d) $\mathcal{C}$ chooses a bit $\alpha \in_R \{0, 1\}$ and sends (c^*, K_α) to $\mathcal{A}_1$.

Phase 2: $\mathcal{A}_1$ adaptively replicates the queries in Phase 1. However, queries about partial key extract or private key request are not performed on an arbitrary challenged identity ID_I^*. Similarly, there is not encapsulation/decapsulation made on an arbitrary chosen ID.

Guess: $\mathcal{A}_1$ outputs a guess α' for α and wins the game if it breaks the proposed algorithm if the guess $\alpha' = \alpha$ then the α can compute the CDH problem by solving $\varphi_i = d_i P - vX$; $(y^* + d_i^*) c^* = (y^* + (\varphi_i + v^* X)) c^*$

$$y^* c^* + d_i^* c^* = y^* c^* + c^* \varphi_i + c^* v^* X$$
$$d_i^* c^* = aP\varphi_i + c^* v^* X = \Gamma + c^* v^* X$$
$$(d_i^* c^* - \Gamma)/v^* = c^* X = abP$$

Analysis: In order to assess the queries of events, we let E_1, E_2, E_3 denote the sequence of events in which the challenger,$\mathcal{C}$ has the success of poses an advantage of aborting the game.

1. E_1 denotes an event in which the adversary$\mathcal{A}_1$ queries the partial key of the target identity ID^*. The probability of E_1 is $(Pr[E_1]) = q_{par}/q_{H_0}$.

2. E_2 denotes an event in which the adversary $\mathcal{A}_1$ makes queries to the private key of the target identity ID^*. The probability of E_2 is $(Pr[E_2]) = q_{sv}/q_{H_0}$.

3. E_3 denotes an event in which the adversary $\mathcal{A}_1$ makes queries to the private key of the target identity ID^* which results in the probability of E_3 as $(Pr[E_2]) = q_{pubR}/q_{H_0}$.

4. E_4 indicates an event in which the adversary $\mathcal{A}_1$ has not queried the target identity ID_i^* during the challenge simulation. The probability of E_3 is given as $(Pr[E_4]) = 1 - \left(\frac{1}{q_{H0} - q_{par} - q_{sv} - q_{pubR}}\right)$. Hence, the probability that the challenger $\mathcal{C}$ does that abort the simulation, thus if event E_n where $(1 \leq n \leq 4)$ does not occur, then $Pr[\neg E_1 \wedge \neg E_2 \wedge \neg E_3 \neg E_4] = \left(1 - \frac{q_{par}}{q_{H_o}}\right) \cdot \left(1 - \frac{q_{sv}}{q_{H_0}}\right) \cdot \left(1 - \frac{q_{pubR}}{q_{H_0}}\right) \cdot \left(\frac{1}{q_{H0} - q_{par} - q_{sv} - q_{pubR}}\right) \cdot \left(\frac{1}{q_{H_1}}\right)$.

Supposed, that $P_i = (\varphi_i, Y)$ and c' be a valid decapsulation query with K be a session key, the likelihood of producing a session key K without making queries $\langle (ID, U), V \rangle$ to H_2.

The probability that $\mathcal{C}$ randomly chooses U from the list L_2 and the result obtained from the CDH problem is $\frac{1}{q_{H_2}}$. Therefore, the probability that the challenger $\mathcal{C}$ is able to solve the CDH problem as follows: $Pr[\mathcal{C}(P, aP, bP) = abP] = \varepsilon \cdot \left(1 - \frac{q_{par}}{q_{H0}}\right) \cdot \left(1 - \frac{q_{sv}}{q_{H0}}\right) \cdot \left(1 - \frac{q_{pubR}}{q_{H0}}\right) \cdot \left(\frac{1}{q_{H0} - q_{par} - q_{sv} - q_{pubR}}\right) \cdot \left(\frac{1}{q_{H_1}}\right)$.

Hence, $Pr[\mathcal{C}(P, aP, bP) = abP]$ is non-negligible if ε is non-negligible.

6   Performance Evaluation

This section compares the performance of the proposed protocol with other related certificateless hybrid protocols existing in literature. The evaluation considers the computational overhead as well as the gas cost complexity of each respective scheme. For computational overhead, we examine the execution time costs of each scheme with respect to the algorithm metric used in the analysis. Hence, the UserKeyGen, Encap and Decap algorithms are used as the key metrics in measuring the performance of each protocol in each analysis. Similarly, the same analytical metrics are used as indicators in analysing the gas cost complexity.

6.1   Computational Overhead Analysis

This subsection determines the computational cost based on pairing, addition, and multiplication operations. Cryptographic hashing and XOR operations are excluded from the analysis as they are not included in the simulation library. The simulation is carried out on an Ethereum pre-compiled pairing library (py-eth-pairing library) defined on a Barreto-Naehrig (BN)128 curve $y^2 = x^3 + 3$ over the finite field $\mathcal{F}_q$ of prime order p. The library is compiled on a 64-bit Mac OS operating system with an Intel dual Core i5 processor running at 3.1GHz and 8 GB of RAM. In accordance with the py-eth-pairing library [13], we represent a curve multiplication is represented as C_{mult}, curve pairing as C_{pair}, and curve addition as C_{add}. A total number of 30 executions are performed for each respective operation. Since the running times of the cryptographic operations in the py-eth-pairing library [13] are minimal, the outcome of each simulation trials are not averaged. From [13], the running time of a C_{mult} operation takes 0.001606 s, a C_{add} operation takes 0.001018 s, and a C_{pair} operation takes 0.090162 s. We evaluate each scheme's computational cost from our experimental findings and compare the efficiency of the proposed protocol with that of the existing methods utilizing the efficiency metrics in [22].

Table 2. Computational costs and Execution times of schemes.

Scheme	UserKeyGen	Encap	Decap
IC-CHS [4]	$4C_{add} + 6C_{mult} \approx 0.013708$ s	$2C_{add} + 2C_{mult} + 1C_{pair} \approx 0.09541$	$1C_{pair} \approx 0.090162$ s
NP-IoT [26]	$1C_{mult} \approx 0.001606$ s	$4C_{mult} + 1C_{add} + 1C_{pair} \approx 0.097604$ s	$2C_{mult} + 1C_{add} + 1C_{pair} \approx 0.094392$ s
IH-IoT [23]	$1C_{pair} \approx 0.090162$ s	$2C_{add} + 2C_{mult} \approx 0.005248$ s	$1C_{pair} + 2C_{add} \approx 0.092198$ s
Proposed	$2C_{mult} \approx 0.003212$	$5C_{mult} + 4C_{add} \approx 0.012102$	$2C_{mult} + 4C_{add} \approx 0.007284$

The execution times of each scheme w.r.t User key generation (UserKeyGen), encapsulation (Encap) and decapsulation (Decap) is represented in Table 2. According to the graph in Fig. 1 while using Table 2 as reference, execution time for User key generation was lower in NP-IoT scheme and Higher in IH-IoT scheme. While IH-IoT scheme performed better in the encapsulation algorithm. With respect to decapsulation, the proposed method surpassed the rest of the schemes in terms of execution times. In comparison, the proposed protocol achieved the lowest execution time w.r.t UserkeyGen, Encap and Decap. In total, the proposed method achieved the least amount of running times compared to that of the relative schemes. Since the computational cost is lesser in the proposed method, we can conclude that, it takes less time to finish a key exchange transaction on the blockchain network.

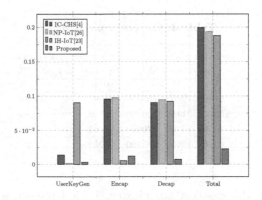

Fig. 1. Computational overhead

Comparing the efficiency of the proposed method to the relative schemes, it is realized that, the proposed protocol is 88.66% improved in IC-CHS [4]'s scheme, 88.33% improved in NP-IoT [26]'s scheme and 87.95% improved in IH-IoT [23]'s scheme.

6.2   Analysis of Gas Cost Complexity

In this subsection, we evaluate the gas cost complexity for the schemes based on addition operation-ECADD (at address 0x06), multiplication operation-ECMUL (at address 0x07), and pairing operation (at address 0x08) on the elliptic alt_bn128 curve and compare the results with the existing schemes. The updated gas costs benchmark values of the Ethereum Improvement Proposals (EIPs) library (eip-1108.md), as shown in Table 3, are employed to evaluate the gas cost complexity of the schemes.

Table 3. Precompile gas costs.

Operation	Addition operation	Multiplication operation	Pairing operation
Updated Gascost	150	6000	34 000 * k + 45 000

K represents the number of pairings.

The eip-1108 pre-compile gas cost, as represented in Table 3, shows that pairing operations are computationally expensive and attract higher gas values than multiplication and addition operations. Moreover, Sanuel et al. [19] also asserted that a higher-complexity transaction attracts higher gas costs, depending on the transaction type employed to determine the gas costs. As a result, a transaction in an addition operation has a lower gas cost than a transaction in a multiplication or pairing operation.

Table 4. Gas cost complexity

Scheme	Algorithm generation gas cost				Precompile gas costs of schemes		
	UserKeyGen	Encap	Decap	Total	Updated Gascost (Total)	Block period (in seconds)	Gas per second
IC-CHS [4]	36600	91300	79000	206900	206900	2 s	103450
NP-IoT [26]	6000	103150	91150	200300	200300	2 s	100150
IH-IoT [23]	79000	12300	79300	170600	170600	2 s	85300
Proposed	12000	30600	12600	55200	55200	2 s	27600

In determining the gas cost complexity, Table 4 measures the gas costs of each respective scheme according to key generation (UserKeyGen), encapsulation (Encap) and decapsulation (Decap) and generates the total gas cost values for UserkeyGen, Encap and decap combined. It is seen that, schemes using consuming time operations such as pairing and multiplication accrued higher gas costs than schemes than schemes that used less consuming time operations. Referring to Table 2, it is obvious that schemes that used pairing computations, as well as increased number of operations in the algorithm generation achieved higher running times than schemes that used a lesser number of operations in the algorithm generation. Following from Table 4 and Fig. 2a, it is realized that the proposed protocol consumed the least gas in the algorithm generation than IC-CHS. [4], NP-IoT [26] and IH-IoT [23] schemes respectively.

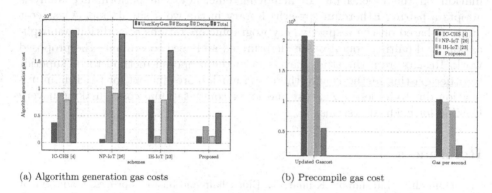

(a) Algorithm generation gas costs   (b) Precompile gas cost

Fig. 2. Gas cost complexity

Consequently, using the total gas cost to be the updated gas cost from the same Table 4, while setting the block period to 2 s as used in Sameuel et al.'s [19] paper, the gas cost per second is evaluated using Eq. 2.

$$\text{Gas per second} = \frac{\text{Updated Gascost (in gas)}}{\text{Block period (in seconds)}} \tag{2}$$

Figure 2b shows the updated gas cost and gas per second is the least in the proposed method than the rest of the schemes. This is due to the fact that the proposed method did not incorporate time consuming operations such as pairings in the algorithm generation. Moreover, the number of cryptographic operations used in the protocol generation of the proposed method was reduced compared to the existing schemes. Based on the analysis conducted so far, we determine that higher gas cost values significantly produces higher gas per second values. Furthermore, increased number of cryptographic operations as well the type of operations used increases the gas cost execution process on the blockchain. It is noteworthy that, computationally intensive operations attract higher gas costs which delays the overall execution process of transactions on the blockchain. Therefore, the authors conclude that the intensity of the computational operation is directly proportional to a higher gas cost and delay in a blockchain transaction process. Thus, $O(n \log crypt_{opt}) \propto O(n \log gas_{cost})) \propto O(delay_{block_{trans}})$

where $crypt_{opt}$, $gascost$ and $delay_{block_{trans}}$ represent cryptographic operations, gas costs and delay in transaction process on the blockchain respectively.

7   Conclusion

There have been countless blockchain research regarding healthcare. Given many fundamental management mechanisms, this article presented a blockchain key encapsulated method for the medicalized blockchain network. In the proposed method, participants exchange derived encapsulated keys to access shared information on the blockchain. In achieving efficiency, the performance analysis adopts a pairing Ethereum (py-eth) library in the work simulation. A gas cost analysis based on the respective cryptographic operations of addition, multiplication, and pairing operations is determined and used to evaluate the proposed work. Results from the study have shown the proposed method to be superior to other existing methods and, therefore, much more efficient for blockchain utilization due to its lesser gas cost and lower computational costs, making it very feasible for medical systems.

References

1. Abunadi, I., Lakshmana Kumar, R.: Blockchain and business process management in health care, especially for Covid-19 cases. Secur. Commun. Netw. **2021** (2021)
2. Akinyele, J.A., et al.: Charm: a framework for rapidly prototyping cryptosystems. J. Cryptographic Eng. **3**(2), 111–128 (2013)
3. Al-Riyami, S.S., Paterson, K.G.: Certificateless public key cryptography. In: Laih, C.-S. (ed.) ASIACRYPT 2003. LNCS, vol. 2894, pp. 452–473. Springer, Heidelberg (2003). https://doi.org/10.1007/978-3-540-40061-5_29
4. Aravind Vishnu, S.S., Praveen, I., Sethumadhavan, M.: An IND-CCA2 secure certificateless hybrid signcryption. Wirel. Pers. Commun. **119**(4), 3589–3608 (2021)
5. Badr, S., Gomaa, I., Abd-Elrahman, E.: Multi-tier blockchain framework for IoT-EHRs systems. Procedia Comput. Sci. **141**, 159–166 (2018)
6. Badshah, A., et al.: LAKE-BSG: lightweight authenticated key exchange scheme for blockchain-enabled smart grids. Sustain. Energy Technol. Assessments **52**, 102248 (2022)
7. Daemen, J., Rijmen, V.: The Design of Rijndael, vol. 2. Springer, Heidelberg (2002)
8. De Caro, A., Iovino, V.: JPBC: Java pairing based cryptography. In: 2011 IEEE Symposium on Computers and Communications (ISCC), pp. 850–855. IEEE (2011)
9. El Majdoubi, D., El Bakkali, H., Sadki, S.: SmartMedChain: a blockchain-based privacy-preserving smart healthcare framework. J. Healthcare Eng. **2021** (2021)
10. Hylock, R.H., Zeng, X.: A blockchain framework for patient-centered health records and exchange (healthchain): evaluation and proof-of-concept study. J. Med. Internet Res. **21**(8), e13592 (2019)
11. Konstantinou, E., Stamatiou, Y., Zaroliagis, C.: A software library for elliptic curve cryptography. In: Möhring, R., Raman, R. (eds.) ESA 2002. LNCS, vol. 2461, pp. 625–637. Springer, Heidelberg (2002). https://doi.org/10.1007/3-540-45749-6_55
12. Liu, X., Wang, Z., Jin, C., Li, F., Li, G.: A blockchain-based medical data sharing and protection scheme. IEEE Access **7**, 118943–118953 (2019)

13. Lucienoa.py-eth-pairing 0.1.4 (2020). https://github.com/Lucieno/py_eth_pairing
14. McGhin, T., Choo, K.-K.R., Liu, C.Z., He, D.: Blockchain in healthcare applications: research challenges and opportunities. J. Netw. Comput. Appl. **135**, 62–75 (2019)
15. Mwitende, G., Ye, Y., Ali, I., Li, F.: Certificateless authenticated key agreement for blockchain-based WBANs. J. Syst. Architect. **110**, 101777 (2020)
16. Nakamoto, S.: Bitcoin: a peer-to-peer electronic cash system. Decentralized Bus. Rev. 21260 (2008)
17. Nguyen, D.C., Pathirana, P.N., Ding, M., Seneviratne, A.: A cooperative architecture of data offloading and sharing for smart healthcare with blockchain. In: 2021 IEEE International Conference on Blockchain and Cryptocurrency (ICBC), pp. 1–8. IEEE (2021)
18. Pal, O., Alam, B., Thakur, V., Singh, S.: Key management for blockchain technology. ICT Express **7**(1), 76–80 (2021)
19. Samuel, C.N., Glock, S., Verdier, F., Guitton-Ouhamou, P.: Choice of Ethereum clients for private blockchain: assessment from proof of authority perspective. In: 2021 IEEE International Conference on Blockchain and Cryptocurrency (ICBC), pp. 1–5. IEEE (2021)
20. Sato, M.: The biggest problem of blockchains: key management. In: Matsuo, S., Sakimura, N. (eds.) Blockchain Gaps. FBF, pp. 75–84. Springer, Singapore (2021). https://doi.org/10.1007/978-981-33-6052-5_9
21. Sun, Z., Han, D., Li, D., Wang, X., Chang, C.-C., Zhongdai, W.: A blockchain-based secure storage scheme for medical information. EURASIP J. Wirel. Commun. Netw. **2022**(1), 1–25 (2022)
22. Ullah, I., Amin, N.U., Khan, M.A., Khattak, H., Kumari, S.: An efficient and provable secure certificate-based combined signature, encryption and signcryption scheme for internet of things (IoT) in mobile health (M-health) system. J. Med. Syst. **45**(1), 1–14 (2021)
23. Wu, Y., Gong, B., Zhang, Y.: An improved efficient certificateless hybrid signcryption scheme for internet of things. Wirel. Commun. Mob. Comput. **2022** (2022)
24. Yao, H., Wang, C., Hai, B., Zhu, S.: Homomorphic hash and blockchain based authentication key exchange protocol for strangers. In: 2018 Sixth International Conference on Advanced Cloud and Big Data (CBD), pp. 243–248. IEEE (2018)
25. Zhang, G., Yang, Z., Liu, W.: Blockchain-based privacy preserving E-health system for healthcare data in cloud. Comput. Netw. **203**, 108586 (2022)
26. Zhang, W., et al.: Certificateless hybrid signcryption by a novel protocol applied to internet of things. Comput. Intell. Neurosci. **2022** (2022)
27. Zhao, H., Bai, P., Peng, Y., Ruzhi, X.: Efficient key management scheme for health blockchain. CAAI Trans. Intell. Technol. **3**(2), 114–118 (2018)

Cryptography

A Universal Lightweight Privacy-Preserving Multifunctional Data Handling Scheme

Yulian Li and Hua Shen[✉]

School of Computer Science, Hubei University of Technology, Wuhan 430068, China
nancy78733@126.com

Abstract. Most previous studies leverage homomorphic encryptions to execute arithmetic operations (e.g., summation, average) on encrypted data. However, these schemes are designed for a specific application environment and just achieve secure computation of a limited number of functions. Therefore, we propose a new privacy-preserving multifunctional data handling scheme with three main contributions. Firstly, it can efficiently complete plenty of rich, secure arithmetic operations through homomorphic encryption techniques to destroy the one-to-one relationship between data and its source. Secondly, it can resist differential attacks launched by the data processing entity by adding random noise. Meanwhile, it enables data analyzing entities to obtain accurate results by removing random noise. Ultimately, we conduct the security analysis, performance analysis, and comparison. These analyses show that the proposed scheme can preserve data privacy and differential privacy and is efficient regarding computation cost and communication overhead.

Keywords: Privacy protection · Differential privacy · Multifunctional data handling · Lightweight · Universality

1 Introduction

Currently, sensors and smart devices are popularly applied in various fields, such as smart meters are applied in Smart Grids [1–3], biosensors and actuators are applied in Wireless Body Area Networks (WBANs) [4, 5]. Therefore, analyzing and utilizing the data collected by these devices can help policymakers make reasonable decisions and aid people in improving the quality of their life. For example, analyzing the physiological data captured by biosensors and actuators can help physicians provide accurate diagnoses and real-time monitor their health status. Nevertheless, these data contain many users' sensitive information. For instance, if adversaries eavesdrop or steal the data transmitted by biosensors or actuators, they may use it for illegal purposes, which will cause many threats to users. Hence, privacy-preserving data handling is worth studying. To achieve this requirement, one of the commonly adopted techniques is homomorphic encryption [6, 7]. The homomorphic property implies that the efficient manipulation of ciphertexts yields the ciphertext of the result of executing some arithmetic operations on the corresponding plaintexts.

© The Author(s), under exclusive license to Springer Nature Singapore Pte Ltd. 2022
E. Ahene and F. Li (Eds.): FCS 2022, CCIS 1726, pp. 261–274, 2022.
https://doi.org/10.1007/978-981-19-8445-7_17

Some works [6–11] utilize additively homomorphic encryptions to implement the secure computation of some linear functions (such as summing, averaging, and comparing operations) meanwhile maintaining the privacy of users' data. The Paillier cryptosystem and the Lifted ElGamal Encryption [12] have appealing additive homomorphism. [6–9] used the Paillier cryptosystem, and the homomorphic encryption adopted by [10] is the Lifted ElGamal Encryption. In [11], the authors first construct a variant ElGamal encryption with additive homomorphism, then use it to design a privacy-preserving data handling scheme. We need more powerful homomorphic encryption tools to implement more complicated functions (like variance, Euclidean Distance, Manhattan Distance, and Correlation Coefficient.) while meeting the given privacy-preserving requirements. [12–15] used the BGN (Boneh-Goh-Nissim) to realize more complicated secure calculations. In [16], the authors organically combined the Paillier cryptosystem (which has additive homomorphic properties) and the ElGamal cryptosystem (which has multiplicative homomorphic properties) to securely compute variance and Correlation Coefficient. The BGV encryption scheme [17] is currently the most efficient fully homomorphic encryption scheme. [18] uses it to encrypt private data and enables cloud servers to train deep computation models efficiently. However, these works design and implement privacy-preserving data handling schemes by ciphertext computation, which restricts the scope of functions that can be achieved and application domains of these schemes and results in expensive computation costs and communication overhead. This paper proposes a universal, lightweight, privacy-preserving, multifunctional data handling scheme.

2   Problem Modeling

In this section, we want to accurately expound the problem we are trying to solve and the main idea of the corresponding solution. We want to construct a processing node capable of outputting expected results without knowing anything about inputs, as shown in Fig. 1. The Processing Node (PN) does not know anything about the input $(x_1, x_2, \ldots, x_n)$ but can return the input's average, variance, minimum and maximum, etc., as shown in Fig. 1(a). If the inputs are more than one data set, suppose that there are two data set X_1 and X_2, PN knows nothing about X_1 and X_2 but can output the statistic results about X_1 and X_2, such as the covariance, the correlation coefficient and so on, as shown in Fig. 1(b). The covariance and coefficient of X_1 and X_2 can be computed as following

$$Cov(X_1, \ X_2) = E[(X_1 - E[X_1])(X_2 - E[X_2])] \tag{1}$$

$$\rho(X_1, \ X_2) = Cov(X_1, \ X_2)/\sqrt{Var(X_1)Var(X_2)} \tag{2}$$

According to Eq. (1) and Eq. (2), we find that two random variables' covariance and correlation coefficient can be calculated based on each variable's mathematical expectation and variance. Therefore, we can use the outputs shown in Fig. 1(a) to gain the results shown in Fig. 1(b). Therefore, we focus on the problem model shown in Fig. 1(a).

Our main idea to solve the above problem is as shown in Fig. 2. Providers' data are organized as a vector, the No.1 provider's data is the first item of the vector, the No.2 provider's data is the second item, ..., and so on. After being encrypted, the vector is used as the input of PN. PN's outputs are various functions' results (with noise). In order to obtain the exact results, the noise should subsequently be removed. The handling procedure of PN consists of two parts:

- Part I: Add noise into the input vector, and then ruin the one-to-one relationship between items and their providers, finally aggregate all items of the vector.
- Part II: Decrypt and parse the aggregated data to recover the input vector (with noise), and then calculate its average, variance, maximum and minimum etc..

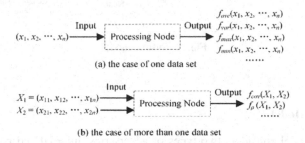

(a) the case of one data set

(b) the case of more than one data set

Fig. 1. Problem description

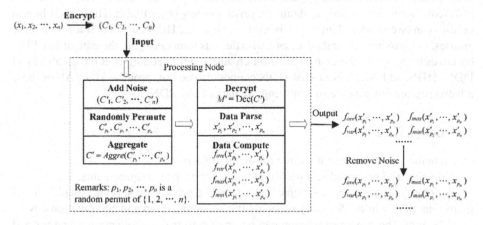

Fig. 2. The main issues that our scheme solves

2.1 System Model

To implement the above idea, we design a system model (as shown in Fig. 3). There are four entities: Providing Data Node (PDN), Disturbing Data Node (DDN), Handling Data Node (HDN) and Analyzing Data Node (ADN).

PDNs are responsible for providing input data; DDN and HDN form a PN, where DDN undertakes the Part I processing task of PN and HDN takes on the Part II task of PN (please see the Sect. 2.2); ADN can remove noise from the outputs of PN to gain the precise results and is in charge of analyzing these results based on the semantic environment under the corresponding application scenario. For the sake of simplicity, assume that there are n PDNs, one DDN, one HDN, and one AND.

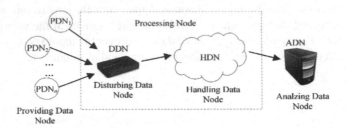

Fig. 3. System model

2.2 Security Model

Our security model considers two types of adversaries: internal and passive external. DDN, HDN, and ADN are honest-but-curious. They follow the protocol properly but keep all input intermediate computation results and try to infer PDNs' privacy. PDN is also semi-honest and strives to obtain the privacy of any other PDNs. These semi-honest entities can be considered internal adversaries. Note that HDN cannot collude with other entities. is a passive external adversary who does its utmost to gain the data of any PDN by eavesdropping on the communication channels and intruding into the databases of DDN, HDN, and ADN. Note that HDN cannot also be compromised by . All of these adversaries are not capable of acquiring the data of any PDN.

2.3 Design Goal

Our scheme should achieve the three following objectives:

Security: The proposed scheme should meet the security requirements.

Efficiency: The proposed scheme can realize the privacy-preserving calculations of many functions while effectively reducing the communication and computation costs.

Ubiquity: The proposed scheme can be applied to many application scenarios and can achieve secure computation of plenty of linear and non-linear functions.

2.4 Our Contributions

Our contributions are summarized as follows:

- We propose a kind of generic system model for security data handling. In our system model, PDNs are responsible for collecting data, DDN and HDN take charge of executing operations on the data, they all need not to know the semantics of the data. ADN is the only one entity that be required to be associated with application domains. ADN combines domain knowledge to analyze the results that be returned by HDN. Thus, our system model has notable commonality which can be well suit for plenty of application scenarios, such as Smart Grids, WBANs, WSNs and so on.
- We present a lightweight privacy-preserving multi-functional data handling scheme. Our scheme enables quite a lot of arithmetic functions to be calculated in the condition of preserving privacy of data. Meanwhile, it realizes significant computation costs and communication overhead savings.
- Aside from achieving differential privacy, the presented scheme can obtain the accurate computed results.

3 Related Works

In this section, we review some privacy-preserving multifunctional data handling schemes. The scheme proposed by [8] employs the Paillier encryption, the Chinese Remainder Theorem and one-way hash chain to compute the average and the variance of the data of hybrid IoT devices without damaging these devices' privacy. However, the data to be encrypted need to be elaborately constructed according to the functions expected to calculate. In [12], authors mainly use BGN cryptosystem to achieve the computation of summation, average, variance and F-test in a privacy-preserving way. The BGN cryptosystem and Shamir's secret share scheme are utilized by [13] and [15] to implement the secure computation of summation, average, min/max, etc.. However, BGN cryptosystem supports only one time multiplicatively homomorphic operation, for this reason, these schemes using BGN cryptosystem can just achieve the secure calculation of the functions that has the maximum degree of 2. Therefore, we choose to design a scheme that can efficiently perform secure computation of a wider range of and more complex functions by breaking the one-to-one relationship between data and its sources. Similarly, [19] presents an efficient scheme to protect privacy of mobile phone users by destroying the relationship between data and its source by using a bit-wise XOR homomorphic cipher system. However, the scheme proposed in [19] doesn't offer the differential privacy of users' data. The schemes presented by [8, 12, 13] and [15] can resist differential attacks by adding appropriate noise, however there is relative error in their results because that they don't eliminate noise from their outcomes. The comparative analysis is shown in Table 1.

Table 1. Comparison with related works

	Scope of functions	Encrypted data for each user	Differential privacy	Noise removing
[8]	Small	More than one, such as x, x^2	Yes	No
[12]	Small	Only one, such as x	Yes	No
[13]	Small	Only one, such as x	Yes	No
[15]	Small	Only one, such as x	Yes	No
[19]	Large	Only one, but the length increases (Suppose x is l-bit long and there are n users, the length of encrypted data is nl-bit long)	No	–
Our work	Large	Only one, such as x	Yes	Yes

4 Preliminaries

4.1 Paillier Cryptosystem

The Paillier homomorphic cryptosystem includes three algorithms:

- *Key Generation*: Let $N = pq$ where p and q are two κ-bit prime numbers, and κ is the security parameter. Let $\lambda = 1 \, \text{cm} \, (p\text{-}1, q\text{-}1)$, and define a function $L(\mu) = (\mu\text{-}1)/N$, pick a random generator $g \in \mathbb{Z}_{N^2}^*$ and calculate $\mu = (L(g^\lambda \bmod N^2))^{-1}$. The public key is $pk = (N, g)$, and the private key is $sk = (\lambda, \mu)$.
- *Encryption*: Choose a random number $r \in \mathbb{Z}_N^*$ and for the message $m \in \mathbb{Z}_N$ calculate the ciphertext $C = g^m \cdot r^N \bmod N^2$.
- *Decryption*: Given C, recover the corresponding message m by computing $m = L(C^\lambda \bmod N^2) \cdot \mu \bmod N^2$.

4.2 ElGamal Encryption

The ElGamal Encryption consists of three algorithms:

- *Key Generation*: Let q_1 is a κ-bit prime number, κ is the security parameter, choose a random generator $g_1 \in \mathbb{Z}_{q_1}^*$, pick a random number $\alpha \in \mathbb{Z}_{q_1}^*$ and set $Y = g_1^\alpha$. The public key is $pk_d = (g_1, q_1, Y)$, and the private key is $sk_d = \alpha$.
- *Encryption*: Given the message $m' \in \mathbb{Z}_{q_1}^*$ and choose a random number $r' \in \mathbb{Z}_{q_1}^*$, calculate the ciphertext $C^* = (\bar{c}_1, \bar{c}_2) = (m'Y^{r'} (\bmod q_1), g_1^{r'} (\bmod q_1))$.
- *Decryption*: Given C^*, recover the message m' by computing $m' = \bar{c}_1/\bar{c}_2^\alpha$.

5 Our Proposed Scheme

Our scheme consists of five phases: System Initialization, Data Encrypted, Data Disturbed, Data Handled and Noise Removed. The flow chart is as shown in Fig. 4.

5.1 System Initialization

In the beginning, the whole system needs to be booted up.

- *Step 1.1*: Choose a security parameter κ, generate $pk = (N, g)$ and $sk = (\lambda, \mu)$ by calling the Paillier *Key Generation* algorithm, generate $pk_d = (g_1, q_1, Y)$ and $sk_d = \alpha$ by calling the ElGamal *Key Generation* algorithm, randomly pick a one-way hash function $H: \{0, 1\}^* \to \mathbb{Z}_N^*$ and a number $R \in \mathbb{Z}_N^*$. Assume the data d_i provided by the PDN_i is less than a constant W_1 ($W_1 < q_1$), the random noise d' is less than a constant W_2 ($W_2 < q_1$), and $W = W_1 + W_2 < N$, then it is should be ensured that $R > nW$.
- *Step 1.2*: Send sk to the HDN and sk_d to the ADN by a secure channel.
- *Step 1.3*: Release parameters $\{pk, pk_d, R, H\}$.

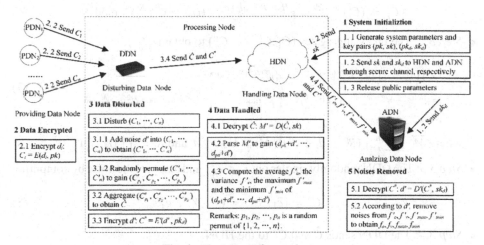

Fig. 4. Flowchart of our scheme

5.2 Data Encrypted

The PDN_i ($i = 1, 2, ..., n$) encrypts its data and then send it to the DDN.

- *Step 2.1*: The PDN_i collects its data d_i at time point t, then chooses a random number $r_i \in \mathbb{Z}_N^*$ and computes

$$C_i = g^{H(t) \cdot R^i \cdot d_i} \cdot r_i^N \mod N^2 \qquad (3)$$

- *Step 2.2*: The PDN_i reports C_i to the DDN.

5.3 Data Disturbed

After receiving n ciphertexts, the DDN makes them into a vector, where the first item is the C_1 from the PDN_1, the i-th item is the C_i from the PDN_i, and so on. That means the position of the ciphertext in the vector $(C_1, C_2, ..., C_n)$ is determined by which PDN it comes from. After appending noises to ciphertexts, their locations in the vector are perturbed.

- *Step 3.1*: The DDN disturbs $(C_1, C_2, ..., C_n)$.
- *Step 3.1.1*: The DDN randomly selects a number $r_i' \in \mathbb{Z}_N^*$ and a noise $d' \in \mathbb{Z}_{q_1}^*$ and adds the noise into each item of $(C_1,..., C_n)$ by computing

$$\Delta C_i = g^{H(t) \cdot R^i \cdot d'} \cdot r_i'^N \mod N^2 \tag{4}$$

$$C_i' = C_i \cdot \Delta C_i = g^{H(t) \cdot R^i \cdot d_i} \cdot r_i^N \cdot g^{H(t) \cdot R^i \cdot d'} \cdot r_i'^N \mod N^2 = g^{H(t) \cdot R^i \cdot (d_i + d')} \cdot (r_i \cdot r_i')^N \mod N^2 \tag{5}$$

- *Step 3.1.2*: The DDN breaks the one-to-one relationship between C_i' and the PDN_i. The DDN randomly picks $p_i \in \{1, 2, ..., n\} - \{p_1, p_2, ..., p_{i-1}\}$ and calculates

$$C_i'' = (C_i')^{R^{p_i}/R^i} = g^{H(t) \cdot R^{p_i} \cdot (d_i + d')} \cdot ((r_i \cdot r_i')^{R^{p_i}/R^i})^N \mod N^2 \tag{6}$$

- *Step 3.2*: The DDN aggregates $(C_1'', C_2'', ..., C_n'')$ to obtain

$$\hat{C} = \prod_{i=1}^{n} C_i'' = \prod_{i=1}^{n} (g^{H(t) \cdot R^{p_i} \cdot (d_i + d')} \cdot ((r_i \cdot r_i')^{R^{p_i}/R^i})^N \mod N^2)$$
$$= g^{H(t) \cdot \sum_{i=1}^{n} R^{p_i} \cdot (d_i + d')} \cdot (\prod_{i=1}^{n} (r_i \cdot r_i')^{R^{p_i}/R^i})^N \mod N^2 = g^{H(t) \cdot \bar{M}} \cdot R'^N \mod N^2 = g^{\hat{M}} \cdot R'^N \mod N^2 \tag{7}$$

where $\bar{M} = \sum_{i=1}^{n} (R^{p_i} \cdot (d_i + d'))$, $\hat{M} = H(t) \cdot \bar{M}$ and $R' = \prod_{i=1}^{n} (r_i \cdot r_i')^{R^{p_i}/R^i}$.

- *Step 3.3*: The DDN randomly singles out $r' \in \mathbb{Z}_{q_1}^*$ and encrypts the noise by computing

$$C^* = (\bar{c}_1, \bar{c}_2) = (d' \cdot Y^{r'}, g_1^{r'}) \tag{8}$$

- *Step 3.4*: The DDN sends $\hat{C}$ and C^* to the HDN.

5.4 Data Handled

The HDN makes efforts to gain $d_i + d'$ $(i = 1, 2, ..., n)$ and calculates the average, the variance, the maximum and the minimum of these data.

- *Step 4.1*: The HDN carries out the Paillier Decryption algorithm with $sk = (\lambda, \mu)$ to obtain $\hat{M}$ and computes $\bar{M} = \hat{M}/H(t)$.
- *Step 4.2*: The HDN parses $\bar{M}$ based on the following observation

$$\bar{M} = \sum_{i=1}^{n} (R^{p_i} \cdot (d_i + d')) = \sum_{i=1}^{n} (R^i \cdot (d_{p_i} + d')) = (d_{p_1} + d')R + (d_{p_2} + d')R^2 + \cdots + (d_{p_n} + d')R^n$$
$$= ((d_{p_1} + d') + (d_{p_2} + d')R + \cdots + (d_{p_n} + d')R^{n-1})R$$
$$= ((d_{p_1} + d') + ((d_{p_2} + d') + (\cdots + (d_{p_n} + d')R) \cdots)R)R \tag{9}$$

The HDN can acquire $\{d_{p_1} + d', d_{p_2} + d', ..., d_{p_n} + d'\}$ by executing

$$\bar{M}_1 = \bar{M}/R = (d_{p_1} + d') + ((d_{p_2} + d') + (\cdots + (d_{p_n} + d')R)\cdots)R; \quad d_{p_1} + d' = \bar{M}_1 \bmod R;$$
$$\bar{M}_2 = \bar{M}_1/R = (d_{p_2} + d') + ((d_{p_3} + d') + (\cdots + (d_{p_n} + d')R)\cdots)R; \quad d_{p_2} + d' = \bar{M}_2 \bmod R; \quad (10)$$
$$\cdots\cdots; \quad d_{p_n} + d' = \bar{M}_n \bmod R$$

- Step 4.3: The HDN obtains the average and the variance of $\{d_{p_1} + d', d_{p_2} + d', ...,$
  $d_{p_n} + d'\}$ by computing $f_a' = \frac{1}{n}\sum_{i=1}^{n}(d_{p_i} + d'), f_v' = \sqrt{\frac{1}{n}\sum_{i=1}^{n}(d_i + d' - f_a')^2}.$

  The HDN can easily find the maximum f_{max}' and the minimum f_{min}' of $\{d_{p_1} + d', ...,$
  $d_{p_n} + d'\}$ by invoking a sequential search algorithm of the running time $\Theta(n)$ only
  once. Because the data of each PDN is less than a constant W_1 ($W_1 < q_1$), HDN
  produces the ciphertexts of f_{max}' and f_{min}' by randomly choosing r'', $r''' \in \mathbb{Z}_{q_1}^*$ and
  computing $C_{max} = (\bar{c}_{max\,1}, \bar{c}_{max\,2}) = (f_{max}' \cdot Y^{r''}, g_1^{r''}), C_{min} = (\bar{c}_{min\,1}, \bar{c}_{min\,2}) =$
  $(f_{min}' \cdot Y^{r'''}, g_1^{r'''}).$
- *Step 4.4*: The HDN transmits $f_a', f_v', C_{max}, C_{min}$ and forwards C^* to ADN.

5.5 Data Noise Removed

The ADN removes noises from f_a', f_v', f_{max}' and f_{min}' by using C^*.

- *Step 5.1*: The ADN recovers the noise d' by decrypting C^*.
  The ADN holds d' securely, and deletes it forever when the removing noise
  operations are finished.
- *Step 5.2*: The ADN eliminates noise of f_a', f_v', f_{max}' and f_{min}' by computing

$$f_a = f_a' - d' = \frac{1}{n}\sum_{i=1}^{n}(d_i + d') - d' = \frac{1}{n}\sum_{i=1}^{n}d_i \qquad (11)$$

$$f_v = \sqrt{\frac{1}{n}\sum_{i=1}^{n}(d_i - f_a)^2} = \sqrt{\frac{1}{n}\sum_{i=1}^{n}(d_i - (f_a' - d'))^2} = \sqrt{\frac{1}{n}\sum_{i=1}^{n}(d_i + d' - f_a')^2} = f_v' \qquad (12)$$

$$f_{max} = f_{max}' - d' = \bar{c}_{max\,1}/(\bar{c}_{max\,2})^{sk_d} - d' \qquad (13)$$

$$f_{min} = f_{min}' - d' = \bar{c}_{min\,1}/(\bar{c}_{min\,2})^{sk_d} - d' \qquad (14)$$

After that, the ADN can analyze these results according to their semantic in a particular
application scenario.

6 Security Analysis

Theorem 1: *In the proposed scheme, the ADN knows nothing about any PDN's data.*

Proof: The data received by the ADN from the HDN are f_a', f_v', f_{max}' and f_{min}' which
are, respectively, the average, the variance, the maximum and the minimum of noised
data of PNDs. After clearing up noises through Eq. (11) – Eq. (14), the ADN has the
precise results f_a, f_v, f_{max} and f_{min}. Obviously, the f_a', f_v', f_a and f_v are statistics results

from which the ADN cannot obtain any PND's data. Besides, the ADN just only know f_{max} and f_{min} are the maximum and the minimum among all PDNs' data, and has no idea about which one PDN's data is f_{max} or f_{min}. In other words, the target PDN and a random PDN are undistinguishable for the ADN. As a consequence, the ADN cannot obtain any information about any PDN's data from f_{max} and f_{min}. For the similar reason, the ADN knows nothing about any PDN's data from f'_{max} and f'_{min}.

Theorem 2: *In the proposed scheme, any PDN knows nothing about the other PDNs' data, and the DDN knows nothing about any PDN's data.*

Proof: Each PDN's data is encrypted by Eq. (3), the ciphertext C_i ($i = 1, 2, ..., n$) is a valid ciphertext of Paillier cryptosystem. Based on the received $(C_1, C_2, ..., C_n)$, the DDN calculates C'_i, C''_i and $\hat{C}$ by Eq. (5), Eq. (4), and Eq. (5), respectively, where $i = 1, 2, ..., n$. Since the DDN don't know the secret key sk and Paillier cryptosystem is semantic secure against the chosen plaintext attack, it has no capability to know something about any PDN's data. Because the PDN doesn't obtain any other PDN's ciphertext in executing the protocol, it cannot obtain any other PDN's data, and even if it obtains the ciphertext it also has no ability to gain the other PDNs' data for lack of the secret key sk to decrypt the ciphertext.

Theorem 3: *In the proposed scheme, the HDN knows nothing about any PDN's data.*

Proof: The HDN has the secret key sk, which is the reason we suppose that it cannot collude with the PDN or the DDN or the adversary . By decrypting $\hat{C}$ and parsing $\overline{M}$, the HDN obtains a vector $(d_{p_1} + d', d_{p_2} + d', ..., d_{p_n} + d')$. It is impossible that the HDN knows the precise value of d_{p_i}, because that the noise d' is unobtainable for the HDN. In addition, $d_{p_i} + d'$ does not necessarily correspond to the i-th PDN, and may be correspond to any one PDN, which means that the target PDN of $d_{p_i} + d'$ and a random PDN are undistinguishable for the HDN. Summary of the above, the HDN knows nothing about any PDN's data.

Theorem 4: *In the proposed scheme, the adversary knows nothing about any PDN's data.*

Proof: According to the Theorem 1–3, it is not hard to find that even if the adversary steals $(C_1, C_2, ..., C_n)$, d', $(C'_1, C'_2, \cdots, C'_n)$, $(C''_1, C''_2, \cdots, C''_n)$, $\hat{C}$, $(d_{p_1} + d', d_{p_2} + d', ..., d_{p_n} + d')$, $f'_a, f'_v, f'_{max}, f'_{min}, f_a, f_v, f_{max}$ and f_{min}, it cannot obtain any PDN's data.

7   Performance Analysis and Comparison

In this section, we compare our scheme with MuDA [12] and PPM-HDA [13]. Suppose the length of ciphertext of our scheme is same with that of MuDA and PPM-HDA. Let T_e denote the time of modular exponential calculation in $\mathbb{Z}^*_{N^2}$, T_m is a indication of the time of modular multiplication, T_b is a sign of the time of bilinear pairing operation and T_p refer the time of using Pollard's lambda method to compute the discrete logarithm. Let the security parameter $\kappa = 512$ and the plaintext space is $[0, 2^{13}-1]$. According to [15], $T_e = 10.082$ ms, $T_m = 0.016$ ms, $T_b = 21.823$ ms, and T_p is directly proportional to $\sqrt{n(2^{13} - 1)}$, when $n = 10,000$, $T_p = 42.875$ ms.

7.1 Efficiency Comparison on Variance Computation

The comparison results between MuDA and our shceme are shown in Table 2. The computation time costs are shown in Table 3. Figure 5. Illustrates the computation cost of our scheme is less than that of MuDA.

Table 2. Comparison on variance operation

	Communication overhead	Computation cost				
		Encryption	Decryption	Multiplication	Bilinear pairing	Exponentiation
MuDA	$n+3$	n	3	$4n$	$n+1$	–
Our scheme	$n+1$	n	1	n	–	n

Table 3. Quantized results of computation time cost

	Encryption	Decryption	Multiplication	Bilinear pairing	Exponentiation
MuDA	$n(2T_e + T_m)$	$O(\sqrt{n(2^{13}-1)} + n(2^{13}-1) + \sqrt{n}(2^{13}-1))$	$4n \cdot T_m$	$(n+1) \cdot T_b$	–
Our scheme	$n(2T_e + T_m)$	$O(\sqrt{n(2^{13}-1)})$	$n \cdot T_m$	–	$n \cdot T_e$

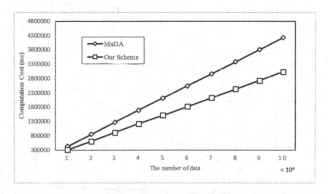

Fig. 5. Comparison of computation costs for secure variance calculation

7.2 Efficiency Comparison on Maximum/Minimum Computation

Here we only consider the comparison of minimum computation, the comparison of maximum calculation is similar. For computing the minimum of n data, PPM-HDA needs $O(n \log_2^W)$ data ciphertexts, but our scheme just needs n data ciphertexts and one aggregated ciphertext. Clearly, the communication cost of our scheme is far less than that of PPM-HDA. After decrypting, PPM-HDA performs an algorithm of $O(n \cdot (\log_2^W)^3)$ to return the minimum, but our scheme just needs to invoke a simple search algorithm of $O(n)$ to find the minimum. These comparison results are shown in Table 4. As can be observed from Table 4, except the encryption and decryption operations, the calculation cost of PPM-HDA is $O(n \cdot (2 \log_2^W + (\log_2^W)^3))$, nevertheless, our scheme is only $O(n)$. The quantified computation time of encryption and decryption is shown in Table 5. According to Table 5, we describe the variation of computation time cost in Fig. 6. The above analyses show that our scheme is more efficient than PPM-HAD.

Table 4. Comparison on minimum operation

	Communication overhead	Computation cost				
		Prefix family	Prefix numeralization	Encryption	Decryption	Search algorithm
PPM-HDA	$n \cdot O(\log_2^W)$	$n \cdot O(\log_2^W)$	$n \cdot O(\log_2^W)$	$n \cdot O(\log_2^W)$	$n \cdot O(\log_2^W)$	$O((\log_2^W)^3 \cdot n)$
Our scheme	$n + 1$	–	–	n	1	$O(n)$

Table 5. Quantized results of computation time computation time of encryption and decryption

	Encryption	Decryption
PPM-HDA	$n \cdot O(\log_2^{2^{13}}) \cdot (2T_e + T_m)$	$n \cdot O(\log_2^{2^{13}}) \cdot O(\sqrt{n(2^{13} - 1)})$
Our Scheme	$n(2T_e + T_m)$	$O(\sqrt{n(2^{13} - 1)})$

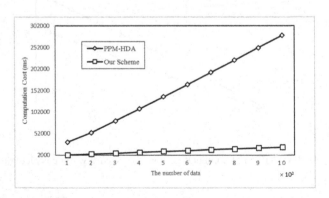

Fig. 6. Comparison of computation costs for secure minimum calculation

8 Conclusion

This article proposes a universal lightweight privacy-preserving multifunctional data handling scheme. Our scheme can be applied to many scenarios like WSNs, Smart Grids, and WBANs, and can achieve secure computation of plenty of arithmetic functions. Moreover, our scheme requires that each provider just offers one ciphertext of its data for actualizing the security computation of many functions. In plaintext space, our scheme implements the calculation of functions. By destroying the relationship between data and its source and adding random noise, our scheme protects the privacy and differential privacy of the data owner. For future works, we will focus on studying privacy-preserving data handling problems of multiple multivariate functions.

References

1. Anoh, K., Maharjan, S., Ikpehai, A., Zhang, Y., Adebisi, B.: Energy peer-to-peer trading in virtual microgrids in smart grids: a game-theoretic approach. IEEE Trans. Smart Grid **11**(2), 1264–1275 (2019)
2. Wang, J., Wu, L., Zeadally, S., Khan, M.K., He, D.: Privacy-preserving data aggregation against malicious data mining attack for IoT-enabled smart grid. ACM Trans. Sens. Netw. (TOSN) **17**(3), 1–25 (2021)
3. Farao, A., Veroni, E., Ntantogian, C., Xenakis, C.: P4G2Go: a privacy-preserving scheme for roaming energy consumers of the smart grid-to-go. Sensors **21**(8), 2686 (2021)
4. Ghamari, M., Janko, B., Sherratt, R.S., Harwin, W.S., Piechocki, R.J., Soltanpur, C.: A survey on wireless body area networks for eHealthcare systems in residential environments. Sensors **16**(6), 1–33 (2016)
5. Hu, C., Li, H., Huo, Y., Xiang, T., Liao, X.: Secure and efficient data communication protocol for wireless body area networks. IEEE Trans. Multi-Scale Comput. Syst. **2**(2), 94–107 (2016)
6. Shen, H., Zhang, M., Shen, J.: Efficient privacy-preserving cube-data aggregation scheme for smart grids. IEEE Trans. Inf. Forensics Secur. **12**(6), 1369–1381 (2017)
7. Zhang, M.W., Song, W.X., Zhang, J.X.: A secure clinical diagnosis with privacy-preserving multiclass support vector machine in clouds. IEEE Syst. J. **16**(1), 67–78 (2022)
8. Lu, R., Heung, K., Habibi Lashkari, A., Ghorbani, A.A.: A lightweight privacy-preserving data aggregation scheme for fog computing-enhanced IoT. IEEE Access **5**, 3302–3312 (2017)
9. Zhang, M.W., Chen, Y., Ling, J.K.: A privacy-preserving optimization of neighborhood-based recommendation for medical-aided diagnosis and treatment. IEEE Internet of Things J. **8**(13), 10830–10842 (2021)
10. Ni, J., Zhang, K., Alharbi, K., Lin, X., Zhang, N., Shen, X.: Differentially private smart metering with fault tolerance and range-based filtering. IEEE Trans. Smart Grid **8**, 2483–2493 (2017)
11. Shim, K., Park, C.: A secure data aggregation scheme based on appropriate cryptographic primitives in heterogeneous wireless sensor networks. IEEE Trans. Parallel Distrib. Syst. **26**(8), 2128–2139 (2015)
12. Liu, J., Asokan, N., Pinkas, B.: Secure deduplication of encrypted data without additional independent servers. In: Proceedings of the 22nd ACM SIGSAC Conference on Computer and Communications Security, Association for Computing Machinery, pp.874–885, New York, NY, USA (2015)
13. Chen, L., Lu, R., Cao, Z., AlHarbi, K., Lin, X.: MuDA: multifunctional data aggregation in privacy-preserving smart grid communications. Peer-to-Peer Networking and Applications **8**(5), 777–792 (2014). https://doi.org/10.1007/s12083-014-0292-0

14. Han, S., Zhao, S., Li, Q., Ju, C., Zhou, W.: PPM-HDA: privacy-preserving and multifunctional health data aggregation with fault tolerance. IEEE Trans. Inf. Forensics Secur. **11**(9), 1940–1955 (2016)
15. Wang, X.: One-round secure fair meeting location determination based on homomorphic encryption. Inf. Sci. **372**, 758–772 (2016)
16. Ren, H., Li, H., Liang, X., He, S., Dai, Y., Zhao, L.: Privacy-enhanced and multifunctional health data aggregation under differential privacy guarantees. Sensors **16**(9), 1–27 (2016)
17. Yi, X., Bouguettaya, A., Georgakopoulos, D., Song, A., Willemson, J.: Privacy protection for wireless medical sensor data. IEEE Trans. Dependable Secure Comput. **13**(3), 369–380 (2016)
18. Brakerski, Z., Gentry, C., Vaikuntanathan, V.: (Leveled) Fully homomorphic encryption without bootstrapping. ACM Trans. Comput. Theory **6**(3), 1–36 (2014)
19. Zhang, Y., Chen, Q., Zhong, S.: Privacy-preserving data aggregation in mobile phone sensing. IEEE Trans. Inf. Forensics Secur. **11**(5), 980–992 (2016)

New Trapdoor and Preimage Sampling on NTRU Lattice

Chengrong Liu[1], Chunming Tang[1,2], and Huiwen Jia[1,2(✉)]

[1] Key Laboratory of Information Security, Guangzhou University,
Guangzhou, People's Republic of China
hwjia@gzhu.edu.cn
[2] Guangzhou Center for Applied Mathematics, Guangzhou University,
Guangzhou, People's Republic of China

Abstract. Despite the importance of preimage sampling algorithm in lattice-based cryptography, its low efficiency limits its applications. In this study, we propose a family of gadget-based trapdoors on NTRU lattice. Our construction is compatible with existing efficient preimage sampling algorithms and offer compact secret. Comparison with two trapdoor schemes of [10], the hash-and-sign signature scheme based on our trapdoor scheme has better security and the sizes of secret and signature are reduced. In the first scheme, the sizes of public key and secret key are 6.25 kB and 5.0 kB for an estimation of 63.95-bit security. In the second one, they are 6.25 kB and 5.0 kB for an estimation of 75.92-bit security. Our proof-of-concept shows that the sizes of secret key and public key can be reduced to 0.88 kB and 3.06 kB for an estimation of 86.72-bit security.

Keywords: Preimage sampling · NTRU lattice · Trapdoor

1 Introduction

The development of quantum computer has brought widespread attention to post-quantum cryptography. In recent decades, lattice-based cryptography has become one of the most attractive areas. The preimage sampling algorithm plays an important role in lattice-based cryptography, since a large fraction of lattice-based constructions use lattice trapdoors to invert the (ring) short integer solution (RSIS) problem. In practice, structured lattices are used for higher efficiency. Let $R(R_q)$ be a polynomial ring with coefficients in $\mathbb{Z}(\mathbb{Z}_q)$. Given a random vector $\mathbf{a} \in R_q^m$ and element $u \in R_q$, it is known that finding a short vector $\mathbf{x} \in R^m$ such that $\mathbf{a} \cdot \mathbf{x} = u \in R_q$ is hard. However, one can easily sample short preimages in polynomial time with the help of a trapdoor [3,6].

According to the underlying structure, preimage sampling algorithms can be instantiated on hard random lattices and NTRU lattices. The security of the former is based on the hardness of the ring learning with errors problem (RLWE), while the latter is based on the NTRU learning problem [19]. RSIS trapdoors

© The Author(s), under exclusive license to Springer Nature Singapore Pte Ltd. 2022
E. Ahene and F. Li (Eds.): FCS 2022, CCIS 1726, pp. 275–287, 2022.
https://doi.org/10.1007/978-981-19-8445-7_18

based on RLWE were introduced in [6] (MP12), in which the preimage sampling task is related to the task on the "gadget" lattice by Peikert's convolution technique. The study of RSIS trapdoors based on NTRU lattice was initiated in [18]. Ducas and Prest [7] improved the efficiency of the preimage sampling on NTRU lattice through the Fast-Fourier Transform algorithm. Cheon et al. [2] introduced a generalized note of NTRU lattices to solve the dimension inflexibility of trapdoors based on NTRU lattice. Recently, Genise and Li have introduced two similar families of gadget-based RSIS trapdoors based on the inhomogeneous NTRU problem (iNTRU). The first trapdoor is a noisy version of a RSIS trapdoor which is entirely parallelized, while the second one has short key size.

1.1   Our Contributions

In this study, we construct a new related family of gadget-based RSIS trapdoors whose security is based on the hardness of the NTRU learning problem [19]. Our trapdoor construction is entirely parallelized as well, and improves on the one in [10] in terms of key sizes and security. Compared to [10], we have smaller public key and secret key when we fix the parameters n, m and R, because we only need a smaller modulus q.

From an application perspective, our trapdoor can be applied to any cryptographic primitive that relies on RSIS trapdoors. Lastly, we rely on the hash-and-sign signature scheme to implement our trapdoor scheme and compare it with the two trapdoor schemes of [10] (Table 1).

Table 1. Here is the detailed data comparing our trapdoor scheme with the two schemes of [10]. The two trapdoor schemes of [10] are recorded as Tra-1 and Tra-2. τ is the standard deviation of the trapdoor $\widetilde{\mathbf{R}}$. The public key and secret key size are measured in kB. Signature sizes are also measured in kB. "RSIS" references to the security level of breaking the RSIS problem. "RLWE" references to the security level of the pseudorandomness of the public key.

Params	Ours	Ours	Tra-1 [10]	Tra-2 [10]	Ours	Ours	Tra-1 [10]	Tra-2 [10]
n	512	512	512	512	1024	1024	1024	1024
$\lceil \log_b q \rceil$	13	7	10	10	15	8	10	10
b	2	4	4	4	2	4	4	4
τ	0.55	0.55	32	32	1.15	1.15	32	32
$|\text{pk}|$	10.56	3.06	6.25	6.25	12.5	8.0	12.5	12.5
$|\text{sk}|$	1.63	0.88	5.0	5.0	2.5	2.0	10.0	10.0
$|\text{sig}|$	6.5	3.94	8.13	8.13	12.5	10.0	17.5	17.5
RLWE	89.64	86.36	117.38	117.38	211.7	200.6	274.55	274.55
RSIS	90.81	86.72	63.95	75.92	212.58	200.9	152.72	176.37

1.2 Technical Overview

The preimage sampling algorithm based on our trapdoor is similar to MP12. The sampling can be divided into online sampling and offline sampling. Offline sampling relies on trapdoors, which is not affected by the RSIS image.

Now, we discuss our trapdoor mechanism in detail. Recall that, given a uniform random vector $\mathbf{a} \in R_q^m$ and an image $u \in \mathbb{Z}_q$, RSIS asks to find a short preimage $\mathbf{x} \in R^m$ such that

$$\mathbf{a}^t \cdot \mathbf{x} = u \mod q.$$

Let $k = \lceil \log_b q \rceil$ and $\mathbf{g}^t = [1 \ b \ b^2 \ \cdots \ b^{k-1}] \in R^k$. Given RSIS instance $\mathbf{a}^t = \mathbf{g}^t \cdot \mathbf{R}^{-1} \in R_q^k$ whose pseudorandomness is based on the NTRU learning problem, we have $\mathbf{a}^t \cdot \mathbf{R} = \mathbf{g}^t$, where $(f, g_1, g_2, \cdots, g_{k-1}) \leftarrow \chi^k$ is drawn from a distribution with small entries and

$$\mathbf{R} = \text{diag}\left(1, \frac{g_1}{f}, \frac{g_2}{f}, \cdots, \frac{g_{k-1}}{f}\right) \in R^{k \times k}.$$

Hence, the matrix $\mathbf{R}$ can reduce inverting RSIS on $\mathbf{a}$ to the gadget $\mathbf{g}$ to solve. We first sample a discrete Gaussian $\mathbf{x}$ such that $\mathbf{g}^t \cdot \mathbf{x} = u \mod q$, and then return $\mathbf{y} = \mathbf{R} \cdot \mathbf{x}$. It's obvious that $\mathbf{y}$ leaks information about the matrix $\mathbf{R}$. We can prevent information leakage by adding a perturbation vector. Since $f^{-1} \cdot g_i$ may not be an element of ring R, we can let $\widetilde{\mathbf{a}} = f^{-1} \cdot \mathbf{a}$, $\widehat{\mathbf{R}} = f \cdot \mathbf{R}$. If the returned preimage $\mathbf{x}$ such that $\widetilde{\mathbf{a}}^t \cdot \mathbf{x} = \widetilde{u} \mod q$, it satisfies $\mathbf{a}^t \cdot \mathbf{x} = u \mod q$. It's easy to know that the matrix $\widehat{\mathbf{R}}$ is the trapdoor of the new RSIS problem, $\widetilde{\mathbf{a}}^t \cdot \mathbf{x} = \widetilde{u} \mod q$. Actually, it is also the trapdoor for original RSIS problem.

In terms of application, lattice based cryptographic schemes that rely on our trapdoor can be statistically hidden. We later describe the preimage sampling algorithm provided by our trapdoor scheme and demonstrate its security under the random oracle model (ROM).

1.3 Related Works

NTRU lattice has a good property with using the Fast-Fourier Transform algorithm to improve sampling efficiency. The most natural trapdoor is Falcon [20], which implemented efficient the hash-and-sign signature scheme based on NTRU lattice. In [10], Genise and Li proposed two related families of lattice trapdoors based on the inhomogeneous NTRU problem (iNTRU). The first trapdoor is an entirely parallelized and noisy version of a RSIS trapdoor, but it requires a large modulo q, which makes it impossible to use the ring structure to sample perturbations as in [7,9], and the second one is not a parallel version. Our trapdoor overcomes their shortcomings.

2 Preliminaries

Notations. We denote by $\mathbb{C}, \mathbb{N}, \mathbb{R},$ and $\mathbb{Z}$ the set of complex numbers, natural numbers, real numbers, and integers, respectively. Bold lowercase letters and bold uppercase letters indicate vectors and matrices, such as $\mathbf{a}$ and $\mathbf{A}$, whose transposes are denoted as $\mathbf{a}^t$ and $\mathbf{A}^t$ respectively, where $\mathbf{a}^t$ is a row vector. The complex number $\bar{z}$ represents the conjugate of the complex number z. The Euclidean norm of matrix $\mathbf{A}$ is defined as $\max\|\mathbf{a}_i\|$, where $\mathbf{a}_i$ is a column vector of $\mathbf{A}$. The probability distribution of the set S is written as χ, where $\chi(x)$ denotes sampling from S with probability $P(x \leftarrow \chi)$. We denote U as the uniform random distribution. For different probability distributions X and Y in the same set S, whose statistical distance is represented by

$$\Delta_{ML} = \max_{x \in S} |\log(X(x)) - \log(Y(x))|.$$

2.1 Linear Algebra

A symmetric matrix $\Sigma \in \mathbb{R}^{n \times n}$ is a (semi) positive definite matrix, represented as $\Sigma > 0 (\geq)$, if $\mathbf{x}^t \Sigma \mathbf{x} > 0 (\geq)$ for all non-zero $\mathbf{x} \in \mathbb{R}^n$. We denote $\Sigma_1 - \Sigma_2 > 0 (\geq)$ as $\Sigma_1 > \Sigma_2 (\geq)$. We write $\Sigma > s\mathbf{I} (\geq)$ as $\Sigma > s (\geq)$, where s is a scalar. For any matrix $\mathbf{A}$, $s_1(\mathbf{A}) = \max_{\|\mathbf{x}\|=1} \mathbf{A}\mathbf{x}$ is denoted as the largest singular value of $\mathbf{A}$. If $\Sigma = \mathbf{A}^t \mathbf{A} \geq 0$, $\sqrt{\Sigma}$ is the square root of Σ. Let $\mathbf{M} = \begin{bmatrix} \mathbf{A} & \mathbf{B} \\ \mathbf{B}^t & \mathbf{D} \end{bmatrix}$ be a block matrix. The Schur complement of $\mathbf{A}$ is matrice $\mathbf{M}/\mathbf{A} = \mathbf{D} - \mathbf{B}^t \mathbf{A}^{-1} \mathbf{B}$ when $\mathbf{A}$ is a nonsingular matrix. The Schur complement of $\mathbf{D}$ is matrice $\mathbf{M}/\mathbf{D} = \mathbf{A} - \mathbf{B}\mathbf{D}^{-1}\mathbf{B}^t$ when $\mathbf{D}$ is a nonsingular matrix. Here, we introduce the fact that for a block matrix $\mathbf{M} = \begin{bmatrix} \mathbf{A} & \mathbf{B} \\ \mathbf{B}^t & \mathbf{D} \end{bmatrix} \in \mathbb{R}^{n \times n}$, $\mathbf{M}$ is a positive definite matrix if and only if both $\mathbf{D}$ and the Schur complement of $\mathbf{D}$ are positive definite matrices. Further, if $\mathbf{M}$ is a positive semi-definite matrix and $\mathbf{D} > 0$ if and only if $\mathbf{M}/\mathbf{D} > 0$.

2.2 Lattices and Gaussians

Given m linearly independent vectors $\mathbf{b}_1, \mathbf{b}_2, \cdots, \mathbf{b}_m \in \mathbb{R}^n$, we define a lattice by

$$\Lambda = \{z_1 \mathbf{b}_1 + z_2 \mathbf{b}_2 + \cdots + z_m \mathbf{b}_m | z_1, z_2, \cdots, z_m \in \mathbb{Z}\},$$

where these vectors are called the basis of the lattice. The span of a lattice Λ is the linear space spanned by its vectors, $\mathrm{span}(\Lambda) = \{\mathbf{B}\mathbf{y} | \mathbf{y} \in \mathbb{R}^m\}$, where matrix $\mathbf{B} = \{\mathbf{b}_1, \mathbf{b}_2, \cdots, \mathbf{b}_m\} \in \mathbb{R}^{n \times m}$ is a basis of the lattice. For a basis $\mathbf{B} = \{\mathbf{b}_1, \mathbf{b}_2, \cdots, \mathbf{b}_m\}$, we define its Gram Schmidt orthogonalization as the matrix $\widetilde{\mathbf{B}} = \{\widetilde{\mathbf{b}}_1, \widetilde{\mathbf{b}}_2, \cdots, \widetilde{\mathbf{b}}_m\}$ defined by $\widetilde{\mathbf{b}}_i = \mathbf{b}_i - \sum_{j=1}^{i-1} \mu_{ij} \widetilde{\mathbf{b}}_j$, where $\mu_{ij} = \dfrac{\langle \mathbf{b}_i, \widetilde{\mathbf{b}}_j \rangle}{\langle \widetilde{\mathbf{b}}_j, \widetilde{\mathbf{b}}_j \rangle}$. The dual of a lattice is defined as a set $\Lambda^* = \{\mathbf{x} \in \mathrm{span}(\Lambda) | \langle \mathbf{x}, \mathbf{y} \rangle \in \mathbb{Z}, \mathbf{y} \in \Lambda\}$.

Given a matrix $\mathbf{A} \in \mathbb{Z}^{n \times m}$ and a vector $\mathbf{u} \in \mathbb{Z}_q^n$, we define a m-dimensional lattice

$$\Lambda_{\mathbf{u}}^{\perp} = \{\mathbf{e} \in \mathbb{Z}^m : \mathbf{A} \cdot \mathbf{e} = \mathbf{u} \mod q\}.$$

Given a vector $\mathbf{c} \in \mathbb{R}^n$ and a matrix $\Sigma > 0$, the n-dimensional Gaussian function is defined as

$$\rho_{\sqrt{\Sigma},\,\mathbf{c}}(\mathbf{x}) = \exp(-\pi(\mathbf{x} - \mathbf{c})^t \Sigma^{-1}(\mathbf{x} - \mathbf{c})),$$

where the domain of definition is $\mathbb{R}^n$. For a scalar matrix $\Sigma = s^2 \cdot \mathbf{I}$, we abbreviate the Gaussian function by $\rho_{s,\,\mathbf{c}}(\mathbf{x})$, where $s > 0$. We define the discrete Gaussian distribution over a lattice Λ as

$$D_{\Lambda,\sqrt{\Sigma},\mathbf{c}}(\mathbf{x}) = \frac{\rho_{\mathbf{B},\sqrt{\Sigma},\mathbf{c}}(\mathbf{x})}{\rho_{\mathbf{B},\sqrt{\Sigma},\mathbf{c}}(\Lambda)}.$$

For any $\epsilon > 0$, the smallest $s > 0$ that satisfies $\rho(s \cdot \Lambda^*) \le 1 + \epsilon$ is called the smoothing parameter, denoted by $\eta_\epsilon(\Lambda)$.

Lemma 1 ([3]). *Let $\Lambda \subset \mathbb{R}^n$ be a lattice with basis $\mathbf{B}$. For any $\epsilon > 0$, we have*

$$\eta_\epsilon(\Lambda) \le \|\widetilde{\mathbf{B}}\| \cdot \sqrt{\ln\left(2n(1 + 1/\epsilon)\right)/\pi}.$$

Lemma 2 ([10]). *Let $\Lambda' \subset \Lambda \subset \mathbb{R}^n$ be a full rank lattice. For any $\epsilon > 0$, we have*

$$\Delta_{ML}(D_{\Lambda,\,s} \mod \Lambda',\ U(\Lambda/\Lambda')) \le \frac{2\epsilon}{1 - \epsilon}.$$

Lemma 3 ([10]). *Let $\Lambda \subset \mathbb{R}^n$ be a lattice with basis $\mathbf{B}$ and let $\mathbf{c} \in \operatorname{span}(\mathbf{B})$. Let $\epsilon > 0$ and let $s \ge \eta_\epsilon(\Lambda)$, we have*

$$\Pr\left[\|\mathbf{x} - \mathbf{c}\| \ge s\sqrt{n}\right] \le 2^{-n} \cdot \frac{1 + \epsilon}{1 - \epsilon}.$$

Lemma 4 ([10]). *Let $\Lambda \subset \mathbb{R}^n$ be a lattice, and let both $\mathbf{S} \in \mathbb{R}^{n \times n}$ and $\mathbf{T} \in \mathbb{R}^{n \times n}$ be nonsingular matrices. For any $\epsilon > 0$, $\eta_\epsilon(\Lambda) \le \mathbf{S}$ if and only if $\eta_\epsilon(\mathbf{T} \cdot \Lambda) \le \mathbf{T} \cdot \mathbf{S}$.*

Lemma 5 ([5]). *For a matrix $\Sigma > 0$ and a lattice coset $A = \Lambda + \mathbf{a} \subset \mathbf{c} + \operatorname{span}(\Sigma)$, if $\Lambda_{\mathbf{T}} = \Lambda \cap \ker(\mathbf{T})$ satisfies $\operatorname{span}(\Lambda_{\mathbf{T}}) = \ker(\mathbf{T})$ and $\eta_\epsilon(\Lambda_{\mathbf{T}}) \le \sqrt{\Sigma}$, we have*

$$\Delta_{ML}(\mathbf{T}(D_{A,\,\sqrt{\Sigma},\,\mathbf{c}}),\ D_{\mathbf{T}A,\,\mathbf{T}\sqrt{\Sigma},\,\mathbf{Tc}}) \le \frac{2\epsilon}{1 - \epsilon},$$

where $\mathbf{T}$ is a linear transformation.

2.3 Polynomial Ring

This article uses $R = \mathbb{Z}[x]/f(x)$ to denote a polynomial ring, where $f(x)$ is an irreducible polynomial over the field of rational numbers $\mathbb{Q}$. The polynomial ring R is called a cyclotomic polynomial ring, if $f(x)$ is a cyclotomic polynomial. We let $R_q = R/(qR)$ denote the coefficients modulo q of the elements of the polynomial ring R. R_q^* represents the polynomials of R_q which have multiplicative inverses. Let $\Phi_n(x)$ be a cyclotomic polynomial of degree n. We have $\Phi_{2n}(x) = x^n + 1$ if $2n$ is a power of two. For a cyclotomic polynomial

$f = \sum_{i=1}^{n} f_i x^{i-1} \in R = \mathbb{Z}[x]/\Phi_{2n}(x)$, we define its coefficient embedding as its vector of coefficients $(f_0, f_1, \cdots, f_{n-1})$. The norm of all coefficient embeddings is the l_2 norm. Further, we define the element embedding of the ring $R = \mathbb{Z}[x]/\Phi_{2n}(x)$ into an inverse cyclic matrix as

$$\varphi(f) = \begin{bmatrix} f_0 & -f_{n-1} & \cdots & -f_1 \\ f_1 & f_0 & \cdots & -f_2 \\ \vdots & \vdots & \ddots & \vdots \\ f_{n-1} & f_{n-1} & \cdots & f_0 \end{bmatrix} \in \mathbb{Z}^{n \times n}.$$

where n is the power of two. There is a fact that the matrix transpose of an element $f(x)$ on the ring corresponds to the inverse circular matrix of its conjugate element, $\varphi^t(f) = \varphi(\overline{f})$. Further, we can know that $\varphi(f\overline{f})$ is a positive definite matrix.

Definition 1 ([19]). *For an invertible $s \in R_q^*$ and a distribution χ on R, define $N_{s, \chi}$ to be the distribution that outputs $e/s \in R_q$ where $e \leftarrow \chi$. The NTRU learning problem is: given independent samples $a_i \in R_q$ where every sample is distributed according to either: (1) $N_{s, \chi}$ for somerandomly chosen $s \in R_q^*$ (fixed for all samples), or (2) the uniform distribution, distinguish which is the case (with non-negligible advantage).*

2.4   G-Lattices

For a positive integer $q \geq 2$ and a integer base $2 \leq b < \sqrt{q}$, $\mathbf{g}$ is generally used as the "gadget" in the RSIS problem, since we can reduce the problem to the gadget $\mathbf{g}$ to solve, that is, Gaussian sampling in the lattice,

$$\Lambda_u^\perp(\mathbf{g}^t) = \left\{ \mathbf{z} \in R^k : \mathbf{g}^t \cdot \mathbf{z} = u \in R_q \right\}$$

where $\mathbf{g}^t = [1, b, b^2, \cdots, b^{k-1}] \in R^k$ and $k = \lceil \log_b q \rceil$. Here, $D_{\Lambda_u^\perp(\mathbf{g}^t), \, \sigma_g}$ is used to represent discrete Gaussian sampling with variance σ_g^2 and the origin as the center point on lattice $\Lambda_u^\perp(\mathbf{g}^t)$.

3   Trapdoor Based on NTRU Lattice

Let $R = \mathbb{Z}[x]/f(x)$ be a finite dimensional polynomial ring of degree n and its quotient ring modulo q for some modulus $q \in \mathbb{N}$, $R_q = R/qR$. Given an integer base $b > 1$, $k = \lceil \log_b q \rceil$, and a gadget $\mathbf{g}^t = (1, b, b^2, \cdots, b^{k-1}) \in R^k$. Let χ be a distribution over R with small entries. We set $\mathbf{R} = \text{diag}(1, \frac{g_1}{f}, \frac{g_2}{f}, \cdots, \frac{g_{k-1}}{f})$, where $(f, g_1, g_2, \cdots, g_{k-1}) \leftarrow \chi^k$. Let $\mathbf{a}^t = \mathbf{g}^t \cdot \mathbf{R}^{-1} \in R_q^m$ be the RSIS instance, and we have $\mathbf{a}^t \mathbf{R} = \mathbf{g}^t$.

Below, we discuss preimage sampling based on our trapdoor. Similar to MP12, the inversion of our scheme has online sampling and offline sampling. Given $u \in R_q$, we try to construct a preimage. First, we sample a vector $\mathbf{x} \in R^m$

that satisfies $\mathbf{g}^t \cdot \mathbf{x} = u \bmod q$, and return to the preimage $\mathbf{y} = \mathbf{R} \cdot \mathbf{x}$. Then, we have

$$\mathbf{a}^t \cdot \mathbf{y} = u \bmod q.$$

Since $\mathbf{y}$ leaks information about R, we use Peikert's perturbation method to hide the information about R. When we use the method, there is a problem that $f_{-1} \cdot g_i (i = 1, 2, \cdots, k - 1)$ may not belong to the ring R so that the sampling of the perturbation vector cannot be performed. For this problem, our solution is to transform the original RSIS problem during the inversion process, $\widetilde{\mathbf{a}} = f^{-1} \cdot \mathbf{a} \in R_q^m$, $\widetilde{R} = f \cdot \mathbf{R} \in R^{k \times k}$ and $\widetilde{u} = f^{-1} \cdot u \in R_q$. Obviously, $\widetilde{\mathbf{a}}^t \cdot \widetilde{\mathbf{R}} = \mathbf{g}^t$. The preimage sampling algorithm steps of $\widetilde{\mathbf{a}} \cdot \mathbf{x} = \widetilde{u}$ perform the following:

1. Sample a perturbation, $\mathbf{p} \leftarrow D_{R^m, \sqrt{\Sigma_p}}$, where $\Sigma_p = s^2 \cdot \mathbf{I}_m - \sigma_g^2 \cdot \widetilde{\mathbf{R}} \cdot \widetilde{\mathbf{R}}^t$;
2. Let $v = \widetilde{u} - \widetilde{\mathbf{a}}^t \cdot \mathbf{p}$;
3. G-lattice sampling, $D_{\Lambda_v^\perp(\mathbf{g}^t), \sigma_g}$;
4. Output $\mathbf{y} = \widetilde{\mathbf{R}} \cdot \mathbf{x} + \mathbf{p}$.

Due to $\mathbf{a}^t \cdot \mathbf{y} = f \cdot \mathbf{g}^t \cdot \mathbf{x} + \mathbf{a}^t \cdot \mathbf{p} = u$, we get the fact that $\mathbf{y}$ is the solution to RSIS problem $\mathbf{a}^t \cdot \mathbf{y} = u \bmod q$. From the previous analysis, we can know that the matrix $\widetilde{\mathbf{R}} = \mathrm{diag}(f, g_1, g_2, \cdots, g_{k-1})$ is the trapdoor for the inversion of the original RSIS problem, $\mathbf{a}^t \cdot \mathbf{y} = u \bmod q$.

As our trapdoor is diagonal matrices, offline sampling can be parallelized. In addition, our trapdoor can be applied to the cyclotomic polynomial ring. Compared with the two trapdoors of [10], our secret key has smaller size.

The hardness of our trapdoor is similar to the NTRU assumption that as, for two small random polynomials f and g in R, their quotient $h = f \cdot g^{-1} \in R_q$ is indistinguishable from uniform element in R_q. For our case, we can establish a similar NTRU assumption, saying

$$\mathbf{H} = f^{-1} \cdot \mathrm{diag}(f, g_1, g_2, \cdots, g_{k-1}) \in R_q^{k \times k}$$

is indistinguishable from a uniform matrix in $R_q^{k \times k}$.

3.1 Trapdoor Inversion

Here, we present the preimage sampling algorithm based on our trapdoor scheme, which is described in Algorithm 1 and Algorithm 2 in detail. We also prove that the RSIS trapdoor structure based on NTRU lattice is secure in the random oracle model.

We first give the parameters for our trapdoor structure. Let $\eta = \eta_\epsilon(R^m) = \eta_\epsilon(\mathbb{Z}^{nm})$ be the smoothing parameter of the integer lattice for some $\epsilon \in (0, 1)$ and denote the largest singular value of the trapdoor $\widetilde{\mathbf{R}}$ as $s_1(\widetilde{\mathbf{R}})$. By Lemma 1, we know $\sigma_g = \sqrt{b^2 + 1} \cdot \eta \geq \eta_\epsilon(\Lambda_v^\perp(\mathbf{g}^t))$. In this paper, we assume the upper bound of RSIS-β is $s\sqrt{nm}$ and the preimage Gaussian width is

$$s = \sqrt{\frac{\sigma_g^4}{\sigma_g^2 - \eta^2} s_1^2(\widetilde{\mathbf{R}}) + \eta^2 \mathbf{I}_m}.$$

Algorithm 1 is the trapdoor generation and Algorithm 2 is the preimage sampling. The sampling of perturbation does not depend on the target u, which means they can be sampled in offlin phase. s is the preimage Gaussian width and σ_g is the G-lattice preimage Gaussian width.

Algorithm 1. TRAPGEN
___
Input: The security parameter λ.
Output: A trapdoor and a verification key.

1: Sample $(f, g_1, g_2, \cdots, g_{k-1}) \leftarrow \chi^k$.
2: Let $\widetilde{\mathbf{R}} = \mathrm{diag}(f, g_1, g_2, \cdots, g_{k-1})$.
3: Let $\mathbf{a}^t = \mathbf{g}^t \cdot (f^{-1} \cdot \widetilde{\mathbf{R}})^{-1}$.
4: **return** $\widetilde{\mathbf{R}}$ and $\mathbf{a}$.

Algorithm 2. SAMPLEPRE$(\mathbf{a}, u, s, \sigma_g)$
___
Input: A target $u \in R_q$ and a trapdoor $\widetilde{\mathbf{R}}$.
Output: A preimage of u.

1: Sample a perturbation $\mathbf{p} \leftarrow D_{R^m, \sqrt{\Sigma_p}}$.
2: Let $\widetilde{\mathbf{a}}^t = f^{-1} \cdot \mathbf{a}^t$, $\widetilde{u} = u \cdot f^{-1}$ and $v = \widetilde{u} - \widetilde{\mathbf{a}}^t \cdot \mathbf{p}$.
3: G-lattice sample $\mathbf{x} \leftarrow D_{\Lambda_v^\perp(\mathbf{g}^t), \, \sigma_g}$.
4: **return** $\mathbf{y} = \widetilde{\mathbf{R}} \cdot \mathbf{x} + \mathbf{p}$.

3.2   Security Proof

The security of our trapdoor structure in the random oracle model is summed up in Theorem 1. In the process of proving Theorem 1, we first introduce a lemma. Then, we give Theorem 1 and its proof.

Lemma 6. *Let $\eta = \eta_\epsilon(R^m) = \eta_\epsilon(\mathbb{Z}^{nm})$ be the smoothing parameter of the integer lattice for some $\epsilon \in (0, 1)$ and let $\sigma_g = \sqrt{b^2 + 1} \cdot \eta$. Let $\Sigma_p = s^2 \cdot \mathbf{I}_m - \sigma_g^2 \cdot \widetilde{\mathbf{R}} \cdot \widetilde{\mathbf{R}}^t$, $\mathbf{L} = \left[\mathbf{I}_m \mid \widetilde{\mathbf{R}} \right] \in R^{m \times 2m}$, and $\Lambda^\perp = \left\{ \mathbf{x} \in R^{2m} : \mathbf{L} \cdot \mathbf{x} = \mathbf{0} \right\}$. If*

$$s^2 \mathbf{I}_m \geq \frac{\sigma_g^4}{\sigma_g^2 - \eta^2} \cdot \widetilde{\mathbf{R}} \cdot \widetilde{\mathbf{R}}^t + \eta^2 \cdot \mathbf{I}_m,$$

we have $\sqrt{\Sigma_p \oplus \sigma_g^2 \mathbf{I}_m} \geq \eta_\epsilon(\Lambda^\perp)$.

Proof. First, considering that a basis of $\Lambda^{\perp} = \left\{ \mathbf{x} \in R^{2m} : \mathbf{L} \cdot \mathbf{x} = \mathbf{0} \right\}$ is

$$\mathbf{B} = \begin{bmatrix} -\widetilde{\mathbf{R}} \\ \mathbf{I}_m \end{bmatrix} \in R^{2m \times m}.$$

One can see the definition of $\Lambda^{\perp}$,

$$\Lambda^{\perp} = \left\{ \mathbf{B} \cdot \mathbf{x} \in R^{2m} : \mathbf{x} \in R^m \right\}.$$

Let

$$\mathbf{E} = \begin{bmatrix} \mathbf{I}_m & \widetilde{\mathbf{R}} \\ \mathbf{0} & \mathbf{I}_m \end{bmatrix} \in R^{2m \times 2m},$$

and we have

$$\mathbf{E}\Lambda^{\perp} = \begin{bmatrix} \mathbf{0} \\ R^m \end{bmatrix} \in R^{2m \times 2m}.$$

By Lemma 4, we can know that $\sqrt{\Sigma_p \oplus \sigma_g^2 \mathbf{I}_m} \geq \eta_{\epsilon}(\Lambda^{\perp})$ if and only if

$$\mathbf{E}\sqrt{\Sigma_p \oplus \sigma_g^2 \mathbf{I}_m} \geq \eta_{\epsilon}(\mathbf{E}\Lambda^{\perp}) = \eta_{\epsilon}(R^{2m}) = \eta.$$

Let

$$\Sigma = \mathbf{E}(\Sigma_p \oplus \sigma_g^2 \mathbf{I}_m)\mathbf{E}^t = \begin{bmatrix} \Sigma_p + \sigma_g^2 \cdot \widetilde{\mathbf{R}} \cdot \widetilde{\mathbf{R}}^t & \sigma_g^2 \cdot \widetilde{\mathbf{R}} \\ \sigma_g^2 \cdot \widetilde{\mathbf{R}}^t & \sigma_g^2 \cdot \mathbf{I}_m \end{bmatrix}.$$

To prove $\sqrt{\Sigma_p \oplus \sigma_g^2 \mathbf{I}_m} \geq \eta_{\epsilon}(\Lambda^{\perp})$, we just need to prove $\Sigma - \eta^2 \mathbf{I}_{2m} \geq 0$. Let

$$\Sigma' = \Sigma - \eta^2 = \begin{bmatrix} \Sigma_p + \sigma_g^2 \cdot \widetilde{\mathbf{R}} \cdot \widetilde{\mathbf{R}}^t - \eta^2 \mathbf{I}_m & \sigma_g^2 \cdot \widetilde{\mathbf{R}} \\ \sigma_g^2 \cdot \widetilde{\mathbf{R}}^t & \sigma_g^2 \cdot \mathbf{I}_m - \eta^2 \cdot \mathbf{I}_m \end{bmatrix}.$$

Since $\sigma_g > \eta$, we have $\mathbf{D} = \sigma_g^2 \cdot \mathbf{I}_m - \eta^2 \cdot \mathbf{I}_m$. Below, we use the fact that Σ' is a positive definite matrix if and only if both $\mathbf{D}$ and Schur complement of $\mathbf{D}$ are positive definite matrix.

Notice that

$$\Sigma'/\mathbf{D} = (\Sigma_p + \sigma_g^2 \cdot \widetilde{\mathbf{R}} \cdot \widetilde{\mathbf{R}}^t - \eta^2 \cdot \mathbf{I}_m) - (\sigma_g^2 \cdot \widetilde{\mathbf{R}}) \cdot \frac{1}{\sigma_g^2 - \eta^2} \cdot (\sigma_g^2 \cdot \widetilde{\mathbf{R}}).$$

In other words

$$\Sigma'/\mathbf{D} = (s^2 - \eta^2) \cdot \mathbf{I}_m - \frac{\sigma_g^4}{\sigma_g^2 - \eta^2} \cdot \widetilde{\mathbf{R}} \cdot \widetilde{\mathbf{R}}^t.$$

Since

$$s^2 \mathbf{I}_m \geq \frac{\sigma_g^4}{\sigma_g^2 - \eta^2} \cdot \widetilde{\mathbf{R}} \cdot \widetilde{\mathbf{R}}^t + \eta^2 \cdot \mathbf{I}_m,$$

we have $\Sigma'/\mathbf{D} \geq 0$. Therefore, we proved that $\sqrt{\Sigma_p \oplus \sigma_g^2 \mathbf{I}_m} \geq \eta_{\epsilon}(\Lambda^{\perp})$.

Theorem 1. *Sample* $(f, g_1, g_2, \cdots, g_{k-1}) \leftarrow \chi^k$ *and let* $\sigma_g = \sqrt{b^2 + 1} \cdot \eta$, *where*
$\eta = \eta_\epsilon(R^m) = \eta_\epsilon(\mathbb{Z}^{nm})$. *Let* $\mathbf{R} = \mathrm{diag}(1, \dfrac{g_1}{f}, \dfrac{g_2}{f}, \cdots, g_{k-1})$, $\mathbf{a}^t = \mathbf{g} \cdot \mathbf{R}^{-1} \in R_q^m$,
$\widetilde{\mathbf{a}} = f^{-1} \cdot \mathbf{a}$ *and* $\widetilde{\mathbf{R}} = f \cdot \mathbf{R}$. *Then, the following distributions are within a max-log*
distance of $\dfrac{2\epsilon}{1-\epsilon}$:

$$\{(\mathbf{a}, \mathbf{y}, u), \ \mathbf{y} \leftarrow D_{R^m, s}, \ u = \mathbf{a}^t \cdot \mathbf{y} \mod q\},$$

$$\{(\mathbf{a}, \mathbf{y}, u) : u \leftarrow U(R_q), \ \mathbf{y} \leftarrow \mathrm{SAMPLEPRE}(\mathbf{a}, u, s, \sigma_g), 0 = u - \mathbf{a}^t \cdot \mathbf{y} \mod q\},$$

where $s = \sqrt{\dfrac{\sigma_g^4}{\sigma_g^2 - \eta^2} \cdot s_1^2(\widetilde{\mathbf{R}}) + \eta^2 \cdot \mathbf{I}_m}$.

Proof. Let $(\mathbf{a}, \mathbf{y}, u)$ be the real distribution in the random oracle model and it
is equivalent to $(\widetilde{\mathbf{a}}, \mathbf{y}, \widetilde{u})$. That is $u \leftarrow U(R_q)$, $\mathbf{p} \leftarrow D_{R^m, \sqrt{\Sigma_p}}$, $\widetilde{u} = f^{-1} \cdot u$,
$v = \widetilde{u} - \widetilde{\mathbf{a}}^t \cdot \mathbf{p}$, $\mathbf{x} \leftarrow D_{\Lambda_v^\perp(\mathbf{g}^t), \ \sigma_g}$, and $\mathbf{y} = \widetilde{\mathbf{R}} \cdot \mathbf{x} + \mathbf{p}$.

Hybrid 1: Instead of sampling uniformly random $u \leftarrow U(R_q)$ directly in
the real distribution, we first sample uniformly random $\widetilde{u} \leftarrow U(R_q)$ and then
compute $u = f \cdot \widetilde{u}$. Others remain the same. We know that the real distribution
and *Hybrid 1* are same.

Hybrid 2: First sample $\widetilde{u} \leftarrow U(R_q)$ and perturbation $\mathbf{p} \leftarrow D_{R^m, \sqrt{\Sigma_p}}$ in
Hybrid 1, then compute $v = \widetilde{u} - \widetilde{\mathbf{a}}^t \cdot \mathbf{p}$. Here, we first sample uniformly random
$v \leftarrow U(R_q)$ and perturbation $p \leftarrow D_{R^m, \sqrt{\Sigma_p}}$, then compute $\widetilde{u} = v + \widetilde{\mathbf{a}}^t \cdot \mathbf{p}$. Others
remain the same. We know that *Hybrid 2* and *Hybrid 1* have same distribution.

Hybrid 3: First sample uniformly random $v \leftarrow U(R_q)$ and then G-lattice
sample $\mathbf{x} \leftarrow D_{\Lambda_v^\perp(\mathbf{g}^t), \ \sigma_g}$ in *Hybrid 2*. Here, we first G-lattice sample $\mathbf{x} \leftarrow$
$D_{\Lambda_v^\perp(\mathbf{g}^t), \ \sigma_g}$ and then compute $v = \mathbf{g}^t \cdot \mathbf{x}$. Others remain the same, $\mathbf{p} \leftarrow$
$D_{R^m, \sqrt{\Sigma_p}}$, $\widetilde{u} = v + \widetilde{\mathbf{a}}^t \cdot \mathbf{p}$, and $\mathbf{y} = \widetilde{\mathbf{R}} \cdot \mathbf{x} + \mathbf{p}$. By Lemma 2 and Lemma 6,
we know that the max-log distance between *Hybrid 3* and *Hybrid 2* is less than
$\dfrac{2\epsilon}{1-\epsilon}$.

Hybrid 4: First G-lattice sample $\mathbf{x} \leftarrow D_{\Lambda_v^\perp(\mathbf{g}^t), \ \sigma_g}$ and sample $\mathbf{p} \leftarrow D_{R^m, \sqrt{\Sigma_p}}$
in *Hybrid 3*, then compute $\mathbf{y} = \mathbf{L} \cdot \begin{bmatrix} \mathbf{R} \\ \mathbf{x} \end{bmatrix}$, where $\mathbf{L} = \begin{bmatrix} \mathbf{I}_m \mid \widetilde{\mathbf{R}} \end{bmatrix} \in R^{m \times 2m}$. Here, we
sample directly $\mathbf{y} \leftarrow D_{R^m, s}$ and then compute $\widetilde{u} = \widetilde{\mathbf{a}}^t \mathbf{y} \mod q$. That is $u = \mathbf{a}^t \mathbf{y}$
mod q. By Lemma 5, we can know that the max-log distance between *Hybrid 4*
and *Hybrid 3* is less than $\dfrac{2\epsilon}{1-\epsilon}$.

4 Instantiation

We conducted some experiments to compare the performance of the hash-and-
sign signature scheme using our trapdoor versus the RSIS based exact trapdoor

in [10]. The detailed data of the experiment are summarized in Table 2. We now describe security estimation of the scheme and discuss the results of the experiment.

4.1 Concrete Parameters

In this study, we estimated the security by estimating the pseudorandomness of the public-key(RLWE security) and the hardness of solving the RSIS problem(RSIS security). RLWE security is determined by parameters q, n and standard deviation τ of trapdoor $\widetilde{\mathbf{R}}$.

RSIS security depends on β, the upper bound of $\|\mathbf{x}\|$. The estimate of RSIS security was carried out through the hardness of $\mathrm{RSIS}_{n,m,q,\beta}$. We estimated the security level of $\mathrm{RSIS}_{n,m,q,\beta}$ by estimating how long it would take the BKZ algorithm to break the scheme. The BKZ algorithm is a basis reduction algorithm which is expected to find a basis with the shortest vector length $\delta_0^m \cdot det(\Lambda)^{1/m}$ in the block size κ, where δ_0 is the root-heuristic factor. Here, we assume that the BKZ algorithm uses $2^{0.292\kappa}$ as the time complexity of the SVP oracle. We got root-heuristic factor δ_0 from $\beta = \delta_0^m \cdot det(\Lambda)^{1/m}$, where δ_0 has the following relationship,

$$\delta_0 \approx (\frac{\kappa}{2\pi e}(\pi\kappa)^{1/\kappa})^{1/2(\kappa-1)}.$$

Further, we got the time complexity of BKZ algorithm to break the $\mathrm{RSIS}_{n,m,q,\beta}$.

4.2 Conclusion

In this paper, compared with the scheme in [10], our trapdoor scheme improves both security and efficiency(smaller secret sizes). The sizes of our public key and secret key are shorter than the second scheme of [10], and secret key is also smaller than the first scheme of [10]. In the first scheme, the sizes of public key and secret key are 6.25 kB and 5.0 kB for an estimation of 63.95-bit security. In the second one, the sizes of public key and secret key are 12.5 kB and 10.0 kB for an estimation of 176.37-bit security. Our proof-of-concept shows that the sizes of secret key and public key can be reduced to 0.88 kB and 3.06 kB for an estimation of 86.72-bit security. For an estimation of 200.9-bit security, the sizes of secret key and public key can be reduced to 2.0 kB and 8.0 kB. In terms of security, the hash-and-sign signature scheme based on our trapdoor scheme has better security. Our scheme has an estimation of 200.9-bit security for n = 512 when the number of q bits is 14. However, for the larger modulus q, the security estimation of [10]'s two schemes is lower than 80 bits When n remains unchanged.

In terms of sampling speed, our scheme has a faster speed from the algorithm point of view. Ours can be fully parallelized to the ring level in offline stage. Although the first trapdoor scheme of [10] is a parallel version, our trapdoor needs to sample one perturbation ring element less than it, m perturbation ring elements. The second scheme of [10] compared with our scheme, it not only needs more perturbation ring elements than we do, but is not spherical Gaussian sampling.

Table 2. The two trapdoor schemes of [10] are recorded as Tra-1 and Tra-2. τ is the standard deviation of the trapdoor $\widetilde{\mathbf{R}}$. s is the preimage Gaussian width. The public key and secret key size are measured in kB. Signature sizes are also measured in kB. "RSIS" references to the security level of breaking the RSIS problem. "RLWE" references to the security level of the pseudorandomness of the public key.

Params	Ours	Ours	Tra-1 [10]	Tra-2 [10]	Ours	Ours	Tra-1 [10]	Tra-2 [10]
n	512	512	512	512	1024	1024	1024	1024
$\lceil \log_b q \rceil$	13	7	10	10	15	8	10	10
b	2	4	4	4	2	4	4	4
τ	0.55	0.55	32	32	1.15	1.15	32	32
s	229.19	421.76	7229.5	7229.5	665.92	1190.44	10224.00	10224.00
$\|\mathbf{x}\|_2$	7832.43	10576.58	216691.87	216691.87	28227.31	45133.79	433381.32	433381.32
|pk|	10.56	3.06	6.25	6.25	12.5	8.0	12.5	12.5
|sk|	1.63	0.88	5.0	5.0	2.5	2.0	10.0	10.0
|sig|	6.5	3.94	8.13	8.13	12.5	10.0	17.5	17.5
RLWE	89.64	86.36	117.38	117.38	211.7	200.6	274.55	274.55
RSIS	90.81	86.72	63.95	75.92	212.58	200.9	152.72	176.37

Acknowledgement. The authors thank the anonymous reviewers for helpful comments and suggestions. This study was supported by the National Key Research and Development Program of China (Grant No. 2021YFB3100200), the National Key Research and Development Program of China through Project 2021YFA1000600, and Natural Science Foundation of China through Projects 12171114.

References

1. Gentry, C.: Fully homomorphic encryption using ideal lattices. In: STOC, pp. 169–178. ACM (2009)
2. Cheon, J.H., Kim, D., Kim, T., Son, Y.: A new trapdoor over module-NTRU lattice and its application to ID-based encryption. IACR Cryptology ePrint Archive, 2019/1468 (2019)
3. Gentry, C., Peikert, C., V aikuntanathan, V.: Trapdoors for hard lattices and new cryptographic constructions. In: STOC, pp. 197–206. ACM (2008)
4. Ajtai, M.: Generating hard instances of lattice problems. Quaderni di Matematica **13**, 1–32 (2004)
5. Chen, Y., Genise, N., Mukherjee, P.: Approximate trapdoors for lattices and smaller hash-and-sign signatures. In: Galbraith, S.D., Moriai, S. (eds.) ASIACRYPT 2019. LNCS, vol. 11923, pp. 3–32. Springer, Cham (2019). https://doi.org/10.1007/978-3-030-34618-8_1
6. Micciancio, D., Peikert, C.: Trapdoors for lattices: simpler, tighter, faster, smaller. In: Pointcheval, D., Johansson, T. (eds.) EUROCRYPT 2012. LNCS, vol. 7237, pp. 700–718. Springer, Heidelberg (2012). https://doi.org/10.1007/978-3-642-29011-4_41
7. Ducas, L., Prest, T.: Fast fourier orthogonalization. In: ISSAC, pp. 191–198. ACM (2016)

8. Jia, H., Hu, Y., Tang, C.: Lattice-based hash-and-sign signatures using approximate trapdoor, revisited. IET Inf. Secur. **16**(1), 41–50 (2022)
9. Genise, N., Micciancio, D.: Faster gaussian sampling for trapdoor lattices with arbitrary modulus. In: Nielsen, J.B., Rijmen, V. (eds.) EUROCRYPT 2018. LNCS, vol. 10820, pp. 174–203. Springer, Cham (2018). https://doi.org/10.1007/978-3-319-78381-9_7
10. Genise, N., Li, B.: Gadget-based iNTRU lattice trapdoors. In: Bhargavan, K., Oswald, E., Prabhakaran, M. (eds.) INDOCRYPT 2020. LNCS, vol. 12578, pp. 601–623. Springer, Cham (2020). https://doi.org/10.1007/978-3-030-65277-7_27
11. Lyubashevsky, V.: Lattice signatures without trapdoors. In: Pointcheval, D., Johansson, T. (eds.) EUROCRYPT 2012. LNCS, vol. 7237, pp. 738–755. Springer, Heidelberg (2012). https://doi.org/10.1007/978-3-642-29011-4_43
12. Hu, Y., Jia, H.: A new Gaussian sampling for trapdoor lattices with arbitrary modulus. Des. Codes Crypt. **87**(11), 2553–2570 (2019). https://doi.org/10.1007/s10623-019-00635-8
13. Alkim, E., et al.: The lattice-based digital signature scheme qTESLA. IACR Cryptology ePrint Archive 2019/85 (2019)
14. Chuengsatiansup, C., Prest, T., Stehlé, D., Wallet, A., Xagawa, K.: Modfalcon: compact signatures based on module NTRU lattices. IACR Cryptology ePrint Archive 2019/1456 (2019)
15. Peikert, C.: An efficient and parallel gaussian sampler for lattices. In: Rabin, T. (ed.) CRYPTO 2010. LNCS, vol. 6223, pp. 80–97. Springer, Heidelberg (2010). https://doi.org/10.1007/978-3-642-14623-7_5
16. Clear, M., McGoldrick, C.: Multi-identity and multi-key leveled FHE from learning with errors. In: Gennaro, R., Robshaw, M. (eds.) CRYPTO 2015. LNCS, vol. 9216, pp. 630–656. Springer, Heidelberg (2015). https://doi.org/10.1007/978-3-662-48000-7_31
17. Gentry, C., Sahai, A., Waters, B.: Homomorphic encryption from learning with errors: conceptually-simpler, asymptotically-faster, attribute-based. In: Canetti, R., Garay, J.A. (eds.) CRYPTO 2013. LNCS, vol. 8042, pp. 75–92. Springer, Heidelberg (2013). https://doi.org/10.1007/978-3-642-40041-4_5
18. Ducas, L., Lyubashevsky, V., Prest, T.: Efficient identity-based encryption over NTRU lattices. In: Sarkar, P., Iwata, T. (eds.) ASIACRYPT 2014. LNCS, vol. 8874, pp. 22–41. Springer, Heidelberg (2014). https://doi.org/10.1007/978-3-662-45608-8_2
19. Peikert, C.: A decade of lattice cryptography. Found. Trends Theor. Comput. Sci. **10**(4), 283–424 (2016)
20. Kirchner, P., et al.: Falcon: fast-fourier lattice-based compact signatures over NTRU. Post-Quantum Cryptography Standardization Round2 Submissions (2019)

Secure EHR Sharing Scheme Based on Limited Sanitizable Signature

Yang Yang[1,2(✉)], Bixia Yi[2], Yonghua Zhan[2], and Minming Huang[1,2]

[1] Fujian Provincial Key Laboratory of Information Security of Network Systems, Fuzhou University, Fuzhou 350108, China
yang.yang.research@gmail.com
[2] College of Computer and Data Science, Fuzhou University, Fuzhou 350108, China
200320103@fzu.edu.cn

Abstract. Many sanitizable signature schemes have been proposed to facilitate and secure the secondary use of medical data. These schemes allow a patient, authorized by the doctor, to modify and re-sign his/her electronic health record (EHR) to hide sensitive information and the new signature can be verified successfully. However, this may lead to fraud because patients may forge medical records for profit. To further standardize sanitization and reduce the sanitizers power, this paper proposes a new limited sanitizable signature scheme, which allows the signer to not only decide which message blocks can be modified but also determine the maximum of modifiable blocks and the expiration time for sanitization. We also propose a secure EHR sharing scheme suitable for medical scenarios based on the above limited sanitizable signature to realize privacy preserving medical data sharing. Finally, the security analysis and experimental results show that the security and efficiency of our scheme can be accepted.

Keywords: Sanitizable signature · Privacy preserving · Data sharing · Sensitive information hiding

1 Introduction

EHRs are widely used in scenarios such as hospital management, scientific research, and insurance claims as a convenient way to improve the efficiency and quality of medical services [1]. To prevent sensitive information in patients' EHR from leakage in medical data sharing, recent research tends to apply sanitizable signatures to anonymize and desensitize medical data [2,3].

Sanitizable signature schemes allow a potential third party (Sanitizer) to alter signed data in a controlled and non-interactive way, and the resulting signature can still be successfully verified [4], which is more suitable than traditional digital signatures for some scenarios that do not require a complete electronic medical record. In this scheme, the doctor can grant the patient permission to delete sensitive data from the original EHR before disclosing or processing it.

Sanitizable signatures allow flexible and efficient manipulation of medical data while also leading to modification abuse, which will lead to fraud. For example, patients may forge medical records to defraud high insurance premiums [5], and healthcare fraud and commercial insurance fraud will seriously endanger the order of the industry and bring burdens to society. Therefore, it is necessary to restrict the capacity of the sanitizer.

Only a few works have focused on reducing the sanitizer power [6–9], proposing Extended Sanitizable Signatures (ESS) to restrict the ability to modify messages by limiting the set of possible modifications, forcing the same modifications on different admissible blocks, limiting the number of modifications of admissible blocks and the number of versions of signed messages. However, most of these schemes are not suitable for medical scenarios because the signature algorithm requires interaction with the sanitizer, moreover, they do not take into account unlinkability and invisibility, which are important in the secure sharing of EHRs. Unlinkability prevents receivers from colluding with each other to reconstruct a complete EHR. In other words, assuming that a medical institution and an insurance company respectively have the sanitized EHRs of the same patient, they cannot tell that the two EHRs have the same origin. Invisibility ensures that the receiver cannot determine which blocks of a given message are admissible, preventing the receiver from inferring sensitive information about the patient [10]. γ-Sanitizable Signature (γSaS) [6] satisfies both unlinkability and invisibility, and limits the number of blocks that can be modified to no more than γ. Since creating a false medical record usually involves a large number of fields, limiting the maximum of modifiable fields can prevent the sanitizer from forging medical records to a certain extent.

However, none of the above work takes into account the time limit. If a patient retains the right to modify the EHR after discharge, it will result in inconsistencies in medical records, which will lead to medical disputes. Therefore, to further ensure the security and correctness of medical data and restrict the sanitizer's power, this paper proposes a time-bound sanitizable signature, which embeds the expiration time, denoted with τ, into the signature, and only allows modifications to the medical record before the expiration time. In practical applications, the expiration time can be set for actual usages, such as the time of medical record filing.

Contribution. The main contributions of this paper are as follows:

– We propose a secure EHR sharing scheme suitable for medical scenarios. In this scheme, the doctor generates and signs the patient's medical record, and specifies the patient to modify some fields before the expiration time τ, and the number of modified fields does not exceed the limit γ. The patient can convert the signature of the original record into a new one for the modified record without interacting with the doctor, and the new signature is indistinguishable from the original one. The scheme satisfies accountability, can trace malicious patients who forge records, and distinguish whether the generator of a given signature is a doctor or a patient.

- We design a limited sanitizable signature scheme to construct a secure EHR sharing scheme. In such a limited sanitizable signature, the signer can decide which blocks and how many blocks at most of a message can be modified in sanitization. In addition, the sanitizer can only execute sanitization before the expiration time.
- Most current sanitizable signatures with accountability only allow the signer to prove the origin of a message/signature pair, which makes it impossible to tell whether the message is sanitized when the signer cannot produce proof due to losing his/her secret key or other reasons. Our scheme allows the signer and the sanitizer to independently prove which party generated the message/signature pair, achieving strong accountability.
- We present the security analysis, which proves the proposed scheme is secure. Moreover, the performance analysis shows the proposed scheme achieves desirable efficiency.

2   System Model and Security Goals

2.1   System Model

The system model of the secure EHR sharing scheme is shown in Fig. 1. There are four types of entities: the Trust Authority (TA), the Signer, the Sanitizer, and the Verifiers.

- **Trust Authority** is fully honest and responsible for generating the key pairs for the signer and the sanitizer.
- **The signer** can be the doctor, who is responsible for generating and signing the patient's EHR. The Signer can define what can be modified, the maximum of modifiable fields, and the expiration time for sanitization.
- **The sanitizer** is usually a semi-trusted third party authorized by the signer, such as a patient or the EHRs information system administrator, who can modify the admissible part of the record within a certain period and generate a new valid signature for the modified record.
- **Verifiers** are usually other medical data sharing entities, such as medical institutions, insurance companies, and scientific research institutions. They verify whether a given record is valid or not. Verifiers can access medical data but cannot modify it.

In this model, the doctor generates the patient's original EHR and signs it. Then he/she specifies the modification rules of the record. The patient can sanitize data based on the secondary use of the record, such as hiding identity-related information for analysis, and hiding other sensitive conditions unrelated to the claims when the record is provided to insurance companies. When the modification reaches the limit, the record is "locked" and no further modification is allowed. In the event of a dispute about the origin of the message/signature pair, both the doctor and the patient can generate proof and send it to the TA, who will judge the identity of the generator.

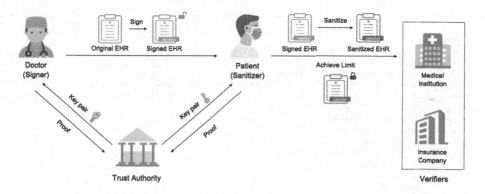

Fig. 1. System model

2.2 Security Goals

To securely support the secure sharing of EHRs in medical scenarios, our scheme aims to achieve the following goals:

- **Immutability.** The Patient cannot modify non-admissible fields in his/her EHR, and cannot produce a valid signature if the expiration time has passed. Moreover, the number of modified fields cannot exceed the limit.
- **Transparency.** Verifiers cannot distinguish between the patient's new signature on the sanitized EHR and the doctor's signature on the original EHR.
- **Unlinkability.** Verifiers cannot link a sanitized signature with the original one.
- **Invisibility.** Verifiers cannot tell which fields are admissible, how many are allowed to be modified, and the time limit for sanitization.
- **Strong Accountability.** Neither the doctor nor the patient can deny the self-generated message/signature pair, nor can they blame each other.

3 The Proposed Scheme

3.1 Notation

Table 1 gives the notations used in our scheme.

3.2 Overview

To realize the secure sharing scheme of EHRs that has a limit of time and number for modifications, and satisfies strong accountability, we consider the γSaS scheme proposed in [6] and further improve it. To satisfy both unlinkability and invisibility, we choose the Equivalence Class Signature (EQS) of Fuchsbauer et al. [11], which allows re-randomizing the signed content and signature, to sign commitments that imply information about admissible blocks and limits, and

Table 1. Notations.

Notation	Meaning
m, σ	The message and the signature on it
m', σ'	The sanitized message and the new signature on it
(mpk, msk)	The system public parameter and the master private key
ADM	The description of the admissible modification. If $m_i \in ADM$, then m_i is allowed to be modified
MOD	The description of the desired modification. It contains elenments like (i, m_i'), which indicates m_i will be replaced with m_i'
(pk_S, sk_S)	The key pair of the signer
(pk_Z, sk_Z)	The key pair of the sanitizer
(χ_{TA}, vk_{TA})	The BBS+ key pair for TA
(χ_{Sig}, vk_{Sig})	The BBS+ key pair for the signer
γ	The maximum of blocks that can be modified
τ	The expiration time for sanitization
t	The current time
λ	The security paramete
l	The length of the equivalence class representative
ℓ	The length of time
π_1	The proof that modified blocks are admissible
π_2	The proof that the number of modifications is below the limit γ
π_3	The proof that the expiration time has not passed
π_{sig}/π_{san}	The proof produced by the signer/sanitizer and indicates the origin of a given message/signature pair
$a \xleftarrow{R} A$	Randomly choose an element a from set A

use the Fujisaki-Okamoto CCA-transformation on ElGamal as the Public-Key Encryption (PKE) to encrypt commitments and other useful information for the sanitizer. [6] did not focus on accountability, but it indicates the property can be achieved by using the generic transformation given in [10]. Therefore, we use the Verifiable Ring Signature (VRS) given in [12] to make our scheme accountable.

To realize a time-bound sanitizable signature, we consider the idea in [13,14] and associate the signature with the expiration time. During the signing phase, the signer embeds the expiration time into the signature. Both the signer and the sanitizer need to prove the current time t is earlier than the expiration time τ (i.e. $t < \tau$) when signing a message. We choose 0/1-Encoding to encode time, then obtain $\{\tau_j\}_{j \in [1,\ell]} \leftarrow 1 - \mathsf{ENC}(\tau)$ and $\{t_j\}_{j \in [1,\ell]} \leftarrow 0 - \mathsf{ENC}(t)$. To prevent the sanitizer from forging time, we use the Boneh-Boyen+ Signature (BBS+) [15] to sign the above results. The signer and TA respectively signs $\{\tau_j\}_{j \in [1,\ell]}$ and $\{t_j\}_{j \in [1,\ell]}$, and obtain BBS+ signatures $\{A_j\}_{j \in [1,\ell]}$ and $\{B_{j,t}\}_{j \in [1,\ell]}$. According to lemma 1 in [14], if $t < \tau$, then $\{\tau_j\}_{j \in [1,\ell]} \cap \{t_j\}_{j \in [1,\ell]} \neq \emptyset$, there exists an index $k \in [1,\ell]$ that satisfies $t_k = \tau_k$, and we have corresponding A_k and $B_{k,t}$. Therefore, the proof of $t < \tau$ can be reduced to prove the knowledge of A_k and $B_{k,t}$. We realize it using Non-Interactive Zero-Knowledge Proof (NIZKP).

3.3   Detail

This section presents the specific construction of our scheme. It consists of the following 10 algorithms:

$(mpk, msk) \leftarrow$ **Setup**$(1^\lambda, 1^l, 1^\ell)$. On input the security parameter λ, the length of the equivalence class representative l and the time length ℓ, TA generates mpk and msk. Choose a bilinear pairing $\hat{e} : G_1 \times G_2 \rightarrow G_T$, where

G_1, G_2 and G_T are multiplicative cyclic groups of prime order p, and pick generators $g_1, \mathsf{g}_1, \tilde{\mathsf{h}}, \mathsf{h}_0, \mathsf{h}_1, \mathsf{h}_2, g, \hat{g} \xleftarrow{R} G_1$, $\mathsf{g}_2, \mathsf{g}_2 \xleftarrow{R} G_2$. Select secure hash functions $H, F : \{0,1\}^* \to G_1^*$. Generate the BBS+ key pair (χ_{TA}, vk_{TA}). Choose $\chi_{TA} \xleftarrow{R} Z_p$, then compute $vk_{TA} = \mathsf{g}_2{}^{\chi_{TA}}$.

Output $mpk = \{G_1, G_2, G_T, \hat{e}, g_1, g, \hat{g}, \mathsf{g}_2, p, H, F, l, \mathsf{g}_1, \tilde{\mathsf{h}}, \mathsf{h}_0, \mathsf{h}_1, \mathsf{h}_2, \mathsf{g}_2, \ell, vk_{TA}\}$ and hold $msk = \chi_{TA}$ locally.

$(pk_S, sk_S) \leftarrow \mathbf{KGen_{sig}}(mpk)$. On input the public parameter mpk, TA respectively generates key pairs of the EQS, VRS and BBS+ for the signer, and finally obtains the key pair (pk_S, sk_S).

- *Generate the EQS key pair.* Choose $(x_i)_{i \in [1,l]} \xleftarrow{R} (Z_p^*)^l$, set $sk_{EQS} = (x_i)_{i \in [1,l]}$ and compute $pk_{EQS} = (g_2^{x_i})_{i \in [1,l]}$.
- *Generate the VRS key pair.* Choose $\alpha \xleftarrow{R} Z_p$, set $sk_{VRS} = \alpha$ and compute $pk_{VRS} = g^\alpha$.
- *Generate the BBS+ key pair.* Choose $\chi_{Sig} \xleftarrow{R} Z_p$, and compute $vk_{Sig} = \mathsf{g}_2{}^{\chi_{Sig}}$.

  Output the public key $pk_S = (pk_{EQS}, pk_{VRS}, vk_{Sig})$ and the private key $sk_S = (sk_{EQS}, sk_{VRS}, \chi_{Sig})$.

$(pk_Z, sk_Z) \leftarrow \mathbf{KGen_{san}}(mpk)$. On input the public parameter mpk, TA respectively generates key pairs of the PKE and VRS for the sanitizer, and finally obtains the key pair (pk_Z, sk_Z).

- *Generate the PKE key pair.* Choose $\beta \xleftarrow{R} Z_p^*$, set $ssk_{PKE} = \beta$ and compute $spk_{PKE} = \hat{g}^\beta$.
- *Generate the VRS key pair.* Choose $\bar{\alpha} \xleftarrow{R} Z_p$, set $ssk_{VRS} = \bar{\alpha}$ and compute $spk_{VRS} = g^{\bar{\alpha}}$.

  Output the public key $pk_Z = (spk_{PKE}, spk_{VRS})$ and the private key $sk_Z = (ssk_{PKE}, ssk_{VRS})$.

$(m, \sigma) \leftarrow \mathbf{Sign}(mpk, sk_S, pk_Z, m, ADM, \gamma, \tau, t)$. On input mpk, the signer's private key sk_S, the sanitizer's public key pk_Z, message m, ADM, the limit γ and τ, and the current time t, the signer generates the signature σ for m. Let $m = m_1 \| \cdots \| m_n$.

- *Compute commitments.* Choose $\delta \xleftarrow{R} Z_p^*$, compute $C_1 = H(\gamma)^\delta$. For every m_i, compute $C_{2,i} = H(i\|m_i)^\delta$. If $i \in ADM$, then compute $C_{3,i} = F(i)^\delta$, otherwise $C_{3,i} = F(i\|m_i)^\delta$. Set $C = (C_1, \{C_{2,i}\}_{i \in [1,n]}, \{C_{3,i}\}_{i \in [1,n]})$.
- *Prove that the signing process is legitimate.* We adopt Signature based on Proof of Knowledge (SPK), which is a NIZK protocol with the Fiat-Shamir transformation [16], to generate π_1, π_2 and π_3, where

$$\pi_1 = SPK\left\{\delta : \bigwedge_{i=1}^{n}\left(C_{3,i} = F(i)^\delta \vee C_{3,i} = F(i\|m_i)^\delta\right)\right\}$$

proves that modified blocks are admissible, and

$$\pi_2 = SPK\left\{\delta : \bigvee_{i=1}^{n}\left(\begin{array}{c}(C_1 = H(i)^\delta) \wedge (\exists J \subseteq [n], (|J| = n - i)\wedge \\ (\forall j \in J, C_{2,j} = H(j\|m_j)^\delta))\end{array}\right)\right\}$$

proves that the number of modifications is below the limit γ. π_2 involves proof of partial knowledge and we use transformation in [17] and Shamir's (k,n)-threshold secret sharing scheme [18] to obtain it.

π_3 proves that the current time is earlier than the expiration time. i.e. $t < \tau$. Before computing it, the signer needs to encode τ. Run $\{\tau_j\}_{j\in[1,\ell]} \leftarrow 1 - \mathsf{ENC}(\tau)$, and sign $\{\tau_j\}_{j\in[1,\ell]}$ using χ_{Sig}. Then obtain $\{(A_j, \xi_j, \zeta_j)\}_{j\in[1,\ell]}$, where $A_j = \left(g_1 h_0{}^{\zeta_j} h_1{}^{\tau_j}\right)^{1/(\xi_j + \chi_{Sig})}$ is the BBS+ signature of τ_j. g_1, h_0 and h_1 are public values, ζ_j and ξ_j are random values. Set the expiration time information $ei = (\{(A_j, \xi_j, \zeta_j)\}_{j\in[1,\ell]}, \tau)$. Download the current time information $ci_t = (\{(B_{j,t}, \xi'_{j,t}, \zeta'_{j,t})\}_{j\in[1,\ell]}, t)$ from TA, where $B_{j,t} = \left(g_1 h_0{}^{\zeta'_{j,t}} h_1{}^{t_j} h_2{}^{t}\right)^{1/(\xi'_{j,t} + \chi_{TA})}$ is a BBS+ signature of t_j and t, and $\{t_j\}_{j\in[1,\ell]} \leftarrow 0 - \mathsf{ENC}(t)$. This is known from Sect. 3.2, if $t < \tau$, there exists an index $k \in [1, \ell]$ that satisfies $\tau_k = t_k$, and obtain $A_k = \left(g_1 h_0{}^{\zeta_k} h_1{}^{t_k}\right)^{1/(\xi_k + \chi_{Sig})}$ and $B_{k,t} = \left(g_1 h_0{}^{\zeta'_{k,t}} h_1{}^{\tau_k} h_2{}^{t}\right)^{1/(\xi'_{k,t} + \chi_{TA})}$. Compute commitments about A_k and $B_{k,t}$. Choose $\rho_1, \rho_2 \overset{R}{\leftarrow} Z_p$, compute $\mathcal{W}_1 = A_k \tilde{h}^{\rho_1}$ and $\mathcal{W}_2 = B_{k,t}\tilde{h}^{\rho_2}$. Set $\beta_1 = \rho_1 \xi_k$ and $\beta_2 = \rho_2 \xi'_{k,t}$. Generate π_3 as follows.

$$\pi_3 = SPK\left\{\begin{array}{c}(\beta_1, \beta_2, \rho_1, \rho_2, \zeta_k, \xi_k, \zeta'_{k,t}, \xi'_{k,t}, t_k, \tau_k) : \\[4pt] \dfrac{\hat{e}(\mathcal{W}_1, vk_{Sig})}{\hat{e}(g_1, g_2)} = \dfrac{\hat{e}(\tilde{h}, g_2)^{\beta_1}\hat{e}(\tilde{h}, vk_{Sig})^{\rho_1}\hat{e}(h_0, g_2)^{\zeta_k}\hat{e}(h_1, g_2)^{t_k}}{\hat{e}(\mathcal{W}_1, g_2)^{\xi_k}} \wedge \\[10pt] \dfrac{\hat{e}(\mathcal{W}_2, vk_{TA})}{\hat{e}(g_1, g_2)\hat{e}(h_2, g_2)^t} = \dfrac{\hat{e}(\tilde{h}, g_2)^{\beta_2}\hat{e}(\tilde{h}, vk_{TA})^{\rho_2}\hat{e}(h_0, g_2)^{\zeta'_{k,t}}\hat{e}(h_1, g_2)^{\tau_k}}{\hat{e}(\mathcal{W}_2, g_2)^{\xi'_{k,t}}}\end{array}\right\}$$

- *Generate the EQS signature for commitment C.* Map C to the equivalence class representative $M_{EQS} \in (G_1^*)^l$, and sign M_{EQS}. Then obtain σ_{EQS}.
- *Encrypt necessary information for the sanitizer.* To make sure that each sanitization is based on the original commitments rather than potentially sanitized ones, the signer encrypts the expiration time information ei, commitment C, exponent δ and signature σ_{EQS}, respectively and obtain e.
- *Generate the VRS signature for the above content.* Set $M_{VRS} = (m\|C\|\pi_1\|\pi_2\|\pi_3\|\sigma_{EQS}\|e)$. Choose $r \overset{R}{\leftarrow} Z_p^*$, compute $h = H(M_{VRS}\|r)$ and $w = h^{sk_{VRS}}$. Compute $\pi_{VRS} = SPK\left\{sk_{VRS} : w = h^{sk_{VRS}} \vee w = h^{ssk_{VRS}}\right\}$, then obtain $\sigma_{VRS} = (r, w, \pi_{VRS})$.

Finally, output the signature $\sigma = (C, \pi_1, \pi_2, \pi_3, \sigma_{EQS}, \sigma_{VRS}, e)$.

$b \leftarrow$ **Verify**$(mpk, pk_S, pk_Z, m, \sigma, t)$. On input mpk, pk_S, pk_Z, a message/signature pair (m, σ) and time period t, a verifier checks whether the message/signature pair is valid.

- *Verify whether* π_1, π_2 *and* π_3 *are valid.* If one of them is invalid, then output 0.
- *Verify whether* σ_{EQS} *is valid.* If σ_{EQS} is invalid, then output 0.
- *Verify whether* σ_{VRS} *is valid.* If σ_{VRS} is invalid, then output 0.
  Otherwise, output 1.

$(m', \sigma') \leftarrow$ **Sanit**$(mpk, pk_S, sk_Z, m, \sigma, MOD, t')$. On input mpk, the signer's public key pk_S, the sanitizer's private key sk_Z, (m, σ), MOD and the current time t', the sanitizer updates the message $m' \leftarrow MOD(m)$ and generates a new valid signature σ' for m'.

- *Decrypt and Re-encrypt.* To prevent verifiers from linking two signatures via e, the sanitizer decrypts e to obtain the original expiration time information ei, commitment C, exponent δ and signature σ_{EQS} and re-encrypt them.
- *Re-randomize commitments.* Choose $\mu \xleftarrow{R} Z_p^*$ and set $\delta' = \mu \cdot \delta$. Compute $C_1' = C_1^\mu$, $\{C_{2,i}'\}_{i \in [1,n]} = \{C_{2,i}^\mu\}_{i \in [1,n]}$ and $\{C_{3,i}'\}_{i \in [1,n]} = \{C_{3,i}^\mu\}_{i \in [1,n]}$. Set $C' = (C_1', \{C_{2,i}'\}_{i \in [1,n]}, \{C_{3,i}'\}_{i \in [1,n]})$.
- *Adapt* σ_{EQS} with above μ for new commitments and obtain σ_{VRS}.
- *Prove that the sanitization is legitimate.* Generate π_1', π_2' and π_3' following the idea of the **Sign** algorithm. Note that this is to prove the knowledge of new commitment C' and $t' < \tau$.
- *Generate the VRS signature for the above content.* Set $M'_{VRS} = (m'||C'||\pi_1'||\pi_2'||\pi_3'||\sigma_{EQS}'||e')$. Choose $r' \xleftarrow{R} Z_p^*$, compute $h' = H(M'_{VRS}||r')$ and $w' = h'^{sskv_{RS}}$. Compute $\pi_{VRS}' = SPK\{sskv_{RS} : w' = h'^{skv_{RS}} \vee w' = h'^{sskv_{RS}}\}$, then obtain $\sigma_{VRS}' = (r', w', \pi_{VRS}')$.
  Finally, output the signature $\sigma' = (C', \pi_1', \pi_2', \pi_3', \sigma_{EQS}', \sigma_{VRS}', e')$.

$\pi_{sig} \leftarrow$ **Proof**$_{sig}(mpk, sk_S, pk_S, m, \sigma)$. On input mpk, the signer's key pair (pk_S, sk_S) and (m, σ), the signer proves the origin of the message/signature pair.

- Parse $\sigma_{VRS} = (r, w, \pi_{VRS})$, compute $\bar{h} = H(M_{VRS}||r)$ and $\bar{w} = \bar{h}^{skv_{RS}}$.
- Compute $\pi = SPK\{skv_{RS} : pkv_{RS} = g^{skv_{RS}} \wedge \bar{w} = \bar{h}^{skv_{RS}}\}$.
  Output $\pi_{sig} = \{\bar{w}, \pi\}$.

$\pi_{san} \leftarrow$ **Proof**$_{san}(mpk, sk_Z, pk_Z, m, \sigma)$. The sanitizer proves the origin of the message/signature pair following the idea of **Proof**$_{sig}$. Compute $\pi = SPK\{sskv_{RS} : spkv_{RS} = g^{sskv_{RS}} \wedge \bar{w} = \bar{h}^{sskv_{RS}}\}$. Output $\pi_{san} = \{\bar{w}, \pi\}$.

$d \leftarrow$ **Judge**$_{sig}(mpk, pk_S, pk_Z, m, \sigma, \pi_{sig})$. On input mpk, pk_S, pk_Z, (m, σ) and a proof of origin sent by the signer π_{sig}, TA captures the identity of the generator for the message/signature pair.

- Parse $\sigma_{VRS} = (r, w, \pi_{VRS})$.
- Verify whether $\pi_{sig} = \{\bar{w}, \pi\}$ is valid. If it is invalid, output $\bot$. Otherwise, if $w = \bar{w}$, then output *Signer*, else output *Sanitizer*.

$d \leftarrow \textbf{Judge}_{\textbf{san}}(mpk, pk_S, pk_Z, m, \sigma, \pi_{san})$. For the proof π_{san} sent by the sanitizer, TA captures the identity of the generator for the message/signature pair following the idea of $\textbf{Judge}_{\textbf{sig}}$. If π_{san} is invalid, output $\bot$. Otherwise, if $w = \bar{w}$, then output *Sanitizer*, else output *Signer*.

4   Security Analysis

Before performing security analysis, we first explain the *Correctness*. As can be known from the **Verify** algorithm, the property is based on the correctness of the underlying NIZKP, EQS scheme, and VRS scheme.

Our limited sanitizable signature is an improvement of the γSaS scheme proposed in [6] and our changes to the γSaS itself do not affect the properties of the underlying scheme, such as soundness and zero-knowledge property of the NIZK, IND-CCA security of the PKE, unforgeability and anonymity of the VRS, and EUF-CMA security and adaptation of the EQS. Therefore, we can follow the proof of immutability, transparency, unlinkability, and invisibility in [6] based on the above requirements. In this section, we focus on the impact of the time limit on the above security attributes, i.e. focus on the elements π_3 and e, which are related to the time limit. The following proof only gives the idea, the specific details will be given in the full version.

Theorem 1. *Our scheme satisfies immutability, if the proof π_3 satisfies soundness, and the underlying BBS+ satisfies unforgeability.*

Proof. We consider how the adversary $\mathcal{A}$ can produce a valid signature in case of violating the time limit. To achieve this condition, $\mathcal{A}$ must forge the expiration time information ei or the current time information ci (we have the latter as an example), i.e. forge the BBS+ signature. If the BBS+ signature cannot be forged, $\mathcal{A}$ can only forge the NIZKP π_3. We adopt a classical game-hops strategy to simulate this process. Note that except for what is listed, the games are the same.

Game 0. The challenger $\mathcal{B}$ runs $(pk_S, sk_S) \leftarrow \textbf{KGen}_{\textbf{sig}}(mpk)$ and $(pk_Z, sk_Z) \leftarrow \textbf{KGen}_{\textbf{san}}(mpk)$, then sends (pk_S, pk_Z) to adversary $\mathcal{A}$. $\mathcal{A}$ can query the oracle **Sign** and get the message/signature pair as response. Then $\mathcal{A}$ outputs (m^*, σ^*) produced with $t > \tau$ and the pair can be verified successfully.

Game 1. Build an adversary $\mathcal{B}$ against the unforgeability of the BBS+. Let $\mathcal{B}$ be the challenger of $\mathcal{C}$, and $\mathcal{B}$ injects its challenges as the ci_t in $\mathcal{A}$'s queries and records it. Finally $\mathcal{B}$ extracts t^* from $\mathcal{A}$'s output and return ci_{t^*} to $\mathcal{C}$.

Game 2. Build a secondary adversary $\mathcal{B}$ against the soundness of the NIZKP. In this game, $\mathcal{B}$ runs **Sign** algorithm, extracts π_3^* from $\mathcal{A}$'s output and returns it to $\mathcal{C}$.

The advantage of $\mathcal{A}$ winning Game 1 and Game 2 are respectively bound by the unforgeability of the BBS+ and the soundness of π_3. After Game 2, $\mathcal{A}$ cannot produce a valid signature. Thus, immutability is proven.

Theorem 2. *Our scheme satisfies transparency, if the underlying PKE satisfies IND-CCA security and the proof π_3 is zero-knowledge.*

Proof. We consider the adversary $\mathcal{A}$ can distinguish whether a signature is sanitized via e and π_3. We progressively replace them with random ones.

Game 0. The challenger $\mathcal{B}$ runs $(pk_S, sk_S) \leftarrow \mathbf{KGen_{sig}}(mpk)$ and $(pk_Z, sk_Z) \leftarrow \mathbf{KGen_{san}}(mpk)$, then sends (pk_S, pk_Z) to adversary $\mathcal{A}$. A can query the oracles **Sign** and **Sanit**, and **Sig/San** and get the corresponding responses, where **Sig/San** is responsible for signing and sanitizing a given message and outputs the original signature or the sanitized one based on a random bit b picked by $\mathcal{B}$. Finally $\mathcal{A}$ guesses the value of b.

Game 1. Build a secondary adversary $\mathcal{B}$ against the IND-CCA security of the encryption and $\mathcal{B}$ injects its challenges as the e in $\mathcal{A}$'s queries.

Game 2. Build a secondary adversary $\mathcal{B}$ against the zero-knowledge property of π_3. $\mathcal{B}$ returns the encryption of a random message rather than the real commitments and injects the response of its challenger as π_3 in $\mathcal{A}$'s queries.

Each hop from Game 0 to Game 2 cannot be distinguished by $\mathcal{A}$ with a non-negligible advantage because PKE is indistinguishable from random under adaptive chosen ciphertext attack (IND-CCA) and the zero-knowledge property of NIZKP, and in Game 2, $\mathcal{A}$ cannot get any useful information from π_3 and e. Thus, transparency is proven.

Theorem 3. *Our scheme satisfies unlinkability, if the underlying PKE satisfies IND-CCA security and the proof π_3 is zero-knowledge.*

Proof. Suppose there are two signatures to be sanitized with the same condition, we replace π_3 and e with random ones like the proof of transparency to break the link between the sanitized signature and the original one. Because of the zero-knowledge property of π_3 and the IND-CCA security of e, $\mathcal{A}$ cannot distinguish between the result and random, and cannot determine which signature was sanitized. Thus, unlinkability is proven.

Theorem 4. *Our scheme satisfies invisibility, if the underlying PKE satisfies IND-CCA security and the proof π_3 is zero-knowledge.*

Proof. Suppose there is a message to be signed with different ADM, γ and τ, we alter π_3 and e in the previous manner. According to the zero-knowledge property of NIZKP and the IND-CCA security of PKE, $\mathcal{A}$ can only guess which ADM, γ and τ the signature is based on. Thus, invisibility is proven.

Theorem 5. *Our scheme satisfies strong accountability, if the underlying VRS satisfies strong accountability and strong non-seizability.*

Proof. The signatures from **Sign** and **Sanit** contain verifiable ring signature [12], which is strongly accountable and strongly non-seizable. According to Theorem 2 in [10], a non-accountable sanitizable signature can be transformed into an accountable one while preserving all other properties using a verifiable ring signature satisfying the above two properties. Thus, strong accountability is proven.

5   Performance Analysis

In this section, we present the functionality comparison among the proposed scheme and other editable signature schemes [6,8,10,12,19,20]. Because ours is similar to [6], we focus on comparing them in terms of computational overhead. Then we evaluate the efficiency of [6,20] and ours, which are of the same complexity $\mathcal{O}(n^2)$, and discuss the influence of two variable factors.

Before the analysis, we define the notations used in the following sections. Since the computational overhead mainly includes exponentiation operation and bilinear pairing operation, we only consider these two. Let Exp_{G_1}, Exp_{G_2} and Exp_{G_T} represent one exponentiation operation on G_1, G_2 and G_T respectively. *Pair* represents one pairing operation.

Theoretical Analysis. Table 2 shows the functionality comparison. Our scheme is the only one that satisfies immutability, transparency, unlinkability, invisitability and strong accountability (both strong sanitizer-accountability and strong signer-accountability) and achieves modification limitations.

- Imposing modification restrictions on the sanitizer can greatly prevent malicious modifications. [6] sets the maximum number of message blocks that can be modified to γ (LimitNbModif), [8] limits modifications to a specific set (LimitSet), [20] prohibits a consecutive third party from removing blocks. We introduce the expiration time of sanitization (LimitTSanit) to further ensure the security of the signed content.
- Immutability ensures that the sanitizer cannot violate the rules set by the signer when sanitizing the message. In [10,12,19], this property requires that the sanitizer cannot sanitize non-admissible blocks. In [6,8,20] and ours, the rules are extended to the limits defined in the scheme respectively.
- Transparency ensures that verifiers cannot decide whether a message has been sanitized or not. Non-interactive public accountability defined in [19] allows anyone to determine the origin of a message/signature pair, and it is mutually exclusive with transparency.
- Unlinkability ensures that verifiers cannot link the sanitized signature to the original one. Invisibility ensures that verifiers cannot infer which blocks are admissible, [6] and ours also requires that limits are also invisible to verifiers. Satisfying both unlinkability and invisibility is an important requirement for the secure sharing of medical data. Except for [6,10] and ours, the other options can only satisfy one of them at most.

– Accountability ensures that the malicious signer/sanitizer cannot deny the signature generated by itself. Strong accountability as defined herein allows the signer and the sanitizer to independently prove the origin of a given message/signature pair, and it is stronger than that defined in [8,20], which only allows the signer to produce proof. Non-interactive public accountability defined in [19] is too strong to be applied to medical scenarios.

Therefore, our scheme is the most complete and comprehensive in terms of functionality compared with the existing scheme, and it is also the most suitable for the secure sharing of EHRs.

Table 2. Comparison of functionality.

Schemes	Limit	Immutability	Transparency	Unlinkability	Invisibility	Accountability
[6]	LimitNbModif	Yes	Yes	Yes	Yes	Strong Accountability
[8]	LimitSet	Yes	Yes	Yes	No	Accountability
[10]	No	Yes	Yes	Yes	Yes	Strong Accountability
[12]	No	Yes	Yes	Yes	No	Strong Accountability
[19]	No	Yes	No	Yes	No	Non-Interactive Public Accountability
[20]	Consecutive Redaction Control	Yes	Yes	No	No	Signer-Accountability
Ours	LimitNbModif+LimitTSanit	Yes	Yes	Yes	Yes	Strong-Accountability

LimitSet: limiting possible modification of an admissible block to a specific set.
LimitNbModif: limiting the sanitizer to modify at most γ admissible blocks.
Consecutive Redaction Control: prohibiting a consecutive third party to remove certain blocks.
LimitTSanit: limiting the time of sanitization.

Table 3 shows the theoretical comparison of computation complexity between [6] and ours. The overhead of them is constant in the **KGen**, **Proof** and **Judge** phase, and the cost of $\mathbf{KGen_{sig}}$ is determined by the length of the equivalence class representative l. In the **Sign**, **Verify** and **Sanit** phase, [6] and ours both require $\mathcal{O}(n^2)$, and the overhead mostly comes from the zero-knowledge proof. In our scheme, the generation and verification of π_1 respectively require $3nExp_{G_1}$ and $4nExp_{G_1}$, and [6] requires $6nExp_{G_1}$ and $8nExp_{G_1}$. The overhead of generating and verifying π_2 in ours is respectively $(2n^2 + n - 1 + \gamma)Exp_{G_1}$ and $(2n^2 + 2n)Exp_{G_1}$, while that in [6] is $(3n^2 - n)Exp_{G_1}$ and $4n^2 Exp_{G_1}$. Since we have less overhead than [6] in terms of zero-knowledge proof, then we have a smaller quadratic term coefficient and a lower growth rate in running time. In the $\mathbf{KGen_{sig}}$, **Sign**, **Verify** and **Sanit** phase, our scheme has an additional overhead about the time limit, which comes from generating the BBS+ key pair and signatures, generating and verifying the proof π_3 and encrypting expiration information. It is only related to the length of time ℓ, and is constant and not dominant. Therefore, ours generally has a lower computation overhead than [6].

Note that we apply Lagrange polynomials to produce zero-knowledge proof π_2. As the increase of n, the resulting computation overhead can not be ignored. Let Mul_{Z_p} denote one multiplication operation on Z_p. The overhead introduced by computing the Lagrange polynomial in the **Sign** and **Sanit** phase is $(\sum_{i=1}^{n}(n-i)i + (n-\gamma)(\gamma-1)\gamma)Mul_{Z_p}$ and that in the **Verify** phase is

Table 3. Comparison of computation overhead.

	Ours	γSaS [6]
KGen$_{sig}$	$(l+1)Exp_{G_2} + Exp_{G_1}$	$lExp_{G_2} + Exp_{G_1}$
KGen$_{san}$	$2Exp_{G_1}$	$2Exp_{G_1}$
Sign	$(2n^2 + 10n + 22 + l + 9\ell + \gamma)Exp_{G_1} + 7Pair + 10Exp_{G_T} + Exp_{G_2}$	$(3n^2 + 7n + 13 + l)Exp_{G_1} + Exp_{G_2}$
Verify	$(2n^2 + 6n + 8)Exp_{G_1} + (l + 14)Pair + 13Exp_{G_T}$	$(4n^2 + 8n + 8)Exp_{G_1} + (l + 3)Pair$
Sanit	$(2n^2 + 14n + 34 + 12\ell + \gamma)Exp_{G_1} + 7Pair + 10Exp_{G_T}$	$(3n^2 + 7n + 12)Exp_{G_1}$
Proof$_{sig/san}$	$3Exp_{G_1}$	$3Exp_{G_1}$
Judge$_{sig/san}$	$4Exp_{G_1}$	$4Exp_{G_1}$

$(\sum_{i=1}^{n} ni + n\gamma(\gamma - 1))Mul_{Z_p}$. We can find that the cost of this part is affected by n and γ. When n is constant, the trend of the cost is determined by the second item of the above two formulas. Therefore, the performance of ours is not only related to n, but also to γ.

Practical Analysis. To evaluate the performance of our scheme, we simulate our construction and the ones in [6,20] based on the Java Pairing-Based Cryptography (JPBC) library. The experiment platform is set to be: Intel(R) Core(TM) i7-10875H CPU @ 2.30 GHz, 16 GB of RAM and Windows 10 (64bit) OS. We use the supersingular curve SS768 for the Type-1 pairing in [20], and use MNT224 for the Type-3 pairing in [6] and ours. Both SS768 and MNT224 provide approximate 96-bit security level [21]. We use "YYMMDD" as the date format, and we need 16 bits to represent a date, where 5 bits for 31 days, 4 bits for 12 months, and 7 bits for 99 years. To improve the efficiency, we optimize the implementation of our scheme as follows: First, we preprocess the hash values related to the commitment C, which include $H(\gamma)$, $H(i||m_i)$ and $F(i_i)/F(i||m_i)$ to reduce the overhead of exponentiation operations. In addition, for $i = 1, 2, \cdots, n$, we construct the Lagrange polynomial with consecutive points if $i \neq \gamma$, reducing the complexity from $\mathcal{O}(i^2)$ to $\mathcal{O}(i)$ by preprocessing.

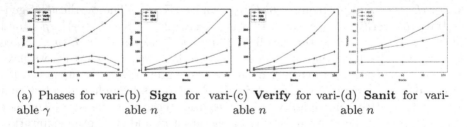

(a) Phases for vari-able γ (b) **Sign** for vari-able n (c) **Verify** for vari-able n (d) **Sanit** for vari-able n

Fig. 2. Computation overhead of different phases for variable γ and n

Figure 2(a) presents the computation overhead of **Sign**, **Verify** and **Sanit** phase with γ is respectively 0, 25, 50, 75, 100, 125 and 150 when n is fixed to be 150. We note that in the **Sign** and **Sanit** phase, when $\gamma < 100$, the cost increases slightly with γ, and when $\gamma > 100$, the cost decreases with γ. It is consistent with the trend of the above $(n - \gamma)(\gamma - 1)\gamma$. When $\gamma = 100$, the cost of computing Lagrange polynomials reaches its peak. In the **Verify** phase, the cost increases clearly with γ, which is also consistent with the trend of $n\gamma(\gamma - 1)$, that is, the computation overhead of the Lagrange polynomials increases with γ.

Figure 2(b), Fig. 2(c) and Fig. 2(d) present the computation overhead of the **Sign**, **Verify** and **Sanit** phase of γSaS [6], RSS [20] and our scheme. We vary the number of blocks from 20 to 80 and fix γ to be 5.

Figure 2(b) shows the overhead of **Sign** for three schemes with the complexity of $\mathcal{O}(n^2)$. Due to [20] is built with the Type-1 pairing, its cost and its growth rate are much higher than [6] and ours, which are built with the Type-3 pairing. As shown in Table 2, to realize the time limit, our scheme needs an extra about 0.4s to execute 7 pairing operations, 10 exponentiation operations on G_T and $3\ell + 2$ (i.e. 50) exponentiation operations on G_1 than [6], which is almost negligible for the total, and we have n^2 fewer exponentiation operations on G_1, the efficiency improvement is significant.

Figure 2(c) shows the overhead of **Verify** for three schemes. It is similar to the trend in Fig. 2(b). The cost of [20] is significantly higher than [6] and ours. When $n = 100$, [20] is about 3 times slower than [6] and 9 times slower than ours. Compared to [6], we need to execute additional 11 pairing operations and 13 exponentiation operations on G_T to produce the proof related to the time limit, which also takes about 0.3s, while ours has $2n^2$ fewer exponentiation operations on G_1 than [6] and performs better.

Figure 2(d) shows the number of blocks n has no impact on the **Sanit** overhead of [20], because **Redact**[1] defined in this scheme only needs to remove the admissible blocks or relation between the blocks and update the aggregated signature, and the resulting computation cost is always 1ms, which is negligible. Note that **Redact** is similar to **Sanit**, and we equate the two here. The overhead of [6] and ours still increase quadratically by n. The process of producing zero-knowledge proof in **Sanit** and **Sanit** is the same, therefore the overhead gap between [6] and ours in this phase is similar to that in Fig. 2(b).

Performance analysis shows that our scheme introduces the time limit for sanitization based on [6] to further protect the privacy of medical data without resulting in a large amount of additional overhead, and has lower computation complexity. In practical performance, ours is more efficient than [6] and [20].

6 Conclusion

Most current sanitizable signature schemes cannot achieve the needs of the medical field. To solve this problem, this paper proposes a secure EHR sharing scheme based on a limited sanitizable signature, which introduces the time limit, and combines γ-sanitizable signatures to realize the sensitive information

---

[1] **Redact** in [20] is also responsible for modifying the message m based on the MOD, but it allows to remove blocks rather than change, and can be considered a special case of **Sanit**.

hiding while restricting the patient's power as much as possible. At the same time, our scheme is unlinkable, invisible and strongly accountable. The security analysis and performance analysis show that the scheme is feasible.

References

1. Xu, Z., Luo, M., Kumar, N., Vijayakumar, P., Li, L.: Privacy-protection scheme based on sanitizable signature for smart mobile medical scenarios. Wireless Commun. Mob. Comput. **2020** (2020)
2. Shen, W., Qin, J., Yu, J., Hao, R., Hu, J.: Enabling identity-based integrity auditing and data sharing with sensitive information hiding for secure cloud storage. IEEE Trans. Inf. Forensics Secur. **14**(2), 331–346 (2018)
3. Xu, Y., Ding, L., Cui, J., Zhong, H., Yu, J.: PP-CSA: a privacy-preserving cloud storage auditing scheme for data sharing. IEEE Syst. J. **15**(3), 3730–3739 (2020)
4. Ateniese, G., Chou, D.H., de Medeiros, B., Tsudik, G.: Sanitizable signatures. In: di Vimercati, S.C., Syverson, P., Gollmann, D. (eds.) ESORICS 2005. LNCS, vol. 3679, pp. 159–177. Springer, Heidelberg (2005). https://doi.org/10.1007/11555827_10
5. Thornton, D., Brinkhuis, M., Amrit, C., Aly, R.: Categorizing and describing the types of fraud in healthcare. Procedia Comput. Sci. **64**, 713–720 (2015)
6. Bossuat, A., Bultel, X.: Unlinkable and invisible γ-Sanitizable signatures. In: Sako, K., Tippenhauer, N.O. (eds.) ACNS 2021. LNCS, vol. 12726, pp. 251–283. Springer, Cham (2021). https://doi.org/10.1007/978-3-030-78372-3_10
7. Canard, S., Jambert, A.: On extended sanitizable signature schemes. In: Pieprzyk, J. (ed.) CT-RSA 2010. LNCS, vol. 5985, pp. 179–194. Springer, Heidelberg (2010). https://doi.org/10.1007/978-3-642-11925-5_13
8. Derler, D., Slamanig, D.: Rethinking privacy for extended sanitizable signatures and a black-box construction of strongly private schemes. In: Au, M.-H., Miyaji, A. (eds.) ProvSec 2015. LNCS, vol. 9451, pp. 455–474. Springer, Cham (2015). https://doi.org/10.1007/978-3-319-26059-4_25
9. Klonowski, M., Lauks, A.: Extended sanitizable signatures. In: Rhee, M.S., Lee, B. (eds.) ICISC 2006. LNCS, vol. 4296, pp. 343–355. Springer, Heidelberg (2006). https://doi.org/10.1007/11927587_28
10. Bultel, X., Lafourcade, P., Lai, R.W.F., Malavolta, G., Schröder, D., Thyagarajan, S.A.K.: Efficient invisible and unlinkable sanitizable signatures. In: Lin, D., Sako, K. (eds.) PKC 2019. LNCS, vol. 11442, pp. 159–189. Springer, Cham (2019). https://doi.org/10.1007/978-3-030-17253-4_6
11. Fuchsbauer, G., Hanser, C., Slamanig, D.: Structure-preserving signatures on equivalence classes and constant-size anonymous credentials. J. Cryptol. **32**(2), 498–546 (2019)
12. Bultel, X., Lafourcade, P.: Unlinkable and strongly accountable sanitizable signatures from verifiable ring signatures. In: Capkun, S., Chow, S.S.M. (eds.) CANS 2017. LNCS, vol. 11261, pp. 203–226. Springer, Cham (2018). https://doi.org/10.1007/978-3-030-02641-7_10
13. Emura, K., Hayashi, T., Ishida, A.: Group signatures with time-bound keys revisited: a new model, an efficient construction, and its implementation. IEEE Trans. Dependable Secure Comput. **17**(2), 292–305 (2017)
14. Liu, J.K., Chu, C.K., Chow, S.S., Huang, X., Au, M.H., Zhou, J.: Time-bound anonymous authentication for roaming networks. IEEE Trans. Inf. Forensics Secur. **10**(1), 178–189 (2014)

15. Camenisch, J., Drijvers, M., Lehmann, A.: Anonymous attestation using the strong Diffie Hellman assumption revisited. In: Franz, M., Papadimitratos, P. (eds.) Trust 2016. LNCS, vol. 9824, pp. 1–20. Springer, Cham (2016). https://doi.org/10.1007/978-3-319-45572-3_1

16. Fiat, A., Shamir, A.: How to prove yourself: practical solutions to identification and signature problems. In: Odlyzko, A.M. (ed.) CRYPTO 1986. LNCS, vol. 263, pp. 186–194. Springer, Heidelberg (1987). https://doi.org/10.1007/3-540-47721-7_12

17. Cramer, R., Damgård, I., Schoenmakers, B.: Proofs of partial knowledge and simplified design of witness hiding protocols. In: Desmedt, Y.G. (ed.) CRYPTO 1994. LNCS, vol. 839, pp. 174–187. Springer, Heidelberg (1994). https://doi.org/10.1007/3-540-48658-5_19

18. Shamir, A.: How to share a secret. Commun. ACM **22**(11), 612–613 (1979)

19. Brzuska, C., Pöhls, H.C., Samelin, K.: Efficient and perfectly unlinkable sanitizable signatures without group signatures. In: Katsikas, S., Agudo, I. (eds.) EuroPKI 2013. LNCS, vol. 8341, pp. 12–30. Springer, Heidelberg (2014). https://doi.org/10.1007/978-3-642-53997-8_2

20. Samelin, K., Pöhls, H.C., Bilzhause, A., Posegga, J., de Meer, H.: Redactable signatures for independent removal of structure and content. In: Ryan, M.D., Smyth, B., Wang, G. (eds.) ISPEC 2012. LNCS, vol. 7232, pp. 17–33. Springer, Heidelberg (2012). https://doi.org/10.1007/978-3-642-29101-2_2

21. Huang, Q., Chen, L., Wang, C.: A parallel secure flow control framework for private data sharing in mobile edge cloud. IEEE Trans. Parallel Distrib. Syst. **33**(12), 4638–4653 (2022)

A Rotating Multi-secret Color Visual Cryptography Scheme Based on Meaningful Shares

Yanyan Han[1,2], Yikun Zhou[1(✉)], Peng Li[1], and Xinyang Liu[1]

[1] Beijing Electronic Science and Technology Institute, Beijing 100070,
People's Republic of China
945883178@qq.com

[2] Xidian University, Xi'an 710071, People's Republic of China

Abstract. The multi-secret visual cryptography scheme (MVCS) can recover different secret images according to multiple stacking methods of shares. The rotating multi-secret visual cryptography scheme can restore additional secrets by stacking the share with another share after rotating a specific angle. The existing rotating multi-secret scheme is associated with the problem of meaningless noise-like shares, shares poor camouflage and security risks in the process of storage and transmission. At the same time, there are many problems in the existing schemes, such as no color image, low contrast of the recovered image and poor scalability of the algorithm. Therefore, this paper proposes a rotating multi-secret color visual cryptography scheme based on meaningful shares. The secret images are encrypted respectively, and the secret information is embedded into the cover images, and the cover images are processed by halftoning technology to obtain the meaningful shares, which improves the security of the rotating multi-secret scheme. The experimental results show that the scheme has the characteristics of gray and color secret images and cover images, the recovered images have no cross interference of cover images and extra secret, the shares and the recovered images have good visual effect, and the scheme meets the security requirements.

Keywords: Rotating visual cryptography scheme · Multi-secret · Color image · Meaningful shares · Halftone technology

1 Introduction

The basic theory of visual cryptography was proposed by Naor et al. [1], which opened a new research direction of secret sharing theory. The basic idea is to set the threshold k to recover the secret, encrypt the original secret and get $n(n \geq k)$ shares, and then distribute these shares to the corresponding participants. Every share is a cluttered and meaningless noise-like image, so it is impossible to get any secret information from a single share. When decrypting, the secret can be recovered by choosing $k'(k' \geq k)$ shares and stacking them, while less than k shares cannot be decrypted. Since the decryption process does not require any calculation and the participants do not need any cryptographic knowledge,

© The Author(s), under exclusive license to Springer Nature Singapore Pte Ltd. 2022
E. Ahene and F. Li (Eds.): FCS 2022, CCIS 1726, pp. 304–323, 2022.
https://doi.org/10.1007/978-981-19-8445-7_20

the secret information can be identified by the human visual system (HVS), which greatly reduces the requirements of the participants. Therefore, visual cryptography has been widely concerned by researchers since it was proposed and has been extended to a variety of application forms.

The shares generated by traditional visual cryptographic schemes are meaningless noise-like images, which have poor camouflage and may arouse the suspicion of attackers during transmission, thus threatening these shares. Zhou et al. [2] first proposed halftone visual cryptography (HVC) based on halftone technology, which embedded the secret information of the encrypted secret image into the cover image, processed the cover image by halftone technology, and finally generated meaningful shares. It solves the problem of meaningless shares in traditional schemes. The scheme proposed by Wang et al. [3] introduces the concepts of secret information pixels (SIPs) and auxiliary black pixels (ABPs), and proposes three pixel-allocation methods, so that the recovered secret does not have visual interference of meaningful shares, and the recovery quality is better. Ahmad et al. [4] proposed a novel enhanced halftoning-based VC scheme is proposed that works for both binary and color images, both colored and black images can be processed with minimal capacity using the proposed scheme. The halftone visual cryptography scheme based on Stucki error diffusion proposed by Wang [5] extends the image type to color images, and the recovered images have good visual effects.

With the development of visual cryptography, the traditional visual cryptography scheme which encrypts a single secret image cannot meet the current application needs. Multi-secret visual cryptography scheme (MVCS) can enable participants to recover specific secret images according to different stacking methods of shares when they only have one share. Shen et al. [6] proposed a XOR-based multi-secret (k, n) visual cryptography based on cylindrical shares. Rotating the shares to different angles can restore the corresponding secret image and reduce pixel expansion. Wang et al. [7] proposed a visual cryptography scheme based on flip operation and halftone technology, which can generate meaningful shares, and flip shares can recover additional secrets. Huang et al. [8] proposed a multi-secret visual cryptography scheme based on random-grids to recover additional secrets after horizontally shifting the shares, achieving efficient image management. Similarly, based on halftone technology, Yan et al. [9] proposed a meaningful-shares and no pixel expansion visual cryptography scheme, which embeds additional watermarks for authentication in addition to secret images, and watermarks can be recovered by translating the shares.

In addition to the above stacking method to recover additional secrets, the rotating multi-secret visual cryptography scheme based on rectangle and ring shares can recover additional secrets after rotating it by a specific angle. Wu et al. [10] first proposed the rotating multi-secret visual cryptography scheme, which encrypts two secret images in two rectangular shares, and the shares rotate by 90° to recover additional secrets. The rotation angle of this scheme can be easily modified to 180° or 270°. To overcome the rotation angle limitation in rectangular shares, Wu et al. [11] designed a rotating multi-secret visual cryptography based on ring shares, and the rotation angle is no longer limited to a multiple of 90. The scheme proposed by Gao et al. [12], which is based on random-grids, the number of shares and the visual quality of the last recovered images are positively correlated, and it has better robustness. Fu et al. [13] proposed the idea of shares design for status equivalence based on ring shares, with regional marking of shares to increase the number of participants. Dong et al. [14] designed an operational visual multi-secret sharing scheme facing a threshold structure to divide and mark the longitudinal region on secrets when sharing secrets, which realized all shares status equivalence and improved the number of secrets. Askari et al. [15] designed a scheme based on the balanced block replacement algorithm, which made the local black-and-white pixel ratio in the processed image close to the local black-and-white pixel ratio in the original halftone secret image, and the obtained recovered image was closer to the original gray image in quality. It alleviates the problems of pixel expansion and contrast loss in traditional schemes. Li [16] proposed a scheme based on XOR operation for the number of encryption secrets, pixel expansion and the contrast of the recovered image, which can generate ring shares without pixel expansion, and can be applied to color images, improve the contrast of the recovered image, and expand the application scenario of the scheme. Zhao et al. [17] proposed a new deception immune visual cryptography scheme based on the rotating multi-secret scheme, which generates n original shares based on the random grid and stamps the authentication mode on the original shares to obtain verifiable shares. In the authentication stage, stacking any two verifiable shares according to different rotation angles can display the corresponding authentication modes respectively.

In the existing rotating multi-secret visual cryptography schemes, research often focuses on expanding the angle of shares rotation, expanding the number of encrypted secrets, improving the quality of recovered images, etc. However, including the above rotating multi-secret schemes, the shares generated by the schemes are meaningless noise-like images with poor visual quality and low camouflage, which may cause the attacker to suspect and be alert during the transmission in the channel. The attacker may think that these meaningless noise-like images contain some secret information, thus hijacking these images and possibly obtaining the secret information therein, so the transmission process of shares is not secure, and the existing rotating multi-secret visual cryptography schemes have potential security risks. At the same time, the existing schemes are mostly limited to binary images. Compared with gray-scale images and color images, better visual quality is missing, and more image details cannot be presented. In addition, the recovery quality of binary secret images is poor, reducing the application scenario of the rotating multi-secret scheme.

To solve these problems, a rotating color visual cryptography scheme based on meaningful shares is proposed. The scheme combines rotating multi-secret visual cryptography and halftone visual cryptography, using secret image and cover image as input, divides the cover image into non-overlapping blocks of size $Q \times Q$, encrypts the secret image pixel by pixel, and embeds the encrypted information into the shared blocks corresponding to the location of the cover image. Then, the halftone technology is used to process the cover image carrying secret information. In the process, factors such as the number of global auxiliary black pixels and the number of local auxiliary black pixels are considered, so that the cover image has the minimum number of auxiliary black pixels evenly distributed, and finally meaningful shares with good visual quality are obtained. The scheme solves the problem that shares are meaningless in the rotating multi-secret scheme, improves the security of the scheme, can be applied to gray-scale images and color images, expands the application scene of the scheme, and the recovered secret has no cross interference between the cover image and the additional secret, and the recovered image has good visual effect. Finally, the effectiveness and security of the scheme are verified experimentally and theoretically, and the possible application scenarios of the scheme are analyzed.

2 Introduction of Halftone Technology

The traditional visual cryptography scheme is only suitable for binary images. If you want to extend the black and white binary image to the gray and color levels, you need to use halftone technology.

Error diffusion was proposed by Floyd et al. [18]. It is a widely used method in halftone technology, which first quantifies the threshold of the pixels of the grayscale image, and then spreads the quantized error to the adjacent pixels of the current pixel according to a certain proportional weight. The specific process of the error diffusion method is shown in Fig. 1 (a). Let X be a pixel quantified by the current threshold in the image, and the number of error filter weights at X is shown in Fig. 1 (b).

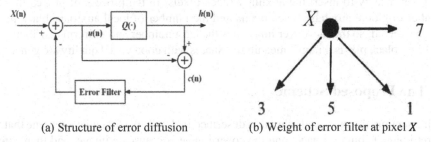

(a) Structure of error diffusion   (b) Weight of error filter at pixel X

Fig. 1. Error diffusion

The void and cluster algorithm is another commonly used halftone method proposed by Robert [19]. It uses the Gaussian filter to calculate the pixel density of each black point and white point in a certain area of the binary black and white image. The higher the pixel density is, the more black pixels around the pixel point in the area are, and the more 'cluster' it is. Conversely, the fewer black pixels around the pixel in the area, and the more 'void' it is. The black pixel with the highest density and the white pixel with the lowest density in the selected area are selected, and the pixel positions of the two are exchanged. Then the above density calculation and pixel exchange process are iterated, and finally the black pixels in the area are evenly distributed. Figure 2 is the legend before and after the void and cluster algorithm. Figure 2 (a) is a randomly generated 64 × 64-sized binary image with 300 black pixels. Figure 2 (b) is an image processed by void and cluster algorithm. It can be seen that the black pixel distribution of the latter is more uniform.

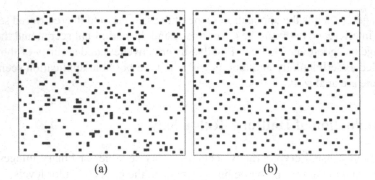

(a)   (b)

Fig. 2. The illustration of void and cluster algorithm.

In the process of recovering the secret by stacking the shares, in order to make the recovered secret free from the visual interference of the meaningful information of the shares, this paper uses the halftone technology to process the cover image carrying the secret information. Firstly, the error diffusion method is used to convert the cover image into binary image, and then the void and cluster algorithm is used to calculate the pixel density to insert the auxiliary black pixels. In the process of processing, the number of global auxiliary black pixels and the number of local auxiliary black pixels are considered, so that the cover image has the least number and uniform distribution of auxiliary black pixels. Finally, meaningful shares with good visual quality are generated.

3   The Proposed Scheme

In this section, the proposed scheme is described in detail. We first give a scheme that the secret image is binary image, and the cover image is grayscale image, and then extend the image to the color level.

3.1   The Rotating Visual Cryptography Scheme with Meaningful Shares for Gray-Scale Image

We select the secret image as binary image, which is represented by SI_1 and SI_2 respectively; The cover image is selected as grayscale image, represented by C_1 and C_2 respectively, and the size is $M_C \times N_C$; The scheme takes the secret image and the cover image as inputs, and finally generates meaningful shares, which is represented by S_1 and S_2 respectively.

Determining the Position of the Pixels
For two cover images, we divide them into non-overlapping blocks of size $Q \times Q$, then the number of blocks contained in each cover image is $\left\lfloor \frac{M_C}{Q} \right\rfloor \times \left\lfloor \frac{N_C}{Q} \right\rfloor$, and each block contains Q^2 pixels. We call it a shared block, where the shared block corresponds to the pixels of the secret image in position one by one, and the shared block is used to encrypt the pixels of the corresponding position of the secret image, so the size of the secret

images SI_1 and SI_2 should be $\left\lfloor \frac{M_C}{Q} \right\rfloor \times \left\lfloor \frac{N_C}{Q} \right\rfloor$. The pixels in the shared block are divided into two types: one is secret information pixels (SIPs), which carry encrypted secret information; The other is non secret information pixels (non-SIPs), which carry cover image information. SIPs are divided into two types, respectively representing the pixel position of different secret images in the shared block. Auxiliary Black pixels (ABPs) and auxiliary information pixels are set in non-SIPs to avoid the cross interference between the cover image and additional secrets. ABPs is used to overlap the cover image information and auxiliary information pixels are used to overlap additional secret information. For the shared block corresponding to the positions of the two cover images, the positions of SIPs and non-SIPs in the block are the same. Let the number of SIPs in the shared block be α, and the pixel expansion of the encrypted secret image be m, then $\alpha = 2m$, and to balance the number of SIPs and non-SIPs in the shared block, the value of α should meet $0 \le \alpha \le \frac{Q^2}{2}$.

We use the following algorithm to determine the location distribution of SIPs and non-SIPs. We define the function $\mathcal{F}(\circ)$ as the operation of rotating the matrix or image by 180°, where "$\circ$" represents any matrix or image, such as $\mathcal{F}\left(\begin{bmatrix} 0 & 1 & 0 & 1 \\ 1 & 0 & 1 & 1 \end{bmatrix}\right) = \begin{bmatrix} 1 & 1 & 0 & 1 \\ 1 & 0 & 1 & 0 \end{bmatrix}$. Let P_1 and P_2 be the SIPs position matrices corresponding to the secret images SI_1 and SI_2 on the cover images C_1 and C_2, $\boldsymbol{p}$ be the vectors randomly generated by Q^2 numbers from 1 to Q^2, K be the two-dimensional matrix of size $Q \times Q$, coordinate $((\boldsymbol{x}(\circ), \boldsymbol{y}(\circ)))$ represent the relative positions of the random numbers in K, K_1 and K_2 be the two-dimensional all zero matrices of size $Q \times Q$. The pixel position determination algorithm is shown in Table 1.

Illustrate the algorithm in Table 1. Let $Q = 4$, $\alpha = 4$, $m = 2$, and randomly generate a vector $\boldsymbol{p} = (3, 9, 8, 10, 7, 16, 13, 11, 1, 4, 15, 2, 5, 12, 6, 14)$. Let the row index and column index of the algorithm in the current pixel block be i and j, respectively. According to the algorithm in Table 1:

$$K = \begin{bmatrix} 1 & 5 & 9 & 13 \\ 2 & 6 & 10 & 14 \\ 3 & 7 & 11 & 15 \\ 4 & 8 & 12 & 16 \end{bmatrix}, K_1 = \begin{bmatrix} 0 & 0 & 1 & 0 \\ 0 & 0 & 0 & 0 \\ 1 & 0 & 0 & 0 \\ 0 & 0 & 0 & 0 \end{bmatrix}, K_2 = \begin{bmatrix} 0 & 0 & 0 & 0 \\ 0 & 0 & 1 & 0 \\ 0 & 0 & 0 & 0 \\ 0 & 1 & 0 & 0 \end{bmatrix} \tag{1}$$

According to the algorithm in Table 1 and equation (1):

$$P_1(i, j) = \begin{bmatrix} 0 & 0 & 1 & 0 \\ 0 & 0 & 0 & 0 \\ 1 & 0 & 0 & 0 \\ 0 & 0 & 0 & 0 \end{bmatrix}, P_1\left(\left\lfloor \frac{M_C}{Q} \right\rfloor - i + 1, \left\lfloor \frac{N_C}{Q} \right\rfloor - j + 1\right) = \begin{bmatrix} 0 & 0 & 1 & 0 \\ 0 & 0 & 0 & 0 \\ 0 & 1 & 0 & 0 \\ 0 & 0 & 0 & 0 \end{bmatrix} \tag{2}$$

$$P_2(i, j) = \begin{bmatrix} 0 & 0 & 0 & 0 \\ 0 & 0 & 1 & 0 \\ 0 & 0 & 0 & 0 \\ 0 & 1 & 0 & 0 \end{bmatrix}, P_2\left(\left\lfloor \frac{M_C}{Q} \right\rfloor - i + 1, \left\lfloor \frac{N_C}{Q} \right\rfloor - j + 1\right) = \begin{bmatrix} 0 & 0 & 0 & 0 \\ 0 & 0 & 0 & 1 \\ 0 & 0 & 0 & 0 \\ 0 & 1 & 0 & 0 \end{bmatrix} \tag{3}$$

From equations (2) and (3), the pixel position distribution of the shared block at (i, j) and $\left(\left\lfloor \frac{M_C}{Q} \right\rfloor - i + 1, \left\lfloor \frac{N_C}{Q} \right\rfloor - j + 1\right)$ of the cover images C_1 and C_2 is shown in Fig. 3.

Table 1. The pixel position determination algorithm.

Input:
   Size $Q \times Q$ of the shared block, size $M_C \times N_C$ of the cover image, number α of SIPs in the shared block, pixel extension m of the encrypted secret image.
Output:
   SIPs position matrices $\mathcal{A}_1$ and $\mathcal{A}_2$ of secret images SI_1 and SI_2 on the cover image.

1. Define $\mathcal{A}_1$ and $\mathcal{A}_2$ as all zero two-dimensional matrices of size $M_C \times N_C$, and define two-dimensional

$$\text{matrix } \mathcal{M} = \begin{bmatrix} 1 & Q+1 & \cdots & Q(Q-1)+1 \\ 2 & Q+2 & \cdots & Q(Q-1)+2 \\ \vdots & \vdots & \ddots & \vdots \\ Q & 2Q & \cdots & Q^2 \end{bmatrix}.$$

2. for $i \leftarrow 1$ to $\left\lfloor \frac{M_C}{Q} \right\rfloor / 2, j \leftarrow 1$ to $\left\lfloor \frac{N_C}{Q} \right\rfloor$

3. Generate random vector p, coordinate $\big((x(\circ), y(\circ)) \big)$ is the relative position of random number in vector p in $\mathcal{M}$, and generate two-dimensional all zero matrices $\mathcal{M}_1$ and $\mathcal{M}_2$ with size $Q \times Q$.

4. for $l \leftarrow 1$ to m $\mathcal{M}_1 \big(x(p(l)), y(p(l)) \big) = 1$ end for

5. for $l \leftarrow m+1$ to α $\mathcal{M}_2 \big(x(p(l)), y(p(l)) \big) = 1$ end for

6. $\mathcal{A}_1(i,j) = \mathcal{M}_1$

7. $\mathcal{A}_1 \left(\left\lfloor \frac{M_C}{Q} \right\rfloor - i + 1, \left\lfloor \frac{N_C}{Q} \right\rfloor - j + 1 \right) = \mathcal{F}(\mathcal{M}_2)$

8. $\mathcal{A}_2(i,j) = \mathcal{M}_2$

9. $\mathcal{A}_2 \left(\left\lfloor \frac{M_C}{Q} \right\rfloor - i + 1, \left\lfloor \frac{N_C}{Q} \right\rfloor - j + 1 \right) = \mathcal{F}(\mathcal{M}_1)$

10. end for

11. Output $\mathcal{A}_1$ and $\mathcal{A}_2$.

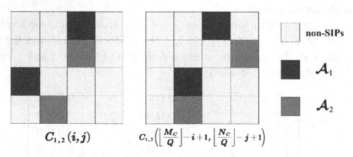

non-SIPs

$\mathcal{A}_1$

$\mathcal{A}_2$

$$C_{1,2}(i,j) \qquad C_{1,2}\left(\left\lfloor \frac{M_C}{Q} \right\rfloor - i + 1, \left\lfloor \frac{N_C}{Q} \right\rfloor - j + 1 \right)$$

Fig. 3. Example of SIPs location distribution.

Encryption of Secret Images

When determining the positions of the cover images SIPs and non-SIPs, we divide the cover images into non-overlapping $Q \times Q$-size shared blocks. In this section, we encrypt the two secret images pixel by pixel into the corresponding SIPs in the shared block at the corresponding position.

Let B_0 and B_1 be the $2 \times m$ basic matrices of encrypted white pixels and black pixels respectively, Π_{B_0} and Π_{B_1} be the matrix sets after random column permutation of B_0 and B_1, M_0 and M_1 be the matrices arbitrarily obtained from Π_{B_0} and Π_{B_1}, $M_0 \in \Pi_{B_0}$, $M_1 \in \Pi_{B_1}$, respectively. When the recovered secret is stacking by two shares. Let $\mathcal{B}$ be the position matrix of the auxiliary information pixels on the cover image to protect the recovered secret from the visual interference of the additional secret. The secret image encryption algorithm is shown in Table 2.

Table 2. The secret image encryption algorithm.

Input:
 Secret images SI_1 and SI_2, cover images C_1 and C_2, size $Q \times Q$ of the shared block, size $M_C \times N_C$ of the cover image, location matrix P_1 and P_2 of secret image SIPs, basic matrix B_0 and B_1.
Output:
 Cover images C'_1 and C'_2 carrying secret information.

1. Define as a two-dimensional matrix of size $M_C \times N_C$, let $= P_2$.
2. for $i \leftarrow 1$ to $\lfloor \frac{M_C}{Q} \rfloor$, $j \leftarrow 1$ to $\lfloor \frac{N_C}{Q} \rfloor$
3. if $SI_1(i,j) = 0$ $M = M_0$ else $M = M_1$ end if
4. Embed line l of M into position P_1 of $C_1(i,j)$, where $l = 1, 2$.
5. end for
6. for $i \leftarrow 1$ to $\lfloor \frac{M_C}{Q} \rfloor$, $j \leftarrow 1$ to $\lfloor \frac{N_C}{Q} \rfloor$
7. if $SI_2(i,j) = 0$ Copy the pixel value of $\mathcal{F}(C_2)(i,j)$ at position P_1 to position P_2 in $C_1(i,j)$.
 else   Copy the complementary of the pixel value of $\mathcal{F}(C_2)(i,j)$ at position P_1 to position P_2 in $C_1(i,j)$.
8. end if
9. Set the pixel value of $C_2(i,j)$ at the position of   to 1.
10. end for
11. Output C'_1 and C'_2.

Illustrate the algorithm in Table 2. Let $Q = 4$, $\alpha = 4$, $m = 2$, and randomly generate a vector $p = (3, 9, 8, 10, 7, 16, 13, 11, 1, 4, 15, 2, 5, 12, 6, 14)$. Let the row index and column index of the algorithm in the current pixel block be i and j, respectively. According to the algorithms in Table 1 and Table 2, the pixel position distribution of the shared block at (i, j) and $\left(\left\lfloor \frac{M_C}{Q} \right\rfloor - i + 1, \left\lfloor \frac{N_C}{Q} \right\rfloor - j + 1 \right)$ of the cover images C'_1 and C'_2 is shown in Fig. 4.

When we stack C'_1 and C'_2, SI_1 is recovered by P_1's secret information, and the auxiliary information pixels will overlap SI_2's secret image information, so the process of recovering SI_1 is not disturbed by SI_2's vision; Similarly, when we stack C'_1 and $\mathcal{F}(C'_2)$ (or $\mathcal{F}(C'_1)$ and C'_2), SI_2 will be recovered under the joint effect of P_1 and P_2, and the auxiliary information pixels $\mathcal{B}$ will overlap the secret image information of SI_1, so the process of recovering SI_2 will not be disturbed by SI_1's vision.

With the above process, we encrypt the secret image, embed the secret information into the cover image, and achieve the goal that the recovered secret is not disturbed by additional secret vision.

Insert Auxiliary Black Pixels ABPs

From the process of the above scheme, we get the cover images C'_1 and C'_2 carrying secret information and stack them according to a specific angle to recover a specific secret. However, the recovered image at this time will be affected by the meaningful information of the cover image, thus reducing the restoration quality. Therefore, in this section, we use halftone technology to process C'_1 and C'_2, add auxiliary black pixels

ABPs to C'_1 and C'_2, generate meaningful shares with good visual quality, and make the recovered images have no cross interference of cover images.

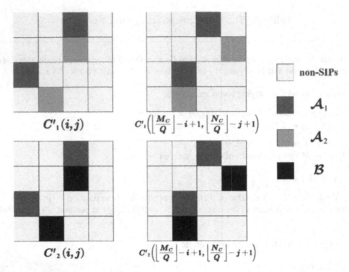

Fig. 4. Example of SIPs and auxiliary information pixels location distribution.

Firstly, C'_1 and C'_2 are processed by the error diffusion method to generate binary intermediate shares S'_1 and S'_2. Since the SIPs positions in C'_1 and C'_2 are fixed, there are constraints in the process of error diffusion processing. Let $F(k, l)$ be a function indicating whether error diffusion is allowed at the pixel point $C'(k, l)$, let $F(k, l) = 0$ if and only if $C'(k, l)$ is the SIPs, otherwise $F(k, l) = 1$. Let $h_{k,l}(x, y)$ be the number of error filter weights at $C'(k, l)$. Since the error diffusion process is constrained, the number of error diffusion weights after correction is $h_{k,l}(x, y) = h_{k,l}(x, y) \cdot F(x, y)$, that is, if the adjacent pixel $C'(x, y)$ of the pixel $C'(k, l)$ is SIPs, the number of error diffusion weights from $C'(k, l)$ to $C'(x, y)$ is 0. The quantization process formula of error diffusion is as follows:

$$S'(k, l) = [1 - F(k, l)] \cdot S'(k, l) + F(k, l) \cdot \mathcal{Q}(C'(k, l)) \tag{4}$$

where $\mathcal{Q}(C'(k, l))$ quantizes the pixel $C'(k, l)$ using a binary quantizer with a threshold of 127.

Secondly, the void and cluster algorithm is used to insert the minimum number of evenly distributed ABPs into S'_1 and S'_2, and finally generate meaningful shares S_1 and S_2, because some black pixels are generated at the non-SIPs position by the error diffusion method, which can overlap some but not all of the meaningful information of the cover image after S'_1 and S'_2 are stacking. Define $DA(k, l)$ as the pixel density function of the calculated pixel point at (k, l), and its expression is as follows:

$$DA(k, l) = \sum_{x'=-Q/2}^{Q/2} \sum_{y'=-Q/2}^{Q/2} BP(x, y) \cdot G(x', y') \tag{5}$$

where $BP(x, y)$ is the pixel value of the pixel point at (x, y), and the pixel points (k, l) and (x, y) are in the same shared block. $BP(x, y) = 1$ if and only if $BP(x, y)$ is a black pixel, otherwise $BP(x, y) = 0$. x' and y' is the relative distance between (k, l) and (x, y) on the horizontal axis and the vertical axis based on the $Q \times Q$ region of the shared block, which satisfies:

$$x' = (Q + k - x) \bmod Q, \, y' = (Q + k - y) \bmod Q \tag{6}$$

And $G(x', y')$ is a Gaussian filter, which satisfies:

$$G(x', y') = \exp\left(-\frac{x'^2 + y'^2}{2\sigma^2}\right) \tag{7}$$

where σ is a constant, generally $\sigma = 1.5$. To make the inserted ABPs evenly distributed, let n_{11} and n_{21} be the number of global ABPs inserted in S'_1 and S'_2, n_{12} and n_{22} be the number of local ABPs inserted in the current shared block of S'_1 and S'_2. The auxiliary black pixel ABPs insertion algorithm is shown in Table 3.

Table 3. The auxiliary black pixel ABPs insertion algorithm.

Input:
　　The intermediate shares S'_1 and S'_2, size $Q \times Q$ of the shared block, size $M_C \times N_C$ of the cover image, location matrix P_1 and P_2 of secret image SIPs.
Output:
　　The meaningful shares S_1 and S_2.

1. Let n_{11} and n_{21} be the number of global ABPs inserted in S'_1 and S'_2, let $n_{11} = 0$, $n_{21} = 0$.
2. for $i \leftarrow 1$ to $\lfloor \frac{M_C}{Q} \rfloor, j \leftarrow 1$ to $\lfloor \frac{N_C}{Q} \rfloor$
3. Let n_{12} and n_{22} be the number of local ABPs inserted in the current shared block (i, j) of S'_1 and S'_2, let $n_{12} = 0$, $n_{22} = 0$.
4. for $k \leftarrow i \times Q - Q + 1$ to $i \times Q, l \leftarrow j \times Q - Q + 1$ to $j \times Q$
5. if $S'_{1,2}(k, l) = 0$ and $P_{1,2}(k, l) \neq 1$
6. The pixel densities $DA_1(k, l)$ and $DA_2(k, l)$ of the pixel points $S'_1(k, l)$ and $S'_2(k, l)$ can be obtained from equations (5) ~ (7).
7. $DA_1(k, l) = DA_1(k, l) + n_{11} + n_{12}$
8. $DA_2(k, l) = DA_2(k, l) + n_{21} + n_{22}$
9. if $DA_1(k, l) \leq DA_2(k, l)$ $S'_1(k, l) = 1$, $n_{11} = n_{11} + 1$, $n_{12} = n_{12} + 1$
   else $S'_2(k, l) = 1$, $n_{21} = n_{21} + 1$, $n_{22} = n_{22} + 1$
10. end if
11. end if
12. end for
13. end for
14. Take S'_1 and $\mathcal{F}(S'_2)$ as inputs, execute the algorithm from step 2) until step 13), and output the meaningful shares S_1 and S_2.

According Table 3, it is first judged whether the pixel points at (k, l) of S'_1 and S'_2 meet the four conditions of being white and do not belong to P_1 and P_2. If they all meet the four conditions, the pixel densities $DA_1(k, l)$ and $DA_2(k, l)$ at (k, l) of S'_1 and S'_2 are calculated. The smaller the value of $DA(k, l)$ the sparser the black pixels around (k, l) in the share. Therefore, the shares of the pixel points with smaller $DA(k, l)$ value is selected and ABPs are inserted and set to black. In this process, the number of global ABPs and the number of local ABPs are taken as influencing factors to jointly determine the size of $DA(k, l)$ value, so that the number of inserted ABPs is the least and can be evenly distributed, and finally meaningful shares S_1 and S_2 with good visual quality are generated. Compared with C'_1 and C'_2, the shares processed by the error diffusion method and the void and cluster algorithm does not suffer from the cross interference of the meaningful information of the cover image.

Recovery of Secret Image

Meaningful shares S_1 and S_2 based on the rotating multi-secret visual cryptography scheme of gray-scale images are generated by the above process. Specific secrets can be recovered by stacking S_1 and S_2 from different angles, and the recovered secret does not suffer from the cross interference between the cover image and additional secret. However, due to the introduction of auxiliary black pixels ABPs and auxiliary information pixels, the brightness of the recovered image is dark, which affects the visual quality of the recovered image. In order to improve the contrast and quality of the recovered image, it is necessary to reconstruct the recovered image.

Suppose that the recovered image after S_1 and S_2 are stacked is SI'_1, and the recovered image after S_1 and $\mathcal{F}(S_2)$(or $\mathcal{F}(S_1)$ and S_2) are stacked is SI'_2, then the steps of reconstructing the recovered image are as follows:

1. Divide SI'_1 and SI'_2 into non-overlapping blocks with size $Q \times Q$, and calculate the number of black pixels in each block.
2. If the number is less than the set threshold, all Q^2 pixels in the block are set to white, otherwise, they are set to black.
3. Repeat the above steps until all the blocks in SI'_1 and SI'_2 are processed to obtain reconstructed recovered images.

Comparing SI'_1 and SI'_2, the reconstructed recovered image eliminates the problem of dark brightness caused by ABPs and auxiliary information pixels, maintains the characteristics of no cover image and additional secret interference, and improves the contrast and visual quality of the recovered image.

3.2 The Rotating Visual Cryptography Scheme with Meaningful Shares for Color Image

In this section, we extend the gray-scale scheme to the color level. We select the secret image as color image, which is represented by SI_1 and SI_2 respectively; The cover image is selected as color image, represented by C_1 and C_2 respectively, and the size is $M_C \times N_C$; The scheme takes the secret image and the cover image as inputs, and finally generates meaningful shares, which is represented by S_1 and S_2 respectively.

For the color scheme, the basic idea is to decompose the secret image and the cover image into three channels of gray-scale images according to the RGB color model, and then process them separately based on the gray-scale image scheme proposed above, and finally synthesize them into color shares according to the RGB color model. Therefore, the color scheme is designed as follows:

1. SI_1 and SI_2 are decomposed into three-channel grayscale images according to RGB color model and converted into binary images by error diffusion method of halftone technology. The converted images are set as R_1, G_1, B_1 and R_2, G_2, B_2 respectively.
2. According to Table 1 and Table 2, the SIPs and auxiliary information pixel positions P_1, P_2, and $\mathcal{B}$ of the cover images C_1 and C_2 are determined, and the cover images is decomposed into three channels of gray-scale images according to the RGB color model, which are respectively set as $C_1^R C_1^G C_1^B$ and $C_2^R C_2^G C_2^B$.
3. According Table 2, encrypt R_1 and R_2 into C_1^R and C_2^R, G_1 and G_2 into C_1^G and C_2^G, B_1 and B_2 into C_1^B and C_2^B to obtain $C_1'^R, C_1'^G, C_1'^B$ and $C_2'^R, C_2'^G, C_2'^B$
4. According to Table 3, the auxiliary black pixel ABPs are inserted based on the halftone technology Firstly, the cover image carrying secret information is processed according to the error diffusion method to obtain the intermediate images $S_1'^R, S_1'^G, S_1'^B$ and $S_2'^R, S_2'^G, S_2'^B$. Secondly, the ABPs are inserted according to the void and cluster algorithm to generate S_1^R, S_1^G, S_1^B and S_2^R, S_2^G, S_2^B.
5. According to the RGB color model, S_1^R, S_1^G and S_1^B arc synthesized into S_1, and S_2^R, S_2^G and S_2^B are synthesized into S_2 to obtain meaningful shares of color scheme. Specific secrets can be recovered by stacking at different angles, and the recovered secret does not interfere by the meaningful information of the cover image and additional secret.
6. In order to eliminate the influence of ABPs and auxiliary information pixels, the recovered image can be reconstructed. Let the recovered image after S_1 and S_2 are stacked is SI'_1, and the recovered image after S_1 and $\mathcal{F}(S_2)$(or $\mathcal{F}(S_1)$ and S_2) are stacked is SI'_2. According to the above gray-scale scheme, SI'_1 and SI'_2 are divided into non-overlapping blocks with size $Q \times Q$, and the number of black pixels in each block of each image is calculated in three channels according to the RGB color model. If the number is less than the set threshold, all pixels in the block are set to white, otherwise, they are black, until all channel images are processed, and the reconstructed recovered image is obtained.

4 Experiments and Analysis

4.1 Experiment for Gray-Scale Images

In this section, the cover images C_1 and C_2 are shown in Fig. 5 (a)–(b), and the size is 512×512; The secret images SI_1 and SI_2 are shown in Fig. 5 (c)–(d), and the size is 512×512. If the parameters $Q = 4$, $\alpha = 4$, $m = 2$ are selected, then the basic matrix $B_0 = \begin{bmatrix} 1 & 0 \\ 1 & 0 \end{bmatrix}$, $B_1 = \begin{bmatrix} 1 & 0 \\ 0 & 1 \end{bmatrix}$. According to the above gray-scale scheme, the experimental results are shown in Fig. 6, where Fig. 6 (a)–(b) are meaningful shares S_1 and S_2, Fig. 6 (c)–(d) are recovered images SI'_1 and SI'_2 after S_1, $S2$ and $S1$, $\mathcal{F}(S_2)$(or $\mathcal{F}(S_1)$, S_2) are stacked, and Fig. 6 (e)–(f) are reconstructed recovered images.

(a) Cover image C_1 (b) Cover image C_2 (c) Secret image SI_1 (d) Secret image SI_2

Fig. 5. Cover image and secret image of gray-scale scheme.

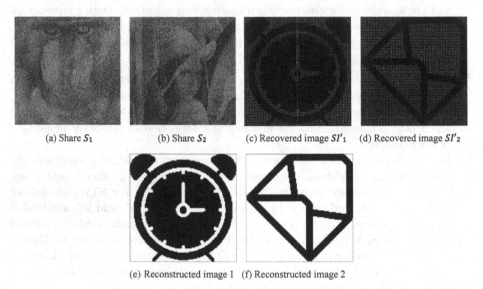

(a) Share S_1 (b) Share S_2 (c) Recovered image SI'_1 (d) Recovered image SI'_2

(e) Reconstructed image 1   (f) Reconstructed image 2

Fig. 6. Experimental results of gray-scale scheme.

In order to measure the quality of the image generated by the scheme, we use contrast, peak signal-to-noise ratio (PSNR) and structural similarity SSIM to quantify and study.

1) Contrast

For the recovered image before reconstruction, the contrast is the "1" relative difference between black pixels and white pixels in the block. When the size of the shared block is $Q \times Q$ and the number of SIPs in the block is α, it is easy to obtain that the contrast of the secret image before reconstruction is $\alpha/4Q^2$ (or $m/2Q^2$). When $Q = 4$, $\alpha = 4$, $m = 2$ are taken, the contrast of the recovered image before reconstruction is 1/16. If you want to improve the contrast of the recovered image before reconstruction, you can take the method of improving the α value. When you take $Q = 4$, $\alpha = 8$, $m = 4$, the contrast of the recovered image before reconstruction is 1/8. However, this will compress the number of non-SIPs, thereby reducing the visual quality of the shares.

For the reconstructed recovered image, it has no obvious difference from the original secret image, significantly improves the brightness of the recovered image, and achieves the best black-and-white pixel contrast, with a contrast value close to 1.

2) Peak signal to noise ratio (PSNR)

PSNR is an objective standard for evaluating image quality. It can measure the quality of reconstructed image relative to the original image. The higher its value, the lower the distortion and the better the re-constructed image quality. We measured the PSNR values of the shares S_1 and S_2 relative to the original images C_1 and C_2, and used a Gaussian filter to eliminate the influence of noise before the measurement. Finally, we determined that the PSNR value of S_1 was 62.4380, and the PSNR value of S_2 was 60.5624.

3) Structural similarity (SSIM)

SSIM is an objective standard for evaluating image quality by measuring the similarity of two images. The range of its value is. The larger the value, the more similar the reconstructed image is to the original image. If the two images are the same, the value of SSIM is 1. We measured the SSIM values of the shares S_1 and S_2 relative to the original images C_1 and C_2. Similarly, Gaussian filters were used to eliminate the influence of noise before the measurement. Finally, the SSIM values of S_1 and S_2 were determined to be 0.2683 and 0.4795 respectively.

4.2 Experiment for Color Images

In this section, the cover images C_1 and C_2 are shown in Fig. 7 (a)–(b), and the size is 512×512; The secret images SI_1 and SI_2 are shown in Fig. 7 (c)–(d), and the size is 512×512. If the parameters $Q = 4$, $\alpha = 4$, $m = 2$ are selected, then the basic matrix $B_0 = \begin{bmatrix} 1 & 0 \\ 1 & 0 \end{bmatrix}$, $B_1 = \begin{bmatrix} 1 & 0 \\ 0 & 1 \end{bmatrix}$. According to the above color scheme, the experimental results are shown in Fig. 8, where Fig. 8 (a)–(b) are meaningful shares S_1 and S_2, Fig. 8 (c)–(d) are recovered images SI'_1 and SI'_2 after S_1, S_2 and S_1, $\mathcal{F}(S_2)$(or $\mathcal{F}(S_1)$, S_2) are stacked, and Fig. 8 (e)–(f) are reconstructed recovered images.

(a) Cover image C_1 (b) Cover image C_2 (c) Secret image SI_1 (d) Secret image SI_2

Fig. 7. Cover image and secret image of color scheme.

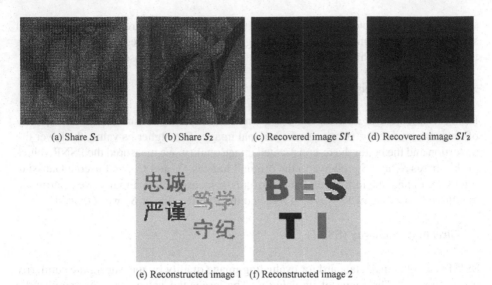

(a) Share S_1 (b) Share S_2 (c) Recovered image SI'_1 (d) Recovered image SI'_2

(e) Reconstructed image 1   (f) Reconstructed image 2

Fig. 8. Experimental results of color scheme

Similarly, we use peak signal-to-noise ratio PSNR and structural similarity SSIM to quantify and study the quality of the image generated by the scheme. We measured the PSNR values of the shares S_1 and S_2 relative to the original images C_1 and C_2, and used the Gaussian filter to eliminate the influence of noise before the measurement. Finally, the PSNR value of S_1 was 61.0943, and the PSNR value of S_2 was 59.6898. Subsequently, we measured the SSIM values of the shares S_1 and S_2 relative to the original images C_1 and C_2. Similarly, the Gaussian filter is used to eliminate the influence of noise before the measurement. Finally, the SSIM value of S_1 is 0.3419, and the SSIM value of S_2 is 0.6080.

From the simulation results and analysis of the above two experiments, it can be concluded that the scheme can generate shares based on gray-scale or color. From the measured PSNR value and SSIM value, the shares quality is good, and there is no significant difference from the original cover image and no secret information can be seen from it. The specific secret can be recovered by stacking the shares in different angles, and the recovered image has no cross interference of cover image and additional secret. Then, the recovered image is reconstructed. The reconstructed image eliminates the adverse effects of auxiliary black pixels ABPs and auxiliary information pixels, and significantly enhances the brightness and contrast of the recovered image. The contrast value is close to 1, which is not significantly different from the original secret, and the image quality is better.

Compared with other rotating visual cryptography schemes, this scheme can generate meaningful shares with good visual quality, improve the camouflage of shares, enable shares to escape the monitoring of attackers in the transmission process of the channel, and make the transmission process more secure, thus enhancing the security of the scheme. Compared with the schemes of Wu et al. [11], Gao et al. [12], Dong et al. [14], Zhao et al. [17], the scheme can be extended to gray-scale images and color images, which enriches the application scenarios of rotating visual cryptography schemes. Compared with the schemes of Askari et al. [15] and Li [16], this scheme greatly improves the contrast of the recovered image through reconstruction operation, and the visual quality is better. This scheme is compared with other rotating visual cryptography schemes in terms of the shape of shares, whether the shares are meaningful, whether it can be applied to color images, and restoring image contrast. The comparison results are shown in Table 4.

Table 4. Comparison with related papers.

Paper	Shape of shares	Meaningful shares	Color	Secrets number	Contrast
[11]	Ring	N	Binary	2	1/4
[12]	Rectangle	N	Binary	m	< 1
[14]	Ring	N	Binary	m	α/m
[15]	Rectangle	N	Gary-scale	2	1/4
[16]	Ring	N	Color	m	< 1
[17]	Rectangle	N	Binary	$3C_n^k + 1$	< 1
Proposed	Rectangle	Y	Color	2	1

4.3 Security Analysis

In the scheme proposed in this paper, the secret image is encrypted into the SIPs position of each shared block of the cover image, and the position of the SIPs is determined by the random vector p, the size of the shared block $Q \times Q$ and the number of SIPs in the block α. Therefore, the position of the SIPs is completely random. It is extremely difficult for the attacker to know the position of the SIPs so that the secret information is obtained without knowing α, Q and the corresponding p of each shared block. Even if the attacker knows the values of α and Q, the probability of completely guessing the location distribution of SIPs in a shared block is $C_{Q^2}^\alpha$, and the probability of guessing the location distribution of SIPs in a share is $2 \cdot \left(C_{Q^2}^\alpha \right)^{\left\lfloor \frac{M_C}{Q} \right\rfloor \times \left\lfloor \frac{N_C}{Q} \right\rfloor}$, and the probability of the latter infinitely approaches 0. Therefore, the attacker cannot obtain the location distribution of all SIPs when α and Q are obtained, and the secret information cannot be obtained from the shares.

If an attacker intercepts one of the two shares, he can modify the share. If the attacker knows the size Q of the shared block and the number α of SIPs in the block, and when the location distribution of SIPs in the shared block is fixed, it is easy to find the exact location of SIPs, and then set all SIPs to black. At this time, when the share is stacked with another unmodified share, neither secret image can be recovered. In proposed scheme, since the location distribution of SIPs is random, the attacker cannot know the exact pixel distribution location, so the most efficient attack method is to randomly select α pixels in each shared block and set it to black. In this case, we stack two shares at different angles to recover specific secrets. Figure 9 shows the visual effect and reconstruction secret image before and after share S_1 under this kind of attack. The PSNR value and MSSIM value of Fig. 9 (c) are 59.4207 and 0.2154 respectively, and the PSNR value and MSSIM value of Fig. 9 (g) are 59.5094 and 0.3070 respectively. The share still has better visual effect after S_1 is attacked, and the recovered image can still be well recognized. Therefore, this scheme also has certain robustness.

In addition, the scheme encrypts the secret image using the fundamental matrix with provable security and embeds the secret information into SIPs. For each secret pixel, the random column transformation matrices $M_0 \in \Pi_{B_0}$ and $M_1 \in \Pi_{B_1}$ of the basic matrix are used. For any subset $\{q_1, ..., q_t\}$ in the set $\{1, ..., t\}$, by restricting each matrix in Π_{B_0} and Π_{B_1} to the row $q_1, ..., q_t$, the two $t \times m$-size matrix sets Γ_{B_0} and Γ_{B_1} contain the same matrix at the same frequency and are therefore indistinguishable.

In summary, the distribution of SIPs is random, and the base matrix used to encrypt the secret image satisfies security, so this scheme satisfies security.

4.4 Application Scenario Analysis

Since the proposed scheme can encrypt two secret images at the same time, it has advantages in some application scenarios that require mutual authentication. For example, biometrics is a technology that uses the inherent physiological characteristics or other behavioral characteristics of the human body to perform personal identification through high-tech means. This scheme combines visual cryptography with biometric technology to identify multiple physiological features such as fingerprints, faces, and irises of participants and encrypt them as secrets at the same time, and then uploads the shares to the cloud. After recovering all the secrets, the cloud compares the secret with its stored participant feature information data, and only all successful participants can pass. Because the shares are disguised, the possibility of tampering with the shares are reduced.

Similarly, visual cryptography technology is often used in military maps, QR codes, cloud computing and other scenes with strong timeliness and high security requirements. Therefore, this scheme can be used to encrypt a secret image as a label information or watermark information and use it as a security mark of another secret image, in which the label or watermark can have a certain timeliness. The sender encrypts the secret together with the label or watermark to generate shares and transmits it to the receiver through a communication link. If the recovered label or watermark does not match the secret image at the receiver, it indicates that the time is lost, or the shares has been attacked and tampered with during transmission. In this way, an anti-spoofing verification mechanism is established between participants, thereby improving the security of the application scenario.

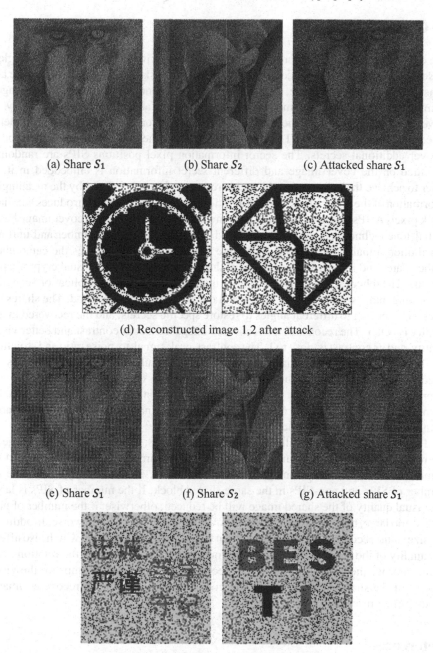

(a) Share S_1 (b) Share S_2 (c) Attacked share S_1

(d) Reconstructed image 1,2 after attack

(e) Share S_1 (f) Share S_2 (g) Attacked share S_1

(i) Reconstructed image 1,2 after attack

Fig. 9. Experimental results of share S_1 being attacked.

5 Conclusions

The existing rotating multi-secret scheme is associated with the problem of meaningless noise-like shares, shares poor camouflage and security risks in the process of storage and transmission. At the same time, the existing schemes are mostly limited to binary images. Compared with gray or color images, binary images have advantages in visual quality. To solve these problems, this paper proposes a rotating color visual cryptography scheme based on meaningful shares. The scheme is based on the characteristics of rotation to recover additional secrets. The secret information pixel positions SIPs are randomly allocated on the cover image and different secret information is embedded in it. In order to achieve the purpose that the recovered secret is not interfered by the meaningful information of the cover image and the additional secret, the scheme introduces auxiliary black pixels ABPs and auxiliary information pixels, and processes the cover image based on halftone technology, so that the inserted ABPs have the least number and uniform distribution. Finally, meaningful shares are obtained, which enhances the camouflage of the shares and improves the security of the rotating multi-secret visual cryptography scheme. The scheme can be applied to color images and extends the application scenarios of rotating multi-secret scheme. The visual quality of the share is good. The shares are stacked according to different angles to restore specific secrets, and the recovered image quality is better. The reconstructed recovered image has better contrast and better visual quality, and its contrast is close to 1. The contrast, peak signal-to-noise ratio and structural similarity of the generated image are measured by simulation tests, which proves the effectiveness of the scheme. The security of the scheme is demonstrated from the aspects of probability, attack situation of shares and construction of basic matrix. The attacker cannot obtain any secret information from the share. Finally, the application scenarios of the scheme are analyzed and conceived.

However, this scheme still has some shortcomings. In this scheme, the edge of the reconstructed image is blurred. Rectangular share limits the rotation angle and the number of encrypted secret images. At the same time, it is necessary to balance the number of SIPs and non-SIPs in the same shared block. If the number of SIPs is large, the visual quality of the shared image will be reduced; otherwise, if the number of non-SIPs is too large, the visual effect of the recovered image will become worse. In addition, the size of the recovered image is larger than the original secret image, which also affects the quality of the recovered image. Therefore, how to break through the rotation angle limit, improve the number of encrypted secret images, and further improve the visual quality of the shares while ensuring the good visual quality of the recovered images needs further research.

References

1. Naor, M., Shamir, A.: Visual cryptography. Lect. Notes Comput. Sci. **950**(9), 1–12 (1994)
2. Zhou, Z., Arce, G.R., Di, C.G.: Halftone visual cryptography. IEEE Trans. Image Proc. A Publ. IEEE Sig. Process. Soc. **15**(8), 2441–2453 (2006)
3. Wang, Z., Arce, G.R., Crescenzo, G.D.: Halftone visual cryptography via error diffusion. IEEE Trans. Inf. Forensics Secur. **4**(3), 383–396 (2009)

4. Ahmad, S., Hayat, M.F., Qureshi, M.A., et al.: Enhanced halftone-based secure and improved visual cryptography scheme for colour/binary images. Multimedia Tools and Applications **80**(21), 32071–32090 (2021)
5. Wang, Y.Y.: Research on Image Encryption and Security Based on Visual Cryptography. Xi'an University of Technology (2021)
6. Shen, G., Yu, B.: (k, n) Multi-secret visual cryptography based on XOR. J. Chin. Comput. Syst. **34**(09), 2116–2119 (2013)
7. Wang, L., Yan, B., Yang, H.M., Pan, J.S.: Flip extended visual cryptography for gray-scale and color cover images. Symmetry **13**(1), 65 (2020)
8. Huang, B., Juan, J.S.: Flexible meaningful visual multi-secret sharing scheme by random grids. Multimedia Tools and Applications **79**(11), 7705–7729 (2020)
9. Yan, B., Wang, Y., Song, L.Y., et al.: Size-invariant extended visual cryptography with embedded watermark based on error diffusion. Multimedia Tools Applications **75**(18), 11157–11180 (2016)
10. Wu, C.C., Chen, L.H.: A study on visual cryptography. [Master dissertation], National Chiao Tung University, Taipei (1998)
11. Wu, H.C., Chang, C.C.: Sharing visual multi-secrets using circle shares. Comput. Stand. Interfaces **28**(1), 123–135 (2004)
12. Gao, J.T., Yue, H., Cao, J.: Visual multi-secrets sharing scheme based on random grid. J. Electron. Inf. Technol. **44**(02), 573–580 (2022)
13. Fu, Z.-X., Yu, B.: Ideal secure multi-secret visual cryptography scheme with ring shares. In: Shi, Y.Q., Liu, F., Yan, W. (eds.) Transactions on Data Hiding and Multimedia Security IX. LNCS, vol. 8363, pp. 42–56. Springer, Heidelberg (2014). https://doi.org/10.1007/978-3-642-55046-1_3
14. Dong, C., Ji, S.T., Zhang, H.Y., et al.: Operational visual multi-secret sharing scheme for threshold structure. Comput. Sci. **47**(10), 322–326 (2020)
15. Askari, N., Heys, H.M., Moloney, C.R.: Novel visual cryptography schemes without pixel expansion for halftone images. Can. J. Electr. Comput. Eng. **37**(3), 168–177 (2014)
16. Li, J.N.: Application of visual cryptography and some research. Hangzhou Dianzi University (2018)
17. Zhao, Y.K., Fu, F.W.: A cheating immune (k, n) visual cryptography scheme by using the rotation of shares. Multimedia Tools and Applications (2022). (prepublish)
18. Floyd, R.W., Steinberg, L.: An adaptive algorithm for spatial gray scale. Proc. Soc. Inform. Display **17**, 75–77 (1975)
19. Ulichney, R.: Void-and-cluster method for dither array generation. John Wiley (1993)

Updatable ElGamal Encryption Scheme with Forward and Backward Security for Cloud Storage

Zhenhua Liu[1,2], Jingwan Gong[1(✉)], Yuanju Ma[1], Yaxin Niu[1],
and Baocang Wang[3]

[1] School of Mathematics and Statistics, Xidian University, Xi'an 710071, China
jwgong0318@stu.xidian.edu.cn
[2] State Key Laboratory of Cryptology, P.O. Box 5159, Beijing 100878, China
[3] State Key Laboratory of Integrated Services Networks, Xidian University,
Xi'an 710071, China
bcwang79@aliyun.com

Abstract. Updatable encryption plays an important role in cloud storage scenario due to providing update functionality for ciphertext data and resisting key compromise attacks. However, most of updatable encryption schemes adopted a type of partitioning strategy: leakage sets or firewalls technique, which prohibited the adversary from querying the key at the challenge-equal epochs and hardly captured forward and backward security. In this paper, we enhance the existing security model by considering a corruption oracle that allows any secret key query and overcomes the dependence on leakage sets, and then present the first updatable public-key encryption scheme with no-directional key updates and uni-directional ciphertext updates on the basis of the classical ElGamal encryption scheme. The proposed scheme can minimize the information leakage of update tokens by using the indistinguishable obfuscation technique of the punctured program. Moreover, under the framework of the enhanced security model, the proposed scheme is proven to be IND-CPA. Finally, compared with the existing updatable encryption schemes, the proposed scheme eliminates leakage sets and firewalls to capture forward and backward security.

Keywords: Updatable public-key encryption · ElGamal encryption ·
Indistinguishability obfuscation · Puncturable pseudorandom function ·
Forward security · Backward security

Supported by the Natural Science Basic Research Plan in Shaanxi Province of China under Grant No.2022JZ-38, the National Natural Science Foundation of China under Grants No.61807026, the Plan for Scientific Innovation Talent of Henan Province under Grant No.184100510012, and the Postgraduate Innovation Fund of Xidian University under Grant No.YJS2215.

1   Introduction

In recent years, the explosive growth of data volume gives rise to a new storage mode – cloud storage. In cloud storage scenario, data owner can store data in the cloud server, and data user can access them via the Internet anywhere and anytime. This storage mode can improve storage efficiency, reduce operation cost, and support flexible access. Although cloud storage can provide the convenience and security guarantee for the clients, it is inevitable that some security incidents occur at the client-side or cloud-side. Therefore, it is important to focus on key life-cycle management to minimize the impact of key compromise on the encrypted data in the cloud.

There are some techniques to resist key compromise attacks. NIST 800-57 [3], PCI-DSS [10] adopted key rotation, which periodically rotates the old key to produce a new key and converts the corresponding ciphertext from the old key to the new key without changing the underlying data. When data owner outsources the ciphertext data to the cloud storage setting, key rotation would turn into something much more complicated: data owner either has to download, decrypt, re-encrypt, and then upload all ciphertexts to the cloud server, or send the secret keys to the cloud server that executes the decryption and encryption. The former makes cloud storage impractical, and the latter violates data security. For the outsourcing cloud storage scenario, it is necessary to seek a novelty update technique, and thus updatable encryption (UE) [5] stands out.

Updatable encryption can be regarded as a new cryptographic primitive tailored for cloud storage environments. The principle [5] is that data user calculates a short token and sends it to the cloud server. Then the cloud server uses the token to update the corresponding ciphertext from the old key to the new key. Although the token relies on the old and new keys, the cloud server can not obtain any information about the keys and messages. In a typical use of updatable encryption, the cloud server receives periodically the update token from data user, updates the stored ciphertexts, and deletes the previous or old ciphertexts. The valid duration of the key is called the epoch. Moreover, the compromised key at the previous epoch cannot be used to decrypt the current ciphertext, and thus the impact of key compromise on the encrypted data can be minimized.

1.1   Related Works

In 2013, Boneh et al. [5] explicitly proposed the concept of updatable encryption for the first time based on incremental cryptography [4]. Furthermore, Ananth et al. [1] carried out a systematic study of updatable cryptographic primitives by adding updatability capabilities into various cryptographic schemes, and introduced updatable randomized encodings to incorporate updatability features. Since then, the upsurge of updatable encryption has been set off [6,11–14].

Furthermore, based on whether or not the update token depends on the ciphertexts, there exist two variants of updatable encryption: ciphertext-dependent and ciphertext-independent. In the ciphertext-independent setting, the update token can be generated only according to the old and new keys, and be used to update all the related ciphertext stored in the cloud server. Such a setting has the advantage of certain universality, and thus has attracted more attentions. Lehmann et al. [13] formally introduced two security notions of ciphertext-independent updatable encryption: encryption indistinguishability (IND-ENC) and update indistinguishability (IND-UPD). Furthermore, Klooß et al. [12] enhanced the confidentiality to CCA security. Subsequently, Boyd et al. [6] gave the definition of update encryption indistinguishable (IND-UE) and obtained a general conclusion: CPA+CTXT$\Rightarrow$CCA.

In 2020, Jiang [11] first considered the impact of the key/ciphertext update direction on the security notions, and presented a shocking conclusion: uni-directional update and bi-directional update are equivalent under the same security notions, and the combination of no-directional key updates and uni-directional ciphertext updates is strictly stronger than other variants. Furthermore, Jiang raised two open problems: how to construct updatable encryption schemes with no-directional key updates and how to bulid updatable encryption schemes with chosen ciphertext post-quantum security. On the other hand, in 2022 Nishimaki [14] subdivided uni-directional key updates into forward-leak and backward-leak, stated a different opinion: the direction of key updates does matter. Although the UE_{iO} scheme proposed by Nishimaki [14] can realize no-directional key updates and uni-directional ciphertext updates, it is an updatable symmetric encryption scheme that is only applies to the single-user scenario.

1.2   Our Motivation and Contributions

The original updatable encryption scheme [5] can be regarded as a variant of proxy re-encryption. In fact, Boneh et al.'s scheme [5] is the type of symmetric encryption, including its subsequent schemes [6,11–14]. However, due to the versatility of update token, these schemes allowed the adversaries to infer some additional information during the update process, and implemented hardly the forward and backward security.

In order to clearly analyze whether the update process would leak information, Lehmann et al. [13] introduced the concept of leakage sets $\mathcal{K}^*$, $\mathcal{T}^*$, and $\mathcal{C}^*$, which are used to track the epochs at which an adversary learned secret keys, tokens and challenge-equal ciphertexts. At the same time, in their security model the intersection of the known challenge-equal ciphertext set $\mathcal{C}^*$ and the known key set $\mathcal{K}^*$ is manually restricted to be an empty set to exclude the trivial win and capture the forward and backward security. Informally, the challenge-equal epochs refer to each epoch at which an adversary knows the current version of the challenge ciphertext. Subsequently, Boyd et al. [5] presented the firewall technique for cryptographic separation in order to more easily demonstrate the security in an epoch-based model with strong corruptibility. The so-called firewall technique described in Fig. 1 is to separate the epoch when the adversary knows the secret key from the epoch at which it knows the challenge-equal ciphertext. Suppose that an adversary $\mathcal{A}$ does ask for a challenge ciphertext at the epoch e^*. Then there exists an unique epoch continuum around e^* such that no keys in the sequence of epochs $(fwl, \ldots, fwr)$ are corrupted, the tokens Δ_{fwl} and Δ_{fwr+1} in the boundaries of this epoch continuum are not corrupted, and all tokens $(\Delta_{fwl+1}, \ldots, \Delta_{fwr})$ are corrupted. They named these epoch ranges as insulated regions and their boundaries to be firewalls.

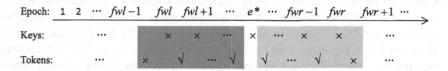

Fig. 1. The firewall proposed by Boyd et al. [6]. fwl indicates the left firewall epoch, and fwr indicates the right firewall epoch. × indicates that the key or token has not been corrupted by the adversary, and √ means the opposite.

The leakage sets or firewall technique played a certain role in reducing the loss caused by key leakage, but they had some inherent defects. Firstly, the two methods severely weakened the security model, requiring that all secret keys at challenge-equal epochs be kept completely secret from the adversary. However, in the real world, an adversary can launch various key corruption attacks, such as side-channel attacks, to obtain partial information about secret keys. Secondly, the security model and proof process are rather redundant and complex, since leakage sets or firewall technology need to be updated whenever an adversary corrupts a key or token. Moreover, at the end of the confidentiality game, it is necessary to check whether a trivial winning condition "$K^* \cap C^* \neq \emptyset$" is triggered. Therefore, it is necessary to seek for a novel technique or method to simplify the model and enhance the security.

In fact, the functionality preserved under puncturing of puncturable pseudorandom function [15] can ensure that the normal secret key and the punctured secret key are indistinguishable. A normal key can correctly decrypt all ciphertext at the current epoch. However, the decryption of challenge ciphertext with a punctured secret key will fail since the first element of challenge ciphertext is set as punctured point. On this basis, an updatable public-key encryption scheme with no-directional key updates and uni-directional ciphertext updates is proposed, which eliminates leakage sets and firewalls, and captures the forward and backward security. To sum up, the main contributions are as follows:

1) **Make ElGamal encryption be updatable.** Based on the classical ElGamal encryption scheme, we propose the first updatable public-key encryption scheme by making full use of the indistinguishable obfuscation technique of the punctured programs. A brief comparison between the proposed scheme and the existing schemes is given in Table 1, which shows that the proposed scheme has obvious advantages in directionality and confidentiality.

2) **Enhance the existing security model and confidentiality.** The enhanced security models overcome the reliance on leakage sets and allow the adversary to corrupt keys and tokens at any epoch. The update token

generated by the secret key SK_e and the public key PK_{e+1} is hidden in the obfuscation program to realize no-directional key updates and uni-directional ciphertext updates, which strengthens the confidentiality of the proposed scheme and solves the open problem left by Jiang [11] in a better way than Nishimaki [14].

3) **Capture forward security and backward security.** We eliminate leakage sets and firewalls to achieve forward and backward security. By combining the update token that cannot be used to degrade key with the corruption oracle that returns a punctured secret key to the adversary, the proposed scheme can easily achieve forward security. Furthermore, the update token cannot be used to upgrade key and degrade ciphertext, which ensures the backward security of the proposed scheme.

Table 1. A brief comparison of our construction with the existing schemes

Scheme	UE/UPKE	Dir. (key)	Dir. (ct)	Leakage Sets	Firewalls Technique	IND-ENC-CPA	IND-UE-CPA
BLMR [5]	UE	bi	bi	✓	–	rand	–
RISE [13]	UE	bi	bi	✓	–	rand	–
E&M [12]	UE	bi	bi	✓	–	–	–
NYUE [12]	UE	bi	bi	✓	–	–	–
SHINE [6]	UE	bi	bi	✓	✓	det	det
LWEPKE [11]	UE	bi	bi	✓	✓	rand	rand
UE_{iO} [14]	UE	no	uni	✓	✓	rand	rand
Ours	UPKE	no	uni	✗	✗	rand[†]	rand[†]

Note: Dir.(key) and Dir.(ct) indicate the key update direction and ciphertext update direction, respectively. The symbol [†] stands for IND-ENC-CPA or IND-UE-CPA security in an enhanced model. We represent "rand" and "det" as randomized and deterministic ciphertext updates, respectively.

2   Preliminaries

2.1   Notations

In this paper, $x \leftarrow X$ denotes the process of uniformly random sampling a value x from a finite set X. Similarly, $y \leftarrow A(x)$ denotes the output of algorithm A on input x to y. Let 1^λ be the security parameter, $a := b$ indicate that a is substituted by b, and PPT represent probabilistic polynomial time.

2.2   Basic Primitives

Pseudorandom Generator (PRG). A PRG [9] is an efficient and deterministic algorithm for transforming a short and uniform string called the seed into a longer and "uniform-looking" (or "pseudorandom") output string. PRG is pseudorandom if no efficient distinguisher $\mathcal{D}$ can detect whether it is given a string output by PRG or a string chosen uniformly at random. More precisely:

Definition 1. *(Pseudorandom Generator) Let l be a polynomial and PRG be a deterministic polynomial-time algorithm such that for any input $s \in \{0,1\}^n$ with any n, the result $PRG(s)$ is a string of length $l(n)$. PRG is called as a pseudorandom generator if the following conditions hold:*

1. *(Expansion) For any n, it holds that $l(n) > n$.*
2. *(Pseudorandomness) For any PPT algorithm, there is a negligible function $negl(\lambda)$ such that*

$$\Big| \Pr \big[\mathcal{D}(PRG(s)) = 1 \big] - \Pr \big[\mathcal{D}(r) = 1 \big] \Big| \leq negl(\lambda),$$

where the first probability is taken over uniform choice of $s \in \{0,1\}^n$ and the randomness of $\mathcal{D}$, and the second probability is taken over uniform choice of $r \in \{0,1\}^{l(n)}$ and the randomness of $\mathcal{D}$. l is referred to as the expansion factor of PRG.

Indistinguishability Obfuscation ($i\mathcal{O}$). As a weakening solution to virtual black-box confusion, $i\mathcal{O}$ was first proposed by Barak et al. [2] in 2001 to ensure that any two circuits with the same functions are indistinguishable after confusion. More accurately:

Definition 2. *(Indistinguishability Obfuscation) A uniform PPT machine $i\mathcal{O}$ is called as an indistinguishability obfuscation for a circuit class $\{C_\lambda\}$ if the following two conditions are satisfied:*

1. *(Preserving functionality) For all security parameters $\lambda \in N$, all $C \in C_\lambda$, and all input x, the following formula holds.*

$$\Pr \big[C'(x) = C(x) : \ C' \leftarrow i\mathcal{O}(\lambda, C) \big] - 1.$$

2. *(Indistinguishability of obfuscation) For any PPT distinguisher $\mathcal{D}$, there exists a negligible function $negl(\lambda)$ of such that the following holds: for all security parameters $\lambda \in N$ and all pairs of circuits $C_0, C_1 \in C_\lambda$ with $|C_0| = |C_1|$, we have that if $C_0(x) = C_1(x)$ for all inputs x, then*

$$\Big| \Pr \big[\mathcal{D}(i\mathcal{O}(\lambda, C_0)) = 1 \big] - \Pr \big[\mathcal{D}(i\mathcal{O}(\lambda, C_1)) = 1 \big] \Big| \leq negl(\lambda).$$

Puncturable Pseudorandom Function (PPRF). As a class of simple constrained pseudorandom functions, PPRF was first presented by Sahai et al. [15] in 2014. Any PPT adversary is allowed to have a polynomial scale input set first. Even if the adversary is given a calculation key that can be used to compute all input function values besides the given set, it is difficult to distinguish between a value that is an input function value in the set and a random element of equal length. More precisely:

Definition 3. *(Puncturable Pseudorandom Function) A PRF $F: \mathcal{K} \times \{0,1\}^k \rightarrow \{0,1\}^m$ is a puncturable pseudorandom function if there is a key space $\mathcal{K}$, an additional punctured key space $\mathcal{K}_p$ and three polynomial time algorithms F.Key, F.Puncture and F.Eval as follows:*

1. *(Functionality preserved under puncturing)* For any PPT adversary $\mathcal{A}$ such that $\mathcal{A}(1^\lambda)$ outputs a set $S \subseteq \{0,1\}^{k(\lambda)}$, then for all $x \in \{0,1\}^{k(\lambda)}$ with $x \notin S$, we have that:

$$\Pr\left[F.Eval(K,x) = F.Eval(K(S),x) : \right.$$
$$\left. K \leftarrow F.Key(1^\lambda), K(S) \leftarrow F.Puncture(K,S)\right] = 1,$$

where $K \in \mathcal{K}$ and $K(S) \in \mathcal{K}_p$.

2. *(Pseudorandom at punctured points)* For any PPT adversary $(\mathcal{A}_1, \mathcal{A}_2)$ such that $\mathcal{A}_1(1^\lambda)$ outputs a set $S \subseteq \{0,1\}^{k(\lambda)}$, considering an experiment with $\forall x \in S$, $F.Eval(K,x) \in \{0,1\}^m$, $K \leftarrow F.Key(1^\lambda)$, and $K(S) \leftarrow F.Puncture(K,S)$, then we have

$$\left| \Pr\left[\mathcal{A}_2(K(S), x, F.Eval(K,x)) = 1\right] \right.$$
$$\left. - \Pr\left[\mathcal{A}_2(K(S), x, y \leftarrow \{0,1\}^m) = 1\right] \right| \leq negl(\lambda).$$

For ease of notation, $F.Eval(K,x)$ and $F.Puncture(K,S)$ are denoted by $F(K,x)$ and $K(S)$, respectively, in the following sections.

3   Updatable Public-Key Encryption and Enhanced Security Models

In this section, we now introduce the formal definition of updatable public-key encryption (UPKE) and the enhanced security models.

3.1   Formal Definition

Definition 4. *(Updatable Public-Key Encryption)* An updatable public-key encryption scheme for message space $\mathcal{M}$ consists of a tuple of efficient algorithms $\{UPKE.KeyGen, UPKE.Enc, UPKE.Dec, UPKE.TokGen, UPKE.Upd\}$ that operate at epochs. These algorithms are defined as:

- *UPKE.KeyGen$(1^\lambda) \rightarrow k_e = (PK_e, SK_e)$: Given a security parameter 1^λ, the key generation algorithm outputs a pair of keys (PK_e, SK_e).*
- *UPKE.Enc$(PK_e, m) \rightarrow C_e$: Given a public key PK_e and a message m, the encryption algorithm outputs a ciphertext C_e.*
- *UPKE.Dec$(SK_e, C_e) \rightarrow m/\bot$: Given a secret key SK_e and a ciphertext C_e, the decryption algorithm outputs a message m or $\bot$.*
- *UPKE.TokGen$(k_e, k_{e+1}) \rightarrow \Delta_{e+1}$: Given two keys k_e, k_{e+1}, the token generation algorithm outputs an update token Δ_{e+1}.*
- *UPKE.Upd$(\Delta_{e+1}, C_e) \rightarrow C_{e+1}$: Given a ciphertext C_e and an update token Δ_{e+1}, the update algorithm outputs an update ciphertext C_{e+1}.*

In the updatable public-key encryption scheme, the total number of epochs is a relatively small integer, and the integer T is specified as the maximum number of epochs.

Correctness. The correctness of an updatable public-key encryption scheme ensures that the update of a valid ciphertext C_e from epoch e to $e + 1$ yields a valid ciphertext C_{e+1}, which can be decrypted under the new epoch key SK_{e+1}.

More formally, for any message $m \in \mathcal{M}$, $1 \leq e_1 \leq e_2 \leq T$, it holds that

$$\Pr\left[UPKE.Dec(SK_{e_2}, C_{e_2}) \neq m\right] \leq negl(\lambda),$$

where $k_{e_1}, k_{e_1+1}, \cdots, k_{e_2-1}, k_{e_2} \leftarrow UPKE.KeyGen(1^\lambda)$, $k_i = (PK_i, SK_i)$, $C_{e_1} \leftarrow UPKE.Enc(PK_{e_1}, m)$, $\Delta_{i+1} \leftarrow UPKE.TokGen(k_i, k_{i+1})$ and $C_{i+1} \leftarrow UPKE.Upd$ (Δ_{i+1}, C_i), for $i \in [e_1, e_2-1]$.

3.2 Enhanced Security Models

In the typical IND-CPA definition of the existing updatable encryption schemes [6,11–14], the adversary $\mathcal{A}$ is granted to access to $\mathcal{O}.Next$, $\mathcal{O}.Upd(C_{e-1})$, $\mathcal{O}.Upd(l, C_{e^*}^*)$ and $\mathcal{O}.Corr$ oracles. To exclude the trivial winning, these existing definitions require that $\mathcal{A}$ has not learned the secret key at any challenge-equal epoch. In other words, it must hold that the leakage sets "$K^* \cap C^* = \emptyset$", i.e., the adversary can not query $\mathcal{O}.Corr$ oracle to corrupt the secret keys or tokens at some epochs.

In order to enhance the capabilities of the adversary, we allow the adversary to access to $\mathcal{O}.Corr$ oracle more freely. In the enhanced definition of $\mathcal{O}.Corr$ oracle, if the adversary requests to corrupt any token, the challenger returns a token at the corresponding epoch. When the adversary asks for a key corruption query, we will return a secret key under the condition that the corrupted secret key cannot decrypt the challenge and challenge-equal ciphertexts. In addition, an identifier $flag$ is used to record whether the adversary has issued a challenge query. We set $flag=1$ if the adversary has issued a challenge query, otherwise $flag=0$. Furthermore, l in $\mathcal{O}.Upd(l, C_{e^*}^*)$ is chosen by the adversary and its range should be larger than the challenge epoch e^* and smaller than the current epoch e. The available oracles are shown in Table 2.

The enhanced security models for updatable public-key encryption contain IND-ENC-CPA and IND-UE-CPA as formally defined in the following.

Encryption Indistinguishability (IND-ENC). The IND-ENC concept requires that the ciphertexts generated by the encryption algorithm $UPKE.Enc$ will not reveal anything about the underlying messages.

Definition 5. *(IND-ENC-CPA security) An updatable public-key encryption scheme is said to be IND-ENC-CPA iff for any PPT adversary $\mathcal{A}$ the advantage function*

$$Adv_{UPKE,\mathcal{A}}^{IND-ENC-CPA} = \left| \Pr[Exp_{UPKE,\mathcal{A}}^{IND-ENC-CPA} = 1] - \frac{1}{2} \right|$$

Table 2. The behavior of oracles in the confidentiality game

$\mathcal{O}.Next(\ )$:

$\quad e := e + 1$

$\quad k_e = (PK_e, SK_e) \xleftarrow{r} UPKE.KeyGen(1^\lambda)$

$\quad \Delta_e \leftarrow UPKE.TokGen(k_{e-1}, k_e)$

$\quad$ if $flag{=}1$ then

$\quad\quad C_e^* \leftarrow UPKE.Upd(\Delta_e, C_{e-1}^*)$

$\mathcal{O}.Corr(model, \hat{e})$:

$\quad$ if $\hat{e} > e$ then

$\quad\quad$ return $\perp$

$\quad$ if $model = key$ then

$\quad\quad$ return $SK_{\hat{e}}$

$\quad$ if $model = token$ then

$\quad\quad$ return $\Delta_{\hat{e}}$

$\mathcal{O}.Upd(C_{e-1})$:

$\quad$ if $UPKE.Dec(SK_{e-1}, C_{e-1}) = \perp$ then

$\quad\quad$ return $\perp$

$\quad$ else $\ C_e \leftarrow UPKE.Upd(\Delta_e, C_{e-1})$

$\quad\quad$ return C_e

$\mathcal{O}.Upd(l, C_{e^*}^*)$:

$\quad$ if $flag{=}0$ or $l > e$

$\quad\quad$ return $\perp$

$\quad$ if $UPKE.Dec(SK_{e^*}, C_{e^*}^*) = \perp$ then

$\quad\quad$ return $\perp$

$\quad C_{i-1}^* := C_{e^*}^*$

$\quad$ for $\ i = e^* + 1, \cdots, l$ do

$\quad\quad C_i^* \leftarrow UPKE.Upd(\Delta_i, C_{i-1}^*)$

$\quad$ return C_l^*

Table 3. The IND-ENC-CPA security notion for UPKE

$Exp_{UPKE,\mathcal{A}}^{IND-ENC-CPA}(1^\lambda)$:

$\quad (PK_1, SK_1) \xleftarrow{r} UPKE.KeyGen(1^\lambda)$

$\quad (m_0, m_1) \xleftarrow{r} \mathcal{A}^{\mathcal{O}.Next, \mathcal{O}.Corr, \mathcal{O}.Upd(C_{e-1})}(\lambda)$

$\quad e^* := e; \ flag := 1; \ b \xleftarrow{r} \{0,1\};$

$\quad$ if $|m_0| \neq |m_1|$ then

$\quad\quad$ return $\perp$

$\quad C^* \xleftarrow{r} UPKE.Enc(PK_{e^*}, m_b)$

$\quad b' \xleftarrow{r} \mathcal{A}^{\mathcal{O}.Next, \mathcal{O}.Corr, \mathcal{O}.Upd(C_{e-1}), \mathcal{O}.Upd(l, C_{e^*}^*)}(C^*, PK_{e^*})$

$\quad$ return 1 if $b' = b$ and the corrupted secret keys cannot decrypt the challenge and challenge-equal ciphertexts.

is negligible, where $Exp_{UPKE,\mathcal{A}}^{IND-ENC-CPA}$ is defined as Table 3.

Update Encryption Indistinguishability (IND-UE). The IND-UE notion ensures that the fresh ciphertext generated by the encryption algorithm *UPKE.Enc* is indistinguishable from the updated ciphertext generated by the updated algorithm *UPKE.Upd*.

Definition 6. *(IND-UE-CPA security) An updatable public-key encryption scheme is said to be IND-UE-CPA security iff for any valid PPT adversary $\mathcal{A}$ the advantage function*

$$Adv_{UPKE,\mathcal{A}}^{IND-UE-CPA} = \Big| \Pr[Exp_{UPKE,\mathcal{A}}^{IND-UE-CPA} = 1] - \frac{1}{2} \Big|$$

is negligible, where $Exp_{UPKE,\mathcal{A}}^{IND-UE-CPA}$ is defined as Table 4.

Table 4. The IND-UE-CPA security notion for UPKE

$Exp_{UPKE,\mathcal{A}}^{IND-UE-CPA}(1^\lambda):$

    $(PK_1, SK_1) \xleftarrow{r} UPKE.KeyGen(1^\lambda)$

    $(m, \bar{C}) \xleftarrow{r} \mathcal{A}^{O.Next, O.Corr, O.Upd(C_{e-1})}(\lambda)$

    $e^* := e; \quad flag := 1; \quad b \xleftarrow{r} \{0,1\};$

    if $\;UPKE.Dec(SK_{e^*-1}, \bar{C}) = \bot\;$ then

        return $\bot$

    if $\;b = 0\;$ then

        $C^* \xleftarrow{r} UPKE.Enc(PK_{e^*}, m)$

    else

        $C^* \xleftarrow{r} UPKE.Upd(\Delta_{e^*}, \bar{C})$

    $b' \xleftarrow{r} \mathcal{A}^{O.Next, O.Corr, O.Upd(C_{e-1}), O.Upd(l, C_{e^*}^*)}(C^*, PK_{e^*})$

    return 1 if $b' = b$ and the corrupted secret keys cannot decrypt

    the challenge and challenge-equal ciphertexts.

The above formal security models define the confidentiality of the fresh and updated ciphertexts. Furthermore, it is essential to consider the impact of the current key leakage on the confidentiality of the previous and future ciphertexts, i.e., forward security and backward security [13].

Forward Security. Forward security ensures that the leakage of the current key can not induce the decryption of the previous ciphertexts. That is to say, an adversary corrupts the key SK_j ($j > e^*$), but would have no advantage of decrypting any ciphertext at the epoch e^* even if he has also corrupted all the tokens from the epoch e^* to j.

Backward Security. Backward security guarantees that the leakage of the current key can not result in the future ciphertext decryption. If an adversary corrupts a secret key SK_i ($i < e^*$) and all the tokens from the epoch i to e^*, he would not gain any advantage of decrypting any ciphertext at the epoch e^*.

Simulating the Punctured Secret Keys in Security Proof. It needs to be emphasized that in the process of security proof the challenger or simulator will return a punctured secret key as a response to key corruption query. In fact, the functionality preserved under puncturing of puncturable pseudorandom function [15] can ensure that the normal secret key and the punctured secret key are indistinguishable. The details are as follows: the key of puncturable pseudorandom function is selected as the secret key, and the auxiliary information of the challenge and challenge-equal ciphertexts, i.e., the first element, is set as the punctured point of secret key. Then the punctured secret key can decrypt only the non-challenge ciphertexts, but not the challenge or challenge-equal ciphertexts. Thus the punctured secret key works as a normal secret key except for decrypting the challenge and challenge-equal ciphertexts.

Moreover, when the adversary requests a key corruption query in the enhanced security models, the challenger can directly return a punctured secret key at the corresponding epoch without the need of distinguishing whether the epoch is a non-challenge epoch or a challenge-equal epoch. For one thing, at the non-challenge epochs, the challenger can honestly simulate the key corruption oracle answer for the adversary by using the punctured secret keys, since the punctured secret keys at these epochs are not different from the normal secret keys. For another thing, the punctured secret keys at the challenge-equal epochs can be distributed to the adversary, which not only ensures that the challenge and challenge-equal ciphertexts cannot be decrypted in a trivial way, but also endows the adversary more power in accordance with the real world, i.e., learning some partial information about secret keys. Therefore, it is believed that the enhanced security models has the advantage over the existing models [6,11–14].

An Intuitive Example About Enhancement. To illustrate that the proposed security notion is stronger than the previous security notions [6,11–14], we give an intuitive example. Suppose the challenge epoch $e^* = 3$, $\mathcal{K}^* = \{1, 2, 5, 7\}$ and $\mathcal{T}^* = \{2, 3, 4, 6\}$. Furthermore assume that an adversary has queried $\mathcal{O}.Upd(6, C_3^*)$ oracle at the epoch 6, which means $\mathcal{C}^* = \{3, 4, 6\}$.

Epoch	1	2	e*	4	5	6	7	...
Keys	√	√	×	×	√	×	√	...
Tokens	√	√	√	×	√	×		...
Challenge ciphertexts	—	—	√	√	×	√	×	...

Fig. 2. An example of allowing an adversary to obtain the maximum information in Jiang's security model [11] for updatable encryption scheme with no-directional key updates and uni-directional ciphertext updates, where × and √ indicates that the keys/tokens/challenge ciphertexts are not corrupted and corrupted, respectively.

In the example depicted in Fig. 2, the difference between the proposed notions and previous notions is mainly embodied at the epochs 3, 4, 5, 6 and 7. In the previous security notions, the secret keys at the epochs 3, 4, and 6 were prohibited from corrupting by the adversary. However, in the proposed security notions, the challenger can return the corresponding punctured secret keys at the epochs 3, 4, and 6 to the adversary, which not only endows the adversary more attack capabilities, but also makes the adversary win hardly. Furthermore, the tokens at the epochs 5 and 7 need to be kept completely secret from the adversary in the existing notions, but these tokens can be distributed to the adversary in the proposed notions. These enhancements make the proposed notions more powerful. In short, the previous notions need leakage sets and the trivial winning conditions to eliminate the trivial winning of the adversaries in security games, while the proposed notions overcomes them by considering a corruption oracle that can return the punctured secret keys.

4   Construction of Updatable Public-Key Encryption

4.1   Scheme Description

Inspired with Sahai et al.'s scheme [15] and Nishimaki's scheme [14], we construct an updatable public-key encryption scheme with forward and backward security based on the classical ElGamal encryption [7] in this section. Let $F : \mathcal{K} \times \{0,1\}^{2\lambda} \to \mathbb{Z}_q$ be a puncturable PRF with key space $\mathcal{K}$, $PRG_1 : \{0,1\}^{\lambda} \to \{0,1\}^{2\lambda}$ be a pseudorandom generator, and $PRG_2 : \{0,1\}^{\lambda} \to \mathbb{Z}_q$ also be a pseudorandom generator. The proposed scheme is described as follows.

Table 5. The description of program $C_{enc}[K_e]$

Program 1 Encryption function $C_{enc}[K_e]$

Constant:

   A punctured *PRF* key K_e.

Input:

   A random seed $s_e \in \{0,1\}^{\lambda}$ and a message $m \in \mathbb{G}$.

   1)   Compute $t_e = PRG_1(s_e)$ and $r_e = PRG_2(s_e)$.

   2)   Compute $x_e = F(K_e, t_e)$ and $y_e = g^{x_e}$.

   3)   Compute $C_{e,1} = t_e$, $C_{e,2} = g^{r_e}$ and $C_{e,3} = y_e^{r_e} \cdot m$.

Output:

   A ciphertext $C_e = (C_{e,1}, C_{e,2}, C_{e,3})$.

Table 6. The description of program $C_{upd}[SK_e, PK_{e+1}, s_e^*, s_{e+1}^*]$

Program 2 Update function $C_{upd}[SK_e, PK_{e+1}, s_e^*, s_{e+1}^*]$

Constants:

   SK_e, PK_{e+1}, s_e^* and s_{e+1}^*.

Input:

   A ciphertext C_e and a fresh random seed $s_{e+1} \in \{0,1\}^{\lambda}$.

   1)   Parse $C_e = (C_{e,1}, C_{e,2}, C_{e,3})$.

   2)   Compute $x_e = F(SK_e, C_{e,1}) = F(SK_e, t_e)$.

   3)   Compute $m = \frac{C_{e,3}}{(C_{e,2})^{x_e}} = \frac{y_e^{r_e} \cdot m}{(g^{r_e})^{x_e}}$.

   4)   If $C_{e,1} \neq PRG_1(s_e^*)$, call the obfuscation program $i\mathcal{O}(C_{enc}[K_{e+1}])(s_{e+1}, m)$. Otherwise, call the obfuscation program $i\mathcal{O}(C_{enc}[K_{e+1}])(s_{e+1}^*, m)$ to receive the updated ciphertext $C_{e+1} = (C_{e+1,1}, C_{e+1,2}, C_{e+1,3})$.

Output:

   An updated ciphertext $C_{e+1} = (C_{e+1,1}, C_{e+1,2}, C_{e+1,3})$.

- **UPKE.KeyGen**(1^λ): Data user runs the group generation algorithm $\mathcal{G}(1^\lambda)$ to obtain $(\mathbb{G}, q, g)$, where $\mathbb{G}$ is a group of order q and g is a generator of $\mathbb{G}$. Data user chooses a key $K_e \in \mathcal{K}$ for puncturable pseudorandom function F and sets a distinguished tag t_e^* as the punctured point, where $s_e^* \in \{0,1\}^\lambda$ is chosen at random and $t_e^* = PRG_1(s_e^*)$. Finally, data user generates an obfuscation of the program $C_{enc}[K_e]$ described in Table 5, where the notation $[K_e]$ indicates that K_e is fixed constant. The secret key SK_e is K_e, and the corresponding public key PK_e is implied by the obfuscation program $i\mathcal{O}(C_{enc}[K_e])$ and not outputted explicitly.

- **UPKE.Enc**(PK_e, m): For the current epoch e and a message $m \in \mathbb{G}$, data owner chooses a random seed $s_e \in \{0,1\}^\lambda$, and then runs the obfuscation program $i\mathcal{O}(C_{enc}[K_e])$ on input $s_e \in \{0,1\}^\lambda$ and $m \in \mathbb{G}$ to obtain a ciphertext $C_e = (C_{e,1} = t_e, C_{e,2} = g^{r_e}, C_{e,3} = y_e^{r_e} \cdot m)$. That is, $C_e \leftarrow i\mathcal{O}(C_{enc}[K_e])(s_e, m)$, where the program $C_{enc}[K_e]$ is described in Table 5. Finally, data owner outputs a ciphertext $C_e = (C_{e,1}, C_{e,2}, C_{e,3})$ to cloud server.

- **UPKE.Dec**(SK_e, C_e): For the current epoch e and the ciphertext $C_e = (C_{e,1}, C_{e,2}, C_{e,3})$, data user firstly computes $x_e \leftarrow F(SK_e, C_{e,1})$ on input the secret key SK_e and the partial ciphertext $C_{e,1}$, and then recovers the message

$$\frac{C_{e,3}}{(C_{e,2})^{x_e}} = \frac{y_e^{r_e} \cdot m}{(g^{r_e})^{x_e}} = m.$$

- **UPKE.TokGen**(SK_e, PK_{e+1}): On input a secret key SK_e at the epoch e and a public key PK_{e+1} at the next epoch $e+1$, data user computes an update token Δ_{e+1} for the epoch $e+1$. The token Δ_{e+1} is implied by the obfuscation program $i\mathcal{O}(C_{upd}[SK_e, PK_{e+1}, s_e^*, s_{e+1}^*])$ and not outputted explicitly, where the program $C_{upd}[SK_e, PK_{e+1}, s_e^*, s_{e+1}^*]$ is described in Table 6, and the notation $[SK_e, PK_{e+1}, s_e^*, s_{e+1}^*]$ indicates that SK_e, PK_{e+1}, s_e^* and s_{e+1}^* are fixed constants.

- **UPKE.Upd**(Δ_{e+1}, C_e): Cloud server firstly chooses a fresh random seed $s_{e+1} \in \{0,1\}^\lambda$, and then runs the obfuscation program $i\mathcal{O}(C_{upd}[SK_e, PK_{e+1}, s_e^*, s_{e+1}^*])(C_e, s_{e+1})$ to obtain an updated ciphertext $C_{e+1} = (C_{e+1,1}, C_{e+1,2}, C_{e+1,3})$, where the program $C_{upd}[SK_e, PK_{e+1}, s_e^*, s_{e+1}^*]$ is described in Table 6. Finally, the cloud server outputs the updated ciphertext $C_{e+1} = (C_{e+1,1}, C_{e+1,2}, C_{e+1,3})$.

Remarks on the Construction. It is necessary to emphasize that indistinguishable obfuscation plays a crucial role in the proposed updatable public-key encryption scheme. In this paper, we believe that efficient $i\mathcal{O}$ [8] would make the proposed updatable public-key encryption scheme more sense. The important ideas behind our approach contain two obfuscated programs as follows.

1) The first program is an obfuscation of the program $C_{enc}[K_e]$. The obfuscated program $i\mathcal{O}(C_{enc}[K_e])$ plays a role of generating a public key. Data user randomly chooses a secret key K_e that is embedded into the program $C_{enc}[\cdot]$. After obfuscation, the program $i\mathcal{O}(C_{enc}[K_e])$ can be reviewed as the public

key PK_e corresponding to the secret key K_e, and would not reveal any information about the secret key. Furthermore, on input of a random seed s_e and a message m, $i\mathcal{O}(C_{enc}[K_e])(\cdot, \cdot)$ is used to encrypt the message and outputs a corresponding ciphertext. In a brief, data owner receives the obfuscated program $i\mathcal{O}(C_{enc}[K_e])$, and then can encrypt any message.

2) The second program is an obfuscation of the program $C_{upd}[SK_e, PK_{e+1}, s_e^*, s_{e+1}^*]$. The obfuscated program $i\mathcal{O}(SK_e, PK_{e+1}, s_e^*, s_{e+1}^*)$ is executed to generate an update token. Data user only need to subtly embed SK_e, PK_{e+1}, s_e^* and s_{e+1}^* into $C_{upd}[\cdot, \cdot, \cdot, \cdot]$, which is obfuscated to output an update token Δ_{e+1} implicitly. The obfuscation program would not reveal any information about SK_e and SK_{e+1}. Furthermore, $i\mathcal{O}(C_{upd}[SK_e, PK_{e+1}, s_e^*, s_{e+1}^*])(C_e, s_{e+1})$ plays a role of updating a ciphertext C_e at the epoch e to a ciphertext C_{e+1} at the epoch $e + 1$. Concisely, cloud server can utilize the obfuscation program $i\mathcal{O}(C_{upd}[SK_e, PK_{e+1}, s_e^*, s_{e+1}^*])(C_e, s_{e+1})$ to obtain a "new" ciphertext C_{e+1} at the epoch $e + 1$.

4.2   Correctness and Directionality

In this section, we will analyze the correctness and directionality of the proposed scheme, including the update direction of key and ciphertext.

Correctness. It is easy to see that the proposed updatable encryption scheme satisfies correctness. To check the decryption success, let $C_e = (C_{e,1} = t_e, C_{e,2} = g^{r_e}, C_{e,3} = y_e^{r_e} \cdot m)$ with $y_e = g^{x_e}$, and then

$$\bar{m} = \frac{C_{e,3}}{(C_{e,2})^{F(K_e, C_{e,1})}} = \frac{C_{e,3}}{(C_{e,2})^{x_e}} = \frac{y_e^{r_e} \cdot m}{(g^{r_e})^{x_e}} = m.$$

Furthermore, the output of the update algorithm $UPKE.Upd(\Delta_{e+1}, C_e)$ is exactly the same as that of the encryption algorithm $UPKE.Enc(PK_{e+1}, m)$. Thus, the correctness of the updated ciphertext decryption also holds.

No-Directional Key Updates. How the tokens are generated determines the update direction of key. In the proposed scheme, the secret key SK_e and the public key PK_{e+1} are subtly embedded in the token by using of the indistinguishable obfuscation technique on the punctured program. Even if the secret key are used to generate the token, it is difficult to infer the relevant key from the token. Intuitively, given the secret key SK_e (resp.SK_{e+1}) and token Δ_{e+1}, there is no way to infer SK_{e+1} (resp.SK_e) due to the obfuscation security. Therefore, in terms of update direction of key, the proposed scheme can implement no-directional key updates.

Uni-Directional Ciphertext Updates. The update direction of ciphertext depends on how the tokens are generated. In the proposed scheme, the token Δ_{e+1} is implied by the obfuscation program $i\mathcal{O}(C_{upd}[SK_e, PK_{e+1}, s_e^*, s_{e+1}^*])$ and not outputted explicitly. The update program $C_{upd}[SK_e, PK_{e+1}, s_e^*, s_{e+1}^*]$ will update a ciphertext from the epoch e to $e + 1$, which is essentially based on the idea of re-encryption. That is to say, firstly decrypt C_e with SK_e to recover the message m, and then re-encrypt m with PK_{e+1} to obtain C_{e+1}. Generally, the re-encryption technique would leak the message m to the cloud server. To avoid the leakage, $i\mathcal{O}$ technique is used to obfuscate the program $C_{upd}[SK_e, PK_{e+1}, s_e^*, s_{e+1}^*]$, and the ciphertext C_e can be updated to C_{e+1}. On the other hand, since the generation of the token Δ_{e+1} does not contain the secret key SK_{e+1}, the token Δ_{e+1} cannot be used to decrypt and convert the ciphertext at the epoch $e + 1$. Therefore, in terms of update direction of ciphertext, the proposed scheme can achieve uni-directional ciphertext updates.

In 2020, Jiang [11] came to the shocking conclusion: the combination of no-directional key updates and uni-directional ciphertext updates is strictly stronger than other variants of the same confidentiality notion. In *BLMR* [5], *RISE* [13], *E&M* [12], *NYUE* [12], *SHINE* [6] and *LWEPKE* [11] schemes, neither no-directional key updates nor uni-directional ciphertext updates can be achieved since the token is generated from the old and new epoch secret keys. Although the $UE_{i\mathcal{O}}$ scheme proposed by Nishimaki [14] can realize no-directional key updates and uni-directional ciphertext updates, it is an updatable symmetric encryption scheme that is only applies to the single-user scenario. However, the proposed scheme is an updatable public-key encryption scheme with no-directional key updates and uni-directional ciphertext updates. Therefore, in terms of the update direction, the proposed scheme has achieved the most desirable goal.

5   Security Analysis

5.1   Confidentiality

In this section, the confidentiality of the proposed scheme can be guaranteed in the following theorems.

Theorem 1. *If PRG_1 and PRG_2 are secure pseudorandom generators, $i\mathcal{O}$ is a secure indistinguishable obfuscator, and F is a secure puncturable pseudorandom function, then the proposed updatable ElGamal encryption scheme is IND-ENC-CPA.*

Theorem 2. *Let $UPKE = \{UPKE.KeyGen, UPKE.TokGen, UPKE.Enc, UPKE.Dec, UPKE.Upd\}$ be an updatable public-key encryption scheme. For any IND-ENC-CPA adversary $\mathcal{A}$ against UPKE, there exists an IND-UE-CPA adversary $\mathcal{B}$ against UPKE such that*

$$Adv_{UPKE,\mathcal{B}}^{IND-UE-CPA}(\lambda) \leq Adv_{UPKE,\mathcal{A}}^{IND-ENC-CPA}(\lambda).$$

Combining Theorem 1 and Theorem 2, we can get the following conclusion: if PRG_1 and PRG_2 are secure pseudorandom generators, $i\mathcal{O}$ is an indistinguishable obfuscator, and F is a secure puncturable pseudorandom function, then the proposed scheme is IND-CPA. The proofs of Theorems 1 and 2 are provided in Appendix A and Appendix B, respectively.

5.2   Forward and Backward Security

In this section, the forward and backward security of the proposed scheme is analyzed below.

Forward Security. Now assume that the adversary corrupts the secret key SK_{e^*+1} and the update token Δ_{e^*+1}. There exist two cases to be considered.

1) The update direction of key is no-directional, so the key SK_{e^*+1} cannot be degraded to SK_{e^*}.
2) The adversary can update the challenge ciphertext to the next epoch by using the token Δ_{e^*+1}. However, the key SK_{e^*+1} corrupted by the adversary is a punctured key or semi-functional key, which can only be used to decrypt the non-challenge ciphertexts at the epoch e^*+1, but cannot be used to correctly decrypt the challenge ciphertext at the epoch e^*+1. Therefore, decrypting the challenge-equal ciphertext at the epoch e^*+1 is just as difficult as decrypting the challenge ciphertext in epoch e^*.

And so on, the adversary who corrupts the key SK_j $(j > e^*)$ will gain no advantage in decrypting the challenge ciphertext at the epoch e^* even if he also corrupts all tokens from epoch e^* to j. Since the adversary can corrupt keys at any epoch, the right firewall in the green box in Fig. 1 is no longer needed, which makes the proposed scheme easily achieve forward security.

Backward Security. Now assume that the adversary corrupts the secret key SK_{e^*-1} and the update token Δ_{e^*}. There exist also two cases to be considered.

1) The update direction of key is no-directional, so the key SK_{e^*-1} cannot be updated to SK_{e^*}.
2) The update direction of ciphertext is uni-directional, so the ciphertext $C_{e^*}^*$ cannot be degraded to $C_{e^*-1}^*$.

By analogy, the adversary corrupts a secret key SK_i $(i < e^*)$ and all tokens from epoch i to e^*, but he would not gain any advantage in decrypting the challenge ciphertext at the challenge epoch e^*. Since the tokens can not upgrade keys and degrade ciphertexts, we can immediately remove the left firewall, where all the keys and tokens in the blue box in Fig. 1 can be distributed to the adversary. Therefore, the proposed scheme cab cleverly realize backward security by utilizing update direction.

6   Conclusions

We have proposed an updatable ElGamal encryption scheme with no-directional key updates and uni-directional ciphertext updates. At the same time, the proposed scheme can achieve forward security and backward security efficiently by modifying the token and corruption oracle. Furthermore, we gave a brief comparison between the proposed scheme and some outstanding schemes in terms of directionality and security, which shows that the proposed scheme has significant advantages. The proposed scheme utilized a complicated $i\mathcal{O}$ tool, so how to construct an efficiently and securely updatable public-key encryption scheme is an interesting research direction in the future.

A   Security Proof of Theorem 1

Proof. In order to ensure that the proof process is clear, the proof of experimental sequence method is given here. Let $\mathcal{A}$ be a probabilistic polynomial-time adversary and the challenge epoch be e^*. Note that the successful events of the adversary $\mathcal{A}$ in experiment **Expt**$_i$ are denoted as $Suc_i (i = 0, 1, 2, 3)$.

Expt$_0$: The first experiment corresponds to the original IND-ENC-CPA security experiment.

1) K_{e^*} is picked as the key for a puncturable pseudorandom function F. A distinguished tag $t_{e^*}^* = PRG_1(s_{e^*}^*)$ is set as the punctured point, where $s_{e^*}^* \in \{0,1\}^\lambda$ is chosen at random. The public key PK_{e^*} is implied by the obfuscation program $i\mathcal{O}(C_{enc}[K_{e^*}])$. The secret key SK_{e^*} is K_{e^*}.
2) After receiving PK_{e^*}, the adversary $\mathcal{A}$ can access a series of oracles $\mathcal{O}.Next$, $\mathcal{O}.Corr$ and $\mathcal{O}.Upd(C_{e-1})$, and then output a pair of messages $m_0, m_1 \in \mathbb{G}$ with the same length to the challenger.
3) The challenger runs the obfuscation program $i\mathcal{O}(C_{enc}[K_{e^*}])$ on input a seed $s_{e^*}^* \in \{0,1\}^\lambda$ and a message $m_b \in \mathbb{G}$ to generate a challenge ciphertext $C_{e^*}^*$, where $b \in \{0,1\}$ is chosen at random. Then $C_{e^*}^*$ is given to the adversary $\mathcal{A}$.
4) The adversary $\mathcal{A}$ can continue to access the $\mathcal{O}.Next$, $\mathcal{O}.Corr$, $\mathcal{O}.Upd(C_{e-1})$ and $\mathcal{O}.Upd(l, C_{e^*}^*)$ oracles. Finally, $\mathcal{A}$ outputs a bit $b' \in \{0,1\}$.

Expt$_1$: This experiment is identical to the experiment **Expt$_0$** except for one difference. The only difference is that the first part of the challenge ciphertext $C_{e^*,1} = t_{e^*}^*$, i.e., $t_{e^*}^* = PRG_1(s_{e^*}^*)$ is replaced by $t_{e^*}^*$ chosen randomly in $\{0,1\}^{2\lambda}$. The following fact can be obtained and will be proved subsequently.

Fact 1. The difference in probability between the event Suc_0 and the event Suc_1 is a negligible function.

Expt$_2$: This experiment is identical to the experiment **Expt$_1$** except for one difference. The only difference is that the second element of the challenge ciphertext $C_{e^*,2} = g^{r_{e^*}^*}$, i.e., $r_{e^*}^* = PRG_2(s_{e^*}^*)$ is replaced by $r_{e^*}^* \in \mathbb{Z}_q$. Note that $s_{e^*}^*$ no longer appears in the adversary's view and does not need to be generated. The following fact can be obtained and will be proved subsequently.

Fact 2. The difference in probability between the event Suc_1 and the event Suc_2 is a negligible function.

Expt$_3$: This experiment is identical to the experiment **Expt$_2$** except for one difference. The difference is that the public key PK_{e^*} is simply replaced with $\widetilde{PK}_{e^*}$ implicitly in the obfuscation program $i\mathcal{O}(\widetilde{C}_{enc}[K_{e^*}(\{t_{e^*}^*\})])$, where the program $\widetilde{C}_{enc}[K_{e^*}(\{t_{e^*}^*\})]$ is described in Table 7. Note that, the program $\widetilde{C}_{enc}[K_{e^*}(\{t_{e^*}^*\})]$ in Table 7 has the same functionality as the program $C_{enc}[K_{e^*}]$ in Table 5, except that the fixed constant K_{e^*} is replaced by $K_{e^*}(\{t_{e^*}^*\})$. The following fact can be obtained and will be proved subsequently.

Fact 3. The difference in probability between the event Suc_2 and the event Suc_3 is a negligible function.

Table 7. The description of program $\widetilde{C}_{enc}\big[K_{e^*}(\{t_{e^*}^*\})\big]$

Program 3 Encryption function $\widetilde{C}_{enc}\big[K_{e^*}(\{t_{e^*}^*\})\big]$

Constants:

A punctured F key $K_{e^*}(\{t_{e^*}^*\})$.

Input:

A random seed $s_{e^*} \in \{0,1\}^\lambda$ and a message $m \in \mathbb{G}$.

1) Compute $t_{e^*} = PRG_1(s_{e^*})$ and $r_{e^*} = PRG_2(s_{e^*})$.
2) Compute $x_{e^*} = F\big(K_{e^*}(\{t_{e^*}^*\}), t_{e^*}\big)$ and $y_{e^*} = g^{x_{e^*}}$.
3) Compute $C_{e^*,1} = t_{e^*}$, $C_{e^*,2} = g^{r_{e^*}}$ and $C_{e^*,3} = y_{e^*}^{r_{e^*}} \cdot m$.

Output:

A ciphertext $C_{e^*} = (C_{e^*,1}, C_{e^*,2}, C_{e^*,3})$.

Expt$_4$: This experiment is identical to the experiment **Expt$_3$** except for one difference. The difference is that the third part of the challenge ciphertext $C_{e^*}^* = (C_{e^*,1}^* = t_{e^*}^*, C_{e^*,2}^* = g^{r_{e^*}^*}, C_{e^*,3}^* = g^{z \cdot r_{e^*}^*} \cdot m_b)$ is modified, where $z \xleftarrow{r} \mathbb{G}$. The following facts can be obtained and will be proved subsequently.

Fact 4. The difference in probability between event Suc_3 and event Suc_4 is a negligible function.

Fact 5. The probability of the event Suc_4 is $\frac{1}{2}$.

The combination of all the above facts leads to the desired conclusion. Let's start proving each of these facts.

Proof of Fact 1. We argue that the probability difference between the event Suc_0 and the event Suc_1 is a negligible function. Otherwise, an algorithm $\mathcal{B}_1$ can be constructed to break the security of the pseudorandom generator PRG_1. $\mathcal{B}_1$ runs the experiment **Expt$_0$** as a challenger and receives a PRG_1 challenge a. Except for setting $t_{e^*}^* = a$, it continues to run the rest of experiment **Expt$_0$**. There exist two cases to be considered:

1) If a is the output of PRG_1, the random variables observed by $\mathcal{A}$ in the algorithm $\mathcal{B}_1$ are distributed identically with those observed in **Expt$_0$**.
2) If a is a random string, the random variables observed by $\mathcal{A}$ in the algorithm $\mathcal{B}_1$ are distributed identically with those observed in **Expt$_1$**.

$\mathcal{B}_1$ outputs exactly 1 when the output b' of $\mathcal{A}$ is equal to b. Since PRG_1 is a secure pseudorandom generator, there exists a negligible function $negl_1(\lambda)$ such that

$$\big|\Pr[Suc_0] - \Pr[Suc_1]\big| = Adv_{\mathcal{B}_1}^{PRG_1} \le negl_1(\lambda). \tag{1}$$

Proof of Fact 2. Similar to the proof of **Fact 1**, we argue that the probability difference between events Suc_1 and Suc_2 is a negligible function. Otherwise, an algorithm $\mathcal{B}_2$ can be constructed to break the security of the pseudorandom generator PRG_2. Therefore, there exists a negligible function $negl_2(\lambda)$ such that

$$\big|\Pr[Suc_1] - \Pr[Suc_2]\big| = Adv_{\mathcal{B}_2}^{PRG_2} \le negl_2(\lambda). \tag{2}$$

Proof of Fact 3. When t_{e*}^* is selected randomly, the input and output behaviors of PK_{e*} and $\widetilde{PK}_{e*}$ are almost identical. Note that, t_{e*}^* is in the range of PRG_1 with probability at most $1/2^\lambda$. If t_{e*}^* is not in the range of PRG_1, the programs PK_{e*} and $\widetilde{PK}_{e*}$ have identical functionality. Therefore, the probabilities of the event Suc_2 and the event Suc_3 must be negligibly close. Otherwise, we can construct an algorithm $\mathcal{B}_3$ that breaks the indistinguishable security of obfuscator. $\mathcal{B}_3$ runs the experiment as a challenger and receives an obfuscation program as a challenge. There exist two cases to be considered:

1) If the challenger chooses PK_{e*}, the observation of $\mathcal{A}$ in the algorithm $\mathcal{B}_3$ and that of $\mathcal{A}$ in experiment **Expt**$_2$ are identically distributed.
2) If the challenger chooses $\widetilde{PK}_{e*}$, the observation of $\mathcal{A}$ in the algorithm $\mathcal{B}_3$ and that of $\mathcal{A}$ in experiment **Expt**$_3$ are identically distributed.

$\mathcal{B}_3$ outputs exactly 1 when the output b' of $\mathcal{A}$ is equal to b. Since iO is a secure indistinguishable obfuscator, there exists a negligible function $negl_3(\lambda)$ such that
$$\left| \Pr[Suc_2] - \Pr[Suc_3] \right| = Adv_{\mathcal{B}_3}^{iO} \leq negl_3(\lambda). \tag{3}$$

Proof of Fact 4. If $\mathcal{A}$ can distinguish **Expt**$_3$ from **Expt**$_4$, then we can build an algorithm $\mathcal{B}_4$ to break the selective security of the puncturable pseudorandom function F at the punctured points. $\mathcal{B}_4$ runs the experiment **Expt**$_3$ as a challenger and receives a challenge c. It continues to run the rest of experiment **Expt**$_3$ in addition to creating the challenge ciphertext as $C_{e*}^* = (t_{e*}^*, g^{r_{e*}^*}, g^{c \cdot r_{e*}^*} \cdot m_b)$. There are two cases to be considered:

1) If c is the output of F at point t_{e*}^*, the random variables observed by $\mathcal{A}$ in the algorithm $\mathcal{B}_4$ are identically distributed as those seen in **Expt**$_3$.
2) If c is chosen at random, the ciphertext obtained by $\mathcal{A}$ in the algorithm $\mathcal{B}_4$ is distributed identically with that in **Expt**$_4$.

$\mathcal{B}_4$ outputs exactly 1 when the output b' of $\mathcal{A}$ is equal to b. Note that, we are able to reduce to selective security since t_{e*}^* is randomly selected by the challenger before the adversary receives the puncturable key $K_{e*}(\{t_{e*}^*\})$, which is not controlled by the adversary. Since F is a secure puncturable pseudorandom function, there exists a negligible function $negl_4(\lambda)$ such that
$$\left| \Pr[Suc_3] - \Pr[Suc_4] \right| = Adv_{\mathcal{B}_4}^{F} \leq negl_4(\lambda). \tag{4}$$

Proof of Fact 5. In the experiment **Expt**$_4$, the challenge ciphertext received by the adversary is a random element, which is independent of m_b. Therefore, the success probability of the adversary in this experiment is $1/2$. That is,
$$\Pr[Suc_4] = \frac{1}{2}. \tag{5}$$

Combining with equations (1)–(5), we have

$$Adv_{UPKE,\mathcal{A}}^{IND\text{-}ENC\text{-}CPA}(\lambda) = \left| \Pr[Suc_0] - \frac{1}{2} \right|$$

$$\leq \sum_{i=0}^{3} \left| \Pr[Suc_i] - \Pr[Suc_{i+1}] \right|$$

$$\leq negl_1(\lambda) + negl_2(\lambda) + negl_3(\lambda) + negl_4(\lambda).$$

B   Security Proof of Theorem 2

Proof. We construct an adversary $\mathcal{B}$ running the IND-UE-CPA experiment, which is used to simulate the response of queries made by the IND-ENC-CPA adversary $\mathcal{A}$. In order to provide a valid challenge query, $\mathcal{B}$ must keep $\mathcal{A}$ out of step with his game. As far as $\mathcal{A}$ is concerned, the epoch 1 is actually the epoch 2 of $\mathcal{B}$, and so on. The configuration of $\mathcal{B}$ is as follows:

1) $\mathcal{B}$ receives the setup parameters from its own challenger, chooses a message m from the message space $\mathbb{G}$, and encrypts this message with PK_1 to obtain a ciphertext C_1. Then $\mathcal{B}$ calls $\mathcal{O}.Next$ oracle to advance for an epoch and finally sends the setup parameters to $\mathcal{A}$.

2) When $\mathcal{A}$ queries $\mathcal{O}.Upd(C_{e-1})$ and $\mathcal{O}.Corr$ oracles, $\mathcal{B}$ sends these queries to its own challenger and returns the corresponding results to $\mathcal{A}$. Whenever $\mathcal{O}.Next$ oracle is called by $\mathcal{A}$, $\mathcal{B}$ randomly chooses a message $m \in \mathbb{G}$ and encrypts this message with PK_e to receive a ciphertext C_e, and then calls $\mathcal{O}.Next$ oracle.

3) At the epoch e^*, $\mathcal{A}$ issues a challenge query (m_0, m_1). $\mathcal{B}$ randomly selects $b \xleftarrow{r} \{0,1\}$ and sends (m_b, C_{e^*-1}) to its challenger as its challenge query. After receiving the challenge ciphertext $C_{e^*}^*$ from its challenger, $\mathcal{B}$ then sends it to $\mathcal{A}$.

4) $\mathcal{B}$ continues to answer $\mathcal{A}$'s queries using its own oracles, now including $\mathcal{O}.Upd(l, C_{e^*}^*)$ oracle.

5) Finally, $\mathcal{A}$ makes a guess and outputs the guess b' to the adversary $\mathcal{B}$. If $b = b'$, $\mathcal{B}$ returns $\delta' = 0$. Otherwise $\mathcal{B}$ outputs $\delta' = 1$.

$\mathcal{B}$ runs in polynomial time since $\mathcal{A}$ does. Here $\delta \in \{0,1\}$ represents the bit selected when generating the challenge ciphertext in the IND-UE-CPA experiment. There exist two cases to be considered.

1) If the challenge ciphertext $C_{e^*-1}^*$ received by $\mathcal{B}$ is the encryption of message m_b, i.e., $\delta = 0$, $\mathcal{B}$ succeeds if and only if $\mathcal{A}$ succeeds.

2) If the challenge ciphertext $C_{e^*}^*$ received by $\mathcal{B}$ is an update of the ciphertext C_{e^*-1}, i.e., $\delta = 1$, $\mathcal{B}$ wins with a probability of $1/2$.

Furthermore, we can easily bound the success probability of the adversary $\mathcal{B}$ in the experimental IND-UE-CPA.

$$
\begin{aligned}
Adv_{UPKE,\mathcal{B}}^{IND-UE-CPA}(\lambda) &= \left| \Pr[Exp_{UPKE,\mathcal{B}}^{IND-UE-CPA} = 1] - \frac{1}{2} \right| = \left| \Pr[\delta' = \delta] - \frac{1}{2} \right| \\
&= \left| \Pr\left[(\delta' = \delta) \wedge \delta = 0\right] + Pr\left[(\delta' = \delta) \wedge \delta = 1\right] - \frac{1}{2} \right| \\
&= \frac{1}{2} \cdot \left| \Pr[\delta' = \delta | \delta = 0] + \Pr[\delta' = \delta | \delta = 1] - 1 \right| \\
&= \frac{1}{2} \cdot \left| \Pr[b' = b | \delta = 0] + \Pr[b' \neq b | \delta = 1] - 1 \right| \\
&= \frac{1}{2} \cdot \left| \Pr[b' = b | \delta = 0] - \Pr[b' = b | \delta = 1] \right| \\
&= \frac{1}{2} \cdot Adv_{UPKE,\mathcal{A}}^{IND-ENC-CPA}.
\end{aligned}
$$

References

1. Ananth, P., Cohen, A., Jain, A.: Cryptography with updates. In: Coron, J.-S., Nielsen, J.B. (eds.) EUROCRYPT 2017. LNCS, vol. 10211, pp. 445–472. Springer, Cham (2017). https://doi.org/10.1007/978-3-319-56614-6_15
2. Barak, B., et al.: On the (Im)possibility of obfuscating programs. In: Kilian, J. (ed.) CRYPTO 2001. LNCS, vol. 2139, pp. 1–18. Springer, Heidelberg (2001). https://doi.org/10.1007/3-540-44647-8_1
3. Barker, E., Dang, Q.: NIST special publication 800–57 part 1, revision 4: recommendation for key management. NIST, Technical report 16 (2016)
4. Bellare, M., Goldreich, O., Goldwasser, S.: Incremental cryptography: the case of hashing and signing. In: Desmedt, Y.G. (ed.) CRYPTO 1994. LNCS, vol. 839, pp. 216–233. Springer, Heidelberg (1994). https://doi.org/10.1007/3-540-48658-5_22
5. Boneh, D., Lewi, K., Montgomery, H., Raghunathan, A.: Key homomorphic PRFs and their applications. In: Canetti, R., Garay, J.A. (eds.) CRYPTO 2013. LNCS, vol. 8042, pp. 410–428. Springer, Heidelberg (2013). https://doi.org/10.1007/978-3-642-40041-4_23
6. Boyd, C., Davies, G.T., Gjøsteen, K., Jiang, Y.: Fast and secure updatable encryption. In: Micciancio, D., Ristenpart, T. (eds.) CRYPTO 2020. LNCS, vol. 12170, pp. 464–493. Springer, Cham (2020). https://doi.org/10.1007/978-3-030-56784-2_16
7. ElGamal, T.: A public key cryptosystem and a signature scheme based on discrete logarithms. IEEE Trans. Inf. Theory 31(4), 469–472 (1985)
8. Gay, R., Jain, A., Lin, H., Sahai, A.: Indistinguishability obfuscation from simple-to-state hard problems: new assumptions, new techniques, and simplification. In: Canteaut, A., Standaert, F.-X. (eds.) EUROCRYPT 2021. LNCS, vol. 12698, pp. 97–126. Springer, Cham (2021). https://doi.org/10.1007/978-3-030-77883-5_4
9. Håstad, J., Impagliazzo, R., Levin, L.A., Luby, M.: A pseudorandom generator from any one-way function. SIAM J. Comput. 28(4), 1364–1396 (1999)
10. Industry, P.C.: Data security standard. Requirements Secur. Assess. Version 3 (2010)
11. Jiang, Y.: The direction of updatable encryption does not matter much. In: Moriai, S., Wang, H. (eds.) ASIACRYPT 2020. LNCS, vol. 12493, pp. 529–558. Springer, Cham (2020). https://doi.org/10.1007/978-3-030-64840-4_18

12. Klooß, M., Lehmann, A., Rupp, A.: (R)CCA secure updatable encryption with integrity protection. In: Ishai, Y., Rijmen, V. (eds.) EUROCRYPT 2019. LNCS, vol. 11476, pp. 68–99. Springer, Cham (2019). https://doi.org/10.1007/978-3-030-17653-2_3

13. Lehmann, A., Tackmann, B.: Updatable encryption with post-compromise security. In: Nielsen, J.B., Rijmen, V. (eds.) EUROCRYPT 2018. LNCS, vol. 10822, pp. 685–716. Springer, Cham (2018). https://doi.org/10.1007/978-3-319-78372-7_22

14. Nishimaki, R.: The direction of updatable encryption does matter. In: Hanaoka, G., Shikata, J., Watanabe, Y. (eds.) PKC 2022. LNCS, vol. 13178, pp. 194–224. Springer, Cham (2022). https://doi.org/10.1007/978-3-030-97131-1_7

15. Sahai, A., Waters, B.: How to use indistinguishability obfuscation: deniable encryption, and more. SIAM J. Comput. **50**(3), 857–908 (2021)

Database Security

A Comparative Analysis of Security Features and Concerns in NoSQL Databases

Evans Ankomah[1], Charles Roland Haruna[2]([✉]),
Francis Xavier Kofi Akotoye[2], Brighter Agyemang[3],
Kwame Opuni-Boachie Obour Agyekum[4], Alexander Asante[5],
Lawrence Ephrim[2], and Alexander N. T. Kissiedu[1]

[1] Information and Technology Training and Support Section,
University of Cape Coast, Cape Coast, Ghana
{evans.ankomah,alexander.kissiedu}@ucc.edu.gh
[2] Department of Computer Science and Information Technology,
University of Cape Coast, Cape Coast, Ghana
{charuna,fakotoye}@ucc.edu.gh
[3] School of Computing and Information Technology, University of Wollongong,
Wollongong, Australia
brighter@uow.edu.au
[4] Department of Telecommunication Engineering, Kwame Nkrumah University
of Science and Technology, Kumasi, Ghana
kooagyekum@knust.edu.gh
[5] Network and Infrastructure Section, University of Cape Coast, Cape Coast, Ghana
alex.asante@ucc.edu.gh

Abstract. Current developments in cloud computing and also distributed internet applications have produced the demand to store huge quantities of data in dispersed databases that offer high availability and scalability. Over the last few years, increasingly more firms are adopting various sorts of non-relational data sources, frequently described as NoSQL data sources. By definition, NoSQL systems are not relational and also do not provide full SQL capabilities. Moreover, unlike relational databases, it uses consistency and security in exchange for performance and scalability. Security issues end up being more important as a growing number of sensitive data is kept in NoSQL databases.

This article, therefore, examines the security features in four of the most preferred NoSQL databases; Cassandra, MongoDB, Redis and Neo4j, one from each category of databases. Unlike in most survey literature on NoSQL security features, that comparisons made excluded the graph database Neo4j, it is inclusive in this work, which makes this survey unique from others. Also, this will give awareness to developers and database administrators and also help them in choosing the best platform for deploying NoSQL databases.

Keywords: NoSQL · Database security · Comparative analysis

© The Author(s), under exclusive license to Springer Nature Singapore Pte Ltd. 2022
E. Ahene and F. Li (Eds.): FCS 2022, CCIS 1726, pp. 349–364, 2022.
https://doi.org/10.1007/978-981-19-8445-7_22

1   Introduction

A NoSQL database also referred to as "Non-SQL" or "Not Only SQL," is a database which stores data in various formats other than relational tables. NoSQL databases were introduced in the late 2000s when the cost of storage drastically reduced, and are now one of the buzzwords of modern data storage systems. This is due to the large amount of data that currently exists and the swiftly growing heterogeneous data sources like sensors, GPS as well as several other types of smart gadgets. Web 2.0 companies (such as Amazon Facebook and Google) are the main drivers of NoSQL databases due to their increasing data and infrastructure demands. Web 2.0 has brought about numerous new apps that rely on the storage and also processing of large amounts of data and require high availability and scalability. This poses additional challenges for RDBs [1]. Primarily, the objective of these databases is to distribute large amounts of data across many cloud servers. There is growing interest in efficiently processing this unstructured data, commonly referred to as «big data» and incorporating it into traditional applications. But recently, NoSQL databases have built-in protection mechanisms to prevent security attacks [2–4].

This white paper analyzes the security features and issues of the four most preferred NoSQL databases-one from each of the four major categories [45] of NoSQL databases [44]. Specifically, Cassandra (column-based database), MongoDB (document database), Redis (key-value store), and Neo4j (graph database). It describes the key security features and issues of these four database systems under vulnerability to authentication, authorization, communication encryption, auditing, and DoS/injection attacks. In most survey literature on NoSQL security features, the comparisons made did not include the graph database Neo4j, which makes this survey unique from others.

2   Overview

2.1   Cassandra

Cassandra is an open-source, distributed, and also decentralized storage system (database) that offers an extremely readily available solution without a single point of failure [5]. Cassandra is a column-oriented database that is consistent, fault-tolerant, as well as scalable, and it runs on a network of hundreds of nodes. Its replication model is based on Amazon's Dynamo [6], and its data design is based on Google's BigTable "column family" data model [7]. Cassandra is thus a hybrid data management system that combines a column-oriented DBMS (e.g., Bigtable) and a row-oriented store. Cassandra was designed to work with Facebook's Inbox Search feature [5]. Cassandra combines BigTable's data structures with Dynamo's high availability to serve over 100 million users daily. Cassandra combines BigTable's data structures with Dynamo's high availability to serve over 100 million users daily. Currently, Twitter, Facebook, Cisco, eBay, Rackspace and Netflix are some of the largest companies using this type of database The following are some of the several outstanding features of Cassandra [5, 8–12].

2.2   MongoDB

MongoDB is a document database created by 10gen that was designed for ease of development and scaling [13]. Written in C++, MongoDB is a schema-free, document-oriented database that manages JSON-like document collections. This enables Data to be nested in sophisticated hierarchical structures while remaining queryable and indexable. As a result of this, it allows many applications to model data more naturally. MongoDB makes use of collections and documents instead of rows and tables as in relational database management systems (RDBMS). Some of MongoDB's key features are as follows: Scalability/sharding, MongoDB Query Language, Indexing, Data Replication and Document Oriented nature [14–18].

2.3   Redis

Remote Dictionary Server, widely recognized as Redis, is a fast, open-source, in-memory key-value data store. It is an in-memory NoSQL database that recognizes a variety of data structures, including strings, lists, sets, hashes, as well as sorted sets. Salvatore Sanfilippo wrote Redis in C Language and released it in 2009. Currently, Redis provides sub-millisecond latency, allowing for countless thousands of transactions per second in real-time applications such as gaming, healthcare, advertising and others. Redis, unlike the other key-value stores, provides data structures for handling any form of binary data, including arrays, bytes, numbers, strings, XML documents, images, and so on [19]. Furthermore, Redis provides hashes for storing and querying the database's objects. Listed here are some of the features of Redis database: Scalability and High availability, In-memory performance, Replication and persistence and Rich Data Structures [20–26].

2.4   Neo4j

Neo4j is arguably the most popular open-source Graph Database in the world. Written in Java, Neo4j adheres to a data model known as the native property graph model. The graph contains nodes (entities), which are linked together (by relationships). Data is stored in key-value pairs known as properties by nodes and relationships. Each piece of data is explicitly linked, resulting in unprecedented speed and scale. Neo4j is powered by a native graph database which stores and manages data in a more natural and connected manner, allowing for ultra-fast queries, a deeper context for analysis, and easily modifiable data relationships. Some of it's Key features includes: Reliability and Scalability, Data model, Cypher Query Language and Indexing [27–30].

Summarized in Table 1 are the features of MongoDB, Casandra, Redis and Neo4j; the NoSQL databases presented in this paper.

Table 1. Features of presented NoSQL databases.

Database features	NoSQL databases			
	Casandra	MongoDB	REDIS	Neo4J
Cypher query language				✓
Data model				✓
Document oriented		✓		
Elastic scalability	✓			
Fast writes	✓			
Fault tolerance	✓			
Indexing		✓		✓
In-memory performance			✓	
Peer to peer decentralized architecture	✓			
Query language	✓	✓		
Reliability and scalability				✓
Replication and persistence		✓	✓	
Rich data structures			✓	
Scalability/sharding and high availability		✓	✓	
Tunable consistency:	✓			

3   Security Features in Cassandra, MongoDB, Redis and Neo4j

Security has been a weakness in all NoSQL databases. There is no NoSQL database that provides complete security. As stated previously in the introduction, the primary concern of NoSQL Database designers was not based on security; hence, there are numerous security concerns in their design. This section focuses on some of the security features and issues with Cassandra, MongoDB, Redis, and Neo4j. Specifically, this section will look at how secure these systems are against vulnerabilities to authentication, authorization, communication encryption, auditing and DoS/Injection attack criteria [43] and possibly outline briefly the main issues in each one.

3.1   Cassandra Security Features

1. Authentication:
   Cassandra supports pluggable authentication and it is configured via «the authenticator»settings in «cassandra.yaml». In Cassandra's default distribution, there are two choices available. This implementation removes the need to authenticate to the database and is thus used to completely disable authentication. The «Password Authenticator»is another option, in which usernames are hashed but unsalted MD5 passwords [31] are saved in the system's «auth.credentials table». To manage security in enterprise Cassandra,

you can also utilize external, third-party packages such as Kerberos authentication. This will necessitate the installation of separate Kerberos servers as well as Kerberos client software on all joining Cassandra hosts.

2. Authorization:
   Similar to Authentication, Cassandra also supports pluggable authorization, which is customizable via the «authorizer»setting inside «cassandra.yaml». It also comes with two major options to choose from. The default distribution enabled is the «AllowAllAuthorizer». This undertakes no checks and thus provides no authorization; hence it gives full permissions to all users irrespective of their roles. The second choice is the «CassandraAuthorizer». This provides full permissions management capability and saves its data in «Cassandra's system tables». By selecting this option, privileged administrators gain the ability to enable any of the privileges on any resource to a selected user by running the CQL. The problem with the Cassandra Authorizer approach is its inability to refresh the file on each access, making it impossible to modify the valid permissions without restarting the entire Cassandra process.

3. Communication encryption:
   Encryption in Cassandra is transparent to all end-user activity. You can read, insert, update, etc. data without changing anything on the application side. Cassandra comes with multiple levels of encrypting data such as auxiliary encrypted mode of communication (client node communication) from the "client machine" to the "database cluster". By default, client node communication is unencrypted, but can be enabled after a valid server certificate is generated. The Client-to-server SSL ensures that data in flight is not compromised and that client machines are securely transferred back and forth. Consequently, "node-to-node encryption" can be used to make sure that data is secured as it is transferred between database cluster nodes. This can also be customized by changing the appropriate settings in "server_encryption_options" in the "cassandra.yaml" file. The SSL feature is deactivated by default, because using these default settings by firms may result in data breaches while sending data over the network in plain text. Finally, in DataStax Enterprise, transparent data encryption (TDE) prevents "data at rest" from theft and unlawful use [32]. Because the data encryption is kept locally, the TDE must be enabled when using a secure file system. Similarly, Cassandra's commit log (the location where the file is edited) is also not secured.

4. Auditing:
   Cassandra 4.0 and higher versions comes with audit Logging [33]. This is used to log all incoming CQL command requests, as well as authentication to a Cassandra node. In the cassandra.yaml file, the custom logger can be implemented and injected with the class name as a parameter. An administrator can use data auditing to determine "who looked at what/when" and "who changed what/when". However, executing prepared statements in Cassandra will log the query as provided by the client in the prepare call, along with the execution timestamp and all other attributes.

5. Vulnerability to DoS/Injection Attack:
Cassandra utilizes a "Thread Per-Client" approach in its network code. With this, an attacker can prevent the Cassandra server from accepting new client connections by causing the Cassandra server to allocate all its resources to fake connection attempts. However, Cassandra offers creating user-defined-functions (UDFs) functionality to perform custom processing of data in the database. But JFrog's Security Research team [34] recently disclosed a remote code execution vulnerability that they said is "easy to exploit and has the potential to wreak havoc on systems." This is possible because even though these new vulnerabilities do not affect Cassandra default installations where UDFs are disabled, many Cassandra configurations enable them, causing the instance to be vulnerable to DoS attack.

3.2   MongoDB Security Features

1. Authentication:
Enabling authentication is essential for MongoDB security because it is not enabled by default. Since MongoDB does not have a distinct user directory, authentication data is kept as part of MongoDB databases. By default, MongoDB employs the Salted Challenge Response Authentication Mechanism (SCRAM) when authentication is enabled. The IETF RFC 5802 standard provides the foundation of this system. With a customizable iteration count and unique random salts for each user, it allows for bi-directional authentication between client and server. It is compatible with both SHA-1 and SHA-256 hashing. In addition, MongoDB has other authentication options such x.509 certificate authentication, Kerberos authentication, Microsoft Active Directory authentication, and Lightweight Directory Access Protocol (LDAP) authentication [35]). Members of replica sets and sharded clusters can use the x.509 certificate authentication for client authentication as well as internal authentication. However, a secure TLS/SSL connection is required to authenticate x.509 certificates. In this situation, MongoDB's authentication feature needs to be active so that each server may be verified before entering the cluster [36].

2. Authorization:
Similar to the authentication described, MongoDB authorization is not enabled by default. You can enable authorization by using "-auth" or "security.authorization" setting [3,37]. You can also enable internal authentication for client authorization. Once MongoDB authorization is enabled, it allows to set permissions that are either explicitly assigned to a role, inherited from another role, or both. You can use the default database roles, or specify new roles if they are insufficient for your purposes. MongoDB also utilizes Role-Based Access Control (RBAC) to regulate access to the system. If a user is assigned one or several roles based on which resources and operations you want the user to perform. But aside from the role assignments, users have no access to the system. Also, MongoDB version 3.4 and higher versions support LDAP authorization, which allows the authenticated user to query the LDAP

server to know the LDAP groups it belongs to. MongoDB links the Distinguished Names (DN) of every corresponding group with roles in the admin database. Following this, the user can then be authorized by MongoDB based on the linked roles and privileges.

3. Communication encryption:
   MongoDB encryption provides robust features, some of which are preinstalled on the MongoDB Atlas Data-as-a-Service platform. MongoDB Atlas includes client-to-server TLS encryption as a requirement. MongoDB's "encryption at rest" is an Enterprise functionality that needs Enterprise binaries to provide a layer of security to ensure that written files or storage are only visible after they have been decrypted by an authorized process/application. MongoDB version 4.2 also provides "encryption in use". This allows MongoDB Clients such as drivers and shell to instantly encode and decode fields using secure keys stored in a secure vault.

4. Auditing:
   For mongod and mongos instances, MongoDB Enterprise has an auditing feature. This auditing facility allows administrators and users to track system activity for deployments with multiple users and applications [38]. To enable audit logging in MongoDB, you need to go to the mongod.conf configuration file. The auditing system, when enabled can record the operations of the schema, replica set and sharded cluster, authentication and authorization, and CRUD operations. MongoDB Atlas also provides support for auditing all M10 and larger clusters.

5. Vulnerability to DoS attack:
   MongoDB by default does not enforce authentication as already stated. In many instances, this can allow anyone on the network to access all data within the database. This leaves MongoDB vulnerable to DoS attacks. An attacker does not need to be an administrator to conduct the attack; because they can use any legitimate user credentials.

3.3   Redis Security Features

1. Authentication:
   Even though Redis doesn't attempt to provide access control, it offers a thin layer of optional authentication that may be activated by modifying the redis.conf file. Redis versions before Redis 6 were only able to understand the one-argument version of the command: AUTH. In this configuration, unless the connection is authenticated by AUTH, Redis will reject any command issued by newly connected clients. In Redis 6, it is possible to use the AUTH command in two-arguments form: AUTH. This technique, however, provides backwards compatibility. Additionally, the AUTH command, like all other Redis commands, is delivered in clear text and is not secure against eavesdropping by an intruder with sufficient access to the network.

2. Authorization:
   Redis comes with an Authorization layer when installed. Once the authorization layer is enabled, any query from an unauthenticated client will be

rejected by Redis. A client can authenticate itself by sending the "AUTH" command preceded by the password provided by the system administrator in clear text inside the Redis.conf file. Although a strong password can be generated using the ACL GENPASS command, hackers can take advantage of Redis' great performance to test many passwords simultaneously in a short amount of time. Also, you would have to restart your Redis server after editing the configuration file.

3. Communication encryption:
   Redis does not by default support any form of encryption. Redis does not support SSL-encrypted connections because it's been created for usage only in trusted private networks. Assuming that encryption is desired in the client-server connection, extra tools are necessary. It does not offer data encryption for Data-at-rest (stored as plain text) and Data-in-transit between Redis client and server is not encrypted. Redis, therefore, uses stunnel to encrypt Redis communication. It is an SSL encryption wrapper between a local client and a local or remote server. This stunnel application can tunnel unencrypted communication via an encrypted SSL tunnel to another server [39]. Although SSL encryption is added by stunnel, this does not completely ensure that unencrypted communication will never be recorded. Any attacker will be able to intercept unencrypted local communication as it is being transmitted to Stunnel if they can breach the server or client-server relationship.

4. Auditing:
   Redis has service logs that compile and document operations taken on various Redis entities. The account itself, users, API Keys, subscriptions, databases, accounts, payment methods, and more are examples of these entities. Syslog and local text log files are the two mechanisms that Redis offers for logging. Syslog takes in log messages, directs them to different on-disk log files, and takes care of rotation and deletion of old logs. This method of logging files can present problems because numerous services are writing to numerous log files.

5. Vulnerability to DoS/Injection Attack:
   Redis is an open-source, in-memory database that persists on disk as already indicated earlier on. By default, Redis can be accessed without credentials and can be exploited to corrupt the heap and potentially result in remote code execution. DoS attack is a key threat that Redis does not address. This attack is possibly done by inserting elements into the input set and changing a constant time-taking algorithm to a linear or exponential time-taking method. This will render the system inoperable, resulting in the Distributed denial of service attack.

3.4   Neo4j Security Features

1. Authentication:
   Neo4j make use of user details such as username and password. Passwords are encoded using the SHA-256 format. It has an authentication

module that utilizes the AuthenticationPlugin interface. In Neo4j, authentication is enabled by default but can be turned off by the setting using dbms.security.auth_enabled. It includes a "native auth provider" that keeps the users and their role information in the database. In addition to the Native auth, LDAP auth Provider is also available. Similarly, Neo4j also provides "Single Sign-On" provider and "Custom-built" plugin auth providers for clients with special requirements that are not handled by either native or LDAP. Again, Neo4j supports Kerberos for authentication with single sign-on.

2. Authorization:
Similar to the authentication, authorization is enabled by default in Neo4j. It comes with the authorization module which utilizes the AuthorizationPlugin interface. Neo4j connects data along with intuitive relations to make identity and access management happen quickly and effectively. Neo4j 3.1 introduced the concept of role-based access control (RBAC). This allows you to possibly create users and grant them specific roles in the database. This was enhanced significantly in Neo4j 4.0 with the inclusion of privileges. However, it is impossible to have different security privileges on different instances of a cluster [40]. As the whole cluster shares the privileges already configured in the database using Cypher administrative commands. This indicates that consumers have the same privileges irrespective of the server they access inside a cluster.

3. Communication encryption:
Neo4j does not currently deal with encryption for data-at-rest explicitly [41]. However, it supports the securing of data-in-transit by using TLS/SSL technology which is implemented by Java Cryptography Extension (JCE), a digital certificate and a set of configuration options provided in neo4j.conf. The SSL framework supports using common SSL/TLS technology to secure the following Neo4j communication channels [42]. Neo4j also provides APIs (OGM) for Java-based Application-Level Encryption [3, 37].

4. Auditing:
Neo4j offers limited auditing facilities in Open source and it offers logging facilities in Enterprise. The systems root directory where the general log files are stored can be configured via "dbms.directories.logs". Queries executed in the database can be enabled or disabled by dbms.logs.query.enabled parameter. Neo4j includes security event logging, which logs all security events. It records login attempts, authorization failures from role-based access control and all administration commands and security procedures that run towards the system database.

5. Vulnerability to DoS/Injection Attack:
Noe4j prevents cypher injection by sending input as a parameter to the query. In a parameterized query, placeholders can be used for parameters and their values supplied at execution time. This means developers do not have to resort to string building to create a query. Moreover, parameters greatly simplify Cypher's caching of execution plans, resulting in quicker query execution times. Parameters can be used for, (literals and expressions) and (node and relationship ids). Since Neo4j uses the Cypher (CQL) declarative graph query,

it makes Neo4j vulnerable to injection attacks by using string concatenation. That is because Cypher is vulnerable to injection.

Table 2. Security features of presented NoSQL databases

Security features	NoSQL databases			
	Casandra	MongoDB	REDIS	Neo4J
Auditing	✓	✓	✓	✓
Authentication	✓	✓	✓	✓
Authorization	✓	✓	✓	✓
Communication encryption	✓	✓	✓	✓
Vulnerability to DoS/injection attack	✓	✓	✓	✓

Table 2 shows the security features of the four databases. However, all databases offer security do the data with respect to all categories of the security features presented in this work. Thus, the next section will throw more emphasis on the strengths of each database with regard to each of the security category.

4   Comparative Findings and Discussions

4.1   Security Assessment Key

The following descriptions are key [43] for assessing the security of the databases for all categories;

* *High*
    A database is considered high with respect to a security category if and only if the features that it provides completely secures the data
* *Medium*
    If the features needed or provided to secure the data are partial or limited, the database is said to provide medium security with respect to the category.
* *Low*
    When databases provide no or low required features to secure data.

4.2   Criteria for Assessing Security

With the key established, a description for the categories of security [43] with respect to the metric values are given as;

1. Authentication

- *High* - Logon authentication such as password-oriented, multifactor, certificate, and SSL-based authentication. Logon makes use of a combination of user identifier and password. Examples of logon authentication are captcha images, pin numbers, and biometrics.
  Network-based authentication uses authenticated user session through drivers and network protocol stack.
  IP-based authentication uses IPsec security modules to validate the source and destination IPs.
- *Medium* - The database supports only one means of logon, network-based or IP-based authentication.
- *Low* - No means of authentication or a basic password requirement.
2. Auditing
   - *High* - NoSQL databases must be able to audit and analyze transaction logs(including external and internal activities), database connections and privilege grants.
   - *Medium* - If database can log all user profile activities
   - *Low* - No mechanism to secure the system or data.
3. Authorization
   - *High* - The three levels; database, content, or object level must be supported by the database with some popular models for authorization such as MAC, discretionary, policy-based, task-based, role-based access control(RBAC) and fine-grained access controls.
   - *Medium* - Database must be able to at least support a level of authorization with any of the models under high as well.
   - *Low* - Little or no authorization support by the database.
4. Communication Encryption
   - *High* - NoSQL databases must provide encryption(two broad categories: data-at-rest and data in transit). Examples the former category are MD5 hashing, Data Encryption Standard (DES), AES, SHA1 and SHA2 hashing. Methods of the latter category include SSL, TLS, SSH, and IPsec. Examples of transport level security methods are SSL Record Protocol, Change Cipher Spec Protocol, Secure Shell (SSH), Handshake Protocol, Alert Protocol and IPsec Protocol.
   - *Medium* - Database provides either of the methods of data-at-rest or the methods of transport layer security.
   - *Low* - Database does not provide any encryption method to secure data.
5. Vulnerability to DoS/Injection Attack
   - *High* - Security assurances by the databases include input validation, least privilege policy and secure coding practices.
   - *Medium* - Databases provide only of the mechanisms stated with high security.
   - *Low* - None of the methods are provided by the databases.

Figures 1, 2, 3, 4 and 5 show the results of comparing the four featured NoSQL databases under the categories of security described. In all the figures, on the Y-axis and X-axis are the metric values and NoSQL databases. The metric values

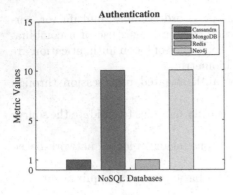

Fig. 1. Comparisons under authentication

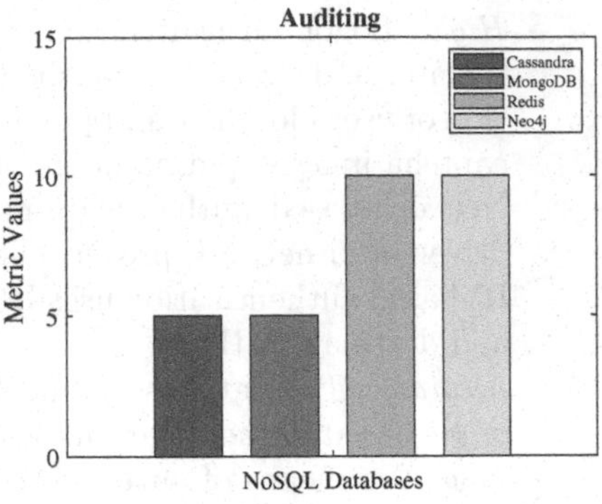

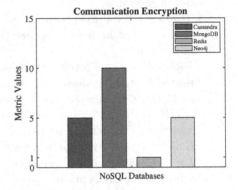

Fig. 2. Comparisons under auditing

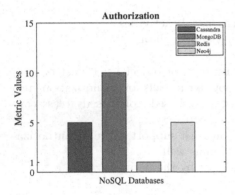

Fig. 3. Comparisons under authorization

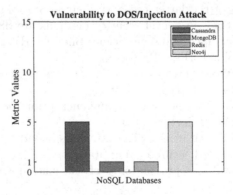

Fig. 4. Comparisons under communication encryption

Fig. 5. Comparisons under vulnerability to DoS/injection attack

are labeled 0, 1, 5, 10 and 15, where labels 1, 5 and 10 represent low, medium and high respectively elaborated in Sect. 4.1. In Fig. 1 where a comparison was made under the category "Authentication", databases MongoDB and Neo4j had high security features to secure data. Both Casandra and Redis databases have little or no authentication features at all. Comparisons were made under the category "Auditing" shown in Fig. 2. It can be seen that databases Redis and Neo4j had high features of protecting data under this category while both Casandra and MongoDB have medium or partial protective features. Thirdly, category "Authorization" represented in Fig. 3 has MongoDB with high features, Casandra and Neo4j having medium security features and only Redis having a low protection of data under this category. Figure 4 shows comparisons of NoSQL databases under the security category "Communication Encryption". In this figure only MongoDB has a high security feature. With Casandra and Neo4j providing medium security features, while Redis is either not able to secure data or does it minimally. Finally, presented in Fig. 5 is category "Vulnerability to DoS/Injection Attack". None of the compared NoSQL databases can fully secure data under this category. They either do it partially by Casandra and Neo4j or not at all by databases MongoDB and Redis.

From all five figures, based on combined features and their power to protect data, Neo4j can be said to have the best protective features to secure data. While Redis database performs the weakest in a collective security features in protecting data.

5   Conclusion, Recommendations and Future Works

Given the various security improvements made by NoSQL database platform vendors to improve their security mechanisms, there is still a paucity of research in discussing the security flaws of NoSQL systems as well as the way forward for resolving them. This paper discussed an extensive overview of various vulnerabilities in four of the most common NoSQL databases (MongoDB, Cassandra, Redis and Noe4j) one from each category. In existing works, the comparisons made either included a few NoSQL databases or excluded Neo4j. The algorithms used by each database to support security features were discussed. Each of these databases discussed has its own set of drawbacks and benefits. Comparisons of the databases under different security categories were made as well. Looking at the features identified and comparisons made, NoSQL system developers and administrators can choose and make a better security plan to make their database systems more secure. Despite making significant improvements to improve NoSQL databases, future studies aimed at designing a more robust security framework are required. This should be targeted at designing and implementing a strong security mechanism against the Vulnerability of DoS attacks. Again, further studies can be conducted to design a standard security framework for each category of the NoSQL databases.

References

1. Stonebraker, M., Madden, S., Abadi, D.J., Harizopoulos, S., Hachem, N., Helland, P.: The end of an architectural era: it's time for a complete rewrite. In: Making Databases Work: the Pragmatic Wisdom of Michael Stonebraker, pp. 463–489 (2018)
2. Rocha, L., Vale, F., Cirilo, E., Barbosa, D., Mourão, F.: A framework for migrating relational datasets to NoSQL. Procedia Comput. Sci. **51**, 2593–2602 (2015)
3. Grolinger, K., Higashino, W.A., Tiwari, A., Capretz, M.A.M.: Data management in cloud environments: NoSQL and NewSQL data stores. J. Cloud Comput. **2**(1), 1–24 (2013). https://doi.org/10.1186/2192-113X-2-22
4. Han, J., Haihong, E., Le, G., Du, J.: Survey on NoSQL database. In: 2011 6th International Conference on Pervasive Computing and Applications, pp. 363–366. IEEE (2011)
5. Lakshman, A., Malik, P.: Cassandra: a decentralized structured storage system. ACM SIGOPS Oper. Syst. Rev. **44**(2), 35–40 (2010)
6. DeCandia, G., et al.: Dynamo: Amazon's highly available key-value store. ACM SIGOPS Oper. Syst. Rev. **41**(6), 205–220 (2007)
7. Chang, F., et al.: Bigtable: a distributed storage system for structured data. ACM Trans. Comput. Syst. **26**(2), 1–26 (2008)
8. Kalid, S., Syed, A., Mohammad, A., Halgamuge, M.N.: Big-data NoSQL databases: a comparison and analysis of "Big-Table", "DynamoDB", and "Cassandra". In: 2017 IEEE 2nd International Conference on Big Data Analysis (ICBDA), pp. 89–93. IEEE (2017)
9. Chebotko, A., Kashlev, A., Lu, S.: A big data modeling methodology for Apache Cassandra. In: 2015 IEEE International Congress on Big Data, pp. 238–245. IEEE (2015)
10. Rosselli, M., Niemann, R., Ivanov, T., Tolle, K., Zicari, R.V.: benchmarking the availability and fault tolerance of Cassandra. In: Rabl, T., Nambiar, R., Baru, C., Bhandarkar, M., Poess, M., Pyne, S. (eds.) WBDB -2015. LNCS, vol. 10044, pp. 87–95. Springer, Cham (2016). https://doi.org/10.1007/978-3-319-49748-8_5
11. Jogi, V.D., Sinha, A.: Performance evaluation of MySQL, Cassandra and HBase for heavy write operation. In: 2016 3rd International Conference on Recent Advances in Information Technology (RAIT), pp. 586–590. IEEE (2016)
12. Abramova, V., Bernardino, J.: NoSQL databases: MongoDB vs cassandra. In: Proceedings of the International C* Conference on Computer Science and Software Engineering, pp. 14–22 (2013)
13. Why use MongoDB and when to use it? MongoDB. https://www.mongodb.com/why-use-mongodb
14. Kookarinrat, P., Temtanapat, Y.: Analysis of range-based key properties for sharded cluster of MongoDB. In: 2015 2nd International Conference on Information Science and Security (ICISS), pp. 1–4. IEEE (2015)
15. Arora, R., Aggarwal, R.R.: Modeling and querying data in MongoDB. Int. J. Sci. Eng. Res. **4**(7), 141–144 (2013)
16. Indexes. https://www.mongodb.com/docs/manual/indexes/
17. Top 5 features of MongoDB: MongoDB. https://www.mongodb.com/what-is-mongodb/features
18. Dipina Damodaran, B., Salim, S., Vargese, S.M.: Performance evaluation of MySQL and MongoDB databases. Int. J. Cybern. Inform. (IJCI) **5** (2016)

19. Bugiotti, F., Cabibbo, L.: A comparison of data models and APIs of NoSQL data-stores. In: SEBD, pp. 63–74 (2013)
20. Redis: in-memory data store. How it works and why you should use it. https://aws.amazon.com/redis/
21. Ji, Z., Ganchev, I., O'Droma, M., Ding, T.: A distributed Redis framework for use in the UCWW. In: 2014 International Conference on Cyber-Enabled Distributed Computing and Knowledge Discovery, pp. 241–244. IEEE (2014)
22. Chen, S., Tang, X., Wang, H., Zhao, H., Guo, M.: Towards scalable and reliable in-memory storage system: a case study with Redis. In: 2016 IEEE Trustcom/BigDataSE/ISPA, pp. 1660–1667. IEEE (2016)
23. Li, S., Jiang, H., Shi, M.: Redis-based web server cluster session maintaining technology. In: 2017 13th International Conference on Natural Computation, Fuzzy Systems and Knowledge Discovery (ICNC-FSKD), pp. 3065–3069. IEEE (2017)
24. Redis replication. https://redis.io/docs/manual/replication/
25. Pan, C., Wang, X., Luo, Y., Wang, Z.: Penalty-and locality-aware memory allocation in Redis using enhanced AET. ACM Trans. Storage 17(2), 1–45 (2021)
26. Redis data structures. https://redis.com/redis-enterprise/data-structures/
27. Jana, T.: Achieve unrivaled speed and scalability with Neo4j. https://neo4j.com/blog/achieve-unrivaled-speed-and-scalability-neo4j/
28. Graph modeling guidelines. https://neo4j.com/developer/guide-data-modeling/
29. Holzschuher, F., Peinl, R.: Performance of graph query languages: comparison of cypher, gremlin and native access in Neo4j. In: Proceedings of the Joint EDBT/ICDT 2013 Workshops, pp. 195–204 (2013)
30. Indexes for search performance. https://neo4j.com/docs/cypher-manual/current/indexes-for-search-performance/
31. Kapadia Gayatri, S., Morena Rustom, D.: Comparative study of role based access control in cloud databases and NoSQL databases. Int. J. Adv. Res. Comput. Sci. 8(5), 51–57 (2017)
32. Savaram, R.: Apache Cassandra data security management. https://mindmajix.com/cassandra/data-security-management
33. Audit Logging: Apache Cassandra documentation. https://cassandra.apache.org/doc/latest/cassandra/new/auditlogging.html
34. Adia: CVE-2021-44521: RCE vulnerability in Apache Cassandra. https://jfrog.com/blog/cve-2021-44521-exploiting-apache-cassandra-user-defined-functions-for-remote-code-execution/
35. Authentication - MongoDB manual. https://www.mongodb.com/docs/manual/core/authentication/
36. Okman, L., Gal-Oz, N., Gonen, Y., Gudes, E., Abramov, J.: Security issues in NoSQL databases. In: 2011 IEEE 10th International Conference on Trust, Security and Privacy in Computing and Communications, pp. 541–547. IEEE (2011)
37. Sahafizadeh, E., Nematbakhsh, M.A.: A survey on security issues in Big Data and NoSQL. Adv. Comput. Sci. 4(4), 68–72 (2015)
38. Auditing - MongoDB manual. https://www.mongodb.com/docs/v4.4/core/auditing/
39. Haber, I.: Using stunnel to secure. https://redis.com/blog/stunnel-secure-redis-ssl/
40. Authentication and authorization - upgrade and migration guide. https://neo4j.com/docs/upgrade-migration-guide/current/migration/surface-changes/auth/
41. Sasaki, B.M.: Neo4j data encryption with OGM [Community Post]. https://neo4j.com/blog/neo4j-data-encryption-ogm/

42. SSL framework - operations manual. https://neo4j.com/docs/operations-manual/current/security/ssl-framework/
43. Zahid, A., Masood, R., Shibli, M.A.: Security of sharded NoSQL databases: a comparative analysis. In: 2014 Conference on Information Assurance and Cyber Security (CIACS), pp. 1–8. IEEE (2014)
44. Nehra, M.: Top 10 NoSQL databases in 2022 (2022). https://www.decipherzone.com/blog-detail/nosql-databases. Accessed 14 Aug 2022
45. Li, Z.: NoSQL databases (2019)

Improving Online Restore Performance of Backup Storage via Historical File Access Pattern

Xingpeng Tang and Jingwei Li[(✉)]

School of Computer Science and Engineering, University of Electronic Science
and Technology of China, Chengdu 611731, China
202021080934@std.uestc.edu.cn, jwli@uestc.edu.cn

Abstract. Online restore reduces the downtime during backup restore,
such that users can operate on the already restored files even if the other
files are still being restored. However, due to the inconsistency between
the access sequence and the restore sequence, the file to be accessed currently is sometimes not restored, thereby leading to long-delay time to
access the file. We propose two approaches, which build on users' historical access sequence to schedule the restore sequence, in order to reduce
users' waiting time to file access: (i) the frequency-based approach, which
restores files based on the access frequencies of historical files; and (ii)
the graph-based approach, which preferentially restores the frequently
accessed files as well as their correlated files. Trace-driven experiments
on two datasets show that our approaches significantly reduce users'
waiting time.

Keywords: Online restore · Access pattern · Correlation graph ·
Cloud backup

1 Introduction

Backup is widely used to increase the reliability of users' data against disasters
[1–4]. However, it brings the problems such as time-consuming restoring and
increasing users' waiting time to access files. Taking offline backup restore as an
example, users need to wait until the entire backup is restored (usually taking
several hours[5–8]) before they can access each file. Online backup restore allows
users to recover backup in the background while performing operations such as
reading and writing in the foreground. In other words, users can now operate on
the already restored files without waiting for the entire backup to be restored,
so as to effectively reduce the waiting time.

However, even with online restore, there is a challenge of *how to schedule
the restore sequence*, so as to make it match users' access sequence as much as
possible. Take a user's backup as an example. It contains files $\langle fID_1, fID_2, \ldots,
fID_{10} \rangle$ (each fID_i represents a file's ID) and the restore sequence is $\langle fID_1,
fID_2, \ldots, fID_{10} \rangle$. If the user's access sequence during restoration is $\langle fID_{10},$

© The Author(s), under exclusive license to Springer Nature Singapore Pte Ltd. 2022
E. Ahene and F. Li (Eds.): FCS 2022, CCIS 1726, pp. 365–376, 2022.
https://doi.org/10.1007/978-981-19-8445-7_23

fID_9, fID_8, fID_7, $fID_6\rangle$, its operations will be delayed until the corresponding files are restored. This does not mitigate the long-delay time. In the contrast, if we adjust the restore sequence to $\langle fID_{10}, fID_9, \ldots, fID_1 \rangle$, the waiting time for access can be significantly reduced.

This paper aims to reduce the waiting time in online restore, so as to improve users' experiences. The main idea is to build on users' historical access sequence to schedule the restore sequence, such that the restore sequence could match the latest access sequence. Specifically, we propose two approaches to this end. First, informed by the observation that the user's file access pattern is highly skewed [9], we propose a *frequency-based approach*, which prioritizes the restore of the frequently accessed files, such that most of user's operations during restore time can be served by the already restored files. Also, inspired by the correlation of accessed files [10], we propose a *graph-based approach*, which establishes a correlation graph based on historical access patterns and generate the restore sequence (of files) via a greedy algorithm.

To sum up, this paper makes the following contributions.

- We show via a case study a baseline online restore approach that restores files in an alphabetical order incurs extremely high waiting time, and hence significantly affects users' experience on foreground operations.
- We propose two approaches to schedule the online restore sequence of files based on historical access patterns.
- We conduct a trace-driven experiment, and show that our approaches can effectively reduce the users' waiting time compared to the baseline approach schedules the restore sequence in an alphabetical order.

2   Background and Problem

Background. We consider a *backup* as a complete copy of the primary data snapshotted from users' home directories or application states. Users periodically generate backups and store them in a storage system, in order to protect their data against disasters, accidents, or malicious actions. Specifically, old backups can be restored either online or offline.

This paper focuses on *online backup restore*, which is widely deployed in existing cloud backup services [11,12]. It allows users to recover backups in the background while performing file access operations in the foreground. Considering that backup restore often takes a long time [6], online restore significantly reduces the downtime since users can operate on the already restored files of the backup even if the whole backup is still under-recovery.

Theoretical Restore Model. One critical requirement for online restore is to *minimize user-perceived performance degradation of the foreground operations*. Specifically, online restore recovers backups gradually in the background, and needs to ensure that the operating files in the foreground have already been restored, in order to hide the performance degradation from the users.

However, to our knowledge, existing approaches (Sect. 5) focus on improving the overall restore speed, yet none of them are aware of minimizing user-perceived performance degradation. We now establish a theoretical restore model (in the contrast, we evaluate the practical online restore performance based on real-world access patterns in Sect. 4) to characterize the availability of users' foreground operations in the online restore procedure, and justify the problem based on the real-world file access trace collected by ourselves.

Specifically, we consider a set of unique files in a backup and define A as a sequence of the files (in the backup) that will be accessed in order by the foreground operations and R as a sequence of the files that will be restored in the background. Note that identical files may repeat in A, since users may access the same files multiple times. On the other hand, each file in R appears only once, since the storage system does not need to restore identical files multiple times. We consider a generic scenario that the metadata (that are small enough and can be recovered quickly) of all unique files, as well as the data contents of $x\%$ unique files in R have already been restored. Then, users start the foreground access in A, while the restore process continues in the background.

Our model makes the following assumptions. First, the restoring of each file in R takes a constant time (called a *time slot*). Our rationale is that many frequently accessed files have small sizes (e.g., hundreds of KBs) [13], and the differences in their restore time can be negligible. For the large files (that are unlikely to be accessed in A), we can divide them into multiple small parts for restoration. Second, the duration that the foreground process stays on each file in A is equal to a time slot, such that the processing speeds of the files in A and R are synchronized. In fact, this captures the *worst availability* of online restore, since the foreground process may stay on a file for a long time (e.g., heavy edits), while the restore process is continuously running on different files. Finally, we do not consider resource contention, since we can limit the resource usage of the restore process.

We characterize two metrics to measure the performance of the foreground operations in A. The first metric is the *availability rate*, which is the number of successfully accessed files (i.e., these files have been restored when they are accessed) divided by the total number of accessed files. In addition, for the file that is unavailable for access, we consider its *delayed time*, which is the number of the time slots that need to be waited to access the file.

Simulation Results. We study the availability of the foreground operations based on the real-world access log of a student (see Sect. 4 for dataset information). We focus on the access sequences of two consecutive days and consider a baseline approach that generates the restore sequence R based on the unique files of the first day *in an alphabetical order*. Also, we use the access sequence of the second day to form A. Note that the files in R may not be in A, since the restored files may not be accessed immediately. Also, the files in A may not be in R, since the user may create and access new files (this implies that such files are available for access by nature). We evaluate the availability rate and delayed time of the baseline approach when the first 0%, 10%, and 30% of files in **R** have already been restored.

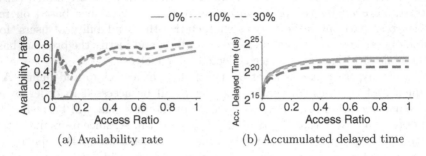

(a) Availability rate   (b) Accumulated delayed time

Fig. 1. Availability rate and accumulated delayed time when 0%, 10%, 30% files have been restored.

Figure 1(a) presents the results for the availability rate when a fraction (i.e., the access ratio in the x-axis) of files in **A** has been accessed. When $x = 0$ (i.e., no files have been restored before), the availability rate keeps low (e.g., below 10%) for a significant fraction (e.g., about 14.0%) of access. This implies that the initial restored files in **R** cannot serve the corresponding file access in **A**. In the contrast, if 10% files have been already restored, the availability rate achieves up to 70.8% when 4.2% files in **A** are accessed. This implies that restoring files in advance helps improve the availability of the accessed files. However, the availability rate then degrades, since the following restored files in **R** do not match the ones that are to be accessed in **A**. Figure 1(b) shows the results for delayed time. We observe that the delayed time first dramatically increases with the access ratio, due to the mismatching of **R** and **A**. Then, the delayed time becomes steady, since most of the files have been restored and are available for file access.

In summary, we observe that the baseline approach incurs a low availability rate (especially for the initial file access in **A**) and extremely high delayed time and hence significantly affects users' experience on foreground operations. This motivates us to improve online restore performance, especially ensuring that users' foreground operations can be served in time.

3   Restore Approaches

We build on previous file access prediction techniques [10,14], and propose two approaches to improve the online restore performance. Specifically, We assume that the sequence of historical access records **H** is known in advance. The frequency-based (Sect. 3.1) generates the sequence of the files to be restored based on the access frequencies of historical files, and the graph-based (Sect. 3.2) approaches further takes file access correlation into account and preferentially restores the corresponding correlated files in addition to the frequently accessed files.

Algorithm 1. Frequency-based approach.

1: **procedure** FREQUENCY-RESTORE
    Input: sequence of historical access records **H**
    Output: restore sequence **R**
2:    Initialize a map **M**
3:    **for** each record r in **H do**
4:       **if** the file ID $r.fID$ is in $fMap$ **then**
5:          $\mathbf{M}[r.fID] = \mathbf{M}[r.fID] + 1$
6:       **else**
7:          $\mathbf{M}[r.fID] = 1$
8:       **end if**
9:    **end for**
10:   Sort **M** by access frequency
11:   **return R** = M
12: **end procedure**

3.1 Frequency-Based Approach

Informed by the previous works [9] that demonstrate that the real-world access distribution is skewed among different files, our idea is to *prioritize the restoration of the frequently accessed files*, such that most of the operations in **A** can be served in time.

Algorithm 1 presents the details of the frequency-based approach. It takes the sequence of historical access records **H** as input and outputs the restore sequence **R** of files. It first initializes a map **M**, which maps each unique file ID to how many times (i.e., frequency) the file is accessed in **H** (Line 2). Specifically, it traverses each record in **H**, and increments the access frequency of a file if the file is indicated to be accessed in the record (Line 5). Otherwise, it inserts the (new) file ID into **M** and initializes the corresponding access frequency with one (Line 7). Finally, the algorithm sorts all file IDs by the corresponding access frequencies and returns **R** that includes the sorted file IDs (Line 11).

3.2 Graph-Based Approach

The frequency-based approach does not capture the correlation of file access, while in practice, users may access a set of files together (rather than each file, individually). For example, when the user launches an application, the application program is likely to access a set of files in a deterministic order for initialization [15]. Previous work [10] builds on the access correlation among files to predict which file will be accessed in the future. Specifically, it partitions the sequence of historical file access records into many non-overlapped fixed-size windows, such that each window includes a number of file access records. It builds a directed graph to model file access patterns. Each node of the graph corresponds to a unique file, and stores how many times the file has been accessed, while each directed edge stores how many windows, in which the corresponding files are accessed in order. Given a currently accessed file, it predicates the file that is likely to be accessed as the one that connects with the current access file with the highest weight.

The insight of our graph-based approach is to *prioritize the restoration of correlated files that are also frequently accessed in a short time*. Specifically, we extend the above graph-based modeling by measuring access correlation based on a sliding window approach. Here, we configure a *sliding window* with a fixed size of five access records and count how likely a file is to be co-accessed with other files in the same sliding window. Also, we construct an undigraph such that each edge stores the number of times that the corresponding files are co-accessed in identical sliding windows. Based on the graph, we use a greedy algorithm to generate the restore sequence **R** of files. Specifically, each time, we choose the edge that has the largest weight and includes the corresponding files into **R**, so as to first restore the frequently accessed correlated files.

Algorithm 2 presents the details of the graph construction algorithm, which takes the sequence of historical records as input. It first initializes an empty queue W (Line 3). For each record r, it adds r into W (Line 5). If W is full, it calls the UPDATE algorithm to update the graph based on the *co-access occurrences* of the file ID in the front of W with each following file ID (Line 7). Our rationale is to avoid repeat counting when the window slides. Then, it removes the front file ID from W (Line 8). It finally returns the graph $\mathcal{G}$ until all records in **H** have been processed (Line 11).

The UPDATE function takes a sliding window W and the graph $\mathcal{G} = (V, \mathbf{E})$ as input, where V is the set of file IDs (as the vertexes of $\mathcal{G}$) and $\mathbf{E}$ is an associate array that maps a pair of file IDs to the weight of the corresponding edge (of $\mathcal{G}$). It first includes the file ID fID_s in the front of W into the graph (Line 15). For any other file ID fID in W, if the edge $\{fID_s, fID\}$ has been stored in the graph, it increments the corresponding weight by one (Line 19). Otherwise, it creates a new edge for $\{fID_s, fID\}$ in the graph and initializes the corresponding weight with one (Line 21).

Algorithm 3 shows the greedy algorithm, which builds on the updated graph $\mathcal{G} = (V, \mathbf{E})$ to gradually generate the restore sequence **R**. Specifically, it initializes **R** as an empty sequence (Line 2). In the main loop, it first chooses the edge $\{fID, fID'\}$ that has the largest weight in $\mathcal{G}.\mathbf{E}$ and appends fID and fID' into **R** (Lines 4-5). It also removes them from $\mathcal{G}.V$ and $\mathcal{G}.\mathbf{E}$ (Lines 6-7). Then, it iteratively finds fID^* in $\mathcal{G}.V$ that connects to existing file IDs in **R** with the largest weight (among other file IDs in $\mathcal{G}.V$). Specifically, if no file ID is found (Line 10), it breaks the loop to find the largest weight edge (see above). Otherwise, it appends such fID^* into **R**, and removes the fID^* and the corresponding edge from $\mathcal{G}.V$ and $\mathcal{G}.\mathbf{E}$, respectively (Lines 13-15). The algorithm finally returns **R** until all file IDs in $\mathcal{G}.V$ have been added into **R** (Line 18).

Algorithm 2. Building graph.

1: **procedure** GRAPH-BUILDING
   Input: sequence of historical access records **H**
   Output: graph $\mathcal{G} = (V, \mathbf{E})$
2:    Initialize $\mathcal{G} = (V, \mathbf{E})$ as an empty graph
3:    Initialize a sliding window queue W with the capacity λ
4:    **for** each record r in **H do**
5:        W.ENQUEUE($r.fID$)
6:        **if** $|W| == \lambda$ **then**
7:            $\mathcal{G} = $ UPDATE($W, \mathcal{G}$)
8:            W.DEQUEUE()
9:        **end if**
10:   **end for**
11:   **return** $\mathcal{G}$
12: **end procedure**

13: **function** UPDATE
    Input: sliding window W, graph $\mathcal{G} = (V, \mathbf{E})$
14:   $fID_s = fID$ in the front of W
15:   $\mathcal{G}.V = \mathcal{G}.V \cup \{fID_s\}$
16:   **for** each fID in $W - \{fID_s\}$ **do**
17:       $\mathcal{G}.V = \mathcal{G}.V \cup \{fID\}$
18:       **if** $\{fID_s, fID\} \in \mathcal{G}.\mathbf{E}$ **then**
19:           $\mathcal{G}.\mathbf{E}[\{fID_s, fID\}] = \mathcal{G}.\mathbf{E}[\{fID_s, fID\}] + 1$
20:       **else**
21:           $\mathcal{G}.\mathbf{E}[\{fID_s, fID\}] = 1$
22:       **end if**
23:   **end for**
24: **end function**

4   Simulation

We now conduct simulation analysis based on two datasets. We first elaborate our datasets, and then present our simulation results.

4.1   Datasets

We use two mixed datasets to drive our evaluation. The first dataset is *mix-1*. We use the process monitor [16] to collect the file system, registry, and process/thread activities of a student's machine (that runs windows 10) in our research group in the period of June 19 to June 25, 2021. We exclude the system directories `Windows`, `ProgramData`, `Intel`, `AMD`, and `Drivers` (if the latter three exist), and focus on the `readFile` and `writeFile` operations that are applied on the remaining files. We merge multiple consecutive reads (writes) on an identical file into one read (write) to the file.

Algorithm 3. Generating restore sequence.

1: **procedure** RESTORE-GEN
   Input: graph $\mathcal{G}$
   Output: restore sequence $\mathbf{R}$
2:    Initialize $\mathbf{R}$ as an empty sequence
3:    **while** $\mathcal{G}.V$ is not empty **do**
4:       Choose $\{fID, fID'\}$ that has the largest weight in $\mathcal{G}.\mathbf{E}$
5:       Append fID and fID' into $\mathbf{R}$
6:       Remove $\{fID, fID'\}$ from $\mathcal{G}.\mathbf{E}$
7:       $\mathcal{G}.V = \mathcal{G}.V - \{fID, fID'\}$
8:       **while** $\mathcal{G}.V$ is not empty **do**
9:          Find $\{fID, fID^*\} \in \mathcal{G}.\mathbf{E}$ that has the largest weight among all $fID \in \mathbf{R}$
   and $fID^* \in \mathcal{G}.V$
10:            **if** $\{fID, fID^*\}$ does not exist in $\mathcal{G}.\mathbf{E}$ **then**
11:               Break
12:            **end if**
13:            $\mathcal{G}.V = \mathcal{G}.V - \{fID^*\}$
14:            Append fID^* into $\mathbf{R}$
15:            Remove $\{fID, fID^*\}$ from $\mathcal{G}.\mathbf{E}$
16:         **end while**
17:      **end while**
18:      **return** $\mathbf{R}$
19: **end procedure**

However, since our collected logs do not contain file metadata, we associate each unique file record in the access log to a file in the FSL snapshots, which are the daily backups of students' home directories from a shared network file system [17]. Specifically, each FSL snapshot is represented by a sequence of file names and corresponding file sizes and access times. We choose two FSL snapshots with as many files as the access logs collected by ourselves. We then map each file record of the access logs to a file in the FSL snapshots based on the principle that small files are likely to be accessed frequently. The mix-1 dataset contains the file access data of the same user for 2 consecutive days, and takes about 59 GiB.

The second dataset is *mix-2*, which maps the access records in the *MSRC* dataset [18] to files in the *MS* dataset [19]. Specifically, the MSRC dataset includes the block-level access records collected from multiple servers, and we focus on the directory *hm_1*. Assuming that each accessed block corresponds to a distinct file, we choose three MS snapshots, and map each block accessed in *hm_1* to a file in the MS snapshots. The mix-2 dataset takes about 333 GiB.

4.2   Simulation Results

We follow the simulation approach (see Sect. 2 for details) to compare the availability ratio and delayed time of our proposed approaches with a baseline approach that directly schedules the restore sequence based on files in an alphabetical order. Note that our approaches generate the restore sequence based on historical access patterns. So, for mix-1, we use access log in the first day as the historical access information, and examine our approaches based on the access sequence in the second day; for mix-2, we equally partition the access log into two parts, and use the first half as the historical access information. Also, unlike our theoretical model (see Sect. 2) that assumes that all files are restored within the same time, we assume that the network bandwidth is 100 MiB/s and estimate the necessary time to restore each file (file size divided by network bandwidth).

We compare the access time of each file with the corresponding restore completion time (see above for how we estimate the time), in order to identify if the file is available to be accessed. We evaluate the *availability rate*, which is the number of successfully accessed files divided by the total number of currently accessed files. In addition, we consider *delayed time rate* as the ratio of the accumulated delayed time of each considered approach by that of the baseline approach.

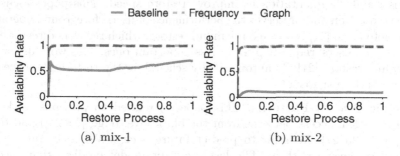

(a) mix-1 (b) mix-2

Fig. 2. Availability ratio in two datasets.

Figure 2 shows the availability rate after a fraction of files have been restored. Our proposed frequency-based and graph-based approaches achieve more than 99% availability rate after restoring about 7% of files, while the baseline approach reaches 50–70% and 12% in the mix-1 and mix-2 datasets, respectively. Note that the availability ratio of the baseline approach differs significantly in the two datasets. This is because the file name of the frequently accessed files in **A** of *mix-1* dataset is at the top of the alphabetical restore sequence.

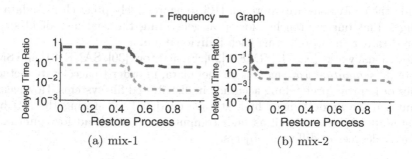

(a) mix-1 (b) mix-2

Fig. 3. Delayed time ratio in two datasets.

Figure 3 shows the delayed time ratio of our proposed approaches. Note that a lower delayed time ratio implies that the considered approach is more effective to reduce the accumulated delay time of the baseline approach. For mix-1, the frequency-based approach reduces the delayed time of the baseline approach by up to 99.7%. For mix-2, the delayed time ratio of the graph-based approach first decreases to 0.01 and then increases to about 0.03.

5   Related Work

Backup Restore. Previous works focus on accelerating restore speed. Cumulus [5] applies segment cleaning to reduce the amount of backup data to be downloaded in the restore procedure. Data deduplication introduces *chunk fragmentation* [6] and degrades restore performance. A large body of works [6–8,20] address chunk fragmentation to improve restore speed. This paper focuses on online restoration and preserves the performance of users' foreground operations.

Nemoto *et al.* [21] propose on-demand restore, which recovers directories and files based on users' requests prior to less important ones. This work differs from on-demand restore [21] for automatically scheduling the restore sequence of all files in a backup snapshot.

Modeling Access Patterns. This paper is related to previous works that model historical access patterns from the block level (e.g., [22–24]) and the file level [10,14,25–27], in order to predict future access. We focus on modeling the file-level access pattern. The last-successor model predicts that access to each file will be followed by the same file that followed the last access to the file. Noah [25] extends the last-successor model by tracking *access locality* (i.e., some files are more likely to be successively accessed followed by each file), and makes predictions only for the files with strong access locality. Amer *et al.* [26] augment Noah with the tunability of the prediction accuracy and the number of predictions made.

In addition to the last-successor model, Kroeger *et al.* [10,27] propose a *context-aware* model to make predictions. It builds a graph to track the frequency counts of file accesses within a sliding window, and predicts future access based on the file that is most likely to be accessed after the current file. Nexus [28] extends the context-aware approach [10] to aggressively prefetch metadata. We highlight that our approaches focus on generating the sequence of files to be restored rather than predicting each individual file.

Additional works (e.g., FARMER [29], SmartStore [30], SANE [31] and SMeta [32]) build *semantic-aware* models on metadata, in order to accelerate metadata queries or improve prefetching accuracy in distributed file systems. However, the semantic-aware models incur high storage overhead for storing the attributes of metadata objects, as well as high computational overhead for counting the similarity degrees of different objects.

6   Conclusion

In this paper, we focus on online restore scenario, and propose two approaches that build users' historical access sequence to schedule the restore sequence. Our first approach restores files based on the access frequencies of historical files, while the second approach further takes the correlation of file access into account. Evaluation shows that both approaches can significantly reduce users' waiting time on file access when the restore process is running in the background.

We pose two directions for future work. First, our proposed approaches are non-adaptive, since they build on the static historical access sequence for prediction and scheduling. One open question is that can we improve our results via an adaptive approach that generates the restore sequence based on users' real-time access patterns in addition to the historical access sequence. Second, it remains open of how to implement the approaches in real backup storage systems.

Acknowledgments. This work was supported in part by the National Natural Science Foundation of China (61972073), the Key Research Funds of Sichuan Province (2021Y FG0167, 2020YFG0298), the Sichuan Science and Technology Program (2020JDTD0 007), as well as the Fundamental Research Funds for Chinese Central Universities (ZYG X2020ZB027, ZYGX2021J018).

References

1. Google cloud. https://cloud.google.com/storage
2. Amazon cloud storage. https://aws.amazon.com
3. Xue, K., Chen, W., Li, W., Hong, J., Hong, P.: Combining data owner-side and cloud-side access control for encrypted cloud storage. IEEE Trans. Inf. Forensics Secur. **13**, 2062–2074 (2018)
4. Gao, Y.: When cloud storage meets RDMA. In: Proceedings of USENIX NSDI (2021)
5. Vrable, M., Savage, S., Voelker, G.M.: Filesystem backup to the cloud. In: Proceedings of USENIX FAST, Cumulus (2009)
6. Lillibridge, M., Eshghi, K., Bhagwat, D.: Improving restore speed for backup systems that use inline chunk-based deduplication. In: Proceedings of USENIX FAST (2013)
7. Fu, M.: Accelerating restore and garbage collection in deduplication-based backup systems via exploiting historical information. In: Proceedings of USENIX ATC (2014)
8. Cao, Z.: ALACC: Accelerating restore performance of data deduplication systems using adaptive look-ahead window assisted chunk caching. In: Proceedings of USENIX FAST (2018)
9. Li, J., Nelson, J., Michael, E., Jin, X., Ports, D.R.K.: Pegasus: Tolerating skewed workloads in distributed storage with In-Network coherence directories. In: Proceedings of USENIX OSDI (2020)
10. Kroeger, T.M., Long, D.D.E.: The case for efficient file access pattern modeling. In: Proceedings of IEEE Workshop on Hot Topics in Operating Systems (1999)
11. CompuVault secure data protection. https://www.compuvaultstl.com/

12. Restore your iphone, ipad, or ipod touch from a backup (2020). https://support.apple.com/en-us/HT204184
13. Douceur, J.R., Bolosky, W.J.: A large-scale study of file-system contents. ACM SIGMETRICS Perform. Evaluat. Rev. **27**, 59–70 (1999)
14. Kroeger, T.M., Long, D.D.E.: Design and implementation of a predictive file prefetching algorithm. In: Proceedings of USENIX ATC (2001)
15. Tang, Y.: Nodemerge: Template based efficient data reduction for big-data causality analysis. In: Proceedings of ACM CCS (2018)
16. Process monitor. https://docs.microsoft.com/en-us/sysinternals/downloads/procmon
17. FSL traces and snapshots public archive (2014). http://tracer.filesystems.org/
18. Microsoft research cambridge target block traces. http://iotta.snia.org/traces/block-io/388
19. Microsoft ubc-dedup traces. http://iotta.snia.org/traces/static/3382
20. Cao, Z., Liu, S., Wu, F., Wang, G., Li, B., Du, D.H.C.: Sliding look-back window assisted data chunk rewriting for improving deduplication restore performance. In: Proceedings of USENIX FAST (2019)
21. Nemoto, J., Sutoh, A., Iwasaki, M.: File system backup to object storage for on-demand restore. In: Proceedings of IEEE IIAIAAI (2016)
22. Liao, J., Trahay, F., Gerofi, B., Ishikawa, Y.: Prefetching on storage servers through mining access patterns on blocks. IEEE Trans. Parallel Distrib. Syst. **27**(9), 2698–2710 (2015)
23. Li, Z., Chen, Z., Srinivasan, S.M., Zhou, Y., et al.: C-Miner: Mining block correlations in storage systems. In: Proceedings of USENIX FAST (2004)
24. Soundararajan, G., Mihailescu, M., Amza, C.: Context-aware prefetching at the storage server. In: Proceedings of USENIX ATC (2008)
25. Amer, A., Long, D.D.E.: Noah: Low-cost file access prediction through pairs. In: Proceedings of IEEE IPCCC (2001)
26. Amer, A., Long, D.D.E., Paris, J.-F., Burns, R.C.: File access prediction with adjustable accuracy. In: Proc. of IEEE IPCCC (2002)
27. Kroeger, T.M., Long, D.D.E.: Predicting file system actions from prior events. In: Proceedings of USENIX ATC (1996)
28. Gu, P., Zhu, Y., Jiang, H., Wang, J.: Nexus: A novel weighted-graph-based prefetching algorithm for metadata servers in petabyte-scale storage systems. In Proceedings of IEEE CCGRID (2006)
29. Xia, P., Feng, D., Jiang, H., Tian, L., Wang, F.: FARMER: A novel approach to file access correlation mining and evaluation reference model for optimizing peta-scale file system performance. In: Proceedings of ACM HPDC (2008)
30. Hua, Y., Jiang, H., Zhu, Y., Feng, D., Tian, L.: SmartStore: A new metadata organization paradigm with semantic-awareness for next-generation file systems. In: Proceedings of IEEE Supercomputing Conference (2009)
31. Hua, Yu., Jiang, H., Zhu, Y., Feng, D., Lei, X.: SANE: Semantic-aware namespace in ultra-large-scale file systems. IEEE Trans. Parallel Distrib. Syst. **25**(5), 1328–1338 (2013)
32. Chen, Y., Li, C., Lv, M., Shao, X., Li, Y., Yinlong, X.: Explicit data correlations-directed metadata prefetching method in distributed file systems. IEEE Trans. Parallel Distrib. Syst. **30**(12), 2692–2705 (2019)

Securely and Efficiently Nearest Neighbor Query Scheme Based on Additive Secret Sharing

Qikai Feng and Bai Liu[✉]

Hubei University of Technology, Wuhan 430068, China
liubai@hbut.edu.cn

Abstract. With the wide application of machine learning algorithms in medical diagnosis, we gradually confronted the problem of computing and storing large-scale data. Outsourcing cloud computing has become the most cost-effective option to address these challenges. However, privacy and security issues have always existed in outsourced computing. Therefore, in this article, we propose an efficient index nearest neighbor query scheme based on Secret Sharing (SS) and Secure Multi-Party Computation (MPC) with the dual-cloud model architecture. For secure and efficient queries, we have designed a comprehensive set of secure index generation algorithms and secure index query algorithms. The cloud server creates indexes for the outsourced data and saves them through index generation algorithms in the offline phase, and uses index query algorithms to complete secure and efficient nearest neighbor query tasks in the online phase where users participate. Security analysis proves that our scheme protects the security of outsourced data and the privacy of query data. Simulation results on real datasets also demonstrate that the proposed scheme has higher efficiency and lower communication overhead compared with existing schemes.

Keywords: Privacy-preservation · Outsourcing computation · Secret sharing · Nearest neighbor(NN) query · k-d tree

1 Introduction

With the development of wearable IoT devices and cloud computing technology, being able to monitor the health of oneself or family members anytime and anywhere is becoming a widespread demand [1]. This monitoring device has the characteristics of frequent requests, simple tasks, limited storage and computing capacity. If we treat such tasks as traditional medical tasks, it will inevitably bring about the problem of medical overload. The rapid growth of medical data will bring computing overhead, so enterprises are more inclined to outsource tasks to cloud services, which have fast data processing capabilities. While outsourcing data, we should also pay attention to potential data privacy. The leakage or improper using of private medical data may cause psychological

© The Author(s), under exclusive license to Springer Nature Singapore Pte Ltd. 2022
E. Ahene and F. Li (Eds.): FCS 2022, CCIS 1726, pp. 377–391, 2022.
https://doi.org/10.1007/978-981-19-8445-7_24

or physical harm to users and bring reputation and economic losses to hospitals [2]. Meanwhile, data processing in cloud servers may also lead to the leakage of private information.

For these security problems, various privacy protection schemes have been proposed. Zhu *et al.* [3,4] designed ML-KNN (multi-label k-nearest neighbor) classification scheme, enables users to diagnose multiple diseases simultaneously and to detect possible relationships between certain diseases. Liu *et al.*. [5] designed a medical pre-diagnosis model base on naive Bayes classifier, and outsourced medical data by adding noise for privacy protection. Wang *et al.* [6] designed a secure SVM (Support Vector Machine) algorithm based on multi-key, realize outsourcing training and evaluation of the medical internet of things. The security schemes adopted by the above pre-diagnosis models have certain deficiencies in data availability and computing efficiency, we need to find other more efficient security schemes.

Secret sharing technology proposed by Shamir [7] can be classified into secret sharing based on polynomial interpolation and additive secret sharing according to different secret splitting methods. Secure multi-party computation based on additive secret sharing (SS-MPC) has widely used due to its high computational efficiency and low communication cost. Therefore, design based on secret sharing has always been the goal of research in practical engineering fields. It completes our needs in efficiency, data availability, and data security.

Exception that, we can also improve the query efficiency from the way of query. Zhu *et al.* [3] combined the K-means clustering algorithm to narrow the query range, but this query has certain deviation. Cheng *et al.* [8] designed a secure KNN query scheme based on the two trapdoors public-key cryptosystem (DT-PKC) [9] and proposed a method to establish a k-d tree index in the optimization stage. But the scheme design does not give the detailed generation algorithm. The index is generated by the data owners in the local plaintext.

Based on the nearest-neighbor (NN) classification algorithm, we design an efficient index Nearest Neighbor query model in dual cloud architecture. We design a series of secure interaction protocols based on additive secret sharing, which can protect data privacy without affecting the computational availability.

Our main contributions can be summarized as follows:

- We propose a new secure indexed nearest neighbor query framework for privacy-preserving classification in preliminary medical diagnosis.
- Our scheme do not rely on computationally intensive cryptographic primitives, so we can significantly improve computational efficiency.
- Theoretical analysis proves that our scheme is secure under the semi-honest security model. Simulation experiments and the performance demonstrate that our scheme outperforms the previous works.

The article is organized as follows. Section 2 introduces some preliminaries. In Sect. 3, we will describe our system architecture, security model. In Sect. 4, we describe the building blocks in our design. Section 5 gives the details of our scheme. Then, in Sect. 6 and 7, we analyze the security and performance of our proposed scheme. In Sect. 8, concludes the whole article.

2   Preliminary

In this section, we introduce some basic preliminary concepts, such as additive secret sharing and k-d tree, which are the basis of our scheme. Table 1 lists the basic notations used in this paper.

Table 1. Basic notation

Notation	Definition
$\langle x \rangle$	Additive secret share of x in $\mathbb{Z}_{2^l}$
$\langle x \rangle_2$	Additive secret share of x in $\mathbb{Z}_2$
$\langle x \rangle^A$	Cloud A's additive secret share of x
$\langle x \rangle^B$	Cloud B's additive secret share of x
Mul	Secure multiplication
SD	Secure squared euclidean distance
SC	Secure squared comparison
SVS	Secure vector sorting
SCT	Secure create tree
$LNNS$	Local nearest neighbor search
$SNNS$	Secure nearest neighbor search

2.1   Additive Secret Sharing

Additive secret sharing is one of the secret sharing schemes for multi-party secure computing (MPC), where the splitting and aggregation of secrets are done using additive methods. We can view additive sharing as a threshold secret sharing scheme (n, n). without loss of generality we set n to be 2. When we additively share an l-bit value a, one party A generates $a_0 \in \mathbb{Z}_{2^l}$ uniformly at random, and sends $a_1 = a - a_0 \ mod \ 2^l$ to the other party B. We denote a_0 as $\langle a \rangle^A$ and a_1 as $\langle a \rangle^B$. To reconstruct Rec an additive shared value, both parties send their share to the recipient and computes $\langle a \rangle^A + \langle a \rangle^B$. Given two shared value $\langle x \rangle$ and $\langle y \rangle$, it is easy to calculate the sum of two secret sharing just need A and B to add their locally held shares: $\langle x \rangle^A + \langle y \rangle^A = \langle z \rangle^A \ mod \ 2^l, \langle x \rangle^B + \langle y \rangle^B = \langle z \rangle^B \ mod \ 2^l$.

In secure multiplication Mul, we need to prepare the pre-computed multiplicative triple proposed by Beaver [11]. a and b are random values on $\mathbb{Z}_{2^l}$ and $c = a \cdot b$, then (a, b, c) is a multiplicative triple. There are two ways to generate triples based on linearly homomorphic encryption (LHE) and oblivious transfer (OT), which can learn more in [12].

Calculating the secret sharing on $\mathbb{Z}_2$ is the same way, except that the addition $(+)$ and multiplication $(\cdot)$ need to be replaced by XOR $(\oplus)$ and AND $(\wedge)$ operations.

Algorithm 1. Secure Multiplication (Mul)

Input: A has $\langle x \rangle^A, \langle y \rangle^A, \langle a \rangle^A, \langle b \rangle^A, \langle c \rangle^A$; B has $\langle x \rangle^B, \langle y \rangle^B, \langle a \rangle^B, \langle b \rangle^B, \langle c \rangle^B$.

Output: A outputs $\langle z \rangle^A$; B outputs $\langle z \rangle^B$.

1: A: $\langle \alpha \rangle^A \leftarrow \langle x \rangle^A - \langle a \rangle^A, \langle \beta \rangle^A \leftarrow \langle y \rangle^A - \langle b \rangle^A$,and sends $\langle \alpha \rangle^A, \langle \beta \rangle^A$ to B.

2: B: $\langle \alpha \rangle^B \leftarrow \langle x \rangle^B - \langle a \rangle^B, \langle \beta \rangle^B \leftarrow \langle y \rangle^B - \langle b \rangle^B$,and sends $\langle \alpha \rangle^B, \langle \beta \rangle^B$ to A.

3: A: $\langle z \rangle^A = \langle c \rangle^A + \langle b \rangle^A \cdot \alpha + \langle a \rangle^A \cdot \beta$

4: B: $\langle z \rangle^B = \langle c \rangle^B + \langle b \rangle^B \cdot \alpha + \langle a \rangle^B \cdot \beta + \alpha \cdot \beta$

2.2 k-d Tree

The k-d tree(k-dimensional tree) is a data structure of k-dimensional Euclidean space points. k-d tree can be used to build a spatial index to improve the search efficiency in multidimensional search. The non-leaf nodes of the tree partition the hyperplane space into two parts, and the left subtree of the node represents the points on the left side of the hyperplane, and the right subtree represents the points on the right side of the hyperplane.

3 System Architecture and Design Goal

3.1 System Architecture

Our proposed system architecture consists of four entities: data owners O, two cloud servers A and B, and users U (Fig. 1)

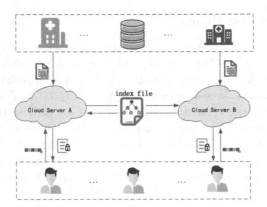

Fig. 1. System architecture.

1) **Data Owner**: O are Hospitals or databases with a large amount of medical data. The outsourced data is secretly divided and uploaded to the cloud A and B.

2) **Cloud Servers**: A and B are two semi-honest cloud servers. Take on computation intensive work. They will receive outsourced data from O and requests from U, and return query results to U.

3) **User**: U will upload the request vector to cloud A and B, and accept the secret share of the query results returned from A and B.

We consider that both the users and data owners are limited computation power and can only undertake simple computational tasks. Moreover, we assume that the dual cloud computing framework exists in realistic environments. They may belong to two different or even competitive service providers.

3.2   Security Model

The cloud server A and B are semi-honest entities. They will follow the protocol process completely, but in the process they try to obtain outsourced data, query vectors, and other private information. Besides, the data owners and users always honest and have secure communication channels with other entities.

We introduce a passive and polynomial-time adversary $\mathcal{A}$. $\mathcal{A}$ can control one of the cloud servers A or B and get its execution view. But $\mathcal{A}$ cannot control two cloud servers at the same time, this limitation is typical in the adversary model.

3.3   Design Goals

In this paper, our scheme will be designed with the following design goals.

1) **Data privacy.** The main concern in our design is to protect the privacy of the outsourced data and query data. The cloud servers or the adversary $\mathcal{A}$ should be prevented from learning any content of the private data.

2) **Correctness.** The interactive computing between cloud servers A and B should be able to return correct query results.

3) **Offline.** Support offline data owners and offline users is quite necessary in terms of the system's scalability.

4   Basic Secure Computation Protocols

In this section, we design a series of secure computation sub-protocol based on additive secret sharing. We emphasize that in the following all secret splitting, secret reconstruction, and secure computation are on $\mathbb{Z}_{2^l}$. For the brevity expression, we omit "$mod\ 2^l$" in the following content.

Algorithm 2. Secure Squared Euclidean Distance (SD)

Input: A has $\{x_1^A \ \ldots \ x_n^A\}, \{y_1^A \ \ldots \ y_n^A\}$; B has $\{x_1^B \ \ldots \ x_n^B\}, \{y_1^B \ \ldots \ y_n^B\}$.
Output: A outputs $\langle D \rangle^A$; B outputs $\langle D \rangle^B$.
1: **for** $i \leftarrow 1$ to n **do**
2:     A, B: $\langle z_i \rangle = \langle x_i \rangle - \langle y_i \rangle$
3:     $A \ \& \ B$: $\{\langle d_i \rangle^A, \langle d_i \rangle^B\} \leftarrow Mul(\langle z_i \rangle, \langle z_i \rangle)$
4: **end for**
5: A, B: $\langle D \rangle \leftarrow \sum_{i=1}^{n} \langle d_i \rangle$

4.1 Secure Squared Euclidean Distance

We design the SD to securely compute the squared Euclidean distance under secret sharing. We first consider the one-dimensional data case where the cloud A holds x^A and y^A, the cloud B holds x^B and y^B. Actually we need to calculate the value of $((x_1 + x_2) - (y_1 + y_2))^2$, then we get the equation $((x_1 - y_1) + (x_2 - y_2))^2$. It is easily calculated by Mul.

As illustrated in Algorithm 4. When we calculate the Euclidean distance of two n-dimensional vectors, we will calculate the data of each dimension in turn. The calculation method is similar for the one dimension.

4.2 Secure Comparison

Our design idea is derived from the secure two-way decomposition protocol in [13,14]. If we restrict the range of input values of x, y to $[-2^{l-2}, 2^{l-2}]$, when calculations on ring $\mathbb{Z}_{2^l}$, we can notice that the value of $x - y$ are distributed on $[2^{l-1}, 2^l - 1]$ and $[0, 2^{l-1} - 1]$. Specifically, negative values are on $[2^{l-1}, 2^l - 1]$, and non-negative values on $[0, 2^{l-1} - 1]$. Based on this observation, we can convert the comparison of x and y into a bit exaction operation on the MSB(most significant bits) of $x - y$. We adopt the calculation principle of *ripple-carry adder* (RCA). According to the calculation characteristics of RCA, we will iteratively calculate to the MSB. Where, for the main iterative object carry c_i, we have formula (1). To implement in the algorithm, we convert the OR ($\vee$) operation to the AND ($\wedge$), then we get the formula (2).

$$c_i = (p_i \wedge q_i) \vee ((p_i \oplus q_i) \wedge c_{i-1}) \tag{1}$$

$$c_i = \neg \, (\neg \, (p_i \wedge q_i) \wedge \neg \, ((p_i \oplus q_i) \wedge c_{i-1})) \tag{2}$$

Since all computations are bitwise operations, so cloud server convert the $\langle a \rangle$ from $\mathbb{Z}_{2^l}$ to $\mathbb{Z}_2$. In our design, the security comparison algorithm SC is a component of another, rather than a separate existence. So we will convert the secret sharing of MSB a_l to $\mathbb{Z}_{2^l}$. We observe the truth table of "$u_1 \oplus u_2$" and find that the value a_l over $\mathbb{Z}_2$ can be expressed through $a_l = (u_1 - u_2)^2$, where the computation is over $\mathbb{Z}_{2^l}$. Therefore, the secret sharing $\langle a_l \rangle$ over $\mathbb{Z}_{2^l}$ can be obtained. If $t_1 + t_2 = 0$, $x \leq y$, if $t_1 + t_2 = 1$ then $x > y$.

Remark: In calculation process we attention that most operation are over $\mathbb{Z}_2$, correspondingly, we need to adjust the *Mul* algorithm, restrict all values including the generation of multiplicative triples in $\mathbb{Z}_2$.

Algorithm 3. Secure Comparison (SC)

Input: A has $\langle x \rangle^A, \langle y \rangle^A$; B has $\langle x \rangle^B, \langle y \rangle^B$
Output: A outputs $\langle t \rangle^A$; B outputs $\langle t \rangle^B$

1: A,B: $\langle a \rangle \leftarrow \langle y \rangle - \langle x \rangle$
2: A,B: Convert $\langle a \rangle^A$ into a bit string $(p_l, p_{l-1} \cdots p_1)$ convert $\langle a \rangle^B$ into a bit string $(q_l, q_{l-1} \cdots q_1)$
3: A: $\langle p_i \rangle_2^A \leftarrow p_i; \langle q_i \rangle_2^A \leftarrow 0$, satisfies $p_i \leftarrow \langle p_i \rangle_2^A \oplus \langle p_i \rangle_2^B$
4: B: $\langle p_i \rangle_2^B \leftarrow 0; \langle q_i \rangle_2^B \leftarrow q_i$, satisfies $q_i \leftarrow \langle q_i \rangle_2^A \oplus \langle q_i \rangle_2^B$
5: $A\&B$: $(\langle c_1 \rangle_2^A, \langle c_1 \rangle_2^B) \leftarrow Mul(\langle p_1 \rangle_2, \langle q_1 \rangle_2)$
6: A,B: $\langle s_i \rangle_2^A \leftarrow p_i, \langle s_i \rangle_2^B \leftarrow q_i$
7: **for** $i \leftarrow 2$ to $l-1$ **do**
8:     $A\&B$: $(\langle m_i \rangle_2^A, \langle m_i \rangle_2^B) \leftarrow Mul(\langle p_i \rangle_2, \langle q_i \rangle_2) + 1$
9:     $A\&B$: $(\langle n_i \rangle_2^A, \langle n_i \rangle_2^B) \leftarrow Mul(\langle s_i \rangle_2, \langle c_{i-1} \rangle_2) + 1$
10:     $A\&B$: $(\langle c_i \rangle_2^A, \langle c_i \rangle_2^B) \leftarrow Mul(\langle m_i \rangle_2, \langle n_i \rangle_2) + 1$
11: **end for**
12: A,B: $\langle a_l \rangle_2 \leftarrow \langle s_i \rangle_2 + \langle c_{l-1} \rangle_2$, denotes $u_1 \leftarrow \langle a_l \rangle_2^A, u_2 \leftarrow \langle a_l \rangle_2^B$
13: A: $\langle u_1 \rangle^A \leftarrow u_1; \langle u_2 \rangle^A \leftarrow 0$
14: B: $\langle u_1 \rangle^B \leftarrow 0; \langle u_2 \rangle^B \leftarrow u_2$
15: A,B: $\langle t \rangle \leftarrow \langle u_1 \rangle - \langle u_2 \rangle$
16: $A\&B$: $(t_1, t_2) \leftarrow Mul(\langle t \rangle, \langle t \rangle)$
17: **return** t_1, t_2

4.3 Secure Vector Sorting

Supposed that two n-dimensional vectors $\langle X \rangle$ and $\langle Y \rangle$ are shared by cloud A and B. Specify a dimension i, by executing the SVS algorithm, cloud sever will get the vector sorted according to the i-th dimension. Before that, we need execution the secure comparison algorithm SC to get the comparison result between two vectors in i-th dimension data.

According to the characteristics of the output results of the security comparison algorithm SC, our calculation is based on the following two formulas: $X_{min} = X_1 + t \cdot (X_2 - X_1)$, $X_{max} = X_2 + t \cdot (X_1 - X_2)$. From the calculation results, during the SVS algorithm, the secret share have been reshared, the cloud server participating in the calculation cannot obtain any private information.

5 Secure Nearest Neighbor Search

This section we will fully introduce our scheme. The outsourced data uploads from O, cloud A and B generate k-d tree index, U uploads the target vector. Cloud servers get the results through interactive calculation. Return the secret shared to U. The U reconstructs the secret share and obtains query result.

Algorithm 4. Secure Vector Sorting (SVS)

Input: A has$\langle X_1 \rangle^A, \langle X_2 \rangle^A, \langle t \rangle^A$; B has $\langle X_1 \rangle^B, \langle X_2 \rangle^B, \langle t \rangle^B$
Output: A outputs $\langle X_{min} \rangle^A, \langle X_{max} \rangle^A$; B outputs $\langle X_{min} \rangle^B, \langle X_{max} \rangle^B$
1: A, B: $\langle S \rangle \leftarrow \langle X_2 \rangle - \langle X_1 \rangle$, $\langle M \rangle \leftarrow \langle X_1 \rangle - \langle X_2 \rangle$
2: **for** $j \leftarrow 1$ **to** n **do**
3: $\quad A \& B$: $\langle z_i \rangle^A, \langle z_i \rangle^B \leftarrow Mul(\langle s_i \rangle^A, \langle t \rangle^A, \langle s_i \rangle^B, \langle t \rangle^B)$
4: $\quad A, B$:$\langle X_{min} \rangle \leftarrow \langle X_1 \rangle + \langle Z \rangle$
5: **end for**
6: **for** $j \leftarrow 1$ **to** n **do**
7: $\quad A \& B$:$\langle z_i \rangle^A, \langle z_i \rangle^B \leftarrow Mul(\langle m_i \rangle^A, \langle t \rangle^A, \langle m_i \rangle^B, \langle t \rangle^B)$
8: $\quad A, B$:$\langle X_{max} \rangle \leftarrow \langle X_2 \rangle + \langle Z \rangle$
9: **end for**

5.1 Data Outsourcing

Data owners O first divide outsourced data locally, $arr \leftarrow \langle arr \rangle^A + \langle arr \rangle^B$. Specifically, for each vector $X_i = (x_{i,1}, x_{i,2}, \cdots, x_{i,m})$ in arr to be outsourced, the data owner will randomly generate a set of values from $\mathbb{Z}_{2^l}$ as $\langle X \rangle^A = (r_{i,1}, r_{i,2}, \cdots, r_{i,m})$, then calculate $\langle X \rangle^B = (x_{i,1} - r_{i,1}, \cdots, x_{i,m} - r_{i,m})$. Similar processing of all vectors in the matrix, data owners upload additive shares to cloud A and B, after that, data owners can remain offline.

Algorithm 5. Secure Create Tree (SCT)

Input: A has $\langle arr \rangle^A, \langle fa \rangle^A, l$; B has $\langle arr \rangle^B, \langle fa \rangle^B, l$
Output: A outputs $\langle rt \rangle^A$; B outputs $\langle rt \rangle^B$
1: **if** $\langle arr \rangle$ is None **then**
2: $\quad$ **return** None
3: **end if**
4: A and B sort the vectors through SC and SVS.
5: A, B: $\langle rt \rangle = \langle arr[mid] \rangle$
6: A, B: $\langle rt \rangle.fa = \langle fa \rangle$
7: $(\langle lef \rangle^A, \langle lef \rangle^B) \leftarrow SCT(\langle arr[0 : mid] \rangle, \langle rt \rangle, l + 1)$
8: $(\langle rgh \rangle^A, \langle rgh \rangle^B) \leftarrow SCT(\langle arr[mid + 1 :] \rangle, \langle rt \rangle, l + 1)$
9: **return** $\langle rt \rangle^A, \langle rt \rangle^B$

5.2 Secure Create Tree

With SCT algorithm cloud A and B can create k-d tree index for the outsourced data. $\langle arr \rangle$ is the secret share of the matrix, contain m vectors of n-dimensional data, $\langle fa \rangle$ is parent node of the current node, its initial value is None, l denotes the dimension of the current vector with an initial value 1.

According to the tree building process, clouds A and B sort the vectors in the matrix by a certain dimension firstly. There are many ways to select dimensions.

In our scheme, we consider order switching. Then, cloud server take the vector of the median index value as the current root node. Finally, cloud A and B will update the input parameters, and index the left (right) subtree according to this generation way. We define the exit in the begin, which returns when the $\langle arr \rangle$ received by cloud A and B is empty. After the algorithm is completed, clouds A and B will obtain the secret share of the index tree and save it locally. Note that cloud A or B locally stored index files do not have indexing capabilities, and A and B do not acquire any private information about outsourced data. Figure 2 is an example of the k-d tree index, in this example, we set $2^l = 16$.

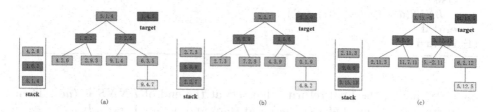

Fig. 2. (a) complete index tree as well as the path stack. (b) Secret share saved by cloud A. (c) Secret share saved by cloud B.

5.3 Query Vector Upload

Users secret sharing the target vector tag into $\langle tag \rangle^A$ and $\langle tag \rangle^B$, the segmentation method is similar to outsourcing data, then send them to A and B, respectively.

5.4 Local Nearest Neighbor Search

After receiving the query request from U, cloud A and B execute nearest neighbor query on the target vector. The complete query divides into two parts, get local nearest neighbors, then adjust to global nearest neighbors.

In the traversal process, Cloud A and B will utilize the local path stack $\langle st \rangle$ to record the visited nodes respectively. After determining the current dimension based on depth d, then they compare the target vector $\langle tag \rangle$ with the currently traversed node $\langle rt \rangle$, if $tag[l]$ is less than $rt[l]$, traversal query in the left subtree, otherwise, traversal query in the right subtree. Figure 2 contains the path stack generated in $LNNS$.

5.5 Secure Nearest Neighbor Search

Though the $LNNS$ algorithm, we get the local nearest neighbor point $\langle ne \rangle$ and path stack $\langle st \rangle$. In $LNNS$ we denote the nearest neighbor as $\langle rt \rangle$ for program

---

Algorithm 6. Local Nearest Neighbor Search $(LNNS)$

Input: A has $\langle rt \rangle^A, \langle tag \rangle^A, d$; B has $\langle rt \rangle^B, \langle tag \rangle^B, d$.
Output: A outputs $\langle rt \rangle^A, \langle st \rangle^A$; B outputs $\langle rt \rangle^B, \langle st \rangle^B$.
1: **if** $\langle rt \rangle$ is None **then**
2:     **return** $\langle fa \rangle^A, \langle fa \rangle^B$
3: **end if**
4: A, B: $\langle rt \rangle$ push in $\langle st \rangle$
5: A, B: $\leftarrow d \% n$
6: **if** $SC(\langle tag[l] \rangle, \langle rt[l] \rangle)$ **then**
7:     $LNNS(d+1, \langle lef \rangle, \langle rt \rangle, \langle st \rangle)$
8: **else**
9:     $LNNS(d+1, \langle rgh \rangle, \langle rt \rangle, \langle st \rangle)$
10: **end if**
11: **return** $\langle rt \rangle^A, \langle rt \rangle^B$

---

integrity, infact, the final return value $\langle rt \rangle$ at the end of $LNNS$ is $\langle ne \rangle$. Then calculate the distance between $\langle ne \rangle$ and $\langle tag \rangle$ and denote it as $\langle nd \rangle$.

Next, we will take the path stack for backtracking queries. Cloud A and B take the top element of their respective stack as current node. Combine the current node to determine the position of the sibling node $\langle br \rangle$. After that cloud A and B calculate the distance $\langle cud \rangle$. Compare it with local nearest neighbor distance $\langle nd \rangle$, if current distance $\langle cud \rangle$ is less than local nearest neighbor distance $\langle nd \rangle$, update the current nearest neighbor $\langle ne \rangle$ and nearest distance $\langle nd \rangle$.

In the following, we will determine whether the nearest neighbor is in the sibling subtree. We denote the dimensional plane divided on the parent node $\langle fa \rangle$ as the hyperplane, $\langle ne \rangle$ is the center of the sphere, and $\langle nd \rangle$ is the radius of sphere noted as hyper-sphere. Determines whether the hyperplane intersects the hyper-sphere, if it intersects, it indicates that there may be a shorter nearest neighbor in the subtree where the sibling node. Specific performance in the algorithm is: to calculate the difference between $\langle tag \rangle$ and $\langle fa \rangle$ in the previous dimension. To avoid the problem of duplicate stack-in and stack-out between sibling nodes, we will mark the visited nodes, and also make intersection judgments only in the unmarked case.

When A and B get the global nearest neighbor $\langle ne \rangle^A, \langle ne \rangle^B$, send them to U. U can recover it by running $ne \leftarrow Rec(\langle ne \rangle^A, \langle ne \rangle^B)$.

6 Security Analysis

In this section, we will analyze the security of our proposed scheme under the generic composable framework [15]. In order to prove the security of our proposed algorithms under the semi-honest model, we need prove that the actual execution images of these sub-protocols are computationally indistinguishable from their simulated execution image. we introduce the following two lemmas, for detailed proofs of *Lemma 1* and *2* refer to [16,17].

Algorithm 7. Secure Nearest Neighbor Search $(SNNS)$

Input: A has $\langle rt \rangle^A, \langle tag \rangle^A, d$; B has $\langle rt \rangle^B, \langle tag \rangle^B, d$.
Output: A outputs $\langle rt \rangle^A$; B outputs $\langle rt \rangle^B$
1: $A\&B$: Run $LNNS$ to get $\langle ne \rangle^A, \langle ne \rangle^B, \langle st \rangle^A, \langle st \rangle^B$
2: $A\&B$: $(\langle nd \rangle^A, \langle nd \rangle^B) \leftarrow SD(\langle ne \rangle, \langle tag \rangle)$
3: **while** $\langle st[top] \rangle$ is not $\langle rt \rangle$ **do**
4:     A,B: $\langle cur \rangle \leftarrow \langle st[top] \rangle$, $\langle fa \rangle \leftarrow \langle cur \rangle.fa$, $\langle st \rangle.pop()$
5:     A,B: $\langle br \rangle \leftarrow \langle fa \rangle.lef$ or $\langle br \rangle \leftarrow \langle fa \rangle.rgh$
6:     $A\&B$:$(\langle cud \rangle^A, \langle cud \rangle^B) \leftarrow SD(\langle cur \rangle, \langle tag \rangle)$
7:     **if** $SC(\langle cud \rangle, \langle nd \rangle)$ **then**
8:         A,B: $\langle ne \rangle \leftarrow \langle cur \rangle$
9:         A,B: $\langle nd \rangle \leftarrow \langle cud \rangle$
10:     **end if**
11:     **if** $\langle cur \rangle$ not visited **then**
12:         A, B : $\langle dis \rangle \leftarrow \langle fa[l-1] \rangle - \langle tag[l-1] \rangle$
13:         **if** $SC(\langle dis \rangle, \langle nd \rangle)$ **then**
14:             A,B: Mark $\langle br \rangle$ as visited
15:             $LNNS(l-1, \langle br \rangle, \langle fa \rangle, \langle st \rangle)$
16:         **end if**
17:     **end if**
18: **end while**

Lemma 1. If a random elements r is uniformly distributed on $\mathbb{Z}_n$ and independent from any variable $x \in \mathbb{Z}_n$, then $r \pm x$ is also uniformly random and independent of from x.

Lemma 2. If all sub protocols are fully simulated, then the protocol is fully simulated.

Theorem 1. *The SC algorithm is secure under the semi-honest model.*

Proof. The execution image of cloud A is $\Pi_A(SC) = \{\langle x \rangle^A, \langle y \rangle^A, \langle p_i \rangle_2^A,$ $\langle q_i \rangle_2^A, \langle c_i \rangle_2^A, \langle m_i \rangle_2^A, \langle n_i \rangle_2^A, u_1, u_2, t_1\}$, we assume that $\Pi_A^S(SC) = \{\langle x' \rangle^A, \langle y' \rangle^A,$ $\langle p_i' \rangle_2^A, \langle q_i' \rangle_2^A, \langle c_i' \rangle_2^A, \langle m_i' \rangle_2^A, \langle n_i' \rangle_2^A, u_1', u_2', t_1'\}$. $\{\langle x \rangle^A, \langle y \rangle^A, \langle p_i \rangle_2^A, \langle q_i \rangle_2^A, \langle m_i \rangle_2^A,$ $\langle n_i \rangle_2^A, \langle c_i \rangle_2^A\}$ are addition secret shares or calculated by Mul algorithm, and $\{\langle x' \rangle^A, \langle y' \rangle^A, \langle p_i' \rangle_2^A \langle q_i' \rangle_2^A, \langle m_i' \rangle_2^A, \langle n_i' \rangle_2^A, \langle c_i' \rangle_2^A\}$ are random value from $\mathbb{Z}_{2^l}$ or $\mathbb{Z}_2$, they are computationally indistinguishable. u_1 and u_2 get locally, and t calculated by Mul. They are computationally indistinguishable from $\{u_1', u_2', t_1'\}$. So $\Pi_A(SC)$ is computationally indistinguishable from $\Pi_A^S(SC)$.

Next, we consider the execution image of cloud B. The interactive part of execution image $\Pi_B(SC)$ is obtained by execute Mul, and local computing part can guarantee security. We can conclude that $\Pi_B(SC)$ is computationally indistinguishable from $\Pi_B^S(SC)$. From the above analysis, we draw a conclusion that the proposed SC algorithm is secure under the semi-honest model.

Theorem 2. *Under the semi-honest model, the SVS, SCT and LNNS are secure.*

Proof. Our SVS, SCT, $LNNS$ and $SNNS$ are composed of SD, SC and Mul, according to *Lemma 2*, it can be demonstrate the security of SVS, SCT and $LNNS$.

Theorem 3. *The $SNNS$ algorithm is secure under the semi-honest model, meanwhile, the adversary $\mathcal{A}$ cannot obtain outsourced data, query data, and query results.*

Proof. In the $SNNS$ algorithm, the interaction between the two clouds mainly exits in $LNNS$, and the security of sub-modules that make up the $LNNS$ algorithm have been proved above. Therefore, it can be known that our $SNNS$ algorithm is secure under the semi-honest model.

Next, we will demonstrate that our proposed security nearest neighbor query scheme can resist the attack of adversary $\mathcal{A}$. $\mathcal{A}$ can intercept all intermediate data exchanged between two cloud servers. Since all intermediate data are random values on $\mathbb{Z}_{2^l}$, they are random and meaningless to $\mathcal{A}$. If $\mathcal{A}$ wants to obtain private information, it needs to control both cloud A and B. However, this is not allowed in our security model. Therefore, our scheme is secure under the semi-honest model and protects outsourced data, query data, and query results from being unknown to $\mathcal{A}$.

7   Evaluation and Performance Analysis

In this section, We present the evaluation results of sub-protocol and our scheme. In addition, we did not consider the overhead of the Beaver triplet generation, as we assumed that sufficient triples were prepared prior to the evaluation.

We develop a Python prototype that implements our scheme. The evaluation was performed on two personal computers in LAN setting. Each computer was equipped with a 6-core AMD Ryzen 5 5600H CPU @ 3.3 GHz and 16 GB RAM.

7.1   Algorithm Performance Evaluation

We will evaluate and analyze our proposed algorithms in controlling different influencing parameters. SD, SC and SVS will be affected by the bit width of the process data, while SD and SVS are more sensitive in vector dimensions, and we will evaluate SCT in different datasets.

We evaluate the computation time and communication cost of SVS, SC and SD at different bit-width of input, shown in Fig. 3(a) and Fig. 3(b). It is easy to conclude that their computation cost rises as the bit-width increase, where the change of SC is obvious, mainly because of the increase in the number of interactions between the two clouds. The number of their interactions grows linearly with the bit width, this will bring more communication delay. Meanwhile, their communication overhead go up in the bit-width. We evaluate the SD and SVS in different dimensions, while we control the bit width of the input value $l=16$. From Fig. 3(c) and Fig. 3(d), we can see that both the running time and communication cost increase with the dimension of the vector.

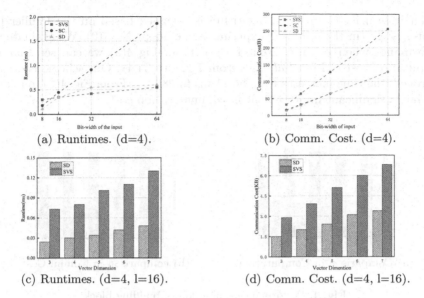

(a) Runtimes. (d=4).   (b) Comm. Cost. (d=4).

(c) Runtimes. (d=4, l=16).   (d) Comm. Cost. (d=4, l=16).

Fig. 3. Performance evaluation of building block

For the index generation algorithm *SCT*, we evaluate the performance in four different sizes of public datasets. Prostate_Cancer[1], bodyfat[2], diabetes[3], car_evaluation[4]. From Table 2, we can conclude that the index establishment time is greatly affected by the size of dataset. Although the computation cost is very high, but the index establishment is belongs the offline part.

Table 2. Performance evaluation of SCT

Datasets	Prostate_Cancer	bodyfat	Diabetes	Car_evaluation
Times (s)	5.515	41.74	394.55	2034.25
Comm. (MB)	0.743	8.193	44.353	246.891

7.2 Scheme Performance Evaluation

Next, we will evaluate our scheme and compare the experimental results with the work of Liu *et al.* [18], because the system structure designed in the scheme of Liu *et al.* is most similar to ours. We adopt the car_evaluation dataset from the public dataset UCI for testing, which contains 1728 records with 6 attribute values every record.

---

[1] https://www.kaggle.com/datasets/sajidsaifi/prostate-cancer.
[2] https://www.kaggle.com/datasets/fedesoriano/body-fat-prediction-dataset.
[3] https://www.kaggle.com/datasets/mathchi/diabetes-data-set.
[4] http://archive.ics.uci.edu/ml/datasets/Car+Evaluation.

Their security comparison algorithm is designed based on the Paillier [19] cryptosystem (in the following experiment, we adopt N=512). We evaluate the performance when K varies from 1 to 5. From Fig. 4(a) we can see that the computation cost of Liu *et al.* rises from 7.12 s to 34.4 s. Our scheme is greatly improved, the time increases from 56.11 ms to 280 ms. From Fig. 4(b), our work also has a significant improvement in communication cost.

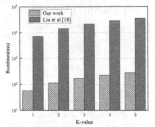
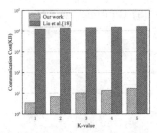
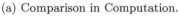

(a) Comparison in Computation.   (b) comparison in Comm. Cost.

Fig. 4. Performance evaluation of building block

The advantages of our scheme are mainly in the following two aspects. Improvements in the security comparison algorithm. The comparison algorithm of Liu *et al.* is designed based on Paillier. In data processing phase, the encryption and decryption steps great reduce the computational efficiency. Our security comparison algorithm is based on secret sharing design, it does not include time-consuming encryption and decryption steps. In addition, we adopted the index query technique, the index is established in the offline phase, which greatly improves the efficiency of the query.

8   Conclusion

We design a secure indexed nearest neighbor query scheme, which can achieve efficient query on outsourced data. Through theoretical analysis, we demonstrate our scheme can achieves outsourced data security and query privacy. From the comparative experimental results, our scheme has better performance. While we note that k-d tree indexing is not effective when dealing with high-dimensional data. We will continue to find a suitable indexing approach for high-dimensional data at later stage.

Acknowledgements. This work was supported by the National Natural Science Foundation of China(62002105, 62072134, U2001205,61902116).

References

1. Hossain, M.S., Ghulam, M.: Cloud-assisted Industrial Internet of Things (IIoT) - Enabled framework for health monitoring. Comput. Netw. **101**, 192–202 (2016)

2. Yi, X., Bouguettaya, A., Georgakopoulos, D., Song, A., Willemson, J.: Privacy protection for wireless medical sensor data. IEEE Trans. Dependable Sec. Comput. **13**(3), 369–380 (2016)
3. Zhu, D., et al.: CREDO: Efficient and privacy-preserving multi-level medical pre-diagnosis based on ML-kNN. J. Inf. Sci. **514**, 244–262 (2020)
4. Zhu, D., Zhu, H., Liu, X., Li, H., Wang, F., Li, H.: Achieve efficient and privacy-preserving medical primary diagnosis based on kNN. In: International Conference on Computer Communication and Networks (ICCCN), pp. 1–9 (2018)
5. Liu, X., Zhu, H., Lu, R., Li, H.: Efficient privacy-preserving online medical primary diagnosis scheme on naive bayesian classification. Peer-to-Peer Netw. Appli. **11**(2), 334–347 (2018)
6. Wang, J., Wu, L., Wang, H., Choo, K.-K.R., He, D.: An efficient and privacy-preserving outsourced support vector machine training for internet of medical things. IEEE Internet of Things J. **8**(1), 458–473 (2021)
7. Shamir, A.: How to share a secret. Commun. ACM **22**(11), 612–613 (1979)
8. Cheng, K., Wang, L., Shen, Y., Wang, H., Wang, Y., Jiang, X., Zhong, H.: Secure kk-NN Query on Encrypted Cloud Data with Multiple Keys. IEEE Trans. Big Data **7**(4), 689–702 (2021)
9. Liu, X., Deng, R.H., Choo, K.-K.R., Weng, J.: An efficient privacy-preserving out-sourced calculation toolkit with multiple keys. IEEE Trans. Inf. Forensics Secur. **13**(10), 2668–2669 (2018)
10. Yao, A.C.: Protocols for secure computations. In: 23rd Annual Symposium on Foundations of Computer Science (sfcs 1982), pp. 160–164 (1982)
11. Beaver, D.: Efficient multiparty protocols using circuit randomization. In: International Cryptology Conference, pp. 420–432 (1991)
12. Mohassel, P., Zhang, Y.: SecureML: A system for scalable privacy-preserving machine learning. In: 2017 IEEE Symposium on Security and Privacy (SP), pp. 19–38 (2017)
13. de Cock, M., et al.: Efficient and private scoring of decision trees, support vector machines and logistic regression models based on pre-computation. IEEE Trans. Depend. Sec. Comput. **16**(2), 217–230 (2019)
14. Zheng, Y., Duan, H., Wang, C., Wang, R., Nepal, S.: Securely and efficiently out-sourcing decision tree inference. IEEE Trans. Depend. Sec. Comput. **19**(3), 1841–1855 (2022)
15. Canetti, R.: Universally composable security: a new paradigm for cryptographic protocols. In: Proceedings 42nd IEEE Symposium on Foundations of Computer Science, pp. 136–145 (2001)
16. Bogdanov, D., Niitsoo, M., Toft, T., Willemson, J.: High-performance secure multi-party computation for data mining applications. Int. J. Inf. Secur. **11**(6), 403–418 (2012)
17. Bogdanov, D., Laur, S., Willemson, J.: Sharemind: A framework for fast privacy-preserving computations. In: European Symposium on Research in Computer Security, pp. 192–206 (2008)
18. Liu, L., Su, J., Liu, X., Cheng, R., Huang, K., Wang, X.: Toward Highly Secure Yet Efficient KNN Classification Scheme on Outsourced Cloud Data. IEEE Internet Things J. **6**(6), 9841–9852 (2019)
19. Paillier, P.: Public-key cryptosystems based on composite degree resid-uosity classes. In: European Cryptology Conference, pp. 223–238 (1999)

Quantum Cryptography

Quantum Information Splitting Scheme of Arbitrary Three-Qubit State by Using a Four-Qubit Cluster State and a Bell State

Dongfen Li[ID], Jie Zhou[✉], Xiaolong Yang, Yuqaio Tan, Yundan Zheng, and Xiaofang Liu

College of Computer Science and Cyber Security (Oxford Brookes College), Chengdu University of Technology, Chengdu, China
zj135888081@163.com

Abstract. With the rapid development of Internet technology, the confidentiality of information content and network security are facing severe challenges, and quantum teleportation ensures the absolute security of information transmission based on its basic characteristics. In this paper, we propose a scheme for quantum information splitting of arbitrary three-qubit state by using a four-qubit cluster state and a Bell state. The scheme only needs to perform two Bell state measurement operations and two single-qubit measurement operations, and Bob can reconstruct the transmitted arbitrary three-qubit state by means of appropriate unitary operations. Compared with other information splitting schemes of arbitrary three-qubit state, our scheme is characterized by higher transmission efficiency. Then we use channel authentication method to ensure the communication security of our scheme under different attack scenarios. Furthermore, we take comparisons with the other quantum information splitting schemes in five aspects of quantum information bits transmitted, necessary operations, consumption of quantum resource, consumption of classical resource and intrinsic efficiency. It is concluded that our scheme has significant advantages of higher intrinsic efficiency and high security.

Keywords: Quantum communication · Communication security · Quantum teleportation · Network information security · Channel authentication

1 Introduction

With the penetration of the Internet into every corner of social and economic life, information security incidents have also increased year by year. In recent years, the constantly exposed monitoring and eavesdropping scandals and user privacy leakage incidents have further intensified the public's concerns about network and information security [13]. Therefore, whether from the level of personal needs or the level of national strategy, the problem of network and

© The Author(s), under exclusive license to Springer Nature Singapore Pte Ltd. 2022
E. Ahene and F. Li (Eds.): FCS 2022, CCIS 1726, pp. 395–409, 2022.
https://doi.org/10.1007/978-981-19-8445-7_25

information security has reached the moment of urgent need to be solved. In traditional digital communication systems, information can be passively monitored or copied. Some eavesdroppers can even change information. In addition, the security of classical cryptographic technology is a computing problem based on mathematical problems. Any breakthrough in solving these mathematical problems or increasing computing power may make cryptographic technology vulnerable [18]. With the emergence of new technologies such as distributed computing, cloud computing and GPU, the computing speed is rapidly accelerated, and the security of classical cryptography will be threatened at any time. Moreover, the existing cryptographic system can not find the threat through a clear method. The emergence of quantum computing technology has exacerbated the uneasiness of classical encryption. For example, Shor [21] designed an algorithm to find prime factors of large numbers. Once quantum computers are available, Shor's algorithm will bring security threats to all classical cryptographic protocols [22]. Quantum communication is based on the principle of quantum uncertainty, the theorem of quantum non cloning and the principle of quantum mechanics of quantum entanglement. Its appearance subverts the security of classical algorithms. In a quantum system, information cannot be copied or read by eavesdroppers. Moreover, any uncontrollable control in quantum information may be detected by legitimate users [15]. Compared with traditional communication methods, the biggest advantage of quantum communication is its absolute security and high efficiency. Quantum communication will encrypt and transmit information. In this process, the key is not certain and full of randomness. Even if it is intercepted by relevant personnel, it is not easy to obtain real information. In addition, quantum communication has strong anti-interference ability, good concealment performance, low noise ratio needs and the possibility of wide application, This means that it is a powerful tool to ensure the security of network information.

Quantum communication includes quantum teleportation (QT), quantum dense coding [1,12,14,31], quantum key distribution (QKD) [6–8], and so on. Among them, the basic idea of quantum teleportation is to use the multi-particle entangled state as a channel to combine a part of classical information to transmit quantum information to the receiver. It has the advantages of high reliability, low communication complexity and resource saving. In 1993, Bennet et al. [2] first proposed this idea. They used Bell states as quantum channels to realize the transmission of arbitrary single-qubit state. Up to now, many researchers are still committed to studying the scheme of quantum teleportation. For example, in 2021, Cao et al. [4]proposed to use the eight-particle entangled state to realize the deterministic quantum teleportation of arbitrary four-qubit state based on the orthogonal basis measurement. In addition, many novel quantum teleportation schemes have been proposed, such as quantum information splitting(QIS), quantum secret sharing(QSS) [3,9,19], controlled quantum teleportation(CQT) [10,11,24] and quantum bidirectional teleportation (QBT) [29,30]. Among them, QIS refers to the sender transmitting quantum information to multiple receivers. These receivers cannot have quantum information alone, and only they help each other can reconstruct the corresponding quantum state. In 2010, Yin *et al.* [25]proposed a quantum information splitting scheme using a simple four-particle cluster state as a channel for arbitrary single-qubit state with two or three receivers. In the same year, Nie *et al.* [17]proposed a scheme for splitting quantum information of arbitrary three-qubit state using two four-particle cluster states as channel. In 2012, Tu *et al.* [26] proposed a scheme for splitting quantum information of arbitrary two-qubit state using the maximum entangled state of six qubits as the channel. In 2013, Li *et al.* [16] proposed a scheme to split the information of arbitrary single-qubit state by using four-qubit entangled state as quantum channel. In 2017, Marlon *et al.* [20]proposed the probability transmission scheme for arbitrary single-qubit state by using the four-qubit cluster state and the information splitting scheme for arbitrary two qubits state by using a four-qubit cluster state and a Bell state. In 2020, Yang *et al.* [28] proposed a quantum information splitting scheme of arbitrary two-qubit state using a five-qubit cluster state and a Bell state as the channel. In 2021, Rajiuddin *et al.* [23]used three groups of GHZ states to split the quantum information of arbitrary three-qubit state, and proved the security of the protocol. In 2022, Xu *et al.* [27] proposed a quantum information splitting scheme for splitting arbitrary three-qubit state based on a five-qubit cluster state and Bell state. Compared with other schemes for splitting arbitrary three-qubit states, this protocol has the advantages of lower resource consumption.

In this paper, we propose a quantum information splitting scheme by using a four-qubit cluster state and a Bell state as the channel to transmit arbitrary three-qubit state, which has higher transmission efficiency than other protocols. In order to achieve information splitting, Alice and Charlie only need to perform two Bell state measurement operations and two single-qubit measurement operations on corresponding qubits. Based on the measurement results of Alice and Charlie, the remaining qubits state will collapse to the corresponding state, and then Bob can obtain the target quantum state by performing the appropriate unitary operation. After proposing the scheme, we completed the verification of the scheme through the IBM quantum simulation experiment platform, and then we analyzed the security of the scheme and compared it with other quantum information splitting schemes.

The structure of this paper is as follows: In Sect. 2, the quantum information splitting scheme based on a four-qubit cluster state and a Bell state is presented in detail. In Sect. 3, the scheme is experimentally verified using the IBM Quantum Experience platform. Section 4 provides the security analysis of our scheme. In Sect. 5, the different quantum information splitting schemes are compared and analyzed. Finally, the conclusion is presented in Sect. 6.

2   Specific Schemes

Network security is the most concerned issue of countries, industry practitioners and academia. As a new network security technology, quantum communication is developing rapidly in recent years, and gradually moving towards industrialization and practicality, which is expected to guarantee the absolute security of network information transmission in principle and technology. In this section, we will describe the quantum information splitting scheme for arbitrary three-qubit state by using a four-qubit cluster state and a Bell state as the channel in detail. The legitimate participants in the scheme are sender Alice, receiver Bob and controller Charlie, and the arbitrary three-qubit state Alice wants to transmit is expressed as follows:

$$|\phi\rangle_{ABC} = (a_1|000\rangle + a_2|001\rangle + a_3|010\rangle + a_4|011\rangle$$
$$+ a_5|100\rangle + a_6|101\rangle + a_7|110\rangle + a_8|111\rangle)_{ABC} \tag{1}$$

where the coefficients $a_1, a_2, a_3, a_4, a_5, a_6, a_7$ and a_8 satisfy the normalization condition of the form $|a_1|^2 + |a_2|^2 + |a_3|^2 + |a_4|^2 + |a_5|^2 + |a_6|^2 + |a_7|^2 + |a_8|^2 = 1$.

To realize the transmission of quantum state information, Alice, Bob and Charlie first need to share a six-qubit state composed of a four-qubit cluster state and a Bell state as the quantum channel. The selected four-qubit cluster state and Bell state can be shown as follows:

$$|\phi\rangle_{1234} = \frac{1}{2}(|0000\rangle + |0101\rangle + |1010\rangle + |1111\rangle)_{1234} \tag{2}$$

$$|\phi\rangle_{56} = \frac{1}{\sqrt{2}}(|00\rangle + |11\rangle)_{56} \tag{3}$$

Then the initial state of the whole quantum system here can be defined as:

$$|\Phi\rangle_{ABC123456} = |\phi\rangle_{ABC} \otimes |\phi\rangle_{1234} \otimes |\phi\rangle_{56}$$
$$= \frac{1}{2\sqrt{2}}[(a_1|000\rangle + a_2|001\rangle + a_3|010\rangle + a_4|011\rangle$$
$$+ a_5|100\rangle + a_6|101\rangle + a_7|110\rangle + a_8|111\rangle)_{ABC}$$
$$\otimes (|0000\rangle + |0101\rangle + |1010\rangle + |1111\rangle)_{1234} \otimes (|00\rangle + |11\rangle)_{56} \tag{4}$$

We describe the whole communication process through quantum logic circuit diagram, as shown in Fig. 1.

After Alice completes the preparation of quantum channel, Alice firstly employs a CNOT operation on qubit pair (C,5) with C as control qubit and 5 as target qubit. Then Alice sends particles 3,4,5 to Bob and particle 6 to Charlie. After preparation, to achieve information splitting, Alice employs a Bell state measurement operation on qubit pairs (A,1) and (B,2) respectively, and a single-qubit state measurement operation on qubit C. Charlie employs a single-qubit state measurement operation on qubit 6. After measurement, Bob can obtain 64 possible state with equal probability. According to measurement result of Alice and Charlie, Bob can choose the appropriate unitary operation to reconstruct the arbitrary three-qubit state transmitted by Alice.

The detail steps are as follows:

Step 1: Alice prepares the four-qubit cluster state and the Bell states via the logical circuit in Fig. 1 and employs a CNOT operation on qubit pair (C,5) with C as control qubit and 5 as target qubit. Then Alice sends particles 3,4,5 to Bob

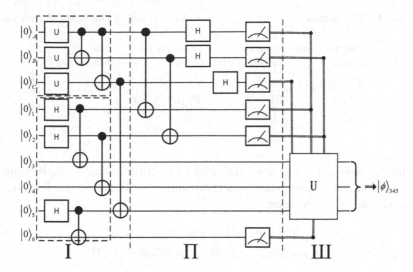

Fig. 1. Quantum logic circuit diagram of the whole process for quantum information splitting. The dotted box at the top of part I represents the preparation of arbitrary three-qubit state, and the dotted box at the bottom represents the preparation of the channel. Part II represents the measurement operation performed by Alice and Charlie and part III represents the operation performed by Bob to reconstruct the state (double real lines represent the classical channel).

and particle 6 to Charlie. Then the quantum state of the whole quantum can be converted into the following form:

$$
\begin{aligned}
|\Phi\rangle_{ABC123456} &= |\phi\rangle_{ABC} \otimes |\phi\rangle_{1234} \otimes |\phi\rangle_{56} \\
&= \frac{1}{2\sqrt{2}}[(a_1|000\rangle + a_3|010\rangle + a_5|100\rangle + a_7|110\rangle)_{ABC} \\
&\quad \otimes (|0000\rangle + |0101\rangle + |1010\rangle + |1111\rangle)_{1234} \otimes (|00\rangle + |11\rangle)_{56} \\
&\quad + (a_2|001\rangle + a_4|011\rangle + a_6|101\rangle + a_8|111\rangle)_{ABC} \\
&\quad \otimes (|0000\rangle + |0101\rangle + |1010\rangle + |1111\rangle)_{1234} \otimes (|10\rangle + |01\rangle)]_{56}
\end{aligned}
\tag{5}
$$

Step 2: Alice makes a Bell state measurement operation on qubit pairs (A,1) and (B,2) respectively, and a single-qubit state measurement operation with the measurement basis $\{|+\rangle, |-\rangle\}$ on qubit C. There will be 32 possible results with equal probability. Alice then encodes her measurement results into five bits classical information and sends those to Bob through the classical channel. And the coding rules are shown in Table 1.

Step 3: Charlie makes a single-qubit measurement operation with the measurement basis $\{|0\rangle, |1\rangle\}$ on the qubit 6. Then Charlie sends measurement result to Bob through classical channel.

Step 4: After the measurement operations taken by Alice and Charlie, the quantum state of the remaining particles 3, 4 and 5 will collapse into 64 corresponding quantum states. Then based on the measurement results of Alice

Table 1. Alice's measurement results and corresponding classical information.

Measurement results	Classical information	Measurement results	Classical information
$\|\Phi\rangle^+_{A1}(\|\Phi\rangle^+_{B2})$	00	$\|\Phi\rangle^-_{A1}(\|\Phi\rangle^-_{B2})$	10
$\|\Psi\rangle^+_{A1}(\|\Psi\rangle^+_{B2})$	01	$\|\Psi\rangle^-_{A1}(\|\Psi\rangle^-_{B2})$	11
$\|+\rangle_C$	0	$\|-\rangle_C$	1

and Charlie, Bob can reconstruct the original quantum state $|\phi\rangle_{345}$ by applying appropriate unitary operations to corresponding collapsed state. The unitary operations can be given below.

$$I = |0\rangle\langle 0| + |1\rangle\langle 1|, \sigma_x = |0\rangle\langle 1| + |1\rangle\langle 0|$$
$$i\sigma_y = |0\rangle\langle 1| - |1\rangle\langle 0|, \sigma_z = |0\rangle\langle 0| - |1\rangle\langle 1| \tag{6}$$

Table 2. The possible results of measurement and the corresponding unitary operations(AMR: Alice's measurement results, CMR: Charlie's measurement results, BS: Bob's state, UO: unitary operations).

AMR	CMR	BS	UO
$\|\Phi\rangle^\pm_{A1}\|\Phi\rangle^+_{B2}\|+\rangle_C$	$\|0\rangle_6$	$a_1\|000\rangle + a_2\|001\rangle + a_3\|010\rangle + a_4\|011\rangle$ $\pm a_5\|100\rangle \pm a_6\|101\rangle \pm a_7\|110\rangle \pm a_8\|111\rangle$	$I \otimes I \otimes I$ $(\sigma_z \otimes I \otimes I)$
$\|\Phi\rangle^\pm_{A1}\|\Phi\rangle^+_{B2}\|-\rangle_C$	$\|0\rangle_6$	$a_1\|000\rangle - a_2\|001\rangle + a_3\|010\rangle - a_4\|011\rangle$ $\pm a_5\|100\rangle \mp a_6\|101\rangle \pm a_7\|110\rangle \mp a_8\|111\rangle$	$I \otimes I \otimes \sigma_z$ $(\sigma_z \otimes I \otimes \sigma_z)$
$\|\Phi\rangle^\pm_{A1}\|\Phi\rangle^+_{B2}\|+\rangle_C$	$\|1\rangle_6$	$a_1\|001\rangle + a_2\|000\rangle + a_3\|011\rangle + a_4\|010\rangle$ $\pm a_5\|101\rangle \pm a_6\|100\rangle \pm a_7\|111\rangle \pm a_8\|110\rangle$	$I \otimes I \otimes \sigma_x$ $(\sigma_z \otimes I \otimes \sigma_x)$
$\|\Phi\rangle^\pm_{A1}\|\Phi\rangle^+_{B2}\|-\rangle_C$	$\|1\rangle_6$	$a_1\|001\rangle - a_2\|000\rangle + a_3\|011\rangle - a_4\|010\rangle$ $\pm a_5\|101\rangle \mp a_6\|100\rangle \pm a_7\|111\rangle \mp a_8\|110\rangle$	$I \otimes I \otimes -i\sigma_y$ $(\sigma_z \otimes I \otimes -i\sigma_y)$
$\|\Phi\rangle^\pm_{A1}\|\Phi\rangle^-_{B2}\|+\rangle_C$	$\|0\rangle_6$	$a_1\|000\rangle + a_2\|001\rangle - a_3\|010\rangle - a_4\|011\rangle$ $\pm a_5\|100\rangle \pm a_6\|101\rangle \mp a_7\|110\rangle \mp a_8\|111\rangle$	$I \otimes \sigma_z \otimes I$ $(\sigma_z \otimes \sigma_z \otimes I)$
$\|\Phi\rangle^\pm_{A1}\|\Phi\rangle^-_{B2}\|-\rangle_C$	$\|0\rangle_6$	$a_1\|000\rangle - a_2\|001\rangle - a_3\|010\rangle + a_4\|011\rangle$ $\pm a_5\|100\rangle \mp a_6\|101\rangle \mp a_7\|110\rangle \pm a_8\|111\rangle$	$I \otimes \sigma_z \otimes \sigma_z$ $(\sigma_z \otimes \sigma_z \otimes \sigma_z)$
$\|\Phi\rangle^\pm_{A1}\|\Phi\rangle^-_{B2}\|+\rangle_C$	$\|1\rangle_6$	$a_1\|001\rangle + a_2\|000\rangle - a_3\|011\rangle - a_4\|010\rangle$ $\pm a_5\|101\rangle \pm a_6\|100\rangle \mp a_7\|111\rangle \mp a_8\|110\rangle$	$I \otimes \sigma_z \otimes \sigma_x$ $(\sigma_z \otimes \sigma_z \otimes \sigma_x)$
$\|\Phi\rangle^\pm_{A1}\|\Phi\rangle^-_{B2}\|-\rangle_C$	$\|1\rangle_6$	$a_1\|001\rangle - a_2\|000\rangle - a_3\|011\rangle + a_4\|010\rangle$ $\pm a_5\|101\rangle \mp a_6\|100\rangle \mp a_7\|111\rangle \pm a_8\|110\rangle$	$I \otimes \sigma_z \otimes -i\sigma_y$ $(\sigma_z \otimes \sigma_z \otimes -i\sigma_y)$
$\|\Phi\rangle^\pm_{A1}\|\Psi\rangle^+_{B2}\|+\rangle_C$	$\|0\rangle_6$	$a_1\|010\rangle + a_2\|011\rangle + a_3\|000\rangle + a_4\|001\rangle$ $\pm a_5\|110\rangle \pm a_6\|111\rangle \pm a_7\|100\rangle \pm a_8\|101\rangle$	$I \otimes \sigma_x \otimes I$ $(\sigma_z \otimes \sigma_x \otimes I)$
$\|\Phi\rangle^\pm_{A1}\|\Psi\rangle^+_{B2}\|-\rangle_C$	$\|0\rangle_6$	$a_1\|010\rangle - a_2\|011\rangle + a_3\|000\rangle - a_4\|001\rangle$ $\pm a_5\|110\rangle \mp a_6\|111\rangle \pm a_7\|100\rangle \mp a_8\|101\rangle$	$I \otimes \sigma_x \otimes \sigma_z$ $(\sigma_z \otimes \sigma_x \otimes \sigma_z)$
$\|\Phi\rangle^\pm_{A1}\|\Psi\rangle^+_{B2}\|+\rangle_C$	$\|1\rangle_6$	$a_1\|011\rangle + a_2\|010\rangle + a_3\|001\rangle + a_4\|000\rangle$ $\pm a_5\|111\rangle \pm a_6\|110\rangle \pm a_7\|101\rangle \pm a_8\|100\rangle$	$I \otimes \sigma_x \otimes \sigma_x$ $(\sigma_z \otimes \sigma_x \otimes \sigma_x)$
$\|\Phi\rangle^\pm_{A1}\|\Psi\rangle^+_{B2}\|-\rangle_C$	$\|1\rangle_6$	$a_1\|011\rangle - a_2\|010\rangle + a_3\|001\rangle - a_4\|000\rangle$ $\pm a_5\|111\rangle \mp a_6\|110\rangle \pm a_7\|101\rangle \mp a_8\|100\rangle$	$I \otimes \sigma_x \otimes -i\sigma_y$ $(\sigma_z \otimes \sigma_x \otimes -i\sigma_y)$
$\|\Phi\rangle^\pm_{A1}\|\Psi\rangle^-_{B2}\|+\rangle_C$	$\|0\rangle_6$	$a_1\|010\rangle + a_2\|011\rangle - a_3\|000\rangle - a_4\|001\rangle$ $\pm a_5\|110\rangle \pm a_6\|111\rangle \mp a_7\|100\rangle \mp a_8\|101\rangle$	$I \otimes -i\sigma_y \otimes I$ $(\sigma_z \otimes -i\sigma_y \otimes I)$

(continued)

Table 2. (*continued*)

AMR	CMR	BS	UO
$\|\Phi\rangle^\pm_{A1}\|\Psi\rangle^-_{B2}\|-\rangle_C$	$\|0\rangle_6$	$a_1\|010\rangle - a_2\|011\rangle - a_3\|000\rangle + a_4\|001\rangle$ $\pm a_5\|110\rangle \mp a_6\|111\rangle \mp a_7\|100\rangle \pm a_8\|101\rangle$	$I \otimes -i\sigma_y \otimes \sigma_z$ $(\sigma_z \otimes -i\sigma_y \otimes \sigma_z)$
$\|\Phi\rangle^\pm_{A1}\|\Psi\rangle^-_{B2}\|+\rangle_C$	$\|1\rangle_6$	$a_1\|011\rangle + a_2\|010\rangle - a_3\|001\rangle - a_4\|000\rangle$ $\pm a_5\|111\rangle \pm a_6\|110\rangle \mp a_7\|101\rangle \mp a_8\|100\rangle$	$I \otimes -i\sigma_y \otimes \sigma_x$ $(\sigma_z \otimes -i\sigma_y \otimes \sigma_x)$
$\|\Phi\rangle^\pm_{A1}\|\Psi\rangle^-_{B2}\|-\rangle_C$	$\|1\rangle_6$	$a_1\|011\rangle - a_2\|010\rangle - a_3\|001\rangle + a_4\|000\rangle$ $\pm a_5\|111\rangle \mp a_6\|110\rangle \mp a_7\|101\rangle \pm a_8\|100\rangle$	$I \otimes -i\sigma_y \otimes -i\sigma_y$ $(\sigma_z \otimes -i\sigma_y \otimes -i\sigma_y)$
$\|\Psi\rangle^\pm_{A1}\|\Phi\rangle^+_{B2}\|+\rangle_C$	$\|0\rangle_6$	$a_1\|100\rangle + a_2\|101\rangle + a_3\|110\rangle + a_4\|111\rangle$ $\pm a_5\|000\rangle \pm a_6\|001\rangle \pm a_7\|010\rangle \pm a_8\|011\rangle$	$\sigma_x \otimes I \otimes I$ $(-i\sigma_y \otimes I \otimes I)$
$\|\Psi\rangle^\pm_{A1}\|\Phi\rangle^+_{B2}\|-\rangle_C$	$\|0\rangle_6$	$a_1\|100\rangle - a_2\|101\rangle + a_3\|110\rangle - a_4\|111\rangle$ $\pm a_5\|000\rangle \mp a_6\|001\rangle \pm a_7\|010\rangle \mp a_8\|011\rangle$	$\sigma_x \otimes I \otimes \sigma_z$ $(-i\sigma_y \otimes I \otimes \sigma_z)$
$\|\Psi\rangle^\pm_{A1}\|\Phi\rangle^+_{B2}\|+\rangle_C$	$\|1\rangle_6$	$a_1\|101\rangle + a_2\|100\rangle + a_3\|111\rangle + a_4\|110\rangle$ $\pm a_5\|001\rangle \pm a_6\|000\rangle \pm a_7\|011\rangle \pm a_8\|010\rangle$	$\sigma_x \otimes I \otimes \sigma_x$ $(-i\sigma_y \otimes I \otimes \sigma_x)$
$\|\Psi\rangle^\pm_{A1}\|\Phi\rangle^+_{B2}\|-\rangle_C$	$\|1\rangle_6$	$a_1\|101\rangle - a_2\|100\rangle + a_3\|111\rangle - a_4\|110\rangle$ $\pm a_5\|001\rangle \mp a_6\|000\rangle \pm a_7\|011\rangle \mp a_8\|010\rangle$	$\sigma_x \otimes I \otimes -i\sigma_y$ $(-i\sigma_y \otimes I \otimes -i\sigma_y)$
$\|\Psi\rangle^\pm_{A1}\|\Phi\rangle^-_{B2}\|+\rangle_C$	$\|0\rangle_6$	$a_1\|100\rangle + a_2\|101\rangle - a_3\|110\rangle - a_4\|111\rangle$ $+a_5\|000\rangle \pm a_6\|001\rangle \mp a_7\|010\rangle \mp a_8\|011\rangle$	$\sigma_x \otimes \sigma_z \otimes I$ $(-i\sigma_y \otimes \sigma_z \otimes I)$
$\|\Psi\rangle^\pm_{A1}\|\Phi\rangle^-_{B2}\|-\rangle_C$	$\|0\rangle_6$	$a_1\|100\rangle - a_2\|101\rangle - a_3\|110\rangle + a_4\|111\rangle$ $\pm a_5\|000\rangle \mp a_6\|001\rangle \mp a_7\|010\rangle \pm a_8\|011\rangle$	$\sigma_x \otimes \sigma_z \otimes \sigma_z$ $(-i\sigma_y \otimes \sigma_z \otimes \sigma_z)$
$\|\Psi\rangle^\pm_{A1}\|\Phi\rangle^-_{B2}\|+\rangle_C$	$\|1\rangle_6$	$a_1\|101\rangle + a_2\|100\rangle - a_3\|111\rangle - a_4\|110\rangle$ $\pm a_5\|001\rangle \pm a_6\|000\rangle \mp a_7\|011\rangle \mp a_8\|010\rangle$	$\sigma_x \otimes \sigma_z \otimes \sigma_z$ $(-i\sigma_y \otimes \sigma_z \otimes \sigma_x)$
$\|\Psi\rangle^\pm_{A1}\|\Phi\rangle^-_{B2}\|-\rangle_C$	$\|1\rangle_6$	$a_1\|101\rangle - a_2\|100\rangle - a_3\|111\rangle + a_4\|110\rangle$ $\pm a_5\|001\rangle \mp a_6\|000\rangle \mp a_7\|011\rangle \pm a_8\|010\rangle$	$\sigma_x \otimes \sigma_z \otimes -i\sigma_y$ $(-i\sigma_y \otimes \sigma_z \otimes -i\sigma_y)$
$\|\Psi\rangle^\pm_{A1}\|\Psi\rangle^+_{B2}\|+\rangle_C$	$\|0\rangle_6$	$a_1\|110\rangle + a_2\|111\rangle + a_3\|100\rangle + a_4\|101\rangle$ $\pm a_5\|010\rangle \pm a_6\|011\rangle \pm a_7\|000\rangle \pm a_8\|001\rangle$	$\sigma_x \otimes \sigma_x \otimes I$ $(-i\sigma_y \otimes \sigma_x \otimes I)$
$\|\Psi\rangle^\pm_{A1}\|\Psi\rangle^+_{B2}\|-\rangle_C$	$\|0\rangle_6$	$a_1\|110\rangle - a_2\|111\rangle + a_3\|100\rangle - a_4\|101\rangle$ $\pm a_5\|010\rangle \mp a_6\|011\rangle \pm a_7\|000\rangle \mp a_8\|001\rangle$	$\sigma_x \otimes \sigma_x \otimes \sigma_z$ $(-i\sigma_y \otimes \sigma_x \otimes \sigma_z)$
$\|\Psi\rangle^\pm_{A1}\|\Psi\rangle^+_{B2}\|+\rangle_C$	$\|1\rangle_6$	$a_1\|111\rangle + a_2\|110\rangle + a_3\|101\rangle + a_4\|100\rangle$ $\pm a_5\|011\rangle \pm a_6\|010\rangle \pm a_7\|001\rangle \pm a_8\|000\rangle$	$\sigma_x \otimes \sigma_x \otimes \sigma_x$ $(-i\sigma_y \otimes \sigma_x \otimes \sigma_x)$
$\|\Psi\rangle^\pm_{A1}\|\Psi\rangle^+_{B2}\|-\rangle_C$	$\|1\rangle_6$	$a_1\|111\rangle - a_2\|110\rangle + a_3\|101\rangle - a_4\|100\rangle$ $\pm a_5\|011\rangle \mp a_6\|010\rangle \pm a_7\|001\rangle \mp a_8\|000\rangle$	$\sigma_x \otimes \sigma_x \otimes -i\sigma_y$ $(-i\sigma_y \otimes \sigma_x \otimes -i\sigma_y)$
$\|\Psi\rangle^\pm_{A1}\|\Psi\rangle^-_{B2}\|+\rangle_C$	$\|0\rangle_6$	$a_1\|110\rangle + a_2\|111\rangle - a_3\|100\rangle - a_4\|101\rangle$ $\pm a_5\|010\rangle \pm a_6\|011\rangle \mp a_7\|000\rangle \mp a_8\|001\rangle$	$\sigma_x \otimes -i\sigma_y \otimes I$ $(-i\sigma_y \otimes -i\sigma_y \otimes I)$
$\|\Psi\rangle^\pm_{A1}\|\Psi\rangle^-_{B2}\|-\rangle_C$	$\|0\rangle_6$	$a_1\|110\rangle - a_2\|111\rangle - a_3\|100\rangle + a_4\|101\rangle$ $\pm a_5\|010\rangle \mp a_6\|011\rangle \mp a_7\|000\rangle \pm a_8\|001\rangle$	$\sigma_x \otimes -i\sigma_y \otimes \sigma_z$ $(-i\sigma_y \otimes -i\sigma_y \otimes \sigma_z)$
$\|\Psi\rangle^\pm_{A1}\|\Psi\rangle^-_{B2}\|+\rangle_C$	$\|1\rangle_6$	$a_1\|111\rangle + a_2\|110\rangle - a_3\|101\rangle - a_4\|100\rangle$ $\pm a_5\|011\rangle \pm a_6\|010\rangle \mp a_7\|001\rangle \mp a_8\|000\rangle$	$\sigma_x \otimes -i\sigma_y \otimes \sigma_x$ $(-i\sigma_y \otimes -i\sigma_y \otimes \sigma_x)$
$\|\Psi\rangle^\pm_{A1}\|\Psi\rangle^-_{B2}\|-\rangle_C$	$\|1\rangle_6$	$a_1\|111\rangle - a_2\|110\rangle - a_3\|101\rangle + a_4\|100\rangle$ $\pm a_5\|011\rangle \mp a_6\|010\rangle \mp a_7\|001\rangle \pm a_8\|000\rangle$	$\sigma_x \otimes -i\sigma_y \otimes -i\sigma_y$ $(-i\sigma_y \otimes -i\sigma_y \otimes -i\sigma_y)$

The possible results of measurement and the corresponding unitary operations are shown in Table 2.

3 Experimental Verification

In Sect. 2, We described the scheme in detail theoretically. In this chapter, we will verify the feasibility of scheme in IBM quantum experience platform. IBM QE is a cloud-based quantum computing platform. We can design quantum circuits on IBM QE and select appropriate quantum simulators or use real quantum computer to test quantum circuits.

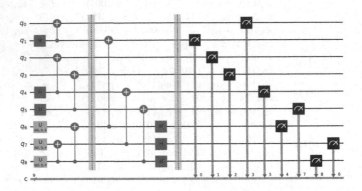

Fig. 2. Quantum Circuit of information splitting of arbitrary three-qubit state using a four-qubit cluster state and a Bell state

First, we draw a quantum circuit diagram on the platform, as shown in Fig. 2, where the inital state of q[0]-q[8] is $|0\rangle$. Three U-gates and two CNOT operations on q[8], q[7], q[6] qubits to prepare arbitrary three-qubit state for transmission. The parameterized matrix form of U-gate is shown in Formula (7). In this experiment, we set the parameters of three U-gates to $(\frac{\pi}{2}, 0, \pi)$, $(\frac{\pi}{2}, 0, \pi)$ and $(\frac{\pi}{4}, 0, 0)$ respectively. Formula (8) represents the three-qubit state we transmit in this experiment.

$$U(\theta, \phi, \lambda) = \begin{bmatrix} \cos\left(\frac{\theta}{2}\right) & -e^{i\lambda}\sin\left(\frac{\theta}{2}\right) \\ e^{i\phi}\sin\left(\frac{\theta}{2}\right) & e^{i(\phi+\lambda)}\cos\left(\frac{\theta}{2}\right) \end{bmatrix} \tag{7}$$

$$\begin{aligned}
|q\rangle_{876} = \frac{1}{2}(&cos\frac{\pi}{8}|000\rangle + sin\frac{\pi}{8}|001\rangle + cos\frac{\pi}{8}|010\rangle + sin\frac{\pi}{8}|011\rangle \\
&+ sin\frac{\pi}{8}|100\rangle + cos\frac{\pi}{8}|101\rangle + sin\frac{\pi}{8}|110\rangle + cos\frac{\pi}{8}|111\rangle)
\end{aligned} \tag{8}$$

Then, we use two H-gate operations and two CNOT operations on qubits q[5], q[4], q[3], q[2] to prepare four-qubit cluster state, and use one H-gate operation and one CNOT operation on qubits q[1], q[0] to prepare Bell state.

Through the IBM QE simulation experiment, we can get all the probability of the measurement results and the state Bob received. Figure 3 shows the probability distribution of Bob's state under different measurement results. When the measurement result of Alice is $|\Phi\rangle_{A1}^+|\Psi\rangle_{B2}^+|+\rangle$ (the classical information is 00011), and the measurement result of Charlie is $|0\rangle$ (the classical information is 0). We get the probability distribution of Bob's quantum state, as shown in Fig. 3. According to Fig. 3, the state Bob received can be written as follows:

$$|\phi\rangle_{345} = \sqrt{0.2048}|000\rangle + \sqrt{0.0288}|001\rangle + \sqrt{0.1939}|010\rangle + \sqrt{0.0416}|011\rangle$$
$$+ \sqrt{0.0384}|100\rangle + \sqrt{0.2093}|101\rangle + \sqrt{0.0371}|110\rangle + \sqrt{0.1978}|111\rangle \tag{9}$$

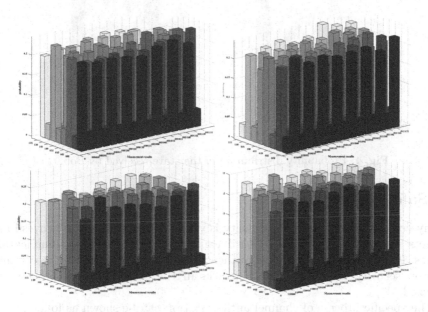

Fig. 3. Probability distribution corresponding to all measurement results.

According to Table 2, the appropriate unitary operation Bob should perform is $I \otimes \sigma_x \otimes I$. Then the state will be change.

$$|\phi\rangle_{345} = \sqrt{0.1939}|000\rangle + \sqrt{0.0416}|001\rangle + \sqrt{0.2048}|010\rangle + \sqrt{0.0288}|011\rangle$$
$$+ \sqrt{0.0371}|100\rangle + \sqrt{0.1978}|101\rangle + \sqrt{0.0384}|110\rangle + \sqrt{0.2093}|111\rangle \tag{10}$$

Using the density operation of $|\phi\rangle_{345}$, $\rho = |\phi\rangle_{345}\langle\phi|$, the fidelity of the scheme is calculated as follows:

$$F =_{876} \langle q|\rho|q\rangle_{876} \approx 0.95075 \tag{11}$$

It can be seen that the fidelity of the teleportation is very high, indicating that the experiment of the scheme is successfully completed (Fig. 4).

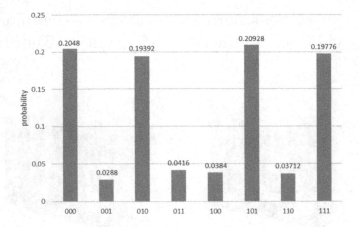

Fig. 4. Probability distribution of the state received by Bob.

4   Safety Analysis

In any communication scheme, security is very important. Once the eavesdropper gets the relevant information, it will cause great losses to the communication parties. In this paper, the channel authentication is used to ensure the communication security, and the possible attacks in the communication process are analyzed.

The specific process of channel authentication can be shown as follows:

1) Alice prepared an arbitrary one-qubit D as a detection particle with quantum state is $|\phi\rangle_D$, which has the form

$$|\phi\rangle_D = (cos\omega|0\rangle + e^{i\mu}sin\omega|1\rangle)_D \tag{12}$$

where, ω, μ is the characteristic parameter of the quantum state.

2) Alice employs a CNOT operation on qubit pairs (1, D),(2, D) respectively with the qubits 1, 2 as the control bits and qubit D as the target bit. The state $|\phi\rangle$ and particle D will become a five-qubit entangled state. Then Alice sents particle D to Bob.

3) Bob makes a CNOT operation on qubit pairs (3, D),(4, D) respectively with the qubits 3,4 as the control bits and qubit D as the target bit to untangle the particle D with the state.

4) Bob performs a CNOT operation on qubit pair (5, D) to entangle particle D with the state $|\phi\rangle_{ABC56}$. Then Bob sends particle D to Charlie, and charlie performs a CNOT operation on qubit pair (6, D). Finally, Charlie sends D to Alice.

5) After Alice receives D, she employs a CNOT operation on (C, H), and then compares the parameters ω, μ. If they are consistent with the initial parameters, we believe that the channel is safe, otherwise the channel has been eavesdropped, and this communication is abandoned.

Next, we will discuss the communication security of the scheme in two cases.

4.1   External Attack

Intercept and Resend Attack. Suppose an eavesdropper Eve intercepted the qubits 3, 4, and 5 which are Alice sent to Bob. Then Eve send a new three-qubit state $|\phi\rangle'_{345}$ to Bob. In the channel authentication state, Bob will conduct disentanglement operation on particle D and $|\phi\rangle_{1234}$. If Bob received the state of Eve, Bob's operation will fail and the parameters of detection particle will also change. So the channel authentication can not pass, Eve's attack is invalid.

Entangle Channel Attack. Suppose the eavesdropper Eve intercepts Bob's qubits 3, 4, 5 and entangles his qubit state $|\phi\rangle_{EFG} = |000\rangle$ into the channel by three CNOT operations to try to steal information. At this time, the state of the whole system changes to as follows:

$$
\begin{aligned}
&|\Phi\rangle_{ABC123456EFG} \\
&= \frac{1}{2\sqrt{2}}[(a_1|000\rangle + a_3|010\rangle + a_5|100\rangle + a_7|110\rangle)_{ABC} \\
&\otimes (|000000000\rangle + |000011001\rangle + |010100010\rangle + |010111011\rangle \\
&\quad + |101000100\rangle + |101011101\rangle + |111100110\rangle + |111111111\rangle)_{123456EFG} \\
&+ (a_2|001\rangle + a_4|011\rangle + a_6|101\rangle + a_8|111\rangle)_{ABC} \\
&\otimes (|000001000\rangle + |000010001\rangle + |010101010\rangle + |010110011\rangle \\
&\quad + |101001100\rangle + |101010101\rangle + |111101110\rangle + |111110111\rangle)_{123456EFG}
\end{aligned}
\tag{13}
$$

Compared with formula (5), we can find that formula (13) is a entangled state with 12 qubits. Eve's CNOT operation entangled state $|\phi\rangle_{ABC56}$ and $|\phi\rangle_{1234}$. So Bob can judge whether he suffered entangled channel attack through qubit 5 in channel authentication phase. Besides, the operation performed by Eve will cause corresponding disturbances on detection particle, resulting in changes in the parameters of the detection particle. So, Alice can not extract the detection particle from the quantum state of the channel. Therefore, entangle channel attack is invalid.

4.2   Internal Attack

It is assumed that Eve has passed the channel authentication with the help of Charlie. And Eve attempts to entangle qubit 6 with his own qubit state $|\phi\rangle_{MN} = \frac{1}{2}(|00\rangle + |01\rangle + |10\rangle + |11\rangle)$ by performing CNOT operation on (6, M) with qubit 6 as the control bit and M as the target bit.

Now the state $|\phi\rangle_{ABC56MN}$ is as follows:

$$
\begin{aligned}
&|\phi\rangle_{ABC56MN} \\
&= \frac{1}{2\sqrt{2}}[(a_1|000\rangle + a_3|010\rangle + a_5|100\rangle + a_7|110\rangle)_{ABC} \otimes (|00\rangle + |11\rangle)_{56} \\
&+ (a_2|001\rangle + a_4|011\rangle + a_6|101\rangle + a_8|111\rangle)_{ABC} \otimes (|10\rangle + |01\rangle)_{56}] \\
&\otimes (|00\rangle + |01\rangle + |10\rangle + |11\rangle)_{MN}
\end{aligned}
\tag{14}
$$

From formula 14, we can see that Eve could not change his state. So we believe Eve can't steal any quantum information with Charlie's help. The internal attack is invalid.

5   Comparison and Analysis

In order to reflect the advantages of the scheme in this paper, we will compare it with the quantum information splitting scheme mentioned in the literature [5,17,20,23,27,28]. It will be compared from five aspects: quantum information bits transmitted, necessary operations, consumption of quantum resource, consumption of classical resource and intrinsic efficiency.

First, the quantum information bits transmitted. The maximum number of qubits transmitted in [5,17,23,27] and ours is three qubits. The other two schemes are two qubits. So our protocol transmits the maximum qubits number.

Second, the consumption of quantum resource. In literature [5,17,20,23,27, 28], the one with the least quantum resource consumption is literature [20], which utilizes a four-qubit cluster state and a Bell state as the channel to realize the quantum information splitting of arbitrary two-qubit state. But in our scheme, we used a four-qubit cluster state and a Bell sate to realize the quantum information splitting of arbitrary three-qubit state.

Third, the necessary operations. Many times multi-particle measurements are used in the scheme proposed in literature [5,17,20,23,27,28], which increases the complexity and difficulty of implementation. In our scheme, Alice and Charlie need to execute two Bell state measurement operations and two single-qubit state measurement operations in total.

Fourth, the consumption of classical resource. In the QIS scheme, the sender and the controller need to inform the receiver their measurement results, so it will produce the consumption of classical resource. In literature [5,17,20,23,27,28], the minimum consumption of classical information is five bits. The consumption of classic resource in our schemes is medium, six bits.

Finally, in order to compare the transmission efficiency of schemes more intuitively, we use the following formula to express the transmission efficiency.

$$\eta = \frac{q_s}{q_u + b_t} \tag{15}$$

where q_s express the number of qubits to be transmitted, q_u express the number of channel qubits(except for those used for security checking), b_t express the number of bits of classical information. According to the above formula, the actual transmission efficiency of each scheme in the literature [5,17,20,23,27,28] is calculated as $\eta_{19} = \frac{3}{8+8} = 18.75\%, \eta_{22} = \frac{2}{6+6} = 16.67\%, \eta_{23} = \frac{2}{5+7} = 16.67\%, \eta_{24} = \frac{3}{9+9} = 16.67\%, \eta_{25} = \frac{3}{7+7} = 21.43\%, \eta_{26} = \frac{3}{7+6} = 23.08\%.$ And in our scheme, $\eta = \frac{3}{6+6} = 25\%$, compared with other schemes, our efficiency is the highest.

Table 3. Comparison of seven schemes.

Reference	QRC	NO	CRC	η
[17]	8	4 BSM	8	18.75%
[20]	6	3 BSM	6	16.67%
[28]	7	1 BSM, 1 GSM	5	16.67%
[23]	9	3 BSM, 3 SM	9	16.67%
[27]	7	3 BSM, 1 SM	7	21.43%
[5]	7	3 BSM, 2 CNOT	6	23.08%
Our scheme	6	2 BSM, 2 SM, 1 CNOT	6	25%

In Table 3, We sort out the comparison of these aspects.

Where QRC represents the consumption of quantum resources, NO represents the necessary operations, and CRC represents the consumption of classical resource, η represents the actual efficiency, BSM represents Bell state measurement, GSM represents GHZ state measurement, and SM represents single-qubit state measurement.

To sum up, we compare our scheme with the scheme proposed in literature [5, 17, 20, 23, 27, 28] in several aspects. We have lower channel resource consumption and classical information resource consumption compared with other schemes. At the same time, through calculation, we can see that our proposed scheme has the highest transmission efficiency of 25%.

6   Conclusion

In summary, the development of quantum communication has been related to the security of national cyberspace and it has been applied in different occasions. In this paper, we have implemented an effective quantum information splitting scheme for arbitrary three-qubit state by using a four-qubit cluster state and a Bell state as quantum channel. In the transmission phase of quantum information, Alice carries out one CNOT operation, one single-qubit measurement operation and two Bell state measurement operations. And Charlie should perform a single-qubit measurement operation. Finally, in the reconstruction phase, Bob adopts corresponding unitary operations to obtain the quantum state information sent by Alice. Moreover, we enhance the security of our scheme by means of channel authentication method, which can resist external and internal attacks. On this premise, compared with the other six quantum information splitting protocols, our schemes also has the prominent advantages of higher transmission efficiency, low complexity, and high security. Therefore, this scheme provides the feasibility for quantum information splitting experiments in this field. At the same time, it has made contributions to ensuring network information security.

Acknowledgements. This work was supported in part by the National Natural Science Foundation of China (62172060), Sichuan Science and Technology Program (2022YFG0316).

References

1. Aili, M., Abulizi, A.: Dense coding in a three-qubit Heisenberg XXZ spin chain with three-site interactions. Int. J. Theor. Phys. **58**(2), 364–371 (2019)
2. Bennett, C.H., Brassard, G., Crépeau, C., Jozsa, R., Peres, A., Wootters, W.K.: Teleporting an unknown quantum state via dual classical and Einstein-Podolsky-Rosen channels. Phys. Rev. Lett. **70**(13), 1895 (1993)
3. Cao, W.F., Yang, Y.G.: Verifiable quantum secret sharing protocols based on four-qubit entangled states. Int. J. Theor. Phys. **58**(4), 1202–1214 (2019)
4. Cao, Z., Zhang, Y., Qi, J.: Quantum teleportation of an arbitrary four-qubit state via three-uniform state of eight qubits. Mod. Phys. Lett. A **36**(05), 2150026 (2021)
5. Chen, Y.: Quantum information splitting of an arbitrary three-qubit state using a seven-qubit entangled state. Int. J. Theor. Phys. **53**(2), 524–532 (2014)
6. Fu, Y., Hong, Y., Quek, T.Q., Wang, H., Shi, Z.: Scheduling policies for quantum key distribution enabled communication networks. IEEE Wirel. Commun. Lett. **9**(12), 2126–2129 (2020)
7. Geihs, M., et al.: The status of quantum-key-distribution-based long-term secure internet communication. IEEE Trans. Sustain. Comput. **6**(1), 19–29 (2019)
8. Guo, Y., Peng, Q., Liao, Q., Wang, Y.: Trans-media continuous-variable quantum key distribution via untrusted entanglement source. IEEE Photonics J. **13**(2), 1–12 (2021)
9. Hao, N., Li, Z.H., Bai, H.Y., Bai, C.M.: A new quantum secret sharing scheme based on mutually unbiased bases. Int. J. Theor. Phys. **58**(4), 1249–1261 (2019)
10. Heo, J., et al.: Implementation of controlled quantum teleportation with an arbitrator for secure quantum channels via quantum dots inside optical cavities. Sci. Rep. **7**(1), 1–12 (2017)
11. Hou, K., Bao, D., Zhu, C., Yang, Y.: Controlled teleportation of an arbitrary two-qubit entanglement in noises environment. Quantum Inf. Process. **18**(4), 1–19 (2019)
12. Hu, X.M., Guo, Y., Liu, B.H., Huang, Y.F., Li, C.F., Guo, G.C.: Beating the channel capacity limit for superdense coding with entangled ququarts. Sci. Adv. **4**(7), eaat9304 (2018)
13. Huang, C.C., Farn, K.J.: A study on e-Taiwan promotion information security governance programs with e-government implementation of information security management standardization. Int. J. Netw. Secur. **18**(3), 565–578 (2016)
14. Huang, Z., Ye, Y., Luo, D.: Simultaneous dense coding affected by fluctuating massless scalar field. Quantum Inf. Process. **17**(4), 1–11 (2018)
15. Kumar, A., Garhwal, S.: State-of-the-art survey of quantum cryptography. Arch. Comput. Methods Eng. **28**(5), 3831–3868 (2021)
16. Li, M., Liu, J., Hong, W.: Quantum information splitting of a single-qubit via genuine four-qubit entangled states. Acta Sinica Quantum Optica **19**(2), 141–145 (2013)
17. Nie, Y., Li, Y., Liu, J., Sang, M.: Quantum information splitting of an arbitrary three-qubit state by using two four-qubit cluster states. Quantum Inf. Process. **10**(3), 297–305 (2011)

18. Pirandola, S., Eisert, J., Weedbrook, C., Furusawa, A., Braunstein, S.L.: Advances in quantum teleportation. Nat. Photonics **9**(10), 641–652 (2015)
19. Qin, H., Tso, R.: Efficient quantum secret sharing based on polarization and orbital angular momentum. J. Chin. Inst. Eng. **42**(2), 143–148 (2019)
20. Ramírez, M.D.G., Falaye, B.J., Sun, G.H., Cruz-Irisson, M., Dong, S.H.: Quantum teleportation and information splitting via four-qubit cluster state and a bell state. Front. Phys. **12**(5), 1–9 (2017)
21. Shor, P.W.: Algorithms for quantum computation: discrete logarithms and factoring. In: Proceedings 35th Annual Symposium on Foundations of Computer Science, pp. 124–134. IEEE (1994)
22. Shor, P.W.: Polynomial-time algorithms for prime factorization and discrete logarithms on a quantum computer. SIAM Rev. **41**(2), 303–332 (1999)
23. Sk, R., Dash, T., Panigrahi, P.K.: Quantum information splitting of an arbitrary three-qubit state by using three sets of GHz states. IET Quantum Commun. **2**(3), 122–135 (2021)
24. Wei, J., Dai, H.Y., Shi, L., Zhao, S., Zhang, M.: Deterministic quantum controlled teleportation of arbitrary multi-qubit states via partially entangled states. Int. J. Theor. Phys. **57**(10), 3104–3111 (2018)
25. Xiao-Feng, Y., Yi-Min, L., Wen, Z., Zhan-Jun, Z.: Simplified four-qubit cluster state for splitting arbitrary single-qubit information. Commun. Theor. Phys. **53**(1), 49 (2010)
26. Xiu-li, T., Ting, Z., Xian-ming, W., Jing, X.: Splitting quantum information via six-qubit maximally entangled state. Chin. J. Quantum Electron. **29**(5), 577 (2012)
27. Xu, G., Zhou, T., Chen, X.B., Wang, X.: Splitting an arbitrary three-qubit state via a five-qubit cluster state and a bell state. Entropy **24**(3), 381 (2022)
28. Yang, Y., Li, D., Liu, M., Chen, J.: Quantum information splitting of arbitrary two-qubit state via a five-qubit cluster state and a bell-state. Int. J. Theor. Phys. **59**(1), 187–199 (2020)
29. Zadeh, M.S.S., Houshmand, M., Aghababa, H.: Bidirectional quantum teleportation of a class of n-qubit states by using (2n+ 2)-qubit entangled states as quantum channel. Int. J. Theor. Phys. **57**(1), 175–183 (2018)
30. Zhang, D., Zha, X.W., Li, W., Yu, Y.: Bidirectional and asymmetric quantum controlled teleportation via maximally eight-qubit entangled state. Quantum Inf. Process. **14**(10), 3835–3844 (2015)
31. Zhou, Y.S., Wang, F., Luo, M.X.: Efficient superdense coding with W states. Int. J. Theor. Phys. **57**(7), 1935–1941 (2018)

Network Security

A Manipulated Overlapped Voltage Attack Detection Mechanism for Voltage-Based Vehicle Intrusion Detection System

Long Yin[ID], Jian Xu[✉], Heqiu Chai, and Chen Wang

Software College, Northeastern University, Shenyang 110169, China
xuj@mail.neu.edu.cn

Abstract. To evade being detected by the content-based or frequency-based IDS, the attack model in the automotive CAN has shifted from the traditional packet flooding and payload modification attacks to stealth attacks such as shutdown attacks. These new types of stealth attacks are difficult to be effectively detected by content-based IDS and frequency-based IDS. The CAN bus physical voltage-based IDS can identify the source of each message and detect these stealth attacks effectively. However, the state of art research has discovered a novel masquerade attack called DUET, which can tamper with the existing voltage-based IDS by generating overlapping voltage signals with an accomplice to distort the fingerprint of the specified ECU. We propose a detection mechanism to prevent the manipulated voltage attacks of overlapping voltage signal samples, which is based on anomaly detection by applying the LSTM autoencoder model. By filtering the overlapped signal and rectifying the voltage fingerprint instance of the original voltage signal, the improved voltage-based IDS can effectively resist the DUET attack. Experiments demonstrated the proposed detection mechanism can authenticate the victim ECU and the accomplice ECU before and after the DUET two-stage attack, and prevent the receiver ECU from being deceived by the forged messages generated by the attacker and accomplice ECUs.

Keywords: Voltage-based IDS · DUET attack · Manipulated overlapped voltage attack · LSTM autoencoder

1 Introduction

The Controller Area Network (CAN) protocol has been applied to in-vehicle networks for many decades. It has many benefits for real-time communication between electronic control units (ECUs). However, security issues are not a concern at the beginning of protocol design. Thus more and more attack methods have been discovered on the in-vehicle automotive CAN in recent years. A lot of attack surfaces are exposed to the adversary which can be penetrated by an OBD diagnosis tool or the telematics control units with vulnerabilities. The adversaries can perform a spoofing attack by sending forged or replayed messages through a connected OBD port or untrusted wireless channels. Although many vehicle manufacturers have firmed the security protection on

© The Author(s), under exclusive license to Springer Nature Singapore Pte Ltd. 2022
E. Ahene and F. Li (Eds.): FCS 2022, CCIS 1726, pp. 413–428, 2022.
https://doi.org/10.1007/978-981-19-8445-7_26

the boundary of the automotive ethernet and the in-vehicle CAN bus network. The threats of spoofing attacks via physical access to the CAN bus remain to be solved.

To cope with the problem CAN bus communication may suffer from spoofing attacks. Some schemes have proposed with a series of CAN bus IDS which are based on measuring the message transmission frequency or the packet payload. But the recent research has demonstrated that a time-aware adversary can evade the frequency-based IDS by blocking the data transmission of legitimate ECU and injecting the masquerade packets after an estimated time offset. In addition, the frequency-based IDS and Payload-based IDS are ineffective to distinguish valid aperiodic CAN packets from normal operations and invalid aperiodic CAN packets from masquerade attacks [1]. Taking these defects into consideration, newly proposed approaches use the physical characteristics of voltage signals generated from each ECU as the distinctive features to detect spoofing attacks. Compared to the frequency-based and payload-based IDS, these voltage-based approaches are hard to evade due to that the fingerprint of physical voltage signals is difficult to counterfeit.

However, In a recent study, Bhatia et al. discovered a new masquerade attack called DUET to bypass the detection mechanisms which are based on voltage signals analysis [2]. In their work, they show how to exploit two compromised ECUs to launch the attack by manipulating the fingerprint of the victim ECU. They generate the overlapping voltage signals on the CAN bus while the voltage-based IDS comes into the retraining phases. By repeatedly executing the above attack and increasing the number of overlapping bits eventually, they can finally use the two compromised ECUs to simulate the corrupt voltage fingerprint profile and deceive the VIDS that the fabricated fingerprint is generated by the legitimate ECU.

To secure the CAN bus against a new data poisoning attack like the DUET, we propose a novel approach. Our proposed approach has some improvements in voltage sample processing and feature extraction. First, we use an LSTM encoder-decoder model to locate and filter the signal portion where the overlaps sit in voltage samples, then we apply an artificial neural network model of CNN with LSTM layers to derive the voltage fingerprint instance based on the filtered voltage waveforms to identify the source ECU of each voltage signal sample. Finally, we set up a CAN bus prototype to simulate the DUET attack and evaluate the performance of the proposed approach in detecting attacks and recognizing the identity of the transmitter ECU in the CAN bus network.

Our main contributions are as follows:

1. We summarize the main categories of intrusion detection systems for the in-vehicle CAN bus network. Especially focus on the physical characteristics-based IDS, namely the voltage-based IDS. We also analyze some defects of existing voltage-based IDS including those that may be affected by the novel data poisoning attack on the training dataset of voltage signal samples.
2. We propose a new approach to detect and resist the two-stage data poisoning attack (the DUET attack). By applying the combined deep learning models of the LSTM autoencoder model and the CNN classifier model, we can easily detect the corrupt voltage samples which contain the overlaps generated by more than two transmitters on the CAN bus and authenticate the identity validity of all ECUs in the CAN bus.

3. We experiment on a CAN bus prototype to prove the effectiveness of the proposed mechanism for the DUET attack detection, by comparing the predicted classification result before and after filtering the overlaps of CAN voltage signals, the predicted accuracy of the retrained model is not degraded by applying the new approach.

2 Related Works

IN this subsection, we summarize some existing voltage-based IDS and identification schemes based on the physical characteristics of CAN networks. The comparisons of these schemes are shown in Table 1.

Table 1. Summary of voltage-based IDS.

	Sampling rate	Features	Method	Compromised ECU	Add new ECU	Overlapped voltage attack detection
Groza et al. [3]	2 GS/s	Raw signal	Signal processing	√	×	×
Viden [4]	50 kS/s	Statistical features	Signal processing	√	×	×
VoltageIDS [6]	2.5 GS/s	Frequency & time domain features	ML (SVM, NN, BDT)	√	√	×
Scission [7]	20 MS/s	Frequency & time domain features	ML(logistic regression)	√	√	×
EASI [8]	2 MS/s	Frequency & time domain features	Signal processing	√	√	×
SIMPLE [9]	50 MS/s	Temperature & Voltage	Statistical analysis	√	×	×
Can Radar [10]	2 GS/s²	Response to sent pulses	Statistical analysis	×	√	×
Xu et al. [11]	N/A	Raw signal	Reinforcement learning	√	×	×
Yang et al. [12]	250 MS/s	Raw signal	ML (deep learning)	√	×	×
Hafeez et al. [13]	2 GS/s	Statistical features	ML (deep learning)	√	×	×
CAN-LOC [14]	500 MS/s	Raw signal	ML (deep learning)	√	√	×
This work	12.5 MS/s	Frequency & time domain features	ML (deep learning)	√	√	√

Groza et al. firstly presented the idea of using simple signal processing techniques on ECU raw voltage signal fingerprinting [3]. They filtered the voltage signal of arbitration fields and examined the mean square errors and convolutions of fingerprints corresponding to each ECU transmitter for identification. Cho and Shin proposed a voltage-based attacker identification scheme called Viden [4], which extracts the statistical features from the transmitter ECU's voltage signal samples from the CAN-L and CAN-H. They exploit these features to construct and update the fingerprint profile of each ECU, hence Viden can modify the fingerprint profile automatically and adapt to environmental changes.

Choi et al. proposed a so-called VoltageIDS, which selects 9 features extracted from the frequency domain and 8 features from time domain characteristics of the external identifier in voltage signal [5, 6]. They employed a variety of machine learning algorithms to create a multi-class classifier for masquerade attack detection and a one-class classifier for bus-off attack detection and applied incremental learning to enhance the robustness of the proposed scheme against environmental changes.

Kneib et al. proposed an improved voltage-based IDS named Scission [7]. They measure a variety of statistical characteristics in the dominant bit set, the falling edges, and the rising edges of the voltage signal samples, and select the 18 most significant features from the time domain and frequency domain features by using the Relief-F algorithm to reduce the training computation cost. They used a simple machine learning algorithm Logistic Regression to create a multi-class classifier to predict the origin of a received frame. And the scheme achieved a high accuracy with these improved measurements and processing techniques.

Subsequently, Kneib et al. proposed an improved version named EASI for resource-constrained automotive platforms [8]. EASI operates at a lower sample rate of 2MS/s, which reduces the computation cost of training and detecting intrusions either. The statistical features are only extracted from one representing edge (rising edge or falling edge) of signals, the 12 most important features in the time domain or frequency domain are selected by the Information Gain algorithm. They chose the SVM to train the identification classifier and achieved a high accuracy of close to 100% either.

Foruhandeh et al. analyzed the shortcomings of CAN voltage-based intrusion detection and identification system that rely on multiple frames processing. They show the Hill-Climbing-style attacks of dominant impersonation on voltage-based IDS and complete impersonation of clock-based IDS. Then they proposed a real-time IDS named SIMPLE [9], which is based on single-frame feature extraction and detection. They applied Fischer-Discriminant Analysis(FDA) algorithm for the feature dimension reduction and calculated the Mahalanobis thresholds for identification. To against the environmental factors changes affection, they employed the statistical analysis and estimation of scaling parameters to compensate for the effect of environmental changes.

Rumez et al. presented an approach CAN-Radar to detect the unknown devices that connect to CAN networks but do not transmit messages [10]. It applied time-domain reflectometry(TDR) technology to measure the response of the pulse sent on the CAN bus and determine the detection threshold, and then it employed an extended coherence analysis technique to derive the existence of unknown connected devices in CAN networks.

Xu et al. proposed a reinforcement learning-based CAN bus authentication scheme to choose the authentication mode such as the protection level and test threshold [11]. Yang et al. proposed an RNN-LSTM-based classifier for sender identity authentication [12]. Hafeez et al. proposed an ECU fingerprinting method by collecting the control-theory-based parameters from feature extraction for each signal pulse and used the artificial neural network to train the classifier to identify the source transmitter [13].

Levy et al. proposed a security hardening system CAN-LOC, which provides the capability of physical intrusion detection and localization for in-vehicle networks. The system uses a deep autoencoder for physical intrusion detection and the convolution neural network classifiers to report the exact location of malicious ECU insertions or replacements [14]. Another usage of CNN classifiers in their system is for detecting spoofing attacks by legitimate ECUs that impersonate peers.

3 Preliminaries

3.1 Some Defects of Voltage-Based IDS

The state-of-the-art voltage-based IDS are susceptible to some external factors or the new stealth attacks: (1) the environmental factors, (2) the Hill-Climbing-style attack, and (3) the two-stage masquerade attack named DUET.

1) Environmental factors: The voltage-based IDS are known to be affected by environmental factors, such as a variation in time and temperature. To address the problem, Choi et al. adopted incremental and decremental learning to their proposed VoltageIDS, which makes it robust against temperature changes [6]. Foruhandeh et al. proposed a single-frame-based physical-layer identification solution SIMPLE, which performs secure updates of the fingerprints to compensate for environmental changes such as temperature and supply voltage [9]. They use a linear regression model for feature training and estimate the scaling parameters to transform the features from each source domain up to the target domain. The adopted linear scaling parameters contribute to removing the effect of change in the voltage level by transferring all the features to the target domain. Zhou et al. proposed to train the classifier with a comprehensive dataset that combines data under various temperatures together [17, 18] to figure out the appropriate range of temperature for training the classifier.

2) The Hill-Climbing-style attack: Choi et al. found a possible imitation of the clock-based intrusion detection system(CIDS) presented by Cho and Shin [19]. They demonstrated that a time-aware adversary can detect the difference between the clock offset of the compromised ECU and that of the target ECU, and delay message transmission at a carefully calculated time by the clock-offset deference. CIDS may not detect this clock skew-imitating intrusions. Foruhandeh et al. discussed two kinds of Hill-climbing-style attacks towards voltage-based IDS, dominant impersonation and complete impersonation [9]. They explained a dominant impersonation example on defeating the voltage-based IDS: an adversary can estimate the maximum injection ratio and inject as many attack frames as possible with it at each step while avoiding detection. With a continuous injection of more and more attack frames at

each future step, the injection ratio will be able to reach 1/2 and the fingerprinting profile of a legitimate ECU is continuously shifting and close to the fingerprinting profile of the compromised ECU even eventually.

3) The two-stage masquerade attack: Bhatia et al. noted that although the ECU fingerprint is difficult to be altered or forged corresponding to its hardware characteristics, however, the voltage-based IDS are vulnerable to training set poisoning. They proposed a novel masquerade attack called DUET, which is launched against a victim ECU by the attacker and accomplice that follow a two-stage training set poisoning-based attack strategy. At the first stage of voltage fingerprint manipulation, they exploit an attacker ECU that has transited into the error-passive state and transmits an attack message simultaneously with the victim ECU. The attack message shares the same front content as the victim's message until a bit location, then the attack message overlaps with the victim's message without hindering it. And at the second stage of voltage fingerprint-based impersonation, they exploit the accomplice ECU to inject the forged victim's message and utilize the attacker ECU transmits simultaneously corrupting the accomplice's voltage samples as they have done in the first stage. The voltage-based IDS would not raise any alarm to these spoofed messages because the corresponding ECU's fingerprint record has been corrupted at the first stage. And the DUET attack is the first manipulated overlapped voltage attack of automotive CAN to the best of our knowledge.

3.2 Attack Strategy of the DUET

To solve the defect lacking resistance to the DUET attack for the most existing voltage-based IDS in the automotive CAN. First, we refer to the introduction of Bhatia et al. about the DUET attack. A complete DUET attack is launched in two stages, which are shown in Fig. 1(a) and Fig. 1(b). In the first stage, the attacker ECU enters the error-passive state with the help of the accomplice ECU, then it sends attack messages simultaneously with the victim's message after the accomplice ECU injects a preceded ID message, The attacker shifts the bit location from the beginning position of the DLC field in the frame to two bytes far from it gradually in each retraining period to corrupt the fingerprint of the victim ECU. In the second stage, the attacker and accomplice synchronize message transmission by using the preceded ID message transmitted by the accomplice, then accomplice ECU transmits a forged victim's message, and the attacker transmits simultaneously corrupting the accomplice's voltage samples as what it has done to the victim in the first stage. The attacker and accomplice play the DUET attack with multiple rounds and increase the one-bit length of the predictable payload prefix (PREP) after the arbitration field in CAN messages at each round. The VIDS suffers a data poisoning attack by the attacker and accomplice ECUs when it enters the retraining stage. Finally, the VIDS will classify the corrupt voltage samples as the victim's samples after manipulating the voltage fingerprint by the attacker and accomplice.

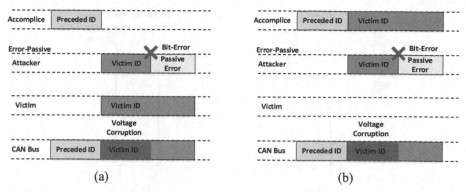

Fig. 1. (a). Voltage fingerprint manipulation (DUET attack Stage 1). (b).Voltage fingerprint-based impersonation (DUET attack Stage 2).

4 Scheme and Construction

The intrusion detection process of this work contains two major phases: (1) overlapped signal detection and filtering, (2) fingerprint feature extraction and identification. Different from the existing Voltage-based intrusion detection schemes for the CAN bus, our proposed mechanism can detect and identify the new type of manipulated overlapped voltage masquerade attack (DUET attack). And we will give a detailed introduction to these processes in the following subsections.

4.1 Overlapped Signal Detection and Filtering

The main reason for existing voltage-based IDS bypassed by the masquerade DUET attack is the lack of resistance to the training dataset poisoning attack. We analyze the signal processing work of the typical VIDS schemes such as the *Viden* and the *Scission*. These schemes ignore the impact of the corrupt voltage samples to distort the detection accuracy of the re-trained classifier model. For the instance of the *Viden*, it updates its voltage fingerprint instance by redrawing the voltage fingerprint curves, which need to calculate the cumulative voltage deviations for its six statistical features after the ACK threshold learning phase. In the phase of ACK threshold learning, it derives the CANH ACK threshold $\Gamma_{ACK}^{H} \approx 3.3\ V$ and CANL ACK threshold $\Gamma_{ACK}^{L} \approx 1.8\ V$, then it discards the voltages which are higher than Γ_{ACK}^{H} or lower than Γ_{ACK}^{L}. The histogram of voltages after filtering the ACK signals presents a unimodal distribution.

However, the voltage distribution of the corrupt voltage samples in the DUET attack is distinct from the normal voltage samples. The corrupt voltage distribution histogram has two peaks in CANH and CANL voltages as shown in Fig. 2(a) by contrasting with normal voltage distribution as depicted in Fig. 2(b). The voltage samples after filtering the ACK signals in normal communication scenarios mostly obey the unimodal distribution(in Fig. 2(b)), while the corrupt voltage samples obey the bimodal distribution. The secondary peak in the corrupt voltage distribution histogram represents an overlapping portion of corrupt voltage samples(in Fig. 2(a)).

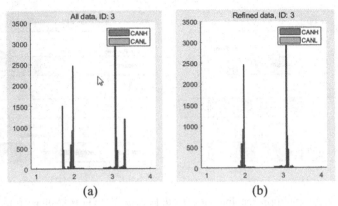

Fig. 2. (a).The voltage distribution of victim ECU during the DUET attack. (b).The normal voltage distribution of victim ECU in normal scenarios.

Another instance of the *Scission*, which calculates 48 features in the time domain and frequency domain from the dominant regions, positive edges, and negative edges of the collecting voltage samples to identify the transmitter ECU. It also neglects the truth that corrupt voltage samples may influence the feature extraction correctness. Figure 3 shows the difference between corrupt voltage samples and general voltage samples. We can easily find there is an abrupt leap in both the dominant and positive/negative edges of the corrupt voltage waveforms. At the same time, these 48 time and frequency domain features have changed a lot as well. According to the thesis of Bhatia et al., once the VIDS accepts the corrupt voltage samples from the first stage of the DUET attack and retrains the model, it will take the falsified voltage fingerprint instance to replace the original fingerprint of the victim ECU. So at the second stage of the DUET attack, when the attacker and accomplice ECUs simulate the corrupt voltage with the same operations in the first stage of the DUET attack, the newly extracted features are identical to what the classifier model has learned from previous corrupt voltage samples. Finally, The VIDS is bypassed by the two-stages DUET attack strategy.

Through the above analysis of the relationship between the characteristics of corrupt voltage samples and the reason caused the existing VIDS have been bypassed, we conclude that the key solution to resolve the problem is to truncate the CAN frame voltage signals and filter the corrupt portion. So we use the LSTM automatic encoder and decoder model to learn the time sequence characteristics of the CAN frame signal transmitted by each ECU in the network, and predict the most likely normal CAN frame voltage signal to detect the overlaps regions in the corrupt CAN voltage signals.

We truncate the voltage signals collected from the CANH and CANL channels and discard the invalid waveforms in which the CAN bus is idle, then we get two sequences S_{CANH} and S_{CANL}, and we calculate the differential voltage sequence $S_{CAND} = S_{CANH} - S_{CANL}$, which represents the actual voltage signals when collected by only one oscilloscope probe. So the input vector of our LSTM autoencoder model is a three-dimensional time sequence.

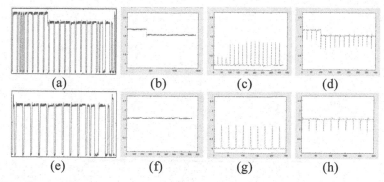

Fig. 3. Waveforms of the victim ECU's CAN frame voltage signals. (a) Corrupt voltage sample. (b) Dominant region of corrupt voltage. (c) The positive edge of corrupt voltage. (d) The negative edge of corrupt voltage. (e) General voltage sample. (f) Dominant region of general voltage. (g) The positive edge of general voltage. (h) The negative edge of the general voltage

The encoder of the model consists of two LSTM layers, it transforms the 3-dimensional input data into a 6-dimensional feature being consistent with the cell dimension of the LSTM. The LSTM stack is constructed with two LSTM with 6-dimensional cell memory for each. The output vector from the first LSTM layer is fed to the second LSTM layer as an input. After many rounds of recursive updates in the two LSTMs, the encoder passes the latest cell state to the decoder. The decoder model also consists of two LSTM layers stacked followed by an FC layer, it uses the cell state vectors passed from the encoder as its initial cell state. The output vector from the first LSTM layer is fed to the second LSTM layer as an input, and the output from the second LSTM is fed to the FC layer. The FC layer contains affine transformation followed by ReLU(Rectified Linear Unit) activation function, it transforms the 6-dimensional input data into 3-dimensional-feature output data which is consistent with the input data dimension of the encoder.

We take the MAE(Mean Absolute Error) as the measurement of the loss between the predicted signal sequence and the actual signal sequence. When the trained model meets the best loss after running multiple epochs, we apply the KDE(kernel density estimation) to plot the density distribution to the loss sequence of the CAN voltage signals and select the inflection point coordinate in the plot as the threshold for discriminating the anomaly(shown in Fig. 4).

The detection result for the overlaps in voltage signal samples is shown in Fig. 5. There is a corrupt voltage sample from the victim ECU (denoted by the red polyline) that is overlapped by the attacker ECU causing a conflict on the CAN bus. After we use the LSTM encoder-decoder model to predict the normal voltage waveform (which is denoted by the blue polyline in Fig. 5), it is clear to find there exists signal disparity in the front portion of the corrupt voltage sample (denoted by the green points). We apply the overlaps detection method to multiple corrupt voltages from the victim ECU, the overlapping signal segments sit on the correct predicted anomaly signal range correctly(denoted by the black points). So we gather the anomaly signal segments and filter them from the

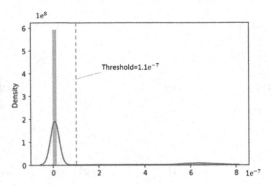

Fig. 4. The threshold of discriminating the anomaly in the CAN voltage signal

corrupt voltage sample, the remains waveform retains the original signal characteristics that we can use for identification.

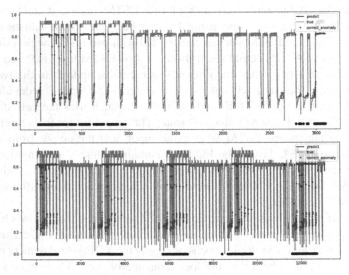

Fig. 5. Voltage signal overlapping segment detection

4.2 Fingerprint Feature Extraction and Identification

After filtering the corrupt portion of collecting voltage samples, we apply an artificial neural network model of CNN with LSTM layers to identify the source ECU of each voltage signal sample. The architecture of the neural network model has a two-dimension convolutional layer with 64 convolution kernels whose kernel size is 6, and two LSTM layers whose output size is 128 and 64 respectively. The size of the input vector satisfies sequential 8×48 matrices, in which 48 represents the number of features extracted from the significant dominant regions, positive edges, and negative edges of the voltage signals. In each significant variation segment of the waveform, we calculate the sixteen features of *Scission* in both time and frequency domains (such as the mean, standard deviation, variance, skewness, kurtosis, root mean square, maximum and energy).

A little Different from the scheme of *Scission*, we divide the whole waveform of a single CAN frame into eight sub-waveforms. We take the sub-waveform length as half of the original waveform and shift the extraction region from the beginning to the end of the waveform. In every shifting process, the position of the extraction region moves at a pace of one-sixteenth whole waveform length. So we get an 8×48 feature matrix for each single CAN frame after the above signal processing. By applying the feature engineering strategy to the voltage signal samples collected within a fixed period, we finally gain the feature dataset as the input for training the classifier model.

The output of the voltage fingerprint instance is a one-hot encoding vector of the n-class, where n presents the number of the ECUs in actual communication scenarios. We will examine the results of the classifier model in Sect. 5.

5 Experiment

To prove our new approach can detect the DUET attack and authenticate the identity of the compromised ECU. We establish the testbed with the same configuration in [2], and we conduct simulation experiments with embedded devices shown in Fig. 6. There are three Arduino devices in the CAN bus network, which play the role of the victim ECU, the accomplice ECU, and the attack ECU either. We use an oscilloscope to collect voltage signal samples on the CAN bus at the sampling rate of 12.5 MS/s. The victim ECU sends cyclical CAN frames with CANID 0x15, while the attacker ECU sends cyclical frames with CANID 0x0B and the forged CAN frame with victim CANID 0x15. The accomplice ECU sends the preceded CANIDs 0x04 and 0x05 to make the attacker ECU transmit the forged frames simultaneously with the victim ECU.

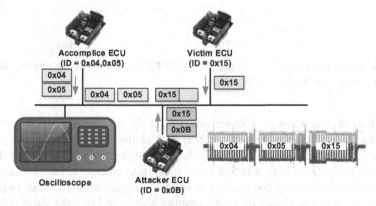

Fig. 6. The CAN bus prototype

At first, we forbade the attacker ECU from transmitting forged victim CANID 0x15, and we collect a considerable amount of voltage samples of three ECUs in the normal communication scenario. We train the proposed neural network model and create the voltage fingerprint instances for each ECU by learning from these benign samples. Then we release the ban of the attacker ECU on sending forged victim CAN message and continue to collect the voltage samples.

When the victim ECU collected voltage signals are overlapped, which means that the voltage fingerprint manipulation has launched. We collect the voltage samples at the first stage of the DUET attack, and we refer to the voltage profile derivation process of *Scission* and select the mean and variance value of dominant regions in the CAN frame voltage signal called *mean-g00* and *var-g00*. We take these two features as the projection of voltage fingerprints on a 2D plane. Figure 7(a) shows the distribution of the three ECUs' feature clusters in the first stage of the DUET attack. In most of these voltage samples (including the benign voltage samples of the victim CANID) whose feature *var-g00* is about 0, however, for the corrupt voltage samples of the victim CANID, the *var-g00* is 0.05. According to the analysis in Sect. 4.2, the corrupt voltage signals contribute to the distortion of the victim voltage cluster. So we filter the overlaps with the LSTM Autoencoder model as in Sect. 4.2. By filtering the overlaps in the corrupted victim CAN frame voltage signals, these distorted voltage samples have restored their fingerprint characteristics and moved closer to the benign victim voltage cluster as in Fig. 7(b).

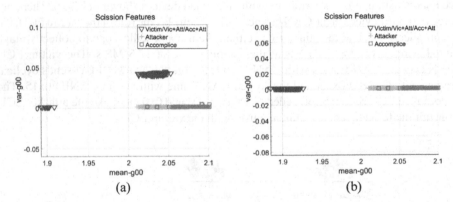

Fig. 7. Feature distribution in the first stage of the DUET attack. (a) Without filtering the corrupt signals. (b) After filtering the corrupt signals

We plot the feature *mean-g00* and *var-g00* of the voltage samples in the second stage of the DUET attack shown in Fig. 8(a). The victim voltage samples are split into two groups: the benign samples sit in the cluster of the accomplice, while the distorted samples sit away from both attacker and accomplice voltage feature clusters. After filtering the overlaps of the corrupt victim voltage samples, all the voltage fingerprints of the victim sit in the cluster of the accomplice shown in Fig. 8(b). So it reflects the truth that the forged victim CAN frame in the second stage of the DUET attack originate from the accomplice ECU.

To prove the effectiveness of the proposed voltage-based intrusion detection system. At first, we train the classifier model by applying the new proposed scheme with the CAN

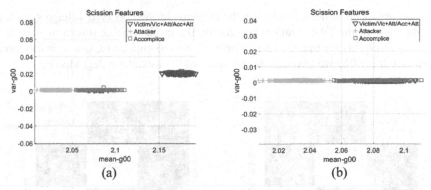

Fig. 8. Feature distribution in the second stage of the DUET attack. (a) Without filtering the corrupt signals. (b) After filtering the corrupt signals

frame voltage samples collected from the normal CAN bus communication scenario, then we predict the classification of collected voltage signal samples from the first and second stages of the DUET attack and plot the confusion matrices for them shown in Fig. 9(a) and Fig. 9(b) respectively. The heatmap in Fig. 9(a) reflects that the proposed scheme can filter the overlaps and identify the real source of all the CAN frames, while the heatmap in Fig. 9(b) proves that the masquerade voltage samples of the victim ECU are generated by the accomplice ECU at the second stage of the DUET attack.

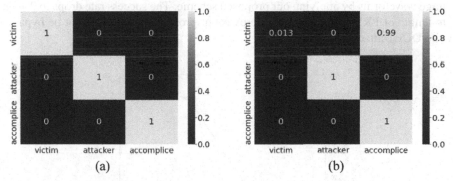

Fig. 9. (a) The heatmap of three ECUs in the DUET attack first stage. (b) The heatmap of three ECUs in the DUET attack first stage

Figure 10(a) shows the predicted accuracy of the retrained model by accepting the corrupt voltage samples without filtering the overlaps. We use the collected voltage samples in the first stage of the DUET attack to retrain the classifier model, then we try to predict the classification of voltage samples collected in the second stage of the DUET attack with the retrained model. The results are listed in Fig. 10(a), in which the falsified victim CAN frame generated by the accomplice and attacker ECUs are categorized into the victim's classification. The phenomenon proves that existing VIDS cannot resist the DUET attack on its classifier model. As a comparison in Fig. 10(b), We apply the proposed approach to detect and filter the overlaps in the collected voltage samples in the first stage of the DUET attack and retrain the model, the confusion matrix of the predicted results shows that the real identity of the accomplice ECU who impersonates the victim. It is effective to retain the accuracy of the model not degraded it.

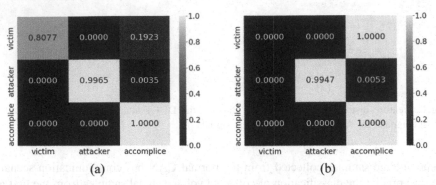

(a)   (b)

Fig. 10. (a) The predicted accuracy of the retrained model without filtering the overlaps. (b) The predicted accuracy of the retrained model after filtering the overlaps

Figure 11 shows the DUET attack success rate against the *Scission* and our proposed scheme. The success rate against Scission reaches 80.77% with the corruption in two bytes length of PREP and 97.20% with three bytes of PREP. After filtering the overlapped voltage waveforms by applying our proposed scheme, The success rate drops to 0 at any byte length of PREP. Thus the result proves our proposed scheme cannot be bypassed by the DUET attack.

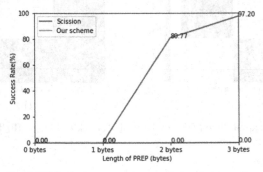

Fig. 11. The DUET attack success rate against scission and our scheme

6 Summary

In this study, we propose a new mechanism to detect the manipulated overlapped voltage attack (DUET attack) and recognize the source of the corrupt voltage samples. We analyze the defect of existing VIDS such as *Viden* and *Scission* and discuss why these schemes can be bypassed by the two-stage DUET attack. According to the characteristics of the corrupt overlapping signal, we improve the process of existing VIDS to detect and filter the overlaps in the collecting voltage signal samples. Our proposed scheme can detect the DUET attack and filter the overlaps in the corrupt voltage samples by applying the LSTM autoencoder. For guaranteeing the predicted accuracy is not degraded, we improve the classifier model by combing the convolutional neural network with LSTM layers. Finally, we examine our new approach by simulating the DUET attack on a CAN bus prototype. The experiment result shows our new approach is effective to detect various masquerade attacks including the DUET attack and recognize the identification of accomplice ECU which impersonates the victim ECU.

Acknowledgements. This research was funded in part by the National Natural Science Foundation of China under grants 61872069, 62072090 and 62173101, and in part by the Fundamental Research Funds for the Central Universities under grant N2017012 and N2217009.

References

1. Jo, H.J., Choi, W.: A survey of attacks on controller area networks and corresponding countermeasures. IEEE Trans. Intell. Transp. Syst. **99**, 1–19 (2021)
2. Bhatia, R., Kumar, V., Serag, K., Celik, Z.B., Payer, M., Xu, D.: Evading voltage-based intrusion detection on automotive CAN. In: Proceedings of the Network and Distributed System Security Symposium, San Diego, CA, USA, pp. 1–17 (2021)
3. Murvay, P.S., Groza, B.: Source identification using signal characteristics in controller area networks. IEEE Signal Process. Lett. **21**(4), 395–399 (2014)
4. Cho, K.T., Kang, S.: Viden: attacker identification on in-vehicle networks. In: Proceedings of the 2017 ACM SIGSAC Conference on Computer and Communications Security, pp. 1109–1123 (2017)
5. Choi, W., Jo, H.J., Woo, S., Chun, J.Y., Park, J., Lee, D.H.: Identifying ecus using inimitable characteristics of signals in controller area networks. IEEE Trans. Veh. Technol. **67**(6), 4757–4770 (2018)
6. Choi, W., Joo, K., Jo, H.J., Park, M.C., Lee, D.H.: Voltageids: low-level communication characteristics for automotive intrusion detection system. IEEE Trans. Inf. Forensics Secur. **13**(8), 2114–2129 (2018)
7. Kneib, M., Huth, C.: Scission: signal characteristic-based sender identification and intrusion detection in automotive networks. In: Proceedings of the 2018 ACM SIGSAC Conference on Computer and Communications Security, pp. 787–800 (2018)
8. Kneib, M., Schell, O., Huth, C.: On the robustness of signal characteristic-based sender identification (2019). arXiv:1911.09881
9. Foruhandeh, M., Man, Y., Gerdes, R., Li, M., Chantem, T.: Simple: Single-frame based physical layer identification for intrusion detection and prevention on in-vehicle networks. In: Proceedings of the 35th Annual Computer Security Applications Conference, pp. 229–244 (2019)
10. Rumez, M., et al.: Can radar: sensing physical devices in can networks based on time domain reflectometry. In: 2019 IEEE Vehicular Networking Conference (VNC), pp. 1–8. IEEE (2019)
11. Xu, T., Lu, X., Xiao, L., Tang, Y., Dai, H.: Voltage based authentication for controller area networks with reinforcement learning. In: ICC 2019–2019 IEEE International Conference on Communications (ICC), pp. 1–5. IEEE (2019)

12. Yang, Y., Duan, Z., Tehranipoor, M.: Identify a spoofing attack on an in-vehicle can bus based on the deep features of an ECU fingerprint signal. Smart Cities **3**(1), 17–30 (2020)
13. Hafeez, A., Topolovec, K., Awad, S.: Ecu fingerprinting through parametric signal modeling and artificial neural networks for in-vehicle security against spoofing attacks. In: 2019 15th International Computer Engineering Conference (ICENCO), pp. 29–38. IEEE (2019)
14. Levy, E., Shabtai, A., et al.: CAN-LOC: Spoofing Detection and Physical Intrusion Localization on an In-Vehicle CAN Bus Based on Deep Features of Voltage Signals (2021)
15. Marchetti, M., Stabili, D.: Anomaly detection of CAN bus messages through analysis of ID sequences. In: 2017 IEEE Intelligent Vehicles Symposium (IV). IEEE (2017)
16. Taylor, A., Japkowicz, N., Leblanc, S.: Frequency-based anomaly detection for the automotive CAN bus. In: 2015 World Congress on Industrial Control Systems Security (WCICSS). IEEE (2015)
17. Zhou, J., et al.: Btmonitor: bit-time-based intrusion detection and attacker identification in controller area network. ACM Trans. Embedded Comput. Syst. **18**(6), 1–23 (2020)
18. Zhou, J., et al.: Clock-based sender identification and attack detection for automotive CAN network. IEEE Access **99**, 2665–2679 (2020)
19. Shin, K.G., Cho, K.T.: Fingerprinting Electronic Control Units For Vehicle Intrusion Detection. US20170286675 (2017)

Author Index

Printed in the United States
by Baker & Taylor Publisher Services

Printed in the United States
by Baker & Taylor Publisher Services